ALWAYS PREPARED

The story of 207 Squadron Royal Air Force

by John Hamlin

This book is dedicated to all who served with 7 and 7A (Naval) Squadrons and 207 Squadron Royal Air Force

AN AIR-BRITAIN PUBLICATION

Published in the United Kingdom by

Air-Britain (Historians) Ltd,
12 Lonsdale Gardens
Tunbridge Wells, Kent TN1 1PA

Sales Dept:
19 Kent Road, Grays,
Essex RM17 6DE

Correspondence to the editor:

R.C.Sturtivant, 26 Monks Horton Way,
St.Albans, Herts, AL1 4HA
And not to the Tunbridge Wells address.

ISBN 0 85130 285 8

Printed by
Hillman Printers (Frome) Ltd
Handlemaker Road
Marston Trading Estate
Frome, Somerset BA11 4RW

Front cover painting by kind permission of Michael Turner.

Back cover photograph by kind permission of the Dean and Chapter of Leicester Cathedral.

CONTENTS

The view from the 'office' of a 207 Squadron Lancaster formating on EM:Z. [via B Goodwin]

FOREWORD

by Air Chief Marshal Sir Neil Wheeler GCB CBE DSO DFC & Bar AFC FRAeS RAF (Retd.)

There can be no finer or more noble reason for publishing the history of a distinguished squadron than as a tribute and memorial to those who gave their lives while serving in that squadron. This is the reason why 207 Squadron authorised this particular history, and I am much honoured to be invited to write the foreword.

Although I was still in Bomber Command at the outbreak of war, I left it quite early in 1940 and therefore I found this history not only very informative but fascinating to read, leaving me full of admiration for the exploits of 207 Squadron during World War Two. Especially humbling is the huge number of casualties this single squadron suffered during that conflict – 954 killed and 173 captured, and the splendid 38 who evaded capture and returned to this country. One very important point which comes out from the history, and something that is often overlooked by the general public, is that the danger was not only enemy action but also weather and the serviceability and reliability of the aircraft, particularly true of the Avro Manchester with which the squadron was equipped in 1941.

I joined 207 Squadron when the squadron returned from the Sudan. My first great surprise was to discover that, apart from the commanding officer, I was the only permanent regular officer in the squadron. Inevitably, therefore, I was soon made adjutant. To the modern pilot in the Royal Air Force, the idea of being the adjutant of a squadron sounds like a gentle sinecure, but it certainly was not so before the war. In those days all the airmen were held on the posted strength of a squadron, and 207, being an emergency or mobile unit, had 350 airmen. In theory, we could operate independently of an established Station and had our own cooks, batmen, stores personnel and accountants to man the appropriate sections. I can, therefore, assure anyone in today's RAF that it was quite a task for a mere Pilot Officer!

Almost the first big task that the CO put on my plate, in the autumn of 1937, was to arrange a squadron reunion dinner. At the time we in the squadron were confident that 7 (Naval) Squadron had been formed in France at Petite Synthe in autumn 1916 and had become 207 Squadron on the formation of the RAF in 1918. Thus we were to celebrate the 21st anniversary of our birth. I soon found myself in great difficulties because one of the earlier commanding officers, Gaskell–Blackburn, wrote to say that we had got the date of formation of the squadron quite wrong. In fact we never resolved the problem because the reunion never took place! I am, therefore, very interested that the history starts with the amazing dilemma that there were two 7 (Naval) Squadrons, and Gaskell–Blackburn, who had been with the unit that started in the Rufiji Delta in East Africa, maintained that the squadron had started there and not at Petite Synthe. I am very pleased, therefore, that the problem seems at last to have been resolved.

When I joined the squadron it was still equipped with the Fairey Gordon, which was rather an old-fashioned single-engined biplane which did not carry much of a bomb load. I recall that in the Army manoeuvres in the Aldershot area in August 1937 we received a complaint that we were flying low and slow over the troops. In fact we were flying into a very strong headwind, but it must have appeared extremely slow to the Army! After the war I was very lucky to meet 207 Squadron again when I was a Wing Commander at Marham and the squadron had a very different aircraft – the Washington. It was therefore extremely interesting to read Chapter 10 of the history, which recounts that period.

I always hoped that a history of 207 Squadron would be produced, because it was one of the great squadrons of the Royal Air Force. As I have said, the reasons that prompted the 207 Squadron Association to commission it are admirable, and I am sure that many people, not only those who served with the squadron during World War Two, will find it fascinating to read about the exploits of a distinguished bomber squadron. It is a story of great skill, courage and determination, for which all who served in 207 Squadron can justly be very proud.

ACKNOWLEDGEMENTS

The author's sincere thanks are due to the following individuals who contributed, directly or indirectly, to the text of this book:

Mr. E. M. Balcombe
Mr. Douglas Barnes
Mr. Paul Bennett
Mr. Dennis Bentley
Sqn. Ldr. Dave Bridger
Sect. Off. Joyce Brotherton MBE WAAF (deceased)
Mr. K. Brown
Mr. W. W. Burke
Mr. E. J. Butler
Mr. D. H. Chandler
Mr. Phillip G. Crawley
Mr. Geoff Cruikshank
Mr. C. Denwood
AVM A. D. Dick CB CBE AFC MA FRAeS
Sqn. Ldr. G. W. O'N. Fisher
Ms. Daphne Forbes
Mr. Alex Gibson MBE JP
Wg. Cdr. 'Goldie' Goldstraw (deceased)
Mr. Barry Goodwin
Mr. Arthur L. Haines
Mr. Norman Hamer
Sqn. Ldr. Ian J. Hampton
Gp. Capt. Charles Hawkins OBE AFC
Mr. Cyril Hewett
Mr. Ken Hunter
Mrs. Irene Jackson
Ms. Sue Kenyon
Mr. Roger Korner
Mr. John A. Laing, for the use of his unpublished manuscript of the Washington period.
Mr. W. H. Lewis
Wg. Cdr. Ken Marwood AFM
Mr. A. Mathieson
Mr. G. E. Moulton–Barrett
Mr. T. Murray
Mr. A. B. Parsons MISM
Mr. John Pearl
Mr. P. M. Rae
Mr. Jim A. Riley
Mr. Fred Rummery (deceased)
Mr. Joseph Scott
Flt. Lt. John Scullard
Mr. Clive Semple, for permission to include selected portions of the diary kept by his father, the late Mr. L. G. Semple
Mr. Charles Smith
Mr. Peter Squirrell (deceased)
Mr. C. B. Sutherland
Mr. James Watts
Mr. G. R. Wheeldon
Sqn. Ldr. A. K. Wolsey

......and not forgetting my ever-helpful wife, Sheila, who provided countless cups of tea while I worked for many hours at my computer; Ron Winton, my day-to-day contact with the 207 Squadron Association, for his never-failing help and advice; and of course Ray Sturtivant of Air Britain, who was responsible for the production of the book.

BIBLIOGRAPHY

'Avro Manchester' by Dr. Robert Kirby (published by Midland Publishing Ltd., 1995)
'For The Duration' – extracts from the diary of George Hawes, published privately in Australia by Denise Roper
'Handley Page Aircraft Since 1907' by C. H. Barnes (published by Putnam, 1976)
'The Lancaster File' by J. J. Halley (published by Air-Britain, 1985)
'On the Wings of the Morning' by Vincent Holyoak (published by the author, 1995)
'Oxford Airport' by Geoff Phillips (published by Bookmarque Publishing, 1996)
'RAF Bomber Command Losses of the Second World War' – 6 volumes, by W.R.Chorley (published by Midland Counties Publications)
'RAF Marham' by Ken Delve (published by Patrick Stephens Ltd., 1995)
'Royal Navy Aircraft Serials and Units, 1911–1919' by Ray Sturtivant and Gordon Page (published by Air-Britain, 1992)
'Tedder' by Roderic Owen (published by Collins, 1952)
'The Green Fields and The Sky' by N. J. Roberson & J. G. Talliss (published by GMS Enterprises, 1991)
'The Squadrons of the Royal Air Force & Commonwealth 1913–1988' by J. J. Halley (published by Air-Britain, 1988)
'Trust To Talk' by Wynford Vaughan–Thomas
'Vickers Aircraft Since 1908', by C. F. Andrews & E. B. Morgan (published by Putnam, 1988)
'Wings Over Suez' by Brian Cull with David Nicholle and Shlomo Aloni (published by Grub Street, 1996)
'207 Squadron, RAF Langar, 1942–1943' by Barry Goodwin and Raymond Glynne–Owen (published by the Langar Airfield 207 Squadron Memorial Committee, 1994)

Documents held at the Public Record Office, Kew:

Relating to 7 (Naval) Squadron:

AIR.1/183/15/213/2

Relating to 207 Squadron:

AIR.1/1914/204/230/5
AIR.1/1914/204/230/7

AIR.27/1233	1916–1942
AIR.27/1234	1943
AIR.27/1235	1944
AIR.27/1236	1944/45
AIR.27/1237	Appendix 1.41–1.45
AIR.27/1238	Appendix 10.43–3.45
AIR.27/2463	1946–1950
AIR.27/2661	1951–1956
AIR.27/2989	1961/62
AIR.27/2990	1963–1965
AIR.27/3179	1967–1971 (not available to the public until 2002)

Relating to Stations on which 207 Squadron was based:

AIR.28/70	Bircham Newton
AIR.28/90	Bottesford
AIR.28/174	Cottesmore
AIR.28/160	Cranfield
AIR.28/1246	Marham
AIR.28/1480	Marham
AIR.28/1612	Marham
AIR.28/538	Methwold
AIR.28/1081	Mildenhall
AIR.28/722	Spilsby
AIR.28/723	Spilsby
AIR.28/1121	Stradishall
AIR.28/1137	Tuddenham
AIR.28/879	Waddington
AIR.28/966	Worthy Down

Documents held in the Royal Air Force Museum:

B.268	Flying logbook of Sqn. Ldr. A. Tedder
B.389	'Army Postal Services' by L. W. C. Pearce–Gervis (unpublished, 1938)
B.431	Army Postal Services (official report)
ARO/1977/241	Private diary of AC2 S. Riches, 1922/23
	Flying logbook of Lt. (RN) J. W. Pearson, 1918

ABBREVIATIONS

AA	Anti-Aircraft
A&AEE	Aeroplane & Armament Experimental Establishment
AC	Aircraftman
AC1	Aircraftman First Class
AC2	Aircraftman Second Class
ACM	Air Chief Marshal
ACW	Aircraftwoman
ADC	Aide-de-Camp
ADGB	Air Defence of Great Britain
AEO	Air Electronics Officer or Operator
AFB	Air Force Base [USAF]
AFC	Air Force Cross
AFM	Air Force Medal
AHQ	Air Headquarters
Air Cdre.	Air Commodore
AM1	Air Mechanic First Class [RNAS]
AM2	Air Mechanic Second Class [RNAS]
AOC	Air Officer Commanding
AOC-in-C	Air Officer Commanding-in-Chief
APS	Army Postal Service
ASC	Aircraft Servicing Chief
ATC	Air Training Corps or Armament Training Camp
ATCC	Air Traffic Control Centre
ATS	Armament Training Station
AVM	Air Vice Marshal
Bart.	Baronet
BCAR	Bomber Command Alert & Readiness plan
BEF	British Expeditionary Force [in France]
Bf	Bayerische Flugzeugbau [Messerschmitt]
bhp	brake horsepower
Bn.	Battalion
BoBMF	Battle of Britain Memorial Flight
Brig.	Brigadier
CAF	Canadian Armed Forces
CB	Companion of the (Order of the) Bath
CBE	Commander of the (Order of the) British Empire
Cdr.	Commander
CFS	Central Flying School
CH	Companion of Honour
Ch. Tech.	Chief Technician
CIE	Companion of the (Order of the) Indian Empire
C-in-C	Commander-in-Chief
cm.	centimetre
CMG	Companion of (the Order of) St. Michael & St. George
CND	Campaign for Nuclear Disarmament
CO	Commanding Officer
Cpl.	Corporal
CU	Conversion Unit
CVO	Commander of the (Royal) Victorian Order
CWGC	Commonwealth War Graves Commission
cwt.	hundredweight [112 lbs. – 50.9 kg.]
DC	District of Columbia
DFC	Distinguished Flying Cross
DH	de Havilland or Direct hit
DSC	Distinguished Service Cross
DSM	Distinguished Service Medal
DSO	Distinguished Service Order
E&E	Escape & Evasion
EAF	Egyptian Air Force
ENSA	Entertainment National Service Association
FE	Far East
Flg. Off.	Flying Officer
Flt. Lt.	Flight Lieutenant
Flt. Off.	Flight Officer [WAAF]
Flt. Sgt.	Flight Sergeant
Flt. Sub-Lt.	Flight Sub-Lieutenant
FN	Frazer–Nash [turrets]
GBE	Knight Grand Cross of the British Empire
GCA	Ground Controlled Approach [a form of radar to assist landings]
GCB	(Knight) Grand Cross of the (Order of the) Bath
Gef.	Gefreiter [Luftwaffe – equivalent to RAF AC1]
GHQ	General Headquarters [Army]
GI	Government issue or general issue (the ordinary US Army soldier)
gm.	gramme
Govt.	Government
GP	General purpose [bombs]
Gp. Capt.	Group Captain
HQ	Headquarters
HM	His or Her Majesty
HMS	His or Her Majesty's Ship
HMT	His Majesty's Troopship
HP	Handley Page
Hptmn	Hauptmann [Luftwaffe – equivalent to RAF Flt. Lt.]
HRH	His or Her Royal Highness
hp	horsepower
IFF	Identification – Friend or Foe
ILS	Instrument Landing System
ISM	Imperial Service Medal
JP	Justice of the Peace
Ju	Junkers
KBE	Knight Commander of the (Order of the) British Empire
KCB	Knight Commander of the (Order of the) Bath
KCVO	Knight Commander of the (Royal) Victorian Order
KD	Khaki drill [tropical clothing]
KG	Knight of the (Order of the) Garter
kg.	kilogramme(s)
KHz	kilohertz [a measure of radio wave frequency]
KIA	Killed in action
km.	kilometres
kph	kilometres per hour
kw	kilowatt

LAC Leading Aircraftman
lb. pounds [weight]
Ldg. Mech. Leading mechanic [RNAS]
Lt. Lieutenant
Lt. Gen. Lieutenant General

m. metres
Maj. Major
MATS Military Air Transport Service [USAF]
MB Bachelor of Medicine
MC Military Cross
MISM Member of the Institute of Supply Management
Mk. Mark
MM Military Medal
MAP Ministry of Aircraft Production
MP Member of Parliament
mph miles per hour
MU Maintenance Unit
MVO Member of the (Royal) Victorian Order

NAAFI Navy, Army & Air Force Institute
NATO North Atlantic Treaty Organisation
NCO Non-Commissioned Officer
NFT Night flying training
NJG Nachtjagdgeschwader [Luftwaffe unit: Night Attack Wing]

OBE (Officer of the) Order of the British Empire
Obfw. Oberfeldwebel [Luftwaffe – equivalent to RAF Flt. Sgt.]
Oblt. Oberleutnant [Luftwaffe – equivalent to RAF Flg. Off.]
OCU Operational Conversion Unit
O/O Observer Officer
ORP Operational Readiness Platform
OTU Operational Training Unit

P&EE Proof & Experimental Establishment, Shoeburyness
PFF Pathfinder Force
PFO Physical Fitness Officer
Plt. Off. Pilot Officer
POL Petrol, oil and lubricants
PT Physical Training
Pte. Private [Army rank]

QMAAC Queen Mary's Army Ambulance Corps
QRA Quick Reaction Alert

RAAF Royal Australian Air Force
RAF Royal Air Force
RAFA Royal Air Forces Association
RAFVR(T) Royal Air Force Volunteer Reserve (Training)
RBSU Radar Bomb Scoring Unit
RCAF Royal Canadian Air Force
Rev. Reverend
RFC Royal Flying Corps
RNAS Royal Naval Air Service
RNVR Royal Naval Volunteer Reserve
RNZAF Royal New Zealand Air Force
RRAF Royal Rhodesian Air Force
R/T Radio Telephony

SAC Senior Aircraftman
SACEUR Supreme Allied Commander Europe
SAM Surface-to-Air Missile
SAP Semi Armour-Piercing [bombs]
SBAC Society of British Aircraft Constructors
SBC Small Bombs Container
Sect. Off. Section Officer [WAAF]
Sgt. Sergeant
Sgt. Maj. Sergeant Major
SHAPE Supreme Headquarters Allied Powers in Europe
SMO Station Medical Officer
SNAFU 'Situation Normal – All Fouled Up'
SNCO Senior Non-Commissioned Officer
SP Service Policeman
Sqn. Cdr. Squadron Commander
Sqn. Ldr. Squadron Leader
SS Steamship
SS Schutzstaffel [the elite police arm of the Nazi party]

TacEval Tactical Evaluation
TOT Time Over Target
TS Troopship

u/s unserviceable
USAAF United States Army Air Force
USAF United States Air Force
u/t under training, or untrained

VC Victoria Cross
VE Victory in Europe
VFR Visual Flight Rules
VHF Very High Frequency [radio]
VJ Victory over Japan

WAAF Women's Auxiliary Air Force
Wg. Cdr. Wing Commander
W/O Warrant Officer
WOp Wireless Operator
WOp/AG Wireless Operator/Air Gunner
WRAF Women's Royal Air Force
WRNS Women's Royal Naval Service
W/T Wireless Telegraphy [using Morse code]
Wt. Off. Warrant Officer
WVS Women's Voluntary Services

YMCA Young Men's Christian Association

Z 'Zulu' time, i.e. Greenwich Mean Time

HP O/100 3118 [B4] of 7 (Naval) Squadron. [Yorkshire Air Museum via P. H. T. Green]

Chapter 1: 7 Squadron RNAS 1915 – 1918

The East Africa campaign

To the military mind, anomalies are generally unacceptable. It is surprising, therefore, to find that during the First World War two squadrons of the Royal Naval Air Service carried the number 7 at the same time, one based for a while in Tanganyika (East Africa) and the other in northern France. The subject of this book, 207 Squadron RAF, undoubtedly descended from the latter, but it is only right that the story of the men who served in Africa during the campaign of General Jan Smuts against German forces is also told.

In May 1916 a number of Royal Navy airmen based off the eastern coast of Africa on the island of Zanzibar but detached to Tanganyika on the mainland were placed under the command of Sqn. Cdr. Eric R. Nanson to support South African forces led by Gen. Van Deventer. Thus assembled, the unit was given the title 7 (Naval) Squadron, and Nanson began to requisition aviation fuel and spare parts to be despatched to Kondoa Irangi, about 250 miles (400 km.) west-north-west of Zanzibar. Four aircraft mechanics, led by Flt. Sub-Lt. Gallehawk, then began the long trek with a thousand native bearers, stopping for four days at Lol Kissale to hack out a rough landing ground before arriving on 28 May at Kondoa.

There the party, now short of three bearers who became a meal for lions on the journey, began to construct an airfield of reasonable standard. Four Voisin Type III pusher biplanes had been shipped out from Avonmouth via Durban and Mombassa aboard SS *Clan Macpherson* for the East Africa Field Force, of which 7 (Naval) Squadron formed a component. Also allocated to the squadron and shipped with the Voisins were two Short 827 seaplanes, but as they were not likely to be of much use in the 'bush' they were taken over by 8 (Naval) Squadron.

While this work was being done, two pilots, Flt. Lt. W. G. Moore and Flt. Sub-Lt. N. G. S. Dawson, took off from Mbuyuni to fly the 180 miles (290 km.) north to Kondoa. Faulty navigation due to poor maps compelled them to land on the Masai plateau, and it was not until 6 June that the Voisins arrived at Kondoa none the worse for their adventure, one of them piloted by Sqn. Cdr. Nanson.

As soon as they appeared, the aircraft and six squadron pilots were put to work on reconnaissance and bombing sorties, many of which caused severe alarm and despondency among native bearers employed by the German forces, who believed such flying machines to be supernatural in origin. Reinforcements in the shape of seven BE.2c biplanes began to arrive at Kondoa in October, but before long the Germans started a withdrawal, during which the RNAS aircraft were used to bomb retreating columns of troops. Other landing grounds in the region were used by the squadron, and around Christmas one Voisin was detached to Dar-es-Salaam and another to Ubena (Njombe).

With the campaign effectively over, orders were given on 12 January 1917 for 7 (Naval) Squadron to withdraw and to be superseded by 26 Squadron RFC, which would take over the aircraft and equipment as well as stored material. About 85,000 miles (136,850 km.) had been flown by 7 (Naval) Squadron during its short time in Tanganyika, without loss of men and with the loss of only one Beardmore-built BE.2c, serial number 8489, which had been wrecked on take-off from Kondoa Irangi on 7 November 1916.

This Voisin Type III 'New Type' pusher biplane of 7 (Naval) Squadron in East Africa seems to be somewhat the worse for wear. [J. M. Bruce & G. S. Leslie collection]

A pair of B.E.2Cs outside a primitive hangar during the East African campaign. [J. M. Bruce & G. S. Leslie collection]

Suitably pith-helmeted, men of 7 (Naval) Squadron set about the task of servicing a BE.2C in East Africa, protected from the worst of the noonday sun by a canvas hangar. [J. M. Bruce & G. S. Leslie collection]

Now for an air test! Mechanics look on as the pilot runs the engine of a B.E.2C of 7 (Naval) Squadron. [J. M. Bruce & G. S. Leslie collection]

A good illustration of the 'sticks-and-string' aircraft flown by 7 (Naval) Squadron in East Africa, a Voisin Type III 'New Type pusher biplane. [J. M. Bruce & G. S. Leslie collection]

Using a convenient tree, men of 7 (Naval) Squadron change the engine of a Voisin at Kondoa Irangi in Tanganyika. [J. M. Bruce & G. S. Leslie collection]

A Caudron G.IV of 7 (Naval) Squadron, with sand dunes in the background, probably at Petite Synthe. [J. M. Bruce & G. S. Leslie collection]

France and the bombing offensive

Even before the disbandment of the unit in Tanganyika, another 7 (Naval) Squadron had been established in France in November 1916 at Petite Synthe near Dunkerque, where it was formed from 'B' Squadron of 4th Wing RNAS. This airfield had come into use in September 1914, when a detachment of RNAS personnel and aircraft under the command of Cdr. C. R. Samson began an attempt to combat the increasing number of raids being mounted by Zeppelin airships against Great Britain. When German forces approached the coast the value of the Petite Synthe base increased, and reconnaissance missions and offensive raids then became part of the task of the small force. Early in 1916 the Dunkerque force was greatly enlarged, and two Wings were established, each to carry out both bombing missions and defensive tasks. 4th Naval Wing had been formed at Eastchurch in August 1915 and moved to Petite Synthe in April 1916, under the command of Sqn. Cdr. C. L. Courtney, while 5th Naval Wing was set up at Coudekerke. More pilots arrived in May, and by mid-June 4th Wing comprised two squadrons, 1 and 2, retitled 'A' and 'B' in July. At this time the title 'squadron' conveyed little more than an administrative function, the operational onus being placed on Flights, usually consisting of six aircraft. In November 1916, however, it was decided that RNAS units should fall more into line with their RFC counterparts, and 4th Wing therefore reorganised its aircraft and crews into two squadrons, 6 (Naval) Squadron, devoted entirely to fighting, and 7 (Naval) Squadron, to carry out bombing missions. 7 (Naval) Squadron was then divided into two Flights, one equipped with twin-engined Caudron G.IV aircraft (soon replaced by Sopwith 1½ Strutters) and the other with Short Bombers. In command of the squadron from 4th Wing HQ was Sqn. Cdr. Courtney, there being no separate squadron headquarters.

Sopwith 1½ Strutter N5504 served with 7 (Naval) Squadron from February to March 1917. [D. M. Hannah]

7 (Naval) Squadron was the first to receive Short Bombers, four of which joined eighteen other aircraft of the 4th and 5th Naval Wings in a raid on Ateliers de la Marine and the Slyken power station at Ostende during the night of 15/16 November. Each Short carried eight 65 lb. (29.5 kg.) bombs, twice the load of the Caudrons which also took part but well inside the Shorts' 900 lbs. (409 kg.) capacity. A long period of very bad weather then settled on the area, preventing any night bombing operations, but on 1 February 1917 a photographic reconnaissance flight revealed that a number of German motor torpedo boats were ice-bound in the harbour at Brugge. Two days later, despite the extreme cold, 4th and 5th Naval Wings made a concentrated attack on the boats, 7 (Naval) Squadron taking part with four aircraft which took off before dawn. Unfortunately, the engines of two of the aircraft succumbed to the temperature, causing forced landings, while the pilot of Short 9339 lost his way and landed at Le Crotoy after four and a half hours in the air. The fourth pilot, Flt. Lt. C. H. Darley, found his objective and dropped six bombs, three of which fell on a group of twelve motor torpedo boats and another on dockside buildings. Next night a follow-up raid was mounted, and this time three squadron aircraft each dropped six 112 lb. (51 kg.) bombs in the dock area. After this raid, Short Bomber 9338, piloted by Flt. Lt. H. G. Brackley with Air Mech. Woolley aboard, hit similar aircraft 9490 while landing, apparently without injury to anyone. Flown by Flt. Sub-Lt. A. L. Thorne with Ldg. Mechanic G.A.Kent, 9490 had found itself nose-down in a ditch after its landing run. These operations were the last flown by the squadron's Caudrons before their withdrawal.

Not an end-of-the-pier pierrot show but members of Petite Synthe-based 7 (Naval) Squadron on the beach at St. Malo in the summer of 1917. C. H. Darley is fourth from the right and second from the right is possibly H.G.Brackley. [E. F. Cheesman]

This type of offensive mission was flown whenever weather conditions during that atrocious winter allowed. Instead of improving, though, weather conditions became even worse, and after a raid on Ghistelles airfield on 16 February no further operations could be flown for six weeks. Instead, the time was spent in practice flying and in testing the aircraft to make sure that they were in top condition. Adding to the squadron's fleet, two more Short Bombers arrived from Dover on 17 March and a third next day from Manston. After trials of a Paulhan propeller fitted to Sopwith N5509 on 23 March, a Vickers gun fitted to the same aircraft was evaluated two days later. Having completed the gun trials, N5509 and N5520 were loaded with four 65 lb. practice bombs each and flew off to drop them on the beach near Fort Mardycke. Short Bomber 9493, meanwhile, was fitted with a new Shorts propeller which took it into the air on 1 April, but it was felt to be less efficient than the original Mann Egerton-made propeller, giving less traction in the climb.

Further organisational developments took place at the end of March 1917, when 4th Wing moved to La Panne and

Short Bomber 9307 was not used by 7 (Naval) Squadron, but this photograph gives an indication of the type's appearance. [J. M. Bruce & G. S. Leslie collection]

Short Bomber 9491 after crashing on the roof of the 5 Wing CO's office on 29 April 1917. Flt. Sub-Lt. L. A. Sands, the erstwhile pilot, may have been hiding his face. [J. M. Bruce & G. S. Leslie collection]

became responsible for all fighter operations, while 5th Wing, commanded by Wg. Cdr. D. A. Spencer Grey DSO, moved to Petite Synthe to administer all day and night bombing. On 2 April, therefore, 7 (Naval) Squadron handed over its Flight of Sopwith 1½ Strutters to 5 (Naval) Squadron and between 2 and 4 April moved to a new base at Coudekerke.

The advent of the 'heavies'

On arrival at Coudekerke, 7 (Naval) Squadron comprised just one Flight of Short Bombers, but immediately took on charge the first three examples of its new equipment, twin-engined Handley Page O/100s, to enable the squadron to carry out its heavy bombing task near Calais. These large aircraft arrived at Coudekerke from Manston as part of the Handley Page Flight, the CO of which, Sqn. Cdr. J. W. K. Allsop, took over the command of 7 (Naval) Squadron on 3 April 1917. Powered by two Rolls–Royce Eagle or Sunbeam Cossack engines of 250 hp, the O/100 had a wing-span of 100'0" (30.48 m.), boasted a cruising speed of 76 mph and normally carried fourteen 112 lb. bombs and twenty Cooper bombs for dealing with enemy searchlights. Three men formed the crew — pilot, observer, and rear gunner, the observer carrying out navigation and bomb-dropping and acting as front gunner if needed.

Bombing raids by the squadron were resumed on 5/6 April, when five Short Bombers attacked a railway junction south of Brugge, each carrying six 65 lb. and two 100 lb. bombs. Considerable damage was believed to have been done to the target, but poor visibility may have misled the crews. A further raid was mounted on 7/8 April, and

Probably amazed by the size of the first HP O/100 to arrive at Coudekerke for 7 (Naval) Squadron, 3116, personnel of the squadron hasten to inspect it. [via R. C. Sturtivant]

A fascinating view from the deck of HP O/100 3116 on approach to Coudekerke on 6 June 1917 with the King of the Belgians in the left of the cockpit. [E. F. Cheesman]

another on 14 April, when four Short Bombers left Coudekerke at about 03.30 to raid the east and west basins at Brugge. Two of the aircraft, however, failed to reach the target – one (9336) force-landing on the beach near Bray Dunes and the other returning to base. Another raided the seaplane base at Ostende and only the fourth reached Brugge to offload its bombs.

Two more HP O/100s arrived from Paris (Villacoublay) toward the end of April, allowing the first mission to be flown on 22 April. That day, three of the 'heavies' took off from Coudekerke at 15.00, each carrying fourteen 65 lb. bombs, to patrol the coastline at an altitude of 5,000 feet, with Flt. Cdr. Buss leading the formation. Seeing nothing of interest, the O/100s returned to base, bombs still aboard, after about 100 minutes. Next day came the first real operation, when three O/100s, seeking enemy shipping which was bombarding English coastal towns and the RNAS airfield at Manston, attacked five destroyers five miles off the coast between Blankenberge and Zeebrugge. The leading aircraft dropped its load of 65-pounders and scored one direct hit, apparently crippling the ship. A hostile seaplane was driven off, and all the aircraft returned safely. On board each O/100 were, in addition to the pilot and observer, two gunlayers rather than the one normally carried.

In the morning of 26 April 1917 three O/100s took off to carry out a bombing patrol over enemy shipping, but low cloud made the patrol ineffective, so the aircraft returned to base. After lunch, four aircraft took off for a similar mission, and at 14.40 spotted four enemy destroyers about seven miles (11 km.) north-east of Ostende. Each O/100 dropped eight 112 lb. bombs, but no direct hits were seen. Unfortunately O/100 3115, piloted by Flt. Sub-Lt. T. S. Hood, was pursued by a large seaplane and was shot down three miles (4.8 km.) north-north-west of Nieuport. It was last seen in the sea with its tailplane vertical, and was the first aircraft of its type to be lost to enemy action. Two French FBA flying-boat crews made a brave attempt at rescue under heavy fire, and although damaged one was able to take off with the wounded observer/gunlayer of the O/100, AM1 F. C. Kirby, on board. The other flying-boat was too badly damaged to take off, and eventually was towed to Ostende by an enemy destroyer. From the Handley Page, Flt. Sub-Lt. Hood drowned, while Ldg. Mech. R. H. Watson and AM2 W. C. Danzey (another gunlayer) were taken prisoner, but both died later. After that, no more daylight missions were flown by the O/100s, and the squadron concentrated on raiding Brugge docks and the canal connecting them with Zeebrugge, along part of which submarines were being repaired. At this stage the squadron relied on moonlight in order to carry out night raids, but training in the art of night-time bombing was beginning to produce results, and before long the crews became proficient in night-flying in all but the worst weather conditions. For the time, the weight of bombs dropped was quite impressive. On a raid on Ostende seaplane base during the night of 1/2 May, for example, sixteen 112 lb. (51kg.), eight 100 lb. (45.5 kg.) and sixteen 65 lb. (29.5 kg.) bombs were dropped by four aircraft, each of which thus carried a bomb-load of 908 lbs. (413 kg.).

The bomb dump at Coudekerke. [E.F.Cheesman]

A Sopwith Triplane and a Nieuport Type 24 Scout, parked beneath 3117, the first of 7 (N) Squadron's HP O/100s to arrive, emphasise the relative difference in size. Seen at Coudekerke on 4 March 1917, the pilot was Sq. Cdr. Spenser Grey, the other crew members being FSL Barker, O/O St.John, W/O Tolly and a Gunlayer. (E.F.Cheesman]

Meanwhile, Flt. Sub-Lt. L. A. Sands had blotted his copybook by crashing Short Bomber 9491 onto the roof of the 5 Wing CO's office on 29 April, writing off the aircraft in the process! Still attempting to put the German navy out of action, 7 (Naval) Squadron sent four Shorts and four O/100s to raid Brugge docks and the seaplane base on the mole at Zeebrugge on 9/10 May 1917, the first mission on which the O/100s had been used at night. Each Short Bomber carried six 65 lb. (29.5 kg.) and two 112 lb. (51 kg.) bombs, while the larger type carried ten 112-pounders. That night, visibility was poor, but anti-aircraft guns and searchlights were very active, precluding any firm claims of damage, although Flt. Lt. Brackley in Short 9338 was aware that his attempt to damage the Zeebrugge mole had not succeeded. Two more O/100s carried out solo bombing patrols over the sea that night. Enemy shipping received more attention from 7 (Naval) Squadron on 26 May, when three O/100s carried a total of 38 65 lb. bombs on a coastal patrol at an altitude of 7,000 feet east of Blankenberge. As no hostile vessels were sighted, the bombs were brought home. On this occasion, each aircraft carried four gunlayers, apart from one which included a supernumerary officer! Further raids on the seaplane base at Ostende were carried out on 27/28 and 29/30 May, and this month of increasing activity ended on 31 May/1 June with attacks on Brugge docks by four Short Bombers, Zeebrugge seaplane base by three O/100s and on the Ateliers de la Marine by another four of the newer type.

At the end of May 1917 German Gotha bombers began a campaign of daylight raids on south-east England, and in retaliation 7 (Naval) Squadron was tasked with attacking airfields used by the Gothas. On what was described in the squadron diary as a flight of inspection but was clearly a tactical reconnaissance, O/100 3126 flew over Belgium on 2 June, piloted by Sqn. Cdr. Babington, with Flt. Cdr. Digby, Flt. Lt. Jones, Flt. Lt. Sieveking and Flt. Sub-Lt. Thompson on board. During the night of 3/4 June, the squadron sent all ten Handley Pages and four Short Bombers, some with French navigators, to raid the airfield at Ghent (St. Denis Westrem). Three O/100s suffered engine trouble and aborted, but nine reached the target while one attacked the secondary target, Zeebrugge mole, but the fourteenth's efforts are not mentioned. Four tons of bombs were dropped and complete success was claimed. Next night, Brugge was the target for four Short Bombers and six O/100s.

Departure of the Short Bombers

It was soon found that the pens used by German submarines were constructed of heavily reinforced concrete, and two weapons had to be developed to overcome the problem, the 520 lb. (236 kg.) 'light case' bomb and the 550 lb. (250 kg.) 'heavy case' bomb. Only the HP O/100s could carry these new weapons, so the squadron's Short Bombers were withdrawn in June 1917, when eight more O/100s were taken on charge, bringing the total to eighteen. The squadron now found itself in the public eye, and on 6 June 1917 was visited by His Majesty the King of the Belgians, who was taken aloft by Wg. Cdr. C. L. Lambe DSO and Wg. Cdr. Spencer–Grey DSO in O/100 3116. On the same day, Flt. Cdr. Buss piloted 3119 with HRH Princess Alexandra of Teck aboard, accompanied by Wg. Cdr. Halahan and Flt. Lt. Digby. Two days later, Her Majesty the Queen of the Belgians was Sqn. Cdr. Babington's passenger in 3127, with Wg. Cdr. Lambe and Sqn. Ldr. Allsop in attendance. Visits were also made to the squadron by high-ranking officers of Allied High Command to inspect the O/100s, which at the time must have seemed the last word in heavy bomber aircraft. The remainder of June was taken up with practice flying, including formations, and on 27 June Sqn. Cdr. J. T. Babington DSO took command of the squadron.

"In Flanders Fields........"

From the end of June 1917 and during August and September the O/100s took part in the new Flanders offensive by making raids on ammunition dumps and on railways being used to move supplies to the Ypres sector during the second battle around that town. Missions also comprised raids on well-established targets such as the docks at Brugge and Ostende, with several airfields as extra objectives. Poor weather in the middle of July gave an opportunity for an experimental flight to be made so that a new parachute flare could be tried out.

In September 1917, adorned with early nose-art, Flt. Lt. Lance Sieveking's 3123 'Split Pin' was one of the O/100s detached to Redcar. [J. M. Bruce / G. S. Leslie collection]

Eight of 7 Squadron's aircraft (one complete flight) were handed over at the end of July to 7A (Naval) Squadron, which was formed at Coudekerke and placed under the control of 7 (Naval) Squadron until it was renumbered 14 (Naval) Squadron in December 1917. The transferred O/100s were replaced by newer aircraft, among them 3116, 3118, 3123, 3125 and 3127.

More unseasonable weather arrived early in August, and a raid on Zuidwedge sidings and Ghistelles airfield on 9/10 August was the only mission in the first half of the month. During the night of 15/16 August, however, a 'maximum effort' was mounted – an attack by seven O/100s of the combined 7 and 7A (Naval) Squadrons on Ostende station and another seven on Thourout station. The aircraft took off at about 00.45, but two soon returned with their bomb loads intact after losing their way, and another bombed the secondary target, Ghistelles airfield. When they returned from the night's task, three airmen learned that they had been recommended for the DSC for their efforts in previous raids. The recipients were Flt. Lt. J. F. Jones, Flt. Sub-Lt. W. A. Scott and Sub-Lt. P. Bewsher, while LM Gunlayer R. W. Bager was put forward for the DSM. Next night the same number of aircraft all went to bomb the railway junction at Thourout, this time in good visibility. A number of direct hits were claimed, fires were started and explosions were caused, including a violent one at an ammunition dump. In all, 189 bombs totalling 9 tons 3 cwt. (9.32 tonnes) were dropped. The remainder of August was devoted to maintaining the pressure on ammunition dumps, railway sites and docks, with bad weather intervening at the end. There was, however, sadness in the 7A Squadron mess when a complete crew was lost during the night of 25/26 August while raiding St. Denis Westrem airfield in aircraft 3137. Piloting the HP O/100 was Flt. Sub-Lt. H. H. Booth, who survived to be captured, as was gunlayer AM1 S. A. Canning, whilst the other crew member, gunlayer ACM2 P. M. Yeatman, lost his life. A similar pattern of missions continued during September, with a week's break in the middle of the month when once again weather conditions prevented any activity by 7 or 7A Squadrons.

Anti-submarine trials

In September one Flight of four of the squadron's O/100s was detached, returning to England to begin inshore anti-submarine patrols from Redcar in Yorkshire. One of the aircraft, 3127, was equipped with a six-pound (2.7 kg.) Davis gun for trials in counteracting the growing threat from submarines close to the coast. The gun was mounted on a bracket fixed to the nose of the HP O/100, and later a similar installation was fitted to the aircraft of 7A Squadron, but the experiment was not deemed successful and no further examples were so equipped. Little more is known about the activities of the detachment except that Flt. Lt. Lance Sieveking, who was to become a well-known figure in BBC Radio in later years, dropped bombs on submarines several times. His nickname, 'Split Pin', was also applied to aircraft 3123, from which he laid four 100 lb. bombs onto an enemy submarine which was stationary on the sea-bed three miles east of North Cheek on 21 September 1917. This Flight never rejoined the squadron but moved south on 2 October to Manston in Kent, where it first became 'A' Squadron and then 16 (Naval) Squadron.

Retaliation against the Naval squadrons' recent activity came in the form of heavy enemy raids on Coudekerke airfield between 23 September and 2 October. Nevertheless, 7 (Naval) Squadron took part in dropping nearly ten tons of weapons on the Thorout—Lichtervelde—Cortemarck railway triangle on 25/26 September. Four nights later, Flt. Cmdr. H. G. Brackley of 7A Squadron was captain of aircraft 3130, which flew 250 miles (402 km.) in bright moonlight to attack the Meuse railway bridge at Namur. Other targets for the squadron, though unsubstantiated, included Antwerp and Hoboken and an attempt is said to have been made to raid Köln (Cologne) on 20 October. Piloted by Flt. Lt. R. G. Gardner, with Flt. Sub-Lt. T. Terrell as observer and AC Beaver as gunner, this O/100 was forced to fly at 2,500 feet altitude for much of its mission due to deteriorating weather conditions. Over Düren, about twenty miles short of Köln, Terrell caught sight of a factory, which the pilot decided to attack instead of pressing on. Twelve 112 lb bombs were dropped, all but one falling on the factory. On the homeward flight the weather grew even worse, and the crew could not see the ground. The aircraft was then fired on when it crossed the trenches on the front line at 2,000 feet, but made a successful landing, without benefit of lighting, on a small airfield at Droelandt after seven hours thirty minutes in the air. It is certain, however, that on the night of 26/27 October 7A Squadron lost HP O/100 3122, which was shot down while bombing St. Denis Westrem airfield. The pilot, Flt. Sub-Lt. G. Andrews, and gunlayer LM G. A. Kent, were taken prisoner, but the third member of the crew, 2nd. Lt. W. W. Hutton, unfortunately lost his life.

During November 1917 bad weather and airfield conditions conspired to keep 7 (Naval) Squadron on the ground for much of the time. One of the few flights made was on 26 November, when Flt. Sub-Lt. Shoebottom took O/100 1459 on a bombing practice flight, with Sqn. Cdr. Chalmers and two ratings on board. A mechanical defect forced the aircraft down on the beach at Fort Mardycke, from where it was flown back to base next day. Missions in December were likewise few and far between. Sqn. Cdr. H. A. Buss took over as CO at the end of the month but on 20 February 1918 was posted to another squadron and was replaced by Sqn. Cdr. H. S. Adams.

It was the middle of February 1918 before 7 (Naval) Squadron could resume the task of raiding enemy submarine and seaplane bases and airfields. During their homeward flight from an attack on St. Denis Westrem airfield on 18 February, Flt. Sub-Lt. F. H. Hudson, the observer of O/100 3119, piloted by Flt. Lt. E. R. Barker DSC, saw an enemy Albatros D.V Scout aircraft, attacked it and sent it down out of control. The last of only four missions flown during the month was by three aircraft to Brugge docks on 25/26 February, after which there was yet more poor weather. Early in March 1918 the squadron's strength was reduced slightly when 15 (Naval) Squadron was formed at Coudekerke from personnel provided by 7 and 14 (Naval) Squadrons. Just before the formation of the Royal Air Force, 7 (Naval) Squadron was withdrawn from RNAS control and placed under the command of Sir Douglas Haig, but in the final days of Naval air operations, the squadron joined 14 (Naval) Squadron in a raid on Valenciennes and other rail targets.

O/400 B8811 [A2] airborne over strip-cultivated fields in 1919. [RAFM P4820]

Chapter 2: 207 Squadron RAF 1918 – 1920

Re-equipment with the HP O/400

During the evening of 31 March 1918 a memorable dinner was held by the officers of 7 (Naval) Squadron to mark the passing of the Royal Naval Air Service. Next day, 1 April 1918, the Royal Air Force came into being by the amalgamation of the RNAS and the RFC, and 7 (Naval) Squadron was renumbered to become 207 Squadron RAF. Displaying a typical 'press on' spirit, 207 Squadron took part in an attack on Zeebrugge on 11 April, after which HP O/100 3119 force-landed and overturned at Vlissingen in Zeeland. Determined not to let the aircraft fall into enemy hands, the crew set fire to it before being taken prisoner. Piloting the ill-fated O/100 was Capt. E. R. Barker DSC, with Lt. E. D. Hudson and 2nd Lt. D. C. Kinmond as the other members of the crew.

207 Squadron then withdrew from the fighting and on 22 April flew to Netheravon in Wiltshire to be re-equipped with the development of the HP O/100, the O/400. This newer aircraft, while of the same overall dimensions, differed from its predecessor in using 360 hp Rolls–Royce Eagle VIII or Sunbeam Maori engines in place of lower-powered versions, giving a speed of 97 mph (156 kph) instead of 76 mph (122 kph). Its normal bomb-load was sixteen 112 lb. (51 kg.) plus a few 25 lb. (11.4 kg.) bombs or, later one 1650 lb. (750 kg.) weapon. At Netheravon ten O/400 aircraft were issued to the squadron, which moved a few miles to Andover on 13 May before returning to France on 7 June to settle at Ligescourt, near Abbeville.

Back to France

At Ligescourt, the two-Flight squadron formed part of 54 (Night) Wing, Independent Air Force, which had its Headquarters at St. André-aux-Bois until 23 June, when it moved to Lambus. Accommodation at Ligescourt was sparse, officers and other ranks alike living in bell tents, only the more important members of the staff using wooden huts as offices. Due to the hectic life led by the squadron, and indeed by many other RAF units at the time, Royal Navy and Royal Flying Corps uniforms were still being worn and the officer ranks of the two services were still in everyday use.

Now commanded by Maj. G. L. Thompson DSO, 207 Squadron resumed its former task of night raids on railway centres, five such attacks being made between 22/23 June and 29/30 June before poor weather set in. Bapaume was the first target, followed by an eight-aircraft raid on Cambrai which produced five direct hits on the station area.

The cockpit of an HP O/400, illustrating the surprisingly comprehensive set of instruments. The airspeed indicator is marked to 160 mph and the altimeter to 15,000 feet, both extremely optimistic figures! [P. H. T. Green collection]

O/400 D5440, seen here in pristine condition, was used by 207 Squadron until written off in a crash-landing on 23 October 1918. The Midland Railway wagon in the background suggests that it was about to be dismantled for over-land shipment. [D. R. Neate via G. S. Leslie]

Bessoneau canvas hangars at Merheim, where 207 Squadron was based from January to May 1919, as part of the Army of Occupation. The aircraft visible are believed to be 'Ninaks' of 25 Squadron. [Capt. Chetwynd–Stapleton via Shuttleworth Collection and P. H. T. Green]

The next three raids in the series were on Tournai station and surrounding tracks. When the weather improved, 207 Squadron took to the air again on 13/14 July, nine aircraft scoring hits on the railway between Blanc Misseron and Thulin and another eight hits on a train, causing a major explosion. One O/400, C9665, failed to return from a raid on the same railway during the night of 18/19 July, but the crew, Lt. F. Kemp, Lt. W. Bayless and Lt. L. Rose, survived as prisoners of war. Maj. T. A. Batchelor took over from Maj. Thompson on 26 July but he was not destined to be in charge for long, as will be seen.

A new arrival, posted to 207 Squadron on 20 July 1918, was Lt. L. G. Semple, fresh from pilot training in England. While he was settling in, he and some new-found friends made use of the squadron tender (motor lorry) for a day out. "Today, ten of us went to Le Tréport, a seaside resort south of the mouth of the Somme," he wrote in his diary. "We passed through Abbeville, which has been very badly bombed......arrived at Le Tréport in time for an excellent lunch at the Grand Café de la Plage, which was very reasonable. After lunch, three others and myself went for a stroll around the town and then called at a little place where we knew there were some girls. Stayed there until 4.30 p.m. Kept a champagne cork in remembrance of same. Had tea and then on tender for home. When we were just out of the town, a tender from 151 Squadron [based at Fontaine-sur-Maye] passed us, as we had stopped owing to the fanbelt breaking. The chaps from 151 were laughing at us and cheered. Well, we put our engine right and raced after them, and after about six kilometres [3.7 miles] came up to them and passed them – our turn to laugh. They raced along after us, but we just kept them in our dust till they could stand it no longer, when they slowed up and we raced on.

We arrived in time for dinner, it being the farewell dinner for Major Thompson, our old CO. We had an excellent dinner and passed our menus round to be signed by everybody." After the dinner, the day's enjoyment ended on a much more serious note when some of the crews left to take part in a raid. "At 10.30 p.m. the eight machines set off on a raid into Germany," noted Lt. Semple. "I stood on the control stand with Lt. Brydon and saw them off, and then waited for their return after two and three quarter hours. Then turned in about 3 a.m."

A few days later, on 29 July, Lt. Semple flew in a Handley Page with Lt. Flavelle. His diary recorded that they "......flew to Desvres and then to Boulogne, thence back to Berck, down along the sands about fifty feet up, zooming at crowds – very good fun." Next day he wrote that the weather was too bad for a raid and there was very little to do, but at about midnight on 31 July he was called upon to take part in his first mission, an attack on Cambrai railway station by eight O/400s. This was, he found "......rather thrilling as a searchlight falls across the machine, hovers on it for a second and then falls away again. 'Archies' burst around and strings of balls of fire known as 'flaming onions' shoot up at one. If these were to wrap themselves around one's tail – well – Amen! On reaching objective, took a line of sight, dropped bombs and came home as fast as possible. Reached aerodrome about 3 a.m., then a meal and bed." Unfortunately, visibility was poor that night, so no results were seen. A further O/400 developed engine trouble and dropped its load at random just north of Bapaume before regaining the Allied lines and making a forced landing, without injury to the crew, at Englebelmer.

Sadly, on 7 August Maj. Batchelor was seriously injured

This unfortunate HP O/100, 3121 [A3], had been passed on to 7A (Naval) Squadron after service with 7 (Naval) Squadron by the time this photograph was taken on 12 December 1917. [J. M. Bruce & G. S. Leslie collection

Outside the Orderly Room at Merheim stand seven of 207 Squadron's officers, clad in a motley collection of uniforms. (Left to right) Purcell, Kennedy, Rowe, Armstrong, Clarke, Champness and Shaw. [C. Box]

Illustrating the rugged nature of the HP O/400, here one of 207 Squadron's aircraft is under tow at Ligescourt. Although most of the ground crew are in posed positions, another is peering around the port undercarriage leg! [via C. Semple]

in the forced landing of D5405 in a field after the aircraft had been badly damaged during a raid on Cambrai. Also on board were Lt. A. W. Robinson and Capt. C. Gilmour, who were only slightly hurt. For this raid, two of the six HP O/400s had each carried a 1,650 lb. bomb for the first time, though apart from a glimpse of five or six explosions results were not verifiable. Maj. Batchelor was then replaced as CO by Maj. G. R. Elliot. Unfortunately, after recovering from his injuries, Maj. Batchelor lost his life on 22 April 1919 when the O/400 he was piloting crashed at Weyhill just after taking off from Andover on a round-Britain navigation training flight .

On 8 August, as part of the Battle of Amiens, four of the squadron's aircraft were assigned to fly above the front line to muffle the sound of a thousand tanks which were massing before a major advance. In the event, the night was very misty, and only two of them took off. Both aircraft, which were piloted by Canadians, Lt. W. J. Peace in D5409 and Lt. G. A. Flavelle in C9657, droned up and down in dense fog for three hours. Subsequently, both men were awarded the DFC for tenacity, the official word for a mixture of boredom and terror! According to Lt. Semple's diary, "GHQ highly commended the squadron for last night's work. The attack was only made possible by the machines drowning the noise of the tanks. We heard today that we have made a great advance in the last twelve hours and are keeping the Huns on the run with the cavalry."

Lt. Semple took part in his second raid on 9/10 August, after enjoying afternoon tea at the British Officers' Club in Abbeville. His diary relates that, acting as the gunner, he took off (in D5404) at 10.45 p.m. to bomb Péronne. "Reached objective but weather extremely thick – so thick that one almost lost all sense of direction" he wrote. "After crossing the line on our way back, the port engine cut out. We endeavoured to keep the machine up on one engine, but as it was not running properly either, we gradually lost height. Seeing a landing T in front, we signalled to it the emergency call to let us land, and immediately the damned fools switched off their lights so that we could see nothing owing to a very thick ground mist. We gradually lost height and tried to land in a field with [the aid of] the Holt flare and the Aldis lamp, but as luck would have it we flew straight into the side of a sunken road and some trees. With a sickening crash we went through it and then bang into the ground. I jumped from the back seat immediately and extinguished the Holt flare, which was burning furiously and might have ignited something. Then I shouted to those in front. Hearing no reply I shouted again and again, gradually worming round to the front of the machine, which I found reduced to matchwood. Both in front were OK but the machine was right over, resting on the leading edge of the bottom plane. Engines were stuck in the ground

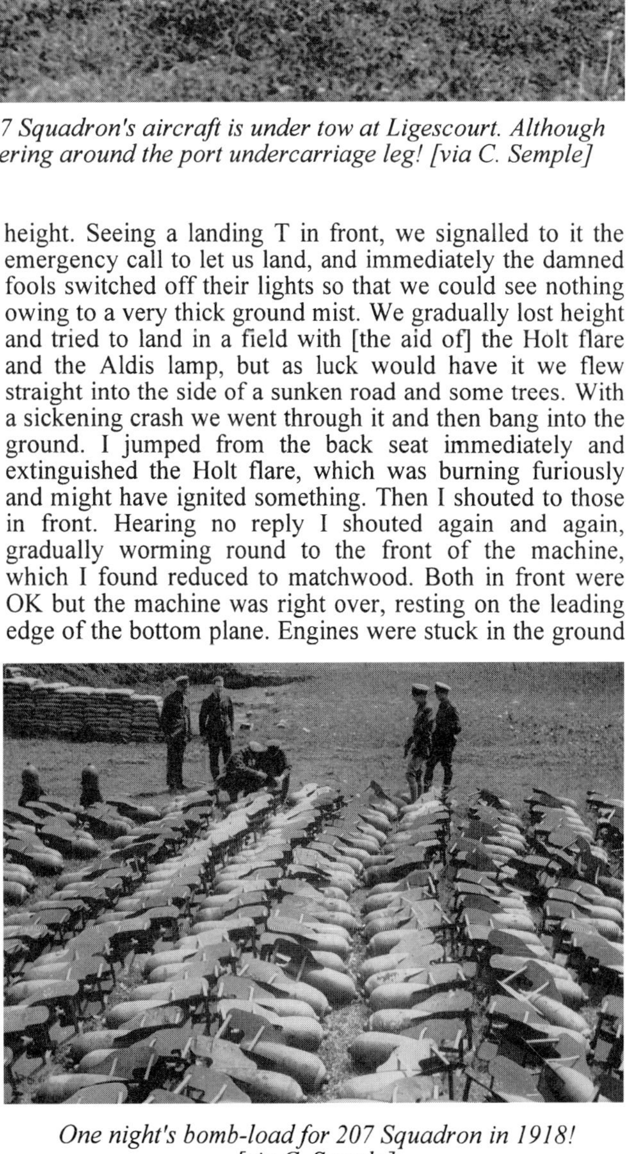

One night's bomb-load for 207 Squadron in 1918! [via C. Semple]

207 Squadron used this solid-tyred lorry during its time in France. [via C. Semple]

and generally smashed up. We then started walking to the searchlight and were met half way by some chaps from 102 Squadron, who took us into their mess, gave us cocoa and biscuits, and then to bed." After this frightening experience, Lt. Semple and his colleagues, Lt. R. J. Mesney (observer) and Lt. G. Roberts (the pilot), ate breakfast and lunch before returning to 207 Squadron, bringing souvenirs of their enforced absence. The site of the crash was near the village of Domart. Another aircraft, C9676, landed near Le Havre after the pilot, Lt. L. Roy, became lost.

Lt. Semple was next assigned aircraft D5422, in which he ferried another pilot to Marquise on 12 August before flying it back down the coast at an altitude of about a hundred feet, giving chase to an FE.2b fighter on the way! On the next three nights he took part in six raids on Péronne, and noted in his diary that since moving to Ligescourt the squadron had dropped over 400 tons of bombs, besides carrying out reconnaissance for the Army. At the weekend, he went into Abbeville and met three QMAAC girls in a café and had a "jolly time" with them. "They gave me a box of powder and a photograph of girls in their nightdresses," says the day's somewhat cryptic entry in his diary. However, he was again in trouble on the Sunday night, 18/19 August, when Mons–en–Chausée airfield was the target. "Started off on raid at 11.30" says his diary. "Very bright moonlight night, but heavy clouds coming up in the distance," he went on. "Reached the objective, dropped bombs and then turned to come back to

Aircrew in front of a Nissen hut, wearing the fur-lined flying clothing which must have been just about adequate for the task. Lt. Boshier, Lt. Semple's observer on the last mission flown by 207 Squadron in the First World War, is on the left. [via C. Semple]

'drome – caught in seven searchlights which held us in spite of turning and stunting. 'Archies' burst directly underneath us with a terrific pop. A Hun scout was on our tail, keeping the back gunner busy. Eventually getting into the clouds, we lost our way and after flying around for an hour and a half I managed to land in a small field [near Beauvais] without any lights at all at 3.15 a.m. Good landing! Some French peasants came up armed with double-barrelled rifles ready to shoot us had we been Huns. After having something to eat and getting to a telephone to find we could not phone up, we managed to start up the machine on our own and then started off at 6.45 a.m., struck the coast at Le Trèport at about 8.10 a.m. and landed at [Ligescourt] 8.40 a.m. Reported, had breakfast and went to bed at 10.00 a.m.; slept until dinner time. After dinner we heard that Lts. Peace and Flavelle had each received the DFC for their little stunt a few nights ago...... Some fellows from 151 Squadron came up – we had a 'blotto' night." And surely they deserved it!

After a raid by eight of the squadron's aircraft on Valenciennes on 22/23 August in good visibility, a major effort was put into sending fourteen loads of bombs to the same target two nights later. Ending the month, six O/400s attacked the town of Marquion and its station on 28/29 August and another one would have done so if the crew had been able to find it. Instead its bomb-load was released over a town thought to be Baralle.

'A LITTLE HELL(P) FROM THE R.A.F.' is the message on this bomb, being pushed on a rail trolley to the aircraft dispersal. [via C. Semple]

Although a shortage of pilots developed in September, the squadron's total bomb-load was as great as in August, many pilots flying up to six hours each night on two sorties. On 1/2 September the target for five O/400s was again Marquion, but this time some of the bombs in one aircraft failed to release, so the pilot flew out to sea off the mouth of the River Somme and after half an hour was able to shake more bombs free. He then landed at Ligescourt, where two groups of bombs fell out and exploded under the aircraft, presumably without injury to the crew, as no such record exists.

Places which the squadron had been bombing as recently as two weeks earlier, such as Bapaume and Peronne, were now in British hands, and the troops on the ground were still advancing. Soon after taking off to raid St. Quentin on 6/7 September, the engines of C9657, crewed by Lt. Semple, 2nd Lt. G. N. Hamilton and Pte. H. H. Phillips, began to overheat.

In his diary, Lt. Semple wrote "Lost height in an attempt to cool the engines. Reached lighthouse at 2,000 feet. Port engine missing. Fired colour of the night and also signalled the letter. 102 Squadron put out a landing searchlight for about one minute and just as I was about to make use of same, extinguished it. Both engines now

Officers of 207 Squadron sat for a group photograph at Ligescourt on 29 August 1918, a 'B' Flight O/400 behind them. In the centre of the front row was Maj.G. R. Elliott, who had become CO of the squadron three weeks earlier. [E. F. Cheesman]

failed. Forced landing in a plantation down the side of a steep hill. Complete crash. Both observer and I pinned under the wreckage – managed to extricate myself and released my observer, who was in great pain. Some men from 101 Squadron, which was also in vicinity, came along with ambulance and helped us. Took Hamilton along to No.2 Stationary Hospital, Abbeville, and then I came on to our own aerodrome. On Saturday morning took a crash party to the crash, near Famechon. Superintended removal of crash all day." Two raids had been made on St. Quentin during the night of Lt. Semple's misfortune, and Lt. J. W. Pearson recorded in his log book that he dropped a 1,650 lb. bomb successfully from 6,000 feet on his first trip and eight 112-pounders on the second.

Not allowing the war to make them too despondent, members of the squadron decided to stage a concert on 14 September, and many of them spent much of their off-duty time in writing and rehearsing the performance. Music and grease-paint were bought by Lt. Semple on a trip to Paris–Plage, and during the concert he sang popular tunes of the time, backed by an impromptu orchestra which used dummy instruments which made a sound similar to a kazoo.

Experiments with a new ground-based sound-locating instrument, regrettably not described in detail in Lt. Semple's diary, took place on 15 September, the 207 Squadron aircraft flying between Pernes and Bruay at a height of 10,000 feet. Another example of perseverance was recorded during the night of 16/17 September, when the only five pilots available dropped nearly eight tons of bombs on or near the airfield at Étreux, south of Valenciennes. Four nights later, the squadron lost another O/400, this time B8804, which crashed and overturned on returning from a raid, luckily without serious injury to the crew, 2nd Lt. L. R. Blacking, Lt. R. J. Mesney and Sgt. J. S. Taylor. Lt. Semple also took part, and landed his aircraft on half its undercarriage, the other half having been shot away, as had the propeller driving the generator for the W/T and part of the trailing edge.

In his diary entry for 20 September, Lt. Semple shows just how angry he was with the perceived foolhardiness of his superiors at Wing HQ. "Tonight we were sent on a raid under disgraceful conditions," he wrote, referring to an attack on Soultain airfield. "The weather report was – wind increasing from 40 to 60 mph with squalls of gale force; overcast; very heavy rain squalls. We crossed the lines, dropped our bombs and turned for home, going against the wind. [We were] caught in searchlights and only doing a ground speed of about 10 mph. Ran into storms and hail and gales and finally landed after three and a half hours of disgusting weather in a storm. Part of the time the machine was out of control, due to the extreme bumpiness of the weather. It was a disgusting shame that we were made to raid, and somebody should be made to suffer. My propellers were so damaged by rain and hail that they had to be changed." Nevertheless, a raid was flown in similar conditions a week later!

A second raid on Soultain was made next night, and a third on 22/23 September. This time, two of the four aircraft each carried a 1,650-pounder, one of which made a direct hit on a large hangar, causing a series of heavy explosions. Another airfield, Bisseghem, was chosen to be subjected to 207 Squadron's attentions on 25/26 September, but bad visibility prevented the four aircraft from finding it, so they dropped their bomb-loads elsewhere, one of them on searchlights near Lille.

On 23 September, while being repaired at 1 Aeroplane Supply Depot, C3490 was destroyed by an enemy aircraft. This run of bad luck involving aircraft ended on 29 September, when an engine of O/400 C9660 failed on take-off. In the hands of Capt. W. A. Scott, the aircraft fell from 100 feet to land on a haystack, complete with its load of bombs! Capt. Scott, Lt. T. G. Fawcett and gunlayer A. H. Vickers all escaped unhurt. That same night, Lt. D. Humphreys took off in D5433, with 2nd Lt. S. A. Garratt and Pte. J. A. Dornan, to take part in a raid on Grimcourt, but when a propeller came off before much distance had been covered, the pilot put the aircraft down on Famechon airfield, where it sustained severe damage. However, the fortunate crew walked away from the wreck unhurt.

Once the Wing officers had decided on a target for 207 Squadron to attack, that target seems to have been concentrated on until it had been thoroughly dealt with.

Thus the first five raids in October 1918 were on Aulnoye railway station, and although not all the O/400s despatched reached it, severe damage was done to the track and nearby ammunition dump by those that did, according to contemporary reports. Lt. J. W. Pearson confirmed this in his log book, remarking that the destruction of the dump was more by luck than judgement! Attacks on Mons station and Tournai junction soon followed, and then on 18/19 October a series of six concentrated attacks on Namur station began. Unfortunately, only one of the four O/400s on the first such raid reached its target, another two dropping their bombs on Charleroi instead and the fourth aborting with engine trouble. Matters were no better on 22/23 October when, of the three aircraft which took off, two aborted. Then came a period of poor weather, and it was 29/30 October before two O/400s made another attempt, but again bad weather prevented one aircraft from attacking.

In those days without radio facilities, the O/400s used a series of light beacons, referred to by the former Naval members of the squadron as lighthouses, as an aid to navigation. The beacon nearest Ligescourt was at Doullens, towards which the aircraft flew as soon as they became airborne, and overhead which the observers set course for their target. Homeward-bound crews pinpointed their position over the lighthouse before beginning their descent to Ligescourt. In the event of an enemy raid on Ligescourt while the 207 Squadron aircraft were airborne, the lighthouse flashed a warning message. Other lighthouses were used for navigational purposes, the relative positions being known to the observers on board the O/400s. On the ground, aids consisted merely of an illuminated landing T and Aldis lamp signals from a 'control officer' on duty in a sandbagged bunker. Thus was today's air traffic control system born! Such refinements did not help Lt. F. B. Champress, the pilot of D5440, which crashed on landing after the raid on Namur on 23 October and careered into the bomb store! Incredibly luckily, he and his crew, 2nd Lt. A. P. Roberts and NCO H. J. Taylor, walked away (or more likely ran!) uninjured.

Following the Allied troops as they advanced, 207 Squadron moved on 26 October 1918 to an airfield at Estrées-en-Chaussée, which had been in German hands a matter of a few days earlier and which 207 Squadron had raided. Lt. Semple, fresh from leave in England, wrote in his diary that the squadron's new base was in "a ghastly position." As far as he could see, not a single house was left standing within thirty miles, and the desolate country was full of water-filled shell holes and abandoned trenches. Whole villages and towns seemed to have been blasted to the ground. "The sad sight of a little white cross sticking up by the roadside marks the lonely grave of some poor lad who fought for his country. All these graves are marked by the Graves Commission and are located so that the relatives may, after the war, visit the graves of their loved ones." No sooner had the move been completed than O/400 D4564 was wrecked when taking off from a field into which it had force-landed with engine trouble earlier. The two crew, 2nd Lts. P. C. Crovat and A. Wichelow, suffered some injuries. On 29 October Lt. A. J. Court, apparently flying solo, managed to stand D4569 in a trench when an engine failed on take-off, but he was unhurt. Another loss to the squadron was Lt. Semple's usual O/400, D5422, which crashed on landing on Famechon airfield on 1 November after attacking Namur, the fourth of the series of raids on that target. The crew, comprising Capt. J. S. Harvey, 2nd Lt. G. N. Hamilton and Sgt. L. C. Boshier, escaped without injury.

Lt. Semple found himself dropping sixteen 112 lb. bombs on Namur's railway junction on the evening of 4 November in company with six more 207 Squadron aircraft. Two of these aircraft returned early with engine trouble, but although high winds were blowing the crews found alternative mounts and set off again, this time successfully! Next day Lt. Semple paid an off-duty visit to Amiens, reached only after a frightful journey. He and his friends saw many of the results of war – crippled tanks, salvage heaps, masses of white crosses, shell holes, derelict buildings and piles of rubble, but an incongruous touch was added in his diary's record of the day's activities. "Had a delightful lunch [in the] hotel next to the Banque de France. Hors d'ouvres, fish, chicken, sweet and coffee – 25 francs and really worth it – most delightfully cooked."

By now, hostilities were drawing to a close, but to make quite sure of this six of the squadron's O/400s dropped just over four tons of bombs on Liege station during the night of 9/10 November, scoring twelve direct hits. In the final raid of the war, on 10/11 November 1918, six O/400s of 207 Squadron paid a final visit to Namur, causing seventeen direct hits. Among those taking part was Lt. Semple, who wrote in his diary "Owing to dud engines I was late in starting, and consequently bombed an hour and a half after everybody else. Very good shooting obtained......gave my observer, Boshier, control on the way home. Went to bed about 11 p.m. At 1 a.m. [on 11 November] news came per wireless that the Armistice had been signed. Cessation of hostilities from 11 a.m. Beautiful news. Lighted a tin of petrol and we kicked it all round the camp. This morning we all had a jolly good drink. Sent somebody to Rouen to buy as much as possible. Have discovered that I was the last pilot to drop bombs on enemy territory during this war. We drove into Amiens tonight and had dinner and lots of champagne......drove around the town firing Verey lights. Jolly fine peace celebrations. Arrived back at camp at 2.30 a.m. [12 November] with a few souvenirs." And who could blame them?

Among the weapons used during the last days of the war were twenty-two 1,650 lb. bombs, which were of such size that they had to be carried below the fuselage of the aircraft. These formed part of the total of 587 tons of bombs dropped by the squadron and its Naval predecessor during the course of 120 raids. Fortunately, since the formation of the RAF in April 1918, not one member of 207 Squadron had lost his life, although several had been injured in crashes and other mishaps. The reason for this is most likely the lack of enemy night-fighters and inaccurate anti-aircraft fire.

The Army of Occupation takes over

207 Squadron moved forward on 1 December 1918 to Carvin, near Lille, and then a month later, on 1 January 1919 took up residence in Germany, at Merheim near Cologne, where it came under the command of the Army's 2nd. Brigade as part of the Army of Occupation. Work now consisted of communications flying, to the apparent pleasure of a number of Army staff officers, who soon realised that aircraft were an exciting and efficient means of transport, and also the task of flying mail for the Army Postal Services.

By 1917 the latter had become highly organised, and the staff prided themselves on being able to deliver mail to and between any units of the BEF in France within 24 hours. Problems had arisen, however, when mines began to break loose in the English Channel and the Germans intensified their submarine operations, factors which combined to interfere with cross-Channel shipping carrying military mail. An NCO in the APS, Sgt. E. E. Gawthawn, had submitted a scheme for the use of aircraft, but it was rejected, as the RFC was by then having difficulty in maintaining air supremacy.

After the end of hostilities, the APS had great difficulty in keeping up with the Army of Occupation, and for a week an experimental air service was flown between Le Cateau, Dinant and Marche. After much discussion, it was decided that two internal air mail services would be commenced on 16 December 1918, and a third service, connecting with England, would begin later.

Inaugural flights were made by D.H.9As of 55 and 57 Squadrons and a sole HP O/400 of 216 Squadron. This was rigged to carry sixty bags of mail, with space allowed for a crew of four. Delivery was to be made at some destinations by dropping the mail by parachute, the ordinary mailbags being placed inside outer bags which were strengthened by wooden battens. 207 Squadron joined in on 5 January 1919 and was allocated to Service A, flying from Marquise to Valenciennes, Namur and Cologne (Bickendorf). The latter sector became a night operation on 10 January, cross-Channel mail having arrived at Marquise at 19.00 by road from Boulogne. On 2 February, however, the squadron ended its participation in the scheme for the time being.

Cyril Box joined the squadron in mid-January 1919 as a pilot after service with 115 and 100 Squadrons. Many years later he recalled that squadron HQ was in the casino at Merheim, from where it was only a short walk to the airfield. "We had to report every morning for routine duties, but the weather was bitterly cold and very little flying was done by our HP O/400s. One day a message came over from Bickendorf that if we had any pilots who could fly FE.2bs they should report there to ferry some of these 'pusher' machines to St. Omer. I had last flown an F.E.2b at Stonehenge during training, but we delivered them safely. We returned to Cologne from Calais in the 'Cologne Express', a converted hospital train which was very popular with anyone going on leave." Even after hostilities had ended, aircraft were still written off in accidents, as on 5 April, when O/400 C9676 hit a goal-post when taking off at Guines.

In April, 207 Squadron rejoined the air mail scheme, and with 216 Squadron now operated Service A from Marquise to Bickendorf and to Aulnoy. Although the RAF maintained that an HP O/400 could carry as much mail as ten D.H.9As, the APS was disappointed with results shown by the Handley Pages. It was claimed that when the O/400s were unable to fly for any reason, the mail had to go by train and was thus severely delayed instead of being speeded up. So at this point it was decided that Service A would be restricted to carrying RAF mail only.

Maj. Elliot left the squadron on 5 May and was replaced by Maj. M. H. Nethersole, five days before the squadron's five O/400s flew in formation to Hangelaar, a few miles from Bonn, where the squadron remained for the next three months. Cyril Box went there, and recalls that the personnel were accommodated in huts and the aircraft in canvas hangars. "This was a big change from Merheim, where I had been lucky with a very friendly family in a good billet", he said. "The weather was now good for flying, and patrols were more frequent, with occasional longer flights to St. Inglevert. One day I was sent up for a height test and reached a ceiling of 11,400 feet, about the limit for the O/400. My last flight was in July 1919, and shortly afterwards I received my demobilisation papers, ending my time in the RFC and RAF. I could not have finished on a happier note than my eight months with 207 Squadron in Germany, which I remember as one of the most interesting periods of my life." He was right about the altitude – the official maximum was 8,500 feet!

To aid the intrepid pilots flying the air mail services, 'compass stations' – direction-finding stations in later parlance – were established at Marquise, Bickendorf and other sites and at each airfield a balloon was tethered and marked with the airfield name. Wireless telegraphy was used extensively, with transmissions on 260 metres (1154 KHz) and reception on 700 metres (428.5 KHz). As an emergency back-up, homing pigeons were carried for release in the event of a forced landing. However, 207 Squadron's short period of flying the mail ended on 9 May 1919, and the whole scheme gradually tailed off until the APS reverted to more conventional transport in August. This left 207 with a diminishing task, and it was clear that the end was close.

On 22 August 207 Squadron pilots sadly flew their HP O/400 aircraft to St. Inglevert to be taken over by 100 Squadron, which was soon intended to embark for the Mediterranean region. In the event, that move never took place, as on 12 September the nucleus of 100 Squadron found itself at Baldonnel in Ireland. Remaining 207 Squadron personnel made their way via Tangmere to Croydon, where they arrived on 8 October. There they stayed until on 16 January 1920 the few remnants of a proud unit moved to Uxbridge, where the squadron was officially disbanded four days later.

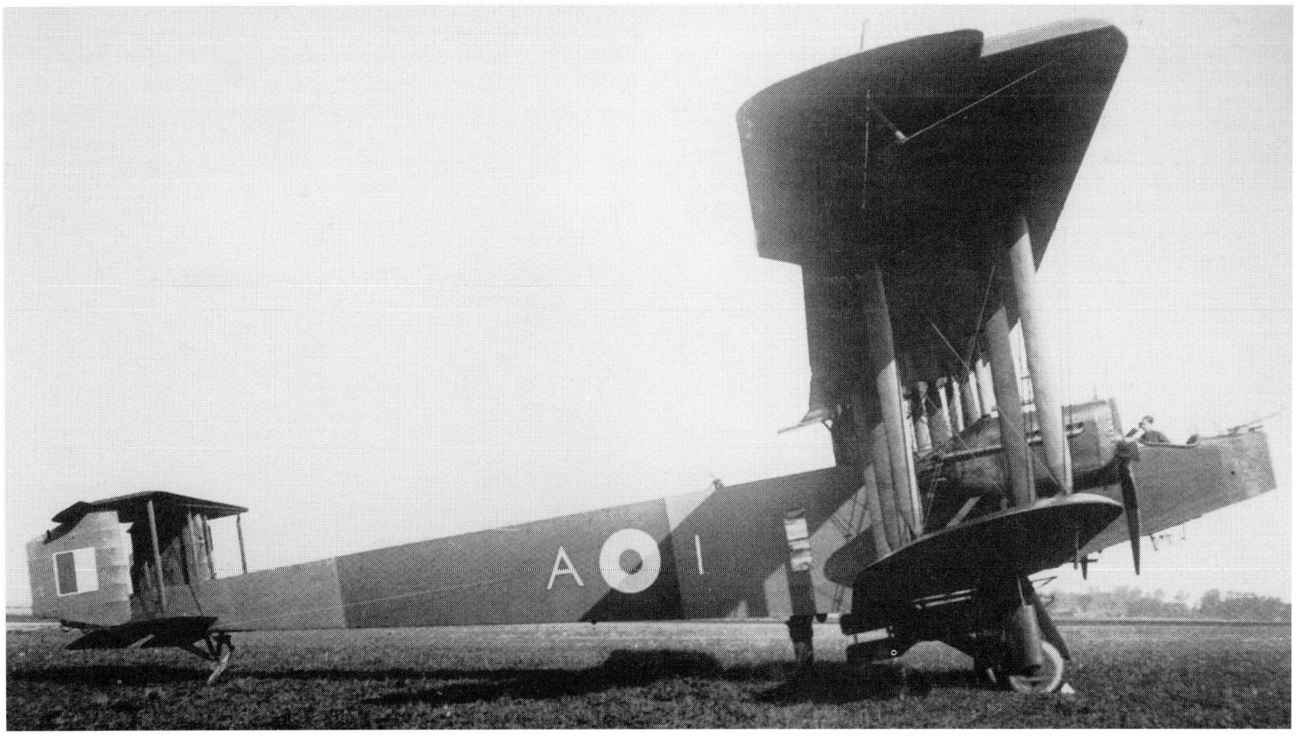

This picture, taken at Ligescourt in 1918, illustrates the method of clinging a 1,650 lb. bomb between the undercarriage legs of a HP O/400, in this case 207 Squadron's A:1, which seems to be lacking a serial number. [E. F. Cheesman]

Tanned members of 207 Squadron pose for the camera at Gebeit just before beginning the long voyage home in the TS Somersetshire in 1936. [D. H. Chandler]

Chapter 3: The inter-war years to 1937

Re-equipment

In the years immediately after the end of the First World War, the task of the Royal Air Force, by then very much a shadow of its former self, was principally to deal with any unrest which might develop in the Colonies or other areas for which Great Britain accepted responsibility. Chosen as the principle light bomber aircraft for this 'policing' role was the Airco D.H.9A, commonly known as the 'Ninak', which had been developed during the latter period of the war from the D.H.9. Problems with the planned Beardmore–Halford–Pullinger engine, which failed to attain its anticipated 300 hp, prompted consideration of the American-built Liberty engine of 400 hp. Before an example could be obtained, a Rolls-Royce Eagle of 375 hp was installed in Westland-built D.H.9 airframe B7664 and flown in March 1918, and a similar engine was flown in C6350 by Airco at Hendon. In addition to the different engine, radical alterations were made to the D.H.9 design to provide a greater wing area. An initial batch of Liberty engines arrived in March 1918, production of the D.H.9A began, and by the end of August 288 'Ninaks' had flown, 579 more following during the next three months.

In compliance with the policy mentioned above, only two squadrons of D.H.9A aircraft were allocated to the RAF in the United Kingdom in the early days. First to be formed was 207 Squadron, which came back to life on 1 February 1920 at Bircham Newton in Norfolk, an airfield which had been opened in 1916 for training purposes. In command of the squadron was Sqn. Ldr. Arthur W. Tedder, an experienced officer who was destined to make a considerable name for himself twenty-odd years later. He had previously served with 274 Squadron, which had been flying Handley Page V/1500 bomber aircraft from Bircham Newton until disbandment a couple of days earlier.

A nucleus of personnel for the re-born 207 Squadron also came from 274 Squadron. Many of the ground crew airmen were not at all happy, as their relationship with their previous CO had become very strained. They gathered in a mutinous frame of mind, and Tedder, who had met a similar revolt while in Egypt, determined to bring the affair to a rapid close. A meeting was arranged, and in a loud voice he told the men that he would give them five minutes to return to their huts before he would discuss their grievances. Clearly reluctant, they moved away, whereupon

D.H.9As at Bircham Newton in 1922: J556, which ditched while on the San Stephano detachment later that year; H3587; and J559, which was also lost in the waters of the Bosphorus in 1922. [via G. A. Jenks and R. C. Sturtivant]

'Ninak' H142 awaiting packing and shipment to San Stephano in 1922 for use by 207 Squadron in the Turkish campaign. H142 later saw service with 84 Squadron. [J. M. Bruce & G. S. Leslie collection]

Sqn. Ldr. A. W. Tedder (on left, in breeches) and one of his Flight COs at San Stephano in 1922. [Quadrant Picture Library / Flight International]

Tedder kept his promise and spoke to each of them before asking for a deputation to bring him the complaints in writing. Among the items were 'proper and just punishment for crime' and 'an enquiry into NCOs' meals in the cookhouse'. Tedder then called the entire personnel of the Station together in the airmen's mess and after some minor problems had been sorted out he was able to deal with all the complaints in an atmosphere of goodwill. From that event developed a happy and efficient squadron with high morale.

The Station had certainly been neglected, so much so that on 20 March Mr. N. P. Jodrell MP stood up in the House of Commons to point out that leaking buildings could have led to an epidemic of pneumonia had the previous winter not been a mild one. For the Air Ministry, Maj. Tryon replied that there was every hope that something would be done by the following winter, for the sake of the personnel. Appropriate action must then have been taken, as conditions at Bircham Newton seem to have improved.

Sqn. Ldr. Tedder's period of command of 207 Squadron, and indeed his life, was almost cut short on 1 August 1922 during an exercise involving bombing the radio-controlled HMS *Agamemnon* to discover whether aircraft could cripple Naval vessels, in the same way that Gen. Billy Mitchell had so effectively demonstrated in the United States on 21 July 1921. Flying in a formation of

Conditions in which the 'Ninaks' had to be serviced while at San Stephano were bad even in fair weather. The only shelter was provided by canvas hangars with earth floors. This one has blown down. [Quadrant Picture Library / Flight International]

'Ninaks' from Gosport, Tedder acted as bomb-aimer, which involved laying prone and pulling on strings attached to the legs of the pilot, Flt. Lt. A. D. Pryor, to indicate the direction to fly for an accurate approach to the target. They spotted *Agamemnon* 12,000 feet below them at about 15 miles (24 km.) off shore, but as they approached the target at 8,000 feet the engine of 'Ninak' J559 failed. There was nothing for it but to 'ditch', but as they came down a wave-crest tore away the undercarriage, causing the 'Ninak' to settle into the trough between two waves, and projecting the pilot out of the cockpit. Tedder, however, remained in the aircraft, and the pilot soon joined him. They were quickly rescued unhurt by a destroyer before the aircraft sank, but Tedder was blamed for the loss of the precious bomb-sight.

The Turkish adventure

At the end of August 1922 Turkish forces launched a major offensive against Greece in an attempt to recover land lost at the end of the First World War. Somewhat overcome by these hostilities, Greece asked for an armistice on 4 September, as Turkish troops advanced toward Smyrna (today known as Izmir). Five days later, all Greeks had been removed from that town, ending their presence on the eastern seaboard of the Aegean. A thousand citizens died as the Turks sacked the town. The rebel Turkish leader, Mustapha Kamel, stated on 19 September that his forces would not advance on the Allied neutral zone if Turkey could be assured that eastern Thrace would be handed over to it.

January 1923 at San Stephano – mud everywhere and a hangar in danger of imminent collapse. [RAFM B.272]

It was to counter the possibility of escalating trouble that four squadrons of the RAF were selected to be sent as a peace-keeping force to San Stephano, on the northern side of the Bosphorus near Istanbul. One of those squadrons was 207, and on 19 September Sqn. Ldr. Tedder received instructions to prepare for shipment overseas nine days' later. Rapid action was taken, and after a visit from the AOC on 23 September an advance party consisting of Warrant Officer Brown and ten other ranks, under the command of Flt. Lt. Trevethan, left on 26 September to board ship at Liverpool. Remaining squadron personnel were addressed by Wg. Cdr. Prettyman on 27 September and listened to a letter of encouragement from Lord Trenchard before leaving next day for Liverpool via London, where they were given an official send-off by AVM Higgins. Sqn. Ldr. Tedder and eight of his officers, together with the advance party, sailed on SS *Eboe* on 29 September, while twelve more officers took to the water next day on SS *Khartoum*. Embarkation was carried out swiftly and smoothly, and on the voyage efforts were made to sort out the hastily-loaded stores, but this was found to be impossible due to the arrival of a relief stores officer who was not of course acquainted with the contents of the crates. While the two ships were on their way to Turkey,

'Ninaks' of 207 Squadron 'A' Flight at San Stephano during the Turkish campaign. Nearest the camera is F2818, then E8681, and third in line is F1616. [J. M. Bruce & G. S. Leslie collection]

two officers had travelled overland to make things ready at San Stephano, where they arrived on 6 October.

Meanwhile, the Allies had on 23 September promised eastern Thrace to Turkey, whose forces arrived at the boundary of the neutral zone at Chanak, on the Asian side of the Dardanelles, on 29 September. This was a situation fraught with danger, as the Turks established observation posts which could easily have been turned into gun positions threatening shipping in the Dardanelles. In London, members of the Cabinet met military chiefs that same day and decided that the position was intolerable. Orders were sent to Lt. Gen. Sir Charles Harrington KCB DSO, the British commander, to insist on an immediate halt to the advance on the neutral zone by Kamel's troops. This was complied with on 1 October, and two days later talks between Turkey and Greece began.

SS *Eboe* arrived at Constantinople (now Istanbul) on 10 October after unloading vehicles at Maidos for 4 Squadron, and SS *Khartoum* docked the following day. The political situation eased somewhat when the Treaty of Mudania was signed by Turkey and the Allies a week later, recognising the right of Turkey to occupy eastern Thrace. Greece signed the Treaty on 15 October, but as there remained a good deal of uncertainty on the future of the area it was decided that the RAF squadrons would become established and remain for the time being.

When the time came to unload the stores from the ships' holds it was found that the crates were poorly stacked, no lighters or flat-bed vehicles were available and there were no stevedores. Furthermore, no facilities for lifting heavy packing-cases existed at the airfield. Hangars were of the canvas-covered Bessoneau type, which were quite unsuitable for the prevailing wintry conditions. In any case, the canvas sheeting was in one hold, the steel framing in another and the screws and pickets in yet another! Some of the equipment and stores were inextricably mixed with those of 25 Squadron, which had travelled on the same ships. All this was not the fault of the squadrons but of the Air Ministry, who had arranged for the packing and loading of the material. Nevertheless, the airmen worked with great keenness, Sgt. Maj. [sic] Brown being notable for his energy and cheerfulness. By 26 October most of the work had been done, and Lt. Gen. Harrington and Gp. Capt. Fellowes paid a visit of inspection. Letters of appreciation from both officers were soon received by the squadron; in his somewhat cumbersome missive Lt. Gen. Harrington said "I was impressed by the workmanlike appearance of 207 Squadron. Just fresh from on board ship, there was evidence of that keen desire to get their machines in the air, and that pleasing spirit of friendly rivalry and keenness. It was a pleasure to see the efforts of all the officers and men, all devoted to getting the machines ready. Whatever may be the future, it will always be clear to me that in recent time of crisis the Royal Navy and Royal Air Force sent their very best to Constantinople to help me."

That letter was probably the result of an unofficial competition between 207 and 25 Squadrons, in which each tried to make its aircraft ready first. Such a contest seems hardly fair, because 25 was flying Sopwith Snipes, a smaller aircraft than the D.H.9A, and in theory won by half an hour. Pointing out that the Snipes were still unarmed and that a fighter without guns was like a tortoise without a shell, Sqn. Ldr. Tedder protested. This was an appropriate comment, as large numbers of tortoises were seen on the airfield. Some of the airmen organised betting on their racing form, which was one way of taking the men's minds off the perpetual mud, the centipedes and the vicious horse-flies which made their lives miserable.

"These little things.............

Owing to the fragile nature of the hangars, the 'Ninaks' were picketed in the open, which caused some deterioration of the fabric covering, as no dope was available. In order to carry forced-landing kits as Wing HQ had authorised, special 'cupboards' were fitted to the aircraft fuselages, while spare wheels were carried underneath. From the first, keeping the 'Ninaks' in the air was a considerable problem. A great deal of difficulty was experienced with propeller blades, which had to be changed after a few flying hours, a five-hour task. Brass sheathing covering the leading edge was found to split easily and sometimes the blade itself cracked. Spare accumulators were in short supply, and undercarriages needed regular adjustment due to the strain imposed on them when taxying over the muddy airfield. Small quantities of water were found in many carburettors and in fuel tanks, all of which had to be drained at frequent intervals.

Nevertheless, all the aircraft had been air-tested and pronounced fit for use by 3 November. Next day 207 Squadron flew its first operation from San Stephano, a photographic reconnaissance of the road from Dodula to Teperan by two aircraft, one taking photographs and the other escorting. However, the camera jammed, resulting in an unsuccessful mission. When weather conditions allowed, the squadron carried out navigational and bombing training exercises, including attacks on a target moored in the Sea of Marmara.

Adding to the problems was the condition of the airfield, which remained muddy and soft, a third of the area being more or less permanently unusable. A violent storm hit San Stephano, doing considerable damage; the canvas on two hangars split and another two were wrecked when their steel framework gave way. Many bell tents were blown down, and the generator providing electric lighting was put out of action. In the domestic area a drainage system, duckboard walkways and cinder paths improved living conditions a little. The officers' mess was set up in a decrepit building called the Hotel Splendide, from the balconies of which the officers could, if they wished, dive into deep water. The bedding provided was riddled with bed-bugs until it was given a rare airing outside the hotel!

Although AC2 S. Riches was not a member of 207 Squadron, his personal diary provides a heart-felt record of life at San Stephano in the winter of 1922/23. His entry for 13 December is typical. "More snow. Scraped some of the mud out of the tent and dug the trench deeper. At 23.30 some of the officers [began] carol singing outside their hut. Threatened to pull the hut down." Quite what he meant by the last remark is open to speculation! Next day he recorded that there was "......more snow, **** it. Strengthening the hangars. French officer and his pusher [sic] came round to have a look at the English 'buses'." On 17 December he paid a visit to 'Stiff Annie' (San Stephano!) and had two suppers. Christmas Day featured a comic football match. "Some game" was his comment. "Dinner was bloody awful, but as good as can be expected under the circs."

Better weather in early January 1923 gave a little respite to the hard-working ground crews, and twenty-two days were suitable for flying, although the month's total was only 65 hours and 40 minutes. On 19 January the long-suffering AC2 Riches wrote in his diary "What a hell of a blizzard! Been shovelling snow off the top of a hangar." Next day, though, he and some mates visited Constantinople in the afternoon but wished they hadn't after falling into several snowdrifts. By now it was so cold that the aircraft engine oil froze, and despondency was rife. That day, Riches wrote "Why the devil don't they have a war or something to liven us up?"

To encourage practice in low-level bombing, a competition was held among the squadrons based in Turkey and cups were presented to the winners of squadron and individual contests. Bombing was carried out at an altitude of four feet (1.2 metres), Flg. Off. Ely claiming the lowest average error, 4.3 yards (3.9 metres) over eight runs.

"..........are sent to try us"

Turkey refused on 7 February to withdraw its warships from off Smyrna, and it was revealed that ten thousand Ottoman Greeks were being held in miserable conditions in Scutari to await deportation to Greece. A warning was issued to Turkey on this subject. Presumably on the assumption the 207 Squadron's aircraft might have to fly longer distances than usual, five of them were fitted with auxiliary fuel tanks, which caused no little dissatisfaction to their pilots, who complained about excessive weight and bad visibility. Two forced landings in February were caused by the adapter cock on the water pump becoming loose, and two more aircraft were badly damaged on landing, one of them being J557, which was written off on 5 February. In addition, J556 was lost when it ditched near HMS *Iron Duke* sixteen miles (26 km.) south of San Stephano on 22 February. Flying time for the month was only 37 hours 50 minutes.

Sqn. Ldr. Tedder's log book reveals that he flew only infrequently during his time at San Stephano, and then usually as a passenger. A cryptic entry for 28 November 1922 records 'Aircraft F2818. Towards Chanak with GC. WO owing to BF forced landing'. If this implies that the aircraft was written off he was wrong, as he flew it again during the following February! He flew a few patrols of the Neutral Zone, including one on 2 June 1923 in 'Ninak' H3501, and a couple of mock attacks on naval targets.

Conditions at San Stephano improved considerably during March, and a successful air display was held, though who attended it is a mystery! The airfield was fully serviceable in April, but flying was restricted by a shortage of aircraft due to the recent spate of forced landings. Squadron members were saddened on 21 April by the death from typhus of the squadron's medical officer, Flt. Lt. H. W. Street MB, in Istanbul, where he had been working among Greek refugees. Three days later Flg. Off. G. H. D. Gossip lost his life in an accident, the circumstances of which are not recorded.

During April 1923 the squadron carried out an experiment with the Royal Navy to determine whether the blast of a 112 lb. (51 kg.) bomb would detonate the warhead of a moving torpedo or divert it from its course. Two torpedoes were fired, but two bombs which were dropped very accurately failed to explode. A second attempt was made a week later, when one bomb with a two-and-a-half second delay was dropped onto a torpedo from 150 feet (45 m.) and appeared to explode as the torpedo

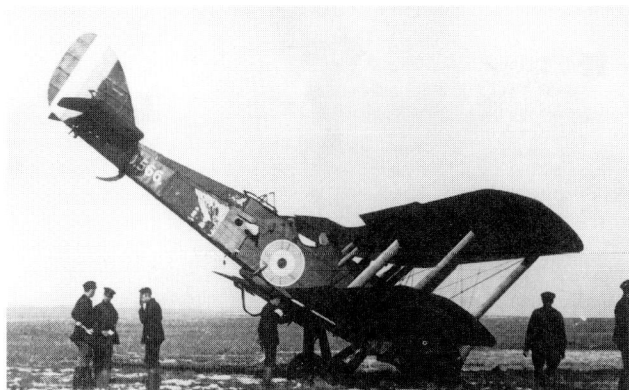

D.H.9A J566 nosed over on landing at San Stephano during the squadron's detachment there in 1922 but survived to fly again. [RAFM P.14797]

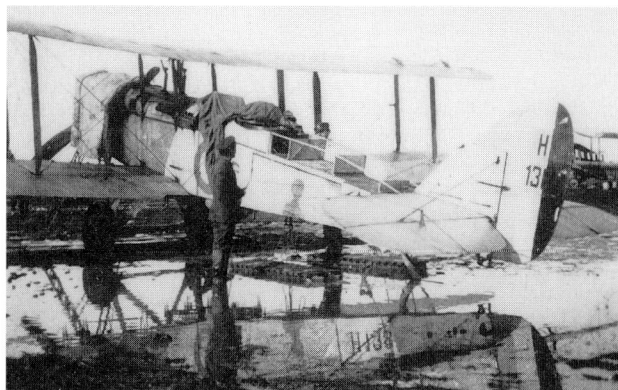

Adding a locker to the upper fuselage of 'Ninak' H138 of 207 Squadron at San Stephano in atrocious conditions. [RAFM B.272]

Appalling conditions at San Stephano during the winter of 1922/23. The canvas-sheeted hangar seems to have given up the struggle. [Quadrant Picture Library / Flight International]

passed six feet away. The torpedo ran on for a few yards before surfacing, leaking oil and smoking. At this point the experiment was stopped.

Summertime routine began on 1 May, when the working hours became 07.15 to 12.00, later extended to 13.00. An inspection of the whole Wing was made by AVM Ellington, who witnessed ceremonial drill which, considering the rough ground on which it was carried out, was regarded as "quite good." On 26 May, Turkey and Greece reached a settlement of their conflict, and it began to seem that the RAF could soon go home.

In June split-axle undercarriages were fitted to some of the 'Ninaks', a move much approved by the mechanics! New wings were fitted to aircraft which had stood in the open all winter, and to add to the work tail skids were in constant need of attention due to the rough, and now hard, surface of the airfield. On 4 June 'Ninak' H19 was destroyed when it spun in after the pilot lost control. This was attributed to the W/T operator, AC2 A. Smith, catching his foot between the dual control and the camera fitting. Smith was unhurt but the pilot, Flg. Off. E. S. Edwards, was seriously injured.

Apart from a congratulatory message resulting from reconnaissance carried out by 'B' and 'C' Flights of the squadron, there was little activity during June and July, but on 24 July a treaty was signed at Lausanne between the Turks and the Allies whereby the Aegaen area lost to Turkey would be restored to that country. This event would mean that British forces could be withdrawn from the area, to the great delight of most of them!

Goodbye to Tedder

Sqn. Ldr. Tedder, who had been 207 Squadron's CO from the time of re-formation in 1920, left on 6 August to go on a Naval Staff College course and was replaced by Sqn. Ldr. V. Gaskell–Blackburn DSC AFC. Tedder had become known as easy-going but efficient, but a man to whom not many people could become close. He had a way of encouraging those under him to want to do things, one of the signs of a true leader. His successor was unique in sporting a beard, and had an intense aversion to walking anywhere.

The main task in August was to begin the process of evacuation to England, and the only operation was a photographic mosaic of Chatalja lines, which had to be attempted four times owing to incomplete information being given to the pilot by the photographic section. Although flying ceased on 23 August more flying was done that month, ironically, than in any other month since the squadron arrived in Turkey!

Orders came from Wing HQ to pack half of 'B' Flight's aircraft and all of 'C' Flight's but to leave 'A' Flight intact for a possible Boundary Commission photographic scheme. As a considerable amount of preparation had begun as soon as the Lausanne Treaty looked likely to be ratified, it was not too difficult to complete the task in good time. Cases had been prepared in readiness, and the intrepid Sgt. Maj. Brown was in charge of a party which worked between 06.00 and 13.00 from 23 to 28 August to pack them. Before the squadron's departure on its way back to 'Blighty', the commander of Turkish troops in Constantinople, Selaheddin Adil Pasha, threw a garden party for officers of the British and Allied forces, and Flt. Lt. L. M. Elworthy was the lucky officer who represented 207 Squadron. Whether his personal charisma or his alcoholic capacity was the criterion for choosing him has been lost in the mists of time!

Many lessons of future value were learned from the experiences of 207 Squadron in Turkey, the most important being the provision of a proper mobile stores organisation. Setting aside the poor planning which had taken place (or had not taken place) before the detachment left the UK, it seemed to Tedder that the idea of a squadron transporting a three-months' supply of stores effectively prevented it from being mobile. What was needed was a mobile holding unit for stores and an aircraft repair depot.

The evacuation of 207 Squadron was completed on 23 September 1923, when the squadron sailed on HMT *Vedic*. A parting shot in the diary of AC2 Riches was written on 22 September: "Burning our beds when told to leave them for the Turks – what a hope! Hell of a march to the naval base. Harrington shed tears. Put out at 17.00. Great doings as we passed San Stephano." One can only imagine the good cheer on board the *Vedic*, which dropped anchor at Southampton on 3 October. There on the dockside the band of the Wiltshire Regt. played to welcome the homesick men, who, with 25 Squadron, paraded on the railway station platform during disembarkation. After being inspected by Gp. Capt. Gerard, 207 Squadron climbed aboard a train and seven hours later arrived at Eastchurch, an RAF Station on the Isle of Sheppey in Kent which had hitherto been used for training purposes and which was to be the squadron's new home.

Back to normal

After settling in at Eastchurch, the members of the squadron spent the months of November and December 1923 in unpacking and assembling the 'Ninaks', not all of which had been made serviceable by the beginning of the Christmas leave period. Equipment for many aircraft was incomplete, adding to the difficulties. Those airmen who were not entitled to a long leave were organised into working parties until the remainder of the personnel returned on 21 January 1924, when the whole squadron was reorganised into Flights. Only 16 hours 15 minutes flying was carried out in January, mainly on air tests.

In February a programme of lectures spread over an eight-month period was inaugurated for the benefit of officers on days when no flying could take place. A new type of RAE silencer was fitted to a number of aircraft, with disappointing results, but in March instructions were received that the 'Ninaks' were to be fitted with Radio Telephones (R/T), a pioneering experiment. A party of civilian engineers supervised by Flg. Off. Jones from 1 Stores Depot at Kidbrooke began the fitting process on 22 March, but it was 16 April before trials, regarded as only partly successful due to limited range and voice distortion, were conducted with one aircraft.

In preparation for the first RAF Pageant, to be held in June 1924, Sqn. Ldr. Gaskell–Blackburn and Flt. Lt. Benge attended a conference on 25 March, after which it was announced that 207 Squadron would take part in the Wing formation drill in conjunction with Spittlegate-based 39 Squadron. At another conference, Flight commanders decided on a standard paint scheme for the aircraft — polished engine and radiator cowlings, aluminium wheel discs, and aluminium-painted interplane struts and 'acorns'. Radiator shutters were to be painted in a chessboard pattern, 'A' Flight in red and white, 'B' Flight blue and white and 'C' Flight black and white. Individual aircraft identification letters would be applied on the forward fuselage.

Possibly to offer their thanks to the squadron for its part in keeping the warring factions apart in Turkey, five Turkish officers visited the Station on 1 April, and 207 Squadron staged a demonstration of formation flying. Present on the same day was Admiral Goodenough, C–in–C the Nore. Later in the month formation practice for the RAF Pageant began, and on 15 May the main body of the squadron moved to Spittlegate to start practising with 39 Squadron.

Meanwhile, two officers, Flt. Lt. Pryor and Flg. Off. Foster, took their aircraft to Gosport for penetration bombing trials targeted on HMS *Monarch.* The bombs used were concrete-filled, and their effect on the ship was recorded, the experiment being regarded a great success. Afterwards, letters of commendation were sent to 207 Squadron by AVM Vyvian, commanding Coastal Area, and Air Cdre. T. I. Webb–Bowen, commanding Inland Area, in praise of the two-crew detachment.

At Spittlegate, those concerned with the RAF Pageant practised formation flying diligently until on 10 June an eighteen-aircraft combined formation with 39 Squadron was attempted. At first all involved despaired of reaching the standard necessary for a successful Pageant, but as time went by the formation flying became excellent. The display was to be held at Hendon, and the two squadrons moved down to Northolt on 25 June to be close at hand. On two successive days the squadrons flew last-minute rehearsals at Hendon and then flew over London to advertise the event. Probably during practice for the display, 'Ninak' J6964 suffered engine failure and force-landed at Wormwood Scrubs on 27 June but was not seriously damaged. The crew, Flg. Off. L. H. Weedon and AC Lines, were not hurt. The big day was Saturday 28 June, when the two squadrons carried out a demonstration of Wing drill with great success, many observers regarding the drill as the most impressive part of the display. After a mass take-off, the formation split into two groups of nine and performed head-on manoeuvres before combining for a V formation which developed into line-abreast. A mock bombing attack on a realistic 'enemy fleet' was featured, and to help rapid tail-up take-offs many of the 'Ninak' gunners stood at full height, leaning forward! The climax came when all eighteen aircraft formed a close circle and orbited the enthralled throng of spectators. Press reports were fulsome in their praise, as was Lord Trenchard, who remarked that it was "............the most wonderful flying yet seen."

This excitement over, 207 Squadron left for Eastchurch on Monday 30 June and immediately began training for bombing trials involving HMS *Agamemnon* to take place on 28 July. Bad weather prevented a successful first raid, but three sorties were flown, each remaining aloft for over four hours and refuelling at Gosport. Monthly flying times had now increased substantially, the total for July being 254 hours 45 minutes.

August was a month of staggered leave for the members of the squadron, a third at a time. There was a visit by Chilean officers, who watched a routine formation bombing practice. Later in the month endurance trials were made during which the longest time spent in the air was 4 hours 15 minutes. This was improved upon in September, however, when five hours was achieved. Another novelty announced that month was a weekly cross-country flight for all pilots.

When the AOC, Air Cdre. Webb–Bowen, inspected the squadron in October he paid particular attention to the progress, if any, being made with Wireless Telegraphy (W/T) [not R/T as previously recorded!] in the 'Ninaks'. As a development from this, Flt. Lt. Oddie gave a lecture to the crews on 16 October on the novel subject of direction–finding, which was listened to with great interest by those present. Afterwards, he gave a practical demonstration in a specially-fitted Bristol Bulldog aircraft. It is interesting, in the light of later technical developments, to learn that the air-to-ground ranges averaged 20 miles (32 km.) for W/T and five miles (eight km.) for R/T, while air-to-air average ranges were, surprisingly, only five miles for W/T and one mile for R/T.

The final competitive endurance test took place on 3 November, when the aircraft involved remained in the air for 6 hours 15 minutes, but an order was then issued prohibiting any longer flights than four hours for the time being. The remainder of November and December were taken up with routing flying practice, and of course the Christmas leave period.

Fortnightly endurance tests began again in January 1925 and tests were made to determine the possible effect of trailing radio aerials when aircraft flew in close formation. A growing amount of time was now being devoted to direction-finding experiments. Possibly interested in such matters, the Under Secretary of State for Air, Sir Phillip Sassoon, paid an informal visit to the squadron on 29 January, transportation from his home at Lympne on the south coast of Kent being provided by one of the 'Ninaks' escorted by two more. He remarked that he was "........delighted with the trip."

In February practice began once more for that summer's RAF Display, and endurance tests ceased. This time, R/T between airborne aircraft was tested, with varying results. During formation landing practice on 21 February, the pilot of 'Ninak' J7354, Flg. Off. H. G. Rowe, was distracted by onlookers and ran into J7352, luckily without injury to anyone. On 30 April, while practising for the Display, 'Ninak' J7112 was written off when it spun out of a formation turn from an altitude of 1,200 feet near Eastchurch and crashed, both the pilot, Flg. Off. B. G. Poole, and the passenger, AC1 W. J. Spare, being seriously injured.

The wreckage of D.H.9A J7112, which spun out of a formation near Eastchurch on 30 April 1925, Flg. Off. B. G. Poole and AC1 W. J. Spare both being seriously injured. [via G. A. Jenks/R. C. Sturtivant]

During May, combined formations of two, three and four squadrons were attempted at Andover and Spittlegate, but the results were not impressive, and inherently poor visibility from the 'Ninak' caused these ambitious plans to be modified. Once again the squadron moved to Spittlegate, where it arrived on 8 June, for final practice with the three other bomber squadrons. This completed, all flew down to Hendon on 24 June in readiness for the Display three days later.

Back at Eastchurch, the squadron recommenced routine endurance tests, though it might be thought that everything possible was known by now! Live bombing tests were carried out in July at Shoeburyness, with a small amount of live gun firing at Leysdown, not far from base. Most pilots flew at night during the month, in the course of which one aircraft was damaged but nobody was injured. Flying times had increased considerably over the past year, July's being recorded as 376 hours 45 minutes.

More bombing trials using HMS *Agamemnon* as the target took place in August after some practice late in July. To create some excitement, the bombing was arranged in competition with 39 Squadron. Each squadron used nine aircraft and employed the Course Setting Bomb Sight. The radio-controlled vessel was very elusive, frequently changing speed and direction. Bombing from altitudes of 14,000, 12,000, 8,000 and 4,500 feet, the 207 Squadron aircraft made only two direct hits, and it was realised

Flg. Off. Brown leaning nonchalantly on the wing of D.H.9A J6967 [A3] at Eastchurch in late 1926. [J. M. Bruce & G. S. Leslie collection]

afterwards that the CSBS compass used was unable to keep pace with the target vessel.

As a change from naval exercises, 207 Squadron was attached to the army of the imaginary country of 'Mercia' during three-day manoeuvres which began on 22 September 1925. Detached to Farnborough for the exercise, the squadron's main task was to carry out long-distance reconnaissance flights and high and low level bombing, which it did successfully when weather conditions allowed. Conditions improved before the decisive part of the proceedings, allowing 207 Squadron to carry out low-level attacks.

After the squadron returned to Eastchurch, preparations began for the annual inspection on 15 October by AVM Webb–Bowen, who congratulated the members of the squadron on their smart turn-out. Routine training then became the order of the day, but in November the issue of new-fangled parachutes to every crew began, an event seen at the time as the greatest single advance in flight safety ever made. Due to bad weather, no practice jumps were allowed, much to the relief of most crew members! As a change from endurance tests, an altitude test was held on 30 November during which a Ninak climbed to 12,000 feet in 32 minutes.

December included the inevitable quiet period when many of the squadron members were on leave, resulting in squadron aircraft being in the air for only 136 hours 45 minutes in total. In February 1926 Sqn. Ldr. Gaskell–Blackburn was posted to command 9 (Bomber) Squadron, and was replaced by Sqn. Ldr. J. B. Graham MC DFC, who arrived from the RAF Depôt. The departing CO had proved himself to be a very able and popular man, and for some time after he left the 207 Squadron drum and bagpipe band

Probably taken at Eastchurch in 1926, this picture shows D.H.9A J7802 [C1] of 207 Squadron to good effect. Note the oleo undercarriage. [P. H. T. Green collection]

An aerial view of Bircham Newton, giving a good illustration of the seven General Service Sheds [hangars] which existed when the photograph was taken in September 1927. The aircraft on the field is thought to have been a Handley Page Hyderabad of 99 Squadron, which was at Bircham Newton between 207 Squadron's two periods of service there. *[P. H. T. Green collection]*

which he had created continued to flourish. Due to bad weather, flying in February was restricted, but spring brought a period of exceptionally good weather, allowing a total of 380 hours 55 minutes to be flown in March and 299 hours 45 minutes in April. Looking ahead, the CO decided to take advantage of these conditions by beginning practice for the annual RAF Display, although no orders on the subject had yet been received. However, in May the General Strike took place, and 207 Squadron was ordered to stand by for possible 'special duties'. In the event, the strike collapsed before any action was required, allowing formation practice with 11, 12 and 39 Squadrons to begin at Spittlegate and Andover. These combined efforts continued until the massed aircraft flew to Hendon on 23 June for a dress rehearsal. Afterwards, they flew back to their respective bases (11 Squadron to Netheravon, 12 Squadron to Andover and 39 Squadron to Spittlegate), only to reassemble at Hendon on 30 June in readiness for the Display on 3 July. 207 Squadron put up an excellent performance, although in the words of a press correspondent "............it was all very pretty and very impressive but it was not new." Nevertheless, in a letter to the squadron the AOC quoted HM King George V, who had said that the formation had showed "..........a commendably high standard of training and flying skill." As soon as the Display was over, the squadron did its best to make up for lost time by carrying out a great deal of bombing practice.

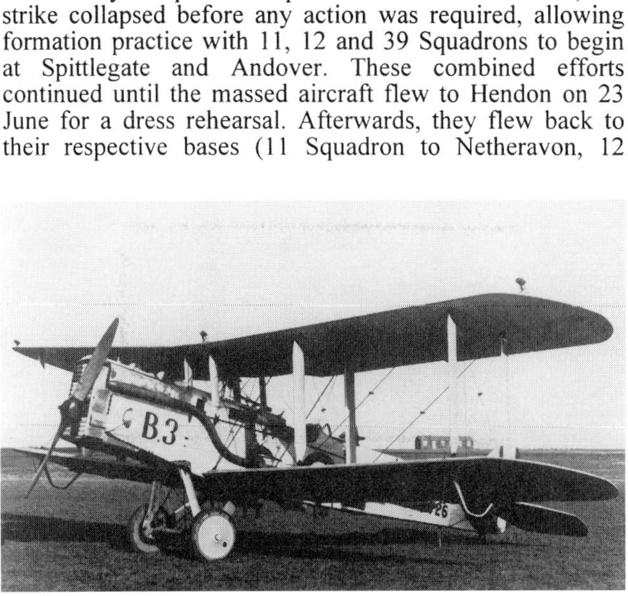

A typical 'Ninak' was E726, coded B3, which was flown by 207 Squadron's 'B' Flight. [RAFM P.17677]

As soon as possible after taking over the command of Wessex Bombing Area, AVM Sir John Steel KCB CMG CBE paid a visit to 207 Squadron on 11 August 1926. For his benefit, all pilots took part in a demonstration in which they were required to land on a mark, while all bomb racks were tested and front guns fired at the butts. Several Flight and Squadron climbs with full war loads were made to a maximum altitude of 14,000 feet, but the time taken to reach that height is not recorded.

Bombing and air firing practice continued in September in readiness for the squadron's detachment to armament training camp at Weston Zoyland in Somerset. Before the ten 'Ninaks' left on 27 September, the AOC–in–C, Sir John Salmond KCB CMG CVO DSO ADC, visited the squadron informally. While in Somerset, the squadron carried out practice raids from altitudes as high as 14,000 feet with good results, and Flg. Off. Brown scored 61% in the front gun contest, the highest score. After inspection by the AOC Wessex Bombing Area, the squadron returned to Eastchurch on 8 October to prepare for the annual inspection by AVM Steel on 2 November. As usual, he remarked that he said that he was very pleased with the squadron's performance and the condition of the aircraft.

The aftermath of the collision between 'Ninak' J7859 of 207 Squadron and Woodcock J7973 of 3 Squadron at Eastchurch on 25 October 1926. The remains of the Woodcock are in the foreground. [via J.J.Halley]

Perhaps he was not aware that 'Ninak' J7859 had been written off when it collided with Woodcock Mk.II J7973 of Upavon–based 3 Squadron while landing at Eastchurch on 25 October!

Members of the squadron received the sad news in November that Flg. Off. E. C. Moon, the officer who had maintained the diary during the time the squadron had served in Turkey, had died of tuberculosis in a private nursing home, where he had been a patient since being invalided out of the service in February 1926. Another sad event took place on 11 November, ironically the eighth anniversary of the Armistice. On that day Sgt. G. F. Taylor and AC2 P. C. Hinton were killed when D.H.9A J7610 crashed at Eastchurch and was burnt out.

Routine flying in connection with the Individual Training Scheme began again after the Christmas leave break, but in February 1927 atrocious weather prevented much activity in the air. Time was therefore devoted to the ground instruction part of the Scheme. The climax of all this training came on 16 March, when the travelling Board visited the squadron to examine all pilots and air gunners, although owing to lack of time only the pilots were subjected to scrutiny. In hindsight, this seems somewhat less than professional, and the gunners must have felt that the concentrated training was to no avail. Only time would tell!

With the spring came 207 Squadron's annual trip to Practice Camp at Weston Zoyland. On Easter Monday, 18 April, a convoy of vehicles drawn from the Wessex Bombing Area pool left Eastchurch on the long journey to Andover, where a night stop was made. It had been intended that nine 'Ninaks' would fly to Weston Zoyland, but at the last minute one had an argument with a Vickers Virginia at Eastchurch and had to be withdrawn, leaving eight to make the trip. Luckily, no 207 Squadron personnel were injured in that incident. At Weston Zoyland, good weather prevailed during the period of the Camp, although for bombing purposes it was not always suitable. The squadron was able to complete all the practices and classification tests laid down for a day bombing squadron, and it was found that although there had been an improvement in front gunnery the bombing results were not as good as those of the previous year. No aircraft force-landed away from the airfield during the Camp, but leaking cylinder jackets gave a great deal of trouble, and three aircraft crash-landed on the airfield. Social events were not overlooked, and on 1 May local residents were invited to the Camp to watch a flying demonstration.

Among the squadron personnel at the time were a number of fine NCOs, of whom several had been working on aircraft since before the late war. Two at least had service numbers of only two digits, signifying their entry into the Royal Flying Corps in 1912. They were the technical warrant officer, Sgt. Maj. Little and the NCO in charge of 'A' Flight, Flt. Sgt. Griggs. 'B' Flight's NCO in charge, Flt. Sgt. Fletcher, had for several years been the coxswain of an airship.

Royal approval

At the end of the Practice Camp, 207 Squadron 'Ninaks' flew on 25 May to Andover to take part in the first of a series of formation practices with 12 and 39 Squadrons in readiness for yet another display at Hendon, where the combined squadrons arrived on 29 May. The display, by now referred to in RAF circles as the 'Taxpayers' Benefit', took place on 2 July, and 207 Squadron was featured in the first event on the programme, Wing Evolutions. Unfortunately, low cloud and rain interfered with the success of this spectacle, and the squadron returned to Eastchurch the same evening. Nevertheless, the Secretary of State for Air sent a message of fulsome praise to all concerned: "His Majesty the King desires me to convey to you and all ranks who took part his appreciation of the very high standard of flying and organisation shown. I congratulate you personally, the Display Committee and all concerned in devising and carrying out an admirable programme on a conspicuously successful afternoon. The smoothness and punctuality with which events proceeded are most satisfactory evidence of the flying skill, staff work and discipline of the Royal Air Force." One wonders whether everything really was that commendable!

July 1927 was indeed a busy month for 207 Squadron, as it participated in both bombing trials at sea and the Air Defence of Great Britain exercises. In all, 403 hours were flown, a post-war record. During trials which began on 4 July attempts were made to bomb a target towed by a destroyer, the 'Ninaks' having been modified to carry both the Fourth Vector Sight and the Back Drift Sight. Considerable difficulties met and overcome included the length and strength of the tow; the depth of water necessary; spotting; suitable weather; and a suitable location. Most of the exercise was carried out by one Flight only due to the demands of the impending ADGB exercise, and results obtained when this Flight led the whole squadron as a forerunner of the pathfinders of the Second World War showed how effective the bomb sights could be, given practice and reasonably good weather. Unfortunately, a potential enemy would not often be generous enough to allow all the criteria considered essential to effectively bomb him!

Taken on 22 July 1927, this aerial picture of the Armament Practice Camp at Weston Zoyland in Somerset imparts some of the easy-going atmosphere of the time. There is some hangarage for aircraft, but personnel accommodation seems to have been entirely in tents. [RAFM P2668]

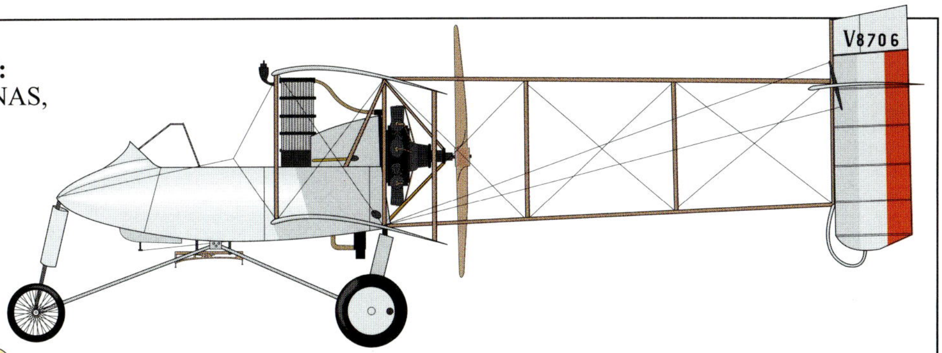

Voisin 3; 1916 - 1917:
8706 of 7(N) Sqn., RNAS,
in East Africa.

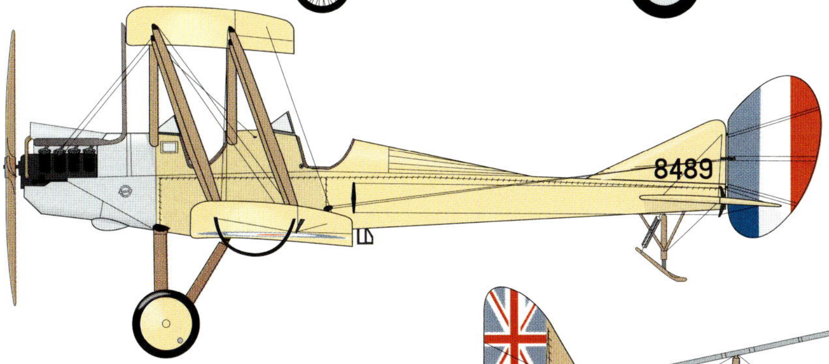

B.E.2C; 1916 - 1917:
8489 of 7(N) Sqn., RNAS,
in East Africa.

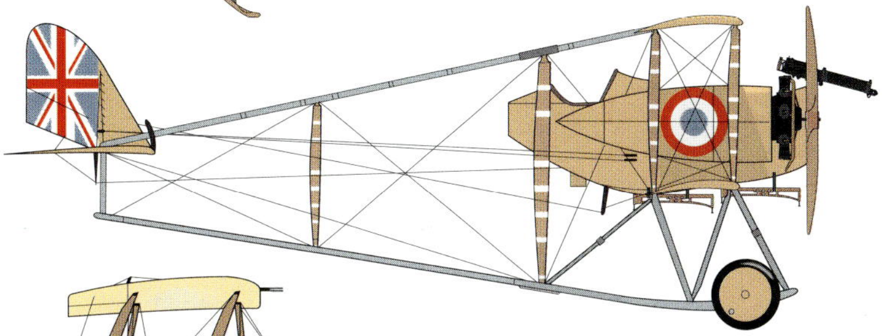

Caudron G.IV; Nov-Dec 1916:
Serial unknown of 7(N) Sqn., RNAS,
Petite Synthe, France.

Sopwith 1½ Strutter; Nov 1916-Apr 1917:
N5504 shown prior to service with 7(N) Sqn.,
RNAS, Petite Synthe, France.

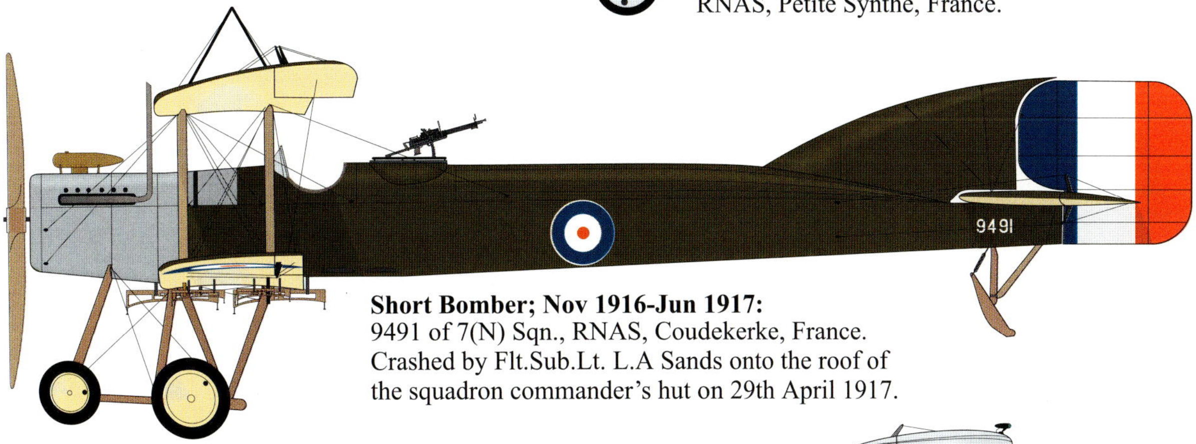

Short Bomber; Nov 1916-Jun 1917:
9491 of 7(N) Sqn., RNAS, Coudekerke, France.
Crashed by Flt.Sub.Lt. L.A Sands onto the roof of
the squadron commander's hut on 29th April 1917.

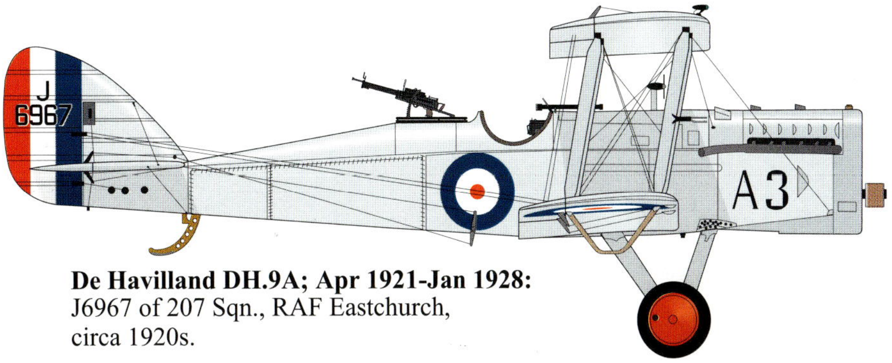

De Havilland DH.9A; Apr 1921-Jan 1928:
J6967 of 207 Sqn., RAF Eastchurch,
circa 1920s.

Approx
1/53 scale

Approx
1/78 scale

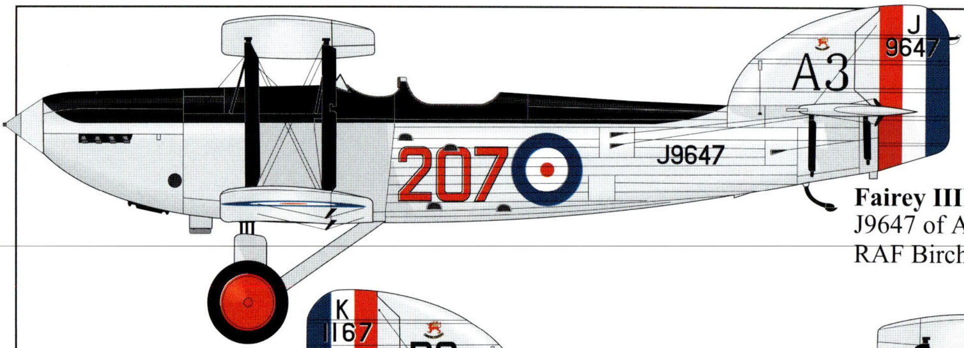

Fairey IIIF; Dec 1927-Sep 1932:
J9647 of A Flight, 207 Sqn.,
RAF Bircham Newton.

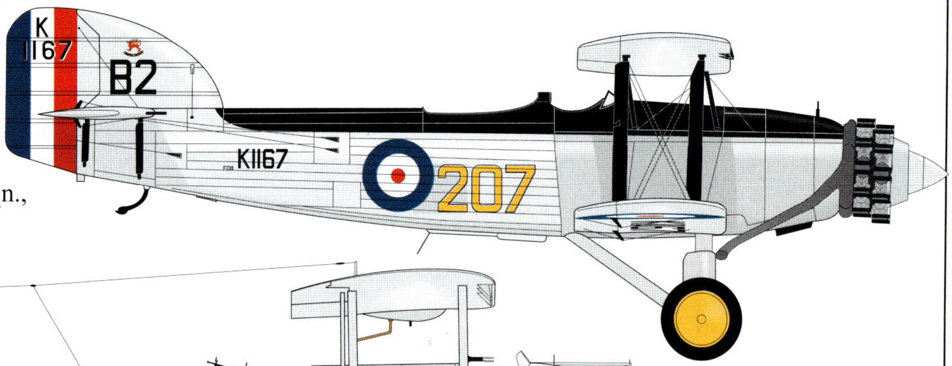

Fairey Gordon;
Aug 1932-Apr 1936;
Aug 1936-Sep 1937:
K1167 of B Flight, 207 Sqn.,
RAF Bircham Newton,
circa early 1930s.

Vickers Vincent; Apr-Aug 1936:
K4687 of B Flight, 207 Sqn.,
Gebeit,Sudan.

Vickers Wellesley; Sep 1937-Apr 1938.
K7758 of 207 Sqn., RAF Worthy Down.

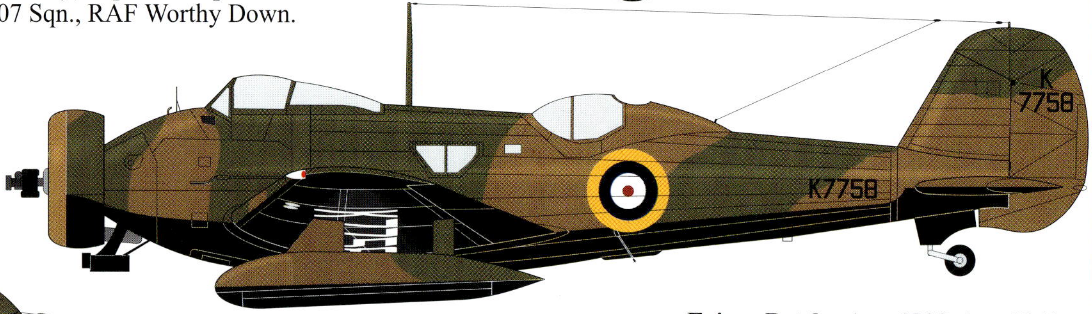

Fairey Battle; Apr 1938-Apr 1940.
K9200/Z of 207 Sqn., RAF
Cottesmore.

Avro Anson I; Jul 1939-Apr 1940.
N5265 of 207 Sqn., RAF
Cottesmore.

Approx
1/135 scale

Handley Page 0/100; Apr 1917 - Apr 1918:
3118 of 7(N) Sqn., RNAS,
Coudekerke, France, 1917-18.

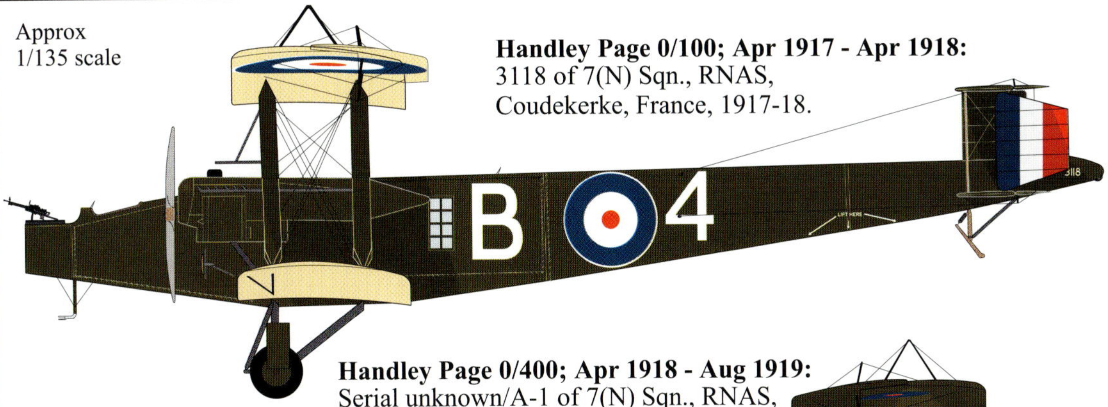

Handley Page 0/400; Apr 1918 - Aug 1919:
Serial unknown/A-1 of 7(N) Sqn., RNAS,
with 1,650lb SN bomb, Coudekerke,
France, 1917-18.

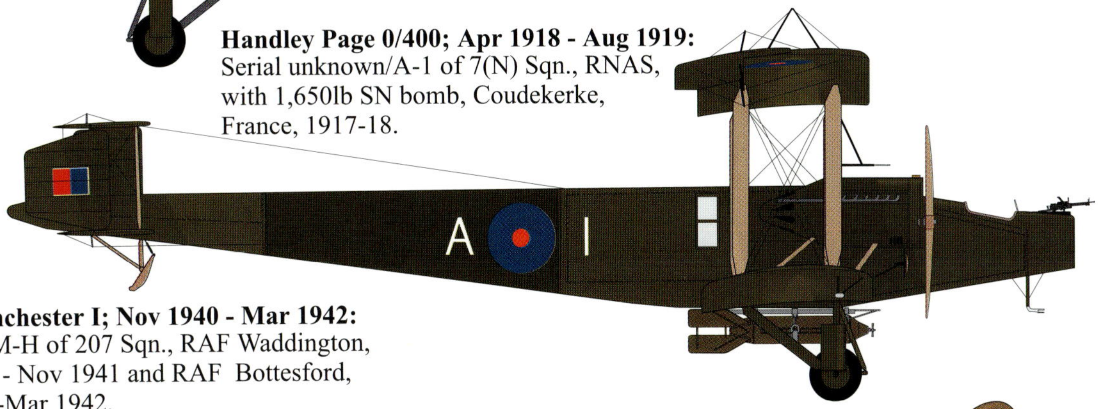

Avro Manchester I; Nov 1940 - Mar 1942:
L7288, EM-H of 207 Sqn., RAF Waddington,
Nov 1940 - Nov 1941 and RAF Bottesford,
Nov 1941-Mar 1942.

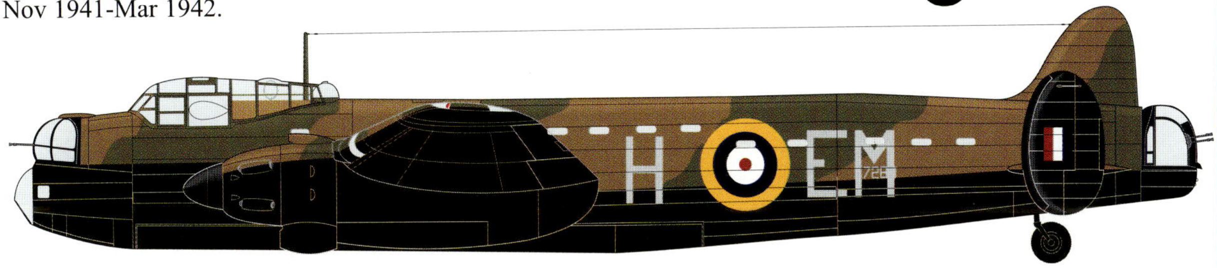

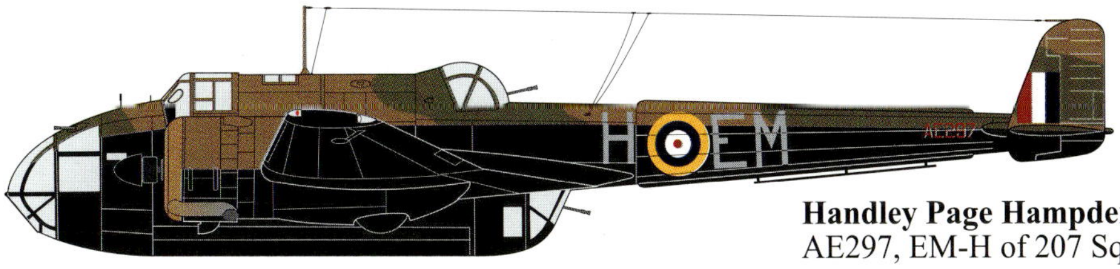

Handley Page Hampden; 1941:
AE297, EM-H of 207 Sqn., RAF
Waddington, July/August 1941.

Avro Lancaster III; Mar 1942-Aug 1949:
ED802, EM-M, flown by Sgt John McIntosh
& Crew, 207 Sqn., RAF Langar, May 1943.

Avro Lincoln B.2; Aug 1949-Feb 1950:
RE324, EM-C of 207 Sqn., RAF Mildenhall.

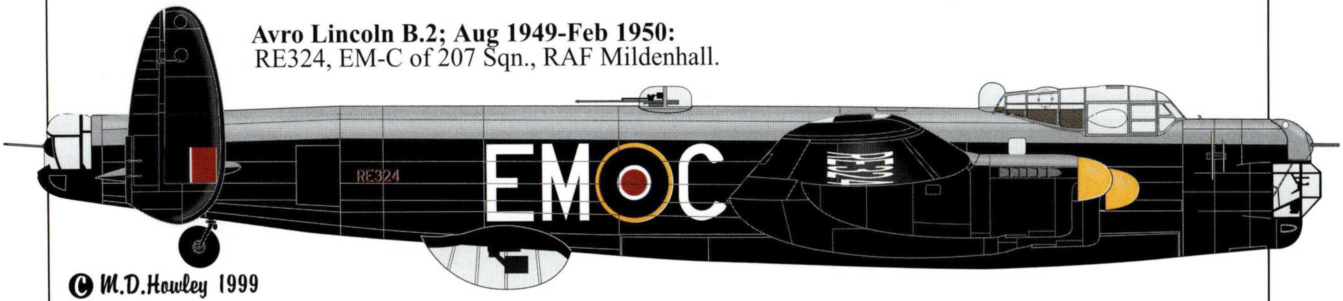

Boeing Washington B.1 (B-29); Jul 1951-Mar 1954:
WF565/B of 207 Sqn., RAF Marham. (An impression of how it may have looked in service).

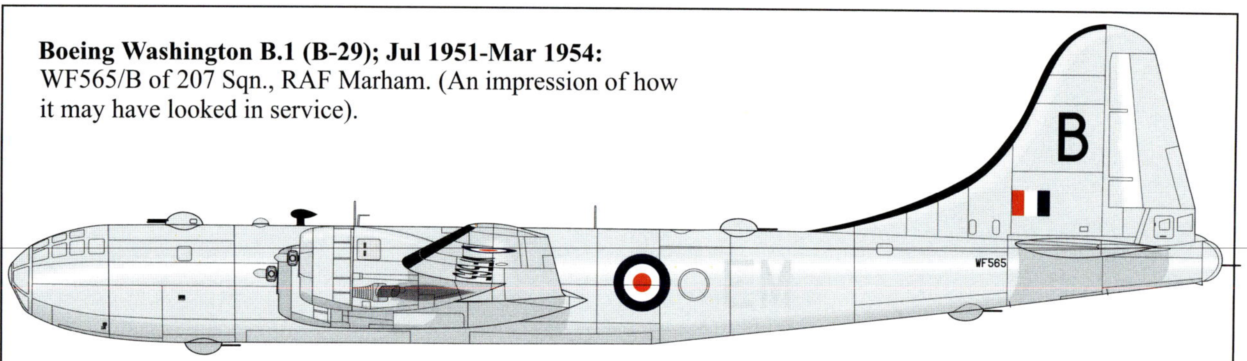

English Electric Canberra B.2; Mar 1954-Feb 1956:
WK102 of 207 Sqn., RAF Marham.

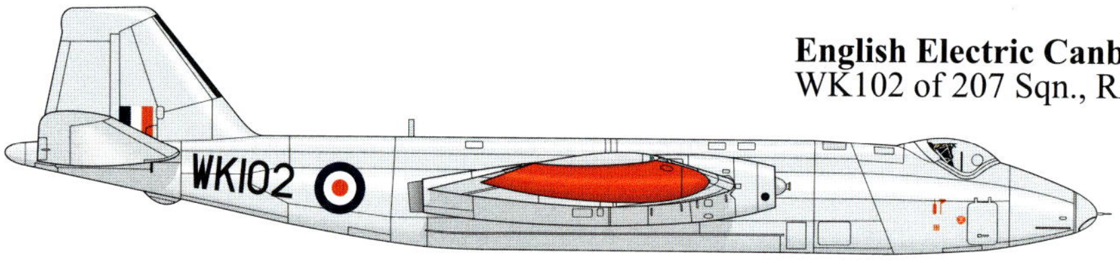

Vickers Valiant B.1; Jun 1956-Dec 1964:
XD873, flown by the CO of 207 Sqn., RAF Marham.

Approx
1/179 scale

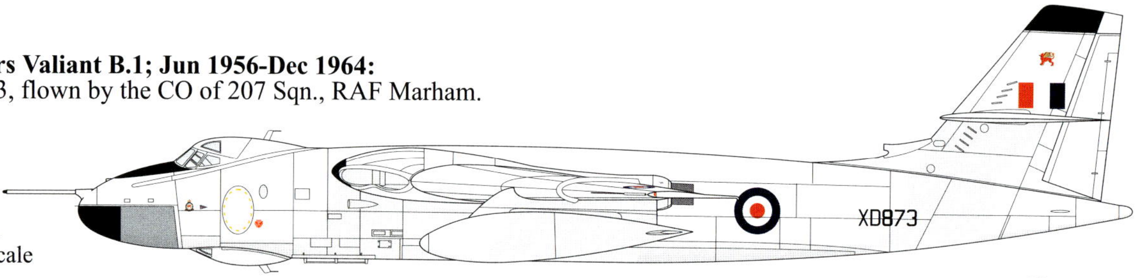

Percival Pembroke C.1; Feb 1969-Nov 1975:
XK884 of 207 Sqn., RAF Northolt.

Approx
1/85 scale

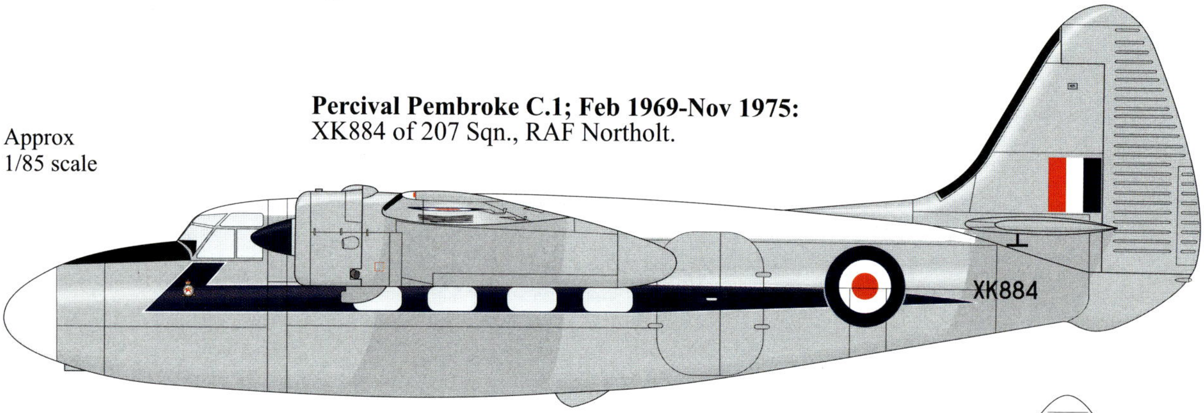

De Havilland Devon C2; Feb 1969-Jun 1984:
VP971 of 207 Sqn., RAF Northolt.

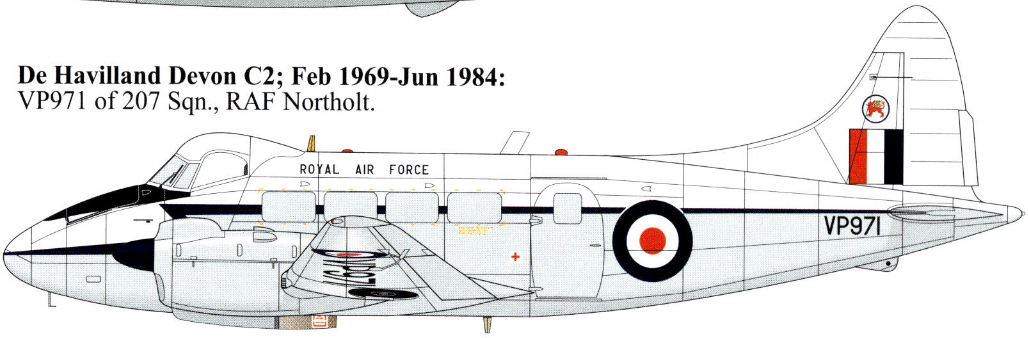

Scottish Aviation Basset; Feb 1969-Jun 1984:
XS784 of 207 Sqn., RAF Northolt. Flown on last sortie 28 May 1974 by OC 207 Sqn., Sqn. Ldr. G.T. West and OC 32 Sqn., Wg.Cdr. G.O. Graydon.

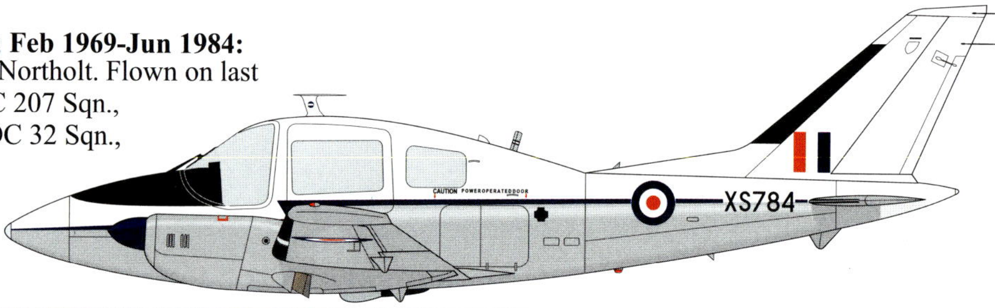

A fine airborne shot of Devon WB530, illustrating the immaculate condition in which they were maintained. After grounding, this Devon saw service as an instructional airframe. [via Sqn. Ldr. I. Hampton]

Two of 207 Squadron's Devons, WB530 and VP971, in formation, the latter carrying a stylised version of the squadron badge on its fin. Paintwork was always immaculate, in view of the squadron's frequent VIP-carrying duties. [Sqn. Ldr. I. Hampton]

It's not often that a pilot has a Spitfire and a Hurricane on the starboard bow! Here two of the aircraft of the Battle of Britain Memorial Flight are being shepherded by a 207 Squadron Devon, a regular duty for the squadron for several years. [Sqn. Ldr. I. Hampton]

The Dakota of the Battle of Britain Memorial Flight flies low overhead during the reburial ceremony at Cambridge cemetery on 25 October 1996. Carrying the Bomber Command Association's standard was Mr. Ron Pearson of Newmarket Branch RAFA. [Cambridge Newspapers Ltd.]

Dedication of the memorial at Langar on 12 May 1994. AVM David Dick salutes, his wife at his side.

The memorial at Brigstock. [R. Winton]

Between October 1943 and October 1945 No.207 Squadron Royal Air Force
was based here at Spilsby aerodrome, whose boundaries encompassed
this Church of All Saints at Great Steeping.
Until 27th April 1945, flying from here the Squadron's Lancaster bombers,
each with seven crewmen, took the battle to the enemy, mostly by night.
Until 6th June 1944 this was the only way in which Great Britain could
strike out from these shores in its own defence and in the
cause of freedom. In this period, 511 men of No. 207 Squadron were killed,
104 of whom have no known grave.
They included men from Great Britain, Canada, Australia, New Zealand,
The USA, The Netherlands, and Eire, and 12 members of the ground staff.
133 more did not return from operations, of whom 109 became Prisoners
of War until May 1945, and 24 evaded capture.
"LEST WE FORGET"

The Spilsby memorial plaque.

The 207 Squadron plot in the cemetery of St. Mary the Virgin church, Bottesford

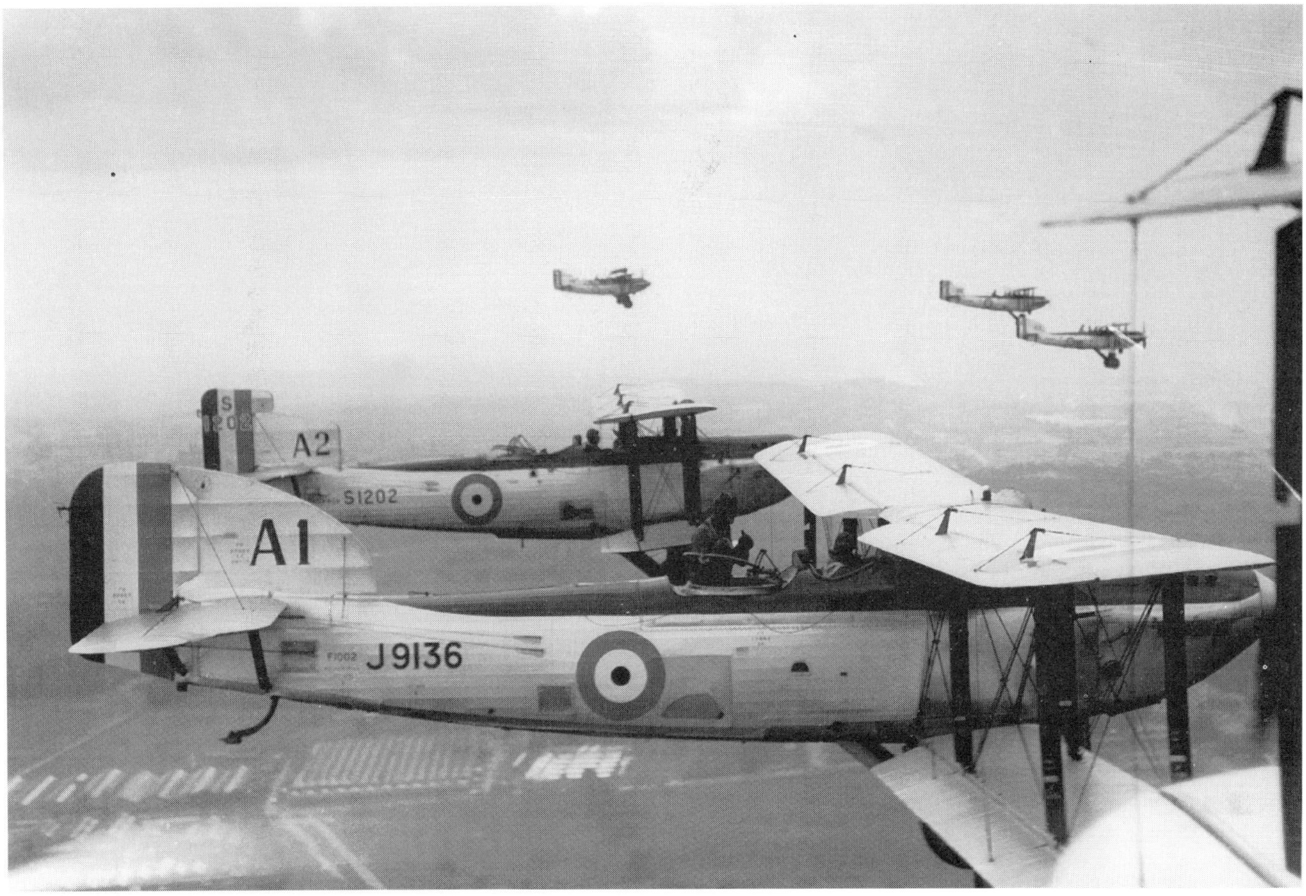

Seen practising for the 1928 RAF Display are Fairey IIIFs J9136 [A1], S1202 [A2] and three others. The difference between the fin shape on aircraft from the Fleet Air Arm (S1202 for example) and those with RAF origins is apparent. [Quadrant Picture Library / Flight International]

From 25 to 31 July the ADGB exercises took up the resources of two Flights of 207 Squadron, which each day carried out mock raids on targets in or near London. On three occasions, however, the mission was unsuccessful due to bad weather which prevented the aircraft reaching their objectives.

In September the squadron competed for the first time, but by no means the last, for the Lawrence Minot Trophy, and the representative crew, Flt. Lt. Foster and LAC Wilson, was placed second. Apart from the AOC's inspection and a spate of rumours circulating round the messes, little else disturbed the even tenor of the squadron's life before Christmas. A move to Bircham Newton was one rumour in which there was an element of truth, but this proposal was cancelled early in December.

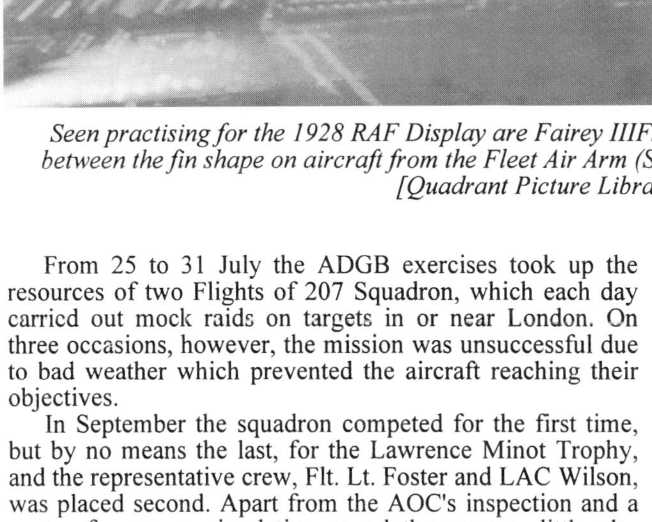

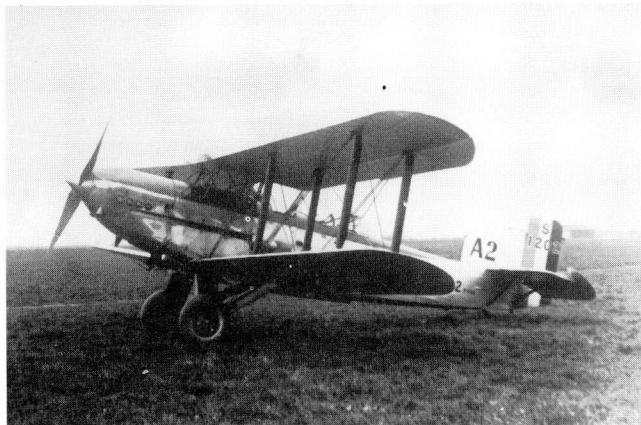

S1202 [A2] was one of the former naval Fairey IIIFs, identifiable by the different fin shape. [RAFM P.4312]

Goodbye to the 'Ninak'

Re-equipment with different aircraft was another rumour, and this became a fact in the last week of the year, when the first two three-seat Fairey IIIF aircraft arrived from the Home Aircraft Depot at Henlow. Grasping the opportunity of a little fine weather, squadron pilots flew the new Faireys and several succeeded in going solo, perhaps not being aware that 207 Squadron was the first UK-based RAF squadron to receive the type. The demise of the 'Ninak' would not have been regretted by the crews, as although it was pleasant to fly it was by now such an outdated design.

Developed from an earlier design, the Fairey IIIF was produced in quantity after the first flight of the prototype in March 1926. Earliest deliveries to the RAF were taken from the Fleet Air Arm pre-production batch and went to squadrons in the Middle East. Those supplied to 207 Squadron were Mk.I aircraft, fitted with Napier Lion Mk.Va engines. Apart from having a better performance, the IIIF sported modern refinements such as streamlining, an oleo undercarriage and a metal propeller.

While many crews were on leave in January 1928, more Fairey IIIFs arrived, some from Henlow and others transferred from the Fleet Air Arm store at Gosport, the latter having a stepped fin and carrying serial numbers in the naval S series. During a ferrying flight from Gosport, the squadron navigation officer, Flt. Lt. Cook, lost himself, and landed at Castle Bromwich, just outside Birmingham, an event which did nothing to improve his status among his peers! Little flying was done in January, however, as difficulties were found in keeping the new aircraft serviceable, and a shortage of spares prevailed. As an added trial, the airfield was not usable for most of the month. The last of the faithful 'Ninaks' were despatched by road and rail during the first week of February, ending eight years of

Fairey IIIF J9074 [B2] was used by 207 Squadron before being sent to 8 Squadron in Aden. [via K. Smy]

Lined up at Hendon for the 1929 RAF show are the Fairey IIIFs of 207 Squadron, with J9147 [A2] and J9146 identifiable. [P. H. T. Green collection]

faithful and arduous service. That month, practice flying in the new aircraft was mainly for the benefit of air gunners, who attempted to perfect their skills in bombing, gunnery, photography and use of the W/T fitted in the Faireys. Sad to say, the squadron suffered a fatal accident on 2 March 1928, when a IIIF (possibly S1195) crashed on the Isle of Grain, with the loss of Sgt. W. Maltman, LAC S. C. Mason and AC1 W. G. Lowman.

April was a busy month for the squadron, which took part in daily mock raids on west London and Birmingham between the 16th and the 20th, using camera obscura targets. On 23 April two Flights were sent to North Weald for the Area Staff Exercises in conjunction with 56 Squadron, exercises in what later became known as fighter affiliation. 56 Squadron, equipped with Siskin Mk.IIIa fighters, attempted interceptions by single and massed aircraft, but a rather smug note in the 207 Squadron diary records that "...........it was obvious that the development of the fighter has not taken place so rapidly as that of the two-seater single-engined day bomber."

By now it was time to prepare for the annual display at Hendon yet again. On 24 May the whole squadron flew to Andover, where combined formation practice was carried out with the Hawker Horsleys of 11 Squadron and the Fairey Foxes of 12 Squadron. This task was completed every week until the end of June, and on 22 June a small display was given at Andover as a dress rehearsal. The squadron flew to Hendon on 27 June, and after final practice the display was held three days later, with the day bombers' formation drill the first item on the afternoon programme. Once again, those involved were congratulated by higher authority for the work they had put in to ensure that the RAF was seen by the general public, in those days of extreme financial stringency, to be a valuable asset.

Hardly had the engines of the Faireys had time to cool after their return to Eastchurch when they took to the air again on 4 July for a month-long Practice Camp at Weston Zoyland. Conditions in the first three weeks were good, but the final period was totally unsuitable for high-level bombing and the squadron therefore concerned itself with

One of the Flight commanders, Flt. Lt. W. Elliott DFC, and his dog pose in front of his Fairey IIIF in 1928. Later he became AOC-in-C Fighter Command. The ground crew airmen seem cheerful, which probably speaks well for 207 Squadron's morale. [Quadrant Picture Library / Flight International]

gun classification and crew assessment. In both of these a considerable improvement over the previous year was noticed, and 207 Squadron was placed first among all the day bomber squadrons taking part in the Camp. Aircraft serviceability in the somewhat spartan surroundings at Weston Zoyland was a problem, oil pipes giving particular trouble, but there were no forced landings away from the airfield. There was one, however, which was seen by the whole squadron. During a bombing sortie, one of the IIIFs developed severe propeller vibration due to shearing of securing bolts. On final approach to Weston Zoyland, the undercarriage hit the edge of a road alongside the airfield and the aircraft belly-landed. Wishing to view the damage, the AOC arrived in a Fairey Fox, the wheels of which hit the same road, causing another ignominious descent! As a way of saying thank you to local residents for their forbearance, an 'At Home' was held on 31 July and was regarded as a great success.

After the squadron returned to Eastchurch on 4 August the AOC made his annual inspection, and then the ADGB exercises began. Between 14 and 17 August mock raids on and around London were made every day between dawn and 09.00 and from 18.00 to dusk. In every case 207 Squadron aircraft reached their objectives, but with heavy theoretical losses at times. Two forced landings in 'enemy' territory were made when oil pipes broke. Afterward, the squadron diarist again remarked that the day bomber had developed more rapidly than had the fighter.

This was certainly a busy year! No sooner had the ADGB exercises been completed than 207 Squadron took part in Sussex Command army manoeuvres, carrying out a reconnaissance and photographic function. For this exercise, which lasted from 18 to 21 August, the Faireys landed at Milton Gate in Sussex (an airstrip which by 1933 had become Wilmington airport), where the Photographic Section was temporarily based, to deliver reports and exposed photographic film. This excitement over, it was time for Flt. Lt. Foster and AC1 Wilson to take part in the contest for the Lawrence Minot Trophy, held that year at North Coates Fitties in Lincolnshire. They were awarded sixth place, a somewhat disappointing result.

In October the squadron found itself back at Hendon, this time to give a display in honour of the Sultan of Muscat while he was on a State visit to England. Afterwards, 'The Aeroplane' magazine reported that the squadron's formation flying was greatly admired by a small but critical crowd of spectators. The AOC–in–C of ADGB, however, was not so happy. He commented that "........I appreciate that the flying efficiency shown by the squadron was of a very high order, but at the same time..............draw your attention to two breaches of flying regulations." What they were was not recorded by the squadron!

As 1928 drew to a close Sqn. Ldr. Graham was promoted and posted, Sqn. Ldr. E. A. Beulah took over as Commanding Officer, and for the next few months routine prevailed. Few unusual events took place to excite the squadron crews until camera obscura exercises were held on Birmingham and London from 3 to 5 April 1929. Accurate reports were in short supply after these missions, and no awards of merit were made.

More fighter affiliation exercises were held between 13 and 25 May, this time with the Siskins of 19 Squadron at Duxford, to where 207 Squadron flew. The exercises consisted of interceptions and tests of Fighting Area experimental attack methods. Unfortunately, the whole exercise proved to be of less value than hoped, as 19 Squadron was handicapped by a shortage of serviceable aircraft and recent changes of personnel. The Siskins were also seen by 207 Squadron as having too small a margin of extra speed over the Fairey IIIFs.

Practice flying for the now-inevitable Hendon display occupied most of June, with some preparation for bombing trials on a naval vessel. The squadron was under canvas at Hendon from 10 to 13 July, when the Faireys took part in the set piece before returning to Eastchurch. One aircraft did not see Eastchurch again, as it had crash-landed at Radlett the previous day, and although it was a write-off the lucky crew members escaped injury.

With scarcely time to draw breath, a road party left for a Practice Camp at Catfoss in Yorkshire at 06.00 on 14 July. Ten of the squadron's aircraft made the journey next day and another two followed within a few days. At Catfoss 207 Squadron took part in bombing practice and rear gun air-to-air firing, but the routine was marred by a fatal accident on 17 July, when K1758 collided with a drogue and crashed into the sea a few hundred yards offshore at Skipsea, with the loss of Flg. Off. S. F. Prince and LAC E. W. Buttenshaw. A demonstration was held on 23 July for the benefit of a party of army officers which included members of the Army Council from the War Office. They witnessed individual and Flight bombing routines and appeared to be most impressed. During August practices continued, until in the second half of the month crew classification began. Visitors to Catfoss that month included the Air Member for Personnel, Sir John Salmond, and the AOC–in–C Wessex Bombing Area, Sir Edward Ellington.

Trials against *Centurion* began on 9 September, when the squadron, in conjunction with a Flight of 7 (Bomber) Squadron, based at the time at Worthy Down and equipped with Vickers Virginias, was placed under the temporary command of Gp. Capt. J. T. Cull DSO, who in 1916 had campaigned with 7 (Naval) Squadron in East Africa. All bombing was by Flights rather than by individual crews. Weather conditions varied during the three days of the trials but were considered to be representative of the weather to be found in England and were thus acceptable. Details of wind speed and direction were determined by the meteorological section established at Catfoss for the purpose or by the Practice Camp's permanent staff and were given to the Flight leader on leaving the coast. New Mk.VII bomb-sights were used by the squadron, and very satisfactory results were obtained. Eighteen of 51 three-bomb salvoes and 29 of 156 single bombs dropped hit Centurion, and photographs were taken throughout. At the end of the exercise, the AOC relayed a message of congratulation from the Chief of the Air Staff, who remarked that "..........as usual, the Royal Air Force had done more than they claimed they would."

Then came the return to Eastchurch on 13 September, but next day Flt. Lt. O'Brien and Cpl. Steel flew to North Coates Fitties to contest the Lawrence Minot Trophy. They were placed sixth overall, but in the Day Bomber squadrons they were awarded second place.

When squadron personnel returned from a month-long leave period on 20 October 1929, they found that all the Fairey IIIFs had been fitted with Handley Page automatic safety slots by the Fairey Aviation Co. They also discovered that 33 (Bomber) Squadron, which in their absence at Catfoss had arrived at Eastchurch from Netheravon, was now sharing 207 Squadron's workshop and office facilities. However, orders were soon received that 207 Squadron was to return to Bircham Newton, where it had been reborn some nine years earlier. The last ten days of October were therefore devoted to preparations for this event, which was viewed by many of the personnel with dismay, as Bircham Newton was thought to be in the back of beyond and unlikely to have the amenities of Eastchurch. Only time would tell.

Back to Norfolk

All the squadron's motor transport facilities were used for the move, in two convoys, one a slow-moving group which took two days on the journey and spent a night at Duxford, and the other a light convoy which arrived at Bircham Newton after a one-day journey. All aircraft were flown to their new base and the move was

Fairey IIIFs of 207 Squadron in a neat line-up at Bircham Newton in 1930, J9172 [B2] nearest, the squadron number being painted just below the rear cockpit. On the buttress of the hangar in the background was an early form of control tower, and below it can be seen a crash rescue vehicle and its shed. [P. H. T. Green collection]

completed on 9 November when the rear party arrived. Two weeks were then spent in settling in, arranging for a number of recently-arrived pilots to solo on the IIIF, and preparing for the AOC's annual inspection. The first part of this was a detailed inspection by departmental staff officers which was completed on 3 December. The AOC himself made his visit on 12 December.

Gp. Capt. Charles Hawkins OBE AFC RAF (Retd.), who joined 207 Squadron in December 1929, recalls that there was time to play golf and enjoy many other sports. “Not everyone got to fly as much as they would like”, he says. “There was practice bombing on a static target with errors of 127 to 200 yards from 10,000 feet and the odd excitement such as a pull-off parachute descent at Henlow from a Vickers Vimy. Night flying was not done, and many flights were of no more than thirty minutes, so that after a year on the squadron I had done 60 hours 30 minutes on Fairey IIIFs and six hours 35 minutes on DH9As.”

Sadly, 1930 began with a fatal accident. While on the way from Bircham Newton to Eastchurch on 21 January in foggy conditions, J9637 hit a tree and crashed at Chilton, just outside Sudbury in Suffolk. In those days when navigational and landing aids did not exist, fog could be a real killer, and according to a contemporary newspaper report the area was shrouded that day in the thickest murk of the winter. At about noon, local residents heard the sound of an aircraft, followed by a terrific thud. Close to the 'Mauldon Grey' public house the wreckage of the Fairey IIIF was soon found in an orchard. In the tangled wreck the body of the pilot, Flg. Off. Donald Mackenzie, could be seen still sitting in his seat, while a few yards away was the headless body of his passenger, Cpl. Leonard E. Barnard. Visibility was so poor that only one of those who heard the approaching aircraft had seen it. Miss Chappell said “I heard it approaching my kennels and just before it got overhead the fog suddenly lifted and I was able to get a clear view of the machine, the engine of which was working beautifully. Just as it approached, the engine began back-firing and spitting. I hoped that they [the crew] would clear my kennels as they were bound to come down. The machine proceeded, flying low in the direction of Sudbury with the engine backfiring, and was lost again in the fog. Then I heard the noise as of a huge hammer hitting a steel drum. Then all was silent.” One can imagine that the other pilots on the squadron were given a salutary lesson by the tragedy suffered by their colleagues.

Another incident early in 1930 was amusing rather than tragic, but again involved fog. One day, fog rolled in from the sea and quickly blanketed the airfield. All the aircraft returned and landed safely except the one piloted by Flt. Lt. 'Fergie' Barrett. He managed to land, but finished his run by hitting the hangar doors head on! Made of asbestos sheeting, they gave way, and the first rescuers to arrive found Barrett standing unhurt by the wreck of his IIIF, his pipe still firmly clenched between his teeth! He always flew with it in his mouth and as a formation leader he exhorted the other pilots to “Put your wingtip in the bowl of my pipe and keep it there.”

February was devoted to routine training, but on 17 March the Wessex Bombing Area individual air pilotage, photographic and signals tests were held. 207 Squadron was placed second, with a score of 83.2 out of a possible 110 marks. Then in April came camera obscura exercises against mock targets in Birmingham and London, and in May 56 Squadron's Siskins flew in from North Weald to take part in fighter affiliation exercises with the squadron. Weather conditions prevented flying on half the allocated days, however. The remainder of the month was devoted to formation flying practice for the forthcoming RAF Display at Hendon. As in previous years, Andover was used as a base for combined practice, and while there the squadron took part in an 'At Home' display on 20 June before flying to Hendon for the Display which took place on 28 June.

After a short period of leave, 207 Squadron took part in a mobilisation exercise which began on 13 July. The squadron was ready to move by noon on 18 July, and three days later a road party set out for Catfoss. The aircraft, however, were grounded at Bircham Newton until 25 July due to bad weather. On arrival at Catfoss, the squadron made use of the Practice Camp facilities until setting off for Duxford, where the four-day ADGB air exercises were held from 11 to 15 August. 207 Squadron formed part of 'Red Colony', under the command of AVM Hugh C. T. Dowding CB CMG, an officer who within a few years became the architect of the air defences of Great Britain. Exactly ten years after his command of 'Red Colony' he was responsible for the operation of Fighter Command in the Battle of Britain. During this exercise 207 Squadron used Hornchurch as an advanced landing ground, and from there carried out reconnaissance patrols of the 'Blue Colony' airfields at Eastchurch, Manston, Hawkinge, Lympne and Tangmere, all of which would accommodate fighter squadrons during the Battle of Britain. The squadron then returned to Catfoss for more practice flying and visits from Air Marshal Sir Edward Ellington KCB CMG CBE, the AOC–in–C of Air Defence of Great Britain, and the Air Member for Personnel, AVM T. I. Webb–Bowen CB CMG, before flying south to Bircham Newton on 1 September with an August total of 616 hours to the crews' credit.

207 Squadron was placed fifth out of eight squadrons taking part in the Armament Officers' Trophy in October, then began preparing for the Annual Inspection by the AOC, AVM Sir John Steel KBE CB CMG, his last inspection before leaving to take command of the RAF in India.

While at Practice Camp at North Coates in 1931, Fairey IIIF J9647 [A3] struck the ground target during a mock attack. It was, however, repaired and flew again. [P. H. T. Green collection]

'C' Flight of 207 Squadron at Bircham Newton in 1931. In the second row were Flt. Sgt. Oakley, Plt. Off. Lucke, Flt. Lt. Brookman, Plt. Off. Cazelet and Plt. Off. Gracie, behind them Cpl. Prestwick, Cpl. (unidentified), Sgt. Durrant, Sgt. Fine, Sgt. Davis and Cpl. French. Airmen of the ground crews made up the remainder. [Wg. Cdr. Davis via AVM A. D. Dick]

1931 seems to have been a year of quiet routine training for 207 Squadron, with only individual tests and camera obscura exercises to break the monotony. The new AOC of Wessex Bombing Area, AVM C. L. N. Newall CB CMG CBE, did pay a visit on 31 March, however. A new CO, Sqn. Ldr. J. W. Woodhouse DSO MC, also arrived, to take command from 23 April. Practice Camp that year was held at North Coates Fitties from 11 May to 21 June, during which twelve crews were completely classified in bombing and air firing. Annual air exercises were held from 20 to 23 July, five mock raids being made on London targets. On 4 August 23 (Fighter) Squadron brought its Bristol Bulldogs from Kenley for fighter affiliation, and between 17 and 23 August 207 Squadron cooperated with the 1st Army Division in the Aldershot area. This was followed by reconnaissance work for the Medium Armoured Brigade on Salisbury Plain until 3 September, for which the squadron was based at Andover.

The first series of camera obscura exercises in 1932 took place in April, when mock raids were made on targets at Avonmouth, Thrapston, Highbridge and Andover. Of twenty-one raids planned, eighteen were attempted, sixteen were carried out and fourteen were successful. Fighter affiliation exercises in 1932 were with 41 Squadron, based at Northolt and equipped with Bristol Bulldogs. They flew to Bircham Newton on 2 May, and in spite of bad weather were able to carry out a large number of mock attacks on 207 Squadron's Fairey IIIFs in Flight and Squadron formations.

June was devoted largely to practice for the Hendon display, for which nine 207 Squadron aircraft were detached to Hornchurch from 22 to 25 June, when they took part in the set piece event. On 4 July the squadron moved to North Coates Fitties, where 2 Armament Training Camp had been formed on 1 January. There air bombing and firing practice was carried out until the squadron returned to base on 13 August. Squadron records created during that period were several. From an altitude of 6,000 feet the bombing error was 37.7 yards (34.5 m.) and from 10,000 feet it was 43 yards (39.3 m.). Best score for front gun firing was 98.5% and for rear gun ground target and towed target firing results were 62% and 99% respectively.

New aircraft on the horizon

While 207 Squadron members were enjoying a well-earned leave in September 1932, new equipment in the shape of the Fairey Gordon aircraft began to arrive at Bircham Newton. In essence, the Gordon was a IIIF with a radial 525 hp Armstrong Siddeley Panther IIa engine in place of the slightly higher-powered in-line Napier Lion of the IIIF; the Gordon prototype had in fact been known as the Fairey IIIF Mk.V. Some of 207 Squadron's Gordons were re-engined IIIFs while others were newly-built. Conversion to the new type presented few problems, although K2692 was written off when it flew into the ground near Docking in foggy weather on 29 November. Normal training continued through the last weeks of 1932 and into 1933, interrupted only by courses in 'air pilotage' and instrument flying — a new technique — for which instructors from the Air Pilotage School at Andover and the Central Flying School at Wittering were attached to the squadron in February. Sqn. Ldr. J. L. Vachell MC took over the command of 207 Squadron on 1 February, but relinquished the post on 29 September on posting to AHQ Iraq, and was superseded by Sqn. Ldr. G. G. Dawson.

For the first time, 207 Squadron did not take part in the annual RAF Display at Hendon in 1933, but this was only due to very bad weather on the day of the event. North

A fine shot of Fairey IIIF Mk.IVM K1169, piloted by Flt. Lt. Brookman in 1931. This aircraft was allocated to 207 Squadron from 24 February that year until going to Home Aircraft Depot on 19 September 1932 for conversion to a Gordon and subsequent service with other units. [via AVM A. D. Dick]

Coates Fitties was again the venue of the Practice Camp in July, after which the squadron was on leave.

In October 1933 three of the squadron's crews took their Gordons to Martlesham Heath to take part in wind velocity trials. Night flying training began on 14 November, and the new CO was attached to Central Flying School for an instrument flying course between 15 November and 7 December. In the past, little or no thought had been given to the problems posed by flying in cloud or at night. Such flying was accepted as a natural hazard, and pilots either learned how to deal with 'blind' flying from their more experienced peers or avoided it at all costs! By 1933 the staff of the CFS had investigated the matter and proposed a standard course of instruction for all pilots, using a hood over the cockpit of an aircraft to simulate the conditions. After sanction by the Air Ministry an Instrument Flying Course was inaugurated, the first students to be squadron commanders. An Avro 504N aircraft was then allocated to each squadron so that pilots could practice flying 'under the hood'. On his return to the squadron, Sqn. Ldr. Dawson began to train all his pilots in the techniques he had learned.

A Royal visit

In April 1934 the squadron flew to Catfoss, which was now known as 1 Armament Training Camp, for the annual air bombing and firing tests, many of which could not be carried out due to low cloud and sea fog. On 19 May the squadron was recalled to Bircham Newton with the news that Their Majesties King George V and Queen Mary were to visit the Station five days later, and intensive preparations were necessary. On the great day, the Royal couple inspected 207 Squadron's aircraft, which were parked on the airfield, and various types of aircraft and equipment inside the hangars. In attendance were the Rt. Hon. the Marquess of Londonderry KG MVO, the Secretary of State for Air; Rt. Hon. Sir Phillip Sassoon Bart. GBE CMG MP, the Under Secretary; Air Marshal Sir Robert Brooke–Popham KCB CMG DSO AFC ADC, the AOC Air Defence of Great Britain; Air Cdre. H. R. Nicholl CBE, the AOC Central Area; Wg. Cdr. Raymond Collishaw DSO OBE DSC DFC, the Station Commander at Bircham Newton; and last but by no means least Sqn. Ldr. Graham G. Dawson, 207 Squadron's Commanding Officer.

A montage of Gordons carefully assembled in a circle, 207 Squadron on the right, 35 Squadron on the left, at an RAF Display at Hendon. Identifiable aircraft are K1758 [A4], J9674 [B4], and J9073 [B3]. [RAFM P7818]

207 was one of many squadrons which had an unofficial badge between the wars. The winged lion statant formed the basis of an official badge awarded in 1936.

The excitement over, 207 Squadron concentrated on its annual task of preparing for the RAF Display, which took place on 30 June. Another display, this time to students of the Imperial Defence College, was given at Andover, to where the squadron was attached from 8 to 10 July. This time, however, the squadron's normal functions in time of war were the object of the demonstration. Rounding off the month, annual three-day exercises began on 23 July and involved mock attacks on London and on the private airfield at Whitley, near Coventry.

Following Sqn. Ldr. Dawson's promotion to Wg. Cdr. in July, Sqn. Ldr. P. A. Maitland AFC took over as CO on 9 August. A sad loss to the squadron occurred on 25 August when Plt. Off. P. H. P. Simonds was killed at Manston in the crash of a civilian aircraft in which he was a passenger. For the remainder of the year routine training and quite frequent inspections by high-ranking officers were the order of the day. Among the latter was a party of Japanese naval officers who witnessed a display given by 35 and 207 Squadrons on 31 August.

A fine shot of Fairey Gordon K1170 of 207 Squadron . [via R. C. B. Ashworth and P. H. T. Green]

The beginning of expansion of the RAF

By now the expansion of the Royal Air Force to meet a perceived threat from Nazi Germany was rapidly gathering pace, and experienced officers found themselves posted at more frequent intervals than in former years. Thus it was that Sqn. Ldr. Maitland was promoted to Wg. Cdr. on 1 January 1935 after just a few months in command of 207 Squadron and on 6 February Sqn. Ldr. R. J. Rodwell took over from the temporary CO, Flt. Lt. B. A. J. Crummy. Flt. Lt. (later Gp. Capt.) Crummy recalls that 207 Squadron had an additional role to play, as it had been selected as the second 'cloud flying' squadron in the RAF, the first being 12 Squadron at Andover. To allow the squadron to practice this role, the aircraft were modified and exposed flying control surfaces were covered in to avoid icing up. Eventually, the squadron could put up a formation of three or four aircraft able to remain in cloud for periods of at least 45 minutes. Ice accretion trials with the RAE were also carried out, and on one occasion an aircraft collected 3.5 inches (90 mm.) of ice, of which 2.5 inches (63 mm.) remained when the aircraft touched down!

For the first time, RAF Bircham Newton was thrown open to the general public on Empire Air Day, 25 May 1935, and 207 Squadron carried out a programme of flying demonstrations. Three days later the crews flew to Abingdon for bombing practice on the nearby Otmoor range, returning to base on 6 June. More hectic days followed when the squadron departed on 11 June for annual armament training at Catfoss, from where the crews returned on 19 July. That month 589 hours in the air were recorded.

Fairey Gordon K2691 [B1] overshot while landing at Bircham Newton and suffered a collapsed undercarriage. Here it is being inspected by RAF personnel, local civilians and the inevitable urchins! [P. H. T. Green collection]

207 Squadron goes to war

Under 'Il Duce', the dictator Benito Mussolini, Italy in the mid-nineteen-thirties developed a desire to acquire colonies, and in July decided to turn the African state of Abyssinia into a sphere of Italian influence. This was of course not to the liking of the Emperor of Abyssinia, Haile Selassie, or to other European countries, which called for a League of Nations conference to settle the dispute. On 18 August Mussolini rejected an Anglo/French plan for a settlement, and after a number of cynical pledges and in the face of economic sanctions Mussolini invaded Abyssinia on 2 October. It was in this situation that the British government decided to send RAF squadrons to neighbouring Sudan (then a British mandate) to prevent possible incursions by Italian forces bent on taking as much territory as possible.

One of the squadrons chosen for this policing role was 207, which received orders on 12 September to proceed overseas for service in Middle East Command. Accordingly, the twelve 'initial equipment' Gordon aircraft were overhauled and flown to the Packing Depot at Sealand

Probably taken in the autumn of 1933, this picture of 207 Squadron personnel in front of a Gordon includes several officers who went on to greater things. The CO, Sqn. Ldr. Graham Dawson, tenth from the left and almost under the propeller boss, became an AVM and Chief Engineering Officer in the MEAF during the Second World War and rapidly improved aircraft serviceability. His hobby while with 207 Squadron was the construction of steam-operated models. Others of note were Flt. Lt. Frank Wright [CO 'C' Flight – ninth from left); Flt. Lt. Ware (CO 'B' Flight – eleventh from left); and Flt. Lt. Basil Crummy (CO 'A' Flight – twelfth from left, later a Gp. Capt.). [Gp. Capt. H. S. Darley via AVM A. D. Dick]

Pilots of 207 Squadron line up for the camera in front of Gordon J9067 in 1933. (Left to right): Sgt. Mitchell, Sgt. Lawton, Plt. Off. Terdrey, Flg. Off. Bax, Flt. Lt. Ware, Sqn. Ldr. Vachell, Flt. Lt. Crummy, Sgt. Gould and Sgt. Goodwin. In the 1950s Gp. Capt. Crummy was Station Commander at RAF Wilmslow, where many members of the WRAF did their basic training. [Quadrant Picture Library / Flight International]

On the voyage to Port Sudan, men of 207 Squadron spotted aircraft carrier HMS Courageous in Alexandria harbour. [D. H. Chandler]

for crating, then loaded on board the SS *Antilochus,* together with an extra twelve aircraft as an immediate reserve. Many postings into and out of the squadron took place, effectively bringing personnel numbers up to establishment. The personnel then went on embarkation leave, after which they were 'kitted up'. Mr. D. H. Chandler, a 'Trenchard brat' who had been serving with 207 Squadron since December 1932, remembers being issued with the unfamiliar clothing and accoutrements. "Our issue of tropical kit included a Wolseley type of helmet, similar to that of the Royal Marines, and a puggaree" he recalls. "This was a long ribbon of linen-like material about 72 inches by 5 inches [183 cm. by 12.5 cm.] which had to be folded to about an inch and a half [38 mm.] wide and cunningly

A view of the Suez Canal from the SS Cameronia, which carried 207 Squadron to the Sudan. [D. H. Chandler]

wrapped around the helmet as a form of heat protection for the temples – a relic of Kitchener's days, perhaps. The camp tailor had no clues, perhaps not surprisingly so in deepest Norfolk. One or two 'old sweats' claimed some knowledge from previous tours in Iraq and India, but results were not encouraging. Most of us were content to give way to the unobtainable, but it was some time before the lightweight working-type pith helmets caught up with us. Another item of kit was a spine pad. Apparently this was supposed to be suspended from the neck and hang down the back to protect the spine. The only time I saw them in use was when, cut in two, they were used as shin guards in impromptu games of football." Before leaving England, all kitbags had to be marked with the identity letters RR, as for security reasons squadron numbers were not to be used.

On 4 October twelve officers, three Warrant Officers and 160 other ranks of the squadron travelled to Liverpool and embarked in SS *Cameronia*, which sailed the same day on its first voyage as a troop transport. Other bomber squadrons embarked in the *Cameronia* were 12 Sqn. from

A troopship in Lake Timsah on its way to Abyssinia with Italian soldiers, seen by the men of 207 Squadron, who were about to prevent incursions into the Sudan by those very troops! [D. H. Chandler]

Andover, which was bound for Aden; 33 Sqn. from Upper Heyford, bound for Aboukir in Egypt; 35 Sqn. from Bircham Newton and going to the Sudan; and 142 Sqn. from Andover, bound for Aboukir. In addition there were three fighter squadrons: 3 Sqn. from Kenley on its way to the Sudan; 29 Sqn. from North Weald bound for Egypt; and 41 Sqn. from Northolt for Aden. Finally, 22 (Torpedo Bomber) Sqn. from Donibristle was being sent to Malta. Personnel of 51 and 52 Maintenance Units, one of which became 4 Aircraft Park and the other went to Aboukir, were on board. After disembarking 22 Squadron at Malta and 29, 33 and 142 Squadrons at Alexandria, *Cameronia* sailed through the Suez Canal. The ship anchored at Lake Timsah to allow other ships to pass, but the secrecy element was ruined when a Lloyd-Triestino liner packed with Italian soldiers moored alongside her! Before long, the ship reached Port Sudan, where it tied up at 19.00 on 20 October.

"It ain't 'alf 'ot, Mum"!

After disembarking, 207 Squadron personnel were accommodated in cotton-storage sheds belonging to Sudan Railways. Early next morning, SS *Antilochus* arrived, and the task of unloading the aircraft began. In conditions of extreme heat and with makeshift facilities, the ground crews worked well, and the uncrated aircraft were taken by road to a hastily-prepared temporary landing ground about a mile from the quayside. There, with the help of engineers and native labourers from Sudan Railways, they were assembled. Without this assistance and the loan of some vital equipment, the work would have taken much longer than it did. To provide some relaxation, an open-air cinema was erected. While the film was being changed, Allsop's

Loading the squadron's possessions onto a train at Port Sudan in October 1935.]

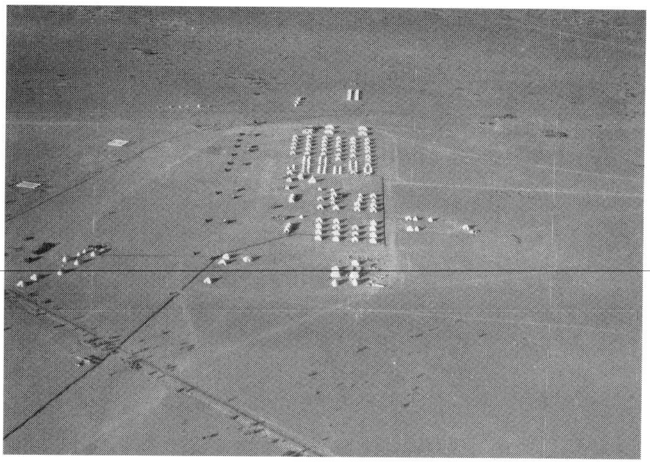

The squadron's home for five months – Ed Damer, near Atabara, in Berber territory.

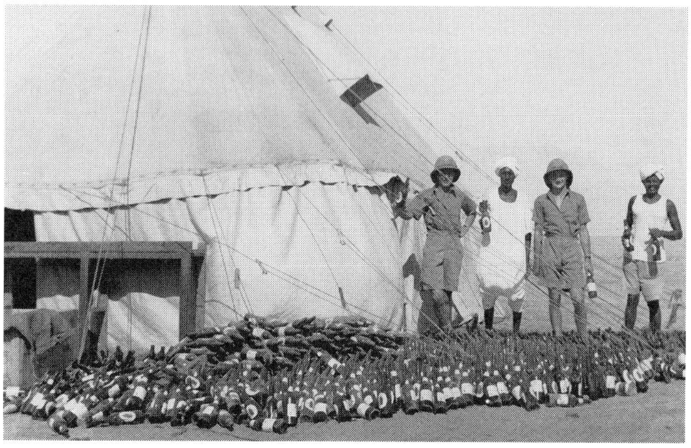

Tom Rouse and D. Chandler shortly after arrivalat Port Sudan. Water was in short supply, but evidently not beer!

Motor transport was also in short supply in the Sudan, so 'ships of the desert' came into favour.

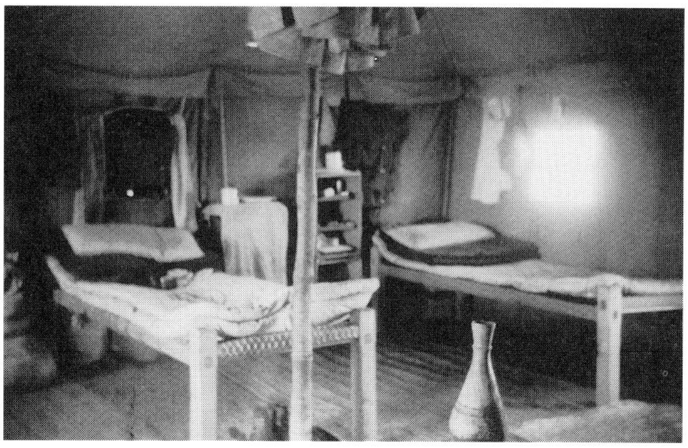

Inside a living tent at Gebeit were wood-framed 'pits' with thin mattresses, but storage space was minimal.

The erecting party at Port Sudan dealing with Gordon K2649 [A3].

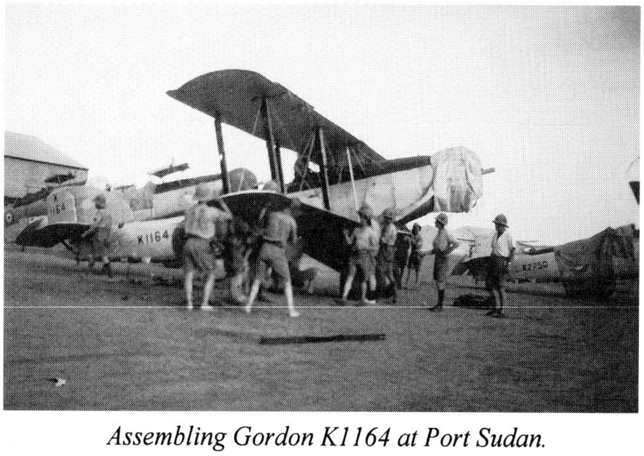

Assembling Gordon K1164 at Port Sudan.

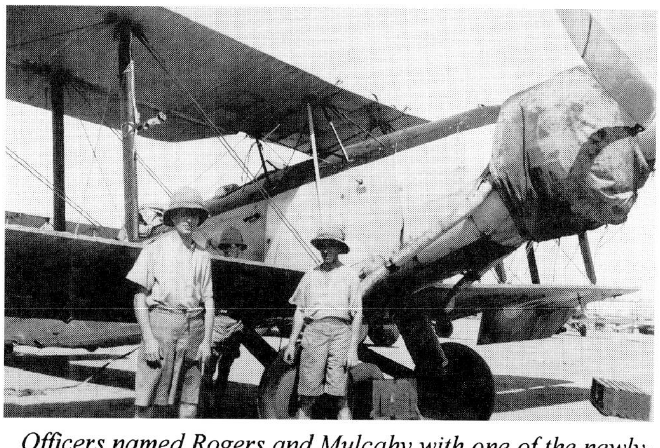

Officers named Rogers and Mulcahy with one of the newly-assembled Gordons at Port Sudan. [all D. H. Chandler]

(1) *The 207 Squadron train, temporary drivers Ross and Northcott on the foot-plate, the regular drivers below. Prominently displayed was the squadron's 'gen' board. (2) Ablutions were, like everything else, somewhat basic in the Sudan. The wash-basins were on the floor! (3) Filling a newly-erected Gordon with fuel from cans at Port Sudan in October 1935.* *[all D. H. Chandler]*

'Red Hand' beer, priced at 5 piastres, equivalent at the time to one shilling (5p.), was brought round by waiters, a service much enjoyed by the thirsty 'erks'.

Meanwhile, in London the Foreign Secretary, Sir Samuel Hoare, said on 22 October that Britain was trying to uphold the League of Nations in its greatest test. "If the League fails" he said "the world will be faced with a period of danger and gloom." How right he was.

By 28 October all the Gordons had been assembled and air tested, and that day the 'initial equipment' aircraft were flown to Ed Damer, about 170 miles (270 km.) north-east of Khartoum on the River Nile, where the squadron would be based. Ground personnel followed that night by train. 'Immediate reserve' aircraft were taken by rail a few days later to Atbara, where 4 Aircraft Park was set up. The squadrons in the Sudan, and 4 Aircraft Park, were administered by 5 Wing, which was formed on 26 October at 2 River Front West, Khartoum, under the command of Gp. Capt. R. Collishaw DSO OBE DSC AFC, who until recently had been Station Commander at Bircham Newton. At Ed Damer a landing ground had been prepared and a tented camp erected by men of the 2nd Bn. Sherwood Foresters, under the supervision of Mr. W. D. Purvis, the Governor of the Northern Province, and Brig. Franklin.

Although each squadron had separate administration, 207 and 35 Squadrons shared messing and other facilities. As there was no Station HQ, the CO of 35 Sqn., Sqn. Ldr. C. W. Hill, was made responsible for discipline of the whole Station. From early November, 207 Squadron was employed on a variety of tasks. A major one was the selection and preparation of advanced landing grounds, some up to 300 miles (nearly 500 km.) from Ed Damer, from which raids on the port of Massawa could be made if necessary. Two officers from the squadron were detailed to set up these landing grounds, one of which was to be 'secret'. For this one, a small island known as Erih, three quarters of a mile (1.2 km.) off shore, was selected. The two officers, accompanied by Sgt. Boggust and a civilian surveyor, laid out this airfield, which could be operational at thirty minutes' notice by setting out portable boundary markers. After a short discussion it was decided that the island should be called Crummy Island after Flt. Lt. Crummy and the channel should be Boggust Channel after the sergeant of that name. Gp. Capt. Collishaw at 5 Wing wanted several more landing grounds to be located alongside the railway line from Port Sudan to Kassala, and ground crews to service aircraft using these airfields were accommodated in a commandeered train defended by anti-aircraft guns. In charge, and sometimes acting as train driver, was Flg. Off. R. Isherwood. Construction of firing and bombing ranges at Ed Damer was also important. Add to this the provision of a daily service carrying official mail to Kassala and Khartoum and a normal training routine and it will be seen that the squadron was fully occupied! It was during a formation flying exercise on 12 November that two of the Gordons, K2697 and K2714, collided over Ed Damer, but both landed without much difficulty and were repaired.

Aircraft were picketed in the open, as no hangars existed at Ed Damer, and were at the mercy of strong sand-laden winds. Engines suffered from sand deposits, which caused a serious increase in oil consumption and excessive wear, but

The Gordons of 207 Squadron's 'A' Flight in formation over the village of Ed Damer, with the River Nile very much in evidence. Nearest to the camera was K1699 [A3].
[D. H. Chandler]

Gordon K1164 [C4] seen from another aircraft when flying through a mountainous pass in the Sudan. [D. H. Chandler]

otherwise they were not harmed. Refuelling was a tedious business, as all fuel came from four-gallon (18.2 litre) drums and had to be decanted into aircraft tanks through a funnel in which a chamois leather acted as a filter. Practical help was still provided whole-heartedly by the Governor and by Sudan Railways, without whose assistance it was regarded as doubtful whether the squadron could have operated. In addition, the Atbara Club was thrown open to all officers, the Atbara Sports Club to senior NCOs and the swimming pool to airmen once or twice a week, although as soon as the airmen left the pool, it was drained for cleaning purposes! There was also a racecourse, to which Chandler and his pals were invited just once to watch camel- and horse-racing.

Hours in the air totalled 295 in November and 404 in December. During November, Italy completed its occupation of the Tigre province of Abyssinia and threatened to leave the League of Nations if sanctions continued. In England, the Foreign Secretary resigned on 18 December after a public outcry over a deal he planned to make with the French Premier, Pierre Laval, for appeasing Mussolini. Under this, Italy's right to keep fertile parts of Abyssinia would have been recognised. Aggression in Abyssinia continued, and the RAF squadrons kept an eye on the situation.

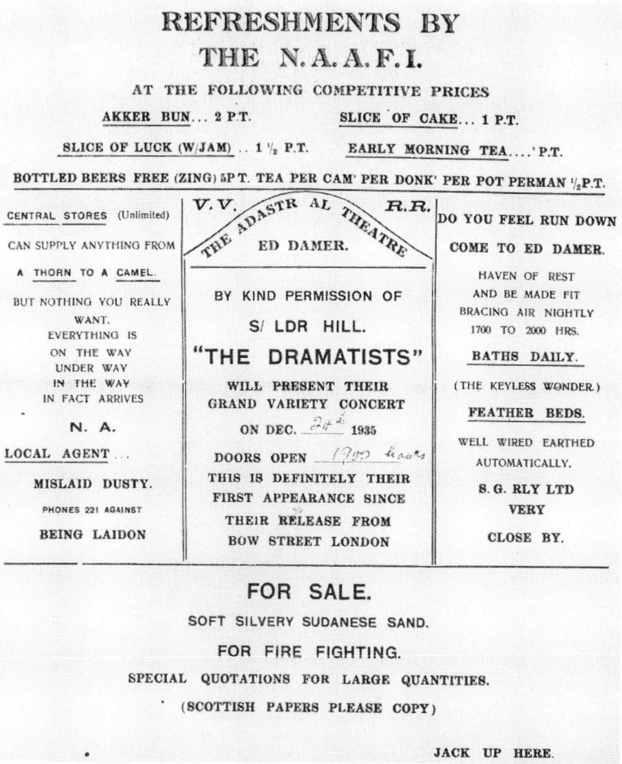

REFRESHMENTS BY
THE N.A.A.F.I.
AT THE FOLLOWING COMPETITIVE PRICES
AKKER BUN... 2 P.T. SLICE OF CAKE... 1 P.T.
SLICE OF LUCK (W/JAM) .. 1 ½ P.T. EARLY MORNING TEA....' P.T.
BOTTLED BEERS FREE (ZING) 5P T. TEA PER CAM' PER DONK' PER POT PERMAN ½P.T.

CENTRAL STORES (Unlimited)
CAN SUPPLY ANYTHING FROM
A THORN TO A CAMEL.
BUT NOTHING YOU REALLY WANT.
EVERYTHING IS
ON THE WAY
UNDER WAY
IN THE WAY
IN FACT ARRIVES
N. A.
LOCAL AGENT ...
MISLAID DUSTY.
PHONES 221 AGAINST
BEING LAIDON

V. V. THE ADASTRAL THEATRE R. R.
ED DAMER.
BY KIND PERMISSION OF
S/ LDR HILL.
"THE DRAMATISTS"
WILL PRESENT THEIR
GRAND VARIETY CONCERT
ON DEC. 24th 1935
DOORS OPEN 1700 hours
THIS IS DEFINITELY THEIR
FIRST APPEARANCE SINCE
THEIR RELEASE FROM
BOW STREET LONDON

DO YOU FEEL RUN DOWN
COME TO ED DAMER.
HAVEN OF REST
AND BE MADE FIT
BRACING AIR NIGHTLY
1700 TO 2000 HRS.
BATHS DAILY.
(THE KEYLESS WONDER.)
FEATHER BEDS.
WELL WIRED EARTHED
AUTOMATICALLY.
S. G. RLY LTD
VERY
CLOSE BY.

FOR SALE.
SOFT SILVERY SUDANESE SAND.
FOR FIRE FIGHTING.
SPECIAL QUOTATIONS FOR LARGE QUANTITIES.
(SCOTTISH PAPERS PLEASE COPY)
JACK UP HERE.

The programme of the first concert to be held at Ed Damer, on 24 December 1935. [D. H. Chandler]

Entering the spirit of Christmas Day 1935. [D. H. Chandler]

Sadly, one of the Gordons (JR9643) crashed near Gebeit on 27 January 1936, with the deaths of the three on board, Flt. Lt. S. G. Connolly, Flt. Lt. P. V. Edwards and LAC F. Campling, and on 2 March K2753 also came to grief when it stalled on the approach to Aqiq landing ground. The new routines were followed in January and February, but in March Sqn. Ldr. Rodwell left for the UK due to ill health. He was succeeded as CO by Sqn. Ldr. J. W. Lissett, who joined from 142 Squadron.

A new landing ground had been prepared at Gebeit, and on 6 April the squadron, with 35 Squadron, took up residence there. About 37 miles (60 km.) from Port Sudan, Gebeit was located in the hills at an altitude of about 2,600 feet (800 m.) with the border of Italian Eritrea about 125 miles (200 km.) to the south-east. Also in residence was 'C' Company of the 2nd Bn. Royal Sussex Regiment, and on 14 April, 5 Wing HQ moved in from Khartoum and took up the duties of a Station HQ in addition to the normal Wing tasks.

The Luftwaffe appeared to have developed some sort of grudge against Waddington-based squadrons, as on 9 May between 00.30 and 02.30 a disastrous raid on the Station took place. Two land mines which fell in the nearby village demolished the church and nineteen houses, causing one death, serious injuries to six people and slight injuries to 43 others. Seventy-one houses were badly damaged and 160 slightly so, leaving 400 residents homeless until repairs could be made. One fortunate escaper was the landlord of the 'Horse & Jockey' public house, a favourite relaxation spot for Waddington-based aircrews, who was asleep when the land mine fell. The situation on the Station was much more serious, as five bombs demolished the NAAFI and a nearby air raid shelter, killing three airmen and seven NAAFI girls, including the manageress, Mrs. Constance Raven. In her memory the Junior Ranks Club and NAAFI is now known as the Raven Club. Flg. Off. Murray and the CO were the last people left in the officers' mess after a party. "Most of the ante-room furniture was upside-down after 'games' between 44 and 207 Squadrons," he remembers. "We were about to sip our last night-cap pint when the parachute land-mine struck the spire of Waddington church. We both dived under the nearest upturned sofa without either of us spilling a drop of beer! Very quickly we drove in the CO's Jeep to the village and spent the rest of the night dealing with casualties – a sobering and harrowing experience." Former WAAF Mrs. Irene Jackson (née Berry), who worked in the pay accounts section, was unable to reach the shelter and lay down in a ditch. "Many of my friends were killed," she says. "I was shattered. Suffering from nervous exhaustion, I was posted to 12 Group." Before the disastrous raid, she had been quite contented with their lot. "We had duty rotas with evenings off duty when we all used to meet and have fun in the 'Horse & Jockey'. On Saturday nights we went on to the Village Hall dances, stayed too late and came back to camp on the floor of the officers' cars, their feet spread over us for concealment. Sometimes we were caught and 'put on the carpet'. Later, when the bombing became constant and every night many of our aircrews failed to return, so many killed, we had to work night and day closing the deceaseds' accounts."

Three Manchester crews were briefed to raid Berlin and one to attack Mannheim on 9/10 May, but the aircraft piloted by Flt. Lt. Taylor DFC returned to base with W/T failure after an hour in the air. Plt. Off. Herring's aircraft, L7316 [EM:U], was attacked by a Bf 110 twin-engined fighter over the North Sea and the crew claimed to have shot it down before continuing to Berlin, where the Manchester was hit by heavy flak while in the process of dropping six 1,000 lb. bombs. The aircraft sent to Mannheim off-loaded a 4,000-pounder into the target area, causing a large fire.

Two Manchesters took to the air on 10 May to raid Berlin again, in conjunction with 97 Squadron. L7309 [EM:J], piloted by Sqn. Ldr. Kydd, was intercepted by two Bf 110s between Rensburg and Husum and damaged, but one fighter was claimed as destroyed by rear gunner Flg. Off. Oliver before the Manchester returned to base. During this engagement, Sgt. Linklater was acting as wireless operator, and with his head poked up into the astrodome gave a running commentary of events, interspersed with a wide range of expletives! Joseph 'Scotty' Scott, who was in the front turret, remembers that Linklater gave instructions to Sqn. Ldr. Kydd which helped him take evasive action. The result of their combined efforts was that Flg. Off. Oliver was awarded an immediate DFC and Sgt. Linklater a DFM. On board this aircraft was Maj. Holmes of the Royal Artillery, the anti-aircraft liaison officer with 5 Group. The other Manchester, flown by Flg. Off. Romans DFC, reached 'the big city' and dropped five 1,000 lb. and three 250 lb. bombs and a package of leaflets on the eastern side of the target. Meanwhile, Flg. Off. Murray DFC in L7381 delivered a 4,000-pounder which caused a large fire in Mannheim. Arriving at Waddington after the mission, Sqn. Ldr. Kydd discovered that he lacked almost all elevator control, which caused the aircraft to fly into the ground rather than make a flared-out touch-down. It was quickly found that almost all the fabric covering of the central fin had been torn off during the fighter attack and there were also about 360 perforations in the airframe.

Mannheim was again visited on 12/13 May, by two aircraft, neither of which was able to locate the primary target. Instead, one dropped six 1,000 lb. bombs on Cologne and the other put down a similar load on a railway junction at Coblenz. While on final approach to Waddington after this raid, Flg. Off. Lewis's L7322 [EM:B] was illuminated by a local searchlight battery, a most undesirable fact as a Luftwaffe intruder dropped a stick of bombs close by. Next came a raid on Berlin by four aircraft on 15 May, each Manchester carrying six 1,000-pounders. However, only two actually dropped their bombs, as one aircraft aborted due to an excessive engine oil temperature and another reached Berlin with bomb doors that refused to open. A third unloaded on Hanover, as the pilot considered that his aircraft was using too much fuel to reach the primary target. This raid was regarded by all as a dismal failure and a reflection on the Manchester's poor design and performance. Not only were lives being lost without good reason, but manpower was being used on what seemed to be an unworthy cause.

Grounded!

Troubles with the Manchester still persisting, on 17 May an order was received prohibiting the use of Manchesters operationally. Intensive training was to be carried out and test flights were to be made to determine engine behaviour. The opportunity was taken to practice Standard Beam Approaches and to carry out practice bombing at Bassingham Fen. During a long cross-country flight on 18 May, the starboard engine of L7393 caught fire, and the pilot, Sqn. Ldr. Mackintosh, had to make a belly-landing at Perranporth airfield on the Cornish coast, damaging the aircraft considerably and injuring the crew slightly. On this occasion a crew of six plus three supernumerary aircrew were on board. Flt. Lt. Taylor was sent down at once in L7280 with Mr. Walker and Mr. Nicholson to investigate the cause. Oil filters seem to have been the problem, as on 22 May all were found to be unserviceable! Sqn. Ldr. Kydd promptly flew to Woodford and brought back 86 new ones, which were quickly fitted, allowing the aircraft to begin air testing. Almost at once, seven aircraft were put on standby to attack the *Bismark* and *Prinz Eugen* but later stood down. Meanwhile, on 21 May, Wg. Cdr. K. Purdon Lewis took command of the squadron.

During that spring, anti-aircraft batteries defending Nottingham were fitted with new radar-operated prediction equipment which was soon under test. Before long, the operators raised doubts about the ability of their new gadget to detect the presence of gliders or an aircraft with engines switched off. As a result, 207 Squadron was asked to carry out a series of tests over Nottingham with engines on the Manchesters cut! The plan consisted of climbing to 20,000 feet (or as high as the aircraft would go) upwind of Nottingham, feathering both propellers and gliding across the city. When a point about twenty miles (32 km.) south of the city at an altitude of about 3,000 feet had been reached, the propellers would be unfeathered, the engines started and a return to Waddington begun. A pilot on two such flights was Flg. Off. W. J. Lewis, who flew L7321 on 23 May and L7377 on 11 June. "These flights were responsible for adding twenty years to my age and covering my head with a fine crop of grey hair!", he wrote years later. "We were experiencing considerable trouble with sticking solenoids on those early feathering props. When this happened the aircraft battery was quickly drained, so that when you came to unfeather there was no power and consequently no unfeathering. These glides were somewhat nerve-racking in themselves. The Manchester did not have any back-up venturi tube, both engines being fitted with pumps to drive the appropriate instruments on the flying panel. When both engines were feathered it was [a case of] 'Look, Daddy! No instruments'. Waiting for a cloudless day would have been comparable to waiting for the Second Coming, so we did glides through the cloud cover, flying by the seat of our pants. It was little wonder that the radar tracks of some of our flights resembled agonised snakes."

At West Raynham on 6 June 1941, examples of Bomber Command aircraft were brought together for inspection by the Prime Minister, Winston Churchill, among them a Manchester Mk.I of 207 Squadron. Behind Churchill, can be seen Sqn. Ldr. Kydd, and from the left the crew was Nunn, Oliver, Goldstraw, Scott and Linklater, and a corporal and two other airmen representing the ground crew. [207 Squadron archives]

Early June saw continued investigation into the Vulture engine malfunctions, with several visits from representatives of Rolls–Royce and from senior RAF engineering officers. To add to the trouble, the port engine of L7318 caught fire soon after being started on 2 June, caused by the failure of the big-end bolt, it was thought. An engine on L7317 had developed a coolant leak the previous day and when the coolant system was pressurised extensive leaks were found, yet another problem adding to the frustration of the engineering staff. This engine was sent to Rolls-Royce for further investigation.

An inspection of examples of RAF aircraft was held at West Raynham on 6 June for the benefit of the Prime Minister, Winston Churchill. 207 Squadron sent a Manchester piloted by Sqn. Ldr. Kydd, with a normal crew plus three groundcrew airmen. On arrival at West Raynham the pilot carried out a beat-up of the airfield, feathered one engine and repeated the trick, then glided past with both engines feathered before restarting the engines and landing! After this show of bravery bordering on recklessness the crew were presented to the great man himself, which pleased them all immensely.

Two Manchesters took off on 10 June with Wg. Cdr. Harris and Lt. Currie RNVR on board on night-time smoke-screen observation flights, and this exercise was repeated on two successive nights. On 13 June a silent approach attack was simulated with Nottingham as the target, the third time that such a ploy had been tried and the first in which the defences had spotted the intruders. During the first such mock raid, on 14 June, Flt. Lt. Burton-Gyles in L7377 made a gliding approach, but when the phase was complete the port propeller failed to unfeather, prompting 'BG' to look for a large field in which to 'pancake'. Fortunately, Harlaxton airfield came into view, and there the Manchester was landed, just missing a flock of Oxford twin-engined training aircraft which were taking off!

Simulated attacks on Manchesters were made on 16 June by Hurricanes of the Air Fighting Development Unit from Duxford, but this experience had to be curtailed due to bad weather. In any case, that day all Manchesters were grounded yet again, for modifications to coolant systems and cabin heating and the thermostat overflow valves. This work was completed in four days, after which seven aircraft were air tested.

Back to operations

On 21 June 207 Squadron was back in business! Eight Manchesters were detailed, with others of 61 and 97 Squadrons, to drop twelve 500 lb. GP bombs each on shipping in Boulogne harbour, and seven took off. Of these, four successfully attacked the target, one attacked the 'last resort' target of Calais docks before landing at Biggin Hill, whereupon one engine caught fire, and one brought its bomb-load back to base after the front gunner had inadvertently pulled the handle on his parachute. Piloted by Flg. Off. J. D. G. Withers, the seventh (L7314 EM:Y) was shot down in flames by a 'friendly' Beaufighter near Wollaston, Northamptonshire, at about 01.55 on 22 June, when the aircraft was outward-bound. Confusion had been caused when the controller in the operations room of 10 Group, Fighter Command, had scrambled Beaufighters of 25 Squadron from Wittering to intercept and destroy a Luftwaffe intruder, which by chance had been flying on a track similar to the Manchester's. The Beaufighter pilot recognised the Manchester but was ordered to shoot down what the controller firmly believed was a hostile aircraft. The unlucky crew had only about twenty minutes of operational flying before losing their lives, and traces of only five of the seven men aboard were found after this sad incident. Another mishap occurred the same day, when L7310 [EM:H] suffered an engine failure on take-off and crashed into trees and an earth bank at Dunston Pillar, on the east side of the Sleaford road; all three on board, including Sqn. Ldr. Charles Kydd DSO DFC, were taken to hospital at Bracebridge Heath with serious injuries, and sadly Sqn. Ldr. Kydd and Flt. Sgt. J. W. Arnott died there later. The flight had been arranged in order to check out Plt. Off. L. Syrett as a potential captain. Sqn. Ldr. Kydd was a courageous and conscientious man who set an example to other aircrew which, in the opinion of 'Scotty' Scott could only be described as superb. His untimely death was a great loss to 207 Squadron and to all others who knew him.

Next target to receive attention from 207 Squadron was Dusseldorf, for which six Manchesters took off on 23 June. Two of them carried one 4,000 lb. bomb only, while the others were loaded with six 1,000 lb. GPs and 180 incendiaries. Much difficulty was experienced by the pilots of these heavily-laden aircraft, partly due to the high air temperature causing overheating and consequent reduction of power output. Two of them failed to reach the target, dropping their loads on airfields at Flushing and Haamstede instead. The same target was raided next night by five aircraft.

After a one-night break, crews of eight Manchesters of 207 Squadron were briefed to attack Kiel, and seven took off, the eighth going unserviceable after its tailwheel burst while taxying. The month's final mission was a raid by eight aircraft on Hamburg on 29 June, but again one suffered a burst tailwheel and another developed an electrical malfunction. During this mission fire broke out in the starboard engine of L7316 [EM:U], captained by Flg. Off. Hills, who jettisoned the bomb-load before restarting the engine and returning safely to base after preparing for what had seemed an inevitable ditching in the North Sea.

German servicemen about to begin salvaging the remains of 207 Squadron Manchester L7380 [EM:W] from the beach at Ameland, where Flt. Lt. Lewis had ditched it in shallow water during the night of 7/8 September 1941. External completeness contrasts with the devastation wrought internally by the crew before they escaped. [207 Squadron archives and G. J. Zwanenburg]

A nice airborne shot of a Handley Page Hampden, although not identifiable as one of those used for a short time by 207 Squadron. [via J. Scutts]

Afterwards, an exhaust manifold was found to have a large hole through which flames played on the engine cowling.

By 27 June all the options on the matter of the mid-upper turret had been investigated, and it was decided that the three fins on the Manchester Mk.I would be deleted and twin fins of the new Lancaster type substituted, allowing the FN.7A turret to be reinstalled. Aircraft on the production line would be fitted with new fins as soon as they became available, and later retrospective alteration to service aircraft would be carried out. In the meantime the turrets would be re-installed to operate with a restricted field of fire, and so the ever-ready ground crews set to work again.

On the last day of the month it was decided that, following two further engine failures in Manchesters belonging to 61 Squadron at Hemswell, all Manchesters would again be grounded. At a conference held at 5 Group HQ that day, attended by Wg. Cdr. Lewis and Flt. Lt. McCabe, intensive flying by four aircraft of each of the three Manchester-equipped squadrons would be commenced. This task began on 1 July but was stopped three days later as a result of further engine failures. On 6 July orders were received for one aircraft with new engines to achieve 240 hours of intensive flying as quickly as possible, but all other Manchesters would remain on the ground while new engines were installed. At the same time, modifications to the oil cooling system were to be made by Avro personnel.

Hampdens to the rescue

To employ the aircrews who were now grounded for lack of aircraft, several were detached to other squadrons, including five crews who flew on operations in Hampdens with 44 Squadron, which was also based at Waddington. On 8 July four second pilots who were qualified as Hampden captains were posted to newly-formed 408 Squadron at Lindholme with six WOp/AGs, while five observers and four WOp/AGs went to 49 Squadron at Scampton, and three observers went with six WOp/AGs to 50 Squadron at Lindholme. Four Hampdens were received by 207 Squadron on 11 July, to be used as an interim measure pending the solution of the Manchester's

An evocative picture of a Manchester of 207 Squadron formating on a 44 Squadron Hampden over Lincolnshire. [Quadrant Picture Library / Flight International]

apparently never-ending troubles. The Manchester chosen as the intensive trials aircraft was L7419, for which two new engines arrived from Rolls–Royce by 13 July and were installed at once, although Avro technicians were still hard at work on their modifications. A decision had, however, been made by the Air Ministry some time previously that Manchester production would be superseded by Lancasters as soon as possible, and at the Avro factory work was proceeding quickly on tooling up for the infinitely-better aircraft.

The Manchester's technical problems added weight to the Prime Minister's avowed intention of providing a force of four thousand heavy bombers for the RAF. On 8 July Churchill wrote "There is one thing that will bring Hitler down, and that is an absolutely devastating exterminating attack by very heavy bombers from this country upon the Nazi homeland." Unfortunately, it would be some time before anything approaching that level of activity could be realised.

During air tests on 16 July, L7419 experienced tail flutter, and the elevator trim tabs were changed. Intensive flying began next day, three crews aiming to fly for five hours per day each, beginning at 06.00 hours. Two corporals who were hoping to become flight engineers flew on alternate trips to advise the captain about the required tests and to record data on engine performance. Whenever the Manchester was airborne, squadrons at Digby were offered the chance of fighter interception practice.

The first operation for the four 207 Squadron Hampden aircraft took place on 19 July, when two of them carried out sea mining ('gardening') in area 'Eglantine' off the mouth of the River Elbe. In addition, they each carried two 500 lb. GP bombs which they off-loaded on land targets. Meanwhile, installation of new engines in all Manchesters continued, and arrangements were made for the trials aircraft to carry out high level bombing practice on each flight. On 23 July two broken saddle bolts were discovered on a starboard engine, and were replaced without grounding the aircraft for long. Daily flight times totalled up to fifteen hours ten minutes, and refuelling was carried out in as little as fifteen minutes.

Four Hampdens took off on 21 July to raid the main post office and telephone exchange at Frankfurt, but found it difficult to pinpoint the target. Three nights later they targetted the shipyards at Kiel in intense flak and searchlight activity, and before the end of the month five more Hampdens were taken on charge, totalling nine. Mining in sea area 'Artichoke' near Lorient was the task for four aircraft on 27 July, and on 30 July four Hampdens set off to raid Cologne, but due to severe thunderstorms and icing conditions only one reached the primary target, two attacked the secondary target, Aachen, and one dropped two 250 lb. GP bombs on the flarepath of Zellick airfield, west of Brussels.

There was no more operational activity until 5 August, when seven Hampdens raided targets in Germany — four on Mannheim in intense flak, two on Karlsruhe and one on Coblenz. Next night one Hampden bombed No. 6 dock at Calais, and on 7 August three Manchesters became operational when with seven Hampdens they were detailed to raid the Krupp works at Essen, with good results. One aircraft suffered tail flutter and bombed Duisburg instead. This was the last raid on which 207 Squadron used Hampdens. By 12 August six Manchesters were available and their crews were briefed to raid 'the big city', where they found searchlights that were very active and troublesome. From this operation two aircraft, L7377 [EM:G] piloted by Sqn. Ldr. G. R. Taylor DFC and L7381 [EM:R] by Flg. Off. W. M. Smith DFC, failed to return, the former crashing near Gros Beeren/Teltow and the latter shot down at Lange Dijk, near Groningen in Holland by Do.215 G9+OM of IV/NJG1 piloted by Oblt. Ludwig Becker, one of the Luftwaffe's night-fighter aces. One aircraft which suffered tail flutter bombed Emden. The Manchesters were again in action on 14 August, when three set off to raid Magdeburg, but only one found the target on this occasion, the others bombing Brunswick and Hanover instead. Sadly, one of the two Manchesters detailed to raid Dusseldorf failed to return from that mission. Captained by Plt. Off. H. G. Keartland, the missing aircraft was L7311 [EM:F]. A superstition involving the last-minute 'watering' of the tail wheel by some pilots had on this occasion been neglected owing to heavy rain at the time the crew boarded the aircraft. During engine run-ups, the grass was found to be so slippery that L7311 was taxied onto the main A15 Lincoln to Sleaford road, where the engines could be run with the Manchester's brakes full on! Road traffic, meanwhile, had to wait its turn. This event may have given rise to local stories of heavy bombers being taxied along the road from the Avro maintenance hangars at Bracebridge Heath. Plt. Off. Keartland had experienced great difficulty in climbing to height, and the Manchester was attacked by a Bf 110 night fighter piloted by Hauptmann Werner Streib of 1 Stab/NJG1 over the Dutch / German border to the extent that a bale-out was ordered. The doomed aircraft came down at Kruchten, just inside Germany, where it blew up, denying the German authorities anything substantial in the way of aircraft components. On the same night, one Manchester attacked the docks at Ostend, re-enacting similar missions carried out in 1918 but with slightly more advanced if less reliable aircraft, while another raided the harbour at Terneuzen.

No more missions were undertaken until 25 August, when seven Manchester crews were briefed to attack Mannheim. Of these aircraft, one suffered a burst tailwheel and another a serious oil leak and had to be 'scrubbed', and some of the five crews who took off complained of tail flutter and a reluctance to climb; one crew actually jettisoned a 1,000 lb. bomb to persuade the aircraft to gain altitude. When the squadron asked Avro to send a test pilot to Waddington to investigate, Mr. Bill Thorn arrived accompanied by Gp. Capt. Roberts, and with Wg. Cdr. Lewis and Flg. Off. Gardiner they carried out a test climb with a full bomb load. It was found that the tail buffeting was caused by climbing at too close to stalling speed, and an optimum setting was then established.

Railway marshalling yards at Duisburg were the target for seven Manchesters on 28 August, but results were not satisfactory. The navigator in L7373 [EM:T] was taken ill and the crew therefore bombed De Kok seaplane base instead, starting large fires. Another aircraft attacked the town of Hamborn as a secondary target, yet another the airfield on Texel island. However, during that night's mission it was found that tail buffeting problem could be overcome by following the most recent climb / rpm / boost parameters and that recently-introduced modifications to the oil cooling outlet were better dispensed with in order to improve general aerodynamic characteristics of the Manchester. Next night Frankfurt inland docks were due to receive the effects of three Manchesters, but two dropped their bomb-loads on the city instead. On the last day of August one Manchester, L7316 [EM:U], piloted by Plt. Off. T. R. Gilderthorp, failed to return from a six-aircraft attack on Cologne, coming to earth at Oberkruechen after some of the crew had baled out. Four members of that crew lost their lives, but two, including the captain, survived to become prisoners of the Germans. Another Manchester on that raid was attacked by fighters and in order to regain control the bombs were jettisoned, allowing the aircraft to return to base, but only after the co-pilot, Sgt. C. J. Marshall, had abandoned ship, to be taken prisoner!

At a conference held at 5 Group HQ on 1 September 1941 it was decided that 'A' Flight of the squadron would be operational and 'B' Flight would be devoted to training. Under Sqn. Ldr. K. H. P. Beauchamp DSO, 'B' Flight made good progress and the crews involved were expected to become operational by the end of the month. There were eight Manchester captains and ten more under training, and the CO was told that 207 Squadron would be given priority for the supply of aircraft and crews. On 2 September four Manchesters were detailed to raid a railway station in Berlin, but one with engine trouble did not take off, while the others, failing to locate the target, dropped their loads on the city. Several formations of enemy fighters were seen, and searchlights and heavy flak made the crews' task particularly tricky. With fuel tanks almost empty, the aircraft piloted by Plt. Off. Pacall DFM landed at Cottesmore. Unfavourable weather forced the return of two aircraft when on their way to attack Brest on 3 September, and on the next three nights operations were cancelled altogether.

Berlin's main telephone exchange was the target for six aircraft on 7 September, but due to technical trouble only four took off. It was during this raid that Flt. Lt. W. J. Lewis sent a W/T message from a point fifty miles short of the target reporting that his Manchester (L7380 EM:W) had been attacked by fighters and that he dropped a 'Cookie' on Wilhelmshaven and was returning to base. After another fifteen minutes he radioed that his port engine was smoking, after which nothing further was heard and he and his crew were posted as missing. The aircraft had, in fact, been cleverly crash-landed on a sandy beach at Ameland in the Frisian Islands, where the crew quickly found that all were safe and set about the task of eating the secret documents printed on rice paper and pressing self-destruct buttons on secret equipment. On wading through shallow water onto the sand dunes they were taken prisoner, their war over. The unfortunate Flt. Lt. Lewis was making an 'extra' trip before posting to 44 Squadron as an instructor on that unit's new Lancasters, and had regarded L7380 with

A fine airborne picture of Manchester L7284 [EM:D]. [207 Squadron archives]

Serious damage was caused to the tail of Manchester L7422 [EM:V] during the night of 31 August/ 1 September 1941. Flg. Off. Peter Birch made an early return, maintaining marginal control by use of the elevator trim tabs, and landed successfully at Waddington. The rear turret was also badly damaged, but fortunately none of the crew was injured. [207 Squadron archives and J. Duncan]

Manchester Mk.I L7380 [EM:W] at Waddington. It carried an interim camouflage scheme with pale grey code letters and red serial. L7380 carried out five missions before it failed to return with Flt. Lt. W. J. 'Mike' Lewis on 7/8 September 1941. [207 Squadron archives]

trepidation, seeing it as a "clunker amongst clunkers". Watching the take-off crash of a 44 Squadron Hampden while awaiting his own departure cannot have helped Lewis's morale. Another Manchester, flown by Flg. Off. W. S. 'Kipper' Herring DFM, suffered flak damage and leaking engine coolant, and avoiding action had to be taken on one engine running at full power all the way through the searchlight belt. By throwing everything not essential out of the aircraft Flg. Off. Herring managed to bring L7432 [EM:Z] back to make a landing at West Raynham after a five-hour journey. Days later, the crew were invited to Avro's factory at Woodford to be congratulated on their performance. Just to bring a Manchester home safely was regarded as something of an achievement! To do so on one unreliable engine was something else!

Matters were, however, showing signs of improvement. 207 Squadron's 'B' Flight was soon working towards becoming operational again, and on 10 September the first two Mk.Ia Manchesters, L7483 and L7484, were received, joined two days later by another three which continued the numerical sequence. They were allocated to 'B' Flight. By this time, the Vulture engine's problems had been cured as far as they were going to be. While performance of the Rolls–Royce Merlin engine was improving rapidly, that of the Vulture had reached its maximum, and it was not enough. As long ago as November 1940 it had been realised that a four-engine version of the Manchester, the Lancaster, powered by four Merlins, was the only option. Further development work on the Vulture was therefore abandoned, and not before time, in the opinion of many.

For a change, Turin in northern Italy was selected as 207 Squadron's target on 10 September, and six Manchesters flew south, one carrying ground crews, to Wattisham airfield in Suffolk, which was to be used as a jumping-off point. However, on arrival it was decided that Wattisham's runway was too short for a loaded Manchester and the operation was 'scrubbed'. One might ask why this elementary fact was not appreciated by the raid planners! Back at Waddington, five Manchesters took off to attack shipyards at Rostock, which they did successfully without loss. On the way, enemy aircraft carrying searchlights were noticed.

The Luftwaffe clearly did not appreciate the squadron's efforts against targets in Germany and elsewhere, as on 12 September one enemy aircraft attacked Waddington, dropping incendiaries on the squadron hangar but not causing any damage to the Manchesters.

Those elusive battle cruisers the *Scharnhorst* and *Gneisenau* at Brest were again the target for 207 Squadron

'B' Flight pilots in front of a new Mk.Ia Manchester in September 1941. (L to R) Wt. Off. K. A. King (unit not known), Flt. Lt. G. Hall (seconded from 61 Sqn), Flg. Off. J. de L. Wooldridge, Plt. Off. G. Crump (killed 15 September 1941), Flg. Off. D. A. Green, Plt. Off. J. C. L. Ruck–Keene (KIA 20/21 October 1941), Plt. Off. B. D. Bowes–Cavanagh (KIA 12/13 October 1941), Plt. Off. Bayley (KIA 8/9 January 1942). [207 Squadron archives]

Manchester L7455 [EM:G] carried out 26 operational sorties with three squadrons. Here seen at Bottesford, with (L to R) Sgt. J. Duncan (1st WOp), Sgt. S. Allen (2nd WOp), Sgt. A. Hall (Obs.), Flg. Off. P. C. Birch (captain), Sgt. N. A. Lingard (co-pilot), Sgt. A. P. Cullerne (mid-upper gunner), Sgt. Boldy (rear gunner) and canine friend. Basic nose-art consists of a stylised bull (?) and a swastika.

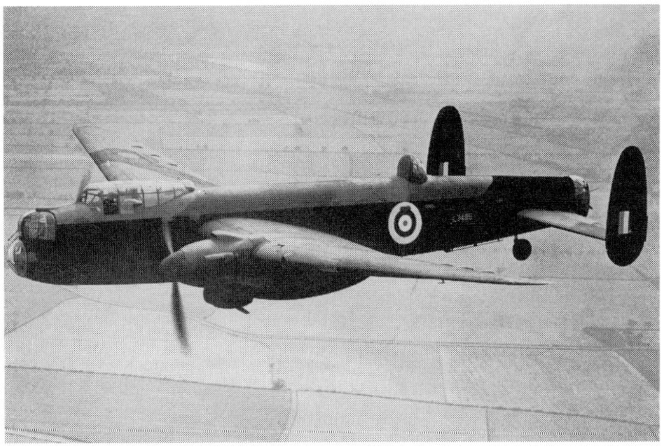

One of 207 Squadron's first Manchesters Mk.Ia was L7486, seen here during an air test soon after delivery to Waddington in early September 1941. Code letters EM:P and EM:Z were carried during its nineteen-sortie operational life with the squadron. [207 Squadron archives and J. Simpson]

Manchester L7319 [EM:X] was one of the triple-finned variety. It was the aircraft flown by Flt. Lt. W. D. 'Babe' Ruth on the night of 23/24 November 1941, the first raid carried out from Bottesford. The target was the port of Lorient. L7319 survived to be passed from 207 Squadron to 106 Squadron and then to other units. [RAFM P.6299]

on 13 September, when four Manchesters left Waddington to do their utmost to put the ships out of action. Owing to dense cloud and a smoke-screen, however, the ships could not be seen, and the Manchester's bomb-loads were dropped on the general area of the target. Next day a Manchester on an navex made a scheduled landing at Millom in what is now Cumbria, only to go unserviceable with hydraulic trouble. Another aircraft, L7318 [EM:K], was flown up with spares by Flg. Off. Crump and on 15 September the two aircraft flew back to Waddington, where the repaired one landed. L7318, however, arrived in the circuit and, with undercarriage down, was seen by many at Waddington to drop its nose and dive straight into the ground at South Hykeham, five miles to the west. An enquiry which followed blamed the fact that lift had been lost when some of the ten men on board, including six ground crew personnel, failed to move out of the nose prior to landing, thus placing the centre of gravity too far forward. All lost their lives in this disaster. A raid on Hamburg by five aircraft took place that night, although one brought its bombs home.

Another distant city, Stettin, was targetted on 19/20 September when, to shorten the distance to carry bombs, six Manchesters flew to Horsham St. Faith, with another one carrying ground crews. Three aircraft then went 'u/s', but the other three took off to find good weather over the target. Stettin was also the planned target on 22 September, but later Berlin became the destination before forecast bad weather for the return trip forced a cancellation.

By late September 1941 a new airfield at Bottesford in Leicestershire, which had opened earlier in the month, was due to be 'christened'. This task was carried out by Sqn. Ldr. K. H. 'Penny' Beauchamp in Manchester R5782, but on preparing to land he found that the undercarriage would not lock down. He therefore decided to land at Waddington instead, and after attempting to use the emergency pneumatic system without success, he made a final approach knowing that the aircraft was likely to go out of control on touch-down. Sure enough, the port oleo leg collapsed and the Manchester settled onto the grass, luckily without major damage.

Horsham St. Faith, the airfield on the northern edge of Norwich which is now Norwich Airport, was again used by 207 Squadron on 26 September, when six Manchesters were detailed for a 'gardening' trip into Baltic waters off Swinemünde. Next day, however, came the cancellation call, bad weather again affecting operations. On 29 September it was possible to take full advantage of better conditions. Early plans involved nine Manchesters of 207 Squadron raiding Stettin, but this was altered to five aircraft for special 'gardening'operations in area Geranium off Swinemunde and four to attack the Blohm und Voss works at Hamburg, where it was found that intensive and accurate flak made evasive action necessary and hampered their efforts. Four of the 'gardeners' completed their task on target, while one laid its mines elsewhere after seven enemy fighters had attacked it. Afterwards, four of the Manchesters returned to land at Horsham St. Faith and one at Waddington.

'B' Flight duly became operational on 1 October although seven crews and two captains were still under training. The first hints of a squadron move were heard on 3 October, when Wg. Cdr. Lewis took a Manchester to make a landing at Bottesford. With an all-up weight of 45,000 lbs. (20.45 tonnes), take-off conditions were judged to be satisfactory. This was one of the last self-imposed tasks for 'K. P.', who handed over the reins of the squadron to Wg. Cdr. C. Fothergill on 10 October.

Waddington weather was still playing havoc with operations, several of which were planned but then cancelled, frustrating all concerned. It was not until 10 October before the next operation could take place, the first involving the Mk.Ia aircraft and the largest participation by 207 Squadron yet. That night crews of twelve Manchesters were briefed for a raid on Stuttgart, but the target was then changed to Karlsruhe and eventually to Essen. Of the ten crews who took off, only six claimed to have found the primary target. Shortage of fuel compelled two of the aircraft to land at Horsham St. Faith on return, one with gauges reading zero! After receiving faulty navigational 'gen' from his navigator which placed the aircraft close to the coast of East Anglia when in reality it was still over Holland, the pilot had been preparing to ditch when the English coast was sighted. Bad weather brought another Manchester down at Spittlegate, where the ground crews were not accustomed to such a large aircraft. Two nights later fourteen crews were detailed for an attack on a vital synthetic rubber factory at Hüls, and eleven aircraft eventually took off. Solid cloud over the target prevented accurate bombing, but fires in the general area were reported. Not all aircraft were able to drop bombs on the primary target: one unloaded four 1,000lb bombs on Hertogenbosch airfield, where the crew saw craters by the lights of flares. Another airfield attacked was ten miles (16 km.) south of Nijmegen where a 4,000 lb bomb fell on the side of the runway. Of one aircraft, L7312 [EM:L], piloted by Flg. Off. B. D. Bowes–Cavanagh, nothing was heard after take-off, and later it was discovered that the aircraft had been shot down at Escen in Belgium by a Bf 110 of II/NJG1 from Leeuwarden piloted by Oberfeldwebel Paul Gildner. Only the observer, Sgt. Jack Cheeseman, survived and was taken prisoner. Tragically, two more Manchester crews were lost next night, when Cologne railway station was raided by nine aircraft. Difficulty was experienced by at least two crews, who jettisoned 1,000 lb bombs in the sea so that a better rate of climb could be attained. The missing aircraft, L7373 [EM:T] and L7321 [EM:D], were captained by Plt. Off. L. A. Paskell and Plt. Off. J. Unsworth. Unsworth's aircraft was held in searchlight beams over Liege and singled out for attention by Oblt. Heinrich Griese, the pilot of a Bf 110C of I/NJG1, based at St. Trond. His attack was devastating, and only two of the crew managed to bale out of the Manchester, which came down and exploded at Horion-Hozemont, 2.5 miles (4 km.) east of Comblain-au-Pont and 10.5 miles (17 km.) south of Liege. Near the target, the other aircraft experienced heavy flak and intense searchlight activity, making target location very difficult. On the return journey 'Jock' Paskell's aircraft was also picked up by the searchlights and attacked by a Bf 110, this one flown by Gefreiter Bruhnke of III/NJG1 from Twenthe in Holland. Two of the crew managed to parachute from the crippled aircraft, which crashed near Lommel, and one, observer Sgt. K. H. Houghton, was self-reliant enough to avoid capture and make his way to Switzerland, where he worked legitimately to acquire enough money for a railway journey to Spain and Portugal and a flight home. After a long period of deprivation he was able to rejoin 207 Squadron.

Next came a 'gardening' mission by four Manchesters in area 'Willow' in the Baltic Sea on 20 October. Again Horsham St. Faith was used in order to shorten the trip. Two aircraft planted their mines in the correct area, one failed to locate it and jettisoned his load and the fourth, L7487 [EM:W], flown by Plt. Off. J. C. Ruck–Keene, came down in the sea about eight miles (13 km.) north-west of

A twin-finned Manchester was L7515 [EM:S], which 207 Squadron passed on to another unit. [via R. C. Sturtivant]

Winterton, Norfolk, for a reason never established. Several Manchesters later carried out a close search of the sea in an attempt to find a dinghy, but without success, and the bodies of the crew remain in the North Sea. Four more aircraft 'planted vegetables' in area 'Forget-me-not' off Kiel on 21 October, as two more raided Bremen docks in heavy flak which damaged one aircraft.

Six Manchesters took off in daylight on 24 October to raid railway workshops at Frankfurt-am-Main, but soon after they crossed the enemy coast heavy cloud was found, and it was impossible to identify the primary target. One crew brought their bomb-load home, two dropped on the city and the others attacked various airfields.

There were no more operations until the last day of the month, but Manchester L7422 [EM:V] crashed at Hardings Farm, Linwood, near Market Rasen on 26 October, luckily without injury to the crew or to the eleven ATC cadets who were being given an air experience flight! That the lives of youngsters had been risked by flying them in Manchesters seems incredible! The apparent reason was engine failure during practice propeller feathering exercises, but for once the fault was not a technical one. On checking the fuel taps to the engine when he deemed it safe to re-enter the cockpit, Sqn. Ldr. Beauchamp found them still in the 'off' position. Honesty prompted him to admit pilot error, caused by the presence of a new direction-finding device which partly obscured the taps. The final mission was by one aircraft which took off from Coningsby to drop mines in area 'Nectarine II' in the Weser area before returning to Coningsby.

The anticipated Movement Order covering a move to Bottesford by the squadron was received on 1 November 1941. That day two Manchesters took off on a mining mission in area 'Willow', but one returned with turret and inter-com failure and the other landed at Docking after completion of the task. With Flt. Lt. W. D. 'Babe' Ruth as captain, this aircraft had started to ice up and had lost both radio aerials, preventing a fix being obtained. On board was WOp/AG 'Scotty' Scott, who at an altitude of about a thousand feet caught sight of a flarepath through the murk and told the captain, who pushed the stick forward and made a straight-in landing. The ground crew at the dispersal point said that they had never seen anything quite so amazing in their lives, particularly when on touch-down there was a shower of ice crystals which were lit up by the Chance light. Three days later it was possible to fly back to Waddington.

During a surprisingly fine period, Cologne's main railway station was the target on 7 November for nine experienced crews, but two turned back when their front turrets became unserviceable. Two Manchesters attacked the primary target in moderate flak and their crews reported that their bombs, some 1,000lb and some 4,000lb, had hit the right spot. All the others dropped their loads on the city of Cologne when they were unable to find the station. At the same time, one new crew raided Boulogne, dropping two sticks of bombs on the dock area. Two 'freshmen' crews gained experience on 8 November by raiding Dunkirk docks and shipping sheltering there, one crew later reporting small fires in the dock area and the other unable to confirm any results.

Targets on 9 November were shipyards at Hamburg and the nearby city, which were attacked by four aircraft; Calais docks, visited by one crew; Wilhelmshaven docks and Borkum seaplane base, to each of which one aircraft paid a visit. Even in the fine conditions, few positive results could be seen. The aircraft which visited Wilhelmshaven, Flg. Off. Wooldridge's L7319 [EM:X], was found to be extremely slow and refused to climb, so in intense flak and searchlight beams the pilot was obliged to dive for the coast, where he levelled out at an altitude of 1,000 feet.

While the squadron was 'stood down' on 11 November, nineteen Air Ministry pressmen paid a call to photograph and film the Manchesters and their crews. Next day Gp. Capt. W. G. Cheshire, the first Station Commander at Bottesford, visited Waddington in connection with the organisation of the forthcoming move. On 15 November Gp. Capt. F. R. D. Swain OBE AFC took over from Gp. Capt. Wheeler, and an advance party of 207 Squadron left Waddington for the new Station. One more operation was mounted from Waddington, however, when that night two 'freshmen' crews raided Emden railway station, causing a large fire.

Goodbye to Waddington

In fine weather on 17 November, 207 Squadron's Manchesters took off for Bottesford at 10.00, but by the time the main road party left at 13.45 rain was falling. By 16.00 the whole squadron had arrived, and all personnel began the job of settling in and preparing to make their presence felt over enemy territory again. However, most of those who made the move were filled with alarm and despondency when they saw their new base — a bleak utility-pattern Station with none of the comforts of Waddington's pre-war amenities. Unlike Waddington, Bottesford's living and domestic accommodation was built on the 'dispersed' pattern, involving a great deal of walking between Nissen-hut sleeping quarters and messes, briefing room, squadron offices and dispersals. Dennis Bentley, an armourer at the time, is a former 207 Squadron member with clear recollections of the move to Bottesford. "We were paraded in the rain at Waddington and then put into trucks," he recalls. "It was only when we stopped to ask a farm labourer where we were that we knew where we were headed. It was dark by the time we reached Bottesford, and still raining heavily. We were in our best blues. In pitch darkness we had to walk up the hill to our billet. Men were calling out and shouting to one another in the blackness, and there was a lot of swearing as uniforms became muddy. Our billet consisted of two Nissen huts near Sewstern Lane. On arrival we discovered that the beds were soaked, there were no proper mattresses, and only two wet blankets each! Worse still, there was only one solitary coke stove with which to try to dry out. This being too much for us, we went to the communal site, found the NAAFI and got drunk! The airfield itself was still a mess, and for the first few months we practically lived in gumboots, the whole area being a sea of mud". Former Flt. Lt. P. C. Ward–Hunt recalls that the Station was not even completed when 207 Squadron arrived. "There was no taxi-track, so all [aircraft] movements had to be done on the runways. Because of the lack of concrete areas we had to bomb up aircraft on the runway, which more or less put the airfield out of action whilst this was going on. I remember we were very much confined to camp at Bottesford; transport was difficult, there were no pubs nearby and Newark was about five miles away". The lack of hardstandings is confirmed by Mr. C. Smith, a former member of Flg. Off. Leland's crew, who mentions that Irish labourers employed by the contractor (George Wimpey & Co. Ltd.) were still working there when the squadron moved in. 'Scotty' Scott comments "..........we lived in mud, we walked in mud, we cycled in mud, we took off in mud, we landed in mud; I have never seen anything like it, and conditions could not have been worse".

Wg. Cdr. W. H. 'Goldie' Goldstraw, then a Sergeant navigator, also remembered the terrible conditions endured by the early arrivals at Bottesford. The room he shared with another sergeant was often awash, the concrete base for the stove was full of water and the stove could not be lit even if there had been any coal! Bedding and clothing were always damp, and he slept in trousers and shirt under blankets, but whenever possible he spent time in the mess, where it was warm and dry. Strangely enough, he considers that it was because of these atrocious conditions that morale among aircrew was so high — it was a case of 'all being in the same boat'. Nobody at Bottesford went sick, because the Sick Quarters were too far from the living quarters! "Bottesford was," said 'Goldie', "a very good character builder if you could adjust to the hardships and, of course, if you lived long enough!"

The first operation from Bottesford took place on 23/24 November 1941, when two Manchesters attacked the docks at Lorient in western France, and the submarines they contained, in cloudless conditions, allowing the dock installations to be identified easily. After dropping ten 500lb (227 kg.) bombs in the target area, these aircraft returned to make a landing at Coningsby. The captain of L7319 [EM:X], Flt. Lt. Ruth, remarked afterwards that his trip had been the "most enjoyable" he had ever had – or did he mean the least unenjoyable?

That same day Manchester L7300 [EM:F] was being flown to Waddington with nine on board, including one officer who was going to join a course and two air traffic controllers. Captain was Plt. Off. W. Hill DFM, who set course to follow the Lincoln–Boston Canal and railway line at an altitude of 500 feet or less, surprising a few engine drivers! Suddenly the port engine stopped, and nearby Cranwell airfield was considered as an emergency diversion. However, the captain decided to press on to Waddington, but then the starboard engine also gave up. With too little altitude it was not long before the Manchester hit the ground, breaking apart before plunging at some speed into Fiskerton Lake, some eight miles (13 km.) east of Lincoln. Fortunately, the tail section had been ripped off, allowing those on board to escape with no more than minor injuries, no doubt thankful to be alive. Around the lake were several anglers, who must have been somewhat surprised to find thirteen tons of Manchester aircraft dropping into the water in front of them! The co-pilot, Plt. Off. Plaistowe, who was standing when the aircraft impacted, sustained a fractured skull, so Charles Smith, the WOp/AG, took him to nearby Applegarth Cottage, where the occupants dried him and wrapped him in a rug to await the arrival of an ambulance from Lincoln. When after nearly an hour it had not arrived, one of the anglers offered to take him and one of the air traffic controllers to hospital by car, so they were made comfortable, Charles Smith sat down next to the driver and off they went. As the car turned into Lincoln High Street, Plt. Off. Plaistowe opened the door and, minus rug, ran naked down the street! Late that Sunday afternoon, there were many RAF men and their girl friends around, and the sight of a bare man, his torso covered with blood, did nothing to improve their mood. Before he had covered many yards, however, a large policeman stopped the runaway officer, who was quickly bundled into a passing ambulance. After some debate, he was taken with the other occupants of the car to Lincoln Hospital, where next day he could be seen doing handstands on his bed until nurses stopped him! The anglers whose activities had been brought to such a dramatic conclusion had the last word. When the Manchester was being salvaged one of them approached the airmen from the MU and said "We want this f***ing wreck out of 'ere by next Saturday – we 'ave a fishing competition on!"

Several times during the next two weeks aircrews were briefed for missions, only to find them cancelled at the last minute. Ground crews, anxious to maintain the Manchesters in top condition, must also have felt frustrated. It was not until 27 November that the next operation took place, a raid on marshalling yards at Dusseldorf by six aircraft which took off soon after 17.00. Two of them, however, dropped their bomb-loads on Ostend docks, one as it was unable to maintain altitude and the other due to engine trouble. The other four crews found ground haze over the target but were satisfied that good strikes had been made. On return, five of the six Manchesters landed at Coningsby and the sixth at Martlesham Heath, this one with radio failure and a burst hydraulic pipe. Finally, two crews who were about to shed their 'freshmen' status raided Emden on 30 November in good weather conditions. One reported fires burning, but the other was too busy taking evasive action to comment!

The daily routine of ground crews in those early days at Bottesford left something to be desired. Dennis Bentley vividly remembers walking across the airfield to the dispersals to carry out a Daily Inspection (DI), the first item of which was to run a long pull-rod through the aircraft's guns. "Another job was to bleed the hydraulic fluid in the turrets, as sometimes an airlock would form, preventing the turret from turning," he recalls. "A job I really didn't like was servicing the Martin cable-cutters on the wing leading edge. This entailed climbing onto the wing itself in muddy boots, which gave little grip. Some twenty feet above the ground, this was not a good prospect! Positioned as comfortably as possible, the armourer would have to lean over the edge and remove the cartridges within the cutters using an internal spanner and working more by feel than by sight. Finally, the mechanism would be oiled and a new cartridge installed; if this was not done correctly the mechanism could easily rust and not work. Worse still from the armourer's point of view, unstable cartridges could sometimes detonate while being handled, causing loss of fingers. A horrible job!"

Early in December poor weather put a damper on operations, until on 7 December twelve crews were briefed for a raid on Aachen. After lunch the number was reduced to six, of which three reached the target, one bombed a secondary target at Dunkirk before returning to land at Manston when low on fuel, and one returned to base with bombs aboard. December turned out to be a poor month for 207 Squadron as far as operations were concerned, as it was not until after Christmas that the next mission was flown. Before that, manifolds on all aircraft had to be changed, which took four days, during which some leave was granted. Then a period of practice formation flying was arranged, and was carried out even on Christmas Day. On 27 December twelve crews were picked for an operation, but five were soon cancelled. Of the remaining seven, the crew of L7483 [EM:O] turned back when their Manchester's starboard engine failed, jettisoned their bombs off Orford Ness and made for Martlesham Heath airfield, where the flare-path lighting was turned on and then, inexplicably, off again! This happened twice more, by which time the pilot was fully committed to a landing, which turned out to be a heavy one, writing the aircraft off but not injuring any of the crew. Meanwhile, five Manchesters bombed the primary target, Dusseldorf marshalling yards, and one dropped its five 1,000lb bombs successfully on Ostend docks. During the homeward flight, Flg. Off. P. C. Birch flew L7455 [EM:G] so low that his gunners were able to use their talents on two factories, a train and two small towns! Afterwards, all six landed at Horsham St. Faith, the weather at Bottesford being poor.

Although an RAF 'liberty bus' ran to and from Nottingham, many of the airmen and WAAFs stationed at Bottesford preferred to use bicycles to visit the local hostelries. The bus was also used by the Irish workmen who were still toiling to complete the finishing touches to the Station, but as they could be amorous most of the WAAFs tried to avoid them. When not under the mild influence of Guinness the Irishmen were generally polite, friendly and generous, however.

Late in the year, one of 207 Squadron's Manchesters made an emergency landing at the de Havilland Aircraft Co. airfield at Hatfield. It was decided to send another Manchester with a spare crew and a ground crew to rectify any faults, carry out the daily inspection and then fly the errant aircraft back to Waddington. An electrician detailed to go to Hatfield was Mr. A. B. 'Joe' Parsons, who remembers a feeling of trepidation as he climbed aboard the second Manchester. "The pilot was a South African, Flg. Off. Kirtland, and I took up station next to the wireless operator, a friend of mine. Fifteen minutes or so into the flight one engine developed a coolant leak, which was relatively common. The pilot took the appropriate action – shutting off the engine and feathering the airscrew. To be on the safe side he issued the command to stand by to bale out." One can imagine 'Joe' Parsons' feelings on this, his first flight! "To say I was petrified would be an understatement. However, I positioned myself near the escape hatch, which was fitted in place of the ventral turret. I doubt very much if I would have been able to jump had the order been given, but no doubt someone would have pushed me. In the event we landed safely, if that is the right description for an emergency landing without brakes due to lack of pressure. We ran the full length of the airfield and through a wooden fence, but everyone got out safely. Hatfield now had two Manchesters, which created a lot of interest, as they were much bigger than anything else there, and if my memory serves me correct, were still on the Secret list. A further crew was to fly down next day, so the 207 Squadron contingent had to spend the night at Hatfield, for which we were ill-prepared. We were allocated beds in a wooden hut, and after working on the two faulty aircraft we decided late in the evening to visit the already famous local hostelry – the Comet. As we were leaving at closing time, we were approached by a Provost Marshal, who took exception to our general appearance – we were all in our working blue, which was of course far less smart than our 'walking-out' dress. After delivering his lecture, he took all our names and said that we would be charged with being improperly dressed. After breakfast next morning we......flew back to Waddington. Although the charges arrived they were, apparently, quashed. I would like to think that the Station Commander, Gp.Capt. John Boothman of Schneider Trophy fame, appreciated our predicament."

The wreck of Manchester L7300 [EM:F] being salvaged by 58 MU on 4 December 1941 after its unplanned descent into a lake at Fiskerton on 23 November. [via H. Holmes]

An example of mistaken identity similar to that suffered by the squadron in its early Manchester days occurred on 23 December, but this time without fatal results. A formation of six Manchesters was flying over the North Sea when they were set upon by Spitfires, which luckily caused slight damage to only one of the six. This flight may have been a practice for the formation flight which took place on Christmas Day, when 207 Squadron aircraft called up as many airfields as possible over the R/T to wish the staff a 'Merry Christmas'!

Whilst food for civilians was strictly rationed, it was plentiful on the Station, although in Dennis Bentley's opinion not of very good quality. He was very young at the time, as were most of the personnel on this and any other RAF Station, and he quickly learned that he had to look after himself in the matter of sustenance. One airman in the same billet as Dennis became friendly with a local girl who often provided bread, eggs and other delicacies, which were cooked and eaten in the billet when a meal was missed or the weather was too bad to venture to the mess.

'Goldie' Goldstraw wrote about the routine at Bottesford during that winter. "We got up at 07.00 to 07.30, took the necessary clothing, towel, soap and razor and walked the mile to the communal site to wash, shave and have breakfast. Then we walked a further mile to the technical site, booked in at the squadron office and checked various items of equipment, maps and flying clothes and got up to date with the latest intelligence information. Usually towards the end of the morning we would be told if operations were on that night. So it was a mile back to the communal site for lunch, [another] mile back to the squadron offices before a take-off on a night-flying test (NFT) on the aircraft we would be flying that night. The

NFT took about half an hour to give every crew member time to check out the equipment he would be responsible for on the raid. Then it was off to the briefing room to be told what the target was, the route, the times on route, bomb load, and anticipated weather on route, over the target and at base on return. After briefing it was back to the communal site for a night-flying supper, then back to the technical site and take-off. After de-briefing and a meal it was back to bed some thirty hours after getting out of it. Usually we were able to get to bed, such as it was, around 02.00 or 03.00 the following morning, but I see from my logbook that time of take-off on one occasion was 01.25 on a six-hour trip to Cologne." He goes on to recall that the steeple of Bottesford church was almost in line with the main runway and presented a disturbing sight on take-off with a full load of bombs and fuel. Happy times in the local pubs were also remembered, as were the forays into Nottingham, after which he and others caught the milk train back to Bottesford in the early hours. "There were happy times also in the mess, when drinks and a sing-song often ended in horse-play and the letting off of high spirits," he said. "We made a lot of our own entertainment, in which everyone seemed to join. One got to know other people a lot better by being isolated as we were, instead of being near a town, where we split into ones and twos. Bottesford was a very good character-builder and morale-builder if you could adjust to the hardships." The late George Hawes, an Australian Flt. Sgt. on the squadron, wrote to his relatives at home in January 1942 to tell them that "......our PT here consists of some wild and woolly games of basketball. Well, they call it basketball but it generally ends up in a free fight. The NCOs play the officers. They are a great bunch of fellows on the whole, with the exception of one officer who is a stinker of the first order. The boys spend their time making up songs about him, most of which I'm afraid would never pass the censor!" Who, one wonders, was that officer?

January 1942 began with a patch of poor weather, but on the second day of the month ten Manchesters took off to raid St. Nazaire. Four were unable to locate the target, four found and bombed it and two attacked alternative targets at Cherbourg, where flak gave the crew a "warm time", and Brest. On the homeward journey two Manchesters landed at Exeter and one at Shrewton on Salisbury Plain, the second 207 Squadron Manchester to visit that tiny grass airfield. As the Manchester was low on fuel, the arrival of a 'bowser' had to be awaited before engines could be restarted for the trip back to base. Three nights later nine aircraft raided Brest, a tenth reporting that the target was obscured. There was similar difficulty on 8 January, when nine aircraft were sent to raid Brest again; none of the crews could find the target, so four bombed an alternative. From this mission Manchester L7322 [EM:Q], flown by Plt. Off. G. R. Bayley, failed to return, having ditched off Crozon, France. Yet again next night the two Manchester crews who took off failed to locate the target ships at Brest.

The situation improved a little on 10 January, when three crews succeeded in bombing the main railway station at Wilhelmshaven and two found the secondary target. On their way home, the crew of Flg. Off. J. 'Dim' Wooldridge DFM 'beat up' anti-aircraft defences on the Frisian Islands which were engaging incoming RAF bombers, as well as searchlights on Nordeney. A heavy-calibre gun was put out of action, as was at least one searchlight, and the ploy would have been even more effective if the hydraulics in the Manchester had not been damaged by flak. Notwithstanding the Manchester's obvious drawbacks, the calibre of the crews was of the highest, especially when using the aircraft in a role for which it had not been designed — that of low-level intruder!

Ablution facilities for ground crews at Bottesford were almost non-existent. "I remember my thighs being almost permanently covered in oil, as baths were not easy to get, the water in the communal site showers rarely being better than lukewarm", said Dennis Bentley. "We rarely wore overalls, uniform being preferred, but unfortunately these quickly became covered in swarf. The answer was to have a fifty-gallon oil drum at dispersal, to be filled with aviation fuel when the bowser came around. Having stripped down to underwear, we put overalls on, then put our uniforms in the drum of fuel and stirred them around with a stick. When they seemed to be clean, we hung them out to dry! Although the swarf would have gone, the uniforms reeked for several days. Men rarely wore greatcoats, even in the coldest weather, but leather jerkins were always in great demand. The nature of the work made it impossible to wear gloves, so our hands became so cold that it was impossible to feel what we were doing." 15 January was a sad day for the squadron, as during the previous night two crews, those of Plt. Off. G. B. Dawkins DFM (L7309 EM:O) and

Flt. Sgt. Basil Courtney Wescombe was one of the pilots who took part in the first raid mounted from Bottesford, after just a few weeks with 207 Squadron. He lost his life on the evening of 14 January 1942 when his Manchester crashed near Holmpton on the Yorkshire coast after disastrous engine failure. [via V. Holyoak]

Flt. Sgt. B. C. Wescombe, had failed to return from a raid on the Blohm und Voss shipyards. It soon transpired that Flt. Sgt. Wescombe and all his crew lost their lives in L7523 [EM:M] when it crashed and burnt out at Cliff House Farm, Holmpton, near Withernsea in Yorkshire. At that position the aircraft was well off course for a return to Bottesford, and it has been surmised that technical difficulties had forced a return across the North Sea with bombs still aboard. Plt. Off. Dawkins and his crew had the misfortune to be shot down by a Bf 110 of II/NJG2, piloted Oblt. Rudolf Schoenert, and baled out, all surviving except the mid-upper gunner, Sgt. J. W. Cadman. The Manchester crashed and blew up at Sandal Moens, near Jever. Only one crew found the primary target that night, the others dropping their loads on Hamburg city instead.

For the night of 15/16 January, the target was Emden harbour, which one 'freshman' crew attacked. Another solitary 'freshman' raided the same target successfully two nights later, and it seemed that experienced crews were being forgotten, as two more 'new boys' were detailed on 21 January, one to visit Emden again and the other to drop leaflets on Paris, but when that city could not be identified the 'nickels' were pushed out to be read by the hapless citizens of Rouen instead.

Even though they were working so hard, the ground crew men often found time to go on drinking expeditions during their off-duty hours, with or without benefit of a pass! After changing, they used a gap in a hedge on the south side of the airfield, where friends would help each other change from the gumboots worn on the airfield side of the hedge to the reasonably good shoes used on the civilian side. From the railway halt at Bottesford it was possible to catch a train to Nottingham, but some hitch-hiked with varying degrees of success and others cycled. Attractions in that city included pubs such as the 'Flying Horse', which inevitably became known as the 'Airborne Nag', the 'Black Boy', the 'Trip to Jerusalem' and a well-patronised Palais de Danse. The return train from Nottingham was at 23.30, and to miss it presented problems. On occasion, Dennis Bentley remembers, he did not arrive at Bottesford until about 05.00, but the ploy used by him and his mates to obtain food was to smear themselves in grease, forge late breakfast chits and pretend that they had worked through the night! At the nearby village of Long Bennington were the 'Reindeer' and the 'Wheatsheaf', the latter a very popular venue for some, particularly the NCO aircrew. For those who were in the landlord's good books there was often the possibility of extended opening hours in the back parlour! From time to time dances would be held in the Sergeants' Mess, to which the Station Commander allowed WAAFs to be invited.

The beginning of the end of the Manchester

The first tangible sign of re-equipment with the new four-engined version of the Manchester, the Lancaster, came about on 16 January 1942, when 207 Squadron Conversion Flight was formed. Its purpose was initially two-fold – to train replacement crews and to convert them to fly four-engined aircraft. In command of the Flight, which was effectively a third Flight of the squadron, was Flt. Lt. P. Ward Hunt DFC, and initial equipment was two Manchesters.

Meanwhile, operations by the Manchesters continued. Munster post office was selected as the target for five aircraft which took off from Bottesford on 22 January, crews recognising the town by its horseshoe shape, which stood out in the snow-covered landscape. On its way home, one aircraft was brought down to 500 feet and machine-gunned a train before shooting out some searchlights and experiencing a 'near miss' with tall radio masts! Three nights later seven aircraft paid another visit to those elusive battle cruisers in Brest Harbour, and just 'Babe' Ruth's crew went there again on 27 January, their aircraft carrying one 4,000lb bomb and four 500-pounders. Much weaving and dodging had to be done to avoid heavy intense flak. The previous night had seen one aircraft over Emden again and another dropping leaflets over Paris. January's penultimate mission was by one 'freshman' crew which dropped six 1,000lb. bombs on Boulogne docks after taking off from Woolfox Lodge, and to end the month two aircraft raided Brest and one St. Nazaire.

Snow also covered Bottesford and its surrounding countryside in January, and all hands were called to help sweep the runways and perimeter tracks clear. It was soon realised that the labourers employed by Wimpey, who were still working on the finishing touches to the Station, were conspicuous by their absence. They were eventually tracked down 'skiving' in their huts, playing cards and generally trying to make themselves invisible in case they were asked to help. They had found themselves very unpopular since they had set fire to a pile of building rubbish on the airfield one night, to the consternation of the RAF personnel, who justifiably expected a raid by Luftwaffe intruders who would undoubtedly see the flames. Luckily this did not happen, and it was mooted at the time that the many Irishmen among the labour force probably believed that since they were officially neutral the Germans would not attack them!

The first Lancaster for 207 Squadron Conversion Flight was the first prototype, BT308, which arrived on 25 January, allowing conversion of operational crews to begin. This aircraft had Merlin X engines and had been built with triple fins, although the centre one had been discarded by the time it arrived at 207 Squadron from 97 Squadron. It is also possible that the second prototype Lancaster, DG595, was used by 207 Squadron, although unlike BT308 it was never on charge to the unit.

A task of a rather different nature came the squadron's way on 31 January, when Sqn. Ldr. T. Murray and his crew, plus twelve ground crew members with kit and equipment took off in L7378 and made for Boscombe Down. Next day they flew to Weston-super-Mare, where experimental mines were loaded by personnel of the Torpedo Development Unit. On 3 February the Manchester took off to carry out a series of trials, but after less than two hours in the air a fault developed and the aircraft had to make an emergency landing at Chipping Warden airfield. Repairs took two days, after which the Manchester returned to Weston–super–Mare to restart the proceedings. The trials completed, a return to Bottesford was made on 8 February. A further detachment to Weston was made on 8 March by Flg. Off. D. Green in L7432 [EM:J] for trials with 30 lb (13.5 kg.) anti-submarine bombs to be dropped from low altitudes at different speeds over Sand Bay. On arrival over Weston, Flg. Off. Green made a shallow dive over the pier to announce his presence as instructed, only to experience the disintegration of the constant-speed unit of the starboard propeller. An experienced fitter who happened to be in the cockpit carried out the emergency drill without fuss, but as a precaution all on board were told to take up

If there wasn't mud there was snow! A Manchester Mk.I of 207 Squadron standing at dispersal at Bottesford in the winter of 1941/42. [207 Squadron archives]

ditching stations. However, the skilful pilot was able to nurse the Manchester back to Weston to make a perfect landing amidst sighs of relief! Clearly, L7432 could not carry out its task, and next day the crew was collected and returned to Bottesford, leaving mechanics to replace the faulty engine. The bombing trials took place between 14 March, when Flg. Off. Green returned to Weston in R5835, and 23 March.

In case the battle cruisers which had for long been the object of so much of 207 Squadron's attention tried to break

Manchester Mk.Ia, L7523 [EM:M] was the aircraft which crashed at Holmpton in Yorkshire returning from a mission on 14 January 1942, with Flt. Sgt. Wescombe at the controls. Here, five ground crew pose during a short break in their never-ending task. [207 Squadron archives]

out of Brest harbour and make a dash for home, three Manchesters stood by on 4 February. When nothing untoward happened, two of them took off to lay mines off the Frisians, but were brought back due to bad weather. Four Manchesters mined area 'Nectarine' on 6 February, and one was intercepted by a Bf 110 fighter on the way home but was unharmed. Afterwards the aircraft were again bombed up to stand by to attack *Scharnhorst* and *Gneisenau*, but without being required.

With the conversion programme in full swing, 207 Squadron managed to carry out a few more operations using the Manchesters to which the crews had eventually become quite attached. Seven crews were briefed for a raid to Mannheim railway station on 11 February, and two did so, another four attacking secondary targets such as Saarbrucken and one, a 'freshman', laying mines off the Frisian Islands. During this operation, crews noticed a large illuminated dummy town north of Mannheim at Biebesheim, consisting of rows of lights laid out on a street pattern and as large as Mannheim itself! Weather conditions on return to England were so poor that one aircraft diverted to Boscombe Down, one to West Malling, two to Manston and two to Horsham St. Faith.

At last, the *Scharnhorst* and *Gneisenau* broke the stalemate which had prevailed for so long and in appalling weather made a dash for freedom on 12 February. Operation 'Fuller' was hastily implemented, and 242 Bomber and Coastal Command aircraft were launched to deal with the problem, the largest number in daylight so far. 207 Squadron was to have put up six aircraft, including two from the Conversion Flight, but in the event four took off and joined the hastily-assembled fleet flying towards the target ships in the prevailing bad weather. Only one of 207 Squadron's contribution actually found any ships, and dropped twelve 500 lb. GP bombs on the *Prinz Eugen* from an altitude of 800 feet, but with no evidence of damage. That aircraft was piloted by Flt. Sgt. J. C. Atkinson, who was awarded the DFM for his part in the operation. The two battle cruisers and their shepherding destroyers managed to pass through the Straits of Dover unscathed apart from minor damage caused by mines, and arrived in north German ports next morning.

At this point in the progress of the war, much thought was being given to the efficacy of bombing operations. The Butt Report had recommended that area bombing of German industrial centres should be undertaken as a direct means of undermining the morale of its citizens, particularly the workers who were turning out munitions and other equipment. This plan was completely endorsed by ACM Sir Arthur Harris when he arrived at High Wycombe on 22 February to take over the control of Bomber Command. Henceforth, the small-scale raids carried out by the RAF since offensive operations began would be discontinued, as it was realised at last that they were no more than a minor irritant to the enemy and did little or nothing to retard his production capacity or affect the country's morale. The answer was to overwhelm the enemy's defences and emergency services by sheer weight of numbers. Harris had made a memorable statement on taking over command at High Wycombe – "There are a lot of people who say that bombing cannot win the war. My reply is that it has never been tried yet. We shall see." It was not long before this plan was put into practice.

Four crews attacked a secondary target, Mannheim, on 14 February, and one crew afterwards commented that the searchlights at Harwich were very useful in pinpointing suitable airfields in Norfolk in case an emergency landing was necessary. Two nights later one crew dropped leaflets on Paris and five others sowed mines. More 'gardening' was done on 21 February by two aircraft neither of which found the target area and so returned to base.

Another brand new airfield, Langar, situated nine miles (14.5 km.) south of Nottingham, came into being as Bottesford's satellite on 17 February, but for the time being did not see any operational use.

Six 207 Squadron armourers pose in front of Manchester Mk.I L7425 [EM:C] of 207 Conversion Flight at a muddy Bottesford in February 1942. This aircraft, inherited from 97 Squadron, retained its wavy demarcation of colours and the white areas of the national markings were darkened. [207 Squadron archives]

Dockyards at Emden were the target for three crews on an early-night raid on 22 February. Two nights later at the same time of day one Manchester took off to drop mines in area 'Rosemary' and another in area 'Yams', one carried out 'nickelling' over Ghent and two more over Paris, all without serious damage, although the crew 'gardening' in area 'Rosemary' reported light damage from a flak ship. The Deutschewerke shipyards at Kiel were the target for four Manchesters on 25 February, but icing conditions forced the return of one aircraft and intercom failure brought another one back; two managed to drop their bomb-loads in the dock area but crews could not see whether they had been successful. Four more Manchesters had another try two nights later, but again the main target, a battle cruiser, could not be identified through 10/10 cloud. That same night, four aircraft went on a mining mission to the Frisians area.

The Conversion Flight was now turning out one trained crew per week to be absorbed into the squadron, and Flt. Lt. Ward Hunt was promoted to Sqn. Ldr. on a temporary basis on 1 March. On 2/3 March seven aircraft were detailed take part in a raid on the Renault vehicle factory at Billancourt, a suburb of Paris, where equipment for the enemy's war effort was being produced. This was the first raid mounted under Harris's new strategy and employed 235 aircraft, the largest force sent to a single target so far.

L7378 in the snow at Boscombe Down on 1 February 1942 when being prepared for the Torpedo Development Unit trials at Weston-super-Mare. [207 Squadron archives]

According to notes made by Flt. Sgt. W. G. Hawes, the only Australian on the squadron at the time, "It was an absolutely wizard show, and we blasted the place off the face of the map. On the run up we counted sixteen huge fires burning in the target area. We attacked as low as we could without getting the blast from our own exploding bombs. You can't imagine the great satisfaction one gets from actually seeing your bombs land smack in the centre of the target and pieces of factory torn from the ground and thrown hundreds of feet into the air." He also remarked "I reckon that if one of these Manchesters was to come to Australia, nothing under a Wg. Cdr. would be allowed near it, but over here Sgt. and Flt. Sgt. pilots are captains, with important duties to carry out and great responsibilities. What's more, they are not riding around for the fun of the business!" Sqn. Ldr. Ward Hunt and the indefatigable Flt. Sgt. Atkinson also took part in this attack with some success, but one aircraft had to return to Bottesford with engine trouble after an hour in the air.

The Intelligence officer at Bottesford was Sqn. Off. Marie Cooper, who arrived early in the proceedings and was billeted out with a local farmer as no WAAF accommodation had become available. She found a certain amount of resentment among the older members of the ground staff, who tended to regard the Officers' Mess and the Intelligence Section as male preserves. Eventually, as more and more WAAFs arrived the situation improved, and as they did everywhere, they made a tremendous contribution to the outcome of the war.

As an airfield, Bottesford was by no means ideally situated, as south of the main runway was Beacon Hill, 199 feet above sea level at its highest point, with the spire of St. Mary's church beyond. By March 1942, Standard Beam Approach equipment was in use as a landing aid, allowing more operations to be mounted in adverse weather conditions than before. While a direction finding service was already available, this only provided a course to steer, leaving the pilot to deal with the approach and landing.

During the many bouts of bad weather experienced at Bottesford, soccer and rugby football teams were formed in several sections and Flights, creating a spirit of competition which helped to boost morale. In addition, small arms were issued when alarming reports of sabotage or the ease with which it could be carried out were published in the Daily Mirror, but nothing actually happened at Bottesford apart from the erection of a barbed wire perimeter fence. Only three more operations by the squadron's Manchesters now remained. The first took place on 8 March, when five crews took off to raid Essen, but the aircraft flown by Flt. Lt. Birch DFC, which was carrying Bottesford's Station Commander, Gp. Capt. Swain, as an eighth crew member, turned back with engine trouble and with 'George' (the automatic pilot) unserviceable. On 9 March four aircraft raided Essen again in clear weather, and finally, on 10 March, six Manchesters took off for Essen again. This time only one reached the primary target, another attacked the secondary and the others all returned to base.

So ended 207 Squadron's pioneering use of the Avro Manchester, a period fraught with difficulties but the source of vital experience in the operation of heavy bombers. The Conversion Flight, however, continued to fly Manchesters as well as Lancasters for some time. By 13 March the squadron had been withdrawn from operations and was converting onto Lancasters, a type which would be used for many years. Manchesters of 207 Squadron had been despatched on 370 bombing sorties, 48 to do 'gardening' and twelve to drop leaflets, a total of 430, and ten different aircraft had each been despatched on fifteen or more sorties. Nineteen aircraft were lost on operations and a further six in accidents. Due in large part to the many periods of grounding, no pilot of 207 Squadron completed a tour of operations exclusively on the Manchester. Pilots who carried out at least ten operations numbered eighteen, as follows:

Flg. Off. W. G. Gardiner	27 operations
Flt. Lt. P. C. Birch	25
Sqn. Ldr. T. C. Murray	20
Flg. Off. W. S. Herring	20
Sqn. Ldr. K. H. Beauchamp	17
Flg. Off. W. J. Lewis	16
Flt. Sgt. G. H. Coles	16
Flg. Off. D. A. Green	15
Plt. Off. A. W. Hills	15
Flg. Off. J. H. Leland	14
Flt. Lt. W. D. Ruth	13
Flg. Off. J. de L. Wooldridge	13
Plt. Off. L. F. Kneil	12
Flt. Lt. P. R. Burton–Gyles	11
Flt. Sgt. J. C. Atkinson	11
Flt. Sgt. G. H. Hathersich	11
Sqn. Ldr. P. C. Ward–Hunt	10
Plt. Off. G. L. Bayley	10

A bowser supplying fuel to 207 Squadron Manchester L7486 at West Malling on 12 February 1942 after the aircraft had taken part in an attack on the Scharnhorst and Gneisenau during the Channel break-out, piloted by Flt. Sgt. 'Ginger' Hathesich. [via V. Holyoak]

A vee formation of Lancasters Mk.I of 207 Squadron in typical night bomber camouflage of 1942. Nearest the camera is R5570 [EM:F], which failed to return from a mission on 9 December 1942. [via B. Goodwin]

Chapter 6: Lancasters at Bottesford and Syerston

As already recorded, 207 Squadron's long association with the Lancaster began on 25 January 1942, when the first aircraft was delivered to the Conversion Flight, allowing conversion of operational crews to begin. As soon as their training was completed, selected second pilots and crews were put through the course, which consisted of about forty hours of day and night flying, culminating in an eight-hour cross-country flight carrying a full war load at an altitude of 20,000 feet. Average monthly output was four or five crews, all of which were absorbed into 207 Squadron. Conversion training proceeded as efficiently as possible during the next few weeks, and on 1 March the Conversion Flight's CO was promoted to Sqn. Ldr. on a temporary basis.

By 14 March five Lancasters had arrived at Bottesford, and nine crews then went on leave while the remainder carried out intensive day and night flying. During the next three days a further five Lancasters were delivered, and training concentrated on landing practice at dusk and during the night, although bad weather often curtailed the programme. Sad to say, it was not long before the first Lancaster training accident occurred. On 28 March R5501 [EM:G] collided with Miles Master DK973 of the RAF College, Cranwell, and crashed on Canwick Hill, near Bracebridge Heath. With Sgt. N. Lingard as captain, the Lancaster was on a daytime cross-country exercise when the student pilot in the Master made an unauthorised mock attack, hitting the Lancaster's tail, and both aircraft came to earth with the loss of all on board. A second mishap happened on 7 April, when Lancaster R5498 [EM:Z] crashed and was destroyed by fire, though luckily no serious injuries were suffered by Flt. Sgt. McCarthy or his crew. This aircraft had been on final approach to land when a booster pump failed, causing starvation of fuel to both starboard engines, which cut out. Now at very low level, the Lancaster's wing-tip hit the chimney stack and corner of Normanton Lodge farmhouse, causing the aircraft to slew and to belly-land nearby. Asleep in the bedroom invaded by the Lancaster was the farmer's daughter!

Daphne Forbes, a newly-trained MT driver, arrived at Bottesford on 26 March and went through the day-long booking-in process. Her first task was to collect the kit of a recently-killed pilot for return to his family. "Suddenly," she says, "the reality of war and the real need of the job came home to me. As drivers, for the first few months most of us were on duty for 36 hours, followed by twelve hours off. This did not mean that we were driving all the time, but we were on call......The type of jobs we did included collecting pigeons from miners and pubs around Nottingham, and consuming gallons of tea and shandy in the process; taking cylinder blocks from the Lancasters back to Rolls-Royce at Derby; taking ground crews out to bomb-up in the afternoon; driving tractors with bomb trolleys; moving goose-necked cranes to winch up the bombs; and carrying aircrews from the messes to briefing and then to dispersal points and in reverse after an operation. Other vehicles we drove included fuel bowsers, the small ambulance, the coal lorry around the living sites,

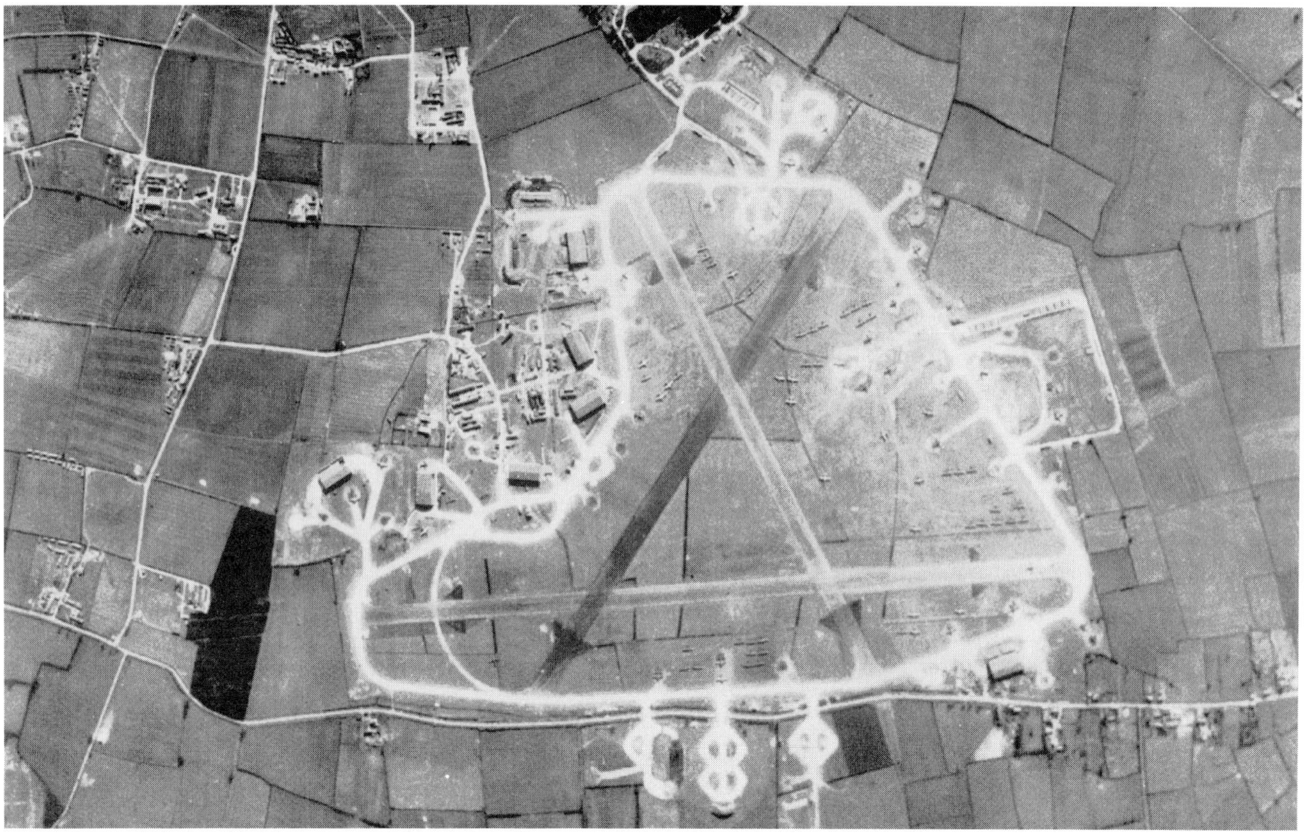

Although taken after 207 Squadron had vacated Bottesford and the US Ninth Air Force had arrived, this air-to-ground view of the airfield illustrates the layout of the runways, technical areas and some of the domestic sites well. [via author]

the ration wagon, the salvage lorry to the dump, the staff car for the CO and for visiting VIPs and cars for any officer or NCO on official business." A busy life indeed! If a driver had no particular job to do, he or she reported to the MT section and waited in the rest room for orders. When a long journey was called for, they had to study and memorise the map, as they were not allowed to carry one or even make notes. Most of the signposts had been taken down, but somehow the drivers always came back! An alternative task for drivers if the work-load was light was to go down into the inspection pit and grease a vehicle's bearings. Daphne goes on to say that she was the regular driver of the small ambulance for some time on a 24 hours on, 24 off basis. "To the right of the main gate, near Sick Quarters, there was a small brick-built hut containing a bed, chair, table and telephone, for use by the ambulance crew," she says. "When on night duty, rations were drawn from the cookhouse – tea and coffee, bread, margarine, bacon, sausage and chips, and there was always a frying pan kicking around. Outside was a hard-standing for the ambulance, the engine of which had to be warmed up every two hours during winter nights."

Into action!

Buoyed up by the excellent characteristics of their new aircraft, 207 Squadron crews attended the briefing for their first operation, on the night of 24 April 1942. The target for four aircraft was the Heinkel aircraft factory at Rostock, and at 23.10 three of the four took off to join 121 other Bomber Command aircraft, the fourth leaving Bottesford's runway six minutes later. Unfortunately, the rear turret of the straggler became completely unserviceable and the captain, Flt. Sgt. Hathersich, brought the aircraft back, complete with its load of one 4,000-pounder and eight SBC bombs. The other three Lancasters found the target in good visibility and dropped their bomb loads, but only Flg. Off Wooldridge DFM in R5507 [EM:Z] was able to confirm that his 4,000-pounder had burst into the workshops and that incendiaries had come down both on the airfield and into the factory buildings. This operation was repeated next night in similar weather conditions by four Lancasters, one of which returned to base on three engines after suffering the effects of light flak. If it had been a Manchester......! Afterwards, the routine post-mission interrogation was attended by the AOC.

There followed a short break from operations due mainly to poor weather over selected targets, so on 29 April six crews were kept busy on daylight formation flying practice, possibly to overcome a deficiency found during the first two Lancaster operations. Such formation flying was repeated on 1 May, during which R5504 [EM:P], piloted by Flg. Off. Wooldridge, struck a line of electrical

Carrying a stylised version of 207 Squadron's crest on its nose, R5908 [EM:B] was Flt. Lt. S. E. Pattinson's usual Lancaster. The official crest features a winged lion, but here it has been transformed into a dragon. [M. Claridge via V. Holyoak]

One of the WAAFs who served so faithfully during the Second World War was ACW Doris George, who worked in the Equipment Section at Bottesford from early 1942 to end of 1943. [via V. Holyoak]

high-tension cables near Cambridge, fortunately without damage to the Lancaster or injuries to the crew.

'Gardening' was indulged in during the night of 2/3 May, when six Lancasters laid their mines in areas 'Radish', 'Spinach' and 'Forget-Me-Not', although three dropped on the last resort target area, 'Hawthorn'. Next night five experienced crews and one 'rookie' crew were briefed for operations, but in the event just two Lancasters took off on leaflet-dropping missions over St. Etienne, Marseilles, Lyons and Toulon while one 'planted vegetables' in area 'Broccoli'. During this operation a submarine was spotted north of Tune Island and was treated to a burst from one of the Lancaster's machine-guns.

The *de facto* elevation of 207 Squadron to the status of a top-rank bomber unit had a great beneficial effect on the morale of all personnel. Entertainment during off-duty hours, which for the ground crews in particular were often few and far between, was made largely by the people stationed at Bottesford, who developed a spirit of friendship not seen so much on Stations closer to civilisation or more permanent in nature. Officers' and sergeants' messes were equipped with billiard and table-tennis tables and there were facilities for 'supping' a quiet drink if that was what one needed. In the officers' mess traditional boisterous games were played, the favourites being 'High Cockolorum', which involved piling furniture to its ultimate height and then climbing the resulting pile and staying there under duress, and 'Are you there, Moriarty?' Sooty hand and foot prints (and sometimes prints of other parts of the anatomy) decorated the ceiling, which was low in comparison with those on permanent Stations like Waddington. Nevertheless, accidents involving broken limbs did occur, and eventually such high jinks became frowned upon. For the other ranks, next to the airmen's mess stood the YMCA, which contained a billiard table and bar and of course a canteen where the mess meals could be supplemented if any cash was available in an airman's pocket. Film shows were put on in the gymnasium, and from time to time an ENSA ('Every Night Something Awful') concert party arrived to stage a show.

Military barracks at Stuttgart were the target for 207 Squadron on 4/5 May, and three Lancasters took off to do their best to eliminate them, but due to low 8/10 cloud over the target they attacked the city instead, each dropping 1,260 four-pound (1.8 kg.) incendiaries. Flak was heavy but not always accurate, causing no significant damage to the Lancasters. They had another try two nights later, but again difficulty in identifying the barracks forced two of the three crews to drop their loads on the town. One aircraft did reach the target and started a large fire, while a fourth had to return to base with an unserviceable engine.

More 'gardening' followed on 7/8 May, when two Lancasters dropped mines in area 'Nasturtium', one in 'Verbena' and one in 'Hawthorn'. Then came the order to make an attack on Heinkel's aircraft works at Warnemunde, and four aircraft left Bottesford at 22.05 on 8 May. One, however, came back an hour later with engine trouble and another just before midnight with electrical problems, leaving two to do what they could to halt the production of Heinkel aircraft. The crew of one of these, L7543 [EM:Z], captained by Flt. Sgt. Walker, managed to unload six 1,000 lb. (455 kg.) general-purpose bombs on the factory, while the other one dropped its load on the nearby town when the captain realised that other aircraft were flying below him over the primary target.

Three 'freshmen' crews carried out 'gardening' on 9/10 May, after which there was a rest until 15 May, when area 'Asparagus' received a batch of mines from Lancaster R5507 [EM:W], piloted by Flg. Off. J. H. Leland. On the outward flight this aircraft had been attacked by a Bf 110, but after retaliation by the Lancaster's gunners it broke away and was not seen again. A very clear sky, the Northern Lights and the dawn breaking had the effect of silhouetting the Lancaster, which had to descend to 800 feet in order not to invite further unfriendly action.

As Daphne Forbes has already recorded, the WAAFs at Bottesford were doing a fine job, but Australian pilot Sgt. George Hawes was somewhat derogatory about them. Writing home in May, he remarked "We now have about a hundred WAAFs on the camp, and I think they must have been hand-picked. Most of them look like ex-bullock drivers or heavyweight champs. The war is hard on the women-folk of the country and this camp is not the place for any girl." In a less contentious letter written soon afterwards, he praised the ground crews of 207 Squadron, which must have included some WAAFs. "I have found (and I think it's only human) [that] if you get to know the ground crew and call them by their first names you will get 100% more work and darn good results out of them," he wrote. "They are as keen as mustard to see you get there and back without any snags and there is quite a lot of rivalry between them as to the performance of their own particular machine."

With the future in mind, the powers-that-be sent thirteen ATC cadets to Bottesford on 16 May for a week of attachment to 207 Squadron. All were regarded as potential pilots and observers and were given a close insight into the working of a major bomber squadron. However, they were not fortunate enough to see the squadron working at full intensity, as no major operations were carried out during their time at Bottesford. On the Conversion Flight, commanded from 18 May by Sqn. Ldr. T.C. Murray DFC, two Lancasters were now in use.

One 207 Squadron aircraft raided Mannheim on 19/20 May, but a second Lancaster had to return to base with several technical problems. On 22 May two aircraft laid mines in area 'Willow', and Sqn. Ldr. 'Penny' Beauchamp and his crew of in R5499 [EM:O], were lucky to return. At an altitude of 200 feet off Aero Island, a port engine failed. After the load of six mines had been jettisoned, course for Bottesford was set, but when crossing the west coast of Denmark at North Ejsberg the aircraft was illuminated by searchlights, and on descending even lower it hit the surface of the sea. This bent both starboard propellers and caused vibration in the starboard inner engine. Flying on two engines at 120 mph, a height of 100 feet was maintained, but the crew made ready to ditch, throwing out the ammunition and oxygen bottles and destroying the TR.1335 radio and the IFF equipment. The Lancaster, released of this impedimenta, had other ideas, and gained altitude to 1,000 feet. Although a fire broke out in one of the flare chutes when there was a short-circuit, the crew managed to coax the Lancaster back to make a landing at Bottesford after six and a quarter hours in the air, the result of a partnership between the crew and the magnificent aircraft.. Also on board was Wg. Cdr. Fothergill as co-pilot, making a final trip before he was posted. Comments made by the 'skipper' on return to base included "Some people *say* they had seaweed in the bomb-doors, but go and have a look for yourself!"

Continuation training including long-distance navigation took place over the next few days, and Lancaster R5617 [EM:T] was lost on the night of 24 May while on such an exercise. Piloted by Sgt. T. K. Paul, it had been recalled due to rapidly-deteriorating weather when it flew into high ground at Standon Hill on Dartmoor, disintegrating, killing four of the crew and seriously injuring Sgt. Paul and Sgt. T. A. Whiteman, a WOp/AG.

Maximum effort!

The next operation was set for 29 May, when two aircraft were detailed for 'gardening' and two to take part in a raid on the Gnome-Rhone aero-engine factory at Gennevilliers, near Paris. Of the latter, one failed to locate the target but the other one dropped a portion of its bomb-load nearby, although it brought back its 4,000-pounder as the bombing height was too low.

Then came the largest effort by Bomber Command so far — the first thousand-bomber raid on Cologne, on the night of 30/31 May 1942. As AOC-in-C Bomber Command, Sir Arthur Harris needed a highly successful operation so that he could stem the allegation of poor performance being levelled at him and his squadrons. Demands were being made in high places for bomber aircraft and crews to be released to Coastal Command for use against the U-boat menace and for others to be sent to the Middle East. The Thousand Bomber plan was Harris's response to these demands, and involved the despatch of at least a thousand aircraft on one night to attack one target. Initially, Coastal Command agreed to take part, but withdrew the offer at the last minute. Harris then ordered experienced crews currently serving as instructors at Operational Training Units to participate, and these brought the total to over the magic thousand. 207 Squadron excelled itself by sending more Lancasters than on any previous squadron operation. For several days, ground crews had been working feverishly to prepare more aircraft than ever before, and although they did not know the reason they realised that something big was about to occur. Twelve crews were briefed at 18.30 and were told by the Station Commander, Gp. Capt. Swain, that they were about to take part in the heaviest raid in the history of air warfare, a remark which prompted much cheering and shouts of approval! All twelve aircraft took off during a thirteen-minute period, and by the time they reached Eindhoven it was possible to see Cologne as a bright glow on the horizon. 207 Squadron formed part of the third and final wave of bombers, and all attacked the primary target. Visibility over Cologne was excellent, and each crew dropped one 4,000-pounder and 720 incendiaries. Those

207 Squadron's CO from May to December 1942 was Wg. Cdr. Francis Russell Jeffs AFC. He was a popular CO, and he and his wife and pet dog became a well-known sight at Bottesford and Langar. Mrs. Jeffs often waited in the Officers' Mess when he was on an operation, a very unusual thing to do, causing WAAF officers a good deal of nervousness. Fortunately, he always returned safely. [via V. Holyoak]

witnessing the raid from the air saw one huge fire raging,with hundreds more scattered around, all visible from a distance of at least 75 miles (120 km.). Local defences seemed completely bewildered, and only moderate flak was experienced by the Lancaster crews, all of which returned to base safely, although Bomber Command as a whole lost 41 aircraft. Of the 207 Squadron crews, only one reported seeing an enemy aircraft, a Ju 88 which did not venture to intercept the Lancasters.

A second 'thousand-bomber' raid was mounted next night, although this time the total number of aircraft was only 956. 207 Squadron provided fourteen aircraft, which were seen off from Bottesford by Wg. Cdr. F. R. Jeffs, who had arrived a few days earlier to take command of the squadron. Three of the Lancasters were forced to return to base with engine trouble and one with failure of the oxygen system, while eight attacked a specific aiming point at Essen and two attacked Essen town in general. No major damage was inflicted upon the Lancasters, and their crews reported a considerable amount of success, although they were less specific than after the previous night's mayhem. Six aircraft went back to Essen on 2/3 June on a comparatively small-scale raid and five attacked the target, but one returned to base with engine trouble.

Until the summer of 1942, there was no separate WAAF cookhouse at Bottesford, so the girls had to walk or cycle to the airmen's mess. According to Daphne Forbes, most of the WAAFs habitually missed breakfast and had to await the arrival of the NAAFI van for 'char and a wad'. Daily routine for WAAFs followed that at other RAF Stations, but is worth recording as a means of demonstrating the way of life the girls had to follow and which undoubtedly had a major effect on them for the rest of their lives. At 06.00 they rose and dressed, plodded to the ablutions hut to wash, returned to stack their bed 'biscuits' (sectional mattresses), blankets and sheets, polished their bed-spaces, and left for working parade. "One of us", said Daphne, "was on hut orderly duty every day, which entailed polishing the centre of the hut, lining up all the stacked bedding and cleaning up generally. We were not allowed to remake our beds until 16.30. Each hut housed thirty 'bods' plus an NCO in a small room by the entrance. There was a kit inspection about every two weeks." This inspection was probably carried out by the WAAF CO, Flt. Off. Kirby. Bottesford meant more to Daphne Forbes than any other Station she was posted to, but she laments that when she attended a Bomber Command Association reunion many years later she felt that ......"the WAAF seemed to be a forgotten and unwanted species, a pity, as many did a really good job."

Bremen was the destination of three Lancasters of 207 Squadron on 3/4 June, and from this trip one, R5847 [EM:Y] piloted by Wt. Off. C. Wathey, failed to return. This was the squadron's first Lancaster lost during an operation. Another two aircraft carried out a 'gardening' mission the same night in the mouth of the Gironde river. More minelaying was done in area 'Nectarine' next night, while five more crews made another attempt to wipe Essen off the map, with some success. Yet more planting of 'vegetables' in 'Nectarine' area followed on 7/8 June. It would be interesting to discover what degree of disablement, or at least annoyance, this bout of mine-laying caused the enemy Naval authorities. We may never know!

Flying over friendly territory for a change must have seemed highly delightful to the crews, and this is what four of them did when they took part in a searchlight and fighter affiliation exercise on the night of 8/9 June. Following a prescribed route, they flew over Hull, Malton, York, Leeds, Halifax, Huddersfield, Sheffield, Doncaster, Scunthorpe and Grimsby before returning to Bottesford.

Mine-laying on 9/10 June was distinctly 'hairy' for the crew of R5500 [EM:B], piloted by Flg. Off. I. Huntley-Wood. After pin-pointing the Hãlsingborg copper works and circling the town twice, the Lancaster dropped its mines and was then fired on when at 1,000 feet altitude by two flak ships and from the waterfront when even lower. With some superficial damage, R5500 made its way back to base. Wt. Off. J. B. Walker DFM and his crew in R5632 [EM:N] were fortunate to survive when both port engines cut out after fuel supply had been switched to the inner tanks after twelve minutes in the air. Return to base was made somewhat lopsidedly but safely! During a mining mission off the Frisian Islands by three aircraft on the night of 11/12 June, four large and six small ships and an enemy submarine were sighted and would no doubt have made tempting targets of opportunity had the appropriate weapon load been carried.

No operations were planned for 15 June, as arrester gear was being fitted to each end of the three runways. Designed to deal with overshooting aircraft, the equipment was a variation of the gear installed on aircraft carriers but was of necessity much strengthened to ensure that it could hold a Lancaster. Made by Mather & Platt Ltd., the gear comprised a large brake drum around which was wound a steel cable which then ran over a series of pulley wheels, across the runway and back again onto another drum. Each Lancaster was to be fitted with hydraulically operated hooks, similar to those on the aircraft of the Fleet Air Arm, which would catch onto the cable stretched at a height of twelve inches (30 cm.) above the runway surface. However, the installation at Bottesford and at nineteen other airfields was never used operationally, as the weight of the additional equipment in the Lancasters and the £21,000 cost per airfield were both considered excessive, and in any case training had improved to the extent that overshoots were becoming rare. Of much more significance were the appearance of the first signs of surface cracking of the runways and perimeter tracks and, in some areas, subsidence. Like so many other airfields, Bottesford had been built in a great hurry on poor ground and had been brought into use too quickly. Plans were made at once for resurfacing to be carried out without, it was hoped, disrupting operational flying.

Essen, that regular target in 'Happy Valley', was once more the focus of 207 Squadron's attention on 16 June, when eight aircraft were detailed to attack. Of these, six made it to the primary target and the other two returned to base, one with a cracked exhaust muffler and the other with electrical failure preventing bomb release. Accurate and heavy flak was experienced over the target but only slight damage was caused to one aircraft.

By now, 207 Squadron was developing into a major participant in the Bomber Command scheme of things. Although technical problems still raised their ugly heads quite frequently, the situation was under infinitely better control than during the Manchester period. Crews had become acclimatised to the Lancaster and had learnt, sometimes by hard experience, that they could rely on this war-horse to bring them home unless damage to the airframe or a couple of engines was just too great. Before long, it would be possible to throw the complete inventory of Lancasters into the nightly battle.

On 20 June thirteen crews were briefed for a raid on target 'A' at Emden, but one was withdrawn later. Take-off was around 23.45, but before long three aircraft turned back, one with a failed hydraulic system and another with engine trouble. R5860 [EM:Y], flown by Flt. Lt. G. Ings, came down in the North Sea about fifty miles (80 km.) off Lincolnshire. When engine trouble had developed after the aircraft left the English coast, the bomb load was jettisoned, but two more engines then failed. Flt. Lt. Ings managed to glide the crippled Lancaster from an altitude of 15,000 feet to make a safe ditching, without injury to the crew. Two aircraft were sent to search for the downed Lancaster, which the crew of a Wellington of 1 Group found next day, and a rescue launch took the crew on board. The remaining eight Lancasters pressed on, and four were able to drop their loads on the primary target while the rest unloaded on the town of Emden. The same city received another visit during the following night, when six aircraft found the primary target and gave it their usual attention. One crew saw a single-engined Luftwaffe fighter 500 feet above their Lancaster, but its pilot chose to ignore them.

It was during the summer of 1942 that air gunner Sgt. Maxwell Riddell DFM received orders to report to the Air Ministry in London. This caused him to be very concerned, as he thought he might be in trouble after exceeding the official number of operations allowed at that time. Having been in the RAF before the war, he had filled his first log book some time before this and had started on his second. More significantly, he had completed more operational sorties than any other NCO in Bomber Command, and was convinced that this was the reason for his summons. He duly departed from Bottesford and did not come back, and it was some weeks before his friends discovered where he was. One day when the newspapers arrived they saw his photograph on the centre page. He was in Hollywood, taking part in the first Parade of Heroes, led by Sqn. Ldr. J. D. Nettleton VC! This was a drive to raise money through War Bonds, and it began with a parade through New York, complete with a hail of ticker-tape, and carried on through the United States to end in Los Angeles. There, he was fêted, and photographed in the company of a bevy of well-known female film stars, a lucky man indeed! On his return to the UK, 'Max' was ordered to meet the AOC of 5 Group, 'Cocky' Cochrane, who told him firmly that he was not to fly on any more operations as an air gunner, and although

Sgt. Maxwell Riddell of 207 Squadron in Hollywood during his publicity tour of the United States in 1942. To his left are Ann Sothern (1) and Donna Reed (2); behind him and to his left, wearing a floppy hat is Loretta Young (3); in the rear row to his right are Eleanor Powell (5) and Joan Bennett (4). [P. M. Rae]

he appealed against this ruling the AOC would not give way. Instead, he arranged for Max to be commissioned and sent to Canada for training as a pilot. This he completed successfully, and eventually became a Sqn. Ldr. and gained the DFC.

Apart from a spot of 'gardening' by one aircraft on 23/24 June and a raid on docks and shipping at St. Nazaire on 24/25 June in which one aircraft took part, things were quiet at Bottesford. But not for long! For a major raid on the important Focke-Wulf aircraft factory at Bremen on the night of 25/26 June nineteen Lancasters of 207 Squadron were detailed. Of these, fifteen made it to the target, as one had been 'scrubbed', two failed to take off and a fourth returned to base with engine trouble. Cloud was solid on the way out, although above cloud the Northern Lights and a full moon shone. Navigation and target-finding was done solely by dead reckoning, and the only indication to the crews of damage caused was through one or two small gaps in the clouds. Flak was heavy but not accurate apart from a few bullet holes sustained by Flt. Sgt. Duxbury's aircraft. A later photographic reconnaissance sortie revealed that one direct hit had been made on a large erecting shed and there were eighteen craters on the airfield. Set against this was the loss of 52 aircraft of Bomber Command – not an acceptable figure. Two nights later ten Lancasters took off to raid Bremen again, but this time two turned back and one crashed on take-off. A third visit to the same city was paid on the night of 29/30 June, when thirteen of the squadron's aircraft dropped their bomb loads on the primary target while three returned to base with engine trouble. One of the Lancasters which reached the target, R5616 [EM:J], was hit by heavy flak, injuring the observer and co-pilot. The captain, Flg. Off. I. Huntley–Wood, succeeded in bringing the aircraft back to Bottesford but on arrival was directed to divert to Wittering because R5616 had no usable flaps due to damage to the hydraulic pipeline and because of the number of aircraft in the Bottesford circuit, which was caused partly by thunderstorms and partly by an air raid in the vicinity.

The young people who made up the great majority of the personnel at Bottesford (and elsewhere) were always hungry, and although the standard of 'grub' in the messes is said to have been reasonable given the shortage of most commodities, efforts were always being made to supplement the supply. MT driver Daphne Forbes remembers a group of airmen and WAAFs standing close to the hedge opposite a farmhouse near the airfield and seeing a woman coming out carrying a pile of fried egg sandwiches which she had cooked to order. "I think they were sixpence [the direct equivalent of 2.5p.] each," she says. "If you wanted to buy eggs at any farm to take on leave, the farmer was not allowed to sell them to you for eating......as all eggs were supposed to go to the Ministry of Agriculture. I think the good woman from the farm was taking quite a risk when Government snoopers might have been around."

Bremen and its aircraft factory were not allowed any respite by Bomber Command in the early part of July 1942. From 207 Squadron, eleven Lancasters of fourteen detailed hit the area during the night of 2/3 July, but apart from one crew who reported seeing a large fire burning at the Focke–Wulf factory no positive results could be ascertained. Three crews planted 'vegetables' in areas 'Brocolli' and 'Asparagus' next night, but for the next few nights the squadron concentrated on formation flying practice, always a crucial skill in mass bombing missions. It was the night of 8/9 July before the next operation was mounted by 207 Squadron, and this time, as a rest from Bremen, the target for nine aircraft was Wilhelmshaven. On this occasion, some crews reported afterwards that while incendiaries were burning over a large area they were not helpful in identifying the target, while other crews maintained that they were! All agreed that the success of this operation was due to the use of target illumination flares.

The confident-looking crew of Sgt. George Hawes (back row, left to right) George Hawes, Percy Hooper, Frank Clarke, Eric Cartwright. (front row) Chiassion, Roddam, 'Bill' Blair. [via V. Holyoak]

The deepest penetration yet

A long-distance mission was next — a raid on Schichau submarine slipways in the port of Danzig on 11 July which involved a round trip of 1,600 miles (2,575 km.) and the deepest penetration of enemy territory yet tried by Bomber Command. Sadly, Lancaster L7543 [EM:Z], with Flt. Sgt. G. H. Duke in command, failed to return from this mission. His was one of ten aircraft which took off at about 17.00, but the mission was not a great success, as formation was lost by several of the aircraft, some of which went on to carry out solo attacks while others abandoned the job in the prevailing poor weather conditions. A United States subject who had volunteered for service in the RCAF, Flg. Off. F. A. Roper DFC remembers that when over Denmark the Lancaster crews could see fighters taking off from Flensburg airfield, so altered course for Sweden, joining a five-aircraft V formation from another squadron. Those crews who did reach the target found themselves welcomed by light but accurate flak, which caused slight damage to some aircraft. Former air gunner Bob Weatherall recorded in his diary "Had dinner and are told that we are going on a daylight raid. Briefed at two [14.00] and what a trip! We are going to Danzig. Well, at last the day has arrived. Right out to our kites after briefing and took off at five [17.00]. Formed up and away we went. Plenty of cloud at first, and then bright sunshine. About half an hour out and we really ran into it. Rain and thunderstorms came our way from then on. Came down to have a look at Sweden. It's a really lovely country. Hit our target in bright sunshine and then it happened. Ran it at 6,000 feet and they really shot hell out of us. I thought my time had come. Dropped our bomb load smack on them and then put the nose down to the tune of 330 mph. Some trip back — rain and lightning. Got back at 2.30 pm [14.30]. We were up for a stretch of 10 hours [in fact they were airborne for twelve and a half hours]. One crew is missing, although only four of us got to the target from here. Had supper, then down to my bunk to thank God for a safe return."

Six aircraft dropped mines in area 'Nectarine' off the Frisian Islands on 12/13 July, after which several operations were planned and then cancelled. On 19/20 July came an attack on the Vulcan submarine works at Vegesack, and this time weather conditions allowed accurate visual bombing by the squadron's six crews, each aircraft carrying 1,250 incendiary bombs. An airfield with a flashing beacon and a double flarepath was seen, the lights of which were extinguished when the Lancasters' engines were heard. For the next mission, on 21/22 July, weather conditions were again good, and twelve Lancasters left Bottesford to raid Duisburg, each carrying five 2,000 lb. (909 kg.) bombs. The same target was the destination for eleven aircraft on 23/24 July, this time with mixed bomb-loads. This time, unfortunately, two aircraft failed to return to base. Missing were the crews of Plt. Off. McCarthy in R5867 [EM:T], which came down at Baerl, on the border between Germany and Holland, and of Flt. Sgt. W. G. Hawes in R5632 [EM:N], which was never traced. Extensive searches only produced the body of one of the gunners aboard R5632, Flt. Sgt. T. C. Blair, recovered from the North Sea near Ijmuiden, Holland, on 12 October, so it is assumed that the Lancaster ditched with the loss of the entire crew. George Hawes was typical of the many thousands of men who came to Great Britain voluntarily to train as aircrew to fight the common enemy and lost their lives in doing so. He had survived 24 of his tour of 30 operations, had just been promoted and was about to apply for a commission. His name is inscribed on the Runnymede Memorial to the 20,455 airmen and airwomen who have no known grave. An extract from the last letter from George to his brother reads: "Things that are everyday affairs now would have scared the daylights out of me once. You cannot imagine what a trip over Hunland is like – the sky lit up by hundreds of searchlights and alive with tracers of every colour; the orange glow of bursting shells and the smell of cordite. It rather shakes you up for a start, but becomes all part of a day's work. Over some parts of 'Happy Valley' (the Ruhr) the flak is almost unbelievable. Bill once described it as being so thick that he had to put his oxygen mask on to breathe....... It's a crazy game, without a doubt. However, we have a good team of chaps, taken all in all – brave boys, devil-may-care chaps and fools, which all go to make good company and a really good squadron."

Holding the propeller blade of his Lancaster at Bottesford is Sgt. George Hawes, who lost his life on 24 July 1942 when R5632 crashed in the North Sea during a raid on Duisberg. [via B. Goodwin]

Duisburg was given more attention on 25/26 July by three aircraft of 207 Squadron while another one laid mines in area 'Deodars'. Heavy flak was experienced over Germany, and Lancaster R5674 [EM:S] came home with a hole in its mid-upper turret but luckily not in its occupant! On 26/27 July Hamburg was the target for seven aircraft, crews of which were able to see the docks clearly by the

'A' Flight of 207 Squadron at Syerston in July 1942. Aircrews from most of the second and third rows, with ground crews in front and rear. 'Babe' Ruth is in the centre of the second row.

light of the moon and drop their bomb loads accordingly. Huge fires were seen to be burning in the town and in the docks. On the way home, the crews could see the conflagration from a distance of sixty miles (nearly 100 km.).

As the end of the month approached, two more raids were planned. For the first, on 29/30 July, the target was Saarbrucken, onto which 4,000 lb. and incendiary bombs were off-loaded with some success. On the outbound trip, Lancaster R5635 was continuously illuminated by our own searchlights, much to the justified annoyance of Flg. Off. M. E. Doble and his crew, who saw themselves in danger in the event of an intruder being in the area. Another crew, that of Sqn. Ldr. W. D. Ruth DFC, complained that their aircraft had been fired upon by our own defences when on the homeward trip. To complete a busy month, 207 Squadron put up sixteen aircraft for a raid on Dusseldorf on 31 July/1 August 1942. All hit the primary target in very good weather and afterwards the crews reported accurate bomb-aiming.

August's first operation was on 5/6, when three aircraft set out to for Essen, using Gee equipment to locate the target. From this mission Lancaster R5761 [EM:T], with Flt. Lt. G. A. Ings as captain, failed to return, having been shot down at Altforst, twelve miles (20 km.) west of Nijmegen in Holland by Oblt. Gerhard Loos of I/NJG1. At the same time, another three aircraft dropped mines in area 'Deodars'. Later the same night, at 05.00, Sgt. F. S. Akerman in Lancaster R5550 [EM:B] was told by Flying Control to taxi back down the main runway after landing, as the perimeter track was under repair. The Lancaster was thought to have cleared the runway, and Manchester L7385 [EM:U] of the Conversion Flight was then given permission to land on the same runway in the opposite direction after a local night sortie. The Manchester landed on top of the Lancaster and burst into flames, with the loss of five men, including Sgt. Akerman, and with injuries to five others, some of them serious. The badly-burned captain of the Manchester was Sgt. A. S. Pearson, who

Flt. Lt. (later Sqn. Ldr.) William David Ruth DFC, known as 'Babe' after the 1930s baseball player, took over as CO of 'A' Flight in June 1942. He was killed in action on his third tour and buried in France. [via V. Holyoak]

underwent treatment by Sir Archibald McIndoe's team of plastic surgeons at East Grinstead. Not a good night for 207 Squadron.

Administration of 207 Squadron Conversion Flight was handed over to Station Headquarters at Bottesford on 8 August, although the policy of the Flight remained that its output was absorbed into the squadron. When Sqn. Ldr. Murray was posted to 9 Squadron's Conversion Flight on 11 August, Sqn. Ldr. Beauchamp took over from him as CO. Instructional staff increased in number at this time, the pilots being the CO with Flg. Offs. Green and Huntley-Wood, air gunners Plt. Off. Waterman and Flt. Sgt. Hall, observers Plt. Off. Ferguson and Flt. Sgt. Knight and WOp/AGs Flt. Sgts. Young and Gilmore.

Osnabruck was the target for six crews of 207 Squadron on 9/10 August, while one inexperienced 'freshman' crew attacked the docks at Le Havre quite successfully. On 10/11 August 'gardening' was the mission for three aircraft, two to drop in area 'Kraut' and one in area 'Silverthorn', both in the Kattegat. The latter, Lancaster R5499 [EM:O] with Flg. Off. J. G. Speir and crew, unfortunately never returned. Another 'freshman' crew attacked Le Havre on 11/12 August, this time using Swinderby as the point of departure, as Bottesford's main runway was still under repair. No results could be observed.

Two more crews and aircraft were lost on 12/13 August, when six were detailed to raid Mainz. Heavy and accurate flak was encountered over Frankfurt, causing damage to several Lancasters and no doubt bringing about the sad demise of the crews of R5760 [EM:Y], piloted by Sgt. M. D. Fry, and R5633 [EM:R], with Flt. Sgt. F. S. Kane at the controls. Swinderby was again the take-off point on 15 August, when six aircraft attacked Dusseldorf without loss. Visibility was moderate, and a mixture of 2,000-pound and 4,000-pound bombs hit the target area. Then came what turned out to be 207 Squadron's final, and sad, mission from Bottesford, when six Lancasters took off on 16 August to drop mines in areas 'Willow' and 'Geranium'. Two failed to return: R5616 [EM:J] captained by Plt. Off. A. J. Southwell, which crashed into the sea off Fano Island, Denmark, and R5509 [EM:G], with Flt. Sgt. N. J. Sutherland and crew, which was also thought to have come down in the sea. A Danish newspaper, 'Nationaltidende', report next day stated that a British aircraft had been shot down by a fighter and had crashed to the south of Fano, four of the crew being dead and the fifth brought ashore injured. This was Sgt. J. Read, flight engineer on R5616, who survived to be captured. The paper also stated that another British aircraft had been shot down off the west coast of Jutland, but not whether fighters or flak were responsible.

Poor weather in the middle of August precluded any more operations but training flights continued. It was while practicing three-engined overshoots on 19 August that Flt. Sgt. W. D. Fordwych's Lancaster R5863 [EM:K] stalled and crashed on the edge of Normanton village. All six on board lost their lives, and it was by sheer good luck that no civilians were harmed, as wreckage was scattered over the main street.

Goodbye to Bottesford.........

The poorly-built runways at Bottesford were now causing such a degree of anxiety that it was decided that 207 Squadron would move elsewhere. On 23 August 1942 the two operational Flights and the gunnery, signals and armaments sections made the short journey to Syerston, while the Conversion Flight moved to Swinderby. There it became a lodger unit and was merged with 61 Squadron's Conversion Flight, the two Flights sharing an orderly room. Meanwhile Squadron HQ and maintenance sections remained at Bottesford while work on runway repairs began.

...........and hello to Syerston

Syerston airfield had been opened in December 1940 as a medium bomber Station in 1 Group, but just one year later had closed to allow the construction of paved runways to commence. This work was finished in May 1942, and the Station then became a heavy bomber airfield in 5 Group. The site was wedged between the main Fosse Way on the east and the river Trent on the west, about 5.5 miles (9 km.) south-west of Newark. No less than nine hangars of various types were available, ensuring that maintenance could be carried out in relatively civilised conditions.

After a break of a week or so, operations by 207 Squadron resumed on the night of 24/25 August 1942, when three aircraft took off, out of five detailed, to raid Frankfurt as part of a fleet led by the newly-established Pathfinder Force. Of these, two returned early with engine troubles, one with its bomb-load still on board. The crew of the third Lancaster managed to identify the target and drop a 4,000-pounder and incendiaries accurately. Next came an attack on Kassel on 27/28 August by seven aircraft, one of which, W4129 [EM:R] piloted by Flg. Off. T. D. Brown, was posted as missing, while the port engine of R5570 [EM:F] failed over the coast of Holland, prompting a return

Lancaster R5632 [EM:N] and its crew on dispersal at Bottesford in the summer of 1942. This aircraft failed to return from a raid on Duisburg on 24 July that year and is thought to have gone down into the North Sea.
[C. Hawes via V. Holyoak]

An evocative picture of 207 Squadron Lancasters at rest during their short period at Syerston. [via B. Goodwin]

to base. Another aircraft, R5635 [EM:L] also returned early, this one with a faulty firing mechanism in the rear turret. Those crews which did reach the target identified it visually and off-loaded their 'cookies', 2,000-pounders and incendiaries with varying degrees of success. W4134 [EM:U] was hit by flak, resulting in damage to glazed areas, bomb doors and engine nacelles, but more importantly the bomb-aimer was wounded in the leg. August's final operation was a trip by four aircraft to Nuremburg, one other Lancaster having returned early with an overheating engine. This was classed as a successful operation, the conflagration being seen up to seventy miles away on the return trip.

Meanwhile, at Swinderby the pace of conversion training was hotting up, and during September the aircraft strength was increased to four Manchesters and four Lancasters. At Syerston, the main body of the squadron carried on with the now well-established pattern of raids on important targets as dictated by Bomber Command, the first one in September 1942 being on Saarbrucken by seven aircraft. Of these, R5674 [EM:S] suffered an electrical failure and being unable to reach the target was diverted to Wittering, where Plt. Off. R. G. Rowlands (Sgt. Warnock in one report!) landed it safely without benefit of brakes, finally colliding with a hangar! Each aircraft dropped either four 2,000-pound bombs or one 4,000-pounder plus a dose of incendiaries onto marker flares placed by pathfinders, although at the time the crews were unaware that their leaders had marked Saarlouis in error, and the result was seen up to 125 miles (200 km.) away.

Raids on Karlsruhe on 2/3 September and on the Focke-Wulf aircraft factory at Bremen on 4/5 September followed, the latter particularly effective in terms of the number of buildings destroyed and damaged. It was on this mission that the squadron lost Plt. Off. R. G. Rowlands and his crew in Lancaster R5755 [EM:N], which was shot down into the Ijsselmeer in Holland by a night-fighter. A night cross-country exercise was held on 5/6 September, and next night Duisburg was the target for two aircraft while another one laid mines in area 'Rosemary II' off Heligoland. On 8/9 September Frankfurt was the target for five aircraft. During the flight, Sgts. R. Boardman and W. E. Lodge, gunners aboard Sgt. Walker's aircraft, made several hits on an enemy fighter and later claimed it as damaged. Two aircraft went mining in area 'Silverthorn' on 9/10 September, and during this mission Sgt. H. B. Einarson and his crew in R5628 [EM:Q] were shot down by a night-fighter, crashing into the sea off Denmark. Next night six of the squadron's Lancasters visited Dusseldorf, one landing at Wittering with brake trouble on returning.

During the morning of 13 September the CO and all the squadron aircrew returned to Bottesford, where the Chaplain of the Forces presided over a church parade held to dedicate the Station chapel. That night nine of the crews were back in action, with Bremen as their target. So successful was this mission that Sgt. R. S. Wilson, the captain of Lancaster W4174 [EM:W], remarked at de-briefing "Good show, well worth missing leave for", though whether the rest of the crew echoed these sentiments is open to conjecture!

Three of 207 Squadron's Lancasters took part in a mission on Wilhelmshaven on 14/15 September and the crews claimed that they had been successful in dropping their loads on the right spot. Essen was the next target, raided on 16/17 September by nine Lancasters, of which L7551 [QR:S], which had been borrowed from 61 Squadron and captained by Flt. Sgt. J. D. Herron, did not return.

News was then received of another squadron move, Syerston having only been a temporary base, whether or not the personnel were aware of the fact. On 20 September 1942 the squadron was to move to Bottesford's satellite airfield, Langar, but on the previous night one more operation took place, an attack on Munich in good visibility by eight aircraft, one of which aborted due to lack of oxygen to the rear gun turret.

Seen here polishing the perspex of his Lancaster before going on a night-flying test is Canadian bomb-aimer Sgt. Timothy 'Bill' Blair. [via V. Holyoak]

Two of 207 Squadron's Lancasters at Syerston on 13 September 1942, a week before moving to Langar. [via R. Winton]

Chapter 7: Langar days

In solitary splendour

207 Squadron's main party left Syerston on 20 September as planned and moved into Langar, a wartime 'temporary' airfield situated nine miles (14.5 km.) south-east of Nottingham. This was a Class A heavy bomber airfield from the time it opened in 1941, although 207 was the only operational squadron of the RAF ever to be based there. On the west side of the airfield were the workshops of Avro, where throughout the war major repairs to and reconditioning of Lancasters were carried out. 207's Lancasters flew in from Syerston next day, and squadron HQ and maintenance sections arrived from Bottesford. So after a month of separation the squadron was in one place again, apart from the Conversion Flight, which remained at Swinderby.

The first offensive operation mounted from Langar was a raid on Wismar, a town on the Baltic coast with a Dornier aircraft factory, on 23/24 September 1942, for which eleven crews were briefed. Ten aircraft took off, of which five attacked the primary target fairly successfully, but the others suffered a variety of misfortunes. Lancaster R5908 [EM:B] developed generator trouble, and Flt. Lt. S. E. Pattison DFC dumped his bomb-load in the Wash before returning to base, while Sqn. Ldr. J. Clift CBE in W4191 [EM:Q] also decided that conditions were too bad and jettisoned his bombs. Sgt. A. J. Parkyn in R5570 [EM:R] reported a bad electric storm which "lit up the aircraft like a Christmas tree." A large piece of the leading edge of this aircraft's starboard wing was shot away by flak, and as it was impossible to pinpoint the target Sgt. Parkyn brought his six 1,000 lb. (455 kg.) bombs home. Lancaster R5745 [EM:T] was struck by lightning when at an altitude of 1,200 feet over the North Sea and went into a steep dive before pulling out at 400 feet. The flight instruments were unreliable, the rear turret ammunition chute jammed and the radio aerials burnt off. All in all, not the most serviceable of aircraft!

Next night, sea mining was the main preoccupation. Seven crews were detailed to drop mines in areas 'Daffodil I', 'Daffodil II', 'Spinach', 'Sweet Pea' and 'Willow', and seven aircraft eventually took off on a trip which was recorded later as being "......unusually peaceful and uneventful." Results were accurate for most of the five crews who reached their targets, and on completion of their sorties they were diverted to Topcliffe in Yorkshire when ground mist obscured Langar and other 5 Group airfields. The squadron then stood down for a week, a rest no doubt welcomed most sincerely by air and ground crews alike, although it is doubtful whether the latter were allowed to have much of a break, as there was always plenty to do around the hangars.

Poor weather conditions characterised 207 Squadron's next mission, which was a return to Wismar on 1/2 October by ten aircraft. Nevertheless, seven were deemed to be successful, while other crews declined to claim success even though they believed they had dropped their bombs in the general target area. On return, five aircraft diverted to Leeming, three to Acklington and one to Linton-on-Ouse before making their way back to Langar. Four out of five crews who attacked Aachen on 5/6 October also considered that they had done a good job, one captain going so far as to report that the 4,000-pounder dropped from his Lancaster had produced "devastating results." One of the five Lancasters went to Woodhall Spa on return and another to Swinderby.

At Swinderby, 207 Squadron's Conversion Flight was still growing. On 6 October 1942 it absorbed 61 Squadron Conversion Flight, after which the Flight was divided into two sub-Flights, 'A' using eight Manchesters and 'B' with eight Lancasters. However, further alterations to the

Outside the Officers Mess at Langar in 1943. 2 unknown, Jimmy Moore, Les Mitchell, David Balme, Ken Letford, Bill De Bardeleben; seated Peter Jennings (CO), F/O Schmeidler (Intelligence Officer). [Squadron archives]

conversion methods used by Bomber Command were in the pipeline and were not long in coming to fruition.

The district around RAF Langar is remembered vividly by Gilbert Haworth DFC DFM, who was a navigator on 207 Squadron. "When I arrived at Langar", he recalls, "I was housed with nine others in a wooden hut, five beds each side. By the time I left six months later no fewer than fifteen men had successively arrived to replace the casualties in my room. Most huts fared no better." He goes on to say "In those days of food rationing we were all invariably hungry despite being relatively well cared for in our messes. Across the road from our Flight offices was Langar Lodge, a farm run by the Gale family, with poultry running around all over the place. Poultry means eggs, which were in very short supply. Each morning we used to flock over to enjoy delicious egg sandwiches at a give-away price. This went a great way to maintaining the light-hearted and comparatively worry-free atmosphere for which 207 Squadron was noteworthy."

Osnabruck was the target for 207 Squadron on 6/7 October, when seven Lancasters took off from Langar and completed their task. After that no more missions were arranged until 13/14 October, when Kiel received 4,000 lb. and incendiary bombs dropped from three aircraft, all of which diverted to Swinderby. Then came a major operation, a daylight raid on the Schneider works at Le Creusot, near the French border with Switzerland. Fifteen Lancasters took off from Langar at about 18.30 on 17 October to join the bomber force, which then totalled eighty aircraft. At an altitude of 1,000 feet, they crossed the coast at Lands End, from where they flew over the Bay of Biscay before turning over the coast of France to make a 300-mile (480 km.) run-up to the target. One Lancaster, L7583 [EM:A], piloted by Sgt. R. S. Wilson, suffered the failure of an engine over the Brest area and when turning back was attacked by three Arado floatplanes. The gunners aboard the Lancaster were able to shoot down two Arados and damage the third before beginning the homeward flight. Langar was reached safely, but in the combat the flight engineer, Sgt. K. S. Chalmers, had been mortally wounded. Other aircraft landed at Upper Heyford, Wyton, Leconfield, Croughton, Tangmere, Gransden Lodge, Castle Camps, Wittering and Abingdon after this mission, which was regarded by those taking part as being highly successful.

The anticipated alterations to the training system took place on 20 October 1942, when the enlarged 207 Squadron Conversion Flight at Swinderby was absorbed

Lancasters of 5 Group squadrons flying in low-level formation over Mon Richard on their way to Le Creusot on 17 October 1942, a raid in which 207 Squadron played its part. [via R. Winton]

into 1660 Conversion Unit, under the command of Wg. Cdr. Oxley DSO DFC. Thus ended the long period of self-provision of aircrews enjoyed by 207 Squadron. In future, ready-converted crews would come from 1660 CU and similar units which now served operational squadrons.

Another daylight raid was arranged on 22 October, although strictly speaking it should be classified as a dusk raid, with take-off at around 18.00 and return in the dark. This time Genoa in northern Italy was the target, a round trip of nearly nine hours. Twelve aircraft took off, but two returned early, one having experienced engine failure over the Alps. The remaining ten reached the target at around 22.00 and crews later reported a successful mission. Diversions at the end of an operation seemed to be becoming the norm, as this time crews found themselves at Gransden Lodge, North Luffenham, Graveley, Abingdon, Wyton and Polebrook! Ten aircraft returned to Italy on 24 October, but this time it was a true daylight raid on Milan, with a take-off from Langar around 12.30. Seven crews reached the primary target and dropped bombs with varying degrees of apparent success, but W4121 [EM:B], with Flt. Sgt. L. R. Wright in command and a crew of nine rather than the usual seven, was lost. Both these Italian raids were set up in support of Operation 'Torch', the Allied landing in Sicily which gave a foothold on the long climb back into Europe from the south. Only one more operation was mounted that month, and by comparison it was simple and easy, involving three Lancaster laying mines in the Kattegat Straits on the night of 27/28 October.

The crew of a 207 Squadron Lancaster concentrating on the task in hand.
[by kind permission of Michael Turner]

While the squadron was at Langar there was an outbreak of gastro-enteritis, which was eventually traced to the MT section. The same vehicle was being used, it was found, for carrying mess salvage in the morning and rations in the afternoon! Needless to say, the MT drivers were not in favour for some time!

Foggy weather early in November prevented operations by 207 Squadron until the night of 6/7 November, when the mist lifted enough to allow five aircraft to set out for Genoa. One returned early with what was described as navigational aid failure, but the other four reached and attacked Genoa in good visibility. A repeat visit was paid next night, and this time 207's contribution was eleven Lancasters, one of which returned to base with an unserviceable intercom and another, L7546 [EM:G], piloted by Sgt. R. S. Wilson, was lost to enemy action and crashed in France. Another Lancaster, R5693 [EM:J], suffered the indignity of a collapsed undercarriage on landing at North Luffenham but was not damaged badly enough to be written off.

An evening raid on Hamburg was organised for seven crews on 9 November, but of these one failed to take off and one aborted with its elevator trimmer out of action. The others found that poor weather over the target meant that the results of their mission could not be seen, and one crew regarded their sortie as a "wasted effort." Mine-laying in area 'Furze' occupied three aircraft on 10/11 November, although one brought some of its mines back to land at Hurn while the other two landed at Tangmere, one after jettisoning its load when the target area became unidentifiable. After this, foggy weather meant that a couple of days were spent on ground training and lectures before the crews could take to the air again.

Genoa was the next target for 207 Squadron, and on 13 November eight crews were briefed for the night's mission. Seven took off between 17.55 and 18.40, but one had to turn back after a short circuit caused a fire in the rear turret. The other six Lancasters carried out a fairly successful raid and returned to the UK, three landing at Ford, one at Tangmere, one at Leconfield and one at base. Next night two aircraft joined in yet another attack on Genoa, one returning to base on three engines and the other landing at Waddington. A 'Bullseye' exercise kept three crews busy on 16/17 November while another crew dropped mines.

Italy was again the chosen area for part of Bomber Command's attentions on the night of 18/19 November, and 207 Squadron sent three of its Lancasters to raid the Fiat factory at Turin, where aircraft and armaments were being produced. This task was repeated two nights later, again with reasonable success, and on this occasion the three aircraft took off from Bottesford instead of Langar, perhaps to test the repair work which had been carried out on the runways and perimeter tracks since the squadron left. Just one Lancaster took off from Langar to join in a raid on Stuttgart on 22/23 November and dropped a 3,000 lb. (1364 kg.) bomb, 810 incendiaries and twenty bundles of leaflets during what the crew regarded as a "quiet trip."

The ill-fated Normanton farmhouse almost suffered again on 20 November, when another Lancaster overshot Bottesford's runway. Sgt. J. K. Banfield was aboard an aircraft flying from Langar and recalls "We encountered very low cloud. After several attempts to see and line up with the runway, we finally landed too far up its length, overshot and ended up in the spinney just short of the Sick Quarters, quite near the Farm House."

Lancaster Mk.III ED413 [EM:P] was one which survived enemy action. During subsequent service with 1651 CU, however, it crash-landed near Barnwell in Huntingdonshire on 27 January 1945 and was written off. [P. H. T. Green collection]

Three Lancasters took part in a 'gardening' mission on 23/24 November, taking off from Bottesford. Two of the four dropped their mines successfully in the Gironde estuary before returning to land at Predannack in Cornwall, and another off Biarritz, where heavy flak from a ship in the mouth of the river was encountered.

A daylight raid provided a change in routine on 25 November, but it turned out to be something of a disaster. Five crews were detailed and took off around 15.00 hours for various destinations. For one the primary target was Quakenbrück, but lack of cloud cover made the captain decide to return, and his aircraft landed at Linton-on-Ouse with seven 1,000 lb (455 kg.) GP bombs still aboard. Another captain turned back for the same reason instead of bombing Friesoythe, and a third landed at Rufforth after dumping bombs in the North Sea on the way to Vechta. Far worse, the crew briefed to raid Haselünne failed to return at all. In command of their Lancaster (R5695 EM:C) was Sgt. A. J. Parkyn. Lancaster R5694 [EM:F] did apparently attack Bad Zwischenahn but on return crashed at Easton in Lincolnshire, with the loss of Flt. Lt. R. J. Hannan DFC and his entire crew.

After this sad episode, four Lancasters took off at about 17.00 on 27 November to raid Stettin, but owing to worsening weather they were recalled while on the outbound flight, after which three landed at Scampton and one at Hemswell. Eight of the squadron crews took part in another raid on Turin on 28/29 November, a very satisfactory trip, according to most crews. Continuing poor weather prevented any more activity until 6/7 December, although a few operations had been planned and then cancelled. The target for the eight aircraft was Mannheim, but the mission was something of a waste of effort due to the weather. One aircraft suffered the failure of its starboard outer engine early in the flight and landed at Docking after jettisoning its bomb load.

Once more, Turin was the target for nine of 207 Squadron's Lancasters which took off on 8 December. This mission was much more successful, and several sets of photographs showing the destruction caused during the raid were brought back. Sadly, the more so because he had taken over from Wg. Cdr. F. R. Jeffs as CO only the previous day, Wg. Cdr. F. G. L. Bain and his crew in Lancaster R5570 [EM:R] were lost during this raid. He was succeeded by Sqn. Ldr. (Wg. Cdr. from 7 February 1943) T. A. B. Parselle on 26 December.

AIR COMMODORE T. A. B. PARSELLE, C.B.E.

Air Cdre. T. A. B. Parselle CBE, who as a Wg. Cdr. was the CO of 207 Squadron from 26 December 1942 to 26 May 1943, when he was shot down and taken prisoner. After the war, he was Commandant of the RAF College, Cranwell, from 1955 to 1958. [207 Squadron archives]

Early in 1943 Lancaster L7580 of 207 Squadron enjoyed a brief rest in Trafalgar Square as part of the 'Wings For Victory' campaign before being transported back to Langar for further service. It was finally struck off charge on 2 November 1945 after use by several other units. [via R. Winton]

Turin received yet another pasting on the night of 9/10 December, when four aircraft of 207 Squadron attacked the primary target, three dropped their loads on Turin town and one aborted with technical difficulties. This was another operation which was seen as a success, with only light and inaccurate flak spoiling the picture a little.

No more operations took place until 14 December, when three Lancasters took off to lay mines off the Frisian Islands, but the aircraft were recalled before they could do so, the weather over the target being too poor. Ten aircraft were detailed to raid Duisburg on 20/21 December, but of these four were withdrawn and two turned back, both with failed starboard outer engines. That left four, all of which reached the target and made a useful contribution to the damage caused by Bomber Command. Next night the squadron put up twelve aircraft to raid Munich, one of which made an emergency landing at North Luffenham two and a half hours after take-off with the starboard inner Merlin on fire and the port inner giving trouble. One of the eleven others on this fairly successful mission, W4191 [EM:Q] with Sgt. J. R. Walker in charge, was shot down over Holland by a night-fighter.

So ended a momentous year for the personnel of 207 Squadron, a year in which the efforts they had all made began to bear more fruit than had been possible before the conversion from Manchesters to Lancasters. During the short time that the squadron had spent at Langar, Lancasters had taken off on 189 sorties and four had been lost, sadly with the deaths of every member of the four crews.

The tide begins to turn

1943 began with an operation against Essen by five aircraft on 3 January during which a new pathfinder marking method was used, involving aiming at flares dropped by radar-equipped Mosquitos. The raid was successful, but Flt. Sgt. J. B. Chaster's aircraft, W4134 [EM:U], was shot down by a Bf 110 night-fighter piloted by Oblt. Manfred Maurer, the CO of NJG1 from Venlo, and four of the crew lost their lives. Sgt. J. K. Banfield was the bomb-aimer, and remembers the starboard wing fuel tank catching fire and his hurried exit. He has no recollection of pulling the ripcord of his parachute on the way down to earth, but was found, hanging from a tree, by Dutchmen and Luftwaffe airmen, and taken to hospital in Amsterdam before being transferred to Stalag VIIIB at Lamsdorf in Upper Silesia. There he was housed with 960 other aircrew, all chained up for twelve hours each day in retaliation for similar treatment given to German prisoners during the Canadian raid on Dieppe in August 1942. The Lancaster had crashed ten miles (16 km.) south of Roermond, near Venlo, and the pilot managed to avoid captivity, eventually returning to 207 Squadron in late March 1943. The other four aircraft on that operation, and two that had been mining in area 'Furze', were safe but landed at other airfields on their return to the UK.

Only one of seven aircraft detailed to raid Essen again on 7/8 January actually took off, and on return landed at Skellingthorpe. The same poor contribution was made next night, when just two of seven aircraft detailed took off to attack Duisburg. Then came a string of four missions to Essen, the first on 9/10 January by five aircraft, two of which returned early. On 11/12 January seven aircraft left Langar but two aborted, and of five aircraft which began the trip on 12/13 January three came back early. Lastly, on 13/14 January, four aircraft took off and one failed to attack the target.

But then came a concerted effort to do some damage to Berlin, in which 207 Squadron joined on 16/17 January by sending thirteen Lancasters, six of which attacked the primary target and one the secondary, while the other five aborted the mission. Next night the target was again the Big City, and 207 Squadron sent ten Lancasters, of which seven hit the primary target while the others aborted. So far only one aircraft had been lost in 1943, but the next one failed to return on 22 January from a four-aircraft contribution to a large attack on Essen. This one was W4365 [EM:B], piloted by Sgt. J. C. Dangerfield, who lost his life, alongside his entire crew. 207 Squadron's input seems to have been restricted then until the middle of February, but no aircraft or lives were lost during that period. Participation in two raids on Dusseldorf, two on Hamburg, two on Lorient and one on Cologne, Turin and Wilhelmshaven, plus a two-aircraft sea-mining mission in area 'Nectarine', kept the squadron busy.

On 13/14 February a larger-scale mission took eleven of 207 Squadron's Lancasters to Lorient, and all returned safely, although W4167 [EM:Q] crashed on landing at Langar. This was not the case next night, unfortunately, as one of the six aircraft which visited Milan, Flt. Sgt. J. H. Whyte's L7547 [EM:M], failed to return. In fact, he and his flight engineer, Flt. Sgt. S. H. Eyre, survived and managed to avoid being captured, but the rest of the crew lost their lives. Lorient received another strike on 16/17 February by five aircraft, and two nights later five aircraft returned to Wilhelmshaven, a mission from which Sgt. N. C. Beer in ED330 [EM:F] did not return. Three more Lancasters of 207 Squadron went there again on 19/20 February without incident. A raid on Vegesack followed two nights later, after which there was a four-night gap before Nuremburg was visited by eight aircraft on 25/26 February. From that raid Flg. Off. M. K. Sexton and his crew failed to return in ED356 [EM:W]. Next night three aircraft went 'gardening' in area 'Nectarine II' while seven joined in an attack on

Cologne, all without loss. To end the month, St. Nazaire was the target for five of 207 Squadron's Lancasters on 28 February.

With the beginning of spring 1943, there seems to have been an upturn in the squadron's participation in the bombing offensive, although the first target, Berlin on 1/2 March, was reached by only three of the seven aircraft which took off from Langar. That night, the bomber force consisted of 42 Lancasters of 1 Group, 50 Stirlings of 3 Group, 52 Halifaxes of 4 Group, 98 Lancasters of 5 Group, 21 Halifaxes of 6 Group and 39 mixed types from 8 (Pathfinder) Group, which laid route-marking flares with great accuracy. Afterwards, reports from all Groups compared the visual spectacle of fiery devastation very favourably with anything previously accomplished elsewhere. A reconnaissance by the PRU found that about twenty acres (eight hectares) of railway workshops at Templehof had been destroyed or put out of action, as was the Kluckner Humboldt Deutz factory and other industrial buildings. A German news broadcast, however, gave another picture. 'British bombers in the night Monday to Tuesday penetrated to Berlin,' the news reader said. 'The concentric attack apparently planned by the enemy was frustrated, however, by the audacity and elan of German night fighters and by well-aimed fire of innumerable AA batteries of heavy and heaviest calibre whose actions were effectively supported by numerous searchlights. Bombs dropped by the raiders over the city were in most cases dropped quite indiscriminately. Fire Brigade squads and the air raid defence formation, with the resolute assistance of the population, soon had the fires under control.' The truth was probably somewhere between the two reports.

Then came another loss, when Sgt. R. Isaacs and his crew in ED533 [EM:N] did not return from a mining operation in area 'Deodars'. On the following night the squadron suffered a further loss, that of Sgt. P. Evison and his crew in ED365 [EM:U], which was one of seven aircraft which had set out to raid Hamburg as part of a major operation. Essen's large Krupp works and Nuremburg were targeted next, but between these two operations Langar received its first visit from the AOC.

Returning with bombs on board was occasionally necessary and was not too much of a problem until the advent of the 4,000 lb. 'Cookie', whereupon the situation changed dramatically. Shaped like a drum, the 'Cookie' was an ominous beast, and crews were told that if for any reason one had to be brought back they should "......evacuate the Lancaster as soon as it stops rolling, run like hell for two hundred yards, hurl yourselves flat on the ground, cover your ears and hope for the best!" Every effort had to be made to avoid damaging any local property, particularly as a number of wives and sweethearts of squadron personnel lived near the airfield. Gilbert Haworth describes an event which could have been very nasty. "We roared down the runway into a filthy black night of pouring rain on 5 March 1943 for an attack on Essen. We were soon dismayed to find that our Lancaster had no climbing ability worth mentioning and managed to clear the boundary by a few inches. Five very long minutes took us up to 500 feet, when we levelled off to collect our wits and consider our extremely serious situation. Landing was out [of the question], as we were well above the safe landing weight; we were carrying a 'Cookie', which could not be dropped without exploding on impact. Unless we reached at least 5,000 feet its blast would wreck our aircraft. Our skipper understood this only too well and [knew] that the 'Cookie' must be dropped into the North Sea. We were not sure that we would reach the coast, but nevertheless headed for the Skegness exit corridor as our pilot strove to increase height, and by the time we reached the Lincolnshire coast our aircraft had been miraculously coaxed up to 4,000 feet. Although the waiting period seemed interminable, we were probably no more that fifteen miles out to sea when I heard Geoff Woodward, in a voice that was a little strained and hoarse, say 'I make it to be just 5,000 feet; bomb doors open, let's get rid of it please'. I let the 'Cookie' and our incendiaries go, noticing the customary bump as the 4,000-pounder parted from us. Looking downward at the same time was an action that was habitual and quite automatic, but I soon regretted it. A vast reddish ball of flame completely filled my entire field of vision, then the tremendous blast wave inflicted a terrific jolt. I expected the wings to part company as they flexed violently......mercifully we emerged unscathed."

One of the squadron's Lancasters, L7580 [EM:O], was taken by road to London on 6 March to be exhibited in Trafalgar Square as part of 'Wings For Victory' Week. The idea was to raise money for new aircraft by encouraging the general public to buy Savings Bonds. Afterwards, 'O Orange' was passed to 9 Squadron and ended its days with a Conversion Unit.

Jack Pegrum thought that this was a "very dodgy period." He says that one did not know many of the other crews, who came in a steady stream and, one way or another, quickly left again. However, Jack retains happy memories of a social life which centred around the 'Plough' inn at Stathern, where the landlady's name was Madge. The WAAFs at Langar and the local Land Army girls, who were "good company despite their heavy boots and breeches", are also recalled with affection. The 'Unicorn' in Langar village is recalled by Gilbert Haworth as another favourite hostelry. "There, the landlady, Mrs. Flint, washed our shirts, underwear and towels at very modest cost. But after a time she announced that she would no longer take in laundry, as so many of her customers went missing and she found it distressing to have to attend to their property. Two months later someone commented that she was still accepting a weekly bundle from Flt. Lt. Haworth, to which she promptly replied 'Ah well, he's different'." Ten years later, Gilbert Haworth revisited the 'Unicorn' and was promptly recognised and addressed by name! Members of the WVS, including a titled lady from Belvoir Castle, also provided a much-appreciated service by touring the dispersals an hangars to dispense 'char and wads' to the ground crews.

A raid on Munich on 9/10 March brought a further loss to the squadron when W4172 [EM:X], piloted by Flt. Sgt. I. Wood, did not return. Although Flt. Sgt. Wood lost his life, one of his crew survived as a prisoner of war and two more avoided capture. A two-aircraft mining mission was flown the same night. Then came participation by five aircraft in a 457-aircraft raid on Stuttgart and on 12/13 March another attack on Essen, this time by six aircraft, of which Flg. Off. M. E. Doble and his crew in W4931 [EM:U] did not return. Mining in area 'Silverthorn' followed, before a week in which no operations were mounted. Then, on 22/23 March, came a large-scale raid on St. Nazaire, to which 207 Squadron contributed eleven aircraft without loss. Berlin was raided twice more and St. Nazaire again felt Bomber Command's force before the end of the month, but Flt. Lt. D. O. Street and his crew failed to see Langar again after the Berlin raid of 29/30 March, although they all survived and were taken prisoner. In a letter to his father, Sir Arthur Street, Flt. Lt. Street wrote "......I cannot obviously tell you the story of how I became a PoW till later, but we were shot up, and despite all our efforts I had to give the order to bale out. I saw all the crew go out, then jumped myself, and you will be pleased to hear that they are all safe and well. They were all glorious and behaved with great fortitude. I wonder if [you] would be so kind as to write a letter to their next-of-kin on my behalf saying they are all OK and were absolutely grand......" Flt. Lt. Street, however, was brutally murdered on 6 April 1944 following the mass break-out from Sagan prison camp, Stalag Luft III.

In the first few days of April 1943 207 Squadron crews joined in raids on St. Nazaire, Essen and Kiel and carried

A panoramic view of Langar airfield in 1944, looking almost due west toward Nottingham. Apart from nine Lancasters standing on 'frying-pan' dispersals, twenty-eight Horsa gliders can be seen, Langar being one of the many Bomber Command airfields on which these aircraft were stored until needed for use in the Arnhem campaign or for the Rhine crossing. On the far side of the public road are the hangars allocated to Avro, while on the airfield itself are four T2 hangars, two of them built specifically for glider storage but perhaps not used for that purpose. [207 Squadron archives]

out small-scale mining missions. On 8 April seven aircraft took off for a raid on Duisburg, but one swung on take-off and its undercarriage collapsed, creating a blockage on the runway. Returning aircraft were diverted to Bottesford. The same target area was raided again next night, this time by all nine aircraft detailed, but sadly ED554 [EM:Q], failed to return. Its pilot was Wt. Off. H. A. Healey, who lost his life with his complete crew. Frankfurt received an attack on the night of 10/11 April by five of six Lancasters of 207 Squadron which left Langar, the other one returning early. A quite spectacular effort was made on 13/14 April, when twelve crews took part in a raid on the Italian port of La Spezia without loss. Several large vessels were said to be in the port and were to be attacked if identified. Only light haphazard flak was experienced, and significant damage was confirmed afterwards. Before a successful return visit to La Spezia was made on 18/19 April by five aircraft, a raid on Stuttgart and a long trek to Pilsen in Czechoslovakia had been made, as well as a small 'gardening' mission. Then came a raid on Stettin by eight aircraft on 20/21 April. In all, Bomber Command put up 339 heavy bombers that night, of which 304 claimed to have attacked successfully.

Visiting Langar on 21 April was a mobile exhibition of German equipment and flying clothing. Although not recorded as such, this may well have been 1426 (Enemy Aircraft Circus) Flight, based at Collyweston, the task of which was to demonstrate to RAF and USAAF units the aircraft in use by the Luftwaffe, so that defensive techniques could be developed. For a visit to a bomber Station such as Langar, examples of Luftwaffe fighters would have been flown so that aircrews could examine them in less intimidating circumstances than normal.

After a short rest from the steady grind of operations, eleven Lancasters of 207 Squadron were detailed for a raid on Duisburg on 26/27 April, and all took off as planned. One of them aborted the mission, however, and another, W4171 [EM:J], with Sgt. I. B. Jones at the controls, was lost, another sad night for the squadron. Two mining operations followed, and even these were not without their dangers, as one aircraft detailed to sow mines in area 'Nasturtium' on 28/29 April did not return. This was W4945 [EM:Z], piloted by Wt. Off. K. R. Rees. A raid on the hard-pressed Krupp works at Essen by seven aircraft on the last night of the month completed April's strenuous efforts by 207 Squadron.

Now that early summer had arrived, with fewer malfunctions caused by poor weather conditions to be expected, it was possible to put more aircraft into the air. On the other side of the coin, more aircraft on a mission meant the probability of heavier losses. April's losses of 207 Squadron aircraft to enemy action had been 2.7 % of those reaching the target, and it was hoped that this figure would not be exceeded, and might even be reduced. May began with a very heavy raid on Dortmund on 4/5 May in which eight aircraft of 207 Squadron took part, but then

A seven-man crew who flew from Langar, survived, and remained in being until Arthur McDavitt died in February 1996. Top row: Ken Bate (bomb aimer); Arthur Barfoot (air gunner); Jack Stephens (pilot); Jack Pegrum(wireless operator). Bottom row: Jim Love (navigator, a Canadian); Nat Bury (flight engineer); Arthur McDavitt (air gunner

there was a lull in the proceedings until 12/13 May, when nine Lancasters were among 480 aircraft which attacked Duisburg, the primary target. It was on this mission that two of 207 Squadron's Lancasters and their crews were lost, W4938 [EM:A], with Flg. Off. D. W. Evans and his crew, and ED418 [EM:G], piloted by Plt. Off. W. D. Hawkes. Ten aircraft paid a return visit to the Skoda armament factory at Pilsen on 13/14 May, but subsequent reconnaissance showed that the target indicators had landed about two miles away from the target and that the bombs had fallen on them. Another gap in the pattern of operations followed before a raid by thirteen aircraft on Dortmund on 23/24 May, but then came another double tragedy, when during a raid by nearly six hundred aircraft on Dusseldorf on 25/26 May another two Lancasters of the twelve put up by 207 Squadron failed to return. This time it was W5001 [EM:J], with none other than the CO, Wg. Cdr. T. A. Parselle, at the controls, and ED600 [EM:P] piloted by Flg. Off. P. C. Drayton. Defences that night were not strong, but the few enemy fighters spotted were seen to be quite ruthless. It was announced later that the CO and the bomb-aimer in his crew, Sgt. R. E. Hood–Morris, had survived to be taken prisoner, but all the other members of both crews lost their lives. Thankfully, those were the only four aircraft lost by the squadron during May, but in percentage terms the loss was 5.5 % – not an encouraging figure. Three more missions were flown at the end of May, targets being Essen and Wuppertal (Elberfeld) and a mining operation.

To replace Wg. Cdr. Parselle as CO of the squadron Wg. Cdr. P. N. Jennings, a former Flight commander on 44 Squadron under Sqn. Ldr. John Nettleton VC, stepped into the breach. A pre-war officer, Peter Jennings was always 'unflappable', and possessed a dry sense of humour, qualities which enabled him to steer the squadron through some very difficult days.

No more operations were carried out by 207 Squadron until the night of 11/12 June 1943, when seventeen crews were briefed to raid Dusseldorf again. In the end, twelve aircraft took off, of which two aborted the mission. One, ED537 [EM:O], failed to return, and the members of its crew under Flt. Sgt. J. H. Elliott have no known graves. Raids on Bochum on 12/13 Jun by fourteen aircraft, on Oberhausen next night by eight and on Cologne on 16/17 June by ten, were successful inasmuch as no aircraft was lost.

The old airship sheds at Friedrichshafen, on the shore of Lake Constance, were the target on 20/21 June for sixty-four heavy bombers, of which five were 207 Squadron Lancasters, and the plan was for this to be the first 'shuttle' mission carried out by the squadron. Plans for the flight and for radar-controlled bombing of the target, which contained a radar equipment factory, were worked out in advance. For several days before the mission, the crews underwent special training at all hours, and were issued with tropical kit, and even received a special briefing from the AOC of 5 Group. On the way south, severe electrical storms over France were experienced, but all aircraft arrived over Lake Constance in bright moonlight. Ground markers were dropped by pathfinder aircraft, and bombs were then released from varying altitudes. The first 'cookie' was seen to fall on a large hangar, and other buildings were also hit. After the raid, four of the aircraft continued in a southerly direction to Algeria, where they landed at Blida to await developments. John McIntosh, one of the pilots on this mission, remembers taking off from Langar and climbing away, only to experience failure of the starboard outer engine at 1,000 feet altitude! As the Lancaster was heavily loaded, landing back at Langar was out of the question, so he decided to fly around to use fuel and lighten the load. He set course for the coast of the English Channel, and after half an hour or so the faulty engine picked up at reduced power, enough to help the aircraft on its way. "Near Selsey Bill, now at 12,000 feet, we held a conference and unanimously decided to go on, even though we were likely to be on three engines", recalled John many years later. "We would lag behind the main force but would be dealing with a relatively undefended area. The Alps were a problem but by then, with half our fuel used, I felt we could make it. We managed to clear the cloud tops across the Channel and set course for Orleans, reducing our altitude......to make up for a little of the time we had lost. Then, as we went to the north of our rendezvous on the Rhine, the starboard outer packed up again. We were now a few minutes late for the target; it was well alight and could be seen miles away.

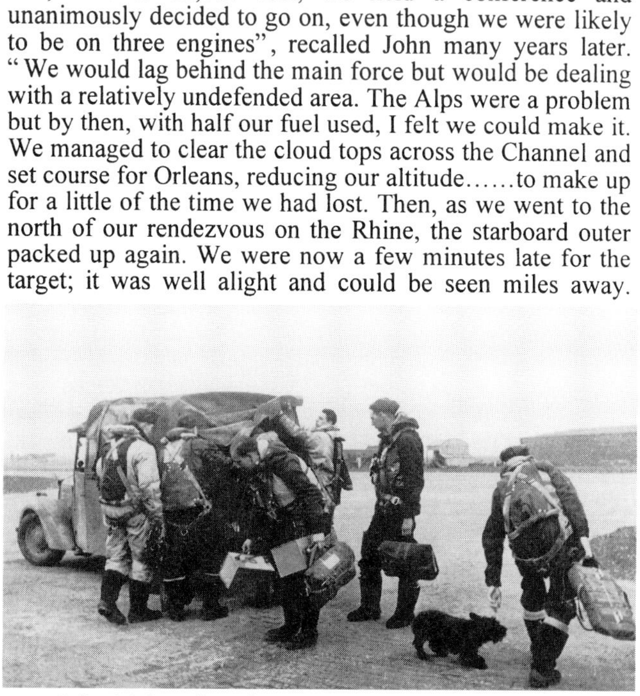

John McIntosh and crew after delivery to a Langar dispersal in one of the ubiquitous Hillman 'gharries' in May 1943. [207 Squadron archives]

Jack 'Dook' Hyde portrayed on the front cover of 'Picture Post' magazine dated 15 May 1943. [via B. Goodwin]

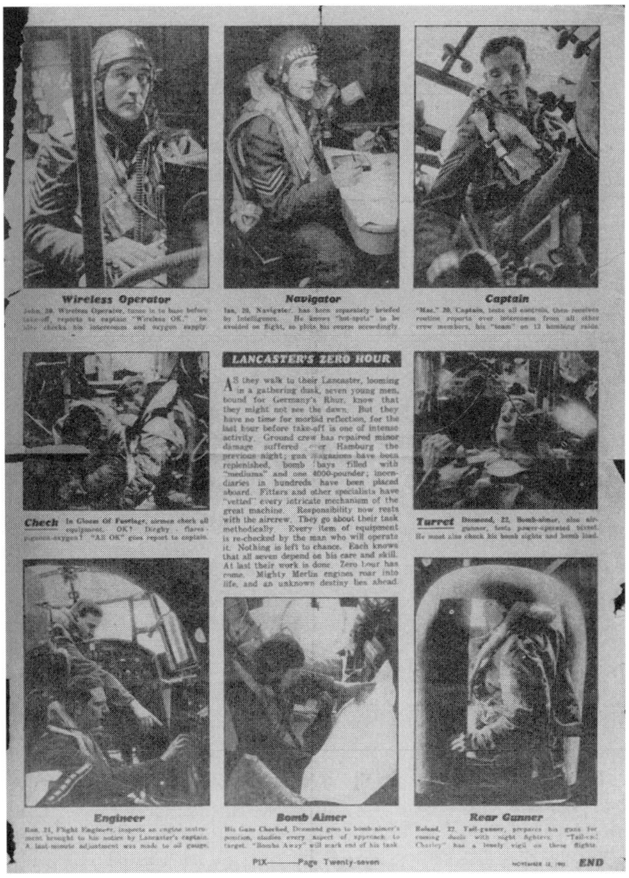

Wireless Operator

John, 20, Wireless Operator, tunes in to base before take-off, reports to captain "Wireless OK." He also checks his intercomm and oxygen supply.

Navigator

Ian, 20, Navigator, has been separately briefed by Intelligence. He knows "hot-spots" to be avoided on flight, so plots his course accordingly.

Captain

"Mac," 20, Captain, tests all controls, then receives routine reports over intercomm from all other crew members, his "team" on 12 bombing raids.

LANCASTER'S ZERO HOUR

AS they walk to their Lancaster, looming in a gathering dusk, seven young men, bound for Germany's Rhur, know that they might not see the dawn. But they have no time for morbid reflection, for the last hour before take-off is one of intense activity. Ground crew has repaired minor damage suffered over Hamburg the previous night; gun magazines have been replenished, bomb bays filled with "mediums" and one 4000-pounder; incendiaries in hundreds have been placed aboard. Fitters and other specialists have "vetted" every intricate mechanism of the great machine. Responsibility now rests with the aircrew. They go about their task methodically. Every item of equipment is re-checked by the man who will operate it. Nothing is left to chance. Each knows that all seven depend on his care and skill. At last their work is done. Zero hour has come. Mighty Merlin engines roar into life, and an unknown destiny lies ahead.

Check

Turret

Engineer

Bomb Aimer

Rear Gunner

PIX——Page Twenty-seven

END

A series of illustrations of 207 Squadron aircrew combined to make a page of 'Picture Post'. [via B. Goodwin]

There was some flak, backed up by searchlights, but I had seen a lot worse......" He went on to say that the bomb-aimer's job was straight forward, and after dropping the bomb load the navigator set up a course over neutral Switzerland to save transit time. On three engines, the Lancaster climbed to orbit Lake Constance before setting course for the Gulf of Genoa. The estimated flight time to reach Algeria was three and a half hours, and the Lancaster touched down a Blida nine hours fifty minutes after leaving Langar. At Blida it was decided that a new engine was needed, and the delay gave the crew a welcome holiday in a hot climate, enjoying a few days in a small hotel at Chrea, a village in the Atlas mountains which was a ski resort in the winter. "We wondered if there really was a war on somewhere!" said John McIntosh, who was awarded an immediate DFC for his part in the operation. Waiting at dispersal to tell Jock about this was the Station

David Balme and crew, with ground crew, standing in front of EM:B in the summer of 1943. [207 Squadron archives]

Commander, Gp. Capt. McKenna, who was fond of winding people up. "You know, McIntosh, I can't have you going on like this," he said to a mystified Jock. "Something will have to be done about it. Group are on about it, and I've had a signal from them about you." And then he handed out the signal congratulating Jock on his DFC!

Meanwhile, seven aircraft attacked Krefeld without loss on 21/22 June, but next night one of the eight Lancasters taking part in a raid on Mulheim failed to return. This was ED692 [EM:W], with Flg. Off. P. G. Herrin in command, and he and his crew were never found. Then came the return of three of the four aircraft from Blida, via La Spezia, which they attacked on their way home. Medium-sized contributions were made by the squadron to raids on Wuppertal, Gelsenkirchen and Cologne before June ended, but the loss of ED569 [EM:B] and its crew headed by Flg. Off. P. C. Russell, who were lost on the Cologne mission, saddened the squadron. Statistically, June had been a month of lower losses than May, but of course to those involved the loss of every crew member was keenly felt.

The Lancaster which had been given an engine change at Blida began its journey home on 3 July by flying to Gibraltar, where the crew bought bunches of bananas, an almost unheard-of luxury in Britain at the time. Keeping clear of the Spanish coast, John McIntosh and his crew brought the Lancaster over the Bay of Biscay to land safely at Langar, bringing with them two Polish Air Force officers of Gen. Sikorsky's staff. Ironically, Gen Sikorsky himself lost his life when his Liberator crashed on take-off from Gibraltar just after the Lancaster had left. The Liberator's captain was Sqn. Ldr. 'Kipper' Herring, a former member of 207 Squadron who had earned a DSO for bringing a Manchester back to base on one engine.

Two raids on Cologne were mounted early in July, followed by a visit to Gelsenkirchen, all without loss. Then came the long journey to Turin on 12/13 July by nine aircraft, of which ED412 [EM:Q] failed to make it to base.

Lancaster ED586 [EM:F], seen here at Langar in the summer of 1943, was the aircraft in which Wynford Vaughan-Thomas and Reg Pidsley were flown over Berlin to make the memorable BBC radio broadcast. It was lost during a raid on Stettin on 5/6 January 1944 when operating from Spilsby. [via R. Winton]

One of the favourite 'watering holes' of 207 Squadron personnel (and of many other squadrons) was the 'Trip to Jerusalem' Inn, built into the cliff face of Castle Rock in Nottingham. [via B. Goodwin]

Its pilot was Plt. Off. H. Badge, who lost his life with all his crew. He had only just been commissioned from his NCO rank of Sergeant, and this was his fourth operation. That night Bomber Command sent 297 Lancasters to Turin, their route over the Somme, then a straight track to Annecy, 100 miles short of Turin, where pathfinders were to drop marker flares over a lake in order to guide the bomber force clear of Swiss territory. The last leg of the route involved flying at an altitude of 20,000 feet to the right of Mont Blanc. Very bad weather was encountered over France, heavy thunderclouds and electric storms making the navigators' task extremely difficult. Over a hundred Lancasters found themselves over Switzerland, whereupon Swiss anti-aircraft guns opened up from the Jura mountain range. Horace Badge's aircraft was hit by flak at 00.55 and according to witnesses flew straight into the face of Mont Grammont, exploding and setting off a rock-slide which buried the Lancaster's engines. Rescuers reached the scene after two hours to find that there were no survivors. The bodies of the crew were taken down the mountainside next day and were buried with full military honours in the British plot at the cemetery of St. Martin's church in Vevey.

A second 'shuttle' mission took place on 16/17 July, the target this time being Cislago, near Milan, and again three of the four Lancasters involved flew on to Blida. The fourth, unfortunately, was shot down. Apart from the WOp/AG, who was captured alive, all the crew of DV183 [EM:W], headed by Plt. Off. L. E. Stubbs, lost their lives. The three crews at Blida stayed there until the night of 24/25 July, when they were greeted by none other than Marshal of the Royal Air Force Lord Tedder, a past CO of 207 Squadron. On their way back to the UK their target this time was the port of Leghorn. That same night, another twelve of the squadron's Lancasters attacked Hamburg without loss. A raid on Essen by ten aircraft next night was accomplished without loss, but on 27/28 July, during a mission to Hamburg in which fourteen aircraft participated,

A page from the squadron 'line-book' shows entries about Sqn. Ldr. I. McA. Huntley–Wood (KIA 3 September 1943); Sqn. Ldr. Balme; Flt. Lt. Bray; Plt. Off. R. Tibs (KIA 19 July 1944); Flg. Off. Anderson (either J. G., who was KIA 16 November 1944, or P. M., who was KIA 11 April 1945). [via B. Goodwin]

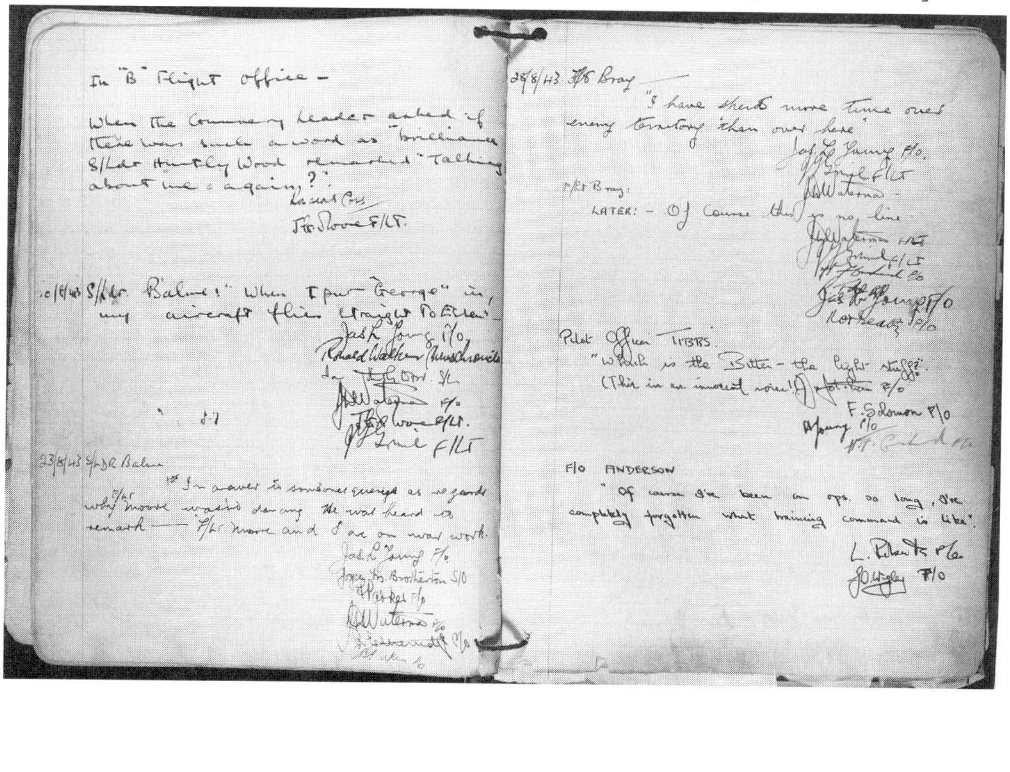

In "B" Flight Office –

When the Commanding Leader asked if there was such a word as "brilliance" S/Ldr Huntly Wood remarked "Talking about me again?".

10/8/43 S/Ldr. Balme: "When I put "George" in, my aircraft flies straight to Essen"

23/8/43 S/LdR Balme

In answer to someone's enquiry as regards why F/Lt Moore wasn't dancing he was heard to remark — F/Lt Moore and I are on war work.

Jack L. Young F/O

Joyce M. Brotherton S/O

28/8/43 F/Lt Bray

"I have spent more time over enemy territory than over here"

F/Lt Bray:

LATER: – Of course this is no line.

Pilot Officer TIBBS.

"Which is the Bitter – the light stuff?".

(This in an innocent voice!)

F. Solomon F/O

F/O ANDERSON

"Of course I've been on ops. so long, I've completely forgotten what training command is like".

L. Roberts F/O

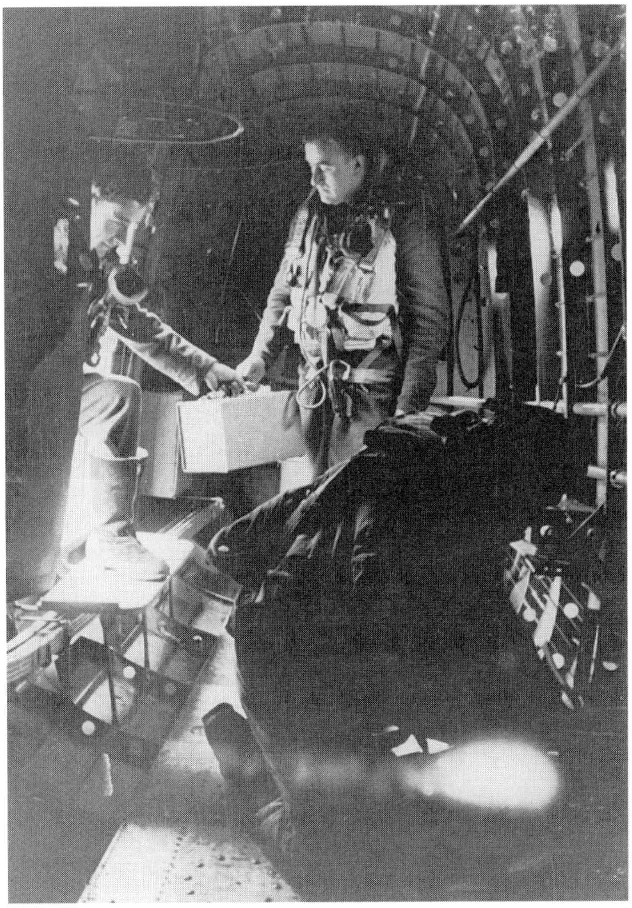

John McIntosh's crew boarding their Lancaster at the beginning of a sortie. [via B. Goodwin]

Navigator Sgt. Iain Nicholson at his post in a Lancaster, making ready for the night's mission. [via B. Goodwin]

W4962 [EM:B] failed to return. Two of the crew survived the ordeal to become prisoners, but the pilot, Flg. Off. C. Burne, and the rest of the crew did not. Raids on Hamburg and Remscheid ended July without further loss to the squadron. Hamburg suffered particularly badly in this series of attacks, as a long period of hot dry weather had meant that fire took hold of the old buildings in the city particularly readily, added to which most of the water mains had been damaged and were unable to provide water for the fire crews. When the fires eventually burnt themselves out, only twenty per cent of the `city's buildings remained unaffected. Forty million tons of rubble blocked the streets and thirty thousand citizens were dead, in some areas amounting to thirty per cent of the inhabitants.

Pressure was maintained during August 1943, but five crews and their aircraft were lost. After raids on Genoa, Mannheim and Hamburg, three attacks on Milan were mounted within four nights. Coming back on 13 August from one of these long trips, Plt. Off. 'Butch' Cartwright in ED361 [EM:R] had the misfortune to collide with another Lancaster, JA844 of Woodhall Spa-based 619 Squadron, over the English coast. His crew wasted no time in jumping from the stricken Lancaster, all of them leaving within fifteen seconds, but the rear gunner (Flt. Sgt. K. E. Goodsell) unfortunately hit a tree and was killed, the others surviving with minor injuries. It was on the last of the Milan trips, on 15/16 August, that Plt. Off. R. G. Pearcey and his crew in ED498 [EM:O] were shot down, although navigator Flg. Off. G. Blakeman lived and was taken prisoner.

Peenemünde experimental station was the target on 17/18 August, and AVM Cochrane made this mission an

Sgt. Ron Sooley, a flight engineer at Langar, concentrating on his vital task. [via B. Goodwin]

John McIntosh and Sgt. Ron Sooley in the 'office' of their Lancaster at Langar. [via B. Goodwin]

inter-squadron competition, according to the late Sqn. Ldr. David Balme, then in command of 'A' Flight. "During our special training, the winning score was 300 yards", he said later, "but this did not perturb us since we assumed that it was to be a method of attacking some large target like Berlin through cloud. But 'Cocky' blew his top and announced that he would take a Lancaster up himself, and went off from Langar with one of our crews. After he had landed, Wainfleet bombing range passed us the news that he had made three attacks with an average error of 38 yards. After that, 'Cocky' could do no wrong in our eyes. When the actual operation was put on we were amazed to find that the target was a tiny research station on the Baltic. Its importance was not explained, but since the attack was to be from 5,000 feet in a full moon and we were gently told that if we missed it we would go again on every subsequent night, regardless of casualties, we got the message. Other Groups would go in first on separate aiming points. 5 Group had the place of honour – last – and our target was the workshops. To overcome the Peenemünde smokescreen, we were to make a timed run down the north/south coast, [which was] surprisingly like the stretch between Mablethorpe and Wainfleet, and then run in from a second pinpoint after finding the wind. 'H' hour was soon after midnight, so we took off at about 20.00." The lower-than-usual altitude increased the danger of accurate flak, and Plt. Off. John McIntosh warned his crew to look out for flak-ships in the Baltic Sea, as he had unpleasant memories of them when in that region before. "However, all was quiet that night as far as Rugen Island", he recalled. "We could see that the target was already well alight; the earlier boys had achieved some success. 'Bomb doors open' and the navigator began counting out the seconds to go to the release point. 'Bombs gone'. Then it happened......a shell burst ahead with a blinding orange flash. We flew straight through and the cockpit filled with acrid fumes. We glumly expected something worse but nothing else happened. We were through unscathed – what luck!" Before long, John's gunners warned of horizontal tracer fire, indicating that night fighters were around, so he began vigorous weaving to evade them, and managed to return safely to base.

The Peenemunde raid was followed by an attack on Leverkusen on 22/23 August. Then came a run of very bad luck, when 207 Squadron lost four aircraft in three consecutive missions. One of the twelve aircraft raiding Berlin on 23/24 August, ED550 [EM:K], with Plt. Off. G. W. Osmer at the controls was shot down, only the navigator surviving. This mission is another of those recalled vividly by Plt. Off. John McIntosh. "I took my usual seat in the briefing room and studied the faces of the others as they entered," he said. "Some of the old ones were still there, but not many. A lot of new faces appeared. Try as they might, they could never disguise how they felt about the night's trip. My crew and I were the only ones present who had been to Berlin before. I didn't feel so great myself, but after a certain number of trips one developed a particular feeling of indifference, the churning in the stomach getting more and more numb with time. I had only one more trip to go after this night and I would have completed my first tour of thirty operations! The usual briefing routine dealt with navigation, intelligence reports, met reports and the CO's remarks, which on this occasion were confined to introducing the AOC 5 Group, AVM Sir Ralph Cochrane. He did not waste words. He emphasised that we were hitting the targets but we had to put in more effort to defeat the night-fighters which were an increasing menace. We had to make every endeavour to profit from our assiduous training in combating fighters."

"Supper, the usual egg and chips, came and went", continued McIntosh. "We collected our gear – parachute, Mae West lifejacket, escape kit, tin of orange juice, packet of glucose sweets, and two packets of chewing gum. I was already in battledress uniform, so on went a pair of long, thick off-white stockings which I always pulled over my knees at 10,000 feet because of the cold. Then on went my front-zipped flying boots...... I made a careful external inspection of the aircraft, making sure that above all else the pitot head cover was removed. Then came the long slow taxying out to the end of the runway to join the queue. A green flash from the Aldis lamp and we were off. It was always a relief to be safely off the deck with such a load of bombs and fuel. For about half an hour we just circled Langar airfield, climbing all the time. I wondered what the locals were doing. Lucky blighters, even birds don't fly at night. I must admit that the sunset looked terrific, but the eastern sky was black and grim, full of foreboding – it always was."

"I set course for Berlin and thought 'Here we go for the fourth time!' The route lay via the island of Texel and the Zuider Zee, then straight on to Berlin and its huge ring of searchlights and guns. Would there still be the black area to the north, with night-fighters lurking in it, I wondered. As we made our way, keeping carefully to our planned track, we could see many aircraft which had strayed a little getting unwelcome attention from gun-defended areas. With sixty minutes to go to Berlin, flying 'M-Mother' as I nearly always did, gently weaving ten degrees or so to each side of the course, suddenly all hell let loose. We had been hit. Charlie [Sgt. Middleton] in the tail shouted 'Dive to port, go!' I went into a corkscrew manoeuvre. This gave both gunners their chance. Charlie shouted 'We've got him!', a Ju 88 on fire diving steeply away. Seconds later a flash from an explosion on the ground told us his fate." It was then found that the self-sealing material covering the inner fuel tank was burning, so more in hope than expectation Plt. Off. McIntosh gave the order for the bombs to be jettisoned and turned for home. Three hundred gallons of fuel remained in the tank, a grim situation, and attempts were made to extinguish the fire by diving, but to no avail. Why the tank did not explode is a mystery. "Listen everyone," said the captain. "Make sure your parachutes are handy and be prepared for a quick exit. As I see it there is no immediate danger, but I could be wrong. The engines are all right so we'll open them up a bit and try to make the Dutch coast as quickly as possible. Once there, we'll think again." The flight to the coast took a long time, and the starboard wing continued to burn. When the sea eventually came into view McIntosh conferred with the crew. He told them that they might just make it to the nearest airfield to the Norfolk coast. If they baled out now, at least they would be in Holland, a lot better than the North Sea, but they had come a long way already and he was confident that they could reach England. The crew made a unanimous decision – stay with 'M-Mother' and take a chance. So the Lancaster flew on over the North Sea. "I always did have a dread of that uninviting area", says John. "My imagination sometimes ran riot on previous crossings. What would I do if I was ever faced with a ditching? Now the possibility was staring me in the face. I checked the swing to port caused by the port inner engine being feathered as we didn't want to risk another fire. This didn't help matters but we had height in hand and the coast of Norfolk was coming up." The nearest available airfield was Little Snoring, where an incomplete but usable lighting system was switched on. Jock made an approach and was about to land when an engine cut out. Instantly he began another circuit, by which time the fire had spread and just a few extra minutes might mean a fatal crash. A fire tender and ambulance stood by while the Lancaster made a second attempt, which was successful, and the crew left the aircraft with great haste! Later, the captain was told that the wing structure was red-hot and that if the aircraft had flown much longer the metal would have burned right through! Such were the trials and tribulations undergone by bomber crews.

Ken Letford and the crew of ED586 [EM:F]. [207 Squadron archives]

At Langar on 3 September 1943 before the Berlin raid were 'Con' Connelly (navigator), Wynford Vaughan–Thomas and Bill Bray (bomb-aimer). [207 Sqn archive]

On the Nuremburg raid on 27/28 August two Lancasters were lost. The entire crews of these, ED627 [EM:N] piloted by Plt. Off. A. M. Fitzgerald, and LM334 [EM:V] with Flg. Off. J. R. Welch in charge, lost their lives. The third loss took place on 30/31 August, when Plt. Off. J. Hickling and his crew in W4120 [EM:L] failed to return from a nine-aircraft participation in a raid on München–Gladbach.

By now the men and women based at Langar had well and truly 'got their knees under the table'. A popular place was Harby Village Institute, where the Secretary for many years was Jack Butcher. His wife, Dora, remembers whist drives and dances arranged for the personnel of 207 Squadron, all for sixpence (2.5p.). "The hall would be an RAF blue mass," she says. "Dancing was almost impossible, four square yards at the most. Music was supplied by gramophone, or by local farmers playing the piano and drums, who were in great demand in the villages around Melton Mowbray."

The BBC takes part

September began with a raid on Berlin by seven aircraft on the first night of the month and another one by ten aircraft three nights later from which Sqn. Ldr. Ian McA. Huntley-Wood and his crew in ED832 [EM:X] did not return. On board was Gp. Capt. A. F. McKenna, who was acting as second pilot. This raid was the one in which Wynford Vaughan-Thomas and sound engineer Reg Pidsley flew with Ken Letford in Lancaster ED586 [EM:F] to make a radio recording for broadcasting by the BBC. Wynford had been briefed at 5 Group Headquarters by the AOC, who told him that all that was wanted was an exact description of what was seen, with no 'window-dressing'. In his autobiography 'Trust To Talk', Vaughan-Thomas wrote "We went into the Officers' mess, where the Wing Commander [Peter Jennings] called out 'Ken, come over and meet your BBC men'. Ken Letford was about twenty-five, handsome, quiet, completely master of himself, a veteran of 52 operational trips across occupied Europe, which had given him a faraway look in his eyes. The whole Station seemed to be interested in our job......beer flowed. We sang RAF songs with no holds barred. We went singing to bed at midnight, and as we stumbled towards our Nissen huts Ken whispered 'I've had the buzz. We're operating tomorrow'." Next morning, 3 September, the two BBC men installed their equipment into the Lancaster and met the rest of the crew. "They were a group who had gone through a lot together," wrote Mr. Vaughan–Thomas. "You felt they acted like a crew even when they were apart, and it was quite obvious that Ken was the mainspring from which they drew their confidence. They were all just over twenty, and we were in our thirties. They nursed us as if we were old men creaking in every limb!" After an air test in the afternoon, the crew and the two BBC men went to the mess for tea, egg and chips. "I said to Bill Bray 'This egg is a bit of a rare treat.' He replied 'Wait till you see what you've got to go through to earn it!' Then we strolled across to the briefing room to learn our fate. Right in front of us was a huge map mounted on rollers. The sergeant pulled down the sections showing the Dutch coast, the Ruhr, and then, to a general groan, Berlin. I felt frightened." The narrative goes on to mention that the atmosphere in the briefing room was like that of a boys' boarding school busily engaged in prep. The 'headmaster' – AOC of 5 Group – entered and spoke briefly, telling the crews that their tactics would be new ones. "Although the first raid was a success," he said "the second went astray, and Air Marshal Harris himself has devised the new plan." The forthcoming raid would be concentrated into ten minutes over the target, and Harris was confident that this would outwit the Luftwaffe fighters. A pilot sitting behind Vaughan-Thomas muttered that he wished he was so sure!

Crew members helped Vaughan Thomas and Reg Pidsley, the sound engineer, into their flying clothing, and escape packets containing Dutch, French and German money were issued. The crew went through the various rituals they used to keep bad luck at bay, and then all trooped out to waiting vehicles, which took them to their Lancaster. Take-off was without incident, and the Lancaster circled and climbed on course towards the North Sea, Mr. Vaughan–Thomas noting a single searchlight stabbing the darkness to provide a final marker for the fleet of heavy bombers. As soon as the coast of Holland was reached, searchlights were illuminated and flak began to burst.

Those involved, after the BBC broadcast of the Berlin raid.. At the rear (left to right) 'Con' Connelly; Wynford Vaughan–Thomas; Mrs. Bray; Bill Bray; Ken Letford and Reg Pidsley, the sound engineer. In front are J. Fieldhouse, W. Sparkes and H. Devenish. [207 Squadron archives]

Lancaster Mk.III LM383 [EM:R] was lost during a raid on Brunswick on 15 January 1944. In command was P/O P. N. Kingston RAAF. [via B. Goodwin]

around the bombers 207 Squadron's aircraft were in the centre of the huge formation, and the early arrivals had already stirred up a hornet's nest. The crew of ED586 watched as an unlucky Lancaster was hit by flak and crippled, soon dropping down into the darkness in flames. Before long, cloud covered Holland, providing something of a sanctuary for the flight across Germany to the target. Arriving over Berlin, the bomber force was met by intense searchlight and flak activity, prompting Ken Letford to weave his way around the beams of light. Bill Bray was now lying in his bomb-aiming position in the nose of the Lancaster, while Mr. Vaughan-Thomas looked down to see Berlin ablaze. No sooner had the 'cookie' been released than a Bf 110 night-fighter circled ED586, but was shot down in flames by the mid-upper gunner, Wt. Off. Fieldhouse DFC. By now the Lancaster had left Berlin fifty miles behind, but the conflagration could still be seen. As the North Sea came into view and the aircraft was brought down to 9,000 feet the tension aboard diminished, and some of the crew began to sing ribald songs, including (to the tune of 'Bless 'em All'),

Peggy Priestley, an MT driver with the squadron at Langar and Spilsby, seems happy with her lot. The utility truck had no headlights but the cruising and maximum speeds were painted on the door for all to see! [via B. Goodwin]

There's many a Lancaster back from Berlin
Bound for old Blighty's shore,
Carrying its cargo of terrified men
S*** scared and prone on the floor.

For we're showing our arse to them all
As back to our billets we crawl,
For Christ's sake give Margate
As our next target
And as for Berlin – Bless 'em all!

As ED586 approached base a clear dawn broke. Wynford Vaughan-Thomas remarked that the gentle bump as the aircraft's wheels touched the runway was the sweetest sound he had ever heard. Even the fact that another Lancaster had landed on the wrong runway and almost collided with ED586 did not matter much! The final task of the BBC men was to rush to London with the recordings they had made during the complete trip and to broadcast them to the nation.

After attacks on Mannheim and Munich there was an interval of sixteen nights before ten aircraft raided Hanover on 22/23 September. From this mission ED442 [EM:W] failed to bring its crew, headed by Plt. Off. G. L. Coxon, back to base. To complete the last full month of 207 Squadron's residency at Langar, raids on Mannheim, Hanover and Berlin were mounted without loss.

At the beginning of October 1943, orders arrived for 207 Squadron to move to Spilsby, an airfield just recently opened, in order to make way for the 435th Troop Carrier Group of the newly-reactivated US Ninth Air Force. However, before the move, six more missions were flown, beginning with one by ten aircraft on Hagen. While taking off for Munich on 2 October, Lancaster DV184 [EM:O], piloted by Flg. Off. A. F. Bremner, crashed, and the entire crew was killed, four of the bodies never being found. 'Jock' Bremner's wife had been staying with him at the 'White Hart' over the weekend, and stood at the airfield gate on the Langar to Harby road with the wife of a member of another crew, Ron Buck, to watch him take off that Monday evening. As the doomed Lancaster began its take-off run, Wg. Cdr. Jennings, watching from close to the control tower, noticed that the pitot head cover was still in position. He told the flying controller, who fired a red Verey light to tell the pilot to abort. 'Jock' Bremner closed his engines down, but it was too late. Being half-way along the runway he realised that he could not pull up in time, so opened up the engines, but with insufficient airspeed the Lancaster stalled and fell fifty feet to the ground. All other crews awaiting take-off closed down their engines and ran to safety, knowing that a 'cookie' was on board. Within minutes, however, they were ordered to take off, as the wreck was not blocking the runway, and after their mission all returned safely. This crew had the sad distinction of being the last one lost by 207 Squadron while at Langar, and were half way through their tour. Finally, raids on Kassel, Frankfurt, Stuttgart and Hanover took place, the last one by nine aircraft on the night of 8/9 October 1943.

207 Squadron was now ready to move to Spilsby, much of the equipment having been packed during the previous few days, and so on 12 October 1943 the last RAF personnel handed over the premises to the incoming USAAF occupants, vacated the buildings and made the short journey to Spilsby, there to continue the seemingly never-ending battle against Germany.

The first Lancaster lost by 207 Squadron on operations from Spilsby was LM326 [EM:Z], which failed to return from a raid on Hanover on 18/19 October 1943. In this picture the airfield seen below the aircraft was Barkston Heath. [via R. Winton]

Chapter 8: Spilsby to VE-Day

At Langar, 207 Squadron personnel prepared themselves for another move, this time to Spilsby in Lincolnshire, which had just opened for business after a hurried construction programme. Located at the southern end of the Lincolnshire Wolds, eight miles (12.5 km.) west of Skegness, Spilsby was a Class A bomber Station with three concrete runways, of which two were 6,000 feet (1,830 m.) in length instead of the usual one. Four officers of 207 Squadron paid a visit on 1 October 1943 to look over the Flight and Squadron accommodation on the technical site, and three days later an advance party from Langar arrived to unload equipment. A further group of airmen made the move on 7 October, but it was another four days before the squadron's Lancasters flew the few miles to their new base. The main party of airmen had all turned up by 18.00 hours on 12 October, ready for a visit to their messes to deal with their hunger, but found that not all the allocated barrack room equipment had arrived. At least it was not as muddy as Bottesford had been! In command of the new Station was Gp. Capt. W. G. Cheshire, who had moved in from Langar, and one of the earliest arrivals was Sect. Off. J. M. Brotherton WAAF, who as an intelligence officer was to become an influential character at Spilsby.

Fog on 13 October prevented an operation, but one crew ventured out on a cross-country exercise, only to be recalled. Six more aircraft carried out cross-countries next day while three made practice bombing runs. Such training exercises increased as the crews settled in, and they were ready on 18 October for the first operation ever flown from Spilsby, but it turned out to be a sad one, as two crews failed to return. The target was Hanover, and fifteen crews were briefed, thirteen eventually taking off, of which one bombed an alternative target due to the navigator being taken ill. Missing were the crews of Flt. Sgt. G. Taylor in LM326 [EM:Z] and Plt. Off. B. L. Negus in W4276 [EM:L].

Next came a raid by twelve aircraft on Leipzig on 20/21 October, and this time all returned safely, although EM:H was afflicted by two iced-up engines! Nevertheless, the crew pressed on and reached the target. Kassel was targeted on 22/23 October by ten aircraft of 207 Squadron, one having aborted with a faulty air speed indicator. EE175 [EM:R] did not return, and it was later revealed that its captain, Sqn. Ldr. A. L. MacDowell, and other members of the eight-man crew had lost their lives. Another Lancaster, DV243 [EM:D], ditched in the North Sea, all the crew except the rear gunner, Flt. Sgt. J. C. Dow, being rescued by two destroyers which carried on searching for him for an hour without success. Captained by Plt. Off. J. A. Kelly, this Lancaster had completed its mission, taken photographs and set course for Spilsby, but major difficulties with the compass had put the aircraft a long way off track. In the belief that they would not reach the English coast, the skipper told the wireless operator to signal that they would have to 'ditch'. Kelly, on his first operation in command, managed to keep the Lancaster in the air for an incredibly long time, giving the air sea rescue service and a naval vessel time to reach the area in which the aircraft was likely to come down. He warned the crew to take up ditching stations, and the aircraft hit the water, quite gently the first time but violently the second. The tailplane broke off, the engines fell out and the front turret shattered. Very soon, water was flooding the fuselage, but all the crew managed to make their way out and into the dinghy, except Sgt. Burleigh, the flight engineer, who remained on the wing of the aircraft, and the unfortunate Flt. Sgt. Dow, who was left behind when the dinghy, which was not attached to the fuselage, floated away. Ironically, he would have survived if he had stayed with Sgt. Burleigh, as the aircraft floated for fourteen hours. As the Lancaster had come down only about forty miles from the English coast, the crew thought that their chances of a rapid recovery would be good, and it was only about ninety minutes before they were picked up by HMS *Windsor,* a destroyer which

Flt. Lt. Ken Letford at Spilsby after receiving his DSO in November 1943. [via R. Winton]

spotted their Very signals. Sgt. Burleigh was plucked from his solitary perch on the Lancaster's wing by HMS *Southdown* half an hour later.

For the remainder of October, thick fog prevented any operations, although briefing did take place on one occasion for an operation which was then 'scrubbed', and it was not until 3 November that the next trip to Germany could be made. Nine aircraft paid a visit to Dusseldorf that night and returned safely. Another week of ground training went by when bad weather kept the Lancasters on the ground, until on 10/11 November ten Lancasters raided Modane while another three carried out 'Bullseye' exercises. Yet more poor weather conditions then affected the squadron's offensive activities, only cross-country navigation exercises, 'Bullseyes' and practice bombing being possible, although on 14 November two crews made a search for the crew of a ditched B-17 aircraft of the US 8th Air Force.

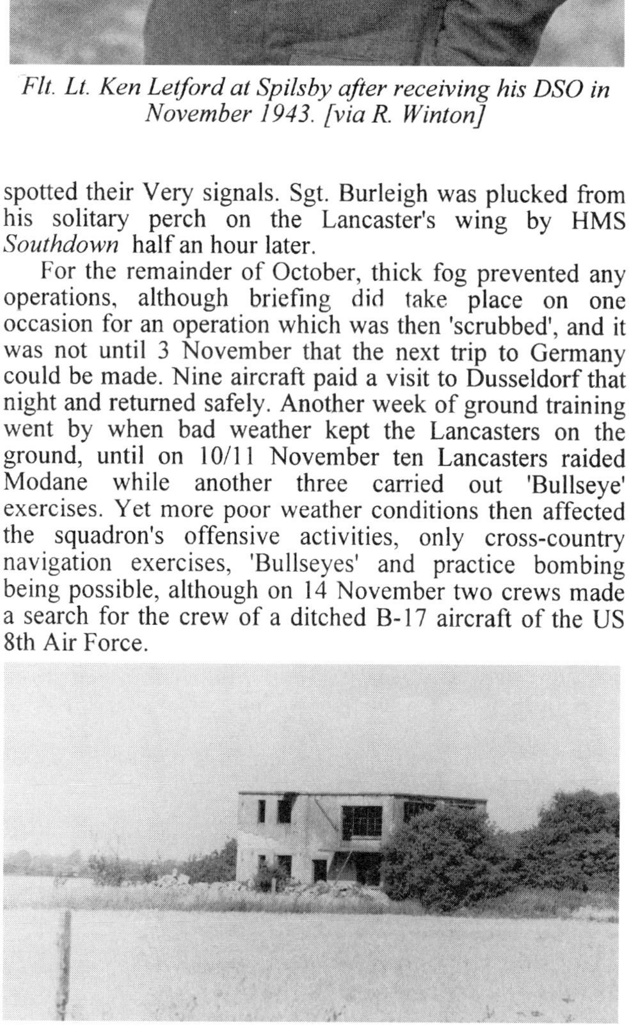

Long since demolished, the control tower at Spilsby is seen here in 1971, by which time it was derelict. It was a standard 'utility' building, and in the picture the front elevation is the one hidden by the tree. [R. Winton]

One of those who still remembers the bad weather at that time is former Wt. Off. Ken Brown, who joined 207 Squadron in November 1943. "Our first action on joining the squadron was to be sent on a diabolical round-Britain cross-country of some scheduled seven hours duration," he says. "It was a terrible night, with storms and cumulo-nimbus cloud up to 25,000 feet in places. It was scary, with blue lights (gremlins) darting across our wings. Subsequent operational flights seemed easier, as you mostly dodged the flak over the target. Anyway, the weather on this cross-country got so bad that we abandoned the exercise after two and a quarter hours. It's one thing being shot at by the Germans but another to be brought down by weather over British soil. It did not enhance our opinion of the Station meteorological forecasters."

Visits to 'The Big City'

Then came a raid on the crews' favourite, and probably most-feared, target – Berlin, which had become 'Bomber' Harris's main target for the forthcoming winter's long nights. Bomber Command had not attacked Berlin properly since January 1942 due to the long distance involved and the city's strong defences, factors which combined to make the attrition rate too high. Now began the most sustained air attack inflicted on the population of any city during the entire war, although in most cases they had access to immensely strong shelters. On 18 November sixteen aircraft took off from Spilsby for this maximum effort, but two aborted with engine trouble and another with an unserviceable rear turret. The others reached the target, where Plt. Off. W. H. 'Bill' Baker's Lancaster, DV361 [EM:V], had the misfortune to collide with another aircraft just as he was about to begin his bombing run. A huge hole was torn on the starboard side of the nose by the impact and

WAAF drivers at Spilsby in October 1943: Peggy Priestley, Joyce Summerscales and another. [via A. G. Pearce]

the bomb-aimer, Sgt. E. H. Shimeild, fell out without his parachute, through the escape hatch, which the impact had forced open. It was fortunate that the collision had not caused the 'cookie' and incendiary bombs to explode, but they had to be jettisoned. Somehow the job was done, and the captain turned and made for base. The outside temperature was about minus 40 degrees Fahrenheit – 72 degrees of frost! In addition to the damage to the nose, through which a bitter gale roared, the propellers of the port engines were bent, the flap jack was missing and the altimeter was out of action. Then one engine failed while they were over the Ruhr, from where flak opened up, but somehow they struggled on, over the coast and the North Sea, until eventually they saw the lights of Spilsby, where Baker's frozen hands managed to put the Lancaster down in one piece. Plt. Off. Baker spent some time in hospital, where his frostbitten fingers had to be amputated at the first joints. Before long he was awarded the DFC and discharged from the Service, marrying the WAAF to whom he had been engaged. Sgt. T. Gedling, the navigator on that fatal trip, was awarded the DFM. Amazingly, DV361 was repaired and flew on more operations.

The same target was attacked again four night later by fourteen aircraft, another one having off-loaded its bombs over Hanover when caught in a heavy box barrage of flak. Determined to do as much as possible to destroy Berlin, the Air Ministry ordered yet another raid on the city on 23/24 November, to which 207 Squadron contributed fourteen Lancasters. From this mission Flg. Off. D. E. Reay and his crew in W4959 [EM:S] failed to return. But the pressure was maintained, as for its final job of the month the squadron sent thirteen aircraft to Berlin on 26 November, all returning safely to Spilsby early next morning.

Statistics can be both boring and misleading, but it may be of interest to note that during that November 169 Lancaster sorties had been detailed, of which 89 were cancelled and five aborted for technical reasons. The remaining 75 attacked the primary target, and one of them was posted as missing.

Berlin seemed to remain the favourite destination for 207 Squadron crews during the early part of December 1943, although in all probability they would rather have stayed at home. Fourteen of them attacked the city on 2/3 December, and one unfortunate crew, headed by Plt. Off. A. Mann, failed to bring Lancaster ED601 [EM:N] back to Spilsby. A raid on Leipzig the following night by ten aircraft followed, and one of the returning crew members, Flt. Lt. K. Letford, had completed his second tour, with 55 sorties to his credit.

It was two weeks before any further raids were detailed. During this period a variety of flying activities were practised, including competitive bombing, air-to-sea gunnery, fighter affiliation with a Martinet aircraft from Syerston, Standard Beam Approach, Gee homing and night landings. All these procedures helped to develop 207 Squadron into an even better and more technically expert fighting force than it already was.

With Christmas no doubt in many people's minds, fifteen crews were briefed on 16 December for a raid on 'the big city', and all but one attacked the primary target. Another crew, headed by Acting Flt. Lt. R. J. Allen, did not survive to see any festivities which may have been planned,

The shattered nose of DV361 [EM:V], which collided with another aircraft on 18 November 1943, with the loss of the bomb-aimer, Flt. Sgt. Jim Schimeild. The pilot, Jim Baker, suffered severe frostbite and never flew again with the squadron. [via R. Winton]

Another recipient of the DSO in November 1943 was Flt. Lt. David Balme. [via R. Winton]

as their aircraft, EE141 [EM:P], was shot down. Among the 'freshmen' who took part in this mission was mid-upper gunner Clarence Sutherland, who flew to replace a member of Flg. Off. Giddens' crew. "On crossing the enemy coast I blasted away at a Ju 88," he says, "and when the pilot dived the gun handle broke off because of the pressure to depress the guns. On returning from Berlin it was the night of the big fog. We were landing wingtip-to-wingtip with another Lancaster, which had to go round again. After landing we found that we were at another airfield – East Kirkby." That night became known as Black Thursday, as many Bomber Command aircraft, unable to locate any airfield in the dense fog, ran out of fuel and crashed. Two more operations followed before Christmas, the first a raid on Frankfurt on 20/21 December by fifteen aircraft. Before take-off, Lancaster ED586 was found to have a coolant leak in the starboard outer engine, which was changed, and W4815 had a leaking port fuel tank, which was replaced in the record time of three hours, a credit to the ground crews concerned. Sadly, before the Christmas break members of two more crews were destined to lose their lives. One incident occurred during a cross-country exercise on 22 December, when an engine caught fire. Sgt. G. A. Baker gave orders for his crew to abandon the aircraft, DV361, the aircraft which had been so badly damaged on 18 November, and they did so, the Lancaster coming to earth near Grafton Underwood in Northamptonshire. Unfortunately, three of the seven men on board lost their lives. The second crew, that of Plt. Off. G. E. Moulton–Barrett, failed to return from a raid on Berlin by twelve aircraft on 23/24 December, their aircraft being DV188 [EM:J]. Of the seven men, all except the rear gunner, Sgt. D. O. Davies, survived the ordeal and became prisoners of war. By way of retribution, a Ju 88 night-fighter was shot down by Clarence Sutherland, on his first trip with his permanent crew, captained by Flg. Off. Doug Smith.

Christmas Day was an official stand-down from operations, and the traditional pattern of events was followed, the officers waiting on the airmen at dinner time. In any case fog permeated Spilsby airfield until 29 December, when twelve aircraft took off to attack Berlin again. All returned safely, and the CO of 'A' Flight, Sqn. Ldr. D. M. Balme DFC, completed his first 30-trip tour of operations and was awarded the DSO. His replacement was Sqn. Ldr. S. Pattinson.

1944 began with a raid by ten aircraft of 207 Squadron on Berlin, but two crews were lost. One, W4892 [EM:T], was captained by a member of the US Army Air Force, Lt.

At Spilsby in late 1943 or early 1944 Flg. Off. Heap and Flt. Lt. Hollings pose with their ground crew in front of Lancaster EE126 [EM:A]. On the right is the derelict farm at the end of Spilsby's east/west runway. [via R. Winton]

F. B. Solomon, who with his navigator was due to revert to flying with his own countrymen on completion of his tour. The other Lancaster, DV370 [EM:L], was captained by Plt. Off. W. J. Bottrell on his seventh sortie. Berlin was again targeted on 2/3 January, and was attacked by six aircraft of 207 Squadron, another three having had to abort with technical defects.

Nine aircraft took off on 5 January to raid Stettin, and eight returned safely. The other Lancaster was ED586 [EM:F], captained by Acting Flt. Lt. G. H. Ebert with Wg. Cdr. A. D. Jackson as second pilot, was posted as missing. Bomb aimer on board the missing aircraft was Flg. Off. P. N. Hodgson, who had been a particularly close friend of Sect. Off. Joyce Brotherton for the previous six months and who was due to be married (but not to Joyce) as soon as he finished his tour. He never did. During the mission a wingtip of Plt. Off. Balfour's aircraft hit a Ju 88, which was seen to go out of control and was therefore claimed as destroyed, a feat which must have cheered the squadron.

By now, an invasion of Europe, code-named Operation 'Overlord', was being planned for the forthcoming summer, but doubts persisted in many minds over the desirability of switching Bomber Command's efforts from German targets to a 'softening-up' campaign against northern France. On 12 January Air Marshal Harris, C-in-C of Bomber Command, wrote:

"It is clear that the best and indeed the only efficient support which Bomber Command can give to [Operation] 'Overlord' is the intensification of attacks on suitable industrial targets in Germany as and when the opportunity offers. If we attempt to substitute for this process attacks on gun emplacements, beach defences, communications or [ammunition] dumps in occupied territory we shall commit the irremediable error of diverting our best weapons from the military function, for which it has been equipped and trained, to tasks which it cannot effectively carry out. Though this might give a spurious appearance of 'supporting' the army, in reality it would be the greatest disservice we could do them."

This summary of 'Bomber' Harris's feelings was, however, to be proved completely without foundation. By now, Bomber Command crews had learned to strike quite small targets accurately, and before long Harris would be over-ruled.

Any feeling of well-being enjoyed by squadron personnel was dashed completely on 15 January, when no less than three of eleven aircraft failed to return from a raid on Brunswick. Captains of the missing Lancasters were Plt. Off. D. C. Balfour (DV369 EM:D), Plt. Off. P. N. Kingston (LM383 EM:R) and Flg. Off. G. W. James (DV191 EM:O). It was later found that James and his navigator, Sgt. E. W. Johnston, had lost their lives, but the other five members of his crew had survived to be taken prisoner. Another aircraft, EE197, captained by Plt. Off. Gallagher, was badly damaged by a FW 190 and made a crash-landing at Spilsby, with minor injuries to the flight engineer. Brunswick was known as a 'hot' target, and crews were not under any delusions about it, although they considered it less horrifying than Berlin. One of the captains, Plt. Off. Gallagher, was awarded the DSO for his part in this mission, which for his crew began to go wrong when their aircraft was approaching the coast of Holland. An engine then failed, and it was the port outer, which on a Lancaster supplied power to the rear turret and to the Gee equipment, which had become a vital navigation aid. 'Gally' decided to dump some of his incendiary bombs, which went down onto a searchlight battery near Den Helder, and then to 'press on regardless'. The lighter load allowed the aircraft to maintain altitude until arrival over the target area. Just as the captain began the final run-in, the rear gunner reported a single-engined fighter 900 yards astern. Undismayed, 'Gally' ordered the gunners to open fire on the FW 190, which was now much closer, and rounds were seen to strike it in the cockpit and port wing. After the welcome call "Bombs away", the fighter returned and opened fire, causing damage to the rudder and elevator trim tabs and rear turret, while 'Gally' put the Lancaster into a corkscrew. A third pass was made by the FW 190, and now the port inner engine was hit and lost power. Flt. Sgt. 'Jock' Stewart, the flight engineer, then feathered the port outer, and the captain began the job of nursing the crippled Lancaster back to friendly shores. Over a twenty-five minute period, the pilot of the FW 190 made eight attempts to destroy the Lancaster, and nearly succeeded. In his final pass, he fired a rocket which almost took off the Lancaster's port wing outboard of the engines, although this was unknown to the crew at the time, which was probably just as well! Even with Stewart's help, Gallagher was hard put to the task of keeping the aircraft on a steady course, as with little power from the port engines the Lancaster wanted to fly in circles. Then the electrical wiring fused and caused a fire which had to be put out with the use of small extinguishers. By now the Lancaster was again losing height and 'Gally' told the crew to jettison everything movable unless it was indispensable. While all this activity was taking place, the navigator, Wt. Off. Young, carried on with his job as though there was no problem. A fix provided by a ground station confirmed the aircraft's position, so there was little chance of being lost. In spite of all his efforts, 'Gally' saw that the Lancaster had descended to 5,000 feet when still forty miles from the coast of England, but before long it came into sight. Gallagher asked his crew whether they wished to bale out over land, as he could not promise to make a smooth landing, but all rejected this idea and took up their crash positions. Several sets of knuckles were white as the Lancaster entered final approach to Spilsby, but at 22.54 it landed. One wheel came off on touch-down, and there was a crunch as the aircraft came to a sudden halt, whereupon the section of wing outboard of the port outer engine fell off! After all that, nobody in the crew was badly hurt. As soon as possible they jumped from the wreck, but 'Gally' had to be helped out as he was so stiff after struggling to counteract the pull of the aircraft for so long. The indefatigable 'Jock' Stewart was awarded the DFM for his part in this sortie.

The next few days were foggy, and no operations were planned. During this period two representatives of Time & Life magazine visited the squadron to record interviews and take photographs for the benefit of their American readers. A homely touch might have been given to their photographs if pictures of the Station's NAAFI and YMCA vans had been included. These vehicles made regular sorties from opposite ends of the technical area to dispense 'char and wads' to ever-hungry airmen. Another facility in great demand from its opening in February was the News

Room, created by Sect. Off. Brotherton for use by all ranks. In this quiet refuge was every type of literature, newspaper and magazine, as well as photographs of every theatre of war, so that everyone could keep up to date on the progress of the war outside their own restricted environment.

Spilsby's fog finally cleared on 20 January, and ten crews were quickly briefed for a raid on Berlin. Of the ten aircraft, ED698 swung off the runway on take-off; on the pilot's second try the same thing happened, and the undercarriage collapsed. A third attempt being impossible, the brave armament officer defused the 'cookie' in the Lancaster's bomb-bay. Two other aircraft returned early, and the remaining seven reached and attacked the target.

Magdeburg was the target for ten crews on 21/22 January, but only five of them reached it, two others dropping their loads on Berlin instead. Another failed to take off, one returned early and the one with Plt. Off. J. M. Read in command, R5895 [EM:B], was posted missing. For an unrecorded reason, six of the eleven Lancasters detailed to raid Berlin on 28/29 January failed to take off. Of those which reached the target LM366 [EM:H] was captained by Acting Flt. Lt. J. G. Taylor, but failed to return. The dreadful losses being suffered by the squadron did not diminish, as on 30/31 January three of eleven Lancasters attacking Berlin never came back to Spilsby. They were piloted by Plt. Off. H. D. Broad (DV371 EM:M), Plt. Off. A. Moore (ED758 EM:V) and Plt. Off. R. Burnett (EE173 EM:K). So ended a very sad month for 207 Squadron's personnel. On board EE173, which was shot down by a Luftwaffe night-fighter using 'Schräge Musik' upward-firing guns, was navigator Wt. Off. Ken Brown, who recounts in his memoirs that he baled out and landed on a building opposite an air raid shelter. He was captured at once and taken to the office of the Burgermeister and from there to a Luftwaffe airfield, where he and some of his crew were fed. Next day they travelled by train to Obereusel, the station for Dulag Luft interrogation centre. That formality over, they were taken to Stalag Luft VI, where Ken became Kriegsgefangener (prisoner) No. 1091, housed in Laager C of the RAF compound. "Some of the chaps used to have terrible nightmares about their flying experiences and being shot down" recalls Ken. "One poor fellow in our hut was in such a bad way that his nightmare became a reality, and one night he baled out from the top of a three-tier bunk, ending up in hospital with severe concussion." He goes on to state that life in Laager C was well-organised. Many of the prisoners were talented, and it was possible to study for professional examinations, though a most popular course was German, considered potentially useful should an escape be arranged. An illicit radio provided BBC broadcasts, and there was a theatre and an orchestra. "In Laager C we were pretty well fed," says Ken. "The Germans provided potatoes, bread, margarine, some foul meat and ersatz coffee made from acorns and rye. We had a cookhouse which provided us with one meal and four brew-ups a day, and everyone received one Red Cross food parcel each week. Many of the contents were exchanged by the guards for essential items such as films and radio parts, as the 'Krauts' were easily corrupted." Eventually, Ken was moved to Stammlaager 357 at Fallingbostel, a new PoW camp, where the regime was much harder. After a number of forced marches, he and his fellow prisoners were released by British tank troops on 2 May 1945 and he was flown back to the UK a few days later. Another member of the squadron who became a PoW was Flt. Lt. G. E. Moulton-Barrett, who in his memoirs reminds us that fifty of his fellow-prisoners were caught while making an escape attempt from the North Camp of Stalag Luft III and on Hitler's orders were murdered by the SS and the Gestapo on 6 April 1944. Among them was Flt. Lt. D. O. Street of 207 Squadron, the pilot of Lancaster W4931 [EM:U], which had been shot down during the raid on Berlin on 29/30 March 1943.

Weather conditions at Spilsby during the first half of February were fine, cold and windy, but only training flights were made. These included night-fighter affiliation sorties and visual Monica exercises with a Martinet and two Beaufighters. The respite gave the hard-pressed ground crews time to bring all the squadron's Lancasters up to their usual high standard, so that on 15/16 February a raid by eighteen aircraft could be mounted. From this mission, Plt. Off. F. W. Cosens DFC and his crew in ND510 [EM:T] failed to return. No less than twenty aircraft were available for the next job, a raid on Leipzig on 19/20 February, and nineteen took off. Sqn. Ldr. Pike's aircraft suffered an engine failure while gaining speed on the runway, but he managed to pull up in time, avoiding a serious accident. Two Lancasters were added to the squadron's mounting total of missing aircraft that night, those of Plt. Off. W. D. Jarvis (ED126 EM:A) and Plt. Off. J. J. Clark (ME633 EM:Y). Later, it was found that Jarvis and three of his crew had survived to be taken prisoner. Stuttgart was the objective for fifteen aircraft on 20/21 February, and during this trip a Bf 110 was claimed as destroyed by Plt. Off. Wright after he shot it down in flames.

The ball-bearing factory at Schweinfurt was the target for fifteen of 207 Squadron's Lancasters on 24/25 February, and all returned safely, to the relief of all concerned. Next night, fifteen aircraft joined in a raid on Augsburg, during which Sgt. Bryden, a gunner in Plt. Off. Walshe's crew, shot down an enemy fighter. On returning to Spilsby, Plt. Off. J. E. Derbyshire's Lancaster overshot the runway, with the loss of the entire crew. So near and yet so far! No more operations took place in February, but at the end of the month there was a change of command when Wg. Cdr. Jennings was posted to 51 Base, Swinderby, being replaced by Wg. Cdr. V. J. Wheeler.

Sqn. Ldr. D. G. Pike and his crew, all lost in ND513 on 10 March 1944 on a mission to Clermont–Ferrand — left to right: Sgt. N. New (flight engineer); Plt. Off. E. H. Moulden (bomb-aimer); unknown; Sqn. Ldr. Pike; Flg. Off. A. A. Boad (navigator); unknown; unknown. [via R. Winton]

March 1944, when the armed forces of the Allied powers were tackling the logistical and tactical problems of the forthcoming invasion of Europe with all their energy, was the month in which Bomber Command and the US 8th and 9th Air Forces were placed under the control of Air Chief Marshal Sir Arthur Tedder, a gentleman famous in the annals of 207 Squadron, for he had been CO when the squadron was re-formed in 1920. The month began for 207 Squadron with a raid on Stuttgart by fifteen aircraft during which no losses were suffered, to the relief of all on the squadron. Changeable weather persisted for the next few days, and any operations for which the crews were briefed were cancelled before take-off time. Opportunities were therefore taken to fly on practice bombing and cross-country exercises.

Then came a raid on a distant target, Clermont-Ferrand, in southern France. For this, eleven aircraft took off, but ND513 [EM:R] failed to return. It had been captained by Sqn. Ldr. D. G. Pike, the CO of 'B' Flight, and Flt. Lt. J. G. Moore, the squadron's gunnery leader, was on board. Seventeen aircraft took off for another raid on Stuttgart on 15/16 March, and this time all came back. Frankfurt felt the impact of Bomber Command's weaponry on 18/19 March, a raid in which 207 Squadron joined with twenty aircraft, a tremendous achievement by the long-suffering ground crews. Plt. Off. G. F. Polley's aircraft was hit by flak over the target, but he managed to reach Spilsby with damaged elevators, rudders and starboard inner propeller.

Sqn. Ldr. J. F. Grey DSO DFC arrived on 19 March to take command of 'B' Flight in place of Sqn. Ldr. Pike, but the horrors of war made themselves felt yet again on 22/23 March when the squadron's CO, Wg. Cdr. V. J. Wheeler, who had been in that position just four weeks, failed to bring ME666 [EM:A] back after taking part in a twenty-one aircraft attack on Frankfurt. Eventually, members of the squadron heard that three of Wg. Cdr. Wheeler's crew had survived to become prisoners of war, but four had lost their lives. It is difficult for most people alive today to imagine and understand the lives, fraught with danger, of the crews of Bomber Command aircraft. It is much easier to understand the displays of high spirits in which they indulged from time to time. Who wouldn't, if one didn't know whether one would return from tomorrow's raid?

The CO's crew. Left to right: Plt. Off. J. Cook (bomb-aimer); Plt. Off. R. Jack (wireless operator); Flg. Off. Hall (navigator); Wg. Cdr. J. H. Grey (pilot and CO); Plt. Off. C. B. Sutherland (air gunner); Flg. Off. W. McIntosh (air gunner). The Lancaster was ND575 [EM:M], which was lost on the raid on Mailly-le-Camp on 4 May 1944. [via R. Winton]

Plt. Off. Polley, who only six nights previously had fought to return to bring a damaged Lancaster back to base, was the next victim of the enemy's defences. His Lancaster (ME680 EM:R) was one of twenty which raided Berlin on 24/25 March. When the other crews returned, they heard that their new CO would be the recently-appointed 'B' Flight CO, Sqn. Ldr. Grey, and to take his place Sqn. Ldr. A. M. Jones arrived next day. Essen was the next city to feel the RAF's strength, and this time 207 Squadron sent fifteen aircraft, all of which came home to Lincolnshire without problems. A feeling of sadness permeated the squadron on 31 March, however, when Plt. Off. J. H. Thornton in ND568 [EM:L] and Plt. Off. B. C. Riddle in LM436 [EM:G] failed to return from the night's raid by eighteen Lancasters on Nuremburg, a raid in which Bomber Command's losses reached the completely unacceptable figure of eleven per cent of aircraft despatched, against an expected five per cent. As bomber crews had to fly a tour of thirty missions before being rested, each crew faced the statistical probability of being shot down before reaching

Leaning on Wg. Cdr. Grey's Hillman service car were an unidentified air gunner, Flt. Lt. J. Wardle (the squadron's gunnery leader), Flg. Off. Wallace McIntosh, and another unknown air gunner. [via R. Winton]

the magic thirty figure. It was found that those who came back unscathed from more than five missions achieved a much higher survival rate than novice crews, who suffered disproportionately high losses, but when the overall attrition rate reached ten per cent even experienced crews were losing their lives. This fact had an inevitable effect on morale.

Much-increased availability of aircraft had contributed to the March total of 131 which attacked their primary targets and returned safely, with 914 hours 35 minutes flying to their credit and 631.75 tons of bombs dropped. Five aircraft were lost during the month.

Poor weather heralded the beginning of April 1944 at Spilsby, and it was 5 April before the next operation was flown. The forthcoming operation, a raid on an aircraft factory on the outskirts of Toulouse, was so 'hush-hush' that only the Intelligence Officers were allowed to know about it, apart from the crews concerned and a few senior officers. Toulouse was reported to be heavily defended, and precision bombing was called for, although the 207 Squadron crews had previously taken part in only one such mission, when the target had been Clermont-Ferrand. This time Flt. Lt. A. Hollings DFC was chosen, with his crew, to carry out a special task which involved remaining over the target for about half an hour, during which his Lancaster would be of course extremely vulnerable. His aircraft was to carry markers to back up those of the Bombing Leader if needed, and in addition he carried a 'cookie' to be dropped after all the others had completed their bombing. In Sect. Off. Joyce Brotherton's estimation, this was one of the most agonising periods of her time at Spilsby, as she was friendly with members of this crew in particular, and she was very concerned about their safety. As things turned out, she need not have worried, as Flt. Lt. Hollings and his crew did return safely, unlike that of Wt. Off. J. R. Senior in ME685 [EM:C], which did not.

A good deal of time was now allocated for cross-country flights involving the use of H2S equipment, and several crews took part. Easter Sunday, 9 April, dawned fine, and six of the squadron's Lancasters took off on a sea-mining mission in area 'Tangerine II'. Unfortunately, Plt. Off. S. A. Edmonds and his crew in ME688 [EM:E] failed to come back. Next day, eleven aircraft attacked Tours and all survived, but a major accident occurred on the ground when the explosion of a delayed-action 1,000 lb. bomb in a fusing shed in the bomb dump caused the deaths of no less than ten armourers, four of them 207 Squadron personnel. These unfortunate airmen were LACs A. G. Barrett, T. E. Davidson and E. T. Rouiller, AC1s J. R. Archer, T. Fleming, I. E. Jones, T. Wright, F. Haworth and W. Clews, and AC2 E. Rourke, and their contribution to Spilsby's campaign is remembered with gratitude. The bodies of at least three of the dead were never found. Strangely, the camp cinema was just in the process of opening for the first time when the explosion occurred, and the traumatic event did not appear to stop the screening of the film "Katrina", starring Sonja Henie.

The recent high level of training on H2S was kept up, and crews were no doubt too busy to be aware (or bothered!) that on 15 April Spilsby became part of the newly-formed 55 Base, with headquarters at East Kirkby. The Base system had originated in March 1943 as a means of co-ordinating operations flown from a geographically close group of airfields, usually three in number. Thus Headquarters 55 Base was allocated East Kirkby, Spilsby and Strubby, each of which could accommodate two squadrons.

Operations resumed on 20 April, when nineteen crews participated in a raid on La Chapelle, from which Plt. Off. T. J. Burgess and his crew in ND564 [EM:H] failed to return. At the same time, ten crews were practising bombing techniques, a fact which indicates the strength of 207 Squadron at that date. Two nights later, another nineteen crews took off to raid Brunswick, and all returned unscathed. After a two-aircraft 'gardening' mission to area 'Geranium', nineteen crews attacked Munich on 24/25 April, and all made their way back to England, although five landed away from base. Pressure was maintained on 26/27 April, when the ball-bearing factory at Schweinfurt was raided by a large Bomber Command force which included fourteen Lancasters of 207 Squadron. Two, unfortunately, did not return, one captained by Sqn. Ldr. A. N. Jones (ME631 EM:K) and the other by Flt. Lt. J. F. Muir (LM526 EM:R). One more operation took place that month, a raid on Clermont-Ferrand by fourteen aircraft on 29/30 April from which all returned safely.

May 1944 was a month of largely fine weather, as indeed one would expect, and 207 Squadron kept up its pace of large-scale participation in Bomber Command's intensive campaign. This was the last month before the planned invasion of Europe, and a range of different locations now became targets. First to receive 207 Squadron's attentions in May was Tours, which twelve aircraft visited on the first night of the month. Then, on the night of 3/4 May, came the attack on the panzer training and maintenance base at Mailly-le-Camp, eighty miles (128 km.) east of Paris, a raid which has been described as one of the most devastating and accurate attacks ever made by Bomber Command. Crews of four Mosquitos of 617 Squadron, led by none other than Wg. Cdr. G. L. Cheshire DSO DFC, were given the task of marking the target, which was close to a centre of civilian population. The plan was that a force of 346 Lancasters would bomb in two waves, sixteen squadrons of 5 Group leading. Bomb loads were to comprise one 4,000 lb. 'cookie' and up to sixteen 500 lb. high-explosive bombs.

For the Mailly raid, 207 Squadron provided seventeen aircraft, and all squadrons were airborne on time. After a slight error in marking by the Mosquitos, the master bomber called in the Lancasters, but only a few responded, due (it was discovered later) to the radio being swamped by a powerful American station. Nine minutes after call-in, however, at least sixty-one crews had dropped their bombs, but then came the order to hold fire until a certain amount of confusion had been sorted out. In the end, though the timetable was not adhered to, very considerable damage was done to the target. Large areas of the camp were destroyed, and some 37 tanks and 65 other military vehicles wrecked. Casualties on the ground amounted to 218 highly-trained soldiers and, unfortunately, fourteen local inhabitants. Fourteen of 207 Squadron's crews had attacked the primary target and one had aborted due to loss of power. Two were lost, those of Plt. Off. C. Bell (ND575 EM:M) and Flt. Sgt. L. H. Lissette (ND556 EM:F), the latter one of the few NCO captains remaining on the squadron. He lost his life, as did rear gunner Sgt. R. Ellis. Eventually, however, four of the Flt. Sgt.'s crew arrived in England after baling out about 30 miles (48 km.) east of Orleans and evading capture, to the delight of those members of the squadron who had known them. One of the four was Sgt. Nicholas Stockford, a 22-year old flight engineer who had been in the RAF since a few days before his sixteenth birthday in January 1938. Like all evaders, he was subjected to debriefing on arrival in the UK, and as his was particularly detailed it is reproduced here in full to show the tribulations suffered by Nicholas and no doubt by the other 37 aircrew of 207 Squadron who avoided being captured during the Second World War. The seventh member of the crew of ND556, Sgt. L. Wesley, was not so lucky, as he was taken prisoner.

"The bomb-aimer baled out first and I followed him. I landed in a wood some miles north of Ferrières. I freed my parachute from the tree in which it had become entangled and buried it, together with my Mae West, in the undergrowth. I set out at once, walking south by my compass, and continued across the fields for about three hours, when I hid in a wood until dawn. While I was resting there I removed my brevet and service chevrons and threw away my loose silver. I could see that I was near a small village, and later that morning (4 May) I moved towards it. About mid-day, as I was hiding by a hedge, two girls passed by, and though they saw me they did not stop. Half an hour later, an old man came straight towards where I was hiding and said that he was the father of the two girls who had seen me and reported my presence. He told me that I had reached Fontenay. When he heard that I intended making my way south, he warned me against going through Montargis, which he said was full of Germans. "

"At 14.00 hours I set out in what I thought was a south-westerly direction, so as to make a detour round Montargis. I crossed the railway and the main road and finally reached a stream, which I followed, thinking it was flowing in the direction in which I wanted to go. After scrambling through some thick undergrowth in my efforts to follow the course of the stream I came out onto a secondary road leading to a bridge across the stream. I crossed the bridge and then realised that I was hopelessly lost. Seeing a man working in a wood yard, I beckoned to him and asked him where I was. He told me that I was on the outskirts of Nargis. I made my way towards the town and hid in some woods for the night. I set out again early next morning (5 May) for Château–Landon. Before I reached the town I decided to seek help at a farm. There were several people working in the fields, but they took no notice of me. Finally I managed to attract the attention of an old man, to whom I declared myself. He took me to the back of the house and gave me some wine to drink. People at once came crowding round and offered me food, which I refused as I was not hungry. They were just discussing the question of providing civilian clothing for me when a woman came running up and told me that I must leave at once, as the farmer had informed the authorities of my presence. I ran down the hill, through some woods and across a stream, finally crawling through the undergrowth on the far side, from where I was able to keep a good look-out for anyone searching for me. About 15.00 hours a man saw me and came towards me. By this time I was feeling extremely hungry, as the only food I had eaten since baling out was some Horlicks tablets from my escape box. The man promised to return in an hour's time with some food. He returned shortly afterwards, however, without the food, which he said he would not give me until I had written in his notebook that he had helped me. I was feeling desperate by this time, so I did as he asked. The man then disappeared for several hours, and it was not until 19.00 hours that he returned with a loaf of bread and some cold potatoes. He was very nervous and asked me to leave at once. I continued on my way towards Chateau–Landon and reached the outskirts that evening. I passed several people, but they took no notice of me. I entered a small coppice and rested there for a while. Shortly afterwards seveal youths passed close by my hiding place whistling 'Tipperary'. I realised that they were looking for me and beckoned to them. They told me that they were members of the Maquis, though I did not believe them as they had no arms. I told them that I wanted to get to Beaumont, whereupon they led me out of the town and left me on the road to Mondreville. That night I lay in a wood just outside the town. Next morning (6 May), I walked through Mondreville and reached the outskirts of Beaumont. I stayed near the town all day, hoping to contact someone who could help me, but I saw no-one. That evening, I walked through Egry and reached the outskirts of Beaune–la–Rolande. I spent half the night in a wood and then hid in a haystack near a farm. Early next morning (7 May) I walked through Beaune-la-Rolande and then continued along the road. I was feeling very weak by this time, so I entered a field and slept for some hours. At 17.00 hours I set off again and walked through Boiscommun, which was deserted. Beyond the town I saw an old man working in the fields and asked him the way to Vitry. He pointed to the road I should take and I continued along it. I passed several people, who completely ignored me, though I heard one man mutter something about 'les Boches' as I passed. A little further on I came to a clearing in the woods by the side of the road. I saw a water trough standing in the clearing and went straight towards it, as I was feeling extremely thirsty. As I was drinking I saw three people standing in front of a small house watching me. I went up to them and asked for something to eat. After they had given me some food, I declared myself to them and was immediately invited inside. The owner of the house said that his son was away at the moment, but when he returned he would be able to put me in touch with an organisation. His son returned shortly afterwards and said that he would be able to help me. I spent the night in the garage attached to the house, and next day the son went to see a member of an organisation. That evening (8 May), I was visited by a young woman, and from this point my journey was arranged for me."

It is a pity that Sgt. Stockford did not divulge the details of his journey through occupied France and Spain to Lisbon, from where he was flown to Bristol (Whitchurch) on 15 July 1944. Nevertheless, this debrief does serve as a typical example of an evader's lot.

Tours was again the target for 207 Squadron on 7/8 May, after which there was a brief respite while squadron offices were moved to new quarters nearer Station HQ. Next came a raid on Annecy by eleven aircraft, then on 11/12 May Bourg Leopold was the objective, but on this trip the crews were ordered to return to base with bomb-loads on board, and all but two did so.

The news that Flt. Lt. Street had been brutally shot while trying to escape from PoW camp was received by the squadron on 19 May, and this fact no doubt stiffened the resolve of the eighteen crews bricfed to attack Amiens that night, their instructions being that they must bomb on markers, in order to avoid civilian casualties. In the hands of Flg. Off. T. Smart, Lancaster EM:P was making its run up to the target when there was a resounding crash, and it was at once obvious that EM:P had collided with another aircraft. Although pieces of metal had been torn off, Flg. Off. Smart managed to regain control and the bomb-aimer released the load, soon after which the Master Bomber ordered cessation of bombing due to bad visibility. It was then possible for the crew of EM:P to take stock of the damage, and it was seen that two or three feet of wing had been torn off and only three feet of port tailplane still survived. In addition, the W/T set was out of action. Damaged as much as this, the Lancaster was well-nigh impossible to control, and at first it wandered around over northern France, but before long Flg. Off. Smart found ways of managing the situation and began to steer towards the emergency runway at Manston, not wishing to make a ditching in the dark. When the crippled aircraft crossed the English coast its altitude was only 400 feet, and moments later it touched down safely, ninety minutes after the collision. After engineers had examined the aircraft they said that in theory it was impossible for it to have remained in the air! Flg. Off. Smart was awarded an immediate DFC for his efforts, only to be posted missing on the night of 21/22 June. After the same Amiens raid, the aircraft flown by Wg. Cdr. Grey hit a tree on the approach to Spilsby, injuring the bomb-aimer, Flg. Off. Casey.

After these raids on French targets, it was back to Germany for the next few operations. Nine of the squadron's aircraft laid mines in Kiel harbour on 21/22 May while another eight were dropping their loads on Duisburg. Lancaster ND522 [EM:J], captained by Flg. Off. P. E. Walshe, never returned to Spilsby. The situation worsened considerably when three of eleven aircraft were lost during the raid on Brunswick on 22/23 May. From this mission Flt. Lt. J. G. Symons, Flg. Off. K. W. McSweeney (LL776 EM:S) and Plt. Off. A. F. Heath (LM540 EM:Q) and their crews did not return, although several of those on board survived to become prisoners of war. Seven aircraft raided Antwerp on 24/25 May, and this time all returned unscathed. Mining was the task for six Lancasters on 26/27 May, and May's final mission for 207 Squadron was an attack on Le Valery by eleven aircraft on 27/28 May, with no loss. However, the visit by the AOC on 31 May may have caused an equal amount of anxiety to some members of the squadron, particularly Flg. Off. G. A. C. Overgaauw, with whom he flew on a bombing practice mission! During this very active month, 190 aircraft had been detailed for offensive sorties, of which 43 were cancelled before take-off, four had aborted and 137 had attacked their primary targets. Six of 207 Squadron's crews had not returned to base; some survived as prisoners of war but others would never see England again. The switch from German targets had resulted in three-quarters of Bomber Command's efforts being directed against France in May 1944, a complete turn-round since March.

In his mcmoirs Flg. Off. D. M. Rose gives great credit to the ordinary 'erks' at Spilsby. "The ground crew boys were the most important in the whole squadron," he claimed. "They always seemed to be working. Day and night they would be crawling all over those Lancasters like a bunch of flies over a piece of rotten meat; a crude way to put it, but it helps to express the way in which those boys stuck to their job. Each aircraft had its own ground crew and they looked after it as if it were a baby. They were always willing to do anything you wanted done to the aircraft, even if it meant missing a meal. They didn't mind,

The crew of Albert Hollings, all tour-expired in July 1944, pose with Lancaster 'A–Able'. (Left to right) Alan Redman (bomb-aimer), John Denton (wireless operator), Joe Blake (mid-upper gunner), Albert Hollings, Bert Hallam (flight engineer), Rex Kenyon (navigator), and Cyril Harper (rear gunner). [C. B. Sutherland]

as long as their aircraft was in A1 condition and would get the crew to the target and back. In fact, they are the boys who, when the aircraft were circling base and coming in, were hoping and praying that their aircraft and crew were OK. No praise can be too high for those boys. When the target was 'pranged' by a thousand bombers of Bomber Command, they were the boys who made it possible, the unsung heroes of the Royal Air Force." Thinking about these sentiments, one can imagine how the ground crew of an aircraft which did not return felt.

The invasion of Europe

At last! June 1944, the month in which the fortunes of war would swing irrevocably to the side of the Allies, began with cold, cloudy, wet weather conditions, but nevertheless 207 Squadron was able to join in Bomber Command's intensified offensive against targets in northern France. The object was to destroy as many road and rail communications centres as possible in order to prevent the enemy's supplies and troops moving to the front. Saumur was the first target of the month, and was visited by thirteen aircraft. Next came raids on two targets near Cherbourg, Ferme d'Urville by ten aircraft on 3/4 June and Maisy by seventeen 'kites' on the next night. La Pernelle was the target for seventeen aircraft on 5/6 June, and although the squadron diarist failed to say so, it is highly probable that the returning crews witnessed, as so many others did, the armada of ships and landing craft making their way in the dawn light toward the coast of Normandy. During the night of 7/8 June, the gunners aboard Wg. Cdr. Grey's Lancaster shot down no less than three enemy fighters during a raid on Balleroi. Clarence Sutherland remembers it: "After leaving the target I saw a fighter in the rear and both of us gunners opened fire. The Ju 88 went down in flames. About ten seconds later another Ju 88 was spotted. We fired and it blew up under our aircraft......Twenty minutes later I spotted a Bf 410 and there were Lancasters with lights on ahead of us. We held course, as we thought he was going after another Lancaster, but he pulled up on our port side. We opened fire and the Bf 410 went down in a glide, on fire, towards the English coast. Next day, Air Marshal Harris phoned Spilsby and talked to the Station Commander, asking 'Who the hell were those guys?' Flg. Off. Wallace McIntosh and I received DFCs [for this action]." This enormous effort was maintained, with raids on Étampes on 9/10 June, Caen on 12/13 June and Anny-sur-Odon on 14/15 June.

A US Army Air Force crew from a neighbouring airfield visited the squadron on 15 June, as did Mr. Kiok, a Dutch reporter who was to fly on an operation with Flg. Off. Overgaauw. But much more significant to 207 Squadron personnel was the arrival at Spilsby that day of Wg. Cdr. Guy Gibson VC, who had just been appointed as Controller of 55 Base.

Nazi Germany's first secret weapon, the V1 flying bomb, came into use against targets in southern England on 16 June, and Bomber Command began a concerted campaign of attacks against the launch sites in northern France. The first in which 207 Squadron was involved was that day, when twenty aircraft attacked Beauvoir, all returning safely. This picture changed for the worse, however, on 21/22 June, when no less than five of the eighteen aircraft which raided Wesseling were lost. In command were Flt. Lt. F. W. 'Gally' Gallagher DSO (the pilot who had struggled so heroically to bring his aircraft back from Brunswick on 14 January 1944), Flg. Off. T. T. Smart DFC, Plt. Off. C. J. Solly, Flg. Off. A. V. D. Corless and Plt. Off. E. A. Goodman. In total, 37 men failed to return, 32 of them having lost their lives. Of the others, three were taken prisoner and two managed to avoid capture. Another sad day for the squadron. Matters improved a little during the next few days, when raids on Pommereval by seventeen aircraft and Marquis

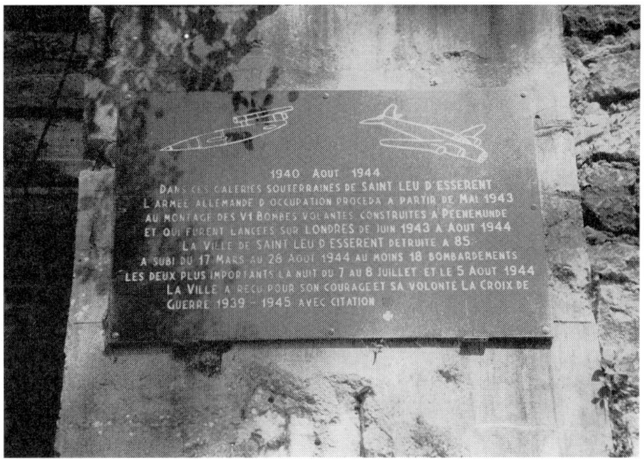

At the main entrance to the former V1 storage depot at St. Leu d'Esserent is this plaque, which records that for the courage maintained by local residents during the heavy raids inflicted on the neighbourhood the village was awarded the Croix de Guerre and Citation.

Mimoyecques by eighteen were staged, all the weary crews returning safely. As the weather at the end of the month was poor, no further missions were flown.

To support the launch sites, the enemy had set up three assembly and storage sites for V1s in France: St. Leu d'Esserent, a town in the Oise valley about thirty miles (48 km.) north of Paris where more than 70% of all V1s launched against England were prepared; Nucourt (in a limestone cavern west of St. Leu); and Rilly–la–Montagne, a railway tunnel south of Rheims. July 1944 was a month of mostly fine weather, and 207 Squadron was kept very busy attacking these assembly sites and transport targets, beginning with a raid on St. Leu d'Esserent by fifteen aircraft on 4/5 July, a mission from which two crews, headed by Plt. Off. J. H. Wilson (LM125 EM:G) and Flt. Sgt. J. W. Gibbs (ND570 EM:Z), did not return. This time 207 Squadron formed part of a force of 229 Lancasters and twelve Mosquitos. Fighter opposition was predicted, as there was a full moon and little cloud cover, and soon after dropping its bombs, Plt. Off. Peter McIntosh's Lancaster was attacked by a Bf 109, which damaged the tailplane and holed the starboard outer fuel tank, as well as severely injuring the rear gunner, Sgt. Burton. The aircraft became very difficult to control, and while attempts were being made to stabilise it the Luftwaffe fighter made another pass. This time the mid-upper gunner, Sgt. Barker, fired a continuous burst, hitting the fighter, which went down in flames. After a time Peter McIntosh found cloud cover and made his way homeward to land at Woodbridge, having warned the crew that they might have to bale out if the situation worsened. The same target was attacked by sixteen aircraft two nights later, and this time the squadron was saddened by the loss of no less than another five of its crews and Lancasters. Flg. Offs. C. E. Stamp, M. N. Milner, M. Alderton, K. A. Boyce and T. J. Hordley were captains of the missing aircraft, and were mourned by all those remaining at Spilsby, especially their fellow aircrews, who when they realised that 35 men were not coming back to Spilsby (nineteen of them having been killed) must have wondered whether it was their turn next. In September, though, Flg. Off. Alderton and five of his crew managed to reach England, having bailed out near Beauvais and avoided being captured. The other two members of the Alderton crew were captured, one becoming an 'ordinary' prisoner of war and the other, Sgt. Len Barham, was managing to evade the enemy when he was betrayed and taken by the SS. Being in civilian clothes, he was classified as a spy. Sgt. Phelps from Flg. Off. Stamp's crew was captured in similar circumstances, and they were both taken to the infamous Frense Prison in Paris, where they joined

An aerial view of the V.1 storage depot in caves at St. Leu d'Esserent after the raid on 4/5 July 1944 in which 207 Squadron took part. [Air Photo Library, University of Keele]

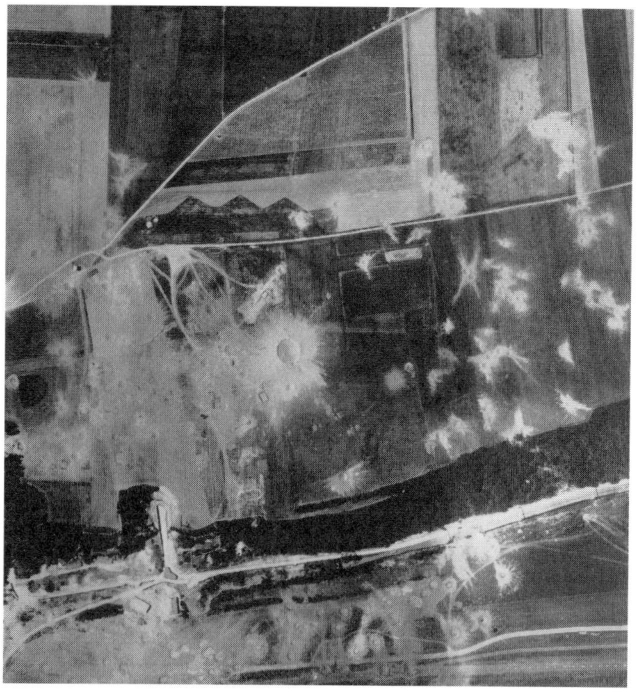

The main entrance to the caves at St. Leu d'Esserent is near the bottom left-hand corner of this photograph. [Air Photo Library, University of Keele]

another 160 or so aircrew who had befallen the same fate. While they were held there in dreadful conditions, they were interrogated under torture, but when Allied troops reached the outskirts of Paris all 168 prisoners were takenby train, under frequent attack by fighters, to Buchenwald concentration camp, where living conditions were even worse than at Frense prison. The two 207 Squadron men found out later that the orders were that none of the 168 was to be transferred to a normal Luftwaffe prison camp, and it was only when the Luftwaffe heard that aircrew were in Buchenwald that their lives were saved. Apparently on direct orders from Goering, all aircrew prisoners were then transferred to Stalag Luft III. The four members of 207 Squadron who spent time in Buchenwald, all Sergeants, were L. P. Barham, A. J. McPherson, L. Wesley and E. K. Phelps.

A poem by a Stalag Luft III inmate sums it all up:

Here we sit in Stalag III,
Drinking at the bar,
With lovely girls to buy the drinks;
Like bloody hell we are!

We travelled here in luxury,
The whole trip for a quid,
A sleeping berth for each of us;
Like bloody hell we did!

Our feather beds are all full up,
Our carpets almost new.
In easy chairs we sit all day;
Like bloody hell we do!

The 'goons' are really wizard chaps,
Their hope of victory good,
We'd take their places any day;
Like bloody hell we would!

When winter comes and snow abounds,
And temperatures are nil,
We'll find hot bottles in our beds;
Like bloody hell we will!

It's heaven on earth in Stalag III,
A life we'd hate to miss,
It's everything we've always missed;
Like bloody hell it is!

And when the war is over,
And Jerry gets the bill,
We'll remember all that's happened here;
My bloody oath we will!

A short patch of cloudy conditions intervened before the next raid could be mounted, and this time the target for twelve crews was Chalindrey. They all returned safely, but had to be diverted when bad weather clamped down at Spilsby. During this attack a Bf 109 fighter was shot down

Lancaster Mk.III ND866 [EM:B] was shot down during the raid on St.Leu d'Esserent on 8 July 1944 and all but one of the crew were lost. Here, however, is a different crew – left to right, back row: Flt. Sgt. G. Hall (air gunner; Plt. Off. L. Daniel (bomb-aimer); Flt. Sgt. K. Dobson (flight engineer); Flg. Off. J. T. Giddens (pilot); Flt. Sgt. G. Walker (wireless operator); E. Rashbrook (navigator); Flt. Sgt. J. James (air gunner). Front row (ground crew): unknown; E. Roberts; K. Maynard; E. Britten; J. Gillespie. [via R. Winton]

Flt. Lt. White and his crew seen shortly after joining 207 Squadron in late July 1944, with Lancaster PB293 [EM:W] as a backdrop. Left to right, back row: Sgt. A. Tweddle (rear gunner); Flg. Off. L. Hahn (mid-upper gunner); Flt. Lt. J. D. White (pilot); Sgt. R. H. Webb (flight engineer). Front row: Sgt. R. S. Winton (wireless operator); Sgt. E. C. Peek (navigator); Sgt. A. E. Wykes (bomb-aimer). [via R. S. Winton]

by a gunner in Wg. Cdr. Grey's crew, providing a boost to squadron morale. Seven crews took off on 14 July to raid Villeneuve St. Georges and all came back, including Sqn. Ldr. S. Pattinson, for whom this had been the final sortie in his second tour of operations. Another loss was felt by the squadron on 16 July, when Flt. Lt. G. L. Jones and his crew in ME807 [EM:S] did not come back from a six-aircraft raid on Nevers. Other crews reported seeing what appeared to be a collision between two aircraft over the target, but there was no proof that it was 207 Squadron's Lancaster.

Daylight operations

Then came a switch to daylight operations, beginning when thirteen crews were briefed at midnight on 17 July for a raid on enemy troop concentrations at Caen. This turned out to be a highly successful mission in which two thousand aircraft of Bomber Command and the USAAF took part, and all 207 Squadron's contribution returned safely. Next to receive attention from Allied bombers was Revigny, to where 207 Squadron sent ten aircraft on 18 July, but this time three crews, headed by Flg. Offs. W. R. McNaughton, N. L. Weekes and J. G. Dallen, failed to return. A V1 launching ramp at Triverny was targeted during daylight hours on 19 July, and this time a fighter escort was provided for the bomber force. 207 Squadron sent seven aircraft, all of which returned unscathed.

The period between 22 June and 19 July was probably the worst 28 days in the squadron's history; 126 aircrew – eighteen crews – did not return from operations and had to be presumed missing, believed killed. 126 bunks had been made empty or had changed occupants; at least as many letters had to be written to next of kin; and all those personal effects and 'Committees of Adjustment' had to be sorted out. We now know, although the squadron would not have known for many weeks, that eleven men were prisoners of war and thirteen had evaded successfully. Eighteen replacement crews would have joined the squadron, with all the administration that involved. Despite this, as before and afterwards, 207 Squadron carried on without a pause, an enormous tribute to the spirit and leadership of the squadron.

After a raid on Courtrai by eleven aircraft on 20 July, two days of intensive continuation training were enjoyed before the next mission, an attack on Kiel by seven aircraft. On 24/25 July crews were briefed for two different targets, nine for Stuttgart and six crews with less experience to strike the railway yards at Donges, a target alleged to be an easy one. Reaching the English coast on his return journey, Flg. Off. P. C. McIntosh called Spilsby to say that he had decided to fly out to sea to jettison a bomb which was 'hung up', but his Lancaster (PB294 EM:G) was then seen to dive into the sea and catch fire. The cause of this crash will never be known; possibly the aircraft had sustained damage of which the crew was unaware. Stuttgart was targeted again the following night, and all fourteen of 207 Squadron's aircraft returned safely. Marshalling yards at Gisors were next to receive 207 Squadron's attention, and during that raid Flg. Off. D. Grant claimed a Bf 410 twin-engined night fighter as destroyed.

This busy month was drawing to a close, but activity on 207 Squadron was maintained at high level. Fifteen aircraft were sent to Stuttgart on 28/29 July, and Wg. Cdr. J. F. Grey claimed that his crew had destroyed two enemy fighters. Flg. Off. D. Grant topped that by claiming three, and Flg. Off. G. H. Montgomery claimed two fighters and a 'doodlebug' (the common name for a V1). Lancaster ND872 [EM:L], however, captained by Flt. Lt. K. Marshall, did not return.

An early morning mission on 30 July was something of a disappointment, as all fifteen aircraft had to bring their bomb-loads back when solid cloud cover prevented their planned attack on Cahagnes. Next day, fifteen crews attended briefing, and eight took off to raid railway yards at La Roche, six attacked V1 sites at Rilly-la-Montagne and one was cancelled. Flak over the launch-ramps was heavy, and Sqn. Ldr. Howes, CO of 'B' Flight, was not amused when Flt. Lt. J. D. White, flying PD209, the aircraft usually allocated to Howes, brought it back liberally peppered with flak holes!

Another case of wasted effort was seen on 1 August, when two aircraft detailed to raid La Roche brought their bombs home when the crews were unable to find the target. Flying bomb sites at St. Maximin were subjected to a daylight raid by twelve of 207 Squadron's aircraft on 2 August, and again fighter cover was provided. This performance was repeated next day by thirteen Lancasters as part of a concerted attempt to rid Europe of these highly dangerous weapons.

Brilliant sunshine on 5 August formed a background for fifteen of the squadron's Lancasters when they left Spilsby for another raid on the flying-bomb depot at St. Leu d'Esserent. Over seven hundred Lancasters and Halifaxes took part in this operation against a vital part of the enemy's effort to retaliate, with Wg. Cdr. Grey leading the 55 Base contribution. Five to ten-tenths cloud over the target made recognition of the aiming point difficult. Wg. Cdr. Grey was about to release his bombs when flak burst under the nose of his aircraft, damaging the port inner and starboard outer engines, but fortunately not causing any injuries. Neither engine would feather, and the Lancaster would not maintain altitude, but its bomb-load was released and the aircraft turned for home. As it was losing height, the crew donned parachutes and made ready to 'hit the silk', at the same time throwing out everything they could to lighten the aircraft. The crippled Lancaster was shadowed by another one as far as the coast of France, a kindness which was greatly appreciated. Just as a little hope was creeping into the minds of the crew, another engine threatened to give up, but thanks partly to the care of the flight engineer, Flg. Off. Young, and partly to sheer luck, the engine kept going for long enough for a landing to be made on the huge emergency runway at Manston. This trip over, Plt. Off. Grant could relax a little, as it was the final sortie of his tour. Next day another daylight raid was undertaken, this time to Bois de Cassan, which was visited by six aircraft. The Lancaster captained by Flg. Off. R. J. Cupit was attacked by an enemy fighter, and his flight engineer and rear gunner were killed and mid-upper gunner seriously injured. Although the aircraft (PD209 EM:V) was badly damaged, Flg. Off. Cupit managed to nurse it back to make a landing at Ford, on the Sussex coast, but having already

Taken by 542 Squadron on 19 November 1945, this vertical photograph shows the damage inflicted on Rilly–la–Montagne railway tunnel's south entrance, where V1s were stored. [Air Photo Library, University of Keele]

The northern entrance to Rilly-la-Montagne tunnel. [Air Photo Library, University of Keele]

Under heavy attack in daylight on 2 August 1944 was the V1 storage depot at St. Maximin, seen here from an altitude of 17,650 feet. [via R. Winton]

suffered the indignity of being damaged on 31 July this Lancaster never returned to 207 Squadron.

Stubbornly-held enemy concentrations in the Caen area had to be dealt with next, and from Spilsby fourteen of 207 Squadron's Lancasters took off during the evening of 7 August to do what they could to rectify the situation. Afterwards, they were all diverted to the small OTU airfield at Moreton-in-Marsh in Gloucestershire, where parking space for these unusually large visitors must have presented a problem. Oil and petrol depots at Fôret de Chatelbrault were targeted by fourteen aircraft during the night of 9/10 August, followed by a raid by five aircraft on Bordeaux next night. Marshalling yards at Givres were given the benefit of 207 Squadron's efforts on 12 August, and then came small-scale participation in a raid on Brunswick.

By now the battle area in Normandy had moved on, but enemy troops were causing mayhem around the town of Falaise. To help deal with this problem, 207 Squadron sent six aircraft on an early-morning attack, and all came back without serious difficulty. Then came a raid on a target well-known to many an earlier member of 207 Squadron during the days of flying the Manchester aircraft — Brest harbour. This time the fourteen crews who took off in daylight on 14 August had faith in the capabilities of their aircraft, with the result that one cruiser was "definitely" sunk. Several of the Lancasters were damaged by flak but all returned to base.

Airfields in the area around Arnhem were the next targets for 207 Squadron. The well-known Dutch member of the squadron, Flt. Lt. G. A. Overgaauw, was captain of the only aircraft lost by the squadron that day, LM263 [EM:N], which exploded in the air. The official reason was that it was hit in the bomb bay by flak, but an eye-witness in another aircraft is certain that bombs from an aircraft of another squadron, flying at higher altitude, caused the explosion. Ironically, Flt. Lt. Overgaauw was only twenty miles from his own home town, and with 32 sorties completed was not far from the end of his tour.

A night-time raid on Stettin followed on 16/17 August, and for this thirteen aircraft took off, although one aborted when the rear gunner was taken ill. Flying bomb sites at Fôret de l'Isle Adam were attacked by thirteen of the squadron's aircraft during daylight hours on 18 August, after which there was a break in activity until 25 August. That night sixteen aircraft took off for a raid on Darmstadt, but Flt. Lt. M. F. Harding and his crew in PD216 [EM:J] failed to return. Another captain, Flg. Off. Watson, collapsed during the flight, but his co-pilot took over and 'pressed on regardless'. Before the end of the month two large-scale attacks on Königsberg were mounted, without loss to the squadron; although this was a very long-distance operation, involving a trip of over eleven hours, most crews brought back about 300 gallons (1,350 litres) of fuel. Finally, on 31 August, a daylight raid on flying bomb sites at Bergeneuse by twelve aircraft was staged.

September 1944 began with another daylight raid on shipping in Brest harbour, this time by twelve aircraft of 207 Squadron. On the fifth anniversary of the outbreak of war, 3 September, seventeen aircraft left Spilsby in cloudy and wet weather to make a daylight attack on airfields at Deelen in Holland, led by Wg. Cdr. Grey. This raid and the earlier one were part of a softening-up process in advance of the planned paratroop drop on the area under Operation 'Market Garden', an operation which was to go so disastrously wrong.

A night raid on München-Gladbach followed on 9/10 September, the eighteen aircraft all returning to Spilsby after what the crews described as a "quiet trip". Early in the morning of 11 September fifteen Lancasters took off to raid the port of Le Havre without any problems, but during the following night Flg. Off. D. C. Cooke and his crew in LM261 [EM:C] failed to return from another raid on Darmstadt. Seventeen aircraft took part in a raid on Stuttgart on 12/13 September, and sadly Sgt. B. V. Bowen and his crew did not bring Lancaster PD267 [EM:G] back to base. Lancaster PD217 had the misfortune to collide with an East Kirkby-based Lancaster, but the captain managed to land it at base with a damaged port wing. A successful daylight raid on Boulogne followed on 17 September, and Bremerhaven was visited next day by eighteen aircraft.

Sgts. Ron Winton and Ted Peek checking over Lancaster LM263 [EM:N] before a daylight raid on Brest on 14 August 1944. On the very next operation, this aircraft, with a different crew, was lost during a raid on Deelen. [via R. Winton]

Flg. Off. A. J. Prescott, who joined 207 Squadron on 12 September 1944, soon made the acquaintance of Sect. Off. Joyce Brotherton, the Intelligence Officer at Spilsby. She was usually referred to by her Christian name, but to some by the nickname 'Blondie'. In Flg. Off. Prescott's experience, she was the only person who could run an Intelligence Room to the standard required by the RAF and at the same time make it interesting enough to entice reluctant aircrews. Often in her spare moments she could be found in the Officers' Mess, darning socks or repairing tunics and shirts for anyone who needed her services.

Proof, if any was needed, of the Lancaster's ability to return home in a less than complete condition! On his thirteenth operation, Flt. Lt. White in PD217 [EM:Z] collided with an aircraft of 57 Sqn. over Stuttgart, but brought the damaged Lancaster home minus a good deal of the outer panel of the port wing. It took just six days to replace the damaged parts of the wing and two fixed aerials. [via R. Winton]

On 19 September, during a daylight raid on München-Gladbach to which 207 Squadron contributed eighteen aircraft, Wg. Cdr. Guy Gibson VC, the Controller of 55 Base who was acting as Master Bomber, and a hero in the eyes of the crews who knew him, lost his life.

An evening take-off for a raid on Handorf by twenty-one of 207 Squadron's Lancasters on 23 September followed, but from this considerable effort Flg. Off. R. T. Kerwin and his crew in PD318 [EM:J] did not come back. Soon after midnight on 26 September no less than twenty-two aircraft left Spilsby on their way to Karlsruhe, and all but one reached the target, dropped their bomb-loads and returned safely. Two crews each claimed that they had destroyed a fighter and two other crews reported combats. Finally, a night raid on Kaiserslauten by eighteen of the squadron's aircraft was made on 27/28 September without loss, completing the month's total of 205 aircraft which had attacked their primary targets.

At the end of September, 207 Squadron was joined at Spilsby by 44 Squadron, another Lancaster unit, which had just spent eighteen months at Dunholme Lodge. Together, the two squadrons would work towards victory in Europe.

Sea mining was undertaken by five aircraft on 4 October in area 'Silverthorn', a type of operation not much undertaken by 207 Squadron over recent months but none the less important for all that. Next day, 21 Lancasters took off after breakfast to raid Bremen, although one returned early with technical troubles. ME667 [EM:X], captained by Flg. Off. J. H. Middleton, did not make it back to base. To the delight of many crews, it was announced that day that a tour of operations was to be reduced to 33 trips, allowing Flg. Off. Giddens to finish his tour unexpectedly!

Many years later, the former Flg. Off. Douglas Rose, a Canadian known to one and all as 'Rosie', gave his impression of life on the squadron. "I must say that at times it was very dull", he remarked, "but we sure made up for those dull moments! None of us gave a damn what happened at any time. We had many a good party together, one night after another if we weren't on ops. Our squadron CO was 'one of the boys', really a top-notch fellow. He could sink more hard Scotch than any man I've known and not show it too much. He was a Scotsman, of course, and very often was with us on our wild sprees. Discipline on the squadron was what you made it. They more or less let us rule ourselves. It worked out very well too. If there were no ops. on and you weren't required for training your time was your own to do with as you pleased. We had a very good Mess considering the Station as a whole. Food was usually 'tops', the staff was friendly and would do almost anything for us. They always called me 'Rosie', in fact that's all I ever got from the whole Station. That, of course, would never do in peacetime – tradition, old boy!"

With 'Rosie' Rose as instigator, a group of 'Colonial' aircrew officers, each with an inbuilt disregard for authority in most of its forms, decided to form a society of those of like persuasion – the 'Crazy Gang'. They went to the extent of having membership cards typed out by Sect. Off. Brotherton, who was made an Associate Member & Chief Sufferer. On the card were listed the three objects of the Gang — 1. To annoy as many people as possible as often as possible in the shortest time possible, with a view to causing them to qualify for membership; 2. To be as crazy as possible with a view to adding to one's own enjoyment; and 3. To get into the maximum amount of trouble in the minimum amount of time with the least possible effort. "Madness is Golden" was selected as the Gang's motto, and their War Song, performed to an unrecorded tune, was

"Now is the time to work,
Do not be lazy,
No member must ever shirk,
Till all the world's crazy!"

There were four Foundation Members – Flg. Off. Douglas M. Rose RCAF, a former ice hockey professional and now a pilot; Flg. Off. T. S. Phelan RCAF; Flg. Off. Arthur 'Paddy' Prescott RNZAF, a pilot; and Flg. Off. Arthur T. Loveless RAAF. There were four other members – Flt. Lt. E. Lawson RAAF; Flg. Off. Paul Flewwelling RCAF, a highly experienced pilot who had been an instructor; Flg. Off. T. O. P. 'Topper' Brown RCAF; and Flg. Off. E. Hudson RAAF, who was 'Topper's' skipper. Underneath this apparent careless attitude, however, were men of high standards who took their operational responsibilities very seriously. Arthur Loveless, for example, was meticulous in carrying out every detail of an operation as instructed. He was in complete charge of his crew and was deservedly popular. 'Rosie' was said to be a very different man when undergoing briefing. "Most men were different in the air",

The complete personnel of 207 Squadron (apart from any who were off sick or on leave) photographed on 26 October 1944 in front of Lancaster PD217 [EM:Z]. [via R. Winton]

said Joyce Brotherton, "but 'Rosie' was more different than most. He was always particularly careful to make sure that he understood what was expected of him and made every effort to carry out his orders. He stood no nonsense from his crew and took pains to see that they knew their jobs. They were always together, and he spoke well of their co-operation with each other, an important matter in any crew."

In her memoirs, Sect. Off. Brotherton refers to an instance of a 207 Squadron captain giving his life to save his crew. "The squadron had lost only one crew and all but the pilot were safe. Flt. Lt. Peter Anderson DFC RCAF – 'Andy' to most of us – had added his name to the long list of pilots who have willingly given their lives by hanging on to their 'kites' too long in order to make sure that the whole crew had time to bale out. It may sound a sweeping statement, but I am firmly convinced that there were few, if any, of the pilots on the squadron who would not have been ready to do the same thing should the occasion demand it. I didn't live with them for two and three-quarter years for nothing." Joyce continued by saying that on an operational Station one acquired the habit of putting aside one's grief for a time. "One had to. Although we were able to laugh and fool about and enjoy being together again, we had none of us forgotten the absent members of the Gang, nor were we ever likely to."

Action over Holland

By early October 1944, Allied forces were making strenuous efforts to control the Scheldt estuary to deny the enemy the use of Antwerp docks, but progress was slow. To speed things up, Bomber Command was asked to help by breaching the sea walls protecting Walcheren. For 207 Squadron's next two missions this was the objective, and after an attempt by sixteen aircraft on 7 October (including a reserve crew flying in a 44 Squadron aircraft) it was achieved on 11 October. That day, nine aircraft made the sea wall their target while another five attacked guns at Flushing, after which they all came back to Spilsby safely. Four coastal gun batteries were submerged and seven others were cut off in Bomber Command's very accurate missions, which included the use of 12,000 lb. (5,455 kg.) 'earthquake' bombs. Then it was back to a night raid on Brunswick, which was attacked by twenty aircraft of 207 Squadron on 14/15 October. All returned to base, although three members of Flg. Off. A. E. Hazel's crew had bailed out when LM123 [EM:Q] was hit by flak. The main operation for 15 October was cancelled due to poor weather conditions, but two aircraft, LM208 [EM:M] captained by

Lancaster PB782 stands at its Spilsby dispersal while being readied for its next operation. [via R. Winton]

A target photograph of the sea wall at Walcheren taken by Flg. Off. P. Passmore from Lancaster LL902 [EM:A] on 7 October 1944. The aircraft below was from 44 Squadron, which had moved into Spilsby from Dunholme Lodge recently. [via R. Winton]

Flt. Lt. G. H. Montgomery and NG143 [EM:R] by Flg. Off. D. W. Ready, left Spilsby to sow mines in area 'Silverthorn'. Neither returned.

Wg. Cdr. J. F. Grey DSO DFC, the squadron's CO since 23 March, was posted to Oakley on 16 October 1944 and Wg. Cdr. H. R. Black AFC took over the reins. Although of course he did not know it, this gentleman was destined to command 207 Squadron through the remainder of the war and beyond.

Sea defences in Holland still occupied the squadron from time to time, and an attempt was made by five aircraft to breach the wall at West Kapelle Dyke during a daylight raid on 17 October. Two days later, an early evening take-off by eighteen aircraft for a raid on Nuremburg was made, and all returned with no more than superficial damage. Back to Walcheren went six Lancasters on 23 October, followed on the night of 24/25 October by a spot of 'gardening' in area 'Kraut' by three aircraft. The next mission was to a completely new target area – Bergen in Norway, for which twenty aircraft took off during the evening of 28 October. Apart from Flg. Off. D. C. Church's LM271 [EM:L], which was lost, the squadron returned to English shores to make a landing at the huge emergency airfield at Carnaby in Yorkshire, from where the crews made their way to Spilsby after refuelling. The final operation in October was another attempt at the West Kapelle Dyke by eight aircraft.

207 Squadron's first mission of November 1944 turned into a disaster before the aircraft had even left the ground. Twenty aircraft were detailed for a raid on Homberg, including PD290, captained by Flg. Off. A. T. Loveless on his first 'solo' mission. Taking off from the short runway, 16/34, he swung violently to port, careered across the grass, demolished a Nissen hut and crashed into a visiting Halifax (MZ824, of Leeming-based 429 Squadron) which was parked on a dispersal. The bombs aboard PD290 exploded, destroying two Halifaxes and damaging another. In addition, the 44 Squadron briefing room and crew room and small buildings around the control tower were badly damaged and it was fortunate that the tower itself was not badly affected. One of the Halifax crew members tried to move his aircraft to safety but was injured and died later. Luckily, Flg. Off. Loveless and his crew were not injured. Lancaster NN724 was just becoming airborne when the explosion occurred, and its wingtip almost touched the runway, but Flg. Off. J. W. Downing, on his first operation, managed to regain control. Only thirteen of the squadron's Lancasters were able to carry out the mission, and all returned to land on a runway which had been cleared during their absence.

Skegness was not too far away for an evening's entertainment, and one day 'Rosie' Rose and 'Paddy' Prescott took Joyce Brotherton there, as they thought she might be taking life too seriously, thus not adhering to the rules of the 'Crazy Gang', a major transgression. Prescott, who for some reason was known by Joyce as Chris, was driving Flewwelling's car, he being on leave at the time, and before long 'Rosie' asked whether the driver knew the way. "Not in the slightest" came the cheerful reply "but I expect we can get there somehow this way". Surprisingly enough, they did, and went to the cinema to see 'Virginia City', a western film in which there was an Intelligence Officer. This caused much ribald comment by the two men at Joyce's expense, but it was all taken in good part.

Members of the crew headed by Flg. Off. Frank Chambers pose in front of PB782 [EM:Y] with 'B' Flight ground crew. By the time this photograph was taken in late 1944 the vertical tailplanes of 207 Squadron's Lancasters had been painted red, without fin flashes. [via R. Winton]

On 1 November 1944 Flg. Off. Loveless in PD290 [EM:N], on his first operation with the squadron, experienced a strong swing to port on take-off, swerved out of control and hit three Halifaxes of 429 Squadron which had been diverted to Spilsby. A fourth Halifax MZ824 (seen here) exploded while being moved, with the loss of one of the crew from burns. [via R. Winton]

Dusseldorf and Dortmund were targeted on 2 and 4 November, and then came an unsuccessful raid on the Dortmund – Ems Canal at Gravenhorst by eighteen aircraft on 6 November, from which Flg. Off. J. E. Adams and his crew in ND555 [EM:D] did not return. Training and sports occupied the crews for the next few days, until on 11 November seventeen aircraft took off for a night raid on Harburg. All reached England safely, but when in the Spilsby circuit two Lancasters collided, with the loss of all on board, LM648 of 44 Squadron and PB428 [EM:T] with Flg. Off. W. A. Sparks in command. Four captains reached the end of their first tours of operations that day and were no doubt very relieved. Advanced troop positions at Düren were targeted on 16 November by sixteen aircraft, but Flg. Off. J. G. Anderson and his crew lost their lives when Lancaster NF979 [EM:B] was shot down. A few days of training and cancelled operations followed, until eighteen aircraft took off on 21 November for another attack on the Dortmund – Ems canal. This time the squadron's Lancasters formed part of a special force of 247 aircraft which between them attacked so successfully that about 15 miles (24 km.) of the Mitteland canal near its junction with the Dortmund – Ems canal and a further 17 miles (27 km.) of the main canal were emptied of water. As a result, these vital waterways, which in 1942 had carried 75,000,000 tons of barge traffic, were put out of action for several months.

In those days, BBC radio was much enjoyed by service people and civilians alike, the fledgling television service having closed down at the outbreak of war. Bob Hope was a favourite among listeners in the Mess at Spilsby, and during the hours proceeding the start of an operation he was nothing less than a godsend to those with nerves on edge. The well-known comedian had the ability to encourage laughter all round, even in times of great stress, of which there were many. In her reminiscences, Joyce Brotherton said "I wished that Bob Hope and those with him could have been with us to see for themselves what a grand help they were to us all."

Norway was again targeted by 207 Squadron on 22/23 November, but this time the raid was on Trondheim. Unfortunately, none of the bombs carried by the twelve Lancasters could be dropped as a smoke-screen covered the target, so home they came. After a small-scale mining mission, Munich was raided very successfully on 26/27 November by seventeen aircraft, and the rest of the month was spent in practice bombing and listening to lectures.

Ground crews were by now working round the clock to maintain a high level of aircraft availability, and the messes were working flat out to 'refuel' tired airmen and WAAFs. "Almost everyone was doing two jobs, and the strain was beginning to tell," said Alec Gibson, a member of the radar section. "Tempers were frayed and relationships became brittle. In an effort to ease the burden of over-taxed ground staff, a Company of the Pioneer Corps was brought in. RAF mess food was ample, even lavish by civilian standards [of the time], but by late 1944 shortages were beginning to occur. All messes were given the choice of a meatless day, with a whalemeat option, and tinned liver was a frequent item on the menu. The catering staff became adept at making a meal out of anything, but despite all their wonderful efforts and much ingenuity, the food was boring."

Sect. Off. Sue Kenyon was the Station catering officer at Spilsby, and recalls that everyone moaned about the food. "It certainly wasn't 'home cooked'," she says, "but it *was* well cooked and there was plenty of it. It was difficult to provide a variety, as we were strictly rationed – one egg per month if you were lucky (although there was plenty of dried egg), half an ounce [14.2 gms.] of sugar and an eighth of an ounce [3.5 gms.] of tea per day. There was, however, plenty of bread and jam." The daily financial allowance per head was one and sevenpence halfpenny (about 8p.) and with that Sue Kenyon had to provide four meals for each man, regardless of rank; the cash allocated to a WAAF was one and fivepence (about 7p.) per day! "We were allowed extra money for flying rations, and aircrews were always served bacon and egg before a flight and on their return," continued Sue Kenyon. "They took with them one small tin of orange juice, a two-ounce [57 gm.] bar of chocolate and some chewing-gum. They were the only ones to receive orange juice; we were lucky to have one orange a month and chocolate for the rest of us was unheard of."

207 Squadron crews reported their first sighting of enemy jet fighter aircraft, an Me 262, during a raid by nineteen aircraft on Heilbronn railway yards on 4 December 1944, but no combats took place. This was regarded as a successful raid, although two Lancasters, captained by Plt. Off. G. L. Wall (PB765 EM:B) and Flg. Off. M. J. Lovett (LL968 EM:K), failed to return and those that did experienced some nasty electrical storms on the way home. With this mission behind him, the squadron's bombing leader, Flt. Lt. Linnett, reached his 100th sortie! Eighteen aircraft took part in a raid on the Giessen

marshalling yards north of Frankfurt on 6/7 December, during which the CO, Wg. Cdr. Black, suffered the indignity of having an engine failure twenty minutes before 'over target' time. On this raid Flg. Off. B. J. Henderson (PD322 EM:C) and his crew were lost, but otherwise it was regarded as a worthwhile mission. In snow showers on 8 December, fourteen aircraft took off at about 08.45 to attack Heimbach Dam, a raid which was not regarded as successful, after which they all diverted to Thorney Island, from where they returned to Spilsby next day. Another attempt to strike the dam was made two days later, this time by sixteen aircraft which took to the air between 04.05 and 04.48, but weather conditions worsened, and they were all recalled. Heimbach was not to be let off the hook, however, as fifteen Lancasters took off at noon on 11 December for another attempt, which this time was carried out according to plan. After six days in which only a minor 'gardening' sortie took place, eighteen aircraft left Spilsby at dusk on 17 December to raid Munich; three returned early, one to land at Woodbridge and one at East Kirkby.

207 Squadron's second participation in a raid on Poland began on 18 December, when twelve aircraft took off in the late afternoon bound for Gdynia. Two crews were lost that night, captained by Flt. Lt. J. D. White (LM671 EM:S) and Flt. Lt. D. G. Buchanan (NG144 EM:G), and all the surviving aircraft landed at Kelstern or Strubby due to fog at Spilsby. It was three days before the mist cleared so that they could return to base, which meant that only six aircraft were ready for a mission to Pölitz that night, and of them two aborted. Fine weather appeared on Boxing Day, allowing five Lancasters to take off at lunch-time for a raid on St. Vith, but they were diverted, and did not return for two days. Apart from an early-morning raid on Houffalize on the last day of the year, a few small-scale mining sorties were all that occupied the squadron just before the beginning of the final year of the War.

Six members of the often-neglected ground crews are prominent in the front row of this group, which also features the crew of Flg. Off. P. A. Curd (fourth from left). Mr. Curd fondly remembers his "......very valiant ground crew, who did sterling work of maintaining our aircraft and became our friends". [P. A. Curd]

Spilsby was still easily recognisable from the air when this picture was taken in 1976, although by then the runways were unusable and some building work had taken place.[via R. Winton]

An interesting impress-ion of the life of an NCO on the squadron was contributed by former Sgt. W.W. Burke, a navigator at Spilsby. "For non-commissioned personnel," he says "lacking the facilities of an officers' mess, life was very basic, especially in the winter months. Keeping the Nissen hut stove going was a problem in itself! Sleep was also a problem, for with a mixture of day and night flying there was no routine pattern to the day. One slept – or tried to sleep – at all hours. But for aircrew it was very much a 'macho', 'Boys Own Paper' life with a moments of extreme danger and a tremendous camaraderie – a sense of being a member of an elite wild-drinking girl-chasing society, with frequent home leave." He goes on to say that he was one of the lucky ones who were never shot down or wounded, but he did have 'hairy' moments. "The most frightening was possibly on the night of 6 October 1944 when raiding Bremen," he recalls. "We were in an early wave of the attack as we were dropping 'window' to confuse enemy radar. Flak was intense as we approached the target and one shell exploded immediately below our aircraft, peppering it with shrapnel. It cut the oil pipe lines to the rear turret, thus immobilising it. At that moment, our rear gunner cried out that a Ju 88 night-fighter was coming in to attack. I then 'knew' that within a second or two the entire fuselage length was going to be raked with cannon and machine-gun fire and that I was about to die. Then, miracle of miracles, we passed into cloud and the fighter pilot could no longer see us. We were reprieved, but it didn't do my nerves any good."

That episode illustrates the pressures under which aircrews lived, but according to Bill it pales into insignificance when compared with that of a mid-upper gunner on the squadron who completed his tour of operations and then agreed to fly one more. Over the target his aircraft was badly hit by flak and the pilot gave the order to abandon it. The gunner in question disconnected his intercom and jumped down from his turret into the fuselage to don his parachute, only to fall through a gaping hole in the floor! Incredibly, his parachute harness caught on projecting pipework and he found himself dangling at an altitude of 20,000 feet minus a parachute! Against all the odds, he managed to drag himself back into the Lancaster, climbed back into the turret, connected his intercom and found that the pilot had cancelled the 'abandon ship' order and was merrily steering back to base! Bill Burke admits that danger, with its surges of adrenaline, can become positively addictive, so much so that he volunteered immediately for a second tour and became a navigator on 627 Squadron, 5 Group's low-level visual marking squadron.

Although by the beginning of 1945 207 Squadron crews, and indeed the armed forces in general, must have been aware that it could be only a matter of time before hostilities in Europe would end, there was still a great deal of work to be done. Dawn on 1 January saw five of the squadron's aircraft leave Spilsby for another raid on Gravenhorst, from which all returned but were diverted to Kinloss in Scotland. Another early morning departure was made on 5 January, when seventeen Lancasters took off for Royan, and again all came back, although one Lancaster, flown by Flg. Off. P. Passmore, lost a wing-tip in a collision over the target. Next day there was a problem with bombing-up, and of the twelve aircraft earmarked for an attack on Houffalize only eight were ready at departure time. One of these, NE168 [EM:F], captained by Flg. Off. M. L. Perez, was lost during the operation, five were diverted and two returned to Spilsby. Later in the day, two more Lancasters took part in a mining operation. Munich was the target for fourteen aircraft which took off before dusk on 7 January, all returning safely, although Flg. Off. Rowell's Lancaster had been attacked by a fighter which was driven off by a short burst from the mid-upper gunner. That operation was the last before a week-long period of snow set in, and the squadron crews took up brooms to help clear Spilsby's runways.

It was 13 January before it was possible to take part in the next mission, a raid by eighteen aircraft on Pölitz, with a dusk take-off. During the afternoon of the next day eighteen crews were briefed for a raid on Merseberg, but when it came to take-off time only eleven aircraft were ready. Two returned early with technical difficulties, eight were diverted elsewhere and just one landed at Spilsby. Brüx was the target on 16 January, when eighteen Lancasters left at dusk, but this turned out to be January's last operation, as snow fell heavily on 19 January, compounded a week later by severe frost and fog. All this added up to an impossible situation, and even more snow fell on 30 January.

On the first day of February a thaw allowed twenty-one crews to be briefed for a raid on Siegen with a reasonable chance of carrying out the mission. Twenty of them took off during the evening, the exception being the CO, whose Lancaster suffered a split hydraulic pipe. Another twenty raided Karlsruhe next evening, after which Flg. Off. Hudson reported that his mid-upper gunner had repelled an attack by a Ju 88, which broke away after a few moments. No losses were sustained during these missions, but when the squadron sent twelve aircraft to take part in a raid on Ladbergen on 8 February Flg. Off. L. J. Fowler's Lancaster (NN724 EM:X) did not return. While that raid was taking place, another three aircraft were sowing mines in Kiel Bay.

Nineteen aircraft took off for Politz on 8 February, but two aborted and all returned safely. Flg. Off. Hazel and his crew claimed to have destroyed a Ju 88, while an inconclusive combat with another of the species was reported by Flt. Lt. Simmons. Dresden, centre of a rail network and a vitally important industrial city, was the target for nineteen aircraft which took part in the heavy Bomber Command assault on 13/14 February, but one of them landed at Melsbroek, near Brussels, with instrument trouble and a build-up of ice. Its captain, Flg. Off. Loveless, contrived to spend five days there, enjoying Continental hospitality to the full! He found that drinks such as Absinthe and Pernod could be bought for five to ten francs (6d to a shilling then or 2.5p to 5p. now) and 1930 vintage champagne was fifteen shillings (£0.75) a bottle. Known to his friends, and there were many of them, as 'Ack Toc' or 'China Plate', Loveless was a 'press on' type who had a technique all his own for being in trouble and yet managing to avoid the consequences. He often took part in recreational sorties to local refreshment establishments, using a Morris 8 car operated by a group of officers of like persuasion. When more than four presented themselves for transportation, Loveless, being short in stature, found himself standing with his head through the sun-roof, the rear wheels grating on the mudguards!

Next night Rositz was attacked by fourteen of 207 Squadron's Lancasters, another three having returned when they failed to catch up with the bomber force. Oil installations at Bohlen were raided during the night of 19/20 February by sixteen aircraft, but an attack on that regular destination, Gravenhorst, on 20/21 February had to be abandoned just before the target was reached, as solid cloud presented too much of a problem. Not to be outdone, 207 Squadron sent twelve aircraft there next evening, but unfortunately two crews, those of Flg. Off. T. B. Phelan (PB814 EM:T) and Wt. Off. C. O. Huntley (PB295 EM:I), failed to return. One more mission brought February to a close, when thirteen aircraft took off at 14.00 on the 24th to raid Ladbergen, but one returned early with its starboard outer engine out of action.

Better weather in March brought early sadness to the squadron, when on the second day of the month Lancaster Mk.III ME473 collided with a Lancaster of 57 Squadron while on a night fighter affiliation exercise near Metheringham. Such exercises were very useful in training evasion techniques, and for the fighter pilots they were of equally good value, but there was a risk involved, as the bomber pilots became proficient in making corkscrew manoeuvres. Both aircraft came to earth near Ruskington, but it was several days before the bodies of all the crew were discovered. Captain of the 207 Squadron aircraft, which was carrying seven crew and one passenger, was Flt. Lt. E. McM. Lawson. At the time only seven bodies could be found, one of which could not be identified. The eighth person on board could only be listed as missing, presumed killed. The two men unaccounted for were the bomb-aimer, Flt. Sgt. A. Henderson, and the mid-upper gunner, Sgt. R. C. Banks, whose names are on the Runnymede Memorial. The body of the unidentified crew member was buried, with some of his fellows, in Cambridge City cemetery and the others near their home towns. Over fifty years later, in August 1995, amateur members of an Aviation Archaeology group secured a licence to permit them to search and excavate at Ruskington Fen for the 57 Squadron

207 Squadron's football team, Flg. Off. P. Passmore wearing top hat, Wg. Cdr. Black at rear. [via R.Winton]

Wg. Cdr. J. F. Grey and crew, with Wallace McIntosh on far right. [via B. Goodwin]

Flg. Off. Heap and crew in front of Lancaster EM:A and a bomb trolley carrying a 4,000-pounder. [A. G. Pearce]

Another photograph taken at the same time shows Flt. Lt. Al Hollins and some of the ground crew. [A. G. Pearce]

Ground crew members of 207 Sqn's 'A' Flight at Spilsby with the WAAF who drove their 'gharry'. [A. G. Pearce]

Three cheerful WAAF drivers at Spilsby with their canine pet. [A. G. Pearce]

Armourers of 207 Squadron and their WAAF driver at Spilsby in 1945. [A. G. Pearce]

Two WAAF members of the Spilsby catering staff – LACWs Emily Rawlings and Doreen Matthews. [A. G. Pearce]

Lancaster, from which all the bodies were known to have been removed. In doing so they revealed the wreckage of ME473 and, to their discomfort, a body in the mid-upper turret. This was quickly identified as that of Sgt. Banks, and this allowed the Coroner and the MoD to accept that the unknown body buried at Cambridge was that of Flt. Sgt. Henderson. On 25 October 1996 the situation was corrected at a reburial ceremony held at Cambridge, details of which can be found in Chapter 13.

Further problems were caused on 3 March when Luftwaffe intruders dropped two bombs near Spilsby's runway while eleven of 207 Squadron's Lancasters were returning from a raid on Ladbergen. One aircraft, NG204 [EM:M], captained by Flg. Off. H. V. Miller, was lost during this mission. More losses were sustained on 5/6 March, when Flg. Off. W. S. De Garis and Flg. Off. A. H. Wakeling and their crews in NG230 [EM:F] and ME386 [EM:G] failed to reach Spilsby after a raid on Bohlen. At midday on 6 March police found the remains of NG230 near the mouth of the River Witham near Boston. The body of one NCO was in Boston mortuary, three of the crew were in Boston hospital with varying degrees of injury, but the bodies of the other three crew members, including the captain, were not recovered until next day.

The Old Post Office at Great Steeping was surrounded by various dispersed domestic sites. [K. Mapley]

In another heartfelt comment, Sect. Off. Joyce Brotherton remarked "The drawback to making friends with people from all over the globe was that when they went you felt that you would never see them again. Ours was an RAF squadron, but it was very mixed, especially among the pilots. In addition to [the countries] already mentioned, we had at one time or another among the aircrews several Americans, a South African, a Belgian, a Dutchman, a couple of Jamaicans and a gunner who had, I believe, some Japanese blood in him. [Author's comment: this probably referred to Flt. Sgt. G. Matsumoto, a bomb-aimer]. Life on an operational Station," she continued, "taught one not to mind being laughed at, for you were liable to be ragged about anything and everything. It was rather a desert island-like existence at times when everyone was confined to camp, standing by for uncertain operations when nobody could get away. Everyone got 'cheesed' with the everlasting hanging-about, interspersed with a few 'scrubs' at unearthly hours. At such times, we were thrown upon our own resources and were entirely dependent upon each other for companionship. On the whole, people stood up to it well, but it was an awful 'bind'. Life on a bomber Station was made up of moments of feverish activity and breathless excitement, followed by suspense and, all too often, heartbreak, interspersed with long periods of boredom – but especially boredom!"

Operations had to continue, no matter what the cost in human life and in aircraft, so during the evening of 6 March eleven aircraft took off to raid Sassnitz and two to sow mines. Next evening thirteen Lancasters raided Harburg, and this mission brought a welcome bonus in the shape of a Ju 88 shot down by Flg. Off. French's crew on their way home. A daylight raid by fourteen aircraft on Essen on 11 March and a fifteen-aircraft mission to Dortmund on 12 March were uneventful, but a raid on Lutzkendorf on 14 March was anything but. Sixteen Lancasters took off at about 17.00, and over the target enemy fighters were much in evidence, doing their best to stave off their country's inevitable defeat. Flg. Off. J. E. Cranston's aircraft (NG399 EM:O) was lost, and all but one of the remaining Lancasters diverted to Downham Market on return. The last aircraft, Flg. Off. M. J. Cooke's LL902 [EM:A], went to Little Rissington in Gloucestershire, where it crash-landed at 02.50, with the deaths of six crew members and serious injuries to the seventh, from which he later died.

This raid on Lutzkendorf was the subject of a detailed analysis compiled by Flg. Off. 'Rosie' Rose, who took part in it. It provides a remarkable insight into the procedures followed by the crews and the emotions felt by individuals, and is therefore reproduced here with only minor editing, mainly standardisation of tense.

Into the valley of death.....

"At 11.00 word comes through from the ops. room that we are at war tonight. All of us are immediately wondering who will be on the crew list. The Flight commander suddenly appears and reads the names off. Good, I'm on, and in my own aircraft, EM:X. I immediately tell my boys and we go out and give our aircraft a good run. As soon as the engines are shut down the bomb trolleys and petrol tankers arrive. 'What's the load, boys?' 'Full tanks', is the reply. Gosh! Another long stooge!"

"We go off to the Flight offices once more and then to lunch. During lunch hour the briefing times are put up. Navigators' briefing 16.30, captains' 17.00, main 17.45. We all wonder where in hell the target is. Many of us are betting it's going to be this one or that, but we are very seldom right. I have often put the third degree on Sect. Off. Brotherton (Joyce – 'The Drip' to the Gang), our Intelligence Officer, but no, she won't give out with the gen. We'll have to wait until briefing time. As it's going to be an all-night session, we go off to our barracks for some sleep. Few ever manage to get any. They can't help wondering what it's going to be like and if they will be coming back. Finally, it's time to go down to the briefing room. As we enter the room we find Joyce looking as if she had been dragged through a rat-hole but twice as nasty. We can always tell what the target is going to be like by looking at her. She can never hide things, for her expression gives it all away."

Members of the crew of Lancaster ED802 [EM:M] climbing aboard for another mission. This aircraft survived its service with 207 Squadron to be passed on to 5 Lancaster Finishing School. [207 Squadron archives]

"She gives us the target. It's Lutzkendorf. An oil target again. She hasn't got the route up on the map yet. One or two of the boys usually give her a hand while the rest of them are busy putting the route down on their maps. A few jokes are passed while waiting for the CO to give us the route plans and target marking. First of all he gives us our bomb weight and the all-up weight of the aircraft. Then come our bombing heights. God! We are bombing low tonight – 8,000 to 10,000 feet. I find myself bombing from the lowest height. That means I have to watch out for our own aircraft bombing me as well as enemy fighters and flak. Oh well, it isn't the first time; my crew won't like it, though. Then comes the route plan. We are to stay low until a few miles from the target and then climb to bombing height. After 'bombs gone' we are to descend again and hug the ground all the way back to friendly territory. Well, that's not always a good plan, but we have done it successfully on other occasions. We then get our R/T communications. They, of course, are code words which will be given out by the Master Bomber. He then asks if there are any questions. Usually there are none, so it's off to the main briefing, where we brief our own crews."

A magnificent photograph of the newly-hung bomb-load of a 207 Squadron Lancaster at Spilsby. Houses in the background were on the road from Great Steeping to Firsby. The aircraft is thought to have been EE173, which ended its days in a Berlin lake after a raid on Brunswick on 15 January 1944. [via A. G. Pearce]

"The boys are sitting round the navigator, who is working like hell on his charts. They don't say anything, but are thinking plenty. The bomb-aimer and navigator watch their notes carefully while I give them the gen. 'All this business should be easy tonight, boys', I tell them. Various remarks come back at me, but I know they are all with me. Now comes the Senior Intelligence Officer with the target defences and methods of escape should we get shot down. There are a hundred heavy and seventy-five light flak guns and approximately fifty searchlights. Not a very healthy effort. The boys start to squirm a bit, but remember other reports of targets somewhat similar when it turned out to be very mild. Still, that isn't saying this one will be the same. 'Christ! This one is going to be hot', says the rear gunner. The met. man says the weather will be favourable at the target, so it is all over now. The CO wishes us a good trip and announces that there will be coffee and sandwiches in the locker room. That isn't so good, going all that way on stinky cheese sandwiches and coffee. Still, what else can we do? We are pushed for time. Everybody makes a dash for the door to be first at the coffee. As the captains pass the door they hand in all notes. Everything has been jotted down in our minds by now, so no need for the notes. We can't take them with us, anyway. Back in the locker room all the crews are busy getting their flying kit out and also their parachutes and Mae Wests. I see that all my boys have emptied their pockets. It takes quite a while to get dressed up in a complete kit, especially for the gunners. They have a pretty cold job back there."

"We finally are ready to go out to the kite – all of us bar the navigator. He stays behind to work out his flight plan and get any last-minute instruct-ions. We get outside and wait for the transport. As our pals pass by, wishes for a good trip are passed by both parties. We wonder as we see them fooling around if they will be around tomorrow. We also wonder if we will be back to join in it. That soon passes when the transport arrives. Ah! It's my favourite gal at the wheel. She pulls up right beside me and I get the front seat. 'X X-Ray, old gal. The best kite in the squadron'. 'OK, Rosie' is the reply. When we get to the aircraft the ground crew are waiting for us. They carry my parachute and put it up in the cockpit for me. Then we all get in and give the engines and turrets a thorough check. Everything is OK so we shut down the engines and climb out for a smoke. This is the worst time for many crews. It's the hanging about waiting for something to happen. Will the trip be scrubbed? Finally, the navigator appears and gives the take-off time right to the minute. That leaves us with about ten minutes before starting up and taxying out. Time for another smoke before getting in."

"The ground crew boys are all around and though very anxious to know where we are going they never ask. They are very good that way. At last it's time to get in and away. The engineer says 'All OK for starting, skipper', and then one by one the four engines roar into life. The navigator checks his DR compass, the rear gunner and mid-upper gunner are in position. By this time nearly all the aircraft are ready to go. 'OK boys, here we go' as I release the brakes. The aircraft starts rolling and we are away on another trip. We taxi down the perimeter [track] to the take-off position in our correct order. It's a very nice sight seeing all the aircraft nose to tail following each other round to the take-off position. Just before turning onto the runway for take-off, I check over the cockpit to see if all is OK. I think

Two Lancasters on the dispersal in early 1945. The one facing the camera, NG245 [EM:R], was decorated with a skull-and-crossbones motif and became known as Jolly Roger. On 3 May 1945 it crash-landed in a potato field near Spilsby and never flew again, although it was not formally struck off charge until 23 March 1949. [via R. Winton]

about the load. 67,000 pounds all-up weight. God! That's a lot of weight to get airborne. Still, a Lancaster will do it. I hope my engines don't fail us. I'm now at the end of the runway. The tail light of the aircraft in front is disappearing fast. 'There it is', says the engineer as we get the green light from the airfield controller. The crowd wave us goodbye as I open up the throttles. The engines sound good. 'OK boys, stand by for take-off'. I release the brakes and we are away. The end of the runway looms up, and then it's 'Full power, engineer'. 'OK, skipper, she's unstuck now'. 'Undercarriage up, engineer'. 'OK, skip'. 'Climbing power after flaps in, engineer'. 'OK' says the engineer and then we set course."

"It's a very clear night over England. The stars are all out and we feel as if the sky belongs to us. That early empty feeling seems to have gone for the moment. Then as time goes by we see aircraft coming from every direction to the concentration point. As we cross the English coast on the way out we hope we are going to see it again. The bomb-aimer breaks the silence. 'Crossing coast, navigator. Bombs selected and fused.' Then silence again. Everyone but the navigator is busy searching the sky for aircraft, as by now our navigation lights are out. The rear gunner reports – 'Aircraft crossing just above.' I look up and see it's a Lancaster. By this time we are well inside France and within an hour and a half of the target. As time draws nearer to H-Hour the tension and strain on our nerves seem greater. I call up the gunners in turn every ten minutes. They answer 'Everything OK back here, skip.' As we cross the front line we keep a very sharp lookout for fighters and flak and any searchlights. Half an hour before H Hour I turn on the VHF [R/T] and listen in for instructions from the Master Bomber. Nothing is heard until about five minutes before the first target indicators go down. Just the usual routine. The Master Bomber calls up his marker leaders and ensures good reception. 'There it goes', says the engineer. The first marker is going down. It's dead ahead of us. 'Good work, navigator. We're dead on track'.

"Suddenly, but right on the minute, the sky is lit up with flares which are over the marking point. Everything seems bright as day. This is the time to really start looking for fighters, as we are silhouetted against the sky now. An easy target for any fighter behind us. I look ahead again and see more markers going down. Visibility on the ground isn't very good, but the PFF boys are doing OK. These boys really have guts. Flak has started coming up. Suddenly all hell lets loose. A stream of tracer bullets is just missing my port wing and crossing the nose. The rear gunner says 'Corkscrew port, go!' but I've beaten him to it! I'm going down in a hell of a dive and just as I start pulling out more tracer starts coming from the starboard side. Hell! I've got two fighters on me. I push it down further and then pull up very tightly. They come at me again. Again I push it down. During all this my gunners are firing like mad. They can't see any results but tell me 'Keep going, skip.' Suddenly the fighters break off. I find myself four thousand feet below my bombing height. The engineer gives me full climbing power, but it's no use. I can't get up there in time. The target is nearly underneath me. I level out for a bombing run. The bomb aimer says 'Steady, skip, you're coming up fine. This marker is right in there.' Suddenly the sky is lit up with a horrible blinding flash. 'An aircraft has just blown up behind us, skip', says the rear gunner. All around us the flak is bursting like mad. They sure are giving us a hot time. 'Just wait a few seconds' I say to myself. 'They will be getting far more than they expect.' 'Bombs gone' says the bomb-aimer, 'steady now for camera run.' I am going through the target at 6,000 feet and the flak is uncomfortably close. At last the camera goes off as there is a hell of a big explosion underneath us. That target sure is catching hell. I then push the nose down and go like hell out of the target area."

"After the heat of action in the target area, the still black night around it has queer things in store. One never knows what is lurking in the darkness waiting to pounce. I call up my crew to see if all are OK. They are, and the engineer reports all engines OK. That's a grand relief to me. So far, so good. Now for the homeward journey. About an hour away from the target, the rear gunner reports an aircraft coming in underneath. He orders me to stand by, as he thinks it's a fighter. Sure enough, it is. For a solid half hour that Ju 88 stays with us, always just a bit in front and below. My gunners have fired all their ammunition on him, so it's just a case of keeping on moving about. I do everything I can to try to shake him off. For brief moments I do, but he comes back again. Aircraft are going down one after another to the port of us. They are being shot down by the same sort of kite that is on me. The boy that is after me is not going to find me an easy target if I can help it. None of his bullets comes very close to us and finally he gives it up. I am very thankful and also mighty tired. This is my worst night yet."

"When over England, diversionary messages are sent out. Only a handful of aerodromes are clear enough to land on. Our petrol is rather low, so we are getting rather anxious. Finally, the aerodrome we are looking for [Downham Market] looms up and in no time we are down on the ground and engines are shut down. We search our aircraft for damage, and on finding it in A1 condition thank God for such a close escape from death. We go into the briefing room and are interrogated by Intelligence Officers. They have so many damn silly questions to ask. We also have a very healthy slug of rum to help quieten our nerves. This works very well for me, because I have three good-sized rations of it. We are given a good meal of bacon and eggs and then a bed. By now it is 09.00 hours."

Ironically, the raid described so graphically above was a failure, as the marker flares had been dropped in the wrong place. This fact nearly broke the hearts of those who had risked their all, for they felt that their tribulations had been in vain. Since only slight damage had been caused to the factory, it was almost certain that a repeat performance would be ordered, but nobody wanted to go, and in fact everyone dreaded the thought.

............rode the five hundred

For the squadron crews, the last few weeks of the war in Europe were not quite as busy as they might have anticipated. Wurzburg was the target for an evening raid on 16 March by thirteen aircraft, but then came a break of a week before an attack on Bohlen by thirteen aircraft and on Halle by another three. That night, 20/21 March, Flg. Off. R. A. Lewis and his crew in PA196 [EM:D] failed to return. Another crew, headed by Flt. Lt. R. L. Werner, was lost in ME522 [EM:X] on 22 March during a raid on Hamburg in which fourteen Lancasters of 207 Squadron participated. An early evening take-off by sixteen aircraft was made on 23 March for a vital raid on Wesel to facilitate the crossing of the river Rhine. During the mission Flt. Lt. W. A. Verrals, not wishing to be left out, flew the entire sortie on three engines! Next day, an airborne force was put down in the Wesel bridgehead in a huge operation. Afterwards, Field Marshal Bernard Montgomery wrote in a letter to Air Chief Marshal Sir Arthur Harris "The bombing of Wesel was a decisive factor in the capture of the town..............the air attack was a masterpiece."

Little did the eighteen crews who flew on the next mission, a daylight raid on Nordhausen on 4 April, imagine that three weeks later 207 Squadron would fly its last operation! Unfortunately, some of them would never reach that wonderful day. All went well for a few days during which raids on Molbis and Lutzkendorf were mounted, but on 10 April during an evening attack on the Wahren railway yards at Leipzig Flt. Lt. P. M. Anderson DFC and his crew were shot down near the village of Burgbrohl, north-west of Koblenz. This mission is remembered vividly by former mid-upper gunner Sgt. John Pearl. "We were airborne at 18.07 in ME472 [EM:O], and except for a malfunction on 'George' [the automatic pilot] the flight proceeded without incident until we reached the target area, where fires were still burning after an earlier raid by Lancasters and Halifaxes of 6 and 8 Groups" he recounts. "We had been briefed to do a support run eight minutes before H-Hour and so began to track across the yards as the PFF markers began to go down. Some light flak appeared ahead of us but it was spread thinly across the sky and did not look too formidable. However, the black puffs of smoke from the predicted heavy flak seemed dangerously close, and it was one of those shells that exploded off to starboard as we continued our run across the target. As the plane was rocked and buffeted by the blast I fell out of the turret and lay for a few seconds as shrapnel rattled on the fuselage like hailstones. The skipper steadied the aircraft and I climbed back into the turret to find it badly holed and most of the perspex dome blown away. A quick check on crew stations established that all crew members were unharmed. Sgt. Ted Nicholls, the flight engineer, walked through the aircraft and reported damage to the fuselage in addition to that sustained by the mid-upper turret. The starboard mainplane had taken some flak and both starboard engines had lost oil pressure and were feathered." Nevertheless, Flt. Lt. Anderson and his crew continued round and made their bombing run. After about ninety minutes the port inner engine began to lose oil pressure, and the crew decided to prepare to abandon the aircraft. There was no panic, as they had practised the drill many times. They jumped into the blackness, and saw their Lancaster hit the ground and explode. Sgt. Pearl landed in a small clearing in a wood and decided to await daylight before deciding what to do. By this stage of the war the area in which the crew had dropped was in American hands, so it was not long before the crew were being looked after by GIs, apart from Flt. Lt. Anderson, who did not survive. The remains of his body were found near the crash site and identified by Flg. Off. Hewitt and Sgt. Eric Matthews, who recognised his boots, nothing more. Cyril Hewett was more than pleasantly surprised by their reception. "I remember one of our rescuers breaking eggs into a pan," he says. "He said 'Say when', but by the time I realised his meaning I had three fried eggs and half a tin of Spam for breakfast! Later that day we were taken to the monastery at Maria Lach, where an RAF unit was based. They were generous in their hospitality, so generous that I can remember little of the evening and night. Next morning they gave us an unlabelled bottle of brandy (from the cellars?) and we were taken to Brussels by Jeep. In the evening we were let loose in the city......picked up by the Military Police and escorted back to our hotel. Next day we flew back to the UK in a Dakota, landing at Down Ampney, where we were picked up by Flt. Lt. Mathieson and taken back to Spilsby in a Lancaster." This crew was in fact the last one of 207 Squadron to be shot down.

A night raid on Pilsen in Czechoslovakia on 16/17 April followed, and on return the fourteen crews were told that the number of sorties per tour had been reduced to 30, which brought an instant end to the proceedings for Sqn. Ldr. Belasco, Flg. Off. Hudson and others. That night sixteen aircraft took off to raid Cham without loss. Flensburg was the target for an afternoon raid by twelve Lancasters on 23 April, but no bombs were dropped after low cloud was found over the target.

Flt. Lt. Peter Anderson DFC and his crew, shot down on 10 April 1945, the last 207 Squadron crew to suffer that fate. Back row: 1st right Flg. Off. Ken Larcombe (bomb-aimer); 2nd right ? (ground crew); 3rd right Flt. Lt. Peter Anderson; others ground crew. Front row: 1st left Sgt. Ted Nicholls (flight engineer); 2nd left Sgt. Eric Matthews (rear gunner); 3rd left ? (ground crew); 4th left Sgt. Vic Collins (WOpAG); 5th left Flg. Off. Cyril Hewitt (navigator); extreme right Sgt. John Pearl (mid-upper gunner). [John Pearl]

John Pearl remembers with affection the Smith family, headed by Bert, an electrical engineer with the Mid-Lincs Electric Supply Co., who was a regular at the 'Bull' in Spilsby. Bert had served in the Royal Navy in the First World War after lying about his age, and had tried to enlist in the second war, but was rejected due to his reserved occupation. At his home he and his wife Winifred and sixteen-year-old daughter Audrey made John and his fellow crew members very welcome, and they went to dances and other functions together. The Smiths even invited the parents of the crew to stay with them, but only Ken Larcombe's were able to take up this offer. "Knowing Bert and his family was a great morale-booster," says John. "They provided a reassuring touch with family and civilian life away from the discipline and routine of the squadron."

Last orders, please!

207 Squadron's final mission was flown on 25 April 1945. During the previous morning a signal had arrived allowing the squadron to stand down until the following day, so the opportunity was taken to arrange a party, the first for a year or so, to celebrate the completion of their tours by a number of aircrew. All was being prepared, the mess was being decorated with flowers, and the cooks, helped by two WAAF officers, were excelling themselves in preparing the supper, when at 17.45 a message came through from 55 Base that an early morning operation was being planned after all. Very soon the details were received – ten Lancasters were to join others in an attack on Hitler's Berchtesgaden chalet, the SS barracks nearby and the Führer's mountain refuge, known as the Eagle's Nest, which 617 Squadron would try to eliminate. A Tannoy message was broadcast confining all aircrews to the Station, but by then the NCOs had left on 'jollies' to such places as Skegness and Boston. Ten Lancasters of 207 Squadron took off at around 04.00, and their crews, approaching the target area, began to look out for the promised proximity markers, which were intended to give some idea of the location of the barracks. They could see no sign of them, and it transpired later that they were never dropped, due to a technical problem. So the crews found themselves flying in a maze of snow-covered mountain peaks and rocky valleys. Captains found it very difficult to identify the target before overshooting, as their track brought them over a mountainside almost before the target became visible. As the briefing instructions laid down that the target must be positively identified before bombs were released and the crews were forbidden to orbit, there was no second chance. It is hardly surprising, therefore, that the bombing pattern was scattered and that two crews brought their bombs back. Accurate flak was another reason not to linger, and three of the squadron's aircraft were hit, but all returned safely. Subsequent reconnaissance showed that three direct hits were made on the chalet, destroying part of the main building, while in the SS barracks one entire block had been demolished and the top storey of another wrecked. 207 Squadron dropped 33.5 tons of hardware on the target, and first aircraft back was EM:X, piloted by Flt. Lt. W. A. Verralls, whose last trip of the tour it was. Although militarily there was not much to be gained by this raid, it boosted morale a great deal. Another raid, this time on Heligoland, was detailed, but weather conditions meant that it was 'scrubbed' at the last minute.

What a feeling of anti-climax there must have been when no more operations were planned! After nearly six years of unremitting effort it was all over in Europe bar the shouting. The thoughts of many of the ground and air crews turned, somewhat prematurely perhaps, to demobilisation, but first the war in the Far East had to be won.

Exodus

There was still a very important task for 207 and many other squadrons to handle – the job of carrying recently-released prisoners of war from the Continent to the UK. To cope with this, Operation 'Exodus' was organised. Each Lancaster was hurriedly fitted with rough-and-ready seating for twenty-four passengers, and reception centres were established on airfields in the south of England. From Germany, C-47 aircraft of the USAAF flew the released men to either Brussels (Melsbroek) in Belgium or to Lille and Juvincourt in northern France, where they were transferred to the Lancasters. Each captain was responsible for checking his passengers on board by means of lists provided to him. At first, it was decided that bomb-aimers and mid-upper gunners would not be carried on 'Exodus' flights, although if the weather was poor a bomb-aimer was included to act as a second navigator. 207 Squadron's first involvement was on 2 May 1945, when seven aircraft flew to Brussels. There the crews found that C-47s had already deposited some of their passengers, and these 48 men were then flown to the reception centre at Westcott in Buckinghamshire.

When the two Lancasters crossed the English coast some of the former prisoners cheered wildly, but others were so worn out by their recent lives that they remained silent. At Westcott, where they were given a great welcome, a good meal was provided in a hangar, where the men could sit in armchairs and listen to a band. Meanwhile, the other five crews waited for three hours, but when their passengers had not arrived they flew home empty. By the time twelve Lancasters took off for Brussels two days later the operation was running smoothly, and 288 men were brought back to Westcott. Among them was Sgt. McCarthy, the rear gunner in Wg. Cdr. Wheeler's aircraft, which had been shot down during the night of 22/23 April 1944 while raiding Brunswick. A member of another squadron, Bill Simmonds had spent some time in Stalag Luft IIIA and was one of those brought home in a Lancaster from Brussels. "It was a thrill to take off and stand in the astrodome and watch as we crossed the English coast and finally to land at Westcott, where I had been an instructor before I had gone back on operations," he said recently. "I soon had a group of WAAFs and airmen around me, shaking hands and hugging me. I was invited to a dance that night in the NAAFI by the WAAFs and to an impromptu party in the Officers' mess, but the powers that be told me that I had to go to Bicester, as per orders."

An unfortunate event took place on 3 May and is recalled by Flt. Lt. Andy Mathieson, who had volunteered to take a new crew on a familiarisation and categorisation flight. On the way out to the aircraft he was hijacked to help the soccer team in a squadron match, so Flg. Off. Loveless said he would take the new crew on a familiarisation flight only and would make sure that the Authorisation Book was altered accordingly. In the air in NG245 [EM:R], he told the new pilot to feather one propeller and then to switch on the fuel to start the engine

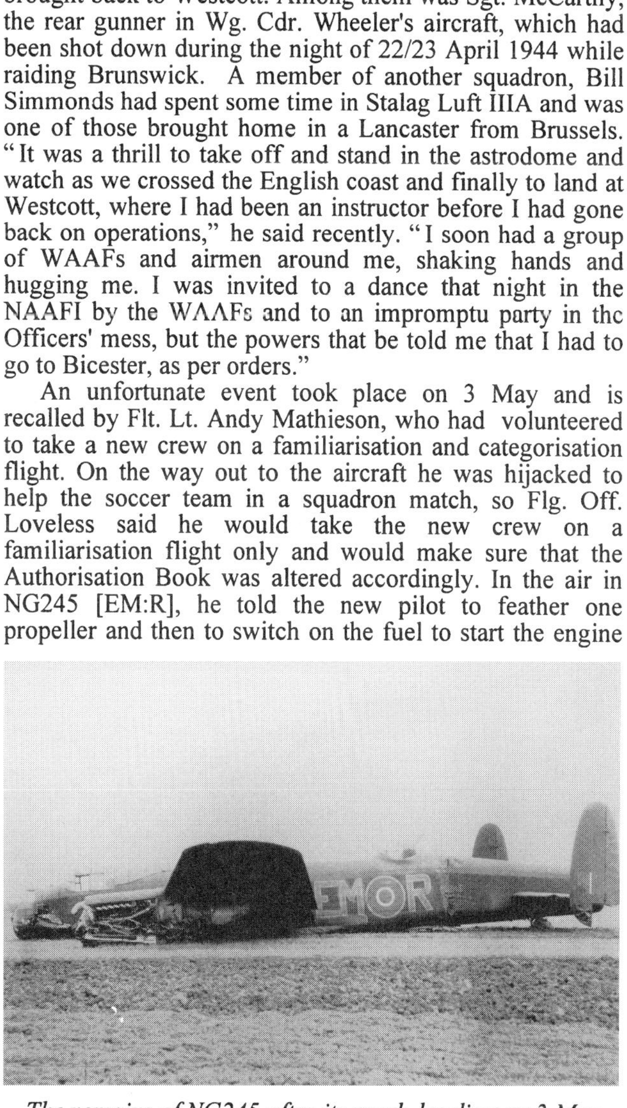

The remains of NG245 after its crash-landing on 3 May 1945. [via R. Winton]

The bombing section of 207 Squadron in April 1945. In the background is a Lancaster of 44 Squadron. [via R. Winton]

No more shots to be fired in anger! 207 Squadron air gunners in May 1945. [via R. Winton]

Wireless operators of 207 Squadron, complete with a radio set, pose for the camera in May 1945. [via R. Winton]

Cheerful because the war in Europe had just ended, the members of the MT section at Spilsby, of which a large proportion were WAAFs, pose in June 1945. [K. Mapley]

An end-of-war photograph of the 207 Squadron navigators, taken at Spilsby in May 1945. [207 Squadron archives]

Lancaster PB764 [EM:L] stands forlornly at Spilsby just after the end of the war, its serial number now displayed under the wing. This aircraft was struck off charge on 2 November 1945. In the background is the 44 Squadron hangar. [via R. Winton]

again. Instead, between them they managed to turn another engine off! This caused the Lancaster to yaw, and it crash-landed in a potato field east of the airfield, crunching over an embankment as it did so. Some six weeks later, Flt. Lt. Mathieson had to see the Base Commander, who blamed him for the incident, but then the matter seems to have been dropped. Furious about taking the blame for someone else's misbehaviour, however, Andy changed his mind about staying in the RAF after the war.

Apart from 'Exodus', a plan was formulated to bomb the surviving guns on Heligoland on 4 May, but when news came through that the island and the whole of northern Germany had surrendered the mission was 'scrubbed'.

Aircrew relaxing at the home of Mr. and Mrs. Bert Smith in June 1945: Back row left to right: Sgt. John Pearl, Sgt. Eric Matthews, Flg. Off. Cyril Hewitt, Mr. Bert Smith, Sgt, Vic Collins. Front row left to right: Sgt. Ted Nicholls, Miss Audrey Smith, Miss Phyllis Codd (an evacuee), Mrs. Winifred Smith. [Ken Larcombe]

It's all over!

When the end of hostilities in Europe finally came most of the squadron personnel were too dazed to take in the news. There was no outburst of excitement, which might have been expected, though many people made for the bar to celebrate by having a drink or two. On 8 May the squadron paraded at 15.00 to hear the VE Day proclamation by the Prime Minister and then to an address by the CO. That day eight Lancasters of the squadron flew to Juvincourt to find that the C-47s which had brought the former prisoners from Germany were still taking off, so 207 Squadron aircraft had to orbit for forty minutes. After another hour, however, they were airborne, this time on their way to Dunsfold in Surrey. Six aircraft went to Brussels on 10 May, with Wg. Cdr. Black flying the spare Lancaster carrying servicing personnel in case of technical trouble. No UK destination is recorded for that day's operation.

Due to the rough condition of the airfields on the Continent, it was decreed on 12 May that only pilots with at least a hundred hours on the Lancaster would be permitted to take part in 'Exodus'. That day, fifteen aircraft made for Brussels, but while still airborne they were recalled due to an impending severe storm. Some, however, had already landed, and to their pleasure were told to stay in Brussels overnight, but this order was soon countermanded, and they flew home without passengers. To speed the process up, new turn-round procedures were implemented on 14 May in an attempt to emplane passengers in ten minutes and thus obviate the stopping of aircraft engines. Passengers would be briefed by two officers who flew with the support aircraft. Seventeen Lancasters of 207 Squadron took part in that day's 'Exodus' by flying to Lille, and all, except one which was damaged while taxying, brought back the usual

Captains of 207 Squadron at Spilsby on 22 May 1945, no doubt very relieved to have survived the war unscathed. Back row, left to right: Flg. Off. R. Watters RNZAF; Flg. Off. F. Chambers RCAF; Flg. Off. Sheenan RCAF; Flg. Off. Blair RCAF; Flt. Lt. Claxton; Flg. Off. Robertson RNZAF. Centre row: Flg. Off. Moore USA; Flg. Off. P. Passmore; Flg. Off. Boyle RCAF; Flg. Off. L. C. French; Flg. Off. Harker; Flg. Off. B. Inglis RAAF; Flg. Off. W. H. Adams. Front row: Flg. Off. King RAAF; Flt. Lt. Chisholm RAAF; Flg. Off. R. Orr RAAF; Sqn. Ldr. Howes ('B' Flt. CO); Wg. Cdr. Black (CO); Flg. Off. Hughes (adjutant); Flg. Off. Morten RAAF; Flg. Off. M. Halewood; Flg. Off. Chambers; Flt. Lt. Downing. [via R. Winton]

AVM H. A. Constantine, who replaced AVM Sir Ralph Cochrane as AOC of 5 Group on 15 January 1945, visited Spilsby on 30 July 1945. 75 (New Zealand) Squadron had recently changed places with 44 (Rhodesian) Squadron, and in this picture the personnel of 75 and 207 Squadrons are on parade. In the background are Lancasters of 75 Squadron. [via R. Winton]

Personnel of 207 Squadron march past the saluting base on the occasion of the AOC's visit on 30 July 1945

complement of passengers. Turn-round time was about forty minutes. That was the last time 207 Squadron was involved in 'Exodus', an operation in which Bomber and Transport Commands between them brought no less than 95,000 former prisoners of war home in a seven-week period, an average of about two thousand every day.

On 15 May five aircraft took selected ground crew members on a four-hour 'Cooks Tour' of Germany to show them the results of the long bombing campaign to which they had contributed so magnificently. Cities seen were Cologne, Dusseldorf, Essen, Gelsenkirchen, Neuss and Duisburg, and one pilot described Cologne as " like a gravel heap". More such flights were made next day.

The squadron's Australian personnel were posted to Skellingthorpe on 1 June 1945 for repatriation, followed a week later by Canadians, who went to Rufforth. In the words of Joyce Brotherton at the time: " And so the Crazy Gang was broken up and scattered to the ends of the earth, but the spirit that inspired it remains. Neither time nor distance can ever really separate us, for we are bound together by a friendship based on a common experience and a common memory, from which has sprung a strong affection which will remain with us – always". Those touching words will be echoed by many.

Although the departure of so many left a marked shortage of both air and ground crews, it was possible to put a maximum effort into dropping surplus incendiary bombs into the North Sea on 9 June. Three details were flown — the first by twelve Lancasters at 08.00, the second at 14.30 by fourteen aircraft, and the last at 20.30 by fifteen aircraft. Apart from a little excitement on 16 June, when five aircraft were detailed for an air/sea rescue search of an area of North Sea, the month was taken up by continuation training, with a total flying time logged of 787 hours 15 minutes.

Plans for the formation of 'Tiger Force' to help bring the continuing war in the Far East to a close were now in hand, and 207 Squadron was notified that it was to be part of the force. When 44 Squadron left Spilsby on 19 July seven of its crews volunteered to transfer to 207 Squadron in exchange for seven of 207's who wished not to take part in the new effort. However, the war against Japan came to a sudden end and, after a VJ-day parade on 15 August marking the end of hostilities, 'Tiger Force' training was discontinued two days later. The squadron retained the modified Lancasters Mk.I (FE) which would have been used in the conflict, and flew them for some years, as will be seen.

Lancasters B.I (FE) TW900 [EM:F] and SW303 [EM:A] of 207 Squadron in formation with TW880 [TL-P] of 35 Squadron.

Chapter 9: Early post-war activities

Operation 'Dodge'

Hostilities were now almost at an end, and a period of anti-climax set in throughout the UK-based Royal Air Force. With the beneficial side effect of helping to maintain a state of readiness and efficiency, 207 and many other squadrons took part in an Operation known as 'Dodge'. The object was to repatriate troops who had been fighting in the Mediterranean area for at least four years and who therefore had priority for leave or demobilisation, a concept which had been raised in the House of Commons as far back as 27 February 1945 by Quentin Hogg MP. It is said that the name 'Dodge' was coined after servicemen in the Middle East adopted the title 'D-Day Dodgers' when somebody erroneously claimed that they were enjoying themselves while those in northern Europe fought the war for them!

Two RAF airfields in Italy, Bari on the Adriatic coast and Pomigliano near Naples, were assigned to handle the flights, although Foggia Main was also used at times. At the UK end, two airfields recently vacated by the US 8th Air Force, Glatton near Peterborough and Tibenham in Norfolk, were chosen as the terminals. Aircraft used were almost all Lancasters, and to carry passengers they were hurriedly modified so that the floor above the bomb-bay could become a rough and ready seating area. The operation began early in August, and 207 Squadron joined in on 28 August, when eight aircraft took off early in the morning bound for Italy. They returned to Spilsby on 1 September, having deposited their loads of twenty soldiers at one of the terminal airfields.

Other activities for 207 Squadron in September included bomb-jettisoning, in which fifteen crews were involved on 6 September, night 'Bullseyes', and Operation 'Spasm' by three crews on 10 September. This Operation was designed to view the damage caused to Berlin during the recent hostilities. Meanwhile ten crews stood by to take part in 'Dodge' on 11 September, but this time the mission was cancelled.

Ten Lancasters of the squadron left Spilsby on 13 September on Operation 'Dodge', and eight returned two days later, the others having landed at Manston and Toulouse. September flying hours were 287 hours 5 minutes on 'Dodge' and 264 hours 40 minutes on general training (which included the disposal of bombs). October began well with twelve aircraft off to Italy on the first day. They returned on 3 October, and four more crews left for Tibenham to pick up replacement army personnel for Italy, only to suffer a cancellation. Nine Lancasters made the trip on 6 October and returned three days later, while a further nine left on 15 October.

Leaving the delights of Spilsby

While the nine crews were in the Italian sunshine, a Movement Order was received at Spilsby instructing 207 Squadron to prepare for a move to Methwold, not far from Kings Lynn, on 30 October 1945. Seven of the nine absent aircraft returned to Spilsby on 18 October, one more having landed at Fulbeck and another at Toulouse. For the time being, no more 'Dodge' flights took place, as packing of equipment and stores was given priority. An advance party under the command of Sqn. Ldr. D. C. Simmons left for Methwold on 26 October and next day ten redundant Lancasters were disposed of to a Maintenance Unit. The main party made the move by air in thirteen Lancasters on 30 October while ground personnel travelled the reasonably short distance by road, taking office equipment with them. Methwold's Station Commander at the time was Gp. Capt. D. H. Burnside DFC, but he was replaced by Gp. Capt. P. G. Chichester on 13 November. Accommodation at Methwold was very cramped, and to make matters worse an increasing rate of demobilisation created a manpower problem.

After the arrival at Methwold of the rear party on 5 November, training began anew. Operation 'Dodge' recommenced when seven aircraft took off on 7 November and flew to Polebrook to pick up personnel for Pomigliano, although one had to land at Woodbridge for attention to its brakes. Two more aircraft left next day for Glatton to collect passengers for Pomigliano but were recalled. Similar SNAFUs were experienced no less than five times in the next few days! It was not until 22 November that five Lancasters left Methwold, this time direct to Bari, only to be diverted to Pomigliano. They returned via Tibenham on 26 and 27 November. Three more left Methwold before the end of the month, and one Lancaster was sent on an organised visit to Berlin (Gatow) via Tibenham, where fifteen passengers were picked up. During the month 220 hours were flown on Operation 'Dodge', 62 hours 25 minutes on training and 5 hours 40 minutes on Operation 'Spasm', the Berlin trip.

207 Squadron's further participation in 'Dodge' flights was then cancelled once more before on 8 December a solitary Lancaster left for Italy and five more flew to Tibenham, only to be recalled to Methwold. Next day another attempt was made by four aircraft which went to Tibenham, where they were immediately stranded by bad weather until 13 December, when they returned to base. The weather also caused several cancellations to further trips to Berlin, although one aircraft did manage it on 19 December, and seven crews made fighter affiliation flights on 20 December. After the Christmas break one Lancaster, captained by Flt. Lt. Oakes, returned from Italy, where it had been grounded for five weeks by poor weather — or so the crew claimed! Flying hours in December totalled only 114 hours 15 minutes, of which 'Dodge' was responsible for 33 and three quarter hours.

Thus ended 207 Squadron's participation in Operation 'Dodge', in which 56 RAF and two SAAF squadrons brought to the UK 55,064 men, mainly soldiers. 207 Squadron had flown 65 sorties, which was an average number, the most (162) being flown by 101 Squadron and the least (1) by 246 Squadron.

The first full year of peace

1946 began with a night-time 'Bullseye' mission for six aircraft, but otherwise the month's 154 hours flying was devoted to continuation training. One minor incident occurred on 29 January when Flg. Off. McGuiness' aircraft, PA304, swung on landing at night on three engines and hit some trees near Station Headquarters, luckily without injury to anyone. The aircraft, however, was a write-off.

Training flights to Italy under Operation 'Jink' began on 5 February when a Lancaster piloted by Flg. Off. McGuiness left Methwold, returning six days later, when another crew carried out the same function. From 12 to 19 February several aircraft were occupied in night-time H2S photography of the city of Hamburg, after which four crews began the disposal of surplus armaments under Operation 'Sincum'. The first such flights were made on 27 February by four aircraft which went to Mildenhall to load the bombs, and seven similar sorties were made in the next few days. On 6 March a start was made on flying Methwold's own surplus away in fourteen sorties spread over ten days. A final mission was flown on 18 March by one aircraft which unloaded its bombs on Heligoland! Two 'Jinks' were also flown in March, a month in which the total flying time was only 188 hours.

An accident befell the CO, the long-serving Wg. Cdr. H. R. Black AFC, on 18 March 1946, when Oxford AB754 of Methwold Station Flight, in which he and Flt. Lt. Linnett were flying, crashed on a hillside near Newton Poppleford in Devon on the way back from Exeter in bad visibility. They were not found until 09.20 next day, after spending over twenty hours in the open, and were taken to the Royal North Devon Hospital to recover. To round off the month, two Lancasters flew to Pomigliano as part of Operation 'Jink' on 26 March, returning two days later. Very little happened in April, as all training was cancelled on 5 April pending a planned move to Tuddenham, near Mildenhall. On 4 April, however, three aircraft went on a special night bombing exercise targeting Heligoland, with three from 149 Squadron. Each Lancaster carried a 500 lb. bomb, and a Master Bomber controlled the attack on target indicators. Shades of 1944!

In view of Wg. Cdr. Black's indisposition, Sqn. Ldr. L. McCracken took over the reins on 18 April. By now the squadron was at a low ebb, with only 44 officers and 113 airmen on the strength. Very little flying had been done that month – just 52 hours – and four Lancasters had been ferried away for disposal. On 25 April what little remained of 207 Squadron began to move by road to Tuddenham, where the same low level of activity continued through May, when a few cross-country navigation flights were made. The summer weather encouraged a few more Lancasters to take to the sky in June, including four on Operation 'Front Line' on 3 June and one on GCA training, probably at nearby Mildenhall. Yet another CO, Sqn. Ldr. G. W. Vowles, took charge of the squadron from 18 June.

Ten aircraft were ferried away in July, when flying hours totalled 262 hours 45 minutes, including two trips to Italy under Operation 'Jink', one on 'Sunbronze' and several on Operation 'Front Line' again. August was quieter, and in September some effort went into ferrying Lancasters to and from Wroughton. October was devoted mainly to various forms of training, principally cross-countries, air-to-sea gunnery, high-level, but on 12 October one Lancaster flew a long-range navigation exercise to Malta, staging through Lyneham before making the journey to Luqa. The first of a series of flights to Malta for affiliation with fighter squadrons based on the island began on 22 October, when one Lancaster flew via St. Mawgan to Luqa, followed on 31 October by another. They returned early in November, in time for the four Lancasters which the squadron now 'owned' to move to Stradishall, a pre-war permanent Station, on 7 November.

207 Squadron's football team won the Bomber Command Trophy in 1946, by which time the squadron was based at Methwold. Unfortunately, no names can be provided for the players. [via R. Winton]

Cheers! The 1946 Christmas party being enjoyed by 207 Squadron personnel, their wives and girl friends. [via J. M. Whitehouse]

Father Christmas paid a visit to Stradishall during the Arctic winter of 1946/47, and is seen here emerging from Lancaster TW880 of 35 Squadron, which was based at Stradishall with 207 Squadron. [via J. M. Whitehouse]

Yet another move!

From their new base three Lancasters flew to Luqa via St. Mawgan on 21 November, returning a week later after useful co-operation with Malta-based fighters. The squadron's aircraft establishment was now six Lancasters Mk.1 (FE) and all six were actually on hand! Due to leave, sickness and demobilisation, however, the average number of crews available to fly was usually in the region of three, and flying in December 1946 totalled a mere 84 in 24 sorties. Three aircraft did take part in Operation 'Wastage', in which eighteen aircraft of 3 Group carried out a formation flight over towns in West Germany at an altitude of 2,000 feet in vics of three in line astern. 207 Squadron's aircraft, SW303 [EM:A] (Sqn. Ldr. Vowles), TW910 [EM:B] (Flg. Off Price), and PB625 [EM:E] (Flt. Lt. Downing) flew in No.3 position for the six-hour flight, which was regarded as useful practice in formation flying and station-keeping.

January 1947 began with a call-out for air/sea rescue duty on the 9th. At 13.23 the squadron crew standing by was notified of wreckage sighted in the Wash, and sixteen minutes later TW869 took off, piloted by Flt. Lt. Downing. After twenty minutes in the air the crew spotted the wreckage but no bodies, and took photographs. The captain was told at 14.22 that Skegness lifeboat was on the way and that he was to orbit over the wreckage, but after nearly two hours of this boring task the recall order came, the lifeboat not having appeared! All concerned were congratulated for their performance.

In the main, the squadron concentrated on cross-country navigation exercises during January, with bomb-dropping whenever possible. Pilots engaged in three-engine approaches and overshoots, with instrument flying in bad weather. Gunnery training over the sea also took place, with affiliation with Meteor aircraft of 56 and 266 Squadrons, based at Wattisham. There was a visit from Air Marshal Sir W. L. Saunders KBE CB MC DFC MM, the AOC-in-C Bomber Command, on 10 January, possibly so that he could see at first hand the poor aircraft serviceability situation. Daily availability was now down to two Lancasters, partly due to a shortage of spare parts and partly to a lack of personnel, particularly instrument and electrical fitters. To occupy those who found themselves unable to carry out their normal tasks, lectures were held daily rather than weekly. Only 26 sorties were flown during the month, a total of 75 hours 30 minutes in the air.

To brighten the situation a little, a highly successful squadron party was held on 15 January as a chance for air and ground crews to fraternise. Music was provided by the Station band, and there was no shortage of dancing partners, particularly nurses from local hospitals.

The Arctic comes to Stradishall!

As far as flying was concerned, February 1947 must go down in the record as being a disaster. The airfield, snow-bound for weeks, was only usable for three half-days at the end of the month, and there was no flying at all until the 28th, when two Lancasters did manage to take off on air tests, four weeks after minor inspections had been completed! Cuts in fuel supply and electricity made most offices almost uninhabitable, while aircraft servicing and ground training were virtually impossible. The only major activities were physical training and snow clearance. To minimise the effects of this Arctic weather, the number of personnel going on leave was increased, but when fuel stocks ran dangerously low it became apparent that the Station might have to close down. The whole Station was then put on a 'super-austerity' status under which no heating was provided during the day, and only the messes were heated after 17.00 hours. Everyone went on a long weekend leave every weekend. All 207 Squadron personnel endured PT three times that month, and on 26 February they took part in a route march, showing surprising enthusiasm for a form of exercise which must have been alien to most. Many remarked that they would like to do it again!

These conditions persisted until 17 March, when the Lancasters began to take to the air again after their enforced idleness. During the previous night a gale had sprung up, gusting to 85 knots. Squadron ground crews were mobilised to sit in aircraft of 207 and other squadrons which had been parked in the open to ensure that control locks remained secure and that the aircraft did not move. None was damaged, and the gale effectively ended the cold spell, much to the relief of all concerned. That very day, Sqn. Ldr. P. J. S. Boggis DFC took charge of 207 Squadron in place of Sqn. Ldr. Vowles. He must have wondered what he had let himself in for!

Although due to a shortfall of twenty-two ground personnel only three of 207's Lancasters were serviceable at once, it was possible on 19 March for the squadron to take part in an exercise with the Home Fleet, of which the flagship was the carrier HMS *Implacable*. The objective was to simulate the conditions of bomber aircraft being homed by Coastal Command aircraft to attack enemy shipping. Watched by students of the Joint Services Staff College, two of 207 Squadron's Lancasters with others of 35, 115 and 149 Squadrons made an attack, and jamming of the ships' R/T was attempted, with unknown results. An effort was made to repulse a fighter, but this was not continued. Afterwards, it was stated that more of these exercises would be welcomed.

An opportunity to indulge in formation flying occurred on 1 April, when two of 207 Squadron's Lancasters joined others from 7, 49, 214 and 148 Squadrons from Upwood, 35, 115 and 149 Squadrons from Stradishall and 90 Squadron from Wyton in a mass fly-past over West Germany. From Marham came a Lincoln and a Mosquito to observe the operation, but an expected fighter interception off Orfordness failed to materialise, to the disappointment of the crews.

Operation 'Wastage' took place again on 13 April, when Lancaster KO:K of 115 Squadron was flown by one of 207 Squadron's five available crews to dump surplus bombs in Cardigan Bay. Although the Met. office had warned the crew that there would be low fog over the sea, they were ordered to proceed. Unable to see the water, they had to bring their bomb-load back, and it was recorded that in future more attention must be paid to the forecasters.

It was now becoming clear that the acute manning situation could no longer be tolerated, and on 15 April the decision was made to pool the ground crews of all squadrons at Stradishall and together with Servicing Wing personnel reallocate them to a Daily Inspection Party, a Handling Party and a detachment at the Major Servicing Unit at Mildenhall. This new system also called for pooling of the aircraft of the based squadrons, and Flying Wing was formed to co-ordinate all flying activity. It was not long before the perceived loss of squadron identity and thus esprit-de-corps was felt. Nevertheless, the 207 Squadron Fund was put on a firm footing at a special meeting during which a committee was elected and a constitution was drawn up, the result being the 'Griffin Club'. This was well supported by all squadron personnel, and visits to London and provincial theatres were organised, parties were thrown, and other activities enjoyed.

Another fleet co-operation exercise, 'Dawn', was held on 27 May, and this time the target consisted of a battleship, an aircraft carrier, three cruisers and several destroyers steaming southward off East Anglia in daylight. Sqn. Ldr. P. J. Boggis DFC led the three 207 Squadron Lancasters, although the H2S equipment in his aircraft soon failed. The ships were not spotted until they were almost underneath the Lancasters, which, although threatened by Meteor and Hornet fighters, dropped bombs from 10,000 feet, presumably being careful that they did not hit anything! After heading out to sea and turning to re-establish the formation, the Lancasters were again attacked by fighters but dropped more bombs from 12,000 feet in poor visibility. By this time the fleet had split into two, going in different directions. At de-briefing, it was felt that in reality the Lancasters would not have been able to penetrate the fighter screen. Valuable lessons were thus learned.

During June 1947 the squadron's strength was again reduced by the demobilisation of many NCO aircrew members, particularly engineers, gunners and signallers. An extra burden was thus placed on those remaining, to several of whom the AOC 3 Group, AVM L. Darvall CB MC, spoke when he paid a visit on the 23rd of the month. Only two crews were available during the June week in which the squadron was on air/sea rescue standby. Nevertheless, a preliminary message came from Bomber Command on 19 June warning that 207 Squadron would be detached to Shallufa in the Canal Zone for Operation 'Sunray' four weeks later.

Before that happened, one 207 Squadron crew, that of Flt. Lt. J. W. Downing, took part in Operation 'Goodwood Bullseye', flying a Lancaster of 115 Squadron to bomb Heligoland from 18,500 feet during the night of 30 June/1

Three Lancasters Mk.I (FE) in white livery fly past during what appears to be an open day at Mildenhall, with a similar aircraft, coded EM:F and therefore probably TW930, on the ground. [via A. Thomas]

July. Most of Bomber Command was involved in this exercise, which was regarded as very successful, although fighter interception expected over Germany and the UK did not materialise. There was also another week of ASR standby for the only two crews to cope with during June.

An administrative change took place on 10 July 1947, when all officers and NCO aircrew except the CO were posted to Station HQ, RAF Stradishall and then detached to any squadron based there, according to demand. This did absolutely nothing to improve morale!

The first 'Sunray'

Then, for four crews, came the excitement of the long trip to Egypt. On 15 July Sqn. Ldr. Boggis in OJ:S of 149 Sqn., Flt. Lt. Downing in KO:J of 115 Sqn. and Flg. Off. Morris in TL:C of 35 Sqn. took off from Stradishall, carrying a spare crew and a few ground crew airmen, bound for Lyneham. After intensive briefing by Transport Command on navigation aids and weather to be experienced during the flight, the crews were frustrated by bad weather, which caused a 24-hour postponement to the next leg. They eventually took off at 09.30 on 17 July for Castel Benito in Libya, and poor weather over France made them use the standard Transport Command 'bad weather route', but when they reached the Mediterranean Sea the sun shone through. The first aircraft landed at Castel Benito at 17.20 local time. Next day two aircraft took off at 10.20, leaving TL:C to follow an hour later after an oil seal problem had been corrected. Over the Libyan desert the air was very turbulent, this not being the best time of day to be in the air. Great interest was shown by the crews when they saw below the remains of battles of four or five years earlier, with burnt-out tanks and trucks strewn over the vastness of the desert. Average flying time was five and a half hours to Shallufa, where the crews were greeted by Gp. Capt. Coates, the Station Commander. As this was a Friday, a weekend in which to become acclimatised was enjoyed.

Training began at Shallufa on 21 July, not helped by the fact that OJ:S needed a carburettor change, which took three days. It was intended that three two-hour details would be flown each day, plus one night flight, but minor snags developed after almost every flight. The hard-pressed ground crews, sixteen men in all, had difficulty in coping, the more so when a Lincoln of 90 Squadron was attached to 207 Squadron for trials of the automatic pilot Mk.9. Fighter affiliation with Spitfires of 32 Squadron, based at Ein Shemer in Palestine but attached to Shallufa, began on 23 July, and keen interest shown by the Spitfire pilots gave

Lancasters of 207 Squadron in formation from Stradishall. Clear plastic H2S radomes are prominent in this picture. [J. Eady via J. M. Whitehouse]

a boost to the 207 Squadron crews. Gp. Capt. Collard, the Station Commander at Stradishall, arrived at Shallufa in a Lancaster that day for a two-day visit. All too soon, the detachment was over, flying ending on Friday 26 July.

At Shallufa, the 207 Squadron crews considered that the food and accommodation were excellent, better in fact than they had anticipated. Their messes were comfortable and fly-proofed, a major consideration in that part of the world. When work finished at 13.30 each day, buses were provided to take swimmers to the Station Lido on the Great Bitter Lake, and on liberty runs to Suez, Fayid and Ismailia. However, the 207 Squadron officers felt and looked a little out of place in the mess as they had been issued with bush shirts instead of the prescribed smart khaki shirt to be worn with a black tie!

The three Lancasters left Shallufa at 07.10 on 29 July and flew in formation with the Lincoln as far as Ismailia, and then singly to Castel Benito, where they landed at 13.05. More technical trouble plagued TL:C, which had to be left behind in the charge of Flt. Lt. W. J. Powell when the others took off next morning at 02.10, bound for Lyneham. They arrived there at 09.10, but bad weather delayed their take-off on the final leg to Stradishall, where they touched down at 13.30. The recalcitrant TL:C (which needed Tender Loving Care!) arrived next day as its pilot had suffered from Montezuma's Revenge!

In general, 'Sunray' was seen as an excellent period of training which provided individuals with the chance to show initiative and allowed the CO to exercise more discretion than usual. It also boosted morale and allowed those involved a glimpse of service life overseas. However, ten days was considered too short; due to two weekends intervening, the 207 Squadron crews had only had five days of flying. Four weeks was proposed as a minimum period. The sixteen ground crew men worked long and hard but were not numerous enough to service the four aircraft. Had a longer time at Shallufa been sanctioned, cross-country flights to such places as Aden and Khartoum could have been made, with on-route bombing practice and fighter affiliation. Even so, the trip gave vital practice in long-range flying outside the range of Gee, with incidental communic-ations problems, as the radio operators found that they were unable to contact 3 Group HQ by W/T after leaving Lyne-ham!

Back at Strad-ishall, August 1947 provided the best weather of the year. Aircrew numbers continued to diminish, however, there being only two effective crews during the second half of the month. These had to stand by for ASR duties for five days and to make three passenger-carrying trips, two of them to Northern Ireland. In addition, preparations for the forthcoming Battle of Britain Day had to be made.

Another alteration to administration was made in August, when the squadron was divided into two Flights for administration, disci-pline and welfare, No.1 under Flt. Lt. A. G. Douglass and No.2 under Flt. Lt. J. S. Pugh DFC. One of the objects of this move was to ensure that junior officers exper-ienced practice in what would today be called man-manage-ment.

Fitting of low-level bombsights Mk.III began in September, and the aircrew situation eased a little when another crew arrived. They were in time to take part in the Stradishall 'Open Day' on 20 September, when squadron members were involved in various activities such as static displays and formation flying. The CO and thirty airmen attended the Battle of Britain church parade at Ely Cathedral next day, while other personnel were at Bury St. Edmunds on similar duty.

The first participation in Exercise 'Ding Dong' took place on 24 September, when Lancaster OJ:Y of 149 Squadron was flown by a 207 Squadron crew to Syerston before setting off to make a dummy attack on the Carfax crossroads in the centre of Oxford. Climbing from a height of 10,000 to 25,000 feet, the aircraft made four 'bombing' runs very successfully at maximum altitude, using H2S. This exercise was in carried out conjunction with the Air Position Plotting Unit, originally known as the Gun Laying Calibration Unit, which had been headquartered at Kidlington airport, just outside Oxford, since January 1946. Sub-sites at Bicester and Oakley each had two trailers, one containing Westex recorders and communications equipment and the other the analysis equipment and staff. On the same day as the initial 'Ding Dong', Flt. Lt. Morris and his crew took part in the Battle of Britain flypast over London in which six Lancasters from Stradishall were featured, along with six of the same type more from Coastal Command.

More of the exercises known as 'Ding Dong' were held in October and November, as well as night fighter

The unlikely venue for the general public to inspect 207 Squadron's Lincoln B. 2 RE324 [EM:C] was Heathrow, where it was photographed in September 1949. [M. J. F. Bowyer via A. Thomas]

affiliation with Mosquitos of 11 and 12 Groups. Crews available increased to five, but one was soon withdrawn when several of its members were demobilised. 207 Squadron's 31st birthday was marked on 26 November by a party at which a superb cake bearing the appropriate number of candles was cut by the CO's wife. Afterwards, rumour had it that this had been the best party ever held at Stradishall!

Routine training continued through December, enlivened by a talk given by the AOC on the subject of the role of Bomber Command in a future war, and the need of intensive training and a high level of efficiency.

For 207 Squadron, 1948 began with the detachment of a navigator and a bomb-aimer to another squadron at Shallufa. 'Bullseye' exercise on Heligoland, more 'Ding Dong' exercises, Rebecca and BABS practice and dummy attacks on Bristol by night and Exercise 'Dawn', a dummy attack on HMS *Implacable,* kept the three available crews busy. On 1 June the squadron reverted to having its own aircraft and ground crews to carry out daily and weekly servicing. Five Lancasters were on strength at this time, of which two or three were serviceable on any day, and each aircrew was allocated an aircraft. With the altered system, morale and general squadron spirit greatly improved, particularly when the AOC inspected the squadron and gave his congratulations.

Sqn. Ldr. G. J. C. Hogan DFC took over as CO on 9 March 1948, and recalls his thoughts about the squadron. "We lived in odd times then," he says. "All our flying was still based on wartime experience and practices. Clashing with this was the desire and intention of higher authority to return to a peacetime Royal Air Force, as they conceived it. Parades again became fashionable, formal cocktail parties had to be given and borne. Formal calling and visiting-cards were reintroduced and Stradling's 'Customs of the Services' became a best-seller. Guest nights were made routine and more formal, but happily still ended in utter chaos. Some idiot redesigned our No.1 uniform without pouch pockets and with golden wings, making us indistinguishable from airline pilots. Another idiot re-categorised our splendid NCO aircrew into ranks called Master, PI, PII, PIII and PIV pilots, navigators, etc., and even gave them a separate mess! However, we generally overcame this sort of nonsense and flew hard, played hard and enjoyed ourselves."

During July 1948 two other Stradishall squadrons left for Shallufa on Exercise 'Sunray', and 207 Squadron had to shoulder an additional load, carrying out an extra ASR standby duty. August was notable for poor availability of aircraft, but in early September the squadron took part in Exercise 'Dagger' — simulated attacks on London. Three crews and four aircraft were made available on each of the three nights, 3-5 September, which reflected well on all concerned. Each crew flew for seven hours every night in variable weather, resulting in a general state of fatigue. Often the cloud was 10/10, and once a piece of ice pierced a perspex windscreen. During 3 September, Marshal of the Royal Air Force Lord Tedder, who had become CO of 207 Squadron in 1920, paid a visit and met Sqn. Ldr. Hogan on his return from an Exercise 'Dagger' flight. Lord Tedder expressed his great interest in the squadron and its progress since he was in charge.

Training in October and November was limited by bad weather, lack of serviceable Lancasters and preparations for a second detachment to Shallufa. Six aircraft and crews flew out, taking off from Stradishall on 7 December after being delayed for several days by the weather. This time ground crews enjoyed the luxury of a Transport Command aircraft. The crews carried out their training schedule at Shallufa, and three crews were able to make a two-day 'Bullseye' flight to Khartoum in the Sudan. Activity on the El Shatt bombing range was restricted to two aircraft at a

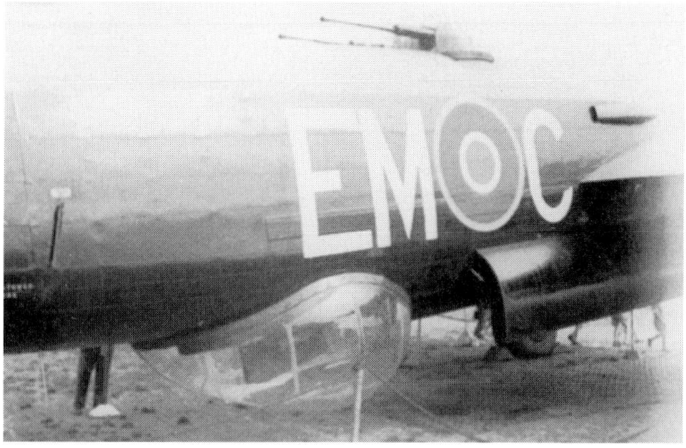

A close-up of the H2S dome on Lincoln RE324 shows that the perspex was completely clear rather than being painted matt black over most of its surface. The mid-upper turret armament is visible in this shot, with the legs of members of the public who are inspecting the aircraft also in evidence. *[M. J. F. Bowyer]*

time, to the disappointment of some crews. The detachment over, five of the Lancasters left Shallufa for Castel Benito on 4 January 1949, leaving EM:B behind for an engine change, and arrived home two or three days later. By this time, all pilots were in possession of the coveted Instrument Ratings.

Another move

At the end of January 1949, three aircraft of 207 Squadron flew to St. Eval in Cornwall to mount a search over the Bay of Biscay, but returned next day. On 1 February the squadron moved to Mildenhall, as Stradishall was now earmarked for use by Flying Training Command. Little activity took place until on 6 March two aircraft took part in the Forth and Clyde exercise, both being diverted to Lossiemouth due to bad weather. This event was repeated six days later, but this time the bomb-loads had to be jettisoned into the sea.

Escape & Evasion exercises took up a good deal of the squadron's time in the spring of 1949, the first being a small-scale training exercise involving a walk of eight to ten miles (13 to 16 km.) on 27 April. On 17 and 18 June a full-scale exercise was held, and was regarded as successful even though the 'escapees' had to contend with service and civilian police, Air Training Corps cadets, reconnaissance aircraft and the rigours of the countryside. A high percentage of those taking part managed to avoid capture.

May 1949 saw the introduction to the squadron of the new Lincoln aircraft which was replacing the venerable Lancaster. All pilots were given dual instruction on the Lincoln, which was from Wyton, and all qualified. Present at the same time was the Bomber Command Categorisation Flight, whose job was to assess standards of efficiency and to make sure that adequate training was being given at squadron level. The squadron's efforts were, however, somewhat diluted by a strike of dock workers, to deal with which Mildenhall sent sixty-six men to be part of 3 Emergency Labour Unit in the London Docks, a task code-named Operation 'Homeland'.

June was largely spent in preparation for Exercise 'Foil', a large operation involving the whole of Bomber and Fighter Commands. During the night of 25/26 June four squadron Lancasters made a dummy attack on Sheffield, and on 28/29 June Battersea power station was the target. Two other nights were spent in dropping 'Window' to confuse ground radars, and the whole exercise, which ended on 3 July, was considered very successful.

Re-equipment at last

On 18 July 1949 the first Lincoln for 207 Squadron was flown in from Lindholme by Flt. Lt. Morris, and others followed. To view the new aircraft, the Minister of Defence, Rt. Hon. A. W. Alexander CH MP, paid a visit to 207 Squadron on 23 July. Training was held up, however, by the absence of a large part of the ground crew, who had been drafted into London docks during the dock workers' strike. A good deal of ferrying of Lincolns back to Lindholme for modifications was also part of the July effort.

Four Lincolns had been taken on charge by the end of August, and three Lancasters remained. To the delight of the aircrews, the Lincolns were equipped with Gee–H Mk.4A, H2S and Rebecca Mk.4. By September, seven Lincolns were in the squadron's hands, and up to five were used in Exercise 'Bulldog', the first large-scale post-war exercise. It lasted three days, during which twelve sorties were flown by the squadron's new Lincolns. All 'targets' were attacked and only one crew reported any fighter interception. From the squadron's point of view the exercise was regarded as highly successful.

Activity in November 1949 was mostly in connection with another 'Sunray' detachment to Shallufa, although two of the Lincolns were used in Exercise 'Porcupine' on 7 and 8 November, making dummy attacks on the fleet. On 2 December a "very enjoyable" 33rd birthday party was held in the old sergeants' mess and was attended by all members of the squadron and their wives. At this event farewells were said to Sqn. Ldr. Hogan, who was replaced temporarily as CO by Sqn. Ldr. E. J. Wicht DSO DFC from 3 Group Headquarters on 5 December.

On 1 January 1950, when the New Year was just two hours old, six of 207 Squadron's Lincolns took off from Mildenhall bound for Shallufa on the direct route. One returned with W/T failure, but the others landed in Egypt twelve and a half hours later. Apart for the usual exercises, two cross-country flights were made, one of five hours to the Fanara oasis and the other of ten hours to Habbaniya in Iraq, no mean feat for the crews. The detachment over, the Lincolns left Shallufa on 30 January on the normal route via Castel Benito, where bad weather held them up until they took off at 06.00 on 1 February for the seven and a half hour flight to Mildenhall.

No sooner had the detachment returned to base than the order was received that 207 Squadron was to be disbanded at the end of February, a surprise decision in view of the fact that it was only six months or so since conversion to the Lincoln had taken place. During its post-war service so far, 207 Squadron had struggled almost constantly against shortage of serviceable aircraft, demobilisation of aircrews and ground crews, and low morale when the squadron's identity had been suppressed. Nevertheless, it had carried out a very useful function as a component of Bomber Command and its members had been looking forward to continued use of the Lincoln. However, this was not to be, and on 1 March 1950 the squadron was formally disbanded and the Lincolns were flown to Upwood for further service.

Four Washingtons of 207 Squadron in formation, three of them carrying large serial numbers on the fin but the nearest one, WF566, displaying a small serial on the fuselage. [via J. Laing]

Chapter 10: The Cold War

Setting the scene

In order to support United States forces in their effort to hold back Chinese-backed Korean troops who had crossed the 38th parallel on 26 June 1950, Prime Minister Clement Attlee decided to send British troops to the area. Speaking in the House of Commons during the following month, Winston Churchill warned of the possibility of a third World War, saying "Once again, America and Britain find themselves associated in a noble cause. When bad men combine good must associate."

The period which came to be known as the 'Cold War' can be traced back to the summer of 1948, when Russia blocked the movement of supplies to Berlin and the United States and Great Britain responded by mounting the Berlin Airlift. Now the Korean campaign added to the danger, and the RAF had to help deal with the perceived threat to world peace. This it did by means of a hectic programme of expansion and modernisation, opening a series of new Flying Training Schools to increase the number of aircrew available to fighter, bomber and transport squadrons with all speed. Some of the trainees were National Servicemen, whose two-year period of service was considered a worthwhile investment in view of the international situation. Appropriate numbers of ground personnel were also absorbed into the Service, and the result was an increase in the number of operational squadrons at readiness should the worst happen.

Nuclear weapons and ways of delivering them had now become vital to both sides of an impending conflict. Although the United States was leading in the development (and indeed the use) of such weapons, the USSR was not as far behind as generally believed. Stalin had ordered a massive programme to bring Russia into the forefront of nuclear technology, aided by a number of spies who were able to penetrate the somewhat lax security maintained by the Allies. The officer who would become 207 Squadron's next CO was attending a course at the RAF Staff College in October 1949 at which a senior Government scientist claimed that it would be a long time before Russia was in a position to test a nuclear device. A young Army officer had the temerity to question this assertion and was ridiculed for his pains. At lunch-time that day came the news over BBC radio that such a test had just taken place! In 1945, Prime Minister Attlee had bravely authorised continued development of a British nuclear weapon, but it was not tested until October 1952.

Lancaster aircraft used by RAF Bomber Command since the end of the second World War had by now been replaced by Lincolns, which in technological terms were only a little more advanced. The promised breakthrough

'A' Flight personnel pose on and around one of the Washingtons. [via J. Laing]

'B' Flight air and ground crews pose in the snow. [via J. Laing]

into the age of the jet bomber had not yet materialised, as the English Electric Canberra was not quite ready to enter service. To bridge the gap, the Air Ministry acquired on loan from the US Government eighty-seven Boeing B–29 Superfortress four-engined heavy bombers, which were quickly taken out of long-term storage, modified and delivered, beginning in March 1950. The first unit to be equipped with the Washington B.1, as it was named in RAF service – although most of the crews referred to it as the B–29 – was the Washington Conversion Unit at Marham, which was formed in July 1950 with eight aircraft on which senior Lincoln crews soon began a course of re-training.

207 Squadron bounces back

Eight squadrons of Washingtons eventually came into being. Almost the last to be formed, on 29 March 1951 at Marham, was 207 Squadron, with Sqn. Ldr. Geoffrey W. O'N. Fisher OBE DFC as Commanding Officer. This officer had a distinguished wartime career and was extremely dedicated and professional. His aims were that everyone on the squadron should try to achieve his own high standards and live up to being members of the RAF's premier bombing squadron. Not all of the personnel appreciated this philosophy, however, and now and then his attention to detail was considered too much. For two months the squadron existed in name only, its eight nine-man crews being attached to the Washington Conversion Unit, but on 27 July they assembled as qualified members of 207 Squadron. All eight Washingtons allocated to the squadron had been delivered by the end of that month.

The Boeing Washington was a very large aircraft by RAF standards, with a wing-span of 141'3" (43.05 m.), a length of 99'0" (30.18 m.) and a height to the tip of the vertical tailplane of 29'7" (9.02 m.). Its fuselage shape led to the B–29 becoming known affectionately as the 'aluminum toob'. Power was provided by four Wright R-3350-23 Cyclone 18 turbocharged radial engines, each turning out 2,200 bhp. The propellers were almost 17'0" (5.18 m.) in diameter, and the power generated could lift 140,000 lbs. from take-off to 35,000 feet. Maximum speed was 358 mph (576 kph), a cruising speed greater than 300 mph (480 kph), a service ceiling of more than 35,000 feet (10,670 m.) and an operational radius of 1,800 miles (2,900 km.). An early fault with the R-3350 engines was that they ran excessively hot, a factor which led to derogatory descriptions such as 'time-bombs' and 'flame-throwers'. However, Sqn. Ldr. Fisher says that the more dangerous engine fires were largely a thing of the past in the versions with which the RAF squadrons were equipped, due to the introduction of fuel injection in place of an induction manifold system on earlier engines. Even so, they were somewhat unreliable and landings 'on three' were commonplace, but thanks to Boeing's fine design and engineering there was a back-up for almost any emergency and the aircraft was inherently safe and a delight to fly.

Former pilot Mike Balcombe agreed. "For us pilots sitting in the greenhouse in front," he said "there was a magnificent all-round view for taxying and take-off, unlike the Lincoln and Lancaster, where the nose obstructed forward visibility until the tail came up on take-off. In fact when I first got into the B–29 cockpit I asked my instructor which window I should look through, and he replied that the one with the wipers would be best. There was no yanking back on the stick to get the thing into the air; the Washington would lift itself off the ground very smoothly without any assistance from the pilot. Violent manoeuvres were forbidden beyond a Rate One turn. If severe turbulence was encountered the auto-pilot could take care of the situation better than us mortals." Arthur Haines added "We used to joke about who worked hardest in a crew, and top of the list were the navigators and flight engineers. The crew were of the opinion that the pilot flung [the aircraft] into auto-pilot at about 1,000 feet and for most flights booked a wake-up call for twenty minutes prior to ETA at Marham!"

A full crew consisted of ten men, most of whom had ample room in which to work. Captain and co-pilot sat side by side in almost armchair comfort with plenty of room for the bomb aimer/front gunner to reach his dickey seat in the nose. The flight engineer sat facing aft behind the co-pilot, while the navigator/plotter was positioned behind him. Diagonally opposite was the wireless operator. The mid-upper gunner sat with his head in an astrodome forward of the aft upper turret, and the two side gunners sat in pits from where they could see through the large waist blisters. In semi-darkness on the port side was the navigator/radar operator's position. Finally, the rear gunner occupied a separate pressurised compartment. About fifteen percent of the crew members had wartime operational experience and a similar number had begun training during the war but had not flown on operations. Few of the navigators who had been trained during the war had covered bomb aiming, but those trained after the war had completed their courses in both 'trades'. Wireless operators were in short supply, and therefore flew more sorties than the other crew members.

Armament of the Washington consisted of two 0.5" (12.7 mm) guns in each of fore and aft dorsal and fore and aft ventral remotely-controlled turrets and with an additional 20 mm cannon in the rear turret. As our Russian allies were becoming more and more unfriendly to us the Washingtons often flew with all guns armed with 1,000 rounds each. Bomb loads could be 6,000 lbs (2,725 kg.)

Sqn. Ldr. Geoffrey Fisher and his Flight commanders, Bill Adams and 'Judy' Garland. The squadron badge is prominent on the fuselage of the Washington. [via J. Laing]

over 3,000 miles (4,830 km.) or 17,500 lbs (7,955 kg.) over 1,000 miles (1,610 km.). The B-29 was the world's first pressurised bomber, and the problem of opening bomb doors at above 8,000 feet was overcome by leaving the bomb bay unpressurised and connecting the two crew compartments, forward and amidships, by a tunnel 33 feet (10 m.) long and 2'10" (0.86 m.) in diameter. Based on the British H2S, the main radar navigational and bombing aid was the AN/APQ–13 system, complemented by a secret Nordern bombsight. Crew comfort was excellent, and thanks to its insulation and pressurisation the aircraft was relatively quiet.

On 1 August the CO, with Flt. Lt. Scott and his crew, made the first sortie in a 207 Squadron Washington, after which two weeks were devoted to air tests, continuation training and mundane tasks such as compass swinging. Training then began for a flypast over London as part of the annual Battle of Britain celebrations. Although the crews had little experience in close formation flying in such a large aircraft as the Washington and the hours available were limited, the dress rehearsal indicated that a high standard had been achieved. However, due to bad weather on the day the flypast was cancelled, an anti-climax for those involved, who at least knew that they had received some good practice.

Early in September, vehicles carrying a strange miscellany of equipment and about four boffin-like characters arrived at 207 Squadron's offices. They began at once to install their gadgetry inside and outside one of the Washingtons, which took off late in the day. John Laing asked one of the navigators where he had been, but the reply was that the crew was not to divulge this information. "Only the flight time is to be recorded in our logbooks, but if I say that our magnetic compass didn't work very well you might have an idea, but keep it to yourself" said John's friend. Next day newspaper headlines announced that Russia had exploded its second atomic bomb.

Some of the ground crew technicians were a little over-awed by the Washington at first, but most relished the challenge. Sqn. Ldr. Fisher remarks that a particularly fine example was set by Flt. Sgt. (later Chief Tech.) Lewis, who was crew chief for Ken Flett's aircraft, WF566, and who inspired ground and air crews alike. "Right from the start" said Sqn. Ldr. Fisher "we tried to create an attitude of mind that the aircraft were there to be flown......and that we expected the ground crews to come up with the goods. It may sound a bit smug, but it is fair to say that this philosophy did not go unnoticed by the older squadrons at Marham, some of whose captains had come from Transport Command, where priorities were sometimes different from those in Bomber Command."

To gain practice in landing the massive Washingtons on comparatively short runways, Flg. Off. Balcombe took WF567 on 4 September to Upwood, where a Battle of Britain open day was due to be held on 15 September. Five days later the first practice bombing sortie since the squadron converted to the Washington was carried out by Sqn. Ldr. Holmes and his crew at Theddlethorpe ranges.

Outside duty hours, the crews' social lives were hampered by a general shortage of money. "Mess functions provided the highlights", recalled Sqn. Ldr. Fisher. "There was also some contact on a semi-official basis with the locals. Names that come to mind include Andrew Fountaine, the local 'squire', and his charming, gentle and beautiful wife. To say that he was right-wing would be an understatement, and this in an era when socialism had been the 'in' thing for some years and had influenced our lives if not our thinking. His extreme views gave us plenty to argue about late into the night and especially when drinks were flowing freely. Another name was Freddie Unwin, the local GP from nearby Fincham, a typical old-fashioned country doctor. He and his vivacious wife Siss were great favourites. She had given up the fleshpots of Switzerland to marry Freddie and settle in Norfolk, yet after twenty years or more in the 'sticks' she remained a shining example of *haut couture* in an otherwise rather drab scene. Among the farming community were the three Wooton brothers, but doing even better was H. O. Crouch, who was involved in

This was the photograph used for the 207 Squadron Christmas card in 1951. A good image for a message of peace and goodwill? [via J. Laing]

cutting and drying grass from several airfields. His already substantial fortune was to increase still further when it was realised that the moisture extracted from the process.........contained chlorophyll in large quantities. Chlorophyll was just becoming a popular ingredient in toothpaste......and he found himself supplying not only the home market but exporting to the USA. One of the very few outside entertainments to which we were invited was to a party at Mr. Crouch's house near Downham Market. Even by today's standards it was an extremely lavish affair at which the drink and everything else flowed freely".

Drawbacks to socialising in the local countryside were the limited public transport and the rarity of private vehicles. A new car, for which there was a waiting list of several years, was almost unheard of, and even the cheapest was beyond the means of most people. If a car was owned, it was usually of the 'old banger' variety, often of dubious reliability. An exceptional owner was Michael Stapleton–Cotton, whose new Jaguar XK120 added a touch of class to the Officers' Mess car park. Some of the 'bangers' included a significant percentage of aircraft parts! More common modes of transport were bicycles, motor-scooters and motor-cycles, particularly for those living off the Station, who often travelled surprising distances in awful weather. An unfortunate motor-cyclist, Sgt. Freeman, was involved in an accident when returning on his motor-bike to Marham one foggy Sunday night, and serious injuries led to the amputation of a leg. Some months later, though, he returned to the squadron sporting a 'tin leg' and resumed his duties as a flight engineer.

Between 29 September and 9 October, 207 Squadron took part in Exercise 'Pinnacle', a large defence exercise designed to test defending fighter squadrons to their limits in mass day and night raids. During 'Pinnacle' twenty-six sorties were flown by the squadron with great success. Normally the Washington carried 500 lb. (227 kg.) or 1,000 lb. (454 kg.) bombs left over from the Second World War, and bombing methods had varied little in the interim period except in terms of scale. Now the intention of Command planners was accurate bombing obtained through precise navigation, rather than sheer weight of bombs dropped. Sadly for him and for the squadron, an armourer who was unloading a practice bomb from a Washington dropped it, it exploded, and he lost an eye. He had to be invalided out of the service, an unfortunate result of the dangers of his trade.

Escape & Evasion exercises were held at intervals during the latter part of 1951 at Marham, and 207 Squadron crews found themselves taking part. A major E&E exercise, 'Cornflit', took place from 17.00 on Friday 24 October to 07.00 on Sunday 26, thirty-four of the aircrew acting as attackers while the remainder of the squadron defended the airfield. This was a new venture for most of them, and they learned a good deal about moving incognito at night, aided by an 'underground' organisation.

An attempt to improve the health and well-being of 207 Squadron personnel! [via J. Laing]

Moves were made in October to improve the squadron's standard of navigation and to simulate operational wartime conditions. After each well-planned exercise, Flying Wing at Marham released a score-card showing the points achieved by each crew, a feature which fostered the spirit of competition, raised morale and encouraged a keen attitude. During November one Bomber Command 'Bullseye' exercise was held but was disappointing as the Master Bomber was unable to direct attacks on the target. At other times in the month, a normal pattern of high-level bombing practice and radar exercises was maintained. It is now clear that some of the 'Bullseyes' were designed to activate Russian defences. During these sorties sophisticated intelligence gathering was carried out intensively, recording every move the Soviet forces made in reaction to a potential threat.

On one such mission which covered almost the whole length of the 'Iron Curtain', Arthur Haines was a navigator. "It was typically foul weather and we maintained radio and radar silence in the sensitive area," he recalls. "We flew in solid cloud, which prevented astro-navigation, and there were minor technical problems which eliminated other navigational aids. Jimmy, the other navigator, and I worked furiously on dead reckoning, double checking each other. It was only on leaving the area, when radar silence had been relaxed, that we got a fix and found out that we weren't where we should have been! When we landed and went through the de-briefing, I think it was the Wingco Flying who announced 'Flt. Lt. Flett and crew, I have a message for you from the Russians, which reads – 'You penetrated Soviet airspace by fifty miles, but we assumed this was a navigational error and therefore did not shoot you down'. I'm rather glad they didn't!"

An anonymous contributor recounts a story which remains a mystery to this day and which involved 207 Squadron. "Late one night, while on a cross-country and bombing exercise......we received a message ordering us to divert to Prestwick immediately to pick up a passenger. Enquiries about who he was and where he was to go produced only one answer: he would tell us his destination himself. On landing at Prestwick we were directed to a dark and remote part of the airport, and our passenger arrived in a Land Rover. He entered our aircraft by the rear hatch, saying 'Good evening, gentlemen, London Airport, please'. I can still see our passenger, sitting opposite me, a very ordinary man dressed in a well-worn raincoat and clutching a battered attaché case, who would not stand out in a crowd. Our arrival at London Airport [Heathrow] was similar to that at Prestwick – we were marshalled to a remote part of the airport, where our passenger climbed out. His only words were 'Thank you, gentlemen'. Arriving at Marham in the early hours of the morning, we were told by air traffic control to remain with our aircraft on dispersal. After a short wait, we were not a little surprised to be confronted by the 'Groupie', who not only impounded all our logs and charts but told us most emphatically that we were neither to record the Prestwick to London detour in our log books nor to discuss with anyone where we had been. Our passenger must have had some remarkable authority. Shades of Le Carré!"

Flying rations in the early days of the squadron's Washington period were very generous, possibly to a USAF specification, but were limited in variety. A large flask of tea or coffee was to be shared, and for each member there was a large tin of fruit juice, sandwiches, a couple of tins of soup, and chocolate and sweets, even for a relatively short flight. For trips of eight hours or more the rations were sometimes difficult to carry! As sweets were still rationed, many of them found their way to the children of the crew members, and other items in short supply travelled with men going on leave. But quite suddenly the rations were greatly reduced and a greater variety of pre-cooked foods such as tins of bacon and egg or liver and bacon, which could be heated on the urn next to the navigator/radar's position, were provided. New rules stipulated that if a flight was aborted, even part-way through, the pro-rata quantity of food was to be returned. John Money, one of the gunners in the same crew as Arthur Haines, had little time for such bureaucracy. Even when leaving on a long flight he usually ate ninety percent of his rations within minutes of taking off!

The other major event before the end of the year was the Bomber Command Blind Bombing competition, in which two squadron crews took part. Flt. Lt. Scott's sortie was successful, but Flg. Off. Bennett suffered bad luck in the form of an unserviceable VHF set, a hung-up bomb and another which failed to explode. These mishaps prevented 207 from any possibility of winning the competition, which was taken by a visiting USAF crew.

As 207 was the last Washington squadron to form at Marham, new arrivals often found themselves in the least popular accommodation. There were so many SNCOs that there were two messes, No.2 Mess being by the roadside just inside the main gate. This building provided catering facilities for personnel located nearby, had a lounge and doubled as a married families' club. "Our food was fairly good" said John Laing "and for a while it was excellent, but the cook in charge was discovered by the Officers' mess and was transferred. My comment on his successor was that he was hired to cut the sports field in the summer and cook the cuttings in the winter. Our relief from poor culinary efforts was to skip off to the Globe in Kings Lynn, where they produced......an excellent duck salad for five shillings [25p.] or perhaps even less. This required time off and someone with a car, plus of course a reasonable supply of cash. But that duck was very tasty!"

Wireless operator Phil Crawley was at first housed in a barrack block which was converted into rooms for SNCOs. Other accommodation was a small complex of former USAF 'Seco' huts built of concrete and asbestos and divided into two-man rooms. It appeared that they had been designed to cook the occupants in summer and freeze them in winter. There was a coke stove in each room which heated the room to the level of a sauna but could not be controlled. The only remedy was to open the windows, but once the stove had cooled down the room rapidly became an ice-box! "How we were supposed to sleep after night-flying I really don't know" said former navigator Arthur Haines. "Luckily, I was spared the 'pleasure' of winter occupation as I was soon able to move into a room for two in the nearby permanent but quaintly named Airmen Pilots' Quarters, which were very acceptable."

The CO presents the prizes at a Sports day, obviously held in chilly weather. [via J. Laing]

Long-range opportunities

As the Washington was a true long-range bomber, squadron training was adjusted to make full use of its capabilities. Routine navigation missions could last up to eight hours by day or night and included both visual and radar-assisted bombing and the dropping of practice bombs. By the end of 1951, flights to such distant places as Germany, Malta, Tripoli and Tunis were being made without landing, outbound and inbound legs being for the benefit of pilots and navigators, with simulated bombing attacks being made on three points. Such sorties often lasted at least fifteen hours, at the end of which the tired pilots no doubt welcomed the sound of the Marham approach controller's voice in their headphones. A detailed debriefing session was then held as part of the categorisation of crews. These sorties were found to be very beneficial for assessing the Washington's capability at various altitudes.

Two Bomber Command exercises were held in January 1952, the first of them successful and the second not. Each aircraft set out to drop twenty 500 lb (227 kg.) bombs on Heligoland, but several faults and hang-ups developed. Mike Balcombe will never forget his participation. "The load that night was ten 500 lb. bombs. I had observed during briefing that the TOTs of the first wave, which included us, were all within a very tight time-scale and that the altitudes we were to fly gave a minimal height separation. Weather that night was clear and we had a nice uneventful flight to the target area, with no irritating slipstream turbulence. As we approached the target I opened the bomb-doors and we set the aircraft onto the bombing run. The bomb-aimer had just given me his predicted 'Twenty seconds to go to release' when I thought I heard a faint voice saying 'Look up'. The message was very clear indeed, so I did look up. Directly overhead, about fifty feet above us, was another Washington on the same heading. Its bomb-doors were open and the bay lights were switched on, which lit up the bombs still in the racks and which were obviously about to be released. Apart from being stunned with horror at what I had seen, my immediate reaction was to get out of the way. Several thing then happened very quickly indeed. I yelled to the bomb-aimer to abort the run and at the same time banged on full left rudder and wound the control column hard over to the left. Being a big aircraft, the Washington shuddered in protest at its pilot's violent behaviour, but slowly, ever so slowly, it turned out of the stream. My crew, who up to then had known nothing of the imminent disaster, were convinced I had gone mad, but they soon calmed down when I explained what had happened. Since we were now clear of all other aircraft we switched on our navigation lights before turning back to the target. This time we dropped our bombs uneventfully, albeit somewhat late!" An attempt to carry out a bombing exercise on Jurby in the Isle of Man was likewise something of a fiasco as target identification by searchlight was poor.

In February, Sqn. Ldr. Fisher, Wg. Cdr. Wheeler and crew in WF565 dropped a practice bomb on Filfla Island, just off the south-eastern corner of Malta, and made a radar run over Bordeaux. Two of the squadron's Washingtons took part in Exercise 'Stratus' on 30 April 1952, with the object of testing NATO defences in the Mediterranean, Malta in particular, but low cloud prevented any success. In any case, one aircraft developed a fault in its bomb shackles.

Sporting activities occupied many off-duty personnel, whose main interest at this time was football. In the Station quarter-finals 207 Squadron beat Station Workshops 9–4, in the semi-finals they trounced 115 Squadron 5–3, finally beating the rival 35 Squadron 3–2. In May a squadron cricket team was organised and a pitch marked out in front of the Operations Block. In the Sergeants' Mess there was a black-and-white TV set with a massive 12" screen, and there were always card games to join in, but as might be expected many took part in the most fundamental activity of all, the pursuit of the opposite sex. An anonymous contributor recalls that one of the sergeants was the proud possessor of a rather ancient van. "He developed a liaison with a very rare species on the camp – a female, to wit one of the NAAFI girls. After an evening in No.1 Mess a couple of us were taking a short cut through the NAAFI compound to return to our quarters......Tucked away in the shadows was Sgt. X's van, which under closer scrutiny seemed to be rocking rhythmically. Discreet observation revealed that Sgt. X had a tryst every night at the same place and time, so a raiding party was organised. When we left the Mess shortly after Sgt.X we sent our scout ahead to keep watch until the appropriate time, when six of us silently descended upon the van, seized it by the sides and repeatedly lifted it bodily and dropped it, before doing a disappearing act. After Sgt. X had been lulled into a false sense of security by the passing of sufficient days, we repeated the performance, but never achieved a third time as we didn't have the mobility to follow him to his new location."

Fuel consumption was restricted in May by a strike in the United States, reducing flying hours to fifteen per captain, but nevertheless 207 Squadron was on air/sea rescue standby at the beginning of the month. This involved the fitting of a rigid lifeboat in one bomb bay and Lindholme gear in the other. On 2 June Flt. Lt. Petheram and crew took off within 28 minutes of being notified that a RCAF Sabre aircraft had ditched in the North Sea, and was soon joined by an aircraft piloted by Flg. Off. Thomas, but although they searched until dawn next day no trace of the missing fighter pilot could be found. Fuel restrictions were lifted on 9 June, allowing practice for the Lawrence Minot Trophy to proceed.

Competition for the Minot Trophy by every squadron in Bomber Command took place in July, each squadron being allowed to enter one aircraft on each of the four nights. Each aircraft had to attack the same three targets. On the first night, 7 July, 207 was very unlucky when Flt. Lt. Adams' aircraft suffered an engine failure less than an hour after take-off, and although he carried on on three engines he was unable to bomb the targets due to cloud cover and a failure of the automatic bomb-door opening mechanism. On the following three nights the squadron was more successful, and in the end came 8th out of eighteen. That year the Trophy, awarded for bombing efficiency, was won by 90 Squadron. Soon afterwards, five of the squadron's Washingtons paid visits to Leuchars for fighter affiliation, high-level bombing practice and air-to-air firing on drogues.

Mess inspections were infrequent, but in 1952 there was one which turned out to be a real blitz, in which every piece of furniture had to be left open. John Laing recalls that Sid Taylor had a room along the corridor from his own. "Sid was not a tidy type" he remembers, "and his room was usually a shambles, but on the day of that inspection it was starkly neat. Unfortunately, to achieve this effect Sid had locked his wardrobe, so the inspecting officer ordered it to be opened, by force if necessary. Out came a deluge of dirty linen, crumpled uniforms, flying kit, sports gear and Lord know what. Sid was in the 'doghouse' again. He was not very popular with the CO, who had him up before the Station Commander......but Sid's return to the Gunnery section was typical of the man. As Sid, a star footballer, told it, he and the 'Groupie' had hit it off well. Sid was the sort of chap who, if he fell off Tower Bridge, would come up clutching a salmon."

In August 1952 Exercise 'Kingpin' was held, involving bombing runs on German targets, notably Osnabruck and the Hamm marshalling yards. What memories this must have awakened in any crew member who might have dropped bombs in anger on those same targets less than ten years before! In addition mock raids were targeted on Larkhill and Berners Heath ranges, but technical faults with the bomb door mechanism were still making themselves felt. Flying time was reduced in August to from 320 to 135 hours per month due to doubts about the life of the Bristol-reconditioned Cyclone engines. However, as Marham as a whole did not take up its quota, 207 Squadron was allowed an extra fifty hours. Steps were taken to reduce the incidence of engine failures by reducing the take-off weight of the Washingtons and operating the engines at lower temperature by using a lower manifold pressure.

Another chance to take part in the Battle of Britain flypast over London came in August, when refresher training in formation flying began, under the eagle eye of the Wg. Cdr. Flying, Wg. Cdr. Fryer. At the first briefing, he told the crews that he wanted a good tight formation and that he would be watching from the astrodome of the leading aircraft. If things were not to his liking he would become very angry, which would cause his bald head to turn bright red, and if it seemed that the sun was setting in the astrodome of his aircraft crews would know they were in trouble! To ensure that a correct spacing between aircraft was maintained, a 'Heath Robinson' type of gadget was designed to fit over each captain's head. This had an arm projecting several inches in front to carry a metal ring through which, when the pilot viewed the neatly-encircled tail of the aircraft ahead, he knew that he was the stipulated distance away. The 'vic' of three 207 Squadron aircraft duly joined the flypast on 15 September, and all went well, and five days later the same pilots, Sqn. Ldr. Fisher, Flt. Lt. McNoble and Flt. Lt. Flett, flew to several airfields which had opened their gates to the public. Permitted flying hours were increased to 210 on 20 September, and greatly-increased activity followed.

Service life in the early 1950s was not easy, and reflected the general pattern of life in Great Britain at the time. Pay in the RAF was poor and married quarters were scarce or non-existent, any priority being given to building houses for NCOs and other ranks rather than officers. Regardless of rank, therefore, personnel lived in what were often really squalid and primitive conditions. Even a town of Kings Lynn's importance was not fully provided with electricity at that time. To add to Marham's housing difficulties, a large number of USAF servicemen were stationed in the area and with a larger disposable income found the pick of the available properties.

An important annual exercise, 'Ardent', was held between 4 and 12 October 1952, and 207 Squadron flew twenty-five sorties as a contribution to the bomber force. Making use of radar bombing techniques, simulated attacks were made on Glasgow and Manchester by night and Liverpool by day during Phase I of the exercise. Phase II involved attacks on Sheffield, London and the Forth Bridge, and Phase III a 'raid' on Bristol after a run-in over France. A passenger on one sortie was AVM W. A. D. Brook CB CBE, the AOC of 3 Group, who flew with the CO to obtain a first-hand impression of the exercise. The final mission involved eight Washingtons creating diversionary raids while the main bomber force attacked London. 207 Squadron participated by making a radar attack on Tangmere airfield and were met by intense fighter opposition. Not for the first time, bomb-doors malfunctioning during the approach to a target were a handicap to success. In December the squadron was unfortunate in gaining only 295 points out of a possible 1,200 in the Sassoon Blind Bombing competition, taking twelfth place out of twenty-nine entrants.

Operation 'Noah'

During the terrible floods in East Anglia in January and February 1953 207 Squadron played a humanitarian role. Under Flt. Lt. A. E. D. Murray, a party of airmen travelled the short distance to Kings Lynn to help evacuate civilians marooned there and at Hunstanton. The airmen were able to provide invaluable aid, rescuing many people by vehicle or by dinghy. From 4 to 9 February, 220 officers, NCOs and airmen helped in the task of rebuilding the bank of the River Ouse at Magdalen, about five miles (eight km.) south of Kings Lynn. After the emergency, Flt. Lt. Murray's efforts were the subject of a commendation by the Chief Constable of Norfolk. Phil Crawley thought the effort was not entirely necessary. "I was detailed with others to help fill sandbags to help stay the flooding," he said. "Some of this was carried out during the night. I couldn't help wondering why I was doing this, as it was completely foreign to what I was in the RAF for, especially when local civilians told me that we were not really required because there was enough civilian manpower to do the job. Fortunately, this didn't go on for long and the floods subsided". John Butler remembers a different aspect. "I was on camp when the airframe bods were roused in the night to go out to dispersals to turn the aircraft into the wind and lash them down. Next morning volunteers were called for to parade on the main square in suitable attire to work on the breach in the river at St. Mary Magdalen. You never saw a more motley shower on parade! There were Wellington boots, denims, jerkins, in fact anything that could be obtained from stores. Initially, regular sandbags were unobtainable, so flour sacks were used......but our guys could not lift them, much less go down a muddy bank to load a barge for the River Board to take across to the gap. Several chaps fell in the mud and got up looking like the Black & White Minstrels. We were fed on greasy stew prepared in the mess and brought to the site in metal churns; you would have thought it was a gourmet meal by the way it was consumed."

Unserviceability of engines in particular had reduced flying hours in January, but by then most crews had almost attained their Bomber Command 'select' category and were expected to reach that standard in February. Aircraft serviceability greatly improved in the latter half of February, and the squadron's routine returned to normal.

One night, two airmen who were on patrol in the 207 Squadron dispersal called out the guard commander, who brought them to the main guardroom in a terrible state. "They swore", said John Butler years later "that they had seen a phantom figure enter one of the Washingtons, WF437 I think, and reappear out of the top hatch and walk along the fuselage. When challenged, the apparition had vanished. The airmen had not been drinking, though at the time de-icing fluid was being drunk by some. It was reported that this aircraft was the one which had killed a wireless operator from Coningsby who had walked into one of its propellers."

With the arrival of spring and an improvement in the fuel situation, 207 Squadron was involved in several exercises, including 'Jungle King', the largest air defence exercise since 1949. Marham was put onto a war footing, the presumption being that West Germany had been over-run, and Bomber Command had been ordered to destroy all major airfields in that country. Among the targets were Wunstorf, Gutersloh and Fuhlsbuttel airfields, and opposition was provided by Meteors, Vampires and Mosquitos of Allied Air Forces Central Europe. Radar bombing results had by now improved dramatically, indicating that the radar operators could at last use their equipment efficiently. Due to postings, however, only six crews were now available. Four of them were designated 'combat' crews, and 207 Squadron was at this time the only Washington-equipped fully operational squadron.

The ultimate deterrent

Nothing official was disclosed at squadron level about the B–29's nuclear capacity, but those at Marham were well aware that the USAF had stocks of nuclear weapons at RAF Stations in Britain. It was assumed that the RAF would, if

The three Washingtons of 207 Squadron in formation over the Royal Review of the RAF at Odiham on 15 July 1953. Below can be seen the serried ranks of aircraft representing every Command of the RAF. Somewhere down there is WF565, 207 Squadron's highly-bulled contribution to the static display. [via J. Laing]

the worst came to the worst, be able to use these stockpiles. At Marham during the Washington period, members of a USAF detachment worked in the bomb dump, close to 207 Squadron's dispersal. Huge C–124 Globemaster aircraft flew in periodically to deliver weapons which were at once covered by sheeting and moved into the dump. The dump was protected with a great deal of barbed wire, trip wires, loose dogs, watchtowers with searchlights and machine guns and a large number of armed sentries, prompting some of the aircrews to christen the area 'Stalag Luft III'. Even though asked to talk about the work they did, none of the Americans ever divulged any secrets. Arthur Haines, who left Marham in 1953 not knowing what mysteries the dump held, returned in 1990, and stopped for evening refreshments in a small country pub not far from the airfield. "We were introduced to the owner, who was an American who had served in East Anglia for most of his twenty years in the USAF. The mystery of the contents came up in the conversation, and he admitted to having worked in the bomb dump for several periods, but he said 'Fancy, after nearly forty years you still don't know, and I ain't going to tell you!' Next day he did, however tell me that he had been an atomic weapons engineer. Those people at Marham who had a good radio were able to hear 'Moscow Molly', who knew far more about the bomb dump than we did!"

At Marham, the airmen's accommodation was in centrally-heated brick-built barrack blocks with plenty of hot water and drying facilities. John Butler, who was an armament mechanic, thought of them as the 'Savoy' after his training at Kirkham. "Apart from sports such as football, rugby, cricket and hockey there were sports day activities for those who were interested. However, one of the most prevalent pastimes, especially after 'credits' had been paid out, was three- or nine-card brag or pontoon. As money was involved, 'schools' were held upstairs so that booted feet could be heard in time for the cash to vanish before the SPs' white hats appeared. The usual format was for the school to finish so that the winners could reach the NAAFI in time to order double everything (sausage, egg and chips) and for the losers to see whether there was any supper to be had in the airmen's mess. Sometimes, blankets were hung over the drying room windows, and 'schools' continued until the early hours. One night we were working late and whiling the time away in the crew room on the flight line by playing brag, when several of us heard the sound of tyres crunching on the gravel outside, followed by the squeak of brakes. Cards and money vanished and we waited for the orderly officer to come in. But he did not, so after a moment or two one of us went to investigate, but there was no one there, and no vehicle. Most weird!" A similar situation could be found in the sergeants' mess, where Flt. Sgt. 'Jock' Gallagher organised a bridge school. An expert player, he soon took substantial winnings from other NCOs, some of whom were married and could not afford to lose the money. The mess President was extremely angry but as a number of Warrant Officers were among Jock's victims no charges were pressed and the affair was hushed up.

A good deal of overseas flying was now taking place, and included a trip in one of 207 Squadron's Washingtons by the AOC, who flew it to Luqa in Malta on 28 March, making a dummy radar attack on Manston in passing, and returned three days later after a spot of sunbathing! 'Lone Ranger' flights to the Near East, North Africa and Germany were sanctioned by Air Ministry in April, with the proviso

Washington WF565, resplendent in highly-polished aluminium finish for the 1953 Royal Review of the RAF, held at Odiham. [via J. Laing]

that all crews must be of 'select' category. Four days were allowed for each round trip. In May one of the 'Lone Rangers' involved a flight to Nicosia in Cyprus via Valley, while four aircraft made dummy radar approaches on Nancy and Dijon airfields as part of Operation 'Horace'.

By now, the squadron was flying about 200 hours per month, allowing preparations for the impending Royal Review of the RAF to proceed. The Coronation of Her Majesty Queen Elizabeth II took place on 2 June, and by way of a contribution 207 Squadron sent Flt. Sgt. R. S. Johnson, one corporal and three airmen to RAF Uxbridge to take part in the Coronation parade. The Flight Sergeant was afterwards presented with the Coronation Medal by the AOC 3 Group.

The Royal Review

The Royal Review of the RAF was held at RAF Odiham on 15 July 1953 and was the largest such review ever seen, before or since. Every type of aircraft then in service – and there were many – was represented in the air or on the ground, or both. 207 Squadron sent Washington WF565 on 2 July for inclusion in the enormous static display, and ten ground crew under the command of Flt. Lt. K. M. Flett to ensure that the aircraft was in tip-top condition on the big day. As navigator Jim Riley says "It was not until we started to polish the aircraft to an acceptable standard that I realised just how big the B-29 was. When not needed for flying, all available bodies were used, and we were working until 21.00 every weekday for several weeks." During WF565's flight to Odiham, an engine failed, spurting oil everywhere. On the evening of the great day a last-minute wipe-down was done, and as many rags as could be found were shoved inside the cowling in the hope that no further seepage of oil would be seen. When the moment for Royal inspection arrived, the Washington stood in a Duraglit-induced pristine condition, and Flt. Lt. Flett is said to have worn sun-glasses for his final check that all was perfect! "As the Queen came by in her Land Rover she did seem to take particular notice of the B-29s" says John Butler. "It made me very proud to have been part of the whole event." Three other squadron aircraft took part in the fly-past in bumpy conditions and maintained the honour of the squadron. Crews comprised the CO and Flg. Off. B. Thomas in WF566, Gp. Capt. O. R. Donaldson, Flt. Lt. C. J. Petheram and Flt. Lt. F. E. Cooke in WF567 and Flt. Lts. E. M. Stewart and R. A. Cunningham in WF569.

Home Run and the New Zealand Air Race

After the Review, Operation 'Home Run' began. This covered the ferrying of 36 surplus Washingtons back to the United States, 35 to Davis-Monthan Air Force Base at Tucson, Arizona, and one to Tinker AFB at Oklahoma City. The set route for Flights of four aircraft was via Prestwick, Ernest Harmon AFB or Goose Bay AFB (Newfoundland) and Dover AFB (Delaware), and the return journey was made on civil airlines to the east coast of the United States and thence by military aircraft of MATS to the UK. Flt. Lt. McNabb's crew were probably the first 207 Squadron crew to take part, and they used Andrews AFB at Washington DC as their port of entry. After six had been despatched, the task was suspended due to the forthcoming England to New Zealand air race, in which 207 Squadron was to provide support facilities.

Two Washingtons carrying passengers and freight, captained by Sqn. Ldr. Fisher and Flt. Lt. Cooke, took off from Marham on 31 August bound for Singapore and Negombo (Ceylon, now Sri Lanka) respectively via Mauripur, their function being to set up servicing facilities for Bomber Command Canberra aircraft competing in the race. In September three more Washingtons followed, and

Members of the Royal Observer Corps visited Marham on 9 August 1953 to see the activities of the squadrons and were greeted by this placard and cartoon showing a hybrid aircraft. [via J. Laing]

all five were at Negombo when the race began. They were also available for any air/sea rescue operations which might be necessary, but luckily no emergency occurred to any of the five Canberras taking part in the race. Sqn. Ldr. Fisher described Negombo airfield as being miles from anywhere. "It was surrounded by coconut palms of great height. Taking off with full payload in the prevailing high temperature required all the power we could muster, and the trees in the take-off path appeared to reach up for us as we struggled for height. They also provided a hazard for the unwary on foot. Steady thuds, like distant bombing, went on by day and night as ripe coconuts fell......and anyone unfortunate to be hit by one would have been seriously injured. The beach was open to the ocean and shelved steeply, producing enormous breakers and a fierce undertow......We were all warned about this. Bathing under these conditions was extremely risky. Sadly, one unfortunate member of the detachment was drowned while we were there. Safer but probably having its own share of nasties was a shallow lagoon just inland of the beach. Here the Station had a motley collection of small sailing boats which we were invited to use." The radio link which it was 207 Squadron's job to provide is described by former navigator Jim Riley. "We flew from Negombo towards the Arabian coast until we reached 20°00'N 64°10'E, where we were to orbit until radio contact with a Canberra was established. After this we were to turn back towards Negombo, keeping in touch with the Canberra until it flew out of range. The timing proved very accurate, as we circled for only about ten minutes before contact was made. When we arrived at Negombo after twelve hours thirty-five minutes in the air we were just in time to hear the Canberra taking off on its next leg. On 17 September we began the homeward trip......and flew the last leg, from Nicosia to Marham on 19 September, Battle of Britain Saturday. We were briefed to arrive after 17.00Z, so that the flying display would be over, but favourable winds brought us to Marham at 15.45Z. We thought we might have to orbit, but Air Traffic Control gave us a landing 'slot' of 15.55Z, and we carried out a Gee homing and caused quite a stir among the thousands of spectators."

Meanwhile, crews at Marham flew five sorties in Exercise 'Momentum', during three of which the Washingtons used Wunstorf airfield in Germany as a base from which to test the defences of the UK. On 14 August a mock raid on Waverley Station, Edinburgh, was made from there after a circuitous route over Beachy Head, Rheims, and the North Sea before turning over the west coast of Scotland and beginning a let-down over north-east England to return to Marham. Five days later they again deployed to Wunstorf to attack Derby, this time returning to Germany. In September Exercise 'Mariner' involved fourteen-hour sorties over Icelandic waters to intercept an 'enemy' fleet.

Despite its other commitments and a lack of continued training, 207 Squadron took part in the Lawrence Minot Trophy contest again in September 1953 and did well by being placed fifth. Training for the annual Bomber Command Blind Bombing competition then began, but in the contest, held between 16 and 20 November, the squadron did not perform very well, finishing sixth out of eleven.

Sqn. Ldr. G. O'N. Fisher remembers an eventful 'Home Run' flight which began on 11 August 1953, when four Washingtons left Marham for Prestwick, where they refuelled in readiness for the next leg, to Stephenville, Newfoundland. On that 1,500-mile flight over the Atlantic, the four crews kept in touch with each other by radio, a wise precaution, as one of the aircraft began to experience trouble with an engine and the pilot expressed concern about the other three. Before long the pilot decided to divert to Bluie West One in Greenland, a USAF base which none of the crews had visited before. From the official charts it was clear that this was a most tricky place to land, consisting of a runway running up a glacial valley, with mountains at one end and water at the other! Even worse, the airfield was at the end of a thirty-mile (48 km.) winding fjord, and final approach demanded a steep descent from 2,000 feet. The troubled Washington was accompanied by Sqn. Ldr. Fisher's aircraft, and both managed to land safely. An engine change was needed, which would delay the crew of the faulty aircraft, so Sqn. Ldr. Fisher and his crew continued their flight, routing direct to Dover AFB, a nine-hour leg. There they were warned about an impending hurricane, so snatched a meal and took off for Davis–Monthan AFB. As soon as they had landed and cleared the runway, they were told to follow the 'Follow Me' vehicle and to keep accurately to the centre-line. "We were on a high-speed chase" recalls Sqn. Ldr. Fisher. "We followed that truck for miles in pitch darkness occasionally broken by arc lights which showed that we were passing through narrow gaps that had been opened in high palisades. It was clear why we had been told to keep to the centre line. On we went, over two main roads with traffic lights until at last we were marshalled to a halt and told to stop engines. Wearily we tumbled out. Our 'Old Faithful' had brought us to the middle of the desert, where she was surrounded by hundreds of her kind. One more elephant had reached her Valhalla."

John Hillier remembers also piloting a Washington on its homeward trip to Davis–Monthan. "20 October 1953 saw me with my crew starting out from Marham to return aircraft WF493 to the USA via Prestwick, Ernest Harmon AFB and Dover AFB. We arrived at Davis–Monthan AFB in Tucson, Arizona, in the early morning. After landing we followed the 'Follow Me' jeep off the runway and through the camp to the public highway, complete with outriders for two or three miles to another airfield, the crew in the blisters saying hello to all the pretty girls in their cars, which had been ushered onto the hard shoulder. It must have been something for them to tell when they arrived in their various offices, that they had been passed on the road by a B-29 in RAF colours! We returned to the UK by MATS to Prestwick and so to Marham by train." The 'other airfield' referred to by John Hillier would have been the desert storage area for which Davis–Monthan was and is justly famous.

The demise of the Washington

Before the year ended, 207 Squadron was given the news that re-equipment with the new English Electric Canberra jet-powered bomber would begin in the following

March. One pilot and eight navigators would convert with the squadron, but all other crews were to be posted. The squadron would then form part of the Canberra light bomber force.

Three more Washingtons were ferried to Tucson in December under Operation 'Home Run', and then in January 1954 the final operations involving 207 Squadron's Washingtons were flown. One aircraft took part in a Bomber Command exercise on 14 January during which its navigation lights were left on, attracting attention from intercepting fighters whose pilots reported being fascinated by the display! Sadly, one of the Washingtons being ferried back to the USA, 35 Squadron's WF495, ditched in Morecambe Bay on 26 January after take-off from Prestwick, and 207 Squadron flew twenty hours in two sorties in an unsuccessful attempt to locate it. Sqn. Ldr. Fisher's second ferry trip was in February, this time via the Azores and Bermuda, where his crew night-stopped. The next leg, from Bermuda to Dover AFB, was not without incident. "The weather seemed perfect", said Geoffrey Fisher. "After the met. briefing we decided to fly at 12,000 feet. With nothing to see but clear blue skies ahead we tucked into our packed lunches. 'George' [the automatic pilot] was flying, and I pushed back my seat and put my feet up on the trunnion carrying the rudder pedals to make myself more comfortable. Ahead of us in the distance at about our height there appeared a small cloud which seemed no bigger than a man's hand and of no vertical extent. Shortly after entering this isolated little puff of cloud there was the proverbial flash of lightning and a thundering roar, accompanied by the smell of ozone and the anguished yell of the radio operator, who had received the worst of the lightning strike via his now vanished trailing aerial. Momentarily stunned, we were relieved to find all four engines turning and nobody hurt. 'George' took it all in its stride, and we continued on course to Dover, where we found that the control surfaces in the vicinity of the static discharge wicks were peppered with tiny holes. Several years later the Bermuda Triangle made the headlines in a big way with reports of a whole Flight of aircraft vanishing and ships being lost without trace. I reckon we were lucky."

207 Squadron Canberra B.2s, WJ718 nearest, in close formation for a Battle of Britain Anniversary flypast over Whitehall on 15 September 1954. [J. Muston]

Just before 207 Squadron's last Washington left on its transatlantic crossing on 16 March, a ceremonial farewell parade was held. All available squadron personnel assembled and were inspected by Air Marshal Sir George Mills KCB DFC and Brig. Gen. P. H. Robey of the United States Air Force. Both officers addressed the parade before the aircraft taxied out on its last flight, and BBC Television, Pathé News and newspapermen were present. Flt. Lt. F. E. Cooke had the honour of piloting the Washington to the desert storage area at Tucson.

207 Squadron in the jet age

Hardly had the last Washington disappeared north-westwards when the first Canberra B.2 for 207 Squadron arrived on 26 March 1954 from Lindholme, piloted by Flt. Lt. D. M. Gossland. Others soon arrived from MUs at Aldergrove and Kinloss. Powered by two Rolls–Royce Avon RA.3 engines, each providing 6,500 lbs of thrust, the Canberra had a wing-span of 63 feet 11.5 inches (19.5 m.) and a length of 65 feet 6 inches (20 m.). Its bomb load was 6,000 lbs (2,722 kg.) and it had a range of 3,000 miles (4,830 km.). Maximum speed was over 600 mph (965 kph), a somewhat different kettle of fish than the Washington it replaced!

The designated eight aircraft had all been taken on charge by 14 April, but in May the establishment was increased to ten, the last of which did not appear until December! Until June, the squadron spent the time in familiarisation and in flying the first navigation and bombing training sorties, involving use of the Gee–H blind bombing equipment with which the new aircraft were fitted. At the end of the month, five aircraft made an over-water navigation flight as far as the Faroe Islands to coincide with an eclipse of the sun, after which the pilots were left not knowing whether to enter a day or a night flight in their log books! During July they took part in a major exercise, 'Dividend', in which they made 44 sorties in attacking UK targets.

John Muston was a navigator / observer with 207 Squadron from June 1954 to May 1955. He joined his crew at Marham direct from the Bomber Command Bombing School at Lindholme, they having gone through 231 OCU at Bassingbourn. Two days later, without any formal conversion training, he had his first flight in a Canberra, during which one bomb was dropped visually, with an error

A typical 207 Squadron Canberra crew in 1954: John Muston (navigator/observer); Barrie Mather (pilot); Tony Norman (navigator/Plotter). [J. Muston]

Flg. Off. Barrie Mather, the pilot of Canberra WH905, which on 25 October 1954 landed with one bomb 'hung up' On landing, there was an explosion, but luckily without injury to the crew. [J. Muston]

of only 55 yards (50 metres), which caused John to be "fairly chuffed." All three members of that crew were under 21 years of age, rare even then and probably impossible now.

Unserviceability plagued the squadron's Canberras in August. In three of them the tailplanes were found to have cracks, while WH905, flown by Flg. Off. W. C. Ford, struck a flock of gulls during its take-off run and was damaged. Adding to the tribulation, two 1,000 lb (455 kg.) bombs exploded on the airfield on 20 September, damaging one of 207's Canberras and others of 90 and 115 Squadrons on dispersals by blast and shrapnel. The CO, Sqn. Ldr. P. H. Gibbs, was for a short time in great danger as he rushed toward the scene of the explosion, and after the dust had settled squadron crews, having been safely esconced below tables in the crew-room, praised him unanimously for the acrobatic way in which he had ducked, sidestepped and dodged the flying debris.

Three of 207 Squadron's Canberras took part in the Battle of Britain flypast over Whitehall on 15 September, and on Sunday 19 September the squadron was represented in a parade in King's Lynn, when the salute was taken by the Mayor of that town.

Only one 'combat' crew yet existed, that of Flg. Off. Conchie, and they took part in Exercise 'Battle Royal' on 24 and 27 September, making attacks on continental targets at night. In October, however, six more crews attained the 'combat' status and were diligently training in long-range navigation. These included a trial 'Lone Ranger' flown by Flt. Lt. D. M. Gossland and crew on 9 November which took the Canberra to Gibraltar, Tripoli and Wunstorf.

A sad loss for the squadron

Further unfortunate incidents to squadron personnel and aircraft occurred before the end of 1954. On 25 October Flg. Off. B. J. Mather in WH905 (an unlucky aircraft) was obliged to return to Marham with a 25 lb. (11.4 kg.) bomb 'hung up'. As he touched down, the bomb was dislodged and exploded in the bomb-bay. Fortunately, nobody was injured and a small fire was quickly extinguished, with some damage to the Canberra. On board was John Muston, who remembers "an anxious few moments." Exactly a month later, Flt. Lt. P. J. F. Halliday was the pilot of a Canberra which was damaged by a flock of starlings while on final approach to Marham. But by far the most serious event is remembered by John Muston. "In the evening of 3 December, we returned to Marham in Canberra WH906, which was then refuelled and taken over by a newish crew of which the pilot was Flg. Off. C. J. Hasler. Later that night [at 00.56] it crashed three miles from the end of Marham's runway, with the loss of all three of the crew. As I recall, the cause was given as pilot error, but we were all convinced that it was a tailplane problem, and later events showed that we were probably right". On the other hand, former Canberra navigator Flg. Off. Terry Grewcock considers that it was probably an error on the pilot's part, and that he may have been confused by the sheer size of Marham's runway. The other officers who lost their lives that night were Flg. Offs. G. Hayes and G. Whitehouse.

During the early part of 1955 207 Squadron crews continued their bombing training, both blind and visual, as frequently as weather conditions and serviceability allowed. In March 322 hours were flown. A novel experience for some crews were the 'Lone Ranger' exercises which began as soon as proficiency had built up. These pleasant missions were designed to provide long-range navigation practice and operation from airfields hitherto unknown to the crews, who might find themselves required to service their own aircraft and to be generally self-reliant over a period of several days. In many cases the airfields were subject to extreme climatic conditions, providing a good test of the crews' personal resources. Among the many destinations were Tripoli/Idris and El Adem (Libya), Wunstorf (Germany), Fayid and Abu Suier (Egypt), Khormaksar (Aden), Luqa (Malta), Habbaniya (Iraq), Amman (Jordan), Gibraltar, and Nicosia (Cyprus).

Exercise 'Sky High' was held in April 1955, and involved a series of mock attacks on targets in the UK and on the Continent of Europe, testing the fighter defences at the same time. Forty-nine sorties were flown by 207 Squadron, reflecting the hard work put in by the ground crews to maintain serviceability.

The AOC's annual inspection was scheduled for 24 May, and rehearsals for a fly-past were arranged. During the rehearsal on 13 May two of the Canberras had the misfortune to collide in mid-air. Luckily the damage was not too serious, and WK142, lacking one tip-tank, was flown by Flg. Off. K. V. O'Rourke to make a safe landing at Marham while Flg. Off. N. Bissell made a belly-landing in WH876 at Wittering after losing most of his aileron control. Although this aircraft suffered extensive damage neither Flg. Off. Bissell nor his navigator, Flg. Off. Campbell, was injured.

Good weather and high serviceability combined during the summer of 1955 to allow 207 Squadron's pilots to fly a large number of hours. In June twenty sorties were flown in the large NATO Exercise 'Carte Blanche', while in July no less than 411 hours 40 minutes were spent in the air. This put the squadron in the position of the first unit in 3 Group to fly more than 400 hours in a month. However, 'Planned Flying & Planned Servicing' had been introduced into the RAF and in August the Station Commander, believing that the ground crews and other technical personnel would not be able to cope with such an intensive programme,

A view of Station Headquarters at Marham, taken from barrack block 33 in 1956. [J. Watts]

restricted each squadron to a maximum of 345 hours per month.

For September's Battle of Britain displays at RAF Stations, four of 207 Squadron's Canberras practised formation flying. A team of five crews, one of them a reserve, had been established for this pleasant task, the leader being Flt. Lt. P. F. J. Hillier. The others were Flg. Off. S. B. Sheppard, Flg. Off. B. J. Mather, Flg. Off. K. V. O'Rourke and Flg. Off. N. Bissell, the last two of whom had experienced the 'prang' on 13 May and no doubt were still wary of each other! On Battle of Britain day they flew to RAF Stations around the country to perform, and also gave a formation display over Huntingdon during a local jubilee. Three exercises were also held in September, all very successful. Code-named 'Beware', 'Air Enterprise' and 'Foxpaw', the exercises were much enjoyed by those crews who enjoyed longer-distance flights, as they involved a detachment of three Canberras to Sola in Norway and five to Geilenkirchen in Germany.

Sometimes members of the squadron were subjected to the rigours of Escape & Evasion exercises in the Stanford Battle Training Area, but even worse were the twelve-mile (19.3 km.) walks which were supposed to be completed within three hours. When first organised, the walks took place on Wednesday afternoons, and nobody managed to return within the stipulated time. Then the Station PFO changed the timing to the morning and the destination to the Old Bell Inn in Marham village, after which nearly everybody put up a good performance! Then someone measured the route and found that it was nearer fourteen miles (22.5 km.) than twelve!

Canberras no more

Apart from involvement in Exercise 'Phoenix' in October, during which fourteen sorties were flown, the remainder of 1955 was spent in routine training, including many 'Lone Rangers' to well-known distant airfields like Habbaniya in Iraq, Khormaksar in Aden and Eastleigh in Kenya. 207 Squadron maintained its place at the very top of the 3 Group Efficiency Ladder, but then came the news that after less than two years the squadron was to be disbanded and then re-formed as part of the new V–Force, flying Vickers Valiant bombers. The routine of continuation training occupied the crews during January and February 1956, although the CO, Sqn. Ldr. Gibbs, left on 14 January to undergo a course with 232 Operational Conversion Unit at Gaydon. He was replaced by Flt. Lt. R. B. McGowan, whose task it was to carry out disbandment procedures. Only three crews remained on 207 Squadron by the end of February, the others having been posted to other Canberra squadrons at Marham, and those three were still present when the squadron disbanded on 27 March 1956.

Canberra B.2 WK102 of 207 Squadron 'B' Flight in the snow at Marham during the winter of 1955. [J. Watts]

This drawing by Michael Turner evokes a feeling of impending action, showing a crew running to board their 207 Squadron Valiant after a Quick Action Alert. [by kind permission of Michael Turner]

Chapter 11: The V-Force

Enter the V–bombers

After only four days in limbo, 207 Squadron was re-formed at Marham as a constituent of the V-bomber force on 1 April 1956, the 38th birthday of the Royal Air Force. Sqn. Ldr. Gibbs returned from Gaydon and assumed command of the squadron temporarily pending the arrival of Wg. Cdr. D. D. Haig DSO DFC, the higher rank having been stipulated for commanders of squadrons in the highly-important V-Force. On Wg. Cdr. Haig's arrival on 28 May, Sqn. Ldr. Gibbs became CO of the squadron's 'A' Flight. Chosen to equip the revived squadron was the Vickers Valiant jet-propelled bomber.

First flown at Vickers' test airfield at Wisley on 18 May 1951, the Valiant B.1 was powered by four Rolls-Royce Avon RA.28 engines of 10,000 lb. static thrust. Crews comprised two pilots, two navigators (one a plotter and the other a radar operator) and an AEO (Air Electronics Officer, or Operator if he was an NCO). The Valiant's maximum speed is given as 567 mph (913 kph) at an altitude of 30,000 feet, but it could climb to a service ceiling of 54,000 feet. With underwing auxiliary fuel tanks (not jettisonable) its range was quoted as 4500 miles (7,245 km.). A conventional bomb-load of 21,000 lbs. (9,545 kg.) could be carried, but no defensive armament was fitted.

While the aircraft were under construction an RAF Chief Technician of the Aircraft Fitter trade was 'attached' to each airframe and watched its progress from that point on. He remained with it as the Aircraft Servicing Chief (ASC) or 'Crew Chief'. Each Crew Chief was responsible for the first-line servicing and maintenance of his aircraft and for the supervision of the airmen working on it. This was one of the most responsible of ground crew tasks and demanded very high standards of technical and managerial skills. Clearly, benefits were to be obtained from being responsible for one aircraft, and a competitive spirit developed among those involved, which was not often the case when resources were pooled.

The first production Valiant had been delivered to the RAF in January 1955. Three of the first VIPs to see the new aircraft were, perhaps surprisingly, Russian – Nikita Kruschev, Marshal Nikolai Bulganin and Mr. A. N. Tupolev, the designer of several Russian bomber aircraft, who arrived at Marham on 23 April 1956 in a Viscount aircraft of British European Airways. Three of Marham's Valiants flew by, as did a Canberra and a Hunter, and as the Russian party was being driven between two rows of Canberras toward the control tower, all the aircraft engines were started by cartridge. When the Russians were on the balcony of the control tower, a Valiant made a very low flypast and as it did so a Vulcan approached, made an almost vertical climb and disappeared into the clouds. All this seems to have failed to impress Kruschev, who remarked later that ".........the RAF was trying to frighten me, but it didn't work".

A fine close-up photograph of a Valiant B.1, though not necessarily a 207 Squadron aircraft.

The Valiant's systems

The Valiant was the largest, heaviest and most complex aircraft that 207 Squadron ever operated. It could fly further, faster, higher and with a heavier bomb load than any other type the squadron had flown. In some ways, especially with regard to its systems, it was unique. Being a first-generation four-jet aircraft, it was relatively unsophisticated compared with later aircraft such as the Vulcan B.2 and the Victor, and this tended to make its operation more difficult for the crew. Instrumentation consisted of large instruments essentially similar to those on previous aircraft, both piston and jet-engined; miniaturised and combined instruments came with second- and later-generation aircraft. One unique aspect was that the aircraft was essentially all-electric. Nearly 100 kW. of power was provided by generators fitted to each engine, and even on those systems which had to be operated hydraulically, such as powered flying controls and wheel brakes, the hydraulic systems were driven by their own electric motors. This resulted in the powered flying controls having three methods of operation – full power, half power and manual reversion. The latter mode gave flying instructors and examiners endless scope for masochistic treatment of pilots, for there cannot have been many aircraft heavier to fly than a Valiant under manual control; neither Vulcan nor Victor had manual reversion.

In the configuration in which 207 Squadron operated it, the 10,000 gallons (45,000 litres) of fuel were carried in ten tanks distributed between wings and fuselage. The fuel state was monitored by the two pilots, who had to track both the consumption and the distribution between tanks to ensure that balance remained within limits. As this was done without an integrating gauge for calculation their mental arithmetic became quite sharp! Management of the vital electrical system depended on the AEO, and as with flight engineers on earlier aircraft, co-operation between pilots and AEOs was particularly close. It is entirely understandable that very comprehensive training was essential to enable all crew members, individually and collectively, to operate an aircraft of this unsophisticated complexity. This training was carried out at 232 OCU at Gaydon.

As an element of Bomber Command's Main Force, 207 Squadron's role was unchanged. Its initial establishment was eight Valiants and eight crews, all of whom had arrived from their conversion course at Gaydon by the end of June, and in early July the eighth Valiant was ferried in. Each aircraft was allocated to a specific crew and was flown as and when it could be made ready. Long hours waiting for an aircraft to become serviceable became the normal way of things, and crews averaged two flights each week, totalling about thirty hours in the air per month.

207 Squadron Valiant B.1 being inspected by the public at an air display

Presentation of the squadron standard

Almost at once, squadron personnel were 'highly chuffed' to receive the news that a squadron standard was to be presented by Her Majesty the Queen. Rehearsals for the parade and other essential preparations were put in hand at once. Selected as standard bearer was Flg. Off. R. C. Haven, and his escorts were Sgts. F. Sears and W. Courtnage, all of whom departed for the home of RAF drill at Uxbridge at the end of June to 'learn the ropes'. Other squadron officers were issued with wooden swords with which to refresh their memories of the intricacies of ceremonial drill. For the next few weeks it was dangerous to enter a squadron office without first checking through the window whether the inmate was practising his swordsmanship!

The big day was 23 July 1956, when Her Majesty the Queen and HRH the Duke of Edinburgh visited Marham to review Bomber Command. On arrival in an aircraft of the Queen's Flight, they were received by the Lord Lieutenant of Norfolk and the Chief of the Air Staff, ACM Sir Dermot Boyle KCVO KBE CB AFC, who presented the AOC-in-C of Bomber Command, AM Sir Harry Broadhurst KCB KBE DSO DFC AFC, the AOC of 1 Group, AVM Sir John Whitley KBE CB DSO AFC, the AOC of 3 Group, AVM K. B. Cross CB CBE DSO DFC, and Marham's Station Commander, Gp. Capt. L. M. Hodges DSO OBE DFC. Her Majesty's first formal function of the day was to present the standard approved by her late father, King George VI, to 207 Squadron, a proud moment for the squadron personnel. The presentation of a standard is the greatest honour which can be given to a squadron, conferable only after 25 years of active and honourable service, and this was the first

Her Majesty the Queen presented its standard to 207 Squadron on 23 July 1956, and is seen here approaching the officer in command of No. 1 Flight on the parade, Sqn. Ldr. P. H. Gibbs. Accompanying Her Majesty was Wg. Cdr. D. D. Haig, the squadron's CO, and behind are HRH Prince Phillip, the Lord Lieutenant of Norfolk and two senior officers, one of them almost hidden.

occasion on which a reigning sovereign had presented a standard to a regular RAF squadron. Accompanied by Wg. Cdr. Haig, Her Majesty inspected a guard of honour, and the standard was paraded in slow time before being marched off. After the ceremony came a review of a static display of Canberra, Valiant, Victor and Vulcan aircraft, followed by a closer inspection of a Valiant with Wg. Cdr. L. H. Trent VC DFC in attendance. The fly-past after lunch consisted of eight Wings of nine Canberras in vics of three and five boxes of four Valiants, including two of 207 Squadron's new aircraft.

The summer of 1956 was devoted to intensive training in navigation and bombing techniques to ensure that the crews quickly became familiar with the Valiant aircraft. During this period the ground crews, which were not up to establishment numbers until August, worked particularly hard. In addition to manpower shortages, the airmen were comparatively inexperienced on the type and had to deal with a significant programme of modifications. To add to their difficulties, on 31 July Flt. Lt. E. A. J. 'Olly' Crooks AFC was alarmed to find that while flying at high altitude the cabin pressurisation in his Valiant had increased to the equivalent of sea level pressure, and then one engine failed. To his immense relief, after landing at Marham he learned that the fuselage showed no signs of damage.

At this time, a typical training sortie entailed three simulated radar attacks flown at high level (35,000 to 45,000 feet) against industrial targets, scored by Radar Bomb Scoring Units (RBSU) located around the United Kingdom. These were followed by 1000+ nautical miles long navigation stages, utilising primary, secondary or limited navigational aids. On return to Marham the sortie would end with several approaches and roller landings in a variety of engine and airframe configurations, with occasional practice diversions to other airfields.

Naturally enough, the Valiant was of immense interest to the general public at this time, and during September two were sent away for static display at Battle of Britain 'Open Days', one to St. Athan and one to Benson. In addition, Wg. Cdr. Haig, Sqn. Ldr. F. C. D. Wright DFC and Sqn. Ldr. J. D. Crook performed fly-pasts at eight airfields open to the public.

Crisis in Suez

In the background, however, was the developing crisis in the Middle East, where on 26 July the Egyptian President, Col. Nasser, had nationalised the Anglo–French controlled Suez Canal Company. France and Britain were extremely angry, and Prime Minister Anthony Eden insisted that "...........a man with Col. Nasser's record cannot be allowed to have his thumb on our windpipe." Within days, British forces embarked for Cyprus, and the aircraft carrier HMS *Theseus* left Portsmouth with troops of the 16th Parachute Brigade. Meanwhile, attempts to persuade Nasser to allow international operation of the canal proved fruitless. On 29 October Israeli forces saw an opportunity, invaded the Sinai peninsula and advanced to within twenty miles (32 km.) of the Suez Canal, but next day Britain and France demanded that Israel must withdraw within twelve hours.

207 Squadron's part in the conflict had started in August, when several squadrons were instructed to stand by for possible operation in the Middle East. Training was at once intensified and included night flying and visual bombing practice. On 24 September the CO flew to Luqa in Malta, taking with him Marham's Station Commander, Gp. Capt. L. M. Hodges DSO OBE DFC, who was to command the Malta Bomber Wing, which had been established at

Two views of 207 Squadron Valiant B.1 WZ404 at Luqa during the short Suez operation. [via John Visanich]

Luqa to be ready for probable action under Operation 'Albert'. By the end of October all the squadron's aircraft and crews were there. Ground crews flew out in noisy Shackleton aircraft of Coastal Command, in which there were no seats, just mattresses laid on the floor. An Elsan closet stood in the centre, but one of the airmen involved, SAC James Watts, is unable to remember anyone using it during the nine-hour flight! When established, crews were briefed on the quite serious threat posed by the Egyptian Air Force, which had a number of modern fighter aircraft of Russian manufacture as well as Meteor NF.11 night-fighters. Top priority was therefore to eliminate the EAF, a task for which a two-day period was considered feasible. Night bombing to crater the runways on the Egyptian airfields was planned, followed by dawn attacks to destroy the aircraft.

A major problem, however, was the condition of the Valiants' bombing equipment, several of the aircraft not having been fitted with a complete Navigational Bombing System, which comprised a H2S Mk.9a with a Navigational Ballistic Computer. It fell upon the Valiant crews, therefore, to make use of the T4 visual bombsights, an expedient considered acceptable if visibility was good. The squadron was briefed to bomb from 28,000 feet, which the crews queried, as they knew that the Meteors could easily reach that altitude. It was then decided that 45,000 feet might be safer!

On 31 October, Raid 3, the first aggressive mission by 207 Squadron, was mounted. Five of the squadron's Valiants, led by Wg. Cdr. D. D. Haig in WZ404 and accompanied by eighteen Canberras, attacked Kabrit airfield that night, together dropping a total of 132 1,000 lb. (455 kg.) bombs, all of which were believed to have fallen within 450 yards (410 m.) of the marker. There was no opposition at all, but many MiG fighters were seen on the ground, and at least three were claimed as destroyed by the four target-marking Canberras. Crews also noticed hundreds of wooden crates containing Russian aircraft to be assembled after delivery by ship in the Bitter Lake. Next night a raid on Kasfareet airfield by two Valiants took place as Raid 9, and hits on the runway intersection were reported as well as large fires in the target area. One of the Valiants with a record of going unserviceable, WP219, suffered a cracked canopy, but as anti-aircraft fire was light this was not thought to have been the cause. On the night of 4/5 November, Raid 18, an attack on fortifications at El Agami Island near Alexandria, was made by four Valiants, each carrying twelve 1,000 lb. (455 kg.) 'iron' bombs, a fifth having returned early with undercarriage problems. In the lead was Sqn. Ldr. F. C. Wright DFC in XD813. This time, anti-aircraft defences made themselves felt, but no RAF aircraft were hit. The object behind this mission was to lead the Egyptians to believe that an Anglo-French amphibious landing was to be made nearby, but it was not a success, as although the target markers fell on the island they bounced into the sea, thus preventing most of the aircraft from bombing.

These eleven sorties were the total of 207 Squadron's activities in the Suez campaign, as the Allied forces gained control of the Canal on 6 November. For ground crews, the operation was a time of very hard work over days of sixteen hours on duty. On 7/8 November the squadron flew back to Marham, where the crews continued to be at readiness, as Kruschev had made a 'Rockets against Britain' threat. The departure of the Valiants coincided with the sighting off Malta of Russian photographic reconnaissance aircraft which were persuaded to leave by Hunters. Kruschev soon calmed down, and December was spent in routine training exercises.

In total, Bomber Command aircraft had flown 49 Valiant and 278 Canberra sorties over Suez, but in a later analysis their contribution was said to have been of limited value, credit for the destruction of the EAF going to the fighter–bomber force. Part of the reason was seen to have been because the bombs carried were restricted to 1,000-pounders, which were unlikely to have much effect on runways and other airfield installations. Although in theory the RAF was using the most sophisticated bomb-delivery system then available, the Valiants were not yet fully equipped and crews were not experienced or combat-ready. They were forced by circumstances beyond their control to bomb from very high altitudes, using rudimentary aiming methods developed before the Second World War. The Suez affair combined with Russia's threatening posture brought the four V-bomber squadrons which comprised the V-Force into focus. A benefit derived from the campaign was thus that it brought home to the powers-that-be the pressing need for the force to be brought up to full operational standard without delay.

While in Malta, James Watts and some of his mates, ready for a few hours of sightseeing, were briefed by an officer (presumably the SMO) to avoid visiting 'The Gut', Valletta's red-light district at that time, and were then told the best way to find it! However, they decided to see Grand Harbour instead, and managed to board the aircraft carrier HMS *Bulwark* without being challenged until they reached the flight deck. On being told in no uncertain terms to leave, they found that their boatman was demanding a much-increased fare for the journey back to the quayside!

To mark Bomber Command's part in the Suez operation, a parade was held at Upwood on 19 February 1957. The reviewing officer was Air Chief Marshal HRH the Duke of Gloucester, and 207 Squadron was represented by Sqn. Ldr. Gibbs.

During February plans were made for 148 and 207 Squadrons to visit the Gold Coast to take part in that country's independence celebrations. Wg. Cdr. Haig was placed in command of the detachment and flew to Accra by civil airliner on 12 February to make the arrangements. The detachment, comprising two Valiants from each squadron and forty ground crew from 207 Squadron, left Marham on 28 February and night-stopped at Tripoli/Idris. Flying with Wg. Cdr. Haig was the AOC 3 Group. On arrival, the four Valiants made flypasts on three consecutive days, the final one on 6 March, when Dr. Nkrumah, the new Prime Minister and self-styled liberator of his people, opened the Parliament of the new country, Ghana. Two days later the Valiants began their homeward flight via Luqa.

In March and April 1957, the squadron was able to take part in Operation 'Goldflake', which was designed to ensure that at least one bomber squadron was at readiness in the Mediterranean area on a rotating basis in case of further trouble. Thus six Valiants returned to Luqa, where the crews concentrated on visual bombing on ranges at El Adem and Tarhuna in Libya and on Filfla Island off Malta in the prevailing fine weather. At the same time, the opportunity of participating in Exercise 'Red Pivot' was taken. This was designed to test the defences of the United States 6th Fleet, and was a great success for 207 Squadron. At the subsequent debriefing, US Navy staff frankly admitted the difficulty they had experienced in intercepting the Valiants.

On return to the base, squadron members began to prepare for the annual inspection by the AOC, soon after which the CO was promoted to Gp. Capt. and posted to Finningley as Station Commander. His place was taken by Wg. Cdr. C. P. N. Newman OBE DFC.

Going for the Trophies

In previous years two separate bombing competitions had been held, the Lawrence Minot Trophy for visual bombing and the Sir Phillip Sassoon Trophy for blind bombing and navigation. In 1957 the two contests were amalgamated as the Bomber Command Bombing Competition, and from 21 to 26 June two 207 Squadron crews, those of Sqn. Ldr. H. A. Smith DFC and Sqn. Ldr. J. D. Cook, competed. Three awards were contested — the Armament Officers' Trophy for the best squadron in bombing; the Sir Phillip Sassoon Trophy for the best squadron in navigation; and the Lawrence Minot Trophy for the best overall results. Each crew had to fly three sorties involving a navigation exercise and three unseen targets. That year 207 Squadron was placed fifth in the overall results.

'Lone Ranger' exercises were reinstated on 1 June, when Flt. Lt. Cook took off on a two-day trip to Tripoli/Idris. Although almost always enjoyable, 'Lone Rangers' were far from mere 'jollies'. They gave crews valuable experience of long flights over new territory, flying into and out of unfamiliar airfields which were often not RAF-controlled or even military. Furthermore, the crew operated without benefit of the usual servicing support and had to carry out the necessary routine turn-rounds and the minor servicing needed after some fifty hours of flying, so that an immediate return to the UK could be made if recalled. For this latter task the crew was increased to six by the addition of the crew chief, that highly experienced senior NCO tradesman.

August and September were occupied by another 'Goldflake'. Again the task was visual bombing, which proved so difficult to carry out in British weather

The bare metal finish to the Valiant is illustrated here by WZ403. [via R. C. B. Ashworth]

conditions. While in Malta, Wg. Cdr. 'Ace' Newman found time to visit Turkey on a 'flag-waving' mission, touching down at Eskeshir and Esenboga and, so rumour has it, greatly enhancing British prestige by his drinking and debating ability! Back in the UK, three of the squadron's Valiants were deployed to Aldergrove, Benson and Leconfield for participation in the static displays at the 1957 Battle of Britain air shows, while the CO gave flying displays at six airfields.

Apart from the effects of a gale in November, when the port wingtip of a Valiant was damaged by a low-flying hut, the remainder of 1957 passed without incident, continuation training being the main task. All pilots spent time in the flight simulator which now formed part of the Station's equipment, learning and practising the art of dealing with emergency situations and equipment malfunctions. In the opinion of the squadron diarist and probably of the crews of 207 Squadron, the flight simulator was the most useful ground trainer ever invented.

In the Bomber Command Bombing Trophy in 1958 the squadron won the Armament Officers' trophy and only missed the Lawrence Minot Trophy by ten points. The individual bombing competition was won by Sqn. Ldr. R. W. Payne and his crew, and in the next list of Queen's Birthday Honours he and his bomb-aimer, Sqn. Ldr. D. S. Collier, were awarded the AFC.

During 1958, a 207 Squadron crew was sent with a Valiant, in some secrecy, to the Royal Aircraft Establishment at Farnborough. After modification to the aircraft and some intensive training for the crew, a two-hour test flight was made to assess the compatibility of the Valiant and its proposed new weapon – a nuclear device. On this flight the crew had the company of an American 'weapon custodian' who carried a loaded side-arm. Eventually, American weapons specialists were based at Marham alongside the RAF squadrons.

Flt. Lt. John Scullard joined 207 Squadron in the early summer of 1958 after flying training at Cranwell, with a mere 330 hours of flying on the piston-engined Provost and the Vampire to his credit. Until that time, Bomber Command had decreed that all V-Force co-pilots must have completed at least one flying tour before joining the Force, but now it was decided that a few men direct from training could be accepted as an experiment. After an interview with the AOC 3 Group, AVM Kenneth 'Bing' Cross, John went to 232 OCU at Gaydon for a four-month conversion course before arriving at Marham. He found that after the youthful environment at Cranwell it was very strange to be among people who were considerably older, and were married, with children. In the mess DSOs and DFCs abounded, and a newcomer felt like a 'sprog' with shiny new 'wings' and a thin Pilot Officer's braid.

At Gaydon, John Scullard had been crewed up with Flt. Lt. Ken Marwood AFM, who had been a co-pilot with 148 Squadron and was now moving to 207 Squadron to take over Sqn. Ldr. Cook's established crew — Flt. Lt. Dave Jeffery (Navigator/Radar), Flt. Lt. Jim Wyld (Navigator/Plotter) and Sgt. John Pagler (AEO). They were brought together at Gaydon and as a crew completed the final conversion exercises before being posted to 207 Squadron at Marham, which was commonly known as 'El Adem with grass'! The Valiant allocated to Ken Marwood's crew was XD813, which none of the other captains liked because they believed that it could not fly a straight line. "Nevertheless", says Ken, "it never let us down." He goes on to say that life on the squadron was relatively easy in those early days, with lots of study periods so that the crews knew their allocated war targets intimately. "We flew about thirty hours per month, with perhaps half by night, although that proportion varied with the time of year. We pilots also had to spend several hours in the flight simulator so that we were capable of handling any emergency in the air."

Wg. Cdr. Newman was promoted to Gp. Capt. on 1 January 1959 and before he left for the RAF Staff College in April he was succeeded by Wg. Cdr. W. D. Robertson. In May of that year, Exercise 'Mayflight' was staged with the aim of practising the procedures for the Bomber Command Alert & Readiness (BCAR) plan. This involved dispersing aircraft elsewhere, in 207 Squadron's case to Filton and the Fleet Air Arm airfield at Yeovilton, with four crews at each. The first period of operation at Yeovilton lasted three days, and crews lived in standard five-berth crew caravans which had been specially designed for the V-Force. Each member of the five-man crew had a private bedroom, and there was a central ablutions caravan. Periodically, the Bomber Controller called the crews to cockpit readiness (Readiness State 05).

In July 1959 Sqn. Ldr. P. P. Coventry was lent to 214 Squadron and flew to Cape Town to act as the RAF liaison officer during the first non-stop air-refuelled flight from the UK, which was captained by Wg. Cdr. M. J. Beetham, the CO of 214 Squadron and later Chief of the Air Staff. A coincidence was that at the time the two squadrons occupied adjoining hangars at Marham, and that 214 Squadron had originally been 7A Squadron RNAS, which had been formed from 7 Squadron RNAS, 207 Squadron's ancestor, at Coudekerke in northern France 43 years before.

In February 1960 Flg. Off. J. W. Blockey, a co-pilot, was selected for the RAF bobsleigh team and spent two weeks at St. Moritz, where he hurtled down the Cresta and other runs at breakneck speed. He was already a fine all-round athlete and hockey-player. Neither did squadron pilots confine themselves to flying Valiants. On 18 June Flt. Lt. G. J. Rondel, flying an Olympia Mk.2B sailplane, reached an altitude of 28,600 feet, and in February of the following year he was awarded the De Havilland Trophy for the greatest gain of altitude in such a machine.

Apart from 'Lone Rangers', 207 Squadron took advantage of the facility whereby selected crews could fly to the United States under the title 'Western Ranger'. Their route was via Goose Bay to Offutt AFB near Omaha, Nebraska, the headquarters of Strategic Air Command. At Goose Bay the Valiant crews used the RCAF section of the airfield and, in the words of Ken Marwood, "...... enjoyed some marvellous thrashes with the RCAF aircrews in the officers' mess, a lovely wooden building." Between Goose Bay and Offutt, three simulated radar-scored bombing runs on selected targets were always made.

A squadron dining-in night on 24 March 1960 proved memorable to those attending, who included former members of the squadron from as long ago as the First World War. After dinner, Wg. Cdr. Robertson welcomed the guests and recalled briefly some of the highlights of the squadron's long and distinguished history. He then played excerpts from the BBC recording made by Wynford Vaughan-Thomas in September 1943 during a raid on Berlin. On behalf of the guests, Gp. Capt. Green replied, and recalled incidents both amusing and hair-raising from his time with the squadron. Throughout the proceedings, the squadron standard stood unfurled behind the CO's chair, its battle honours on display. Speeches over, the assembled throng repaired to the ante-room, there to demonstrate that after-dinner activities and consumption of alcoholic beverages had not altered over the years!

The Lawrence Minot Trophy is ours!

1960 was the first year in which 207 Squadron won the coveted Lawrence Minot Trophy since its introduction in 1927, although it had come very close to doing so on a number of occasions. The Armament Officers' Trophy also came to 207 Squadron that year, for the second time. Two of the six crews who competed performed particularly well, Wg. Cdr. W. D. Robertson being placed second in the individual bombing figures and Flt. Lt. K. M. Marwood

Another picture of WZ403, this time airborne and in white anti-flash paint, now with the squadron badge on the fin.
[207 Squadron archives]

second in bombing and navigation combined, but victory was the result of teamwork in which the ground crews played a major part. Between 10 January and 17 March the squadron devoted a great deal of time to the forthcoming Competition, which lasted for four nights. After the third night, 207 Squadron was not leading but was still well in the running, and Ken Marwood's crew was the 'anchor' crew scheduled to fly on the final night. The format was the standard three radar-scored radar bombing runs followed by a 1,000-mile (1,610 km.) navigation leg using only astro-navigation. "I was flying my beloved XD813," says Ken, "and for the bombing runs I normally disengaged the autopilot because I could fly the aeroplane more smoothly. Our first two bombing runs were scored as DHs, but this time I left her with autopilot connected, as over many practices, and with fine tuning by our crew chief (Ch. Tech. McAlpine) it was flying the aeroplane so smoothly without my assistance. Unfortunately, during the last couple of miles to 'Release' the autopilot started a slow un-noticed descent. Although I disengaged immediately, the small change of height (only some 200 feet) had been detected by the ground radar plotter, and it assessed the score (incorrectly) as 109 yards (100 m.) out. However, the next leg was a navigation leg, when only limited navigation aids were permitted, in this case astro-navigation. Whenever Jim Wyld, the Nav. Plotter, was taking astro shots, I flew the aircraft manually as I knew well by then all of XD813's idiosyncrasies. Unbelievable though it may seem, we aimed to finish the period of the astro shot within half a knot airspeed and a quarter of a degree of heading compared with the figures at the beginning of the shot. There would be no variation of altitude at all. This paid dividends, as usual, and we were scored at the end of the thousand-mile leg as being only 250 yards (229 m.) from the target. These results clinched the prizes for 207 Squadron, which won the Laurence Minot and the Armament Officers' Trophies. My own crew was pipped by only one point by a 148 Squadron crew for the award for the best crew in the competition – if only I'd flown that third run manually!"

Ken Marwood remembers being in Malta for the Battle of Britain celebrations in September 1960. "We operated from Ta Kali, just below the old city of Mdina, adjacent to Rabat," he says. "We were parked on the old fighter operational readiness platform at the end of the longest runway, some 4,800 feet (1,463 m.) or so [long] – a bit on the short side, even for a Valiant. There were three of us – Sqn. Ldr. Pete Coventry, Flt. Lt. Mike Cawsey and myself, and we all had very light fuel loads. We performed our standard Valiant scramble...... and on *the* day we had all three [aircraft] rolling at the same time. Each had a different rôle to play before the crowds; I can't recall exactly what the other two did, but mine was a very steep climb away at minimum speed, not much above stalling speed! The Valiant could match the climb-away *attitude* of the Vulcan, but with less power the rate of climb was not as good. On this occasion I climbed to 2,000-plus feet and did a quick wing-over and descended straight onto 'finals' at Luqa. My flight time was exactly two minutes 35 seconds, so it is in my logbook as five minutes (rounded up). Had I been able to cut the time by six seconds the flight would not have been loggable! Previously, we had had lots of fun during rehearsals. Pete Coventry led us in a tail-chase all round Malta and Gozo, with run-ins and breaks to land at Ta Kali. We also managed to do some illegal close formation flying out of sight of the 'wheels' in Malta."

Operationally, 207 Squadron had been at the disposal of SACEUR since January 1960, but remained under Bomber Command's control for training and administration. Gen. Norstad, SACEUR himself, visited Marham on 13 October 1960 to welcome the squadron to NATO officially and to watch a simultaneous start and scramble by four of 207 Squadron's Valiants. All were in the air within one minute twenty-five seconds, prompting the General to write to the AOC–in–C Bomber Command that "......the scramble was

Valiant B.1 WZ405 slumbers peacefully, protected from possible crowds at an open day by ropes. On its fin is a stylised version of the squadron badge, while in the background is an Auster of the Army Air Corps and a Provost. [via R. C. B. Ashworth]

tremendously impressive and without doubt the best I have witnessed." A significant factor in the rapid take-off was a modification invented by a 207 Squadron Crew Chief – 'Simstart' – which enabled all four engines of the Valiant to be started simultaneously instead of singly in sequence.

Apart from the routine Bomber Command exercises, 207 Squadron's assignment to SACEUR committed the squadron to maintaining an aircraft and crew on Quick Reaction Alert status. QRA duty was for 24 hours on weekdays and 48 hours over weekends, a rota which came round every few weeks. Initially the QRA crew was located in the Operations Block, conveniently opposite 207 Squadron's hangar. Crews ate in the aircrew buffet there and slept in one of the standard aircrew caravans parked behind the block. On duty, crews were permanently dressed in flying kit and were ready to take off at fifteen minutes' notice in their fully-armed Valiant to counter any threat of nuclear attack. From time to time a practice 'scramble' was held to determine reaction times, which helped reduce the boredom and increased the flow of adrenaline!

Later, accommodation was provided next to the highly secure QRA aircraft dispersal on the south-east side of the airfield, diametrically opposite the Operations Block and thus some distance away. 207 Squadron crews were joined by crews from 49 and 148 Squadrons, with four Valiants kept permanently on fifteen minutes' alert (RS 15). Each of the three squadrons was allocated a specific SACEUR war target, the fourth being shared on rotation by all three. Increases in Readiness State from RS 15 to RS 05 (cockpit readiness) was ordered by the Bomber Controller through teletalk, the announcement being preceded by the ringing of particularly loud and intrusive alarm bells – a sound which all those who experienced and reacted to it will never forget! These exercises were known as Exercise 'Edom' and in accordance with Bomber Command Standard Operating Procedures were required to be called at intervals of no greater than 36 hours. The next Readiness State was RS 02 – 'Start engines' – but this was never practised by Valiant QRA crews loaded with American weapons.

While the new QRA accommodation area was more spacious and comfortable than the old aircrew caravans, there were no catering facilities, meals being towed around the airfield in heated trolleys. Former Flt. Lt. Ken Hunter remembers the accommodation without affection. "QRA duty was a miserable affair," he says. "The sordid accommodation next to the QRA aircraft dispersal was permanently swamped with cigarette smoke and although the stigma attached to smoking had not taken effect, if the thickness of the atmosphere was anything to go by a lot of lung cancer started there."

While on the ground, crews spent many hours projecting radar pictures of training targets and studying their allocated war targets and the routes to and from them. For these activities, the crews were locked in secure window-less rooms so that highly classified material could be studied without fear of interruption. The end results of the crews' tasks were kept in a 'Go–Bag' which was locked away in the operations room until an urgent operational requirement developed – which never happened. From time to time, senior staff would check the crews for their knowledge and combat readiness.

On 10 May 1961, Exercise 'Mayflight' began. Crews were permitted to live in the mess in flying kit, but upon receipt of an 'Alpha Blue' alert, they came to 45 minutes readiness. A 'Bravo Blue' alert was given at 18.00, and four Valiants took off for Cranwell, where dedicated dispersal facilities had been provided on the south-eastern side of the airfield. The alert state was altered several times over the next couple of days, the crews living in caravans on the dispersal site, until on the Friday evening HQ Bomber Command issued a stand-down order, with the proviso that there would be a scramble at some time on the following day. Cranwell's Station Commander, Gp. Capt. Hugh Lynch–Blosse, issued an invitation to the four crews for the use of the Trenchard Bar during the evening, sweaty flying suits notwithstanding, an invitation all except one captain who had a heavy cold accepted with alacrity. Ken Marwood remembers the evening well. "As the evening wore on," he says, "207 Squadron rose to the challenge issued by the Cranwell officers, including schooner races involving a circuit of the mess via very prickly rose bushes! Cranwell simply could not beat 207 at any of these events. Then they issued a new challenge. The idea was to pile bar stools on top of one another until they almost reached the quite high ceiling. We were required to climb up this very steep pile and to make contact with our backsides. After a demonstration by the opposition, I went up first of the 207 team, did the necessary and dropped, none too gently, to the floor – my ankle was only slightly twisted. Peter Coventry was next. After making contact with the ceiling he jumped clear. The only snag was that he jumped outwards, still holding a full beer mug. The pile of stools flew in the opposite direction. He landed in a horizontal attitude on his elbows and knees. He got to his feet still holding the beer mug handle – the rest had disintegrated – and rubbing his left elbow, which was 'hurting a bit'. Mike Cawsey was next up the rebuilt pile……and descended in exactly the same manner as Peter……with another painful elbow. Cranwell conceded another victory to 207 Squadron and the evening continued with high fuel consumption until around 04.00 hours, when we were driven back to our dispersal and bed. At about 07.00 I was awakened by Peter, who told me that he thought both he and Mike had broken their arms! It was a beautiful morning, hot and sunny. Before long we were brought to cockpit readiness and there we sat for a long time, ready to fly if needed. When the readiness state was relaxed slightly we were allowed to leave the aircraft. Mike Cawsey felt so ill that he had to go to Sick Quarters, from where he was taken to RAF Hospital Nocton Hall. Several hours later he returned with his arm in plaster; it was well and truly broken at the elbow joint. Robbie Robinson took over as captain but Peter Coventry had no option but to carry on, becoming paler and greener by the hour. Eventually, at 18.47 on 13 May the order was given to scramble. All four Valiants of 207 Squadron were airborne within six minutes and returned to Marham some three and a half hours later. Peter made a typical smooth landing, but was then taken to RAF Hospital Ely to be put in plaster, as he had smashed his elbow joint exactly like Mike Cawsey!" After rehabilitation, the two men returned to the squadron about three months later. While 'Mayflight' was in progress, Exercise 'Matador', Fighter Command's annual air defence exercise, was also under way, involving interception practice which benefited both Commands.

'Lone Rangers' were valuable and much coveted exercises and one of the more interesting destinations was Salisbury, Southern Rhodesia, now known as Harare. The outward route included night stops at Tripoli (Idris), and at Nairobi before landing at the RRAF base and international airport at New Sarum. The return route was similar except that after Nairobi the final stop was at El Adem. Typical times for the legs were four and a half hours to Idris, six hours from there to Nairobi and three and a half hours from Nairobi to New Sarum. On the way back, Nairobi to El Adem was just over six hours and from there to Marham took just over five hours. Valuable experience was gained in several ways, apart from that of the crew operating on their own a long way from base. The aircraft's Crew Chief was carried, as usual, to assist in turn-round and to deal with any servicing problems. Another factor was the experience of using the Valiant's navigation system over long stretches of featureless desert; in particular 'Nasser's Corner' – the point where Egypt, Libya and Sudan meet – had to be navigated accurately in order to avoid Egyptian airspace. A further piece of experience was the need to use parts of the Valiant's Operating Data Manual never used in the UK. It was, of course, used in planning every flight, but when dealing with temperatures of over 80°F, especially in conjunction with the runway at Idris, which was shorter than that at Marham, or at Nairobi, which was 5,500 feet above sea level as well as being hot, the long take-off runs and high rotate and 'V-Stop' and 'V-Go' speeds required careful checking and were quite a revelation.

The Medium Bomber Squadron Efficiency Trophy, which had been donated to Bomber Command by 460 Squadron in memory of the aircrew of that unit who had lost their lives in the Second World War, was won by 207 Squadron in 1961. Awarded to the squadron which had shown the best results in all aspects of its work, the trophy was presented by AVM A. M. Murdoch CB CBE RAAF at a parade and formal luncheon on 27 July.

A factor which, according to former Sqn. Ldr. Ken Hunter, who was CO of 'A' Flight from March 1961, bedevilled training and operations alike was the use of American nuclear weapons. "Although their light weight permitted multiple carriage and they were reputedly of higher yield than their British equivalents," he says, "the restrictive US control procedures associated with them limited reaction times in generation exercises and complicated QRA weapon loading as well as aircraft and crew changeovers. In my time, through a bit of give and take on both sides, these problems decreased in magnitude but were never solved completely."

It seems that members of the squadron were not averse to the occasional practical joke when a suitable situation arose. The story of 'Operation Suncrush' is told by Sqn. Ldr. Dave Bridger, a pilot on the squadron between 1959 and 1964. "One day a new arrival, who we will call Sqn. Ldr. Pippin, was posted in to be the new 'B' Flight commander. This gentleman had no intention of hanging about in the lower ranks. He openly declared that, as this was possibly his last flying tour, he would be first in line for all the goodies on offer, i.e. USA, Nairobi, Germany, etc. Our boss, dear old Wg. Cdr. 'Bill', greeted this statement with a wry smile. Now, even career officers go on leave, and so when Sqn. Ldr. Pippin took his first leave there was a golden opportunity for Flt. Lt. 'Hard', the squadron practical joker, to put Operation 'Suncrush' into effect. A dummy signal was raised announcing a tour of South American countries. Four crews and a standby were nominated by the boss; needless to say Flt. Lt. 'Hard' was one of those crews. Sqn. Ldr. 'Pippin' was tasked to keep the remains of the squadron running in the UK, and as a really nice twist the boss suggested that the good Sqn. Ldr. should draft the Op. Order for approval before contacting Bomber Command HQ. Flt. Lt 'Hard' had somehow enlisted the maximum support from all sections on the Station, so much so that when our man returned from leave his desk was awash with paperwork. OC Supply was requesting details of technical supply requirements, sizes of KD uniforms etc.; the SMO about details of inoculations various that would be needed; OC Engineering with suggestions for engineering support; and OC Catering with advice on food hygiene overseas. Give our boy his due, unhappily, but very progressively, he settled down to put it all together. Days went by until it became essential to contact Command for clarification of a few details. Operation 'Suncrush'? Never heard of it! Gotcha!"

All crews attended a winter survival course in the snows of Bavaria, with greater or lesser degrees of enjoyment. On their return to Marham, Ken Hunter received a report that the captain of one crew was picked up at the end of his stint in the snowbound wilderness very much the worse for wear. He was the only one who had not killed the rabbit which each member was given, together with a bar of chocolate, to aid survival. Furthermore, this normally 'macho' captain had fed his chocolate to the rabbit because it looked hungry!

In September the squadron took part in the SBAC Show at Farnborough on three days, and during Battle of Britain week sent aircraft to Biggin Hill, Waterbeach, Tangmere and Abingdon for static and flying displays. Then followed a dispersal exercise at Cranwell, Exercise 'Kinsman', in which four aircraft took part from 9 to 12 October. From 21 November to mid-December four of the squadron's Valiants were detached to Malta under Exercise 'Sunspot', for which the ground crews flew out in a Britannia aircraft of Transport Command. While there, visual bombing practice on the El Adem range in Libya was carried out. A change of participating crews was made at the half-way point so that everyone could take advantage of the facilities. Although 'Sunspot' was in progress, squadron personnel were stretched by Exercise 'Mickey Finn', which involved crews being at forty minutes readiness. The two aircraft remaining at Marham were flown to Cranwell, and two more crews borrowed aircraft from 49 and 148 Squadrons, as all the others were at Luqa. Two days later the four crews at Cranwell came home. In the sunny Mediterranean, three crews of the Luqa detachment carried out a simulated attack on HMS *Ark Royal* on 12 December, eight passes being regarded as successful as they were not intercepted by Fleet Air Arm fighters before their weapons were released.

Exercise 'Sunspot' was regarded by the aircrews (and probably the ground crews as well) as the highlight of the year. The exercise involved one V-Force squadron relocating to Malta for four to six weeks for visual bombing training. 207 Squadron's turn came round once each year between 1958 and 1961 and fortunately was always a summer allocation. Crews were rotated half way through so that each spent up to three weeks in Malta, and the detachment was always treated as something of a summer holiday. Most of the flying was done either from an early morning take-off or at night, thus leaving the days free for swimming and sunbathing and fraternising with the WRNS billeted in Whitehall Mansions and at HMS *Falcon* (RNAS Hal Far). At least one member of the squadron met his wife there! As the runways at Luqa in those days were too short for Vulcans and Victors, 207 Squadron crews had the airfield to themselves until the main runway was extended in 1961, apart from transit traffic. The purpose behind 'Sunspot' was to practice reinforcement of the still-vital island of Malta, which was also the only place from where the squadron could meet its visual high-level bombing practice commitment. There were three targets, of which the small islet of Filfla (just off the south coast) was the most significant. "Every crew achieved excellent results" says Ken Marwood "because the Malta plotters used waves splashing against the island to score 'Delta Hotels' (direct hits) if they couldn't see the bomb strikes! The other targets were at El Adem and Tarhuna, both in Libya. These, of course, were pre-Ghaddafi days, but the bombing of Tarhuna had to stop when a Canberra dropped a practice bomb into an oil-drilling rig, having mistaken its light for a target. Our bombing was done either very early in the morning so that we could be back in Malta by 11.00 and free for the rest of the day, or early at night so that we were back in time to join in the social life. We struck up a strong liaison with the Fleet Air Arm aircrew at Hal Far and there were many mess exchange visits. Every weekend was spent with them (and with some WRNS!) at one of the many bays in Malta for extended picnics."

A new system known as 'progressive servicing' of the squadron's Valiants began on 1 March 1962. Under this arrangement, minor inspections would be carried out by the squadron, and extra hangar space was allocated for the purpose. Servicing Control offices were provided in the hangars. Inspections would henceforth be carried out in stages, obviating the need for aircraft to be taken off the line for long periods. Major inspections were not affected.

In April the squadron went in for the 1962 Bombing & Navigation Competition, but was placed 14th, largely due to equipment failures. This somewhat poor result did not, however, dampen the enthusiasm of air or ground crews, who were pleased to receive seventeen representatives from SHAPE on 3 July and to provide a Valiant for their inspection. The resident squadrons had been notified at the beginning of June that Marham's main runway would be out of use for some time so that repairs could be made. This meant that the Valiants had to use the shorter runways, and full loads of fuel were not allowed. To aid landings, a mobile GCA unit was brought in.

On the sports field, 207 Squadron provided a substantial number of athletes to the Flying Wing team on 18 July, when the Station Sports Day was held, and Flying Wing won the Inter-Wing Trophy. Four officers represented 207 Squadron at Halton on 31 July, when swimming competitions took place, and were selected to represent 3 Group at Cosford in the finals of the relay race.

From high to low

A significant change of operational status came about in August 1962, under which the Valiant squadrons became a low-level force. Officers from Bomber Command Development Unit then visited 207 and other squadrons to lecture on the subject of low-level flying and to inform the listening crews that special low-level routes had been determined, and would be used from September.

On display at an open day in 1962, Valiant B.1 XD873 was resplendent in white anti-flash paint.
[via R. C. B. Ashworth]

Low-level training then started for 207, 49 and 148 Squadrons. A typical training sortie would involve firstly two or three high-level scored simulated attacks, followed by descent to low altitude at either 500 or 100 feet above the ground by day and later at 1,000 feet by night. Simulated attacks were made on targets along the approved routes and were assessed either by the RBSUs or by analysis of photographs of the Valiant's own H2S radar picture at the moment of simulated bomb release. The low-level stage was normally followed by a climb to high-level for a long navigation stage, the sortie ending as usual with some pilot continuation training in the circuit at Marham.

Initially, there were four approved low-level routes. One started by crossing the coast of West Sussex and following a route west into Devon and Cornwall, but approval was soon withdrawn after numerous complaints from residents below the flight path. On another route, aircraft coasted in over north Cornwall, crossed Devon and Somerset, and then flew into south Wales via Lundy Island and across Wales to the Irish Sea. Due to objections from the populace, this route was also curtailed. A modified version of this route started at Lundy Island from an entry point in the Bristol Channel, turned north to cross Wales, went out over the Irish Sea before turning east to arrive near Morecambe before the aircraft climbed out over the Pennines; this route was eventually known as LL Route Three. A short-lived third route started near Morecambe and went through the Lake District and into Scotland, passing between Glasgow and Edinburgh, through the Highlands and out near Ben Nevis. Ken Marwood flew this route only once before it was cancelled and found it "......very hairy", flying in and out of very turbulent cloud and up and down through the mountains. It was not a comfortable route without the use of terrain-following radar, which of course the Valiant never carried. The fourth route, eventually designated LL Route One, began near Lossiemouth on the Moray Firth in northern Scotland, passed over the Grampians, across the Firth of Forth to the east of Edinburgh, along the Pennines, and through Yorkshire via a simulated radar-scored attack on Moorends Colliery. Continuing through Lincolnshire, the route usually finished with a live attack on Wainfleet or Holbeach ranges using 25 lb. (11.3 kg.) practice bombs. These two low-level routes, LL One and LL Three, remained the only two available for training until the demise of the Valiant.

Cuba and the Valiants

Then came the Cuban crisis. 207 Squadron, with the others of the V-Force, was put on Alert 3 status towards the end of October 1962, and specific crews stood by in the vicinity of the Station, trying to avoid arousing public concern. A navigator/plotter at the time, Roger Korner, remembers being on QRA one lunch-time and watching President Kennedy on television calling Kruschev's bluff, when the hooter sounded. "We did the hundred and fifty yards to the aircraft compound in twenty seconds, dressed in full kit, only for Mike Bryett, whose job it was to check, to call out that it was a practice," he recalls. "We were all ashen-faced because we thought this was really going to be it!" Fortunately, Cuba and its Russian allies backed down before any escalation leading to the Third World War could develop.

A dispersal exercise to Cranwell scheduled for 29 October had been cancelled due to the Cuban crisis, but one Sunday, Marham crews were taken by bus, each man with a packed lunch, to a special storage area near another Class 1 airfield. They entered through a remote rear gate, and even their colleagues at that airfield were not told of their arrival.

Down in a bunker, the crews spent the day learning how to deliver the ultimate weapon – 'Blue Danube'. To see the five-ton bomb for the first time and to realise its awesome potential was felt by all the crews to be a sobering experience. Former navigator Sqn Ldr. John Hamer recalls seeing the nuclear weapon. "I was somewhat bemused by the size of it," he says. "'Blue Danube' was the 'bombiest' bomb one could imagine – very big, very black and very sinister, filling most of the Valiant's bomb-bay. We were told that one such weapon was equivalent to the whole of the tonnage dropped by Bomber Command in World War Two."

Snow lay on the ground at Marham for the whole of January 1963, but a Sno–Flo machine was brought in and in conjunction with snow ploughs was able to clear a strip 150 feet (46 m.) wide down the main runway so that the Marham squadrons' alert commitment could be maintained. At the end of the month fog added to the problem, and routine exercises were cancelled. On the sporting scene, Flt. Lt. F. C. Welles of 207 Squadron captained both RAF and Combined Services hockey teams that winter as well as representing Suffolk.

At the end of March Marham was visited by a team from SHAPE HQ and Bomber Command, including some USAF personnel, to check that the Station was fit to carry out its NATO commitment. This check was known as a TacEval (Tactical Evaluation) and was in the form of an exercise in which the aircraft carried both live and dummy weapons on attacks on simulated targets. Marham passed the test with flying colours, achieving an A1 status. 207 Squadron crews involved were those of Flt. Lt. R. Maclachlan and Flt. Lt. D. H. Clelland in the air and Wg. Cdr. W. E. Martin and Flt. Lt. J. Jones on the ground.

Nuclear capability and the CND

Immediately after the Taceval, 207 Squadron received its first American Mk.43 nuclear weapon, superseding the Mk.28 weapon which the squadron had since 1960. This enhanced the operational low-level target attack missions. The squadron then flew two sorties in Exercise 'Regex', taking off at 03.00 on a seven-hour return trip to the Mediterranean Sea, where vessels of the US Navy were subjected to mock attacks. Later in the month the squadron competed for the Lawrence Minot Trophy, in which it was awarded second place, and in the Bomber Command Bombing Competition, when another second place was achieved.

This was the era of demonstrations by the Campaign for Nuclear Disarmament, and Marham was the subject of their protests on 11 and 18 May 1963. A few hundred of the great unwashed tried to make their presence felt, and succeeded to the extent that the Valiants were moved from 207 Squadron's usual dispersal area to an area closer to the technical site, and the ground equipment was taken into the hangars. To patrol the perimeter fence to prevent trespass, the squadron provided six officers and a hundred airmen as part of a larger force. Ken Hunter remembers that when the CND's plans became known in advance "......there was great excitement at the thought of a forthcoming confrontation with people who were almost universally disliked and despised by all ranks." The RAF Regiment showed a great deal of acumen in identifying weak areas and much ingenuity in deploying limited numbers of men. Despite pleas from several quarters, live ammunition was not issued, but there were those among the guards who improved their powers of deterrence by the judicious display of such weapons as wooden staves! Late in the afternoon a hundred or so of CND formed a mass strong enough to scale the perimeter wire, but when they streamed towards the fence they were confronted by airmen, each equipped with a baton, who rose from behind each tuft of grass. The invaders then decided that discretion was the better part of valour and dispersed. An AOC's parade scheduled for 24 May had to be cancelled due to these fruitless events.

On 30 May 1963, Wg. Cdr. A. D. Dick AFC MA took over command of 207 Squadron from Wg. Cdr. W. E. Martin. David Dick writes "I believe I was the first CO of 207 Squadron who had never been a bomber pilot, and hence to some extent was a bit of an outsider and was perhaps able to form a dispassionate view of the squadron. I had been a flying instructor, a fighter pilot in World War Two, one of the RAF test pilots at Boscombe Down and done a tour with Bloodhound guided weapons. Immediately before joining 207 Squadron I had been on the Directing Staff at Staff College. For the only time in my career I was asked what I would like to do on my next posting; as I regarded the 'V-Force' as doing the most vital role in the service and as I desperately wanted a flying posting and a command of a front-line squadron I asked for such a posting as I had heard of other former fighter pilots following that route."

"A full refresher flying course led to the course at 232 OCU at Gaydon before joining 207 Squadron. Furthermore, as an incoming CO I did not arrive with my crew except for my co-pilot, Flg. Off. Don Audsley, who joined me at Gaydon fresh from flying training. On arrival at Marham I inherited Bill Martin's crew: Flt. Lts. Colin Wilkinson (nav. radar), Jim Kearney (nav. plotter), and 'Dinty' Moore (AEO); they were also the squadron's 'leaders' in these skills. This was hard on them for two reasons: firstly, 'V-Force' crews were strictly constituted, which meant that on any formal Group or Command exercise and for QRA (and hence any operational sortie) those crew members always flew together. Secondly, 'V-Force' crews were strictly categorised by virtue of their achievements in the Force – their skills and experience in bombing and navigation and the captain's Instrument Flying Rating etc.

"These categories varied from 'Combat' to 'Select' and to 'Select Star'. They had to work their way up the ladder together as a crew. So when a total newcomer arrived the whole crew became 'Non-operational' until they had achieved together the minimum qualifications to be rated 'Combat'. They could then go on QRA and would strive to work their way up the classification ladder. My crew therefore not only had to come down from the 'Select Star' rating they had with Bill Martin to 'Non-operational', but they had to cope with a new captain who they had to train to become a bomber captain; for whilst the OCU course had thoroughly trained one to fly the Valiant and manage its complex systems, in just twelve sorties it was not possible to impart more than a little of what was needed to captain the aircraft. The three of them did a splendid job over our first few months together and, because I had to fly regularly with all the squadron's crews I learnt a great deal from them too."

"An impression I will always retain", David says, "is the tremendous professionalism of the Force. The members had enormous dedication to achieve the highest possible standards; they fully comprehended the grim task which they had volunteered to undertake, and indeed most had sought the job because they saw it as the most important role in the Service, as I had done myself. I am also convinced that the dedication was due, at least in part, to the tradition which the Command had built with so much sacrifice during World War Two, which was almost a generation away. The 'V-Force' was then towards the end of a transitional stage in its personnel. When it was formed some six years earlier, the crews were older and very experienced, many having completed wartime tours. By 1963, many captains were in their mid-twenties and had graduated through one successful co-pilot tour immediately after training. Many navigators and AEOs were on their first tour after training, which was extremely thorough."

David Dick continues by commenting "In 1963 the Valiant was a much-loved, effective and reliable aircraft, and 207 Squadron not only had an outstanding record for meeting its tasks and attaining – indeed perhaps in setting – standards, but also had a most enviable reputation as a friendly and 'unstuffy' squadron. This I found was indeed so and I count myself singularly fortunate to have joined it. Many of the members had been on the squadron in 1960, when, under Wg. Cdr. W. D. Robertson, 207 Squadron won both the Lawrence Minot and the Armament Officers' Trophies in the Bomber Command Bombing Competition. Its win reflected the outstanding co-operation between aircrew and ground crew – the spirit of 'belonging' which had always been a feature of the squadron and was strongly in evidence then. Sadly this was destroyed in 1964, when centralised servicing under Technical Wing was introduced and all squadrons lost their first-line servicing personnel, and importantly, their crew chiefs, who in many ways were the bedrock of servicing."

Life with the Valiants

David Dick goes on to provide information on the routine life of 207 Squadron in the early 1960s. "On the squadron life was dominated by two principal factors: the QRA schedule and the demands of the Bomber Command classification scheme. Associated with this was the annual visitation – or 'audit' – by the 3 Group Standardisation Unit. The QRA schedule was inviolate and the essential parameter; the squadron had to meet its commitment to provide one, or on a roster basis with the other two strike squadrons, two 'combat ready' aircraft and crews on QRA. The task of providing the second aircraft on QRA arose because of the need for the three squadrons to provide four Valiants."

"The demands of the classification system were also stringent because each crew had to meet a comprehensive list of training achievements in each six-month period. These ranged from satisfactorily assessed navigation legs at both high and low levels, using all the various permutations of aids; scored bombing runs, also at high and low altitudes, using various bombing methods; a satisfactory number of instrument approaches using GCA and ILS, both manual and on auto-pilot, down to a self-monitored approach by the nav/radar using the onboard H2S. Probably the most difficult to achieve were the necessary number of low-level navigation sorties, especially those required at night; here the weather was the joker in the pack, and towards the end of each hectic classification period it was often difficult to ensure that each crew had been able to have all the squares on the training board filled in. This imposed a great burden on the Flight commanders, who had to juggle the available flying with the many requirements of the crews. 3 Group's annual visit was a trial; as I recall it lasted about a week and amounted to a pretty complete audit of the squadron's work over the preceding period. It involved 3 Group staff trawling through the records and examining several crews on the ground and in the air."

"Once all these parameters had been entered into the programme, crews' leave had to be accommodated. One had to take account of families and other personal commitments – school holidays were an important factor for those with children – and once the leave roster had been finalised it was regarded as inviolate! Also ever present were the Group and Command exercises, many of which could be called on without notice and involved generating as many Valiants and crews as possible. When the sirens sounded everything stopped! On top of all that were the periodic 'No Notice Tactical Evaluations' by SACEUR's NATO staff; these turned the whole Station inside-out, and the reputations of squadrons and Station were on the line – nail-biting stuff! So life on the squadron was extremely busy, but not so busy that squadron members could not enjoy it, and I'm sure that almost universally they look back on it with favour."

On 11 June 1963 six Valiants, with nine others from Marham, took part in Exercise 'Co-op' as a means of testing NATO defences. The main part of their route was flown at low level over Holland and deep into France, and interceptions by NATO fighters was made at several points. Exercise 'Mystic' was new to 207 Squadron, and on 27 July involved five Valiants which made simulated attacks on SAM sites in the UK before landing at designated dispersal airfields. As another element of NATO, the US Air Force was interested in the V–Force, and at the end of August four USAF officers from Upper Heyford, Majors Louslier, Rowe and Dyer and Capt. Maddison, flew as passengers in Valiants of 207 Squadron.

Further exercises and Lone Rangers filled the remainder of 1963, but Chief Tech. Miller, aided by his wife, found time to escort 36 children of squadron personnel to Norwich on 27 December to see the pantomime 'Mother Goose'. For this sortie, fraught with danger, the SNCO was mentioned in despatches, or in the squadron diary, anyway!

Co-pilot of WZ401 on its return flight from Southern Rhodesia in November 1963 was Flg. Off. Don Audsley, seen here at the controls of the Valiant during the final leg from El Adem to Marham. [AVM A. D. Dick]

A civilian Friendship aircraft keeps company with 207 Squadron Valiant WZ401 at Salisbury, Southern Rhodesia, (now Harare) in November 1963.Salisbury was at the end of a 'Lone Ranger' route flown periodically by 207 Squadron crews. [AVM A. D. Dick]

1964 opened with rather better weather than the previous year, and with the arrival from St. Athan of a 'new look' Valiant, WZ403. Resplendent in new grey and green

Valiant WZ401 at Salisbury, Southern Rhodesia, (now Harare) at the end of a Lone Ranger' in November 1963. The aircraft carries the pennant of the CO, Wg. Cdr. A. D. Dick AFC MA. [all AVM A. D. Dick]

A Boeing 707 keeps company with 207 Squadron Valiant WZ401 at Salisbury, Southern Rhodesia (now Harare) in November 1963. Salisbury was at the end of a 'Lone Ranger' route flown periodically by 207 Squadron crews.

An interior shot of the 'office' of Valiant WZ401while at an altitude of 40,000 feet between El Adem and Marham.

Another interior shot of the 'office' of Valiant WZ401while at an altitude of 40,000 feet between El Adem and Marham.

camouflage with a white underside, this Valiant carried the first example of a colour scheme to be applied to all low-level bomber aircraft, replacing the all-white 'anti-flash' livery formerly carried. By the end of January, however, fog was in evidence, and only one of 207 Squadron's Valiants was able to carry out a low-level strike against Navy ships in the Western Approaches on 28 January.

Under radical new arrangements for centralised aircraft servicing which came into force on 1 February, aircraft and ground crew personnel of all three Marham-based squadrons were transferred to Technical Wing. A planning cell was set up in Operations Wing to prepare a weekly flying programme in conjunction with the COs of the three squadrons and to allocate aircraft from a pool as required. 207 Squadron's dispersal at the south-east side of the airfield had to be closed, as all Marham aircraft were to stand on pans near the Operations block. Under the former system, each squadron contained three Sqn. Ldrs. – 'A' Flight CO, 'B' Flight CO and the Training Officer – and there were about three times as many ground crew personnel as air crews. The new system allowed only one Sqn. Ldr. – the 'A' Flight CO. 207 Squadron now consisted, therefore, of the Wg. Cdr. CO, eleven aircrews, a Sgt. personal assistant to the CO, and a clerk. Major teething troubles were soon experienced, the most serious being last-minute changes in aircraft allocation and delayed take-offs.

Disaster strikes

A Royal visit to Marham took place on 5 May, and two of 207 Squadron's Valiants demonstrated scramble procedures. Then disaster struck. At 22.35Z on 6 May 1964 Valiant WZ363 of 148 Squadron, being flown by a 207 Squadron crew, carried out a roller landing at Binbrook on 'Practice Pan' exercise, and then climbed away. Five minutes later it dived into the ground at high speed just south of Market Rasen and exploded on impact, total destruction resulting. All five crew members died instantly. They were Flt. Lt. F. C. Welles (the hockey player, captain); Flt. Lt. G. A. Mills (co-pilot); Flt. Lt. J. R. Stringer (nav/plotter); Flt. Lt. L. R. Hawkins (nav/radar); and Sgt. R. Noble (AEO). All except Flt. Lt. Mills were buried in Marham village cemetery after a funeral service at the Station church which was attended by the complete squadron other than those on Quick Reaction Alert. Flt. Lt. Mills' body was interred at Warrington on 13 May, with the CO and eight officers present.

The loss of a front-line V-bomber was a serious matter and was fully investigated, but the Board of Enquiry had an almost impossible task, as the level of destruction was so severe; most of the wreckage was in a waterlogged crater thirty feet (nine metres) deep, and significant amounts of debris had blown away downwind. Despite a number of wholly credible eye-witnesses, it was possible to establish only that no member of the crew had had time to attempt to eject or bale out and that all engines were working properly on impact. One significant fact was that the tailplane actuator was found in the fully nose-down position, but it was impossible to discover whether it had been driven there deliberately or there had been a malfunction. While some extreme circumstances might have made a runaway possible, on the whole a malfunction seemed unlikely, as, after the investigation and resolution of tailplane runaways on other prominent types at around that time, the Valiant's circuits were very well protected. The crew was very competent and the two pilots were fit and strong. Thus the Board was unable to come to any conclusion, which was disappointing but understandable.

Low-level exercises still kept the squadron busy, and included Exercise 'Maenad', a mock attack on coastal radar installations on 8 June. Exercise 'Co-op' was repeated on 23 June, and this time involved a high-level attack on sites in Norway, followed by a rapid descent over the North Sea and a low-level sector to a point south of Luxembourg.

During the afternoon of 12 August all Marham aircraft were grounded after a Valiant of 232 OCU had suffered a failure of its rear spar in flight. Later that day the aircraft were cleared to fly at high level only and next day for low level operation, although fast dashes were banned. On 25 August it was decided that all Valiants must be inspected for any signs of similar deterioration. This meant that only two of Marham's fleet were serviceable, with the inevitable drastic reduction in flying. The opportunity was taken by 207 Squadron to speed up work on the crew room coffee bar! Fatigue life predictions were recalculated in mid-September and the flying time allocated to each squadron was halved. Co-pilots were then allowed to fly just once per month and captains were to fly together in order to maintain their 'safe' status! No exercises or 'Lone Rangers' were permitted.

On 21 September 1964 Wg. Cdr. Dick was posted to Boscombe Down as Gp. Capt. (Flying) and Sqn. Ldr. R. C. Allen took over on a temporary basis. Five evenings earlier, when saying goodbye to the squadron at a ceremony at which large quantities of beer were available, Wg. Cdr. Dick had been presented with an engraved tankard. Next day, fifteen aircrew members, surely somewhat 'hung over', began an overnight survival exercise in the Stanford Battle Area near Thetford. As they slept in shelters they had devised themselves, it was fortunate that the weather was particularly kind to them! Back in the air, only one Valiant was available for Exercise 'Mickey Finn' from the dispersal airfield at Cranwell and one from Middleton St. George, 207 Squadron's other dispersal.

As the spar problem was now causing serious difficulties, all Valiants were categorised in early October in an attempt to bring the situation to a head. Category A defined aircraft fit to fly; Category B aircraft were grounded for viable repairs; and Category C aircraft were also grounded and might be Struck Off Charge. Marham boasted nine Cat.A Valiants. It was decided that the over-riding requirement was to maintain in each squadron as many crews as possible who could fly often enough to remain 'safe'. As far as 207 Squadron was concerned, the optimum number of such crews was eight, who would fly about ten hours per month in four sorties – two-hour night flights and four-hour trips by day. The number of days on QRA were to be increased for a reduced number of available crews. Bomber Command introduced two means of maintaining competence – a refresher course of one week at 232 OCU Gaydon, and weekly visits to Marham by 232 OCU instructors who would fly with squadron crews. All these changes were taking place when, on 2 November, Wg. Cdr. J. F. Stewart took over from the temporary CO.

On 9 December all Valiants were grounded when defects were found in the front main spar of an aircraft in the hangar for inspection of the rear spar, a much more serious situation. It now became necessary to use a variety of ploys to keep crews as near to an operational status without actually flying in Valiants. These were:

(1) From 4 January 1965 the number of crews on the refresher course at 232 OCU would be increased. Some would fly in Victors.

(2) Navigators would go to Lindholme to fly in Hastings aircraft.

In complete contrast to the silver and white finishes of other 207 Squadron Valiants, WZ404 is seen here at Marham in 1964 in camouflage with a white underside. [V. Flintham via A. Thomas]

(3) Four Valiants per day would practice scrambles from the ORP and would taxi at 50 knots but would not take off!

(4) Maximum use would be made of the simulator.

(5) Ground training would be increased.

(6) There would be visits to other service and civilian units.

(7) Maximum use would be made of the gymnasium.

(8) Pilots would convert to Chipmunk and Anson aircraft.

As might be imagined, these orders, particularly the last one, were seen for what they were – a last-ditch effort to stave off the inevitable, and morale dropped. A 'Shipwreck' party held in the Officers' Mess on 11 December did a little to lighten the gloom, but by Christmas there was little doubt that the end was nigh.

The end of an era

During the first days of 1965 the only training being carried out was not in Valiants but in Chipmunks and Ansons. The final blow came on 26 January, when the order came to cease all use of the Valiant aircraft with effect from midnight, but no information on the future of 207 Squadron was given. Probably nobody knew. Many of the squadron personnel were sent on detachments during February, and on 15 March Wg. Cdr. Stewart was posted to Scampton. He was succeeded on a temporary basis by Flt. Lt. B. A. Sherlock. The 'Chippies' and 'Faithful Annies' carried on flying, and took ATC cadets into the air over the Easter break. Flt. Lt. Sherlock was posted to Bahrain on 6 April, whereupon Flt. Lt. M. J. A. Bryett took over and on 28 April received orders to disband 207 Squadron.

207 Squadron's colours were handed over to the Queen's Colour Squadron at Uxbridge on 5 May 1965 for safe keeping, and next day the squadron silver was taken over by the President of the Messing Committee at Marham pending further instructions. On 10 May the squadron badge and its historical documents were passed to the Air Historical Branch, thus ending officially twenty-five years of almost unbroken squadron service and a span of forty-seven years of existence.

Bomber Command itself was disbanded on 1 April 1968, the fiftieth anniversary of the formation of the Royal Air Force, to be superseded by Strike Command. Ken Marwood relates how he attended the Stand-Down Parade at Scampton, where was seen what must have been the final public flight of a Valiant. XD816, formerly of 214 and 148 Squadrons, had been re-sparred by Vickers as part of an investigation of the feasibility of such a modification, and was flown by test pilot Jock Cochrane (formerly of 214 and 90 Squadrons), who demonstrated the beautiful lines of the much-loved Valiant. On the same day the 207 Squadron standard was laid up in the Chapel at Marham in the presence of several former Commanding Officers of the squadron.

Devon WB533 [DA] of 207 Squadron's detachment taxies past the control tower at Wyton. [via author]

Chapter 12: A communication squadron

Re-equipment

On 1 January 1969 the Southern Communication Squadron, based at Bovingdon, was renamed the Strike Command Communication Squadron, which on 27 January moved to Northolt. There, on 3 February, the unit was retitled 207 Squadron, with Sqn. Ldr. G. Pearson as its Commanding Officer. The squadron's task was to provide transport for high-ranking officers throughout the United Kingdom and sometimes overseas, using the two Devon C.2, seven Pembroke CC.1 and thirteen Basset CC.1 aircraft which 207 Squadron inherited. From the outset, the squadron maintained detachments at Edinburgh (Turnhouse) and at Finningley. Fifteen pilots and fifteen navigators was the establishment, and within a few weeks the Command Examining Unit visited the squadron to check their flying standards.

Throughout its service life, the small twin-engined Beagle Basset aircraft was plagued by technical problems made worse by a perpetual shortage of spare parts. Furthermore, in June 1969 cracks were found in the wings of some of the Pembrokes, which seriously curtailed flying and caused the grounding of one aircraft. The Devons and, with difficulty, the Bassets, maintained the squadron's task during this period, but there was a never-ending struggle to keep in the air enough aircraft to meet operational requirements.

In August 1970, Sqn. Ldr. B.R. Kent MBE took over as CO, and very soon took a Basset to Rygge in Norway on a training flight. Another three refurbished Devons arrived during that year, the greater comfort of the Devon being welcomed by passengers and crews alike. Although older than the other two types used by 207 Squadron, the Devon was by far the most reliable and practical aircraft for the squadron's task.

A most enjoyable task befell the squadron in the summer of 1971 — that of escorting the Spitfires and Hurricanes of the Battle of Britain Memorial Flight to air displays throughout the United Kingdom and Europe. These sorties were known as 'Spitsups', and involved conveying ground crews, spares, toolkits and publicity handouts to the events. Such sorties became a regular and enjoyable task for 207 Squadron every season until final disbandment in 1984.

Social traditions of a former bomber squadron were not forgotten, and after the AOC's formal inspection in July 1971 a luncheon continued until the early hours of the following day, becoming less restrained as the hours went swiftly by, all vestiges of formality having been abandoned! In August a party was held at which beef from Aberdeen and wine from Nice were featured, both having been flown in by squadron aircraft, the wine by the CO himself.

Parked at Kinloss in June 1971 with a Nimrod in the background is 207 Sqn. Basset CC.1 XS782. [R. C. B. Ashworth]

Basset XS779 served with 207 Squadron for a time before being sold and civilianised in 1974 as G–BCJC. [via R. C. Sturtivant]

The squadron continued to range far and wide across north-west Europe, with landings at such places as Copenhagen, Berlin and Munich, although most trips were within the United Kingdom. By the end of 1973 the aircraft fleet comprised two Pembrokes, seven Devons and five Bassets, but soon it was decided that the latter type was not suitable for continued use and was to be taken out of service. Three more Devons would then be taken on charge by 207 Squadron. Although a pleasant aircraft to fly, the Basset was cramped and noisy. The last aircraft was flown to a Maintenance Unit on 29 May 1974, crewed by the COs of 207 and 32 Squadrons. Most Bassets were eventually sold to private owners and subsequently appeared on the civil register.

Devons on the squadron continued to multiply, some of them arriving from far afield. In May 1975, Flt. Lts. M. J. Mercer and A. R. Edmunds brought VP961 from Singapore to Northolt, taking 57 flying hours over a three–week period. Their route sounds like a guide–book; from Singapore they flew to Butterworth, Bangkok, Rangoon, Akyab, Calcutta, Bhubaneshwar, Nagpur, Ahmadabad, Karachi, Muscat, Dubai, Bahrain, Riyadh, Jeddah, Luxor, Cairo, Alexandria, Heraklion, Athens, Brindisi, Bari, Rome, Nice and Orleans before reaching Northolt. The Pembrokes were also being replaced, and the last one left in November 1975 for service with 60 Squadron in Germany, leaving 207 Squadron with a fleet of fourteen Devons, a type now a firm favourite with the crews. When 26 Squadron disbanded on 1 April 1976, 207 Squadron took over its detachment at Wyton in order to continue communications duties for RAF Brampton, the home of Training Command, later Support Command, inheriting four Devons in the process. In addition, flights were made on behalf of the Joint Centre for Photographic Reconnaissance at Brampton and the Joint Air Reconnaissance Intelligence Centre at Wyton.

Former navigator Michael Greenland, who served with 207 Squadron from 1975 to 1983, recalls his surprise when he realised that in a Devon he actually faced the direction of travel! "After years of sitting down the back, facing aft in the dark, I could actually look out", he said. "Then, horror of horrors, I was expected to play at pilot's assistant! I won't say co-pilot, never having been a frustrated pilot – I didn't want to fly the thing anyway. Even so, I had to get used to keeping my head up and look out of the cockpit and to learn unnatural things like engine temperatures and limitations in order to monitor the pilot and confirm his decisions. What a joke, when you consider how experienced our pilots were. Then we had to learn to transmit messages over the R/T……which required the use of the principle of engaging brain before opening mouth. Finally, the duties of steward and Air Loadmaster had to be learned. The Devon didn't have a very big cockpit and I am not too tall, but climbing in and out a couple of times each trip was a bit of a bind, just to chat up the passengers and serve tea. Mind you, one certainly quickly learned a few tricks, such as never offering your passengers anything to drink unless certain that you had brought the flasks on board, and never, never, stirring the passengers' drinks with a pencil, as most VIPs prefer you to use a spoon!"

On 20 November 1976, 207 Squadron celebrated its 60th anniversary with a reception at Northolt. The Commanding Officer, Sqn. Ldr. P. G. Goodman, welcomed over a hundred guests, including twelve of his predecessors, including AVM A. D. Dick, Air Cdre. W. D. Robertson and Air Cdre. N. C. Hyde, the CO in 1940.

One of the 'characters' on 207 Squadron at this time was the fabled Flt. Lt. Jerzy 'Joe' Kmiecik, who was still piloting Devons until he retired in February 1981 at the age of 58. He had made a remarkable escape from a Soviet gulag during the Second World War, found his way to England and joined the RAF. He then flew Spitfires and Mustangs with 303 (Polish) Squadron between 1944 and 1946, after which he transferred to Transport Command to fly Yorks during the Berlin airlift. After that came a period on Lancasters and service with 224 Squadron on maritime reconnaissance duty from Gibraltar before coming to 207 Squadron. Mr. R. E. 'Slim' Pocock, a navigator with 207 Squadron from April 1976 to May 1983, flew with him many times, and remembers them with pleasure. "Flying with 'Joe' was not only an education, it was always fun, and you knew you were in good hands," he says. "Some of his techniques may not have pleased the 'trappers', but he got the job done with skill, a grin and the best will in the world. If a pilot was needed for the weekend for a compassionate airlift and the weather was grotty, Joe was your man! Humour was one of his strengths. I was with him on a visit to Waddington. After lunch, we went to pay our casual meal dues and as usual needed to give our names to the young stewardess at the cash box. My name gave her little trouble, but KMIECIK really threw her! Joe's reaction was quick – 'No problem, I spell' – but she was even quicker. Joe spent the next few hours almost in hysterics as he showed all and sundry his receipt made out in the name 'Flt. Lt. I. Spell'! As always, Joe, off the cuff." Sadly, 'Joe' lost his life in an accident in his home in Gibraltar, to where he had retired.

Sqn. Ldr. Goodman handed over to Sqn. Ldr. M. J. Perrett on 18 April 1977, and in that year of the Queen's Silver Jubilee the squadron proudly displayed its aircraft and its standard in her presence at Finningley on 29 July. The squadron continued to fly to European destinations,

A Hurricane and a Mosquito formate on a 207 Squadron Devon flying in support of the Battle of Britain Memorial Flight. [Sqn. Ldr. I. Hampton]

and in November these included Copenhagen, Cologne, Dusseldorf, Keil, Brussels, Berlin, Paris and Groningen, many of which had been visited under very different circumstances thirty-odd years previously!

The continuing 'Spitsup' task for the BoBMF is well remembered by 'Slim' Pocock. "207 Squadron Devon crews provided the navigation, planning and radio facilities for the longer transit flights and often formed part of the formation on arrival at events, particularly when they were at a considerable distance from the BoBMF base at Coningsby," he says. "This assistance was also welcomed by the Lancaster crew at times! Routes had to be planned to take into account that the Flight has to abide by special rules devised to ensure the safety of its rare and valuable aircraft. Apart from the normal hazards of weather, airspace regulations etc., aircraft in transit have to maintain visual contact with the ground...... and to route via used or disused airfields suitable for emergency landings."

"A normal support sortie" went on Mr. Pocock "started with prepositioning the Devon at Coningsby, briefing the pilots on the suggested route and timings and amending them if necessary. In the air, a close but not tight formation was held, the Devon crew obtaining all the required clearances and weather updates and generally liaising with all the agencies concerned. It was quite amazing how even international airports can be very co-operative when they learn that you have a Spitfire and Hurricane in tow – even a low flypast was [sometimes] suggested! In May 1980 I had the pleasure of planning and carrying out a 'Spitsup' to

Displaying a stylised version of the squadron badge on its fin, Devon C.2/2 VP971 is seen here in August 1981. [R. C. B. Ashworth]

Schipol airport, Amsterdam, to commemorate the anniversary of the liberation of the city in 1945. Getting VP971 into Schipol among the 'Jumbos' and Airbuses was quite a game in itself, particularly when we were required to overfly the terminal buildings before landing! Try that on any other day! Next day we flew a circular route around Holland, taking in the main cities and towns whenever possible, before arriving back over Dam Square at precisely 13.00. At the reception later in the day one would have thought that we had liberated Amsterdam ourselves!"

Flt. Lt. Paul Bennett was posted to 207 Squadron in June 1979 and joined a conversion course which involved very little classroom tuition and a great deal of 'hands-on' learning. After a short time, trainee crews were sent to Benson, where almost all the air familiarisation took place. After scores of 'circuits and bumps' came navigation exercises to RAF and civilian airfields, firstly in the UK and then on the Continent. Finally came certification that a certain standard had been reached. In October 1979 Paul was sent to Wyton, where the squadron detachment consisted of three crews and three Devons, and there was a dedicated engineering team under Flt. Lt. S. Taylor.

Seen at Odiham in September 1972 was Pembroke C.1 XK884. The squadron badge is carried on the cheat line below the cockpit. [R. C. B. Ashworth]

The years between 1978 and 1980 were notable for the number of rumours, counter-rumours, reduced flying and undermanning, all resulting in uncertainty about the future. However, the new CO, Sqn. Ldr. J. H. Easton, responded well to the changing situation and morale remained high, partly the result of soundly beating 32 Squadron at sports. During the Falklands conflict between April and June 1982 no part of the RAF was left untouched in some way, and 207 Squadron flew many sorties within the UK in support of the operation. Several officers of the squadron were detached for operations duties with HQ 38 Group and to Gibraltar and Dakar.

Pride was taken in keeping rigidly to pre-arranged schedules, but on one occasion the newly-appointed WRAF aide-de-camp to the AOC of Support Command spoiled the squadron's record by not checking the facts. The mission was to deliver the AOC on his annual inspection of Southampton University Air Squadron, an almost routine 'bread-and-butter' task. A Devon carrying the great man duly landed at Southampton Airport and taxied to the control tower to arrive dead on time at noon. It was a matter of personal pride that the aircraft's wheels would stop turning just as the second hand touched the 12-o'clock position, but this time there was no red carpet, no reception committee, no nothing! The crew, on calling up the tower to ask what had happened to the UAS party, was told that the unit did all its flying from Bournemouth (Hurn) and it might be a good idea to go there, so engines were restarted and a rapid take-off was made. The red-faced crew landed at Hurn eighteen minutes late!

The compact 'office' of a Devon. [P. Bennett]

Sqn. Ldr. Ian Hampton arrived on the squadron early in 1983 to take the 'in-house' conversion course before becoming CO. "At that time," he recalls "we had a total of fifteen Devons and seventeen crews, including three at Wyton who provided support for the then RAF Support Command HQ at nearby Brampton. There was also one aircraft and crew at Turnhouse as transport for AOC Scotland and his Navy and Army opposite numbers. The detached elements of the squadron were almost exclusively involved in 'run-of-the-mill' VIP transport, while we at Northolt looked after MoD and all the other Commands and Groups as well as picking up the non-routine jobs that came our way. I was conscious that not only were the aircraft the oldest in RAF squadron service (older than the much-publicised Shackletons of 8 Squadron), but that most of the crews were also of the 'old and bold' variety. As I arrived, Flt. Lt. Joe Kmiecik was just retiring as the very last pilot in the RAF who had flown Spitfires during the war. Among the younger element were Larry Chamberlain, who had flown operational Hornets, and Fred Hambly, who had flown Dakotas. General experience included types as diverse as Hunters, Meteors, Sabres, Lincolns, Valettas, Javelins, Vulcans, Belfasts, Hastings, Hercules, VC10s and many more. So they were vastly experienced and a generally 'laid-back' bunch who needed the minimum of supervision." Sqn. Ldr. Hampton, after his conversion course, took over from Sqn. Ldr. Robb Lunn in May 1983.

Devon WB534 on finals at St. Mawgan on 22 July 1983 with starboard engine feathered in response to an indication of fire. At the controls was Flt. Lt. Bill Austin, who continued the sortie next day after an electrical short circuit had been traced. [B. Wallond via P. Bennett]

The 40th anniversary of the flight to Berlin on which Wynford Vaughan-Thomas of the BBC made a sound recording was celebrated on 3 September 1983, when a guest night was held in the Officers' Mess. In addition to Mr. Vaughan-Thomas, the guest list included Sqn. Ldr. K. H. Letford DSO DFC, Mr. C. Stewart from the original crew and Mr. Reg Pidsley, the BBC sound engineer who had been on the Berlin mission. Squadron personnel discovered that all the crew had survived the war except the mid-upper gunner. Ian Hampton remembers that the evening was wonderful, with a great deal of reminiscing. "Sadly, within three years all the crew, Wynford and Reg were dead," he says. "I consider myself fortunate to have met them." A couple of days after the event, Reg Pidsley's son called at the squadron offices and said that his father wished to present 207 Squadron with the original recording of the 1943 mission, and laid an aluminium disc on my desk. "The image of this civilian lying in the bowels of a Lancaster, manually placing a diamond-tipped stylus on the disc to cut the recording over Berlin added a new dimension to my understanding of the air war!" Sqn. Ldr. Hampton then telephoned the BBC and reported what he had. At first the archivist was not easily convinced, but then became excited enough to send a senior man to look at the disc and take it away, wrapped in cotton wool. As a way of expressing thanks, the BBC gave the CO a cassette copy of the original programme as broadcast and an unedited version as recorded.

It was at this celebration that the idea of a 207 Squadron Association was mooted, and Sqn. Ldr. Hampton detailed his colleagues to begin the task of gathering the names and

Sqn. Ldr. Ian Hampton, the last CO of 207 Squadron, and his officers pose in the Mess at Northolt on 10 February 1984. [via Sqn. Ldr. I. Hampton]

whereabouts of as many former personnel as possible in order to judge whether such an organisation was viable. A small committee was soon formed, and since then, as will be described in Chapter 13, the Association has gone from strength to strength.

An interesting insight into the activities of 207 Squadron in its last days is provided by Ian Hampton. "Routine communications and VIP jobs need little comment, other than to say that we operated into any airfield that could give us 2,400 feet (823 m.) of grass or better and with or without a fire engine!" he says. "Many of the airfields had few or no navigation aids and we were adept at finding our way into them, even in fairly dire weather. Ones that spring to mind include Andover, Upavon, Aberporth and Plymouth, the latter being on top of hills, the bad weather approach invariably meaning that at about three miles finals we were still *below* the runway, approaching *up* a valley. This sort of flying was inevitably at variance with the tightly controlled rules of the RAF, but we were often carrying as passengers the very people who had formulated these rules and they seemed to trust us, and anyway, they were keen to get to their destination and never complained. The Devon had little in the way of equipment and the preferred method of navigation was at relatively low level with a map. This was, not least, because if you went into a cloud the Devon leaked and the navigator especially used to end up with a soggy and freezing cold right leg. Also, ice would form on the inside of the windscreen and the navigator would lean across and scrape a clear patch in front of the pilot with the sharp edge of his plastic ruler, invariably just before landing. This was in the mid-eighties, when we were sharing the skies around London with 757s, Jumbos and Concorde! Mind you, the Devon was a robust little aircraft and had 'seen off' the younger Pembrokes and Bassets!"

One of the twenty de Havilland Devon aircraft which served 207 Squadron was C.2/2 VP965. This one carried code letters DE, indicating its use in a four-aircraft detachment to Wyton about 1982. [via R. C. B. Ashworth]

The last fly-past. Devons VP981, VP969, VP965 and VP971 in close formation on 12 June 1984.
[via Sqn. Ldr. I. Hampton]

Between 1982 and 1984, another regular trip for 207 Squadron involved flying Buccaneer crews from Lossiemouth to Honington so that they could use the Buccaneer simulator. Oddly enough, in the Devon they often suffered air-sickness at low level, especially when heading north through the Highlands of Scotland. The Buccaneer rode very smoothly, so they said, compared with the Devon, the big wing of which magnified every bump and roll. Very little sympathy was forthcoming from the Devon crews!

'Spitsup' sorties in support of the Battle of Britain Memorial Flight continued into the 1980s. If they were embarking on a fairly long flight, 207 Squadron supplied a Devon to handle the navigation and communications for the two fighters, and to carry spare parts and a couple of ground crew if required. "I did many such trips," says Sqn. Ldr. Hampton, "and there is no more enjoyable way of spending a day than flying VFR with a Spitfire and Hurricane on your wing! We went as far afield as central Germany, which is just about the limit for the Spitfire......and we had to keep out of cloud or rain, as although not likely to cause critical damage this could shorten the lives of the fighters' propellers. One Battle of Britain Week, the only way I could avoid some 'grotty' weather was to go straight through the middle of the Bonn Control Zone. Even in the eighties, it took some negotiation on the radio, explaining that 'Yes, we are a Royal Air Force formation of Spitfire and Hurricane wanting to fly over the city at five hundred feet. No, this is not a joke.' It was at that stage that Barry Masters leaned across the cockpit and said 'Boss, whatever you do, don't tell them that we are 207 Squadron or we'll never get out of here alive!' Anyway, we managed and eventually landed at a small airfield in the Harz Mountains for a weekend airshow."

Throughout 1983 and into 1984 rumours abounded on the subject of the fate of the Devon, which by now was decidedly 'long in the tooth' but for which no replacement type was available. Sqn. Ldr. Hampton was airborne on the way to Hull one evening in March 1984 when he received a message via air traffic control, instructing him to call Northolt as soon as he had landed. In that way he received the official notification that the squadron was to disband in the summer. He recalls his time with 207 Squadron with pleasure. "While I have enjoyed every tour [in the RAF], there is no doubt that my time on 207 Squadron was the highlight", he says. "Maybe it was the sheer nostalgia of flying aircraft built in the late 'forties, without the hassle of modern technology, knowing that this was the last vestige of 'real' flying in the RAF. Memories of being thrown about in storms and fighting with ice have receded, mostly leaving recollections of quiet summer days. Mind you, I do vividly recall being forced lower and lower during bad weather in central Wales. Discussion of our options with Hamish Grigor produced from him the best definition of low-flying that I have come across – 'When you can see the legs of individual cows, that's OK. When you can seen the legs of individual sheep, that's low flying. When you can tell which sex they are, that's too low!' Crews got around a bit and occasionally had to suffer the rigours of a weekend in some foreign fleshpot. It was late at night in a Munich bar that I rescued George Mitchell. He had been explaining to some locals how fortunate they were to have had our squadron do the site clearance for their car park some forty years earlier and that maybe it was time they paid the bill! However, it was not all fun and frolics – the squadron had a reputation, as ever, for getting on with the job. Eventually, I had the task of telling the chaps that the squadron was to go, and then of organising the disbandment. It was sad, of course, especially for the older guys, for whom this was going to be the end of their flying careers, as it would be uneconomical to train them on a new type. However, we disbanded in style, with much partying."

Towards the end of June 1984 a four-Devon formation took to the air to mark the disbandment of the squadron after 66 arduous years and to pay tribute to the Devon aircraft, which had been in RAF service for 35 of those years. The box formation was led by Sqn. Ldr. Bert Conchie and his navigator, Sqn. Ldr. Mike Rosenorn-Lanng, while the CO, Sqn. Ldr. Ian Hampton, flew in number three position. Between them the eight aircrew taking part had built up a total of 55,000 hours in the air and had flown almost every type of aircraft in RAF service since the late 1940s. Lasting two and a half hours, the sortie overflew Hatfield, where the Devons had been built; Wyton, the base until recently of the 207 Squadron detachment; Benson; Upavon; Strike Command HQ at High Wycombe; and Bentley Priory, before returning to Northolt.

After the squadron had officially disbanded on 30 June 1984, seven of the fifteen Devons were sold at auction, some then finding their way onto the civil register. Of the remainder, one went to the Battle of Britain Memorial Flight at Coningsby to carry on with the task previously performed by 207 Squadron, one was flown to St. Athan for the RAF Museum collection and six were distributed around RAF Stations for use in fire practice.

Such was the final demise of a squadron which had every reason to feel proud of its achievements. But every unit is composed of people, and in 207 Squadron's case those people were not prepared to see the squadron fade away!

Faithful Devon VP952 after the last sortie ever carried out by 207 Squadron, when on 5 July 1984 the aircraft was handed over to the RAF Museum collection at St. Athan. The crew that day was Sqn. Ldr. Ian Hampton (right) and Flt. Lt. Norman Enston (centre), who are seen handing over the Form 700 to the Wg. Cdr. in charge of the collection. [via Sqn. Ldr. I. Hampton]

Sqn. Ldr. Bulpit handing over a cheque from RAF Marham to Wallace McIntosh on 13 March 1993, during the latter's memorial tour. [RAF Marham via W. McIntosh]

Chapter 13: Since then........

Following the disbandment of 207 Squadron at Northolt on 30 June 1984, it was necessary to 'lay up' the squadron standard, in accordance with military tradition. The first gathering of members of the newly-established 207 Squadron Association took place on 13/14 October 1984, when the standard was laid to rest in Leicester Cathedral, which was chosen with the city's long-established connection with the squadron – 'Leicester's Own' – in mind. More than two hundred people gathered for a reunion dinner at the Grand Hotel on the Saturday evening and were present at the ceremony next day. The Provost of Leicester, the Very Rev. Alan Warren, conducted the service, which was attended by the Lord Mayor and Lady Mayoress of the city, Mr. and Mrs. Michael Cufflin. Carrying the treasured standard was Flt. Lt. Norman Enston, late of 207 Squadron at Northolt, with Sgt. James Pennycook and another SNCO in attendance.

Shortly afterwards, the first committee was formed, with AVM David Dick as President and Chairman; Ben Lyon as Secretary; Bill Bray as Treasurer; and Ron Winton as Membership Secretary. They met as a committee for the first time soon after the Leicester event, and set about compiling a Constitution and dealing with other pertinent matters which would help the Association to succeed.

At the reunion in the following year, held at the Petwood Hotel at Woodhall Spa, the first discussion on the subject of a possible memorial to be erected at Spilsby took place, but it turned out to be several years before this project came to fruition. The 1986 reunion was held at the same venue, but in 1987 a move to the Stakis Victoria Hotel in Nottingham was made. There it was announced that earlier in the year an anonymous donor had generously offered to pay for a high-quality Day Book containing the names of every member of 7 (Naval) Squadron and 207 Squadron who lost his life while serving, to be located in Leicester Cathedral. Early in 1988 the Provost of Leicester agreed to allow a glass case to be used for display of the Day Book and to arrange for the pages to be turned daily.

1988's reunion was held at the Ladbroke International Hotel at Leicester and in 1989 the venue was the Penguin Hotel in the same city. On 5 November 1989 the Memorial Day Book, inscribed by a young lady calligrapher on goatskin parchment and bound in blue leather with the 207 Squadron badge on the front, was laid in its case in Leicester Cathedral. A considerable number of VIPs participated in the ceremony, including seven former

The RAF guard of honour at Leicester Cathedral on 5 November 1989, when the squadron's Memorial Book was dedicated

Commanding Officers of the squadron or its flights – Sqn. Ldr. P. J. S. Boggis, Wg. Cdr. G. W. O'N. Fisher, Wg. Cdr. P. Goodman, Gp. Capt. K. P. Lewis, Wg. Cdr. T. C. Murray, Gp. Capt. C. P. N. Newman and Wg. Cdr. M. J. Perrett. The Chaplain-in-Chief of the RAF preached and ACM Sir Lewis Hodges KCB CBE DSO DFC RAF (Retd.) read the lesson. Music was provided by the Band of the RAF Regiment from Catterick, and also present were the Lord Lieutenant of Leicestershire and the Hon. Mrs. Brooks, the Lord Mayor and Lady Mayoress of Leicester; the High Sheriff of Leicestershire and Mrs. De Lisle, the High Bailiff of Leicester, Gp. Capt. O. G. Bunn MBE (the Station Commander at Northolt, representing the AOC-in-C Strike Command); Maj. M. W. Hill CAF and Mrs. Hill; Sqn. Ldr. R. Owen RAAF, representing the Australian High Commissioner; Flg. Off. S. W. Iggo RNZAF and Mrs. Iggo, representing the New Zealand High Commissioner; and ACM Sir Neil Wheeler GCB CBE DSO DFC & Bar AFC RAF (Retd.) and Lady Wheeler. A Guard of Honour was provided by 207 (Cranfield) Squadron of the Air Training Corps, and the Cathedral was filled with Members and local representatives of organisations such as the Royal British Legion and the Royal Air Forces Association, as indeed it was by the magnificent music of the Band of the Royal Air Force Regiment. The service itself was beautifully conducted and had an impressive flow to it, with an exhilarating climax at which AVM A. D. Dick, President of the Association, formally requested the Provost to take charge of the Memorial Book, which was borne by former Sqn. Ldr. J. F. Grime DFC, a wartime Flight commander of 207 Squadron.

Members were much moved. Indeed such was the occasion that in retrospect it can be seen as marking a turning point for the Association. That the squadron's Roll of Honour was permanently recorded and beautifully displayed, resting beneath the squadron's treasured Standard in a way that any former member of 207 Squadron could be proud of was a reality.

At the next AGM, held at the Duke's Head at King's Lynn, sharpened focus turned to forming and implementing a realistic Association policy for Memorials to the Squadron. Members realised that it would happen if they wished to record its service at the principal airfields where 207 Squadron had served, especially during the Second World War, with its appalling casualties. The Committee gave much thought to the matter, and in the next Newsletter proposed a formal policy and balloted all Members for their views. Responses were in favour, and a Memorial Committee was set up, as was a 207 Squadron Memorial Fund to which Members were invited to contribute, with the intention of placing Memorial tablets in the Parish Churches of, firstly, Great Steeping for Spilsby, which suffered the greatest number of casualties; at Bottesford, to include Langar; at Waddington if funds permitted; and at Marham.

Contributions to the Memorial Fund were encouraging, and on 8 May 1992 the Memorial at Great Steeping was unveiled by Wg. Cdr. P. N. Jennings, the sole surviving CO from the Spilsby period. The Rev. Brian Halfpenny, a former Chaplain-in-Chief to the RAF, preached, and a Memorial Book containing the names of the many casualties suffered by the squadron at Spilsby was carried by Wallace McIntosh and deposited in the church. After the service the Battle of Britain Memorial Flight's Lancaster made several low passes, bringing lumps to many throats, and all, including the Lancaster's crew, attended a splendid lunch at the museum at East Kirkby, seated beneath the Lancaster in its hangar.

In 1992 the reunion was held at the Falcon Hotel at Stratford-on-Avon, but in 1993 the Association returned to Woodhall Spa, this time meeting at the Golf Hotel. Attending this reunion was an entire seven-man crew, headed by John Stephens DFC, who completed their operations with 207 Squadron at Langar between March and September 1943! They had flown together on 28 operational sorties, plus a few others when they had to return early with technical trouble and which could not be counted toward the total.

To raise money for memorials, 73-year-old former 207 Squadron member Wallace McIntosh DFC & Bar DFM began a marathon drive from his Aberdeen home in March 1993. Behind the wheel of a car loaned by the Rover Group, he visited the sites of 64 former Bomber Command airfields, the first on his route being Middleton St. George, now Tees-Side Airport. Wallace's mission was to raise enough money to finance three memorials to the 970 men of 207 Squadron who lost their lives during the Second World War. The highlight of his trip came on 25 April, when he attended a reunion at Bottesford at which a number of former RAAF aircrew members were also present. "Unfortunately it poured all day," he told a reporter, "but the rain didn't drench our spirits."

On 13 July 1993, a small group of members gathered at the Langar Hall Hotel to secure positive help in ensuring that a memorial to 207 Squadron be set up at Langar airfield. With the full backing of the Association, a committee was formed, and a budget of £3,000 was agreed.

The seven-man surviving crew (see Chapter 7) met at Langar in 1993. Left to right: Jack Pegrum, Nat Bury, Jack Stephens, Jim Love, Arthur McDavitt, Ken Bate, Arthur Barfoot.

Seen at Langar during his tour of 64 former Bomber Command bases, Wallace McIntosh poses alongside his Rover 827, with the control tower and the parachute club's Islander aircraft in the background. [via W. McIntosh]

Meanwhile, on 10/11 July 1993, a memorial in Switzerland to the crew of 207 Squadron Lancaster ED412, which was shot down in July 1943 by Swiss anti-aircraft fire on its way back from a raid on Turin, was dedicated. Present were the British, French and US military attachés and Swiss military officers. The bodies of the crew had been buried in the cemetery of St. Martin in Vevey, west of Montreux.

The efforts which had gone into the Langar memorial project came to fruition on 12 May 1994, when a Service of Dedication was held. This was the culmination of the dedication of members of the Association in the area and the people of local villages, led by Sqn. Ldr. John Mitchell and Mr. Barry Goodwin, Chairman and Secretary respectively of the Langar Airfield 207 Squadron Memorial Committee.

Exactly fifty years after the series of raids mounted by Bomber Command to obliterate the flying-bomb assembly depots in France, Peter Phelps arranged a visit to the area where 207 Squadron had lost many crew members. On 8 July 1994 forty-seven members took the *Stenna Londoner* ferry boat from Newhaven to Dieppe on their way to the town of Gisors to be the guests of the mayor and citizens of nearby Neufles-St.-Martin, where five of the crew of Lancaster ND866 are buried. Next day a parade of standards, including that of the regional RAFA Branch, was held, followed by a moving church service and a wreath-laying ceremony. The party then moved to Bézu-St.-Eloi, where a splendid monument has been erected on the spot where ND866 came down. After laying a wreath on the graves of four members of a Halifax of 76 Squadron which was shot down at the same time, the party continued to Noyers, where they attended the unveiling of a plaque honouring Mme. Majo Perdereau, who has become an Honorary member of the 207 Squadron Association. In 1940 she was a key member of the resistance movement and in 1943 and 1944 she sheltered twenty-two Allied airmen on their way along the clandestine routes to freedom. What remained of the day was taken up with a *Vin d'Honneur* and a long dinner at Neufles. On the final day of the tour the party visited the National Cemetery at Beauvais before boarding the coach to return to Dieppe for the ferry to Newhaven.

1995's reunion was held at the Moat House Hotel at Nottingham on 16 September, a feature being the newly-published book by Bob Kirby on the subject of the Avro

Manchester. Next day, most of those who had attended the reunion travelled to Bottesford for the Memorial Dedication service in the church of St. Mary the Virgin, where in the churchyard several members of 207 Squadron are buried. In addition to members of the Association, about a hundred local residents attended the ceremony, as did the invited guests, the Duchess of Granby and her son the Marquis, from nearby Belvoir Castle. Flanking the pathway to the church door were cadets from 207 (Cranfield) Squadron of the ATC. After a service conducted by the Rev. G. Spencer, the dedication began with the forming up of an escort party led by AVM David Dick, accompanied by Wg. Cdr. Russell Jeffs, a former CO of 207 Squadron at Bottesford, who unveiled the Westmoreland Greenstone tablet. To complete the dedication, the Last Post was sounded by a trumpeter from the ATC squadron, and one minute's silence was observed.

Later in the year, on 7 July, AVM David Dick, his son and grandsons paid a visit to Neufles cemetery to lay wreaths on the graves of Flg. Off. Milner's crew and then to Bézu to carry out a similar function on the grave of Sgt. Jacques. Next day, David and his family attended a moving ceremony at Sérifontaine, north of Gisors, at which a beautiful granite Memorial stone commemorates the crash of Lancaster ND567 [EM:V], captained by Flg. Off. Trevor Hordley. George Baker, as the only known survivor of the crew, was the honoured guest. So exactly 51 years after the Lancaster was shot down, people including George Baker, who was by then quite infirm, tramped some quarter of a mile across rough stubble fields to lay wreaths on a new stone cross which had replaced an earlier wooden one near the actual crash site in a wood. At the ceremony, some distance from the crash site, near a road and thus visible and accessible, is the granite Memorial. Among about a hundred local people who had come for the ceremony were the Mayor of Sérifontaine, the police chief, members of many ex-Service Associations, representatives of L'Armée de l'Air, a representative from the British Embassy in Paris,

At Langar a very practical memorial in the form of a hardwood seat is used by many visitors. It was donated by Mrs. Dorothy Ware in memory of her late husband, Sgt. Thomas Skelton, aged 19, who failed to return from a raid on Duisburg on the night of 13 May 1943. [Norman Yates, RAFA Eastern Area Director]

The Langar memorial to 207 Squadron personnel who lost their lives while flying from that airfield. [Norman Yates, RAFA Eastern Area Director]

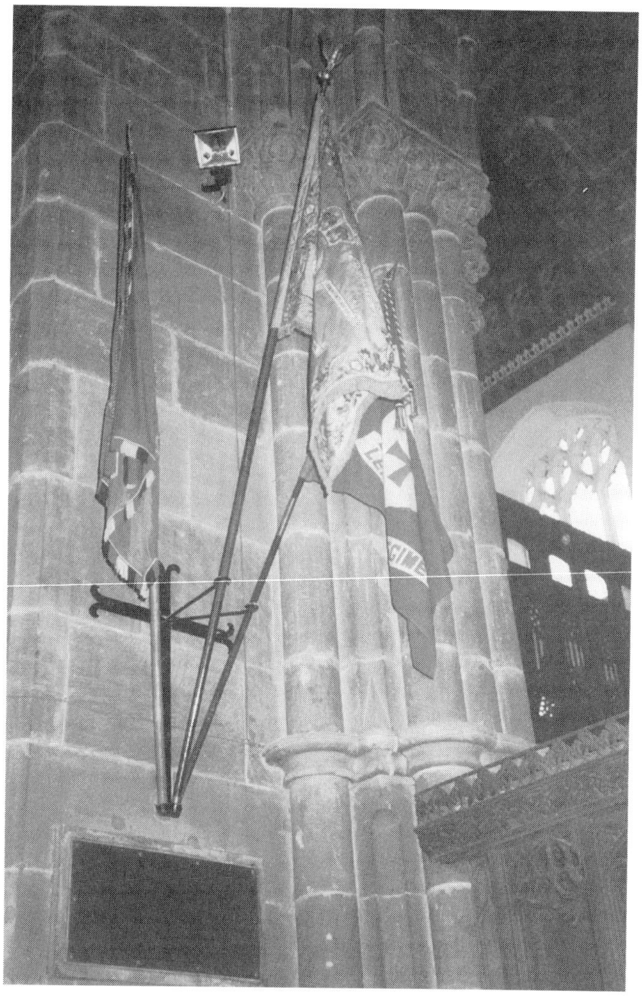

207 Squadron's standard is the centre of three in Leicester Cathedral.

our Honorary Member Claude Le Roux and lots of children. After a *Vin d'Honneur* in the old farmhouse, there was a reception and presentation of souvenirs, and David Dick presented a Certificate of Honorary Membership to M. Yves Desmesliers, who had been responsible for the whole enterprise. The party moved on to the military cemetery in Beauvais, where they laid wreaths on the graves of the crew members who had been killed.

Another moving and memorable occasion took place in 1996, when on 7 September a Memorial service was held at Waddington. A superb Memorial Tablet was unveiled by Wg. Cdr. T. C. Murray DSO DFC & Bar, a former Flight commander who flew twenty operational sorties on Manchesters. In the presence of a splendid gathering of Waddington veterans, the Memorial Book was carried by Sqn. Ldr. Max Riddell DFC DFM, escorted by Wg. Cdr. K. H. P. Beauchamp DSO, another former Flight commander, and Wg. Cdr. W. Goldstraw DFC & Bar, a veteran observer. The Station Commander, Gp. Capt. Mike Remlinger, attended, and the cadets of 207 (Cranfield) Squadron ATC turned out in force, their bugler giving an excellent rendering of the Last Post and Reveille. The fact that the service was held at Waddington, where the squadron had served 55 years previously, added to the impact of the event. On the same day as the Waddington service, the Association's 1996 reunion was held, at the Golf Hotel, Woodhall Spa.

In Chapter 8 mention is made of the collision between two Lancasters on 2 March 1945 and the non-identification of one crew member. When in 1995 the wreckage of the aircraft was excavated a body was found which was immediately identified as that of the mid-upper gunner, Sgt. R. C. Banks. At once this made it possible for the body of the one unidentified crew member, who had been buried as an unknown airman, to be identified as that of Flt. Sgt. Henderson. The appropriate indefatigable department of the Ministry of Defence spent many months in attempting to trace relatives of the two men, sadly with no success for Sgt. Banks. So on Friday 25 October 1996 in a full military funeral fifty-one years after the event, Sgt. Banks was buried alongside some of his other crew members in the RAF section of Cambridge Cemetery.

The day dawned wet and gloomy, but by 12.00, when the service began, the small chapel was filled by several of Flt. Sgt. Henderson's relatives, members of the 207 Squadron Association and representatives of other associations. The Bomber Command Association's standard was carried by Mr. Ron Pearson of Newmarket & District Branch of the RAF Association, and the impeccable Pall Bearers and Escort were provided by the Queen's Colour Squadron. After the service, while the funeral party slow-marched to the burial plot, the sun broke through the gloom. A wreath from the Air Force Board was laid by Gp. Capt. Luke and one for the 207 Squadron Association by Wallace McIntosh DFM DFC & Bar, while other wreaths were laid on behalf of relatives of members of the unlucky crew. No sooner had this been completed than the Dakota aircraft from the Battle of Britain Memorial Flight made two passes in salute. Afterwards, the Cambridge University Air Squadron hosted the party at a buffet lunch. The only disappointment was that it had not been possible to trace any relatives of Sgt. Banks.

A scene on 16 September 1998 during the dedication at Brigstock, Northants, of the memorial to the crew of Lancaster DV361. [R. Winton]

After the Association's successful visit to Neufles St. Martin in 1994, a strong demand for a return trip with an extended itinerary began to develop. It was felt that this should include a visit to the caves at St. Leu d'Esserent, which had been the principal depot for assembly of V1s and the target for 207 Squadron on 8 July 1944. Secondly, the squadron's graves at Creil and Auvers-sur-Oise and the new memorial at Sérifontaine should be visited. So on 6 July 1997 a coach set off from Reading with thirty-one members on board, bound for the Dover to Calais ferry and thence to Senlis, where three more members joined the party. From there the group was able to travel the short distance to Creil to lay a wreath. Next day the members arrived at St. Leu d'Esserent, where a historian and guide joined them. Members who had paid a non-stop visit in July 1944 found it extremely interesting to hear all about the results of their trip! After presenting a squadron badge to the Mayor of St. Leu, the party moved on to Auvers-sur-Oise to lay a wreath and to present yet another badge. Finally, on 8 July, the party drove to Neufles St. Martin to lay a wreath and were welcomed in the traditional style by the local Mayor and veterans. Before heading for Calais the party visited Sérifontaine Memorial.

On Saturday 12 July 1997, a glorious sunny day, some fifty former members of 207 Squadron, many with their wives, gathered at Marham for lunch in the Officers' Mess. But this was not just a reunion; what had encouraged them to attend was a Memorial service in the Station Chapel during the afternoon, during which a Scroll paying tribute to the squadron's fourteen years of service at Marham was presented by the Association. Hand inscribed on goatskin parchment, the Scroll outlines both the essence of the squadron's service at Marham and records the names of the eight squadron members killed while serving there. The Scroll was carried by Wg. Cdr. Geoffrey O'N. Fisher OBE DFC & Bar, who commanded the squadron between May 1951 and May 1953. He was escorted by the Association's Secretary, Wg. Cdr. Ken Marwood AFM, who served at Marham from 1958 to 1961. Once again, the Association's loyal supporters on 207 (Cranfield) Squadron ATC, under Flt. Lt. Marian Rolfe RAFVR(T), provided a guard of honour.

1997's annual Reunion, on 6 September, was held for the first time at the Midland Hotel in Derby, a venue which had been used successfully by other squadrons for similar events. As it proved to be a very suitable meeting-place, the 1998 reunion was held there on 5 September.

A long-standing desire to visit Deelen airfield, the target on 15 August 1944 when Flt. Lt. G. A. C. Overgaauw and his crew lost their lives, was realised on 2 April 1998, when Wallace McIntosh, Alec White, Bill Verralls and Ken Williams arrived by car. Arrangements had been made through Kees Rijken, an honorary member of the Association who lived in Eindhoven, who had also made an unsuccessful attempt to locate members of the Overgaauw family. Next day the small party visited the Moscowa General Cemetery near Arnhem to pay their respects at the graves of Flt. Lt. Overgaauw, Plt. Off. A. L. Brett, Sgt. R. L. Coaker, Plt. Off. H. D. Mackay and Sgt. P. A. Wildsmith, and a wreath was placed on Flt. Lt. Overgaauw's grave for the whole crew, the two Canadian members of which are buried in the Canadian War Cemetery.

At the Aviation Heritage Centre at East Kirkby on 13 July 1998, a small group of members of the Association gathered to dedicate a tree and plaque in memory of the crew of LL973 [EM:M], which was shot down during a raid on Wesseling on 21/22 June 1944. Three of the crew, including pilot Mike Solly, lost their lives, while two were taken prisoner and two evaded capture. One of thirty such trees, the 'Solly' tree stands beside the path from the rear exit of the newly-extended visitors' building and near the control tower.

To honour the memory of the crew of Lancaster DV361, a memorial was dedicated on 16 September 1998. The idea of former RAF electrician Paul Knight and ex-Wg. Cdr. Eric Reeves, it was erected at Brigstock in Northamptonshire, where the aircraft had crashed on 22 December 1943 while on a cross-country practice flight from Spilsby. On board at the time were the pilot, Sgt. G. A. Baker, flight engineer Sgt. P. W. Groom, air gunners Sgt. T. G. Higgins and Sgt. G. C. O'Neill, wireless operator Flt. Sgt. C. E. Ryall, navigator Sgt. R. Wellfare and bomb-aimer Sgt. L. A. Hinch. Four of these men were able to bale out when an engine caught fire and could not be extinguished, but Higgins, O'Neill and Ryall failed to do so and lost their lives in the ensuing crash. Veterans of 207 Squadron attended the ceremony, in which representatives of the Royal British Legion, the Air Gunners Association and the Royal Air Forces Association took part. The memorial in Harley Way was unveiled by Sqn. Ldr. J. Mitchell, who had been a signals leader at Spilsby at the time of the accident. To add the final unbeatable touch to the event, the Lancaster from the Battle of Britain Memorial Flight flew overhead.

The last event up to the time of going to press took place on 9 March 1999, when three committee members of the 207 Squadron Association met a former member of 26 Squadron, from which the 207 Squadron detachment at Wyton had stemmed in 1976. A recently-found board listing the names of the COs of 26 Squadron and the 207 Squadron detachment was handed over and will eventually be placed in the Aviation Museum at Tangmere.

The 207 Squadron Association maintains close contact with its members through a Newsletter, and there is also an Internet site, http://freespace.virgin.net/frank.haslam, from which information on the Association's activities may be obtained.

The new memorial at Brigstock to the crew of Lancaster DV361. [J.N. Smith]

INDEX OF PEOPLE

The Armament Officers' Trophy (The 'Cock') displayed by 207 Squadron at Bircham Newton in 1933, with Flt. Lt. Ware central in the front row. [P. H. T. Green collection]

INDEX OF PLACE NAMES

Appendix I: Squadron Bases

7 (Naval) Squadron

Koanda Irangi (Tanganyika)	June 1916 to 12 January 1917
Petite Synthe (France)	November 1916
Coudekerke (France)	4 April 1917 to 1 April 1918

207 Squadron RAF

Coudekerke (France)	1 April 1918
Netheravon	22 April 1918
Andover	13 May 1918
Ligescourt (France)	7 June 1918
Estrée-en-Chausée (France)	26 October 1918
Carvin (France)	1 December 1918
Merheim (Germany)	1 January 1919
Hangelar (Germany)	10 May 1919
Tangmere	23 August 1919
Croydon	8 October 1919
Uxbridge (as a cadre)	16 January 1920 to 20 January 1920
Bircham Newton	1 February 1920
(left for Turkey)	29 September 1922
San Stephano (Turkey)	11 October 1922
Eastchurch	3 October 1923
Bircham Newton	7 November 1929
Ed Damer (Sudan)	28 October 1935
Gebeit (Sudan)	6 April 1936
Worthy Down	29 August 1936
Cottesmore	20 April 1938
Cranfield	24 August 1939
Cottesmore	9 December 1939
Cranfield	5 April 1940 to 8 April 1940
Waddington	1 November 1940
Bottesford	17 November 1941
detached to Syerston	24 August 1942
Langar	20 September 1942
Spilsby	12 October 1943
Methwold	30 October 1945
Tuddenham	29 April 1946
Stradishall	7 November 1946
Mildenhall	1 February 1949 to 1 March 1950
Marham	29 May 1951 to 27 March 1956
Marham	1 April 1956 to 1 May 1965
Northolt	3 February 1969 to 30 June 1984

207 Squadron Conversion Flight

Bottesford	16 January 1942
Swinderby	23 August 1942 to 20 October 1942

Appendix II: Squadron Commanders

7 (Naval) Sqn., Tanganyika

Sqn. Cdr. E. R. C. Nanson	April 1916

7 (Naval) Sqn., France

Sqn. Cdr. C. L. Courtney	November 1916
Sqn. Cdr. J. W. K. Allsop	5 April 1917
Sqn. Cdr. J. T. Babington DSO	27 June 1917
Sqn. Cdr. H. A. Buss	1 January 1918
Sqn. Cdr. H. S. Adams	20 February 1918 to 31 March 1918

207 Squadron RAF

Sqn. Cdr. H. S. Adams	1 April 1918
Maj. G. L. Thompson DSC	24 May 1918
Maj. T. A. Batchelor	26 July 1918
Maj. G. R. Elliott	7 August 1918
Maj. M. H. B. Nethersole	5 June 1919 to 20 January 1920
Sqn. Ldr. A. W. Tedder	1 February 1920
Sqn. Ldr. V. Gaskell–Blackburn DSC AFC	6 August 1923
Sqn. Ldr. J. B. Graham MC DFC	28 February 1926
Sqn. Ldr. E. A. Beulah	1 December 1928
Sqn. Ldr. J. W.Woodhouse DSO MC	23 April 1931
Sqn. Ldr. J. L. Vachell MC	1 February 1933
Sqn. Ldr. G. G. Dawson	29 September 1933
Sqn. Ldr. P. A. Maitland AFC	9 August 1934
Sqn. Ldr. R. J. Rodwell	6 February 1935
Sqn. Ldr. J. W. Lissett	18 March 1936
Sqn. Ldr. J. N. D. Anderson	6 August 1938 to 8 April 1940
Wg. Cdr. N. C. Hyde	1 November 1940 (PoW 9 April 1941)
Sqn. Ldr. C. J. F. Kydd	9 April 1941
Wg. Cdr. J. N. D. Anderson OBE	30 April 1941
Wg. Cdr. K. P. Lewis	21 May 1941
Wg. Cdr. C. Fothergill	10 October 1941
Wg. Cdr. F. R. Jeffs	28 May 1942
Wg. Cdr. F. G. L. Bain	7 December 1942
Wg. Cdr. T. A. B. Parselle	26 December 1942 (PoW 26 May 1943)
Wg. Cdr. P. N. Jennings	29 May 1943
Wg. Cdr. V. J. Wheeler	26 February 1944 (KIA 22 March 1944)
Wg. Cdr. J. F. Grey DSO DFC	23 March 1944
Wg. Cdr. H. R. Black AFC	16 October 1944
Sqn. Ldr. L. McCracken	18 April 1946
Sqn. Ldr. G. W. Vowles	18 June 1946
Sqn. Ldr. P. J. S. Boggis DFC	17 March 1947
Sqn. Ldr. G. J. C. Hogan DFC	9 March 1948
Sqn. Ldr. E. J. Wicht DSO DFC	5 December 1949 to 1 March 1950
Sqn. Ldr. G. W. O'Neil Fisher OBE DFC	29 May 1951
Sqn.Ldr. P. H. Gibbs	15 February 1954
Flt. Lt. R. B. McGowan	14 January 1956 to 27 March 1956
Sqn. Ldr. P. H. Gibbs	1 April 1956
Wg. Cdr. D. D. Haig DSO DFC	28 May 1956

Wg. Cdr. C. P. N. Newman OBE DFC	12 June 1957
Wg. Cdr. W. D. Robertson	22 April 1959
Wg. Cdr. W. E. Martin DFC AFC	1 June 1961
Wg. Cdr. A. D. Dick AFC MA	20 May 1963
Sqn. Ldr. R. C. Allen	21 September 1964
Wg. Cdr. J. F. Stewart	2 November 1964
Flt. Lt. B. A. Sherlock	15 March 1965
Flt. Lt. M. J. A. Bryett	6 April 1965
	to 1 May 1965
Sqn. Ldr. G. Pearson	3 February 1969
Sqn. Ldr. B. R. Kent MBE	5 August 1970
Sqn. Ldr. L. T. Arthur	January 1972
Sqn. Ldr. G. T. West	27 March 1973
Sqn. Ldr. P. G. Goodman	10 March 1975
Sqn. Ldr. M. J. Perrett	18 April 1977
Sqn. Ldr. J. H. Easton	February 1979
Sqn. Ldr. R. Lunn	5 January 1981
Sqn. Ldr. I. J. Hampton	30 April 1983
	to 30 June 1984

207 Squadron's Wyton detachment

(none)	1 April 1976
Flt. Lt. D. J. Butler	22 November 1976
Flt. Lt. B. J. Alford	12 July 1977
Flt. Lt. A. J. Gault	31 October 1977
Sqn. Ldr. G. Derbyshire	1 January 1978
Sqn. Ldr. L. E. Blackburn MBE	15 July 1980
Sqn. Ldr. B. J. Conchie AFC	14 February 1983
	to 30 June 1984

One of 207 Squadron's Handley Page O/400s, seen here at Hangelaar with its port wing folded. [C. Box]

APPENDIX III: Summary of First World War operations

Raids carried out by 7 (Naval) Squadron

Date	Target	Aircraft	Remarks
15/16.11.16	Ateliers de la Marine and Slyken power station, Ostende	four Shorts ?	
3.2.17	Brugge docks	four Shorts ?	
4/5.2.17	Brugge docks	three ?	
16.2.17	Ghistelles airfield	?	
5/6.4.17	Junction S of Brugge	five Shorts	
7/8.4.17	Objective P.16	four Shorts	
13/14.4.17	East and west basins at Brugge	four Shorts	
22.4.17	(Armed patrol)	three O/100	
23.4.17	Five destroyers	three O/100	
26.4.17	Two bombing patrols over enemy shipping	three + four O/100	3115 ditched
29/30.4.17	Objectives K1 and O	four Shorts	
30.4/1.5.17	Objectives K1 and O	four Shorts	
1/2.5.17	Objectives X14, X15 and X16	four Shorts	
7.5.17	Hostile shipping	three O/100	Mission abandoned
9/10.5.17	Docks at Brugge and seaplane base on mole at Zeebrugge	four Shorts + four O/100	
26.5.17	Bombing patrol over enemy shipping	three O/100	Bombs brought back
27/28.5.17	Ostende seaplane base	four Shorts	
29/30.5.17	Ostende seaplane base	four Shorts	
31.5/1.6.17	Brugge docks	four Shorts	
	Zeebrugge seaplane base	three O/100	
	Ateliers de la Marine, Ostende	four O/100	
3/4.6.17	St. Denis Westrem airfield	three Shorts + eight O/100	
	Zeebrugge mole	one O/100	
4/5.6.17	Brugge	four Shorts + six O/100	
2/3.7.17	Brugge docks	eight O/100	
3/4.7.17	Ghistelles airfield	eight O/100	
	Nieumunster/Houttave airfield	four O/100	
	Trains in Brugge/Ostende area	one O/100	
	Ostende seaplane base	one O/100	
6/7.7.17	Gontrode airship shed	one O/100	
	St. Denis Westrem airfield	seven O/100	
	Ghistelles airfield	one O/100	
	Ostende–Thorout railway	one O/100	
11/12.7.17	Ostende	four O/100	
	St. Denis Westrem airfield	one O/100	
	Ghistelles airfield	four O/100	
	Vassenaere airfield and dump	two O/100	
12/13.7.17	Rail sidings, Ostende harbour	one O/100	
	Nieumunster/Houttave airfield	three O/100	
	Brugge canal and Thorout jct.	two O/100	
	Aertrycke airfield	one O/100	
	Glustalen airfield	one O/100	
	Brugge docks	one O/100	
15/16.7.17	Zeebrugge	three O/100	
	Railway vehicles in naval area	two O/100	
	Ostende sidings and Aertrycke airfield	three O/100	
21/22.7.17	Middelkerke dump	two O/100	
	Railway vehicles in naval area	two O/100	

From this point the records of 7 (Naval) and 7A (Naval) Squadrons were combined, until 10 September 1917, when 7A Squadron became fully independent.

Date	Target	Aircraft	Remarks
27/28.7.17	Railway vehicles in naval area	one O/100	
	Ghistelles airfield	one O/100	
	Ghent (St. Pierre) station	two O/100	
28/29.7.17	Railway vehicles in naval area	four O/100	
	Brugeoise works, Brugge	four O/100	
9/10.8.17	Zuidwedge sidings	three O/100	
	Ghistelles airfield	five O/100	
15/16.8.17	Ostende station	seven O/100	
	Thorout station	seven O/100	
16/17.8.17	Thorout junction	fourteen O/100	
18/19.8.17	Ghent (St. Pierre) station	four O/100	
	Brugge docks	five O/100	
19/20.8.17	Middelkerke dump	four O/100	
	Brugeoise works, Brugge	four O/100	
21/22.8.17	Zeebrugge mole	four O/100	
22/23.8.17	Middelkerke dump	three O/100	
	Raversyde dump	two O/100	
25/26.8.17	St. Denis Westrem airfield	seven O/100	3137 failed to return
31.8/1.9.17	Ghistelles airfield	eight O/100	
2/3.9.17	Brugge docks	eight O/100	
3/4.9.17	Brugge docks	nine O/100	
	Ghistelles airfield	one O/100	
	Vassenaere dump	one O/100	
4/5.9.17	Brugge docks	seven O/100	
	Ghistelles airfield	one O/100	
10/11.9.17	Ghentrode airfield	one O/100	
	St. Denis Westrem airfield	two O/100	
	Brugge docks	one O/100	
11/12.9.17	Thorout airfield	four O/100	
12/13.9.17	Ghistelles airfield	one O/100	
	Thorout junction	one O/100	
20/21.9.17	Thorout junction	five O/100	
21/22.9.17	Courtemarche station	three O/100	
	Thorout junction	two O/100	
25/26.9.17	Lichtenvelde	two O/100	
	Coutenacke	one O/100	
	Thorout junction	four O/100	
27/28.9.17	St. Denis Westrem airfield	three O/100	
	Gontrode airship shed	one O/100	
	Zeebrugge lock gates	one O/100	
29/30.9.17	Zeebrugge lock gates	five O/100	
	Meuse railway bridge, Namur	one O/100	Not confirmed by
	squadron diary		
30.9/1.10.17	St. Denis Westrem airfield	three O/100	
	Zeebrugge	one O/100	Returned early
1/2.10.17	Namur	one O/100	Returned early
2/3.10.17	St. Denis Westrem airfield	two O/100	
9/10.10.17	Thorout junction	two O/100	
	Lichtervelde station	two O/100	
14/15.10.17	Brugge docks	one O/100	
15/16.10.17	Brugge docks	three O/100	
19/20.10.17	Brugge docks	one O/100	
20.10.17	Köln (alternative Düren)	one O/100	Not confirmed by squadron diary
20/21.10.17	Brugge docks	one O/100	
21/22.10.17	Melle sidings and junction	one O/100	
22/23.10.17	Ghent (St. Pierre) station	one O/100	
26/27.10.17	Lichtervelde	two O/100	
	Thorout junction	three O/100	
27/28.10.17	St. Denis Westrem airfield	one O/100	
	Engel airfield	one O/100	
	Lichtervelde sidings	two O/100	
28/29.10.17	Antwerpe	two O/100	
	Duron	one O/100	
	Brugge docks	one O/100	
	railway south of Ghent	one O/100	

Date	Target	Aircraft	Remarks
29/30.10.17	Sparappalhoek airfield	one O/100	
	Vassenaere airfield	one O/100	
30/31.10.17	Thorout	three O/100	
	Lichtervelde	two O/100	
6/7.11.17	Thorout	two O/100	
	Lichtervelde	two O/100	
9/10.11.17	Brugge docks	two O/100	
	St. Denis Westrem airfield	one O/100	
5/6.12.17	St. Denis Westrem airfield	three O/100	
10/11.12.17	Brugge docks	three O/100	
	Oostaker airfield	two O/100	
11/12.12.17	Brugge docks	one O/100	
18/19.12.17	Brugge docks	four O/100	
22/23.12.17	Mariakerke airfield	two O/100	
	St. Denis Westrem airfield	two O/100	
23/24.12.17	Brugge docks	three O/100	
	St. Denis Westrem airfield	one O/100	
16/17.2.18	Mariakerke airfield	two O/100	
17/18.2.18	Brugge docks	three O/100	
18.2.18	St. Denis Westrem airfield	two O/100	
25/26.2.18	Brugge docks	three O/1200	

Any raids which may have been carried out by 7 (Naval) Squadron after this date are not recorded.

Raids carried out by 207 Squadron

NB: in official records the number of aircraft taking part was not always stated and has therefore been calculated from the known number and weight of bombs dropped, with possible slight inaccuracy.

11.4.18	Zeebrugge		
22/23.6.18	Bapaume station, dump and sidings	seven O/400	
23/24.6.18	Cambrai East & West stations	eight O/400	
26/27.6.18	Tournai station, Railway at Cambrai, billets at Lille, Lens station and are abetween Lens and Douai	eight O/400	
28/29.6.18	Tournai bridges and station	ten O/400	
29/30.6.18	Bridge over canal south-east of Tournai	ten O/400	
13/14.7.18	Railway between Thulin and Blanc Misseron on Mons to Valenciennes line	nine O/400	
18/19.7.18	(ditto)	nine O/400	C9665 failed to return
19/20.7.18	(ditto)	seven O/400	
31.7/1.8.18	Cambrai station	eight O/400	
6/7.8.18	Cambrai	six O/400	D5405 failed to return
7/8.8.18	Mission to drown sound of massing tanks	two O/400	
9/10.8.18	Peronne station	seven O/400	
10/11.8.18	Peronne station	twelve O/400	
11/12.8.18	Peronne station	six O/400	
12/13.8.18	Peronne station	seven O/400	
13/14.8.18	Peronne station	thirteen O/400	
14/15.8.18	Peronne station	seven O/400	
	Special patrol between Roye and Chirilly	two O/400	
16/17.8.18	St. Quentin station	six O/400	
18/19.8.18	Mons-en-Chausee airfield	five O/400	
21/22.8.18	Cambrai station	twelve O/400 in two raids	
22/23.8.18	Valenciennes junction	eight O/400	
24/25.8.18	Valenciennes junction and Douai station	fourteen O/400	
28/29.8.18	Marquise town and station	seven O/400	
1/2.9.18	Marquise town and station	five O/400	
3/4.9.18	Cambrai Ville station	eight O/400 in two raids	
6/7.9.18	St. Quentin station	six O/400	C9657 failed to return
13/14.9.18	Le Cateau station	four O/400	
15/16.9.18	Etreux airfield	nine O/400	
16/17.9.18	Etreux airfield	five O/400	
17/18.9.18	Tupigny airfield	five O/400	

Date	Target	Aircraft	Remarks
20/21.9.18	Soultain airfield	one O/400	
	Vitry	one O/400	
	Cambrai	two O/400	
	area around Douai	two O/400	
21/22.9.18	Soultain airfield	four O/400	
22/23.9.18	Soultain airfield	four O/400	
25/26.9.18	Bisseghem airfield	four O/400	
27/28.9.18	Busigny junction	seven O/400	
28/29.9.18	Busigny station	three O/400	
	Bohain station	four O/400	
1/2.10.18	Aulnoye station	eight O/400	
3/4.10.18	Aulnoye station	twelve O/400	
4/5.10.18	Aulnoye station	eight O/400	
6/7.10.18	Aulnoye station	four O/400	
8/9.10.18	Aulnoye station	seven O/400	
13/14.10.18	Mons station	two O/400	
14/15.10.18	Tournai junction	two O/400	
18/19.10.18	Namur station	four O/400	
22/23.10.18	Namur station	three O/400	
29/30.10.18	Namur station	two O/400	
31.10/1.11.18	Namur station	two O/400	
3/4.11.18	Maubeuge junction	five O/400	
4/5.11.18	Namur station	seven O/400	
9/10.11.18	Liege station	six O/400	
10/11.11.18	Namur station	six O/400	

No bowsers in those days! Seen at Manston, this HP O/100 was destined for service with 7 (N) Squadron across the Channel. [E. F. Cheesman]

APPENDIX IV: Summary of Second World War operations

In the 'Failed to return' column in the lists below, aircraft which crashed in the UK on return from, or in one case outbound to, an operation are included.

Waddington — Manchesters

Date	Primary target	Aircraft detailed	Took off	Failed to complete mission	Failed to return
24.2.41	Brest	6	6		
26.2.41	Cologne	5	5	1	
3.3.41	Brest	2	2	2	
12/13.3.41	Hamburg	4	4		
13/14.3.41	Hamburg	5	5		1 (L7313 EM:C)
18.3.41	Kiel	2	2		
20.3.41	Lorient	3	3	1	1 (L7278 EM:A)
27.3.41	Dusseldorf	4	3	1	1 (L7303 EM: P)
30.3.41	Brest	4	4		
4.4.41	Brest	5	4	1	
6.4.41	Brest	4	4	1	
8.4.41	Kiel	8	8		1 (L7302 EM: R)
9.4.41	Vegesack	1	1		
12.4.41	Brest	6	6	2	
2/3.5.41	Hamburg	3	3		1 (L7379 EM: T)
3.5.41	Brest	1	1		
	Cologne	2	2		
5.5.41	Mannheim	4	4		
6.5.41	Hamburg	2	2	1	
8.5.41	Hamburg	6	6		
9.5.41	Mannheim	1	1		
9/10.5.41	Berlin	3	3	1	
10/11.5.41	Berlin	2	2		
12.5.41	Mannheim	3	2		
15.5.41	Berlin	4	4	2	
21/22.6.41	Boulogne	8	6	1	1 (L7314 EM:Y)
23/24.6.41	Dusseldorf	7	6		
24.6.41	Dusseldorf	5	5		
26/27.6.41	Kiel	8	7		
29/30.6.41	Hamburg	7	6		

Waddington — Hampdens
(* = 44 Sqn. aircraft with 207 Sqn. crew)

6/7.7.41	Brest		5		
7/8.7.41	Munchen Gladbach		4	1	
	Dusseldorf		1		
11/12.7.41	Wilhelmshaven		2		
14/15.7.41	Hanover		4		
19/20.7.41	Minelaying in 'Eglantine'	4	4+2*		
21/22.7.41	Frankfurt	4	4+2*		
24/25.7.41	Kiel	6	6		
	Minelaying in 'Nectarine'	1	1		
27/28.7.41	Minelaying in 'Artichoke'	4	4+2*		
30/31.7.41	Cologne	4	4		
5/6.8.41	Mannheim		4		
	Karlsruhe		1		
	Coblenz		1		
6/7.8.41	Calais		1		
7/8.8.41	Essen		7		

Date	Primary target	Aircraft detailed	Took off	Failed to complete mission	Failed to return
		Waddington — Manchesters			
7/8.8.41	Essen	3	2		
	Duisburg		1		
12/13.8.41	Berlin	6	6		2 (L7377 EM: G and L7381 EM: R)
14/15.8.41	Magdeburg	3	3		
16/17.8.41	Dusseldorf	2	2		1 (L7311 EM:F)
	Ostend	2	2		
25.8.41	Mannheim	7	5		
28/29.8.41	Duisburg	7	6	1	
29/30.8.41	Frankfurt	3	3		
31.8/1.9.41	Cologne	6	4	1	1 (L7316 EM: U)
2/3.9.41	Berlin	4	3		
7/8.9.41	Berlin	6	4		1 (L7380 EM:W)
11/12.9.41	Rostock	5	5		
13/14.9.41	Brest	5	4		
15/16.9.41	Hamburg	6	5	1	
19/20.9.41	Stettin	6	3		
29/30.9.41	Minelaying in 'Geranium'	5	5		
	Hamburg	4	4		
10/11.10.41	Essen	10	10		
12/13.10.41	Huls	14	11		1 (L7321 EM: D)
13/14.10.41	Cologne	10	9		2 (L7312 EM: L and L7373 EM:T)
20/21.10.41	Minelaying in Willow	4	4		1 (L7487 EM:N)
21/22.10.41	Bremen	2	2		
	Minelaying in 'Forget-Me-Not'	4	4		
24/25.10.41	Frankfurt	6	6	1	
31.10/1.11.41	Minelaying in 'Nectarine'	2	1		
5.11.41	Cherbourg	4	2		
7/8.11.41	Cologne	10	9	2	
	Boulogne	1	1		
8.11.41	Dunkirk	2	2		
9.11.41	Hamburg	8	7		
	Ostend	1	1		
15.11.41	Emden	2	2		
		Bottesford — Manchesters			
23.11.41	Lorient	1	1		
27.11.41	Dusseldorf		6		
30.11.41	Emden	2	2		
7/8.12.41	Aachen	6	6	1	
27.12.41	Dusseldorf	7	6	1	
2/3.1.42	St. Nazaire	12	10	4	
5.1.42	Brest	11	10	1	
8.1.42	Brest	9	9	1	
9/10.1.42	Brest	5	2	2	1 (L7322 EM:Q)
10.1.42	Wilhelmshaven	5	5		
14.1.42	Hamburg	8	7		2 (L7309 EM:O and L7523 EM:M)
15.1.42	Emden	2	1		
17.1.42	Emden	1	1		
21.1.42	Emden	1	1		
	Paris	1	1		
22.1.42	Munster	5	5		
25.1.42	Brest	7	7		
26.1.42	Emden	3	2		
28.1.42	Brest	5	1		
	Boulogne	1	1		
28/29.1.42	Boulogne	1	1		
31.1.42	St. Nazaire	1	1		
	Brest	2	2		
4.2.42	Minelaying off Frisians	2	2	2	
6.2.42	Minelaying in ' Nectarine'	5	5	1	
11/12.2.42	Mannheim	6	5		
	Minelaying in 'Nectarine'	1	1		

Date	Primary target	Aircraft detailed	Took off	Failed to complete mission	Failed to return
12.2.42	Operation 'Fuller': Channel breakout	6	3	1	
12/13.2.42	Minelaying in 'Nectarine'	4	4	2	
14/15.2.42	Mannhein	5	4		
16.2.42	Minelaying	5	5	1	
19.2.42	Paris	1	1		
21.2.42	Minelaying in 'Yams'	2	2	2	
22.2.42	Sola	2	2	2	
	Emden	3	3	1	
24.2.42	Paris		2		
	Ghent		1		
	Minelaying in 'Yams'		1	1	
24/25.2.42	Minelaying in 'Rosemary'		1	1	
25/26.2.42	Kiel		4	1	
25.2.42	Minelaying in 'Nectarine'		1		
27/28.2.42	Kiel		4		
	Minelaying off Frisians		4	1	
2/3.3.42	Billancourt	7	7	1	
9.3.42	Essen	4	3		
	Minelaying off Lorient	1	1		
9/10.3.42	Essen	6	4	1	
10/11.3.42	Essen	6	5	2	

Bottesford — Lancasters

24/25.4.42	Rostock	4	4	1	
25/26.4.42	Rostock	4	4		
2/3.5.42	Minelaying in 'Radish', 'Spinach' and 'Forget-Me-Not'	7	6		
3/4.5.42	Minelaying in 'Broccoli'	1	1		
	Nickelling St. Ettiene and Marseilles	1	1		
	Nickelling Lyons and Toulouse	1	1		
4/5.5.42	Stuttgart	3	3		
6/7.5.42	Stuttgart	4	4	1	
7.5.42	Minelaying in various areas	4	4		
8/9.5.42	Warnemunde	4	4	2	
9/10.5.42	Minelaying in various areas	3	3	2	
15/16.5.42	Minelaying in 'Asparagus and Hawthorn	6	2		
19/20.5.42	Mannheim	2	2	1	
22/23.5.42	Minelaying in 'Willow'	6	2		
26/27.5.42	Minelaying in 'Pumpkin'	2	2	2	
29/30.5.42	Minelaying in 'Hawthorn' and Nasturtium'	2	2		
	Gennevilliers	2	2	1	
30/31.5.42	Cologne	12	12		
1/2.6.42	Essen	14	14	4	
2/3.6.42	Essen	6	6	1	
3/4.6.42	Bremen	4	3		1 (R5847 EM:Y)
	Minelaying in 'Deodars'	2	2		
5/6.6.42	Essen	6	5		
	Minelaying in 'Nectarine' (took off from Syerston)	2	2		
7/8.6.42	Minelaying in 'Nectarine'	4	4		
9/10.6.42	Minelaying in 'Nasturtium' and 'Geranium'	5	3	2	
11/12.6.42	Minelaying in 'Nectarine'	3	3		
16/17.6.42	Essen	7	8	2	
20/21.6.42	Emden	13	11	2	1 (R5860 EM:Y)
22/23.6.42	Emden	8	6		
23/24.6.42	Minelaying in 'Deodars'	2	2		
24/25.6.42	St. Nazaire (took off from Syerston)	1	1		
25/26.6.42	Bremen	19	16	1	
27/28.6.42	Bremen	10	9	1	
29/30.6.42	Bremen	16	16	2	
2/3.7.42	Bremen	14	14	3	

Date	Primary target	Aircraft detailed	Took off	Failed to complete mission	Failed to return
3/4.7.42	Minelaying in 'Broccoli' and 'Asparagus'	3	3		
	Bremen	1	1		
8/9.7.42	Wilhelmshaven		9		
11/12.7.42	Danzig	11	11	5	1 (L7543 EM:Z)
12/13.7.42	Minelaying in 'Nectarine'	8	7	1	
19/20.7.42	Vegesack	11	10		
21/22.7.42	Duisburg	12	12		
23/24.7.42	Duisburg	13	11		2 (R5632 EM:N and R5867 EM:T)
25/26.7.42	Duisburg	5	4		
26/27.7.42	Hamburg	12	11	3	
29/30.7.42	Saarbrucken	14	13		
31.7/1.8.42	Dusseldorf	17	16		
5.8.42	Minelaying		3		
5/6.8.42	Essen		3		1 (R5761 EM:T)
6/7.8.42	Duisburg	8	7	1	
9/10.8.42	Le Havre	1	1		
10.8.42	Osnabruck	6	6	1	
10/11.8.42	Minelaying in 'Kraut' and 'Silverthorn'	7	3		1 (R5499 EM:O)
12.8.42	Le Havre (took off from Swinderby)	1	1		
12/13.8.42	Mainz	6	6		2 (R5633 EM:R and R5760 EM:Y)
15/16.8.42	Dusseldorf (took off from Swinderby)	6	6		
16/17.8.42	Minelaying in 'Geranium' and 'Willow'	6	6		2 (R5509 EM:G and R5616 EM:J)

Syerston — Lancasters

Date	Primary target	Aircraft detailed	Took off	Failed to complete mission	Failed to return
24/25.8.42	Frankfurt	9	3	2	
27/28.8.42	Kassel	9	9		1 (W4129 EM:R)
28/29.8.42	Nuremburg	5	5	1	
31.8/1.9.42	Minelaying in 'Silverthorn'	2	2	1	
1/2.9.42	Saarbricken	7	7	1	
2/3.9.42	Karlsruhe	5	5	1	
4/5.9.42	Bremen	6	6	1	1 (R5755 EM:N)
6/7.9.42	Duisburg	4	4	2	
	Minelaying in 'Rosemary 2'	1	1		
8/9.9.42	Frankfurt	7	5		
9/10.9.42	Minelaying in 'Silverthorn'	2	2		1 (R5628 EM:Q)
10/11.9.42	Dusseldorf	6	6		
13/14.9.42	Bremen	9	8		
14/15.9.42	Wilhelmshaven	8	3		
16/17.9.42	Essen	9	9		1 (L7571 EM:S)
19/20.9.42	Munich	8	8	1	

Langar — Lancasters

Date	Primary target	Aircraft detailed	Took off	Failed to complete mission	Failed to return
23/24.9.42	Wismar	11	10	3	
24/25.9.42	Minelaying	7	7		
1/2.10.42	Wismar	10	10		
5/6.10.42	Aachen	6	5	1	
6/7.10.42	Osnabruck	7	7		
13/14.10.42	Kiel	3	3		
17.10.42	Le Creusot	15	15		
22/23.10.42	Genoa	13	12	2	
24.10.42	Milan	10	10		1 (W4121 EM:B)
27/28.10.42	Minelaying in 'Silverthorne'	3	3	1	
6/7.11.42	Genoa	5	5		
7/8.11.42	Genoa	11	11		1 (L7546 EM:G)
9/10.11.42	Hamburg	7	5	1	
10/11.11.42	Minelaying	3	3		
13/14.1.42	Genoa	8	7	1	
15/16.11.42	Genoa	3	2		
16/17.11.42	Minelaying	1	1		

Date	Primary target	Aircraft detailed	Took off	Failed to complete mission	Failed to return
18/19.11.42	Turin	3	3		
20/21.11.42	Turin (took off from Bottesford)	4	3		
22/23.11.42	Stuttgart	3	1		
23/24.11.42	Minelaying (took off from Bottesford)	4	3		
25.11.42	Vechta	5	5	1	2 (R6595 EM:C and R5694 EM:F)
27/28.11.42	Stettin	6	4	4	
28/29.11.42	Turin	9	8		
6/7.12.42	Mannheim	8	8	1	
8/9.12.42	Turin	10	9		1 (R5570 EM:F)
9/10.12.42	Turin	8	8		
14/15.12.42	Minelaying	3	3		
20/21.12.42	Duisburg	10	6	2	
21/22.12.42	Munich	12	12	1	1 (W4191 EM:Q)
3/4.1.43	Essen	5	4		1 (W4134 EM:U)
3/4/1/43	Minelaying in 'Furze'	2	2		
7/8.1.43	Essen	5	1	1	
8/9.1.43	Duisburg	7	2		
9/10.1.43	Essen	5	5	2	
11/12.1.43	Essen	7	7	2	
12/13.1.43	Essen	5	5	3	
13/14.1.43	Essen	4	4	1	
16/17.1.43	Berlin	15	13	6	
17/18.1.43	Berlin	12	10	3	
21/22.1.43	Essen	5	4	1	1 (W4365 EM:B)
23/24.1.43	Dusseldorf	5	5	2	
27/28.1.43	Dusseldorf	6	6	3	
27/28.1.43	Minelaying in 'Nectarine'	2	2		
30/31.1.43	Hamburg	8	7	5	
2/3.2.43	Cologne	8	8	2	
3/4.2.43	Hamburg	5	5	1	
4/5.2.43	Turin	3	2		
4/5.2.43	Lorient	2	2		
7/8.2.43	Lorient	6	5		
11/12.2.43	Wilhelmshaven	6	6		
13/14.2.43	Lorient	12	12	1	
14/15.2.43	Milan	9	6	3	1 (L7547 EM:M)
16/17.2.43	Lorient	6	6	1	
18/19/2/43	Wilhelmshaven	6	6	1	1 (ED330 EM:F)
19/20.2.43	Wilhelmshaven	3	3		
21/22.2.43	Vegesack	5	5	2	
25/26.2.43	Nuremburg	9	9	1	1 (ED356 EM:W)
26/27.2.43	Cologne	7	7		
26/27.2.43	Minelaying in 'Nectarine 2'	3	3		
28.2/1.3.43	St. Nazaire	5	5		
1/2.3.43	Berlin	8	7	3	
2/3.3.43	Minelaying in 'Deodar'	5	5	2	1 (ED533 EM:N)
3/4.3.43	Hamburg	8	7	1	1 (ED365 EM:U)
5/6.3.43	Essen	9	9	3	
8/9.3.43	Nuremburg	10	10	2	
9/10.3.43	Munich	7	6		1 (W4172 EM:X)
9/10.3.43	Minelaying	1	1		
11/12.3.43	Stuttgart	6	6	1	
12/13.3.43	Essen	7	7	1	1 (ED604 EM:A)
13/14.3.43	Minelaying in 'Silverthorn'	2	2		
22/23.3.43	St. Nazaire	11	11		
26/27/3/43	Duisburg	7	6	2	
27/28.3.43	Berlin	8	8	1	
28/29.3.43	St. Nazaire	5	5		
29/30.3.43	Berlin	9	7		1 (W4931 EM:U)
2/3.4.43	St. Nazaire	3	3		
2/3.4.43	Minelaying	3	3	1	
3/4.4.43	Essen	10	10	2	
4/5.4.43	Kiel	11	9	1	
8/9.4.43	Duisburg	9	7		
9/10.4.43	Dusburg	9	9		1 (ED554 EM:Q)
10/11.4.43	Frankfurt	6	6	1	

Date	Primary target	Aircraft detailed	Took off	Failed to complete mission	Failed to return
13/14.4.43	La Spezia	12	12		
14/15.4.43	Stuttgart	8	8		
16/17.4.43	Pilsen	10	10	2	
17/18.4.43	Minelaying	4	3		
18/19.4.43	La Spezia	8	6	1	
20/21.4.43	Stettin	8	8		
26/27.4.43	Duisburg	11	11	1	1 (W4171 EM:J)
27/28.4.43	Minelaying in 'Cinnamon'	10	4		
28/29.4.43	Minelaying in 'Nasturtium'	5	5	1	1 (W4945 EM:Z)
30.4/1.5.43	Essen	10	9	2	
4/5.5.43	Dortmund	9	9	1	
12/13.5.43	Duisburg	9	9		2 (W4938 EM:A and ED418 EM:G)
13/14.5.43	Pilsen	10	10	1	
23/24.5.43	Dortmund	13	13	1	
25/26.5.43	Dusseldorf	12	12		2 (W5001 EM:J and ED600 EM:P)
27/28.5.43	Essen	11	11	1	
29/30.5.43	Wuppertal	9	9	1	
30/31.5.43	Minelaying	5	5		
11/12.6.43	Dusseldorf	17	12	2	1 (ED537 EM:O)
14/15.6.43	Oberhausen	11	11	3	
16/17.6.43	Cologne	11	10		
20/21.6.43	Friedrichshaven	5	5		
21/22.6.43	Krefeld	8	8	1	
22/23.6.43	Mulheim	10	10	2	1 (ED692 EM:W)
23/24.6.43	La Spezia (took off from Blida)	4	4		
24/25.6.43	Wuppertal	8	8	1	
25/26.6.43	Gelsenkirchen	6	6	1	
28/29.6.43	Cologne	10	8	1	1 (ED569 EM:B)
3/4.7.43	Cologne	10	10	1	
8/9.7.43	Cologne	14	14	3	
9/10.7.43	Gelsenkirchen	9	9		
12/13.7.43	Turin	10	10	1	1 (ED412 EM:Q)
16/17.7.43	Cislago	5	4		1 (DV183 EM:W)
24/25.7.43	Hamburg	13	13	1	
24/25.7.43	Leghorn (took off from Blida)	3	3		
25/26.7.43	Essen	11	10		
27/28.7.43	Hamburg	15	15	1	1 (W4962 EM:B)
29/30.7.43	Hamburg	12	12	1	
30/31.7.43	Remscheid	10	4	1	
2/3.8.43	Hamburg	10	8		
7/8.8.43	Genoa	15	12		
9/10.8.43	Mannheim	14	14	1	
10/11.8.43	Nuremburg	13	12		
12/13.8.43	Milan	13	12		1 (ED361 EM:R)
14/15.8.43	Milan	6	6	1	
15/16.8.43	Milan	8	8		1 (ED498 EM:O)
17/18.8.43	Peenemunde	10	9		
22/23.8.43	Leverkusen	11	11	1	
23/24.8.43	Berlin	12	12		1 (ED550 EM:K)
27/28.8.43	Nuremburg	11	11		2 (ED627 EM:N and LM334 EM:V)
30/31.8.43	Munchen-Galdbach	9	9		1 (W4120 EM:L)
31.8/1.9.43	Berlin	9	8	1	
3/4.9.43	Berlin	11	10		1 (ED832 EM:X)
5/6.9.43	Mannheim	6	6		
6/7.9.43	Munich	8	8		
22/23.9.43	Hanover	11	11	1	1 (ED442 EM:W)
23/24.9.43	Mannheim	9	9	1	
27/28.9.43	Hanover	11	11	1	
29/30.9.43	Berlin	10	10	2	
1/2.10.43	Hagen	10	10		
2/3.10.43	Munich	11	7		
3/4.10.43	Kassel	10	9	1	
4/5.10.43	Frankfurt	8	8		
7/8.10.43	Stuttgart	10	10		
8/9.10.43	Hanover	11	9		

Spilsby — Lancasters

Date	**Primary target**	**Aircraft detailed**	**Took off**	**Failed to complete mission**	**Failed to return**
18/19.10.43	Hanover	15	13		2 (LM326 EM:Z and W4276 EM:L)
20/21.10.43	Leipzig	12	12		
22/23.10.43	Kassel	11	11	1	2 (EE175 EM:R and DV243 EM:D)
3/4.11.43	Dusseldorf	9	9		
10/11.11.43	Modane	10	10		
18/19.11.43	Berlin	16	16	2	
22/23.11.43	Berlin	15	15	1	
23/24.11.43	Berlin	16	14		1 (W4959 EM:S)
26/27.11.43	Berlin	15	15	2	
2/3.12.43	Berlin	15	15		1 (ED601 EM:N)
3/4.12.43	Leipzig	10	10		
16/17.12.43	Berlin	15	15		1 (EE141 EM:P)
20/21.12.43	Frankfurt	15	15		
23/24.12.43	Berlin	13	13		1 (DV188 EM:J)
29/30.12.43	Berlin	12	12		
2/31.44	Berlin	10	9	3	2 (W4892 EM:T and DV370 EM:L)
5/6.1.44	Stettin	9	9		1 (ED586 EM:F)
14/15.1.44	Brunswick	11	11		3 (DV369 EM:D, DV191 EM:Q and LM383 EM:R)
20/21.1.44	Berlin	10	9	2	
21/22.1.44	Magdeburg	7	6	1	1 (R5895 EM:B)
	Berlin	2	2		
27/28.1.44	Berlin	10	10	1	
28/29.1.44	Berlin	11	5		1 (LM366 EM:H)
30/31.1.44	Berlin	11	11		3 (EE173 EM:K, DV371 EM:M and ED758 EM:V)
15/16.2.44	Berlin	19	19		1 (ND510 EM:T)
19/20.2.44	Leipzig	20	19	2	2 (EE126 EM:A and ME633 EM:Y)
20/21.2.44	Stuttgart	17	15		
24/25.2.44	Schweinfurt	18	18	3	
25/26.2.44	Augsburg	17	16		1 (W4815 EM:C)
1/2.3.44	Stuttgart	15	15		
10/11.3.44	Clermont–Ferrand	11	11		1 (ND513 EM:R)
15/16.3.44	Stuttgart	18	17		
18/19.3.44	Frankfurt	21	21	1	
22/23.3.44	Frankfurt	21	21		1 (ME666 EM:A)
24/25.3.44	Berlin	20	20	1	1 (ME680 EM:R)
26/27.3.44	Essen	16	15		
30/31.3.44	Nuremburg	18	18		2 (LM436 EM:G and ND568 EM:L)
5/6.4.44	Toulouse	11	11		1 (ME685 EM:C)
9/10.4.44	Minelaying in 'Tangerine'	6	6		1 (ME688 EM:E)
10/11.4.44	Tours	13	11		
11/12.4.44	Aachen	6	6		
18/19.4.44	Juvisy	18	18		
20/21.4.44	La Chapelle	19	19		1 (ND564 EM:H)
22/23.4.44	Brunswick	19	19		
23/24.4.44	Minelaying in 'Geranium'	1	1		
24/25.4.44	Munich	19	19		
26/27.4.44	Schweinfurt	17	16		2 (ME631 EM:K and LM526 EM:R)
29/30.4.44	Clermont–Ferrand	14	14		
1/2.5.44	Tours	12	12		
3/4.5.44	Mailly–le–Camp	17	17		2 (ND556 EM:F and ND575 EM:M)
7/8.5.44	Tours	16	16		
9/10.5.44	Annecy	11	11		
11/12.5.44	Bourg–Leopold	17	17		
19/20.5.44	Amiens	18	18		
21/22.5.44	Duisburg	9	8		
	Minelaying in Kiel Bay	9	9		1 (ND522 EM:J)

Date	Primary target	Aircraft detailed	Took off	Failed to complete mission	Failed to return
22/23.5.44	Brunswick	15	13	2	3 (ND871 EM:G, LM540 EM:Q and LL776 EM:S)
24/25.5.44	Antwerp	10	9	2	
26/27.5.44	Minelaying in 'Silverthorn'	3	3		
	Minelaying in 'Nectarine'	3	3		
27/28.5.44	La Valery–en–Caux	11	11		
1/2.6.44	Saumur	15	13		
3/4.6.44	Ferme d'Urville	10	10		
4/5.6.44	Maisy	17	17		
5/6.6.44	La Pernelle	17	17	1	
6/7.6.44	Caen	9	9		
7/8.6.44	Balleroi	19	15		
9/10.6.44	Etampes	17	17	1	1 (ME678 EM:N)
12/13.6.44	Caen	19	19		
14/15.6.44	Aunay–sur–Odon	17	17		
16/17.6.44	Beauvoir	20	20		
21/22.6.44	Wesseling	21	21	3	5 (LM578 EM:C, ME827 EM:I, LL973 EM:M, DV360 EM:U and ME683 EM:W)
24/25.6.44	Pommereval	17	17		
27/28.6.44	Marquis Mimoyecques	18	18		
4/5.7.44	St. Leu d'Esserent	19	15	1	2 (LM125 EM:G and ND570 EM:Z)
7/8.7.44	St. Leu d'Esserent	16	16		5 (ND866 EM:B, ME805 EM:J, LM218 EM:N, ND567 EM:V and LM129 EM:Y)
12/13.7.44	Chalindrey	12	12		
14/15.7.44	Villeneuve–St.–George	7	7		
15/16.7.44	Nevers	13	6		1 (ME807 EM:S)
18.7.44	Caen	13	13		
18/19.7.44	Revigny	14	10		3 (PD210 EM:C, ME814 EM:E and ME681 EM:T)
19.7.44	Triverny	8	7		
20/21.7.44	Coutrai	12	11		
23/24.7.44	Kiel	14	7		
24/25.7.44	Stuttgart	9	9		
	Donges	6	6		1 (PB294 EM:G)
25/26.7.44	Stuttgart	14	14	1	
26/27.7.44	Givors	7	7		
28/29.7.44	Stuttgart	16	15	1	1 (ND872 EM:L)
30.7.44	Cahanges	15	15		
31.7.44	Rilly–la–Montaigne	5	5		
	La Roche	9	9		
1.8.44	La Roche	2	2		
2.8.44	St. Maximin	12	12		
3.8.44	Trossy–St. Martin	14	13		
5.8.44	St. Leu d'Esserent	16	15		
6.8.44	Bois Cassan	6	6		
7/8.8.44	Caen	14	14		
9/10.8.44	Fôret de Chatelbrault	14	14		
10/11.8.44	Bordeaux	15	5		
11/12.8.44	Givors	14	13	1	
12/13.8.44	Brunswick	4	4	1	
	Falaise	6	6		
14.8.44	Brest	14	14		
15.8.44	Deelen	10	8		1LM263 EM:N)
16/17.8.44	Stettin	13	13	1	
18.8.44	L'Isle Adam II	13	13		
25/26.8.44	Darmstadt	16	16	1	1 (PD216 EM:J)
26/27.8.44	Konigsberg	14	12		
	Minelaying	1	1		
29/30.8.44	Konigsberg	12	12	1	
31.8.44	Bergueneuse	12	12		

Date	Primary target	Aircraft detailed	Took off	Failed to complete mission	Failed to return
2.9.44	Brest	12	12		
3.9.44	Deelen	17	17		
9.9.44	Munchen–Gladbach	18	18		
11.9.44	Le Havre	15	15		
11/12.9.44	Darmstadt	19	19		1 (LM261 EM:C)
12/13.9.44	Stuttgart	17	17		1 (PD267 EM:G)
17.9.44	Boulogne	17	17		
18.9.44	Bremerhaven	18	18		
19/20.9.44	Munchen–Gladbach	18	18		
23/24.9.44	Handorf	21	21	1	1 (PD318 EM:J)
26/27.9.44	Karlsruhe	22	22	1	
27/28.9.44	Kaiserslauten	19	18		
4.10.44	Minelaying in 'Silverthorn'	5	4		
5.10.44	Wilhelmshaven	21	21		
6.10.44	Bremen	21	21	2	1 (ME667 EM:X)
7.10.44	Walcheren	16	16		
11.10.44	Walcheren (Veere)	9	9		
	Flushing	5	5		
14/15.10.44	Brunswick	20	20		
15/16.10.44	Minelaying in 'Silverthorn'	2	2		2 (LM208 EM:M and NG143 EM:R)
17.10.44	Walcheren (West Kapelle)	5	5		
19/20.10.44	Nuremburg	18	18		
23.10.44	Walcheren	6	6		
24/25.10.44	Minelaying in 'Kraut'	3	3		
28/29.10.44	Bergen	20	20		1LM271 EM:L)
30.10.44	Walcheren (West Kapelle)	8	8		
1.11.44	Homberg	20	13		
2.11.44	Dusseldorf	18	18	2	
4.11.44	Dortmund	13	13		
6.11.44	Gravenhorst	18	6		1 (ND555 EM:D)
11.11.44	Harburg	17	17		1 (PB428 EM:T)
16.11.44	Duren	17	16		1 (NF979 EM:B)
21/22.11.44	Gravenhorst	19	18		
22/23.11.44	Trondheim	18	12		
23.11.44	Minelaying	5	3		
26/27.11.44	Munich	17	17		
4/5.12.44	Heilbron	19	19		2 (PB765 EM:B and LL968 EM:K)
6/7.12.44	Giessen	18	18	1	1 (PD322 EM:C)
8.12.44	Heimbach	14	14		
10.12.44	Heimbach	16	16	16	
11.12.44	Heimbach	15	15		
14.12.44	Minelaying in 'Silverthorn'	2	2		
17/18.12.44	Munich	18	18	3	
18/19.12.44	Gdynia	12	12		2 (NG144 EM:G and LM671 EM:S)
	Minelaying	3	3		
21/22.12.44	Politz	13	6	2	
26.12.44	St. Vith	10	5		
28/29.12.44	Oslo / Horton	4	4		
29/30.12.44	Minelaying in 'Onions'	3	3		
30/31.12.44	Houffalize	12	12		
31.12.44	Minelaying in 'Yewtree'	2	2		
1.1.45	Ladbergen	10	10		
1/2.1.45	Gravenhorst	5	5		
4/5.1.45	Royan	17	17		
5/6.1.45	Houffalize	12	8		1 (NE168 EM:F)
6/7.1.45	Minelaying	2	2		
7/8.1.45	Munich	15	14	2	
13/14.1.45	Politz	18	18	1	
14/15.1.45	Merseburg	18	11	2	
16/17.1.45	Brux	19	18		
1/2.2.45	Siegen	21	20		
2/3.2.45	Karlsruhe	20	20		
7/8.2.45	Ladbergen	12	11		1 (NN724 EM:X)
	Minelaying in 'Forget-Me-Nots'	3	3		
8/9.2.45	Politz	19	19	2	
13/14.2.45	Dresden	19	18	1	

Date	Primary target	Aircraft detailed	Took off	Failed to complete mission	Failed to return
14/15.2.45	Rositz	17	17	3	
	Minelaying in 'Silverthorn'	1	1	1	
19/20.2.45	Bohlen	18	16		
20/21.2.45	Gravenhorst	11	11		
21/22.2.45	Gravenhorst	13	13		2 (PB295 EM:I and PB814 EM:T)
23/24.2.45	Minelaying	2	2		
24.2.45	Ladbergen	13	13	1	
3/4.3.45	Ladbergen	13	13		1 (NG204 EM:M)
	Minelaying in 'Onions'	1	1		
5/6.3.45	Bohlen	16	16		2 (NG230 EM:F and ME386 EM:G)
6/7.3.45	Sassnitz	11	11		
	Minelaying	2	2		
7/8.3.45	Harburg	13	13		
11.3.45	Essen	14	14		
11/12.3.45	Minelaying in 'Onions'	2	2		
12.3.45	Dortmund	15	15		
14/15.3.45	Lutzkendorf	17	16		2 (NG399 EM:O and LL902 EM:A)
16/17.3.45	Wurzburg	13	13		
20/21.3.45	Bohlen	13	13		1 (PA196 EM:D)
	Halle	3	3		
21/22.3.45	Hamburg	14	14		1 (ME522 EM:X)
23/24.3.45	Wesel	16	16		
4.4.45	Nordhausen	18	18		
7/8.4.45	Molbis	19	13		
8/9.4.45	Lutzkendorf	18	18	1	
10/11.4.45	Leipzig	11	11	1	1 (ME472 EM:O)
13/14.4.45	Minelaying	3	3	1	
16/17.4.45	Pilsen	15	14		
17/18.4.45	Cham	17	16		
23.4.45	Flensburg	12	12		
25.4.45	Berchtesgaden	10	10		

Another view of Manchester L7378 [EM:A] in the snow at Boscombe Down on 1 February 1942. It survived 33 operations before being transferred to 106 Squadron and eventually being relegated to ground instructional duties as 3752M.
[via H. Holmes]

Appendix V: Aircraft of 7 (Naval) and 207 Squadrons

(A) Aircraft used by 7 (Naval) Squadron, 1917/18

❑ Voisin Type III 'New Type' pusher biplanes

Serial No.	Code	Fate
8704		
8705		To 8 Sqn., Zanzibar
8706		
8707		

❑ Sopwith 1½ Strutter Type 9700 Bomber (to April 1918)

Serial No.	Code	Fate
N5153		To 5 Sqn.
N5504		To 5 Sqn.; eventually became G–EAVB
N5509		To 5 Sqn.
N5519		To 5 Sqn.
N5520		To 5 Sqn.

❑ Royal Aircraft Factory BE.2c (to January 1917)

Serial No.	Code	Fate
8424		To 26 Sqn. RAF
8425		To 26 Sqn. RAF
8427		To 26 Sqn. RAF
8428		To 26 Sqn. RAF
8489		Crashed on take-off from Iringa, 7.11.16
8715		To 26 Sqn. RAF
8716		To 26 Sqn. RAF
9970		To 14 Sqn.

❑ Caudron G.IV

Serial No.	Code	Fate
3300		To Air Depot, Dunkerque, 1.2.17; SOC 24.3.17
9113		To Air Depot, Dunkerque, 1.2.17; SOC 24.3.17
9119		To Air Depot, Dunkerque, 1.2.17; SOC 24.3.17
9120		To Air Depot, Dunkerque, 1.2.17; SOC 24.3.17
9121		To Air Depot, Dunkerque, 1.2.17; SOC 24.3.17
9123		To Air Depot, Dunkerque, 1.2.17; SOC 24.3.17
9130		To Air Depot, Dunkerque, 1.2.17; SOC 24.3.17

❑ Short Bombers

Serial No.	Code	Fate
9306		To War Flt., Eastchurch
9313		To Eastchurch workshops
9322		To Eastchurch workshops
9335		SOC 26.6.17
9336		Wrecked 15.4.17; SOC 14.5.17
9337		SOC 23.4.17
9338		SOC 27.6.17
9339		SOC 27.6.17
9490		To Air Depot, Dunkurque, 1.3.17; SOC 24.3.17
9491		Crashed 29.4.17; SOC 14.5.17
9492		SOC 27.6.17
9493		SOC 27.6.17
9494		To Air Depot, Dunkerque, 23.6.17; SOC 27.6.17
9776		To Air Depot, Dunkerque, 20.4.17; SOC 27.6.17
9835		
9836		To Air Depot, Dunkerque, 23.6.17; SOC 27.6.17

❑ HP O/100 (April 1917 to April 1918)

Serial No.	Code	Fate
1455		To 'A' Sqn., Manston
1459		(7A Sqn. only)
1460		Hit by AA fire 18.7.17, force-landed Baizerais
1461		To 207 Sqn. on formation
1462		To 207 Sqn. on formation
1465		To HP Sqn., Manston
1466		To 'A' Sqn., Manston
3115		Shot down into sea off Nieuport 25.4.17
3116	B3	To HP Sqn., Manston
3118		To HP Sqn., Manston
3119		To 207 Sqn. on formation
3120		To 7A Sqn.
3121	A3	To 7A Sqn.
3122		To 7A Sqn. Shot down during raid on St. Denis Westrem, 26/27.10.17
3123	D3	(named 'Split Pin') To 'A' Sqn., Manston (Note 1)
3125		To 207 Sqn. on formation (Note 1)
3126		
3127		To 'A' Sqn., Manston
3128	C1	To 214 Sqn.
3129		To 7A Sqn.
3130		To 7A Sqn.
3131		To 207 Sqn. on formation (Note 1)
3132		To 7A Sqn.
3133		To 7A Sqn.
3134		To 7A Sqn.
3136		To 'A' Sqn., Manston (Note 1)
3137		(7A Sqn. only – shot down by flak near Ghent 25/26.8.17)

(Note 1: these aircraft were the ones sent to Redcar on detachment)

(B) Aircraft used by 207 Squadron, 1918 to 1984

❑ HP O/400 (May 1918 to August 1919)

Serial No.	Code	Fate
B8804		Crashed and overturned 19.9.18
B8810	H, later A	SOC 15.1.19
B8811	A2, later G	To 58 Sqn.
B8813		Scrapped 25.8.19
C3490		Destroyed by hostile aircraft at 1 ASD, 23.9.18
C9649		To 215 Sqn.
C9657	W, later A5	Force-landed after engine failed, 6.9.18; SOC 2.10.18
C9660	D, later N	Force-landed after engine failed, 29.9.18; SOC
C9664		To 215 Sqn.
C9665		FTR from night raid 18/19.7.18
C9674		To 214 Sqn.
C9676	P, later J	Hit goal post on take-off from Guines, 5.4.19
C9684		To 215 Sqn.
C9721	L	
D4563	B1	
D4564	N	Wrecked when taking off from field after landing with engine trouble, 27.10.18
D4565	F, later B, later M	SOC 30.12.18 due to effects of weather
D4569	R	Engine failed on take-off 29.10.18
D4596	D	To 216 Sqn.
D5404		Force-landed Domart 10.8.18 after night raid
D5405		Force-landed after night raid on Peronne, 7.8.18; SOC 20.8.18
D5406		To 58 Sqn.
D5408		Wrecked 20.6.18
D5409	X, later C	
D5422	A, later S	Crashed on landing at a French airfield after night raid, 1.11.18
D5428		
D5429	Z, later L	To Egypt (216 Sqn.?)
D5433	D	Crash-landed Famechon airfield 29.9.18; SOC
D5440		Crash-landed after night raid, 23.10.18; SOC
D8323		To 214 Sqn.
D9683		SOC 19.4.19 due to effects of weather
D9714		

❑ DH.9A (February 1920 to December 1927)

Serial No.	Code	Fate
E726	B3	To 4 FTS, Aboukir
E852		To 30 Sqn., Hinaidi 11.27
E871		To 1 FTS 10.25
E8681		To 14 Sqn.
E8754	A4	
E8758	A4	To DH for reconditioning; eventually to 60 Sqn.
E8805	C4	To DH for reconditioning
F1616		
F2818		To DH for reconditioning for RAF (Cadet) College
F2820		
H19		Pilot lost control; spun in, San Stephano, 4.6.23
H138		To DH for reconditioning; eventually to 84 Sqn.
H142		To 84 Sqn.
H3501		To 4 FTS, Aboukir
H3635		To 47 Sqn.
J556		Ditched near HMS Iron Duke, 16 mls. south of San Stephano, 22.2.23
J557		Crashed in soft ground after fast landing, San Stephano, 5.2.23
J559		Engine failed; ditched 21 mls. off coast, 1.8.22
J560		To DH for reconditioning; eventually to 30 Sqn.
J561		To DH for reconditioning; eventually to RAF (Cadet) College
J566		To 27 Sqn.
J6964		To Royal Aircraft Establishment
J6967	A3	To 4 FTS, Aboukir
J7034	C2	To DH for reconditioning
J7038	C2	To DH for reconditioning
J7039	C4	To 39 Sqn.
J7041	C1	To 39 Sqn.
J7048	C1	To DH for reconditioning; eventually to 84 Sqn.
J7112		Spun out of formation near Eastchurch, 30.4.25
J7352		To 84 Sqn.
J7354		To RAF (Cadet) College
J7355	C3	
J7610		Crashed and burnt out 11.11.26
J7611	C2	
J7612		To 30 Sqn.
J7802	C1	To 2 FTS
J7808		To 4 FTS, Aboukir
J7859		Collided with taxying Woodcock J7973 of 3 Sqn. while landing at Eastchurch, 25.10.26; SOC
J8144		To 39 Sqn.
J8145		To 603 Sqn.

❑ Fairey IIIF (December 1927 to September 1932)

Serial No.	Code	Fate
J9057	C1	
J9058		
J9062		To HAD
J9074	B2	To Packing Depot Ascot for 8 Sqn.
J9135	B3	
J9136	A1	To HAD for conversion to Gordon
J9137		Crashed 10.30
J9139		
J9146		Converted to Gordon
J9147	A2	
J9152		
J9167		To HAD
J9168	B1	Hit hangar on landing at Martlesham Heath,10.30
J9169	A1	
J9170		Crashed 24.7.31
J9172	B2	To HAD for conversion to Gordon
J9637		Crashed nr. Sudbury, Suffolk, 4.1.30
J9638	C1	Undercarriage collapsed on landing, Martlesham Heath, 1931
J9639		
J9647	A3/A1	Converted to Gordon
J9651		To 2 ASU
J9681		To HAD for conversion to Gordon
J9786		
J9790		
K1120		To HAD for conversion to Gordon
K1162		To HAD for conversion to Gordon

Serial No.	Code	Fate
K1163		To A&GS
K1164	C4	To HAD for conversion to Gordon
K1166		To HAD for conversion to Gordon
K1169	C1	To HAD for conversion to Gordon
K1170		To HAD for conversion to Gordon
K1699	A3	To HAD for conversion to Gordon
K1700		To HAD for conversion to Gordon
K1756	C2	To HAD for conversion to Gordon
K1757	C1	To HAD for conversion to Gordon
K1758		Hit drogue during air-to-air firing and crashed, 14.7.33
S1178	B4	
S1179		
S1182	A3	
S1184	A4	
S1196	C1	
S1197		
S1202	A2	
S1203	C2	
S1204	B2	
S1205	B1	
S1461		

❑ Fairey Gordon Mk. I (September 1932 to April 1935 and August 1936 to August 1937)

Serial No.	Code	Fate
(converted from Fairey IIIF) –		
J9073	B3	Became instructional airframe *693M*
J9136	A1	
J9154		To A&AEE
JR9643		Crashed nr. Gebeit, Sudan, 27.1.36
J9647	C3	
J9651		To 2 ASU
J9674	B4	To HQ Central Area
J9784		To 2 ASU
JR9804		To 4 ASU
J9821		
K1161	A4	To 8 ATC
K1164	C4	SOC 7.8.36
K1167	B2	Became instructional airframe *869M*
K1170		SOC 28.8.35
K1699	A3	SOC 7.8.36
K1756	C2	Became instructional airframe *711M*
K1757	C1	To Station Flight Eastchurch
K1758	A4	Hit drogue during air-to-air firing practice and crash-landed, 14.7.33
K1763		SOC 29.8.35
K1765		To 2 ASU
K1771		To 2 ASU
(new production) –		
K2614		Became instructional airframe *1516M*
K2626		To 35 Sqn.
K2628		To 3 ATC
K2641		Became instructional airframe *1523M*
K2649	A3	To 35 Sqn.
K2691	A4/B1	To AAS
K2692		Flew into ground in fog nr. Docking 29.11.32
K2693		Became instructional airframe *1515M*
K2695	A2	SOC 7.8.36
K2696		Became instructional airframe *1512M*
K2697	C3	Became instructional airframe *1105M*
K2698		To 102 MU
K2707	A4	
K2713	B1	
K2714	C4	Became instructional *airframe 1518M*
K2721		Became instructional airframe *1521M*
K2729		To 25 Sqn.
K2731		To 8 FTS
K2732		Became instructional airframe
K2733		To 35 Sqn.
K2734		To 47 Sqn.
K2749	A1	
K2751		Became instructional airframe *1519M*
K2752		

Serial No.	Code	Fate
K2753		Stalled off turn on approach to Aqiq and crashed, 2.3.36
K2761		To 35 Sqn.
K2762		
K2763		To 1 ATC
K2764	V	To 47 Sqn.
K2765		
K2767		To AOS
K2769		Became instructional airframe *1510M*
S1202	A2	

❑ Vickers Vincent Mk. I (April 1936 to August 1936)

Serial No.	Code	Fate
K4707		To AD Aboukir 8.36
K4708		To AD Aboukir 8.36
K4709		To AD Aboukir 8.36
K4710		To AD Aboukir 8.36

❑ Vickers Wellesley (August 1937 to April 1938)

Serial No.	Code	Fate
K7756		To Aboukir for 45 Sqn.
K7757		To Aboukir for 14 Sqn.
K7758		To Aboukir for 14 Sqn.
K7759		To Aboukir for 14 Sqn.
K7760		To Aboukir for 45 Sqn.
K7761		Hit by K7760 while parked at Worthy Down, 22.3.38; DBR
K7762		To Aboukir for 47 Sqn.
K7763		To Aboukir for 14 Sqn.
K7764		To Aboukir for 14 Sqn.
K7765		To Aboukir for 14 Sqn.
K7766		Engine cut, force-landed and hit tree, Abingdon, 13.4.38.
K7769		To Aboukir for 14 Sqn.
K8531		To 76 Sqn.
K8532		To 76 Sqn.
K8533		To Aboukir for 14 Sqn.

❑ Fairey Battle (April 1938 to April 1940)

Serial No.	Code	Fate
K7571		To 54 Sqn.
K7573		To 1 Air Armament School
K7576		To 1 Air Armament School
K7578		To 1 Air Armament School
K7580		To 1 Sqn.
K7581		To 3 Sqn.
K7582		To 3 Sqn.
K7583		To 1 Air Armament School
K7584		To 111 Sqn.
K7585		Undershot and hit tree on night approach, Cottesmore, 13.12.38. Became *1787M* as instructional airframe
K7601		Became *1793M* as instructional airframe
K7628		To 1 Air Armament School
K7690		To 6 Bombing & Gunnery School
K9181		To 105 Sqn.
K9185		To 105 Sqn.
K9186		To 105 Sqn.
K9187		To 105 Sqn.
K9188		To 105 Sqn.
K9189		To 105 Sqn.
K9190		To 105 Sqn.
K9191		To 105 Sqn.
K9192		Engine cut; belly-landed 4 miles west of Wyton 22.11.39; DBR
K9193		To 105 Sqn.
K9194	207:T	To 105 Sqn.
K9195		To 105 Sqn.
K9196	207:A	To 105 Sqn.
K9197		To 105 Sqn.
K9198		To 105 Sqn.
K9200	207:Z	To 105 Sqn.
K9448		Flew into hill in bad visibility, Winchcombe, Glos., 19.9.39; two killed
K9450		To 88 Sqn.

Serial No.	Code	Fate
K9451		To 12 OTU
K9452		To 88 Sqn.
K9453		To 12 OTU
K9454		To 12 OTU
K9455		To 12 OTU
K9458		To RCAF
K9459		To RCAF
K9460		To 63 Sqn.
K9461		To RCAF
K9462		To RCAF
K9463		To 12 OTU
K9464		To 12 OTU
K9465		To RCAF
L4962		To 88 Sqn.
L4963		To 305 Sqn.
L4964		To RCAF
L4965		To 12 OTU
L4966		To 12 OTU
L4967		Stalled and crashed at Litcham, Norfolk avoiding high ground while descending in cloud, 23.3.39
L4977		To 12 OTU
L5228		To 4 Group Target Towing Flight
L5274		To 12 OTU
L5275		To 63 Sqn.
L5276		To 12 OTU
L5277		Undershot landing and undercarriage collapsed, Weston Zoyland, 2.1.40
L5278		To RCAF but then to RAAF
L5279		Engine failed on take-off, Bassingbourn, stalled and crashed, 28.11.39
L5280		To AMDP
L5281		To RCAF
L5282		To 12 OTU
L5283		To 12 OTU
L5284		To RCAF
L5482		To 12 OTU
P2260		To 3 Group Target Towing Flight

❑ Avro Anson Mk. I (July 1939 to April 1940)

Serial No.	Code	Fate
N5111		To 22 OTU
N5113		To 16 OTU
N5163		To 21 OTU
N5166		To 35 Sqn.
N5192		To 9 Air Observers School
N5265		To 7 Sqn.
N5266		To 10 OTU
N5267		To 7 Sqn.

❑ Avro Manchester Mk. I (November 1940 to March 1942)

Serial No.	Code	Fate
L7278	EM:A	Engine caught fire; hit tree in forced landing. 15 miles east of Wymondham, Leics on return from raid on Lorient, 21.3.41
L7279	EM:B	To 61 Sqn.
L7280		To 44 Sqn. Conversion Flt.
L7282		To 97 Sqn.
L7283		To 25 OTU
L7284	EM:D	To 61 Sqn.
L7286		To 61 Sqn. Conversion Flt.
L7288	EM:H	To 97 Sqn.
L7290		To 97 Sqn.
L7291		To 97 Sqn.
L7292		To 97 Sqn.
L7293		To 1660 Conversion Unit
L7294		To 97 Sqn.
L7297		To 1660 Conversion Unit
L7298		To 97 Sqn.
L7299		To 97 Sqn.
L7300	EM:S/F	Engine cut on approach, hit ground and skidded into Fiskerton Lake, 8 miles east of Lincoln, 23.11.41
L7302	EM:R	Crashed at Hostrup, Germany, with flak damage during mission to Kiel, 9.4.41
L7303	EM:P	Missing (Dusseldorf) 28.3.41
L7304		To 61 Sqn.

Serial No.	Code	Fate
L7307		To 97 Sqn.
L7309	EM:J/O	Shot down, crashed at Sandel/Moens, near Jever, Germany during operation on Hamburg 15.1.42
L7310	EM:H	Engine cut after take-off for Boulognecrash-landed and hit bank at Waddington, 21.6.41
L7311	EM:F	Shot down by Bf.110 (?) and crashed at Kruchten, Germany, during operation to Ostend, 17.8.41
L7312	EM:L	Shot down by Bf.110, crashed at Eschen, Belgium, during operation to Cologne, 14.10.41
L7313	EM:C	Shot down by Ju.88 intruder at Whisby, Lincs. after take-off for raid on Hamburg, 13.3.41
L7314	EM:T/Y	Shot down in error at Wollaston, Northants by Beaufighter of 25 Sqn. while on way to raid Boulogne., 22.6.41
L7316	EM:U	Shot down by flak, crashed at Oberkreuchen, Germany, during operation to Cologne, 1.9.41
L7317	EM:C	To 106 Sqn.
L7318	EM:K	Dived into ground at South Hykeham, Lincoln, while in circuit at Waddington, 15.9.41
L7319	EM:X	To 106 Sqn.
L7321	EM:D	Shot down by Bf.110 and crashed at Hozemont, Belgium, while on operation to Hüls, 13.10.41
L7322	EM:B/Q	Hit by flak, crashed in sea near Ile Longue during operation to Brest, 9.1.42
L7373	EM:T	Shot down by Bf.110 (?) and crashed SW of Lommel, Belgium, during operation to Cologne, 4.10.41
L7377	EM:G	Shot down by flak and crashed at Gross-Beeren near Berlin during operation to Berlin, 13.8.41
L7378	EM:A/M	To 106 Sqn.
L7379	EM:T	Missing (Hamburg) 3.5.41
L7380	EM:W	Shot down by night-fighter, crashed on beach at Ameland Is., Frisians, after raid on Berlin,8.9.41
L7381	EM:R	Shot down by Do.215 and crashed at Lange Dijk, Holland, during operation to Berlin, 13.8.41
L7385	EM:O/U	Collided with Lancaster R5550 while landing at Bottesford, destroyed by fire 6.8.42
L7387		To 97 Sqn.
L7389		To 83 Sqn.
L7391	EM:Y	To 106 Sqn.
L7393	EM:V	Engine caught fire, overshot landing at Perranporth and hit truck,18.5.41; became *2660M* as instructional airframe at 25 OTU 7.9.41
L7397		To 1660 Conversion Unit
L7419	EM:H/K	To 50 Sqn.
L7420		to 1660 Conversion Unit
L7422	EM:V	Engine cut, lost height and belly-landed at Hardings Farm, Linwood, one mile south of Market Rasen during feathering test, 26.10.41
L7425	EM:C	To 50 Sqn.
L7432	EM:J/Z	To 50 Sqn.
L7453		To 97 Sqn.
L7454	EM:M	To 61 Sqn.
L7455	EM:G	To 50 Sqn.
L7457		To 97 Sqn.
L7468	EM:Z	To 50 Sqn.
L7476	EM:K	To 50 Sqn.
L7480	EM:L	To 61 Sqn.
L7483	EM:O/H	Became *3749M* as instructional airframe at 12 SoTT 17.6.43
L7484	EM:F/P	To 83 Sqn.
L7485	EM:G/D	To 106 Sqn.
L7486	EM:P/Z	To 50 Sqn.
L7487	EM:N	Ran out of fuel and ditched 10 miles north of Great Yarmouth when returning from mine-laying off Sassnitz, 21.10.41
L7488	EM:Q	To 106 Sqn.
L7491	EM:O	To 50 Sqn.
L7515	EM:S	To 106 Sqn.
L7523	EM:M	Crashed at Cliff House Farm, Holmpton, near Withernsea, Yorks on return from raid on Hamburg, destroyed by fire, 14.1.42
L7526		To 1656 Conversion Unit
R5778		To 50 Sqn.
R5782	EM:R	To 50 Sqn.
R5788		To 83 Sqn.
R5790		To 83 Sqn.
R5791	EM:V	To 1485 Flt.
R5796	EM:S/W	To 106 Sqn.
R5833		To 83 Sqn.
R5835		To 83 Sqn.

❑ Handley Page Hampden Mk. I (July 1941 to August 1941)

Serial No.	Code	Fate
AE186	EM:A	To 61 Sqn.
AE192		To 44 Sqn.
AE219		To 61 Sqn.
AE247		To 61 Sqn.
AE249		To 50 Sqn.
AE264		To 455 Sqn.
AE295		To 5 Group Target Towing Flt.

Serial No.	Code	Fate
AE296		To 455 Sqn.
AE297	EM:H	To 408 Sqn.
AE299		To 106 Sqn.

❑ Avro Lancaster Mk. I (March 1942 to August 1949) (* indicates an aircraft allocated to 207 Squadron post-war, often for a short period only)

Serial No.	Code	Fate
L7530		To 467 Sqn.
L7532	EM:Z	To 1654 Conversion Unit
L7540	EM:O	To 1654 Conversion Unit
L7543	EM:Z	Missing (Danzig) 12.7.42
L7544		To 1667 Conversion Unit
L7546	EM:G	Missing (Genoa) 8.11.42
L7547	EM:M	Caught fire and abandoned over St. Brisson-sur-Loire after raid on Milan, 14.2.43
L7566		To 1660 Heavy Conversion Unit
L7571		Missing (Essen) 17.9.42
L7578		To 83 Sqn. Conversion Flt.
L7580	EM:O/C	To 9 Sqn.
L7582	EM:D	To 106 Sqn.
L7583	EM:A/L	To 1661 Conversion Unit
R5498	EM:Z	Crashed adjacent to Normanton Lodge on approach to Bottesford, 8.4.42
R5499	EM:O	Missing from 'gardening' operation to Kattegat, 11.8.42
R5500	EM:B	To 460 Sqn.
R5501	EM:G	Collided with Miles Master DK973 and crashed on Canwick Hill, 2 mls. south of Lincoln, 28.3.42
R5503	EM:S/X	To 1660 Heavy Conversion Unit
R5504	EM:P	To 1660 Heavy Conversion Unit
R5505	EM:X	To 61 Sqn.
R5507	EM:W/Z	To 97 Sqn. Conversion Flt.
R5509	EM:N/G	Missing ('gardening' operation to Kiel Bay), 17.8.42
R5549	EM:H	To 1661 Heavy Conversion Unit
R5550	EM:B	Destroyed by fire after collision on runway with Manchester L7385, 6.8.42
R5570	EM:F	Missing (Turin) 9.12.42
R5616	EM:J	Shot down by fighters on 'gardening' operation to Kattegat, ditched SSW of Mano Island, Denmark, 17.8.42
R5617	EM:T	Flew into Standon Hill, near Tavistock, Devon, while on training flight in bad weather, 24.5.42
R5628	EM:Q	Shot down into sea 6 mls. SW of Thyboron, Denmark, on 'gardening' operation to Kattegat, 10.9.42
R5632	EM:N	Missing (Duisburg) 24.7.42; believed crashed into North Sea
R5633	EM:R	Missing (Mainz) 13.8.42
R5635	EM:L	To 1661 Heavy Conversion Unit
R5668		To Bombing Development Unit
R5674	EM:S	To 103 Sqn.
R5686	EM:T	To 83 Sqn.
R5693	EM:J	SOC 15.5.47
R5694	EM:F	Hit high ground in bad visibility, Eaton, Lincs., 25.11.42
R5695	EM:C	Missing (Haselunne) 26.11.42
R5736		To 1660 Heavy Conversion Unit
R5745	EM:T	To 460 Sqn.
R5755	EM:N	Shot down into the Ijsselmeer east of Medemblik during operation to Bremen, 5.9.42
R5756	EM:D	To 1667 Heavy Conversion Unit
R5758	EM:Z	To 97 Sqn.Conversion Flt.
R5760	EM:Y	Missing (Mainz) 13.8.42
R5761	EM:T	Shot down at Altforst, Holland, 6.8.42 during operation to Essen
R5847	EM:Y	Shot down at at Zwiggelte, Holland, 4.6.42, during operation to Bremen
R5848		To 106 Sqn. Conversion Flt.
R5851		To 50 Sqn.
R5852	EM:R	To 83 Sqn. Conversion Flt.
R5860	EM:Y	Ditched in North Sea 90 mls. east of Humber estuary on way to operation on Emden, 21.6.42
R5863	EM:K	Crashed at Normanton, Notts. when on overshoot, 19.8.42
R5865	EM:W	To 57 Sqn.
R5867	EM:T	Shot down at Baerl on Dutch / German border during operation on Duisburg, 24.7.42
R5895	EM:B	Missing (Magdeburg) 22.1.44
R5908	EM:B	To 49 Sqn. Conversion Flt.
W4119	EM:K	To 1661 Conversion Unit
W4120	EM:L	Missing (München-Gladbach) 31.8.43
W4121	EM:B	Missing (Milan) 24.10.42
W4129	EM:R	Missing (Kassel) 28.8.42
W4130		To 57 Sqn.
W4134	EM:U	Missing (Essen) 4.1.43
W4164	EM:G	To 9 Sqn. Conversion Flt.

Serial No.	Code	Fate
W4165	EM:K	To 57 Sqn.
W4167	EM:Q	Crashed on landing, Langar, 14.2.43
W4171	EM:J	Missing (Duisburg) 27.4.43
W4172	EM:X	Missing (Munich) 10.3.43
W4174	EM:V	To 1660 Conversion Unit
W4191	EM:Q	Missing (Munich) 22.12.42
W4276	EM:L	Missing (Hanover) 19.10.43
W4365	EM:B	Missing (Essen) 22.1.43
W4383	EM:S	To 1654 Conversion Unit
W4795	EM:B	To 61 Sqn.
W4798		To 61 Sqn.
W4815	EM:C	Overshot landing at Spilsby, 26.2.44
W4892	EM:T	Missing (Berlin) 2.1.44
W4931	EM:U	Missing (Berlin) 30.3.43
W4938	EM:A	Missing (Duisburg) 13.5.43
W4945	EM:Z	Missing (minelaying) 29.4.43
W4952	EM:T	Crashed on landing, Langar, 12.8.43
W4959	EM:S	Missing (Berlin) 24.11.43
W4962	EM:B	Missing (Hamburg) 28.7.43
DV360	EM:U	Missing (Wesseling) 22.6.44
DV361	EM:V	Caught fire in air and abandoned near Grafton Underwood, Northants., 22.12.43
DV369	EM:D	Missing (Brunswick) 15.1.44
DV370	EM:L	Missing (Berlin) 2.1.44
DV371	EM:M	Missing (Berlin) 31.1.44
ED329	EM:T	To 617 Sqn.
ED330	EM:F	Missing (Wilhelmshaven) 19.2.43
ED356	EM:W	Missing (Nuremburg) 26.2.43
ED361	EM:R	Collided with JA844 and abandoned near Dunsfold, Surrey, 13.8.43
ED365	EM:U	Missing (Hamburg) 4.3.43
ED412	EM:Q	Missing (Turin) 13.7.43
ED418	EM:G	Missing (Duisburg) 13.5.43
ED498	EM:O/D	Missing (Milan) 16.8.43
ED533	EM:N	Missing (minelaying) 3.3.43
ED537	EM:O	Missing (Dusseldorf) 12.6.43
ED550	EM:K	Missing (Berlin) 24.8.43
ED554	EM:Q	Missing (Duisburg) 10.4.43
ED569	EM:B	Missing (Cologne) 29.6.43
ED586	EM:F	Missing (Stettin) 6.1.44
ED600	EM:P	Missing (Dusseldorf) 26.5.43
ED601	EM:N	Missing (Berlin) 3.12.43
ED604	EM:A	Missing (Essen) 13.3.43
ED692	EM:W	Missing (Mulheim) 23.6.43
ED758	EM:V	Missing (Berlin) 31.1.44
LL776	EM:S	Missing (Dortmund) 23.5.44
LL902	EM:A	Flew into ground in bad weather, Little Rissingtonwhen returning from raid on Lutzkendorf, 15.3.45
LL968	EM:K	Missing (Heilbron) 5.12.44
LL973	EM:M	Missing (Wesseling) 22.6.44
LM123	EM:Q	SOC 2.11.45
LM125	EM:G	Missing (St. Leu d'Esserent) 5.7.44; crashed at Halby Apremont, 5 km. from Creil, Oise
LM129	EM:Y	Missing (St. Leu d'Esserent) 8.7.44; crashed at Herouville, near Auvers–sur–Oise
LM159 *		SOC 5.12.46
LM208	EM:M	Missing (minelaying) 16.10.44
LM218	EM:N	Missing (St. Leu d'Esserent) 8.7.44; crashed at Haudricourt, 5 km. W of Aumale
LM261	EM:C	Missing (Darmstadt) 12.9.44
LM263	EM:N	Missing (Deelen) 15.8.44; crashed 3 mls. SW of Deelen airfield
LM271	EM:L	Misisng (Bergen) 29.10.44
ME631	EM:K	Missing (Schweinfurt) 27.4.44
ME633	EM:Y	Missing (Leipzig) 20.2.44
ME666	EM:A	Missing (Frankfurt) 23.3.44
ME667	EM:X	Missing (Bremen) 7.10.44
ME678	EM:N	Missing (Etampes) 10.6.44
ME680	EM:R	Missing (Berlin) 25.3.44
ME681	EM:T	Missing (Revigny) 19.7.44
ME683	EM:W	Missing (Wesseling) 22.6.44
ME685	EM:C	Missing (Toulouse) 6.4.44
ME688	EM:E	Missing (minelaying) 10.4.44
ME805	EM:J	Missing (St.Leu d'Esserent) 8.7.44; crashed near Wambez, 20 km. NW of Beauvais
ME807	EM:S	Missing (Nevers) 16.7.44
ME814	EM:E	Missing (Revigny) 19.7.44
ME827	EM:I	Missing (Wesseling) 22.6.44
NF970 *		SS 7.5.47

Serial No.	Code	Fate
NF971 *		SS 23.3.49
NF973 *		SOC 25.3.48
NF979	EM:B	Missing (Duren) 16.11.44
NG138 *		To 90 Sqn.
NG143	EM:R	Missing (minelaying) 16.10.44
NG144	EM:G	Missing (Gdynia) 19.12.44
NG204	EM:M	Missing (Ladbergen) 4.3.45
NG230	EM:F	Missing (Bohlen) 6.3.45
NG245	EM:R	Crash-landed 3.5.45; SOC 23.3.49
NG286		To 619 Sqn.
NG388 *	EM:N	SS 29.8.47
NG399	EM:O	Missing (Lutzkendorf) 15.3.45
NG438 *		SOC 15.5.47
NG462 *		SOC 12.12.46
NN724	EM:X	Missing (Ladbergen) 8.2.45
NN760 *		SOC 19.5.47
NN761 *	EM-D	
NN782 *	EM:E	SOC 17.10.46
NX560 *	EM:D	Became 5845M 3.46
NX570 *		SOC 21.11.46
PA183	EM:K/B	SOC 2.1.47
PA196	EM:D	Missing (Bohlen) 21.3.45
PA230		SOC 28.8.46
PA252 *		To 90 Sqn.
PA253		To 90 Sqn.
PA266 *		SOC 12.3.48
PA275	EM:G	SOC 6.11.45
PA304 *		Crashed on landing, Methwold, 29.1.46
PA418 *		To 138 Sqn.
PA442 *		To 90 Sqn.
PB726 *	EM:G	SOC 29.8.47
PB764	EM:L	SOC 2.11.45
PB765	EM:B	Missing (Heilbron) 5.12.44
PB782	EM:Y	SOC 2.11.48
PB814	EM:T	Missing (Gravenhorst) 22.2.45
PB874	EM:B/K	SOC 2.11.45
PB878	EM:C	To 460 Sqn.
PB905 *		To 9 Sqn.
PD209	EM:V	To 429 Sqn.
PD210	EM:C	Missing (Revigny) 19.7.44
PD216	EM:J	Missing (Darmstadt) 26.8.44
PD217	EM:Z	To 1659 Conversion Unit
PD220	EM:E	SOC 6.11.45
PD267	EM:G	Missing (Stuttgart) 13.9.44
PD280	EM:V	SOC 3.9.47
PD290	EM:N	Swung on take-off, hit Halifax MP954 and blew up, Spilsby, 1.11.44
PD318	EM:J	Missing (Handorf) 24.9.44
PD322	EM:C	Missing (Giesen) 7.12.44
PD334 *	EM:D	SS 29.8.47
PD381	EM:M	To 44 Sqn.
PD433 *		SOC 3.6.47
RA519		To 467 Sqn.
RA588 *		To 149 Sqn.
RA598 *	EM-R	To 138 Sqn.
RA599 *	EM-A	To 90 Sqn.
RF144	EM:H	SOC 20.4.49
RF180 *	EM:H	SS 29.8.47
RF184 *		To 138 Sqn.
RF194	EM:A	To 630 Sqn.
RF195	—	To 57 Sqn.
SW260 *	EM:Q	SOC 3.6.47
SW263 *	EM-P	SS 29.8.47
SW266 *		SOC 2.6.47
SW303 *	EM:A	SOC 10.9.48
TW860 *		To 214 Sqn.
TW869 *	EM:D	To 148 Sqn.
TW887 *		SS 14.11.50
TW891 *		To 138 Sqn.
TW896 *		Became ground instructional *6638M* 2.49
TW897 *		To 138 Sqn.
TW900 *	EM:F	To 115 Sqn.
TW910 *	EM:B	To 115 Sqn.

❑ Avro Lancaster Mk. III (May 1943 to December 1947) (* indicates an aircraft allocated to 207 Squadron post-war, often for a short period only)

Serial No.	Code	Fate
W5001	EM:J	Missing (Dusseldorf) 26.5.43
W5006	EM:G	To 9 Sqn.
BT308		To Rolls-Royce
DV183	EM:W	Missing (Cislago) 17.7.43
DV184	EM:O	Crashed on take-off, Langar, 2.10.43
DV188	EM:J	Missing (Berlin) 24.12.43
DV191	EM:O/Q	Missing (Brunswick) 15.1.44
DV243	EM:D	Ditched off Great Yarmouth when returning from raid on Frankfurt, 23.10.43
DV383	EM:O	SOC 6.11.47
ED371	—	To 57 Sqn.
ED413	EM:P	To 1651 Conversion Unit
ED442	EM:W	Missing (Hanover) 23.9.43
ED623	EM:N	To 626 Sqn.
ED627	EM:N	Missing (Nuremburg) 28.8.43
ED698	EM:S	Swung on take-off, undercarriage collapsed, Spilsby, 20.1.44
ED802	EM:M	To 5 Lancaster Finishing School
ED832	EM:X	Missing (Berlin) 4.9.43
EE126	EM:A	Missing (Leipzig) 20.2.44
EE141	EM:P	Missing (Berlin) 17.12.43
EE173	EM:K	Missing (Brunswick) 15.1.44
EE175	EM:R	Missing (Kassel) 23.10.43
EE197	EM:N	Damaged by Fw.190 over Brunswick and crash-landed at Spilsby, 15.1.44
JB309	EM:B	To 1668 Conversion Unit
LM326	EM:Z	Missing (Hanover) 19.10.43
LM334	EM:V	Missing (Nuremburg) 28.8.43
LM366	EM:H	Missing (Berlin) 29.1.44
LM383	EM:R	Missing (Brunswick) 15.1.44
LM436	EM:G	Missing (Nuremburg) 31.3.44
LM526	EM:R	Missing (Schweinfurt) 27.4.44
LM535	EM:P	SS 7.5.47
LM540	EM:Q	Missing (Brunswick) 23.5.44
LM543	EM:F	To 115 Sqn.
LM578	EM:C	Missing (Wesseling) 22.6.44
LM671	EM:S	Missing (Gdynia) 19.12.44
ME379*	EM:B	SOC 29.8.47
ME386	EM:G	Crashed into River Witham, near Boston, Lincs when returning from raid on Bohlen, 6.3.45
ME389	EM:J	SOC 23.7.46
ME472	EM:O	Hit by flak over Leipzig and crashed near Koblenz, 11.4.45
ME473	EM:H	Collided with Lancaster ND572 of 57 Sqn. near Metheringham and crashed at Ruskington, Lincs., 2.3.45
ME522	EM:X	Missing (Hamburg) 22.3.45
ME532	EM:M	SOC 15.5.47
ME550 *		SOC 14.6.46
ND510	EM:T	Missing (Berlin) 16.2.44
ND513	EM:R	Missing (Clermont Ferrand) 11.3.44
ND521	EM:B	To 576 Sqn.
ND522	EM:J	Missing (minelaying) 22.5.44
ND555	EM:D	Missing (Gravenhorst) 7.11.44
ND556	EM:F	Missing (Mailly) 4.5.44; shot down by night-fighter near Chaintreaux, 12 km. SE of Nemours (Seine–et–Marne)
ND564	EM:H	Missing (La Chappelle) 21.4.44
ND567	EM:V	Missing (St. Leu d'Esserent) 8.7.44; crashed at Champ Muger, Sérifontaine, 30 km. W of Beauvais
ND568	EM:L	Missing (Nuremburg) 31.3.44
ND570	EM:Z	Missing (St. Leu d'Esserent) 5.7.44
ND575	EM:M	Missing (Mailly) 4.5.44; crashed 1 km. E of Donnermarie–Dontilly, 15 km. SW of Provins (Seine–et–Marne)
ND862	EM:D	To 1661 Conversion Unit
ND866	EM:B	Missing (St. Leu d'Esserent) 8.7.44; crashed between Bezu St. Eloi and Neaufles St. Martin
ND871	EM:G	Missing (Brunswick) 23.5.44
ND872	EM:L	Missing (Stuttgart) 29.7.44
NE168	EM:F	Missing (Houffalize) 6.1.45
PB286	EM:U	SOC 30.11.46
PB293	EM:W	SOC 28.11.46
PB294	EM:G	Crashed in sea off Lincolnshire coast when jettisoning bomb-load on return from raid on Donges, 25.7.44
PB295	EM:I	Missing (Gravenhorst) 22.2.45
PB428	EM:T	Colllided with Lancaster LM648 of 44 Sqn. in Spilsby circuit on returning from raid on Harburg, 11.11.44
PB555 *	EM:T	SS 29.8.47

Serial No.	Code	Fate
PB625 *	EM:E	SOC 3.6.47
PB653 *		SOC 13.11.45
PB699		To 619 Sqn.
RE128	EM:X	SOC 14.6.46
RE132 *		SOC 27.8.46
RF208	EM:S	SOC 24.1.47
RF209	EM:T	SOC 8.8.47
RF238 *		To Telecommunications Flying Unit
RF240 *		SOC 12.9.47
RF266	EM:O	To 231 Sqn.

❑ Avro Lincoln B.2 (August 1949 to March 1950)

Serial No.	Code	Fate
RE296	EM-K	To 214 Sqn.
RE301		To 214 Sqn.
RE320		To 214 Sqn.
RE324	EM:C	To 214 Sqn.
RE360		To 214 Sqn.
RE400	EM:E	To 7 Sqn.
RE423		To 214 Sqn.
RF570		To 149 Sqn.

❑ Washington B.1 (July 1951 to March 1954)

Serial No.	Code	Fate
WF437	EM:Y	To 35 Sqn.
WF549		Returned to USAF 19.1.54 as *44-62013*
WF558		Returned to USAF 5.1.54 as *44-61978*
WF559		Returned to USAF 5.1.54 as *44-62014*
WF560		Returned to USAF 19.1.54 as *44-61969*
WF561		Returned to USAF 1.12.53 as *44-62109*
WF564	EM:B	Returned to USAF 15.2.54 as *44-62259*
WF565		Returned to USAF 15.2.54 as *44-62243*
WF566		Returned to USAF 16.3.54 as *44-62135*
WF567		Returned to USAF 16.3.54 as *44-62256*
WF568	EM:W	Returned to USAF 15.1.54 as *44-62265*
WF569	EM:V	Returned to USAF 15.2.54 as *44-62105*
WW342		Returned to USAF 3.11.53 as *44-62242*
WW352	EM:F	Returned to USAF 25.2.54 as *44-62255*

❑ English Electric Canberra B.2 (March 1954 to March 1956)

Serial No.		Fate
WE118		Converted to T.4 for Station Flight Hemswell
WF916		To 44 Sqn.
WH643		Stored until SOC 17.6.63
WH645		To 115 Sqn.
WH870		To 32 Sqn.
WH876		To 73 Sqn.
WH886		To 44 Sqn.
WH904		To 35 Sqn.
WH905		To 115 Sqn.
WH906		Flew into trees on approach to Marham, 3.12.54
WH925		To 18 Sqn.
WJ618		To 32 Sqn.
WJ631		To 115 Sqn.
WJ648		To 18 Sqn.
WJ718		To 35 Sqn.
Serial No.	Code	Fate
WJ978		Transferred from RAF charge 26.2.57
WJ993		To 6 Sqn.
WK102		To 75 Sqn., RNZAF
WK106		Converted to T.11 for 228 OCU
WK117		To 90 Sqn.
WK142		To 90 Sqn.

❑ Vickers Valiant B.1 (July 1956 to February 1965)

Serial No.	Fate
WP210	SOC 1.3.65
WP217	To 7 Sqn.
WP219	SOC 1.3.65; scrapped at Marham
WP221	SOC 5.3.65; to P&EE Shoeburyness
WZ361	SOC 16.6.65
WZ363	Dived into ground S of Market Rasen, 3.5.64
WZ401	SOC 5.3.65
WZ402	SOC 1.3.65
WZ403	SOC 1.3.65; scrapped at Marham
WZ404	SOC 1.3.65; scrapped at Marham
WZ405	To 138 Sqn.
XD812	To 214 Sqn.
XD813	To 90 Sqn.
XD815	To 138 Sqn.
XD828	SOC 5.3.65
XD858	To 214 Sqn.
XD865	SOC 5.3.65
XD873	To 138 Sqn.
XD875	To 138 Sqn.

❑ Beagle Bassett CC.1 (February 1969 to July 1974)

Serial No.	Fate
XS765	To 26 Sqn.
XS775	To 26 Sqn.
XS776	Sold 12.8.74 to become *G-BCJG*
XS777	To 32 Sqn.
XS778	To 32 Sqn.
XS779	Sold 15.7.74 to become *G-BCJC*
XS780	Sold 12.7.74 to become *G-BCIV*
XS781	Sold 19.7.74 to become *G-BCIY*
XS782	Sold 15.7.74 to become *G-BCJD*
XS784	Sold 18.7.74 to become *G-BCIZ*

❑ De Havilland Devon C.2 (February 1969 to February 1984)

Serial No.		Fate
VP952		Became *8820M*; preserved at Cosford
VP955		To storage; sold 12.10.84
VP956		To 26 Sqn.
VP957		Became *8822M*; nose section at 1137 Sqn. ATC, Belfast
VP958	DC	Became *8795M*
VP961		To Air Attaché Bangkok
VP962		To storage; sold 12.10.84
VP963		SOC 5.10.78
VP965	DE	Became *8823M*
VP967		(C.1) To 21 Sqn.; under restoration 1994 at East Surrey Technical College, Redhill
VP968		To A&AEE, Boscombe Down
VP971	DD (?)	Became *8824M*; extant 1994 at Manston
VP974		SOC 5.10.78
VP976		Became *8784M*
VP977		To MoD (PE)
VP981		Eventually in service with Battle of Britain Memorial Flight; sold 24.9.98 to Air Atlantique Historic Flight as *G–DHDV*
WB530		Became *8825M*
WB531		To storage; sold 12.10.84
WB533	DA	To storage; sold 12.10.84
WB534	DB	To storage; sold 12.10.84
WB535		SOC

❑ Percival Pembroke C.1 (February 1969 to March 1977)

Serial No.	Fate
WV735	To Ministry of Technology
WV746	To 60 Sqn.; now preserved at Cosford
WV753	Became *8113M* 3.71; preserved at Cardiff Airport for a time.
XF798	SOC 21.6.72
XK884	To 21 Sqn.
XL929	To 60 Sqn.

Appendix VI: Statistics

Section A – personnel who lost their lives while serving with 207 Squadron and its predecessors.
It has been calculated that less than a quarter of all the aircrew members who began their operational training in Bomber Command finished their tour of duty safely. The statistics may be displayed as follows:

Killed on operations	51%
Killed during training	9%
Survived crashes to become PoWs	12%
Survived crashes and avoided capture	1%
Injured and taken off operations	3%
Completed tour safely	24%

207 Squadron lost 981 members (including ground personnel) between its formation in 1918 and its final disbandment, 954 of them during the Second World War, nineteen between the wars and eight since 1945. Its predecessor, 7 (Naval) Squadron, lost a further three, and in view of the fact that 7A (N) Squadron operated alongside its parent 7 (N) Squadron until December 1917, the two casualties suffered by that unit (one of whom was a member of the RFC) are also included. The grand total of 986 who lost their lives may then be analysed as follows:

Fatalities by service:	
RNAS (WW1)	4
RFC	1
RAF, RAuxAF and RAFVR	791
RCAF	112
RAAF	60
RNZAF	16
USAAF	2
Fatalities by rank:	
Group Captain	1
Wing Commander	3
Squadron Leader	5
Flight Lieutenant	35
Flight Sub-Lieutenant RNAS	1
Flying Officer	124
Pilot Officer	115
1st Lieutenant USAAF	1
2nd Lieutenant RFC	1
Flight Officer USAAF	1
Warrant Officer	26
Flight Sergeant	166
Sergeant	476
Corporal	1
LAC	13
Leading Mechanic RNAS	1
AC1/ACW1	9
AC2	5
Air Mechanic 1st Class RNAS	1
Air Mechanic 2nd Class RNAS	1
Fatalities by role:	
Pilot	188
Navigator	136
Bomb-aimer	98
Flight engineer	105
Air gunner	267
Wireless operator/air gunner	125
Wireless operator	33
Air Electronics operator	1
Gunlayer	4
Engineering officer	1
Medical Officer	1
Fitter	1
Armourer	10
Electrician	1
Instrument mechanic	2
Flight mechanic	2
Batman	1
(not known)	10

Fatalities by year:

1917	5
1923	2
1926	2
1928	3
1929	2
1930	2
1936	3
1938	2
1939 to 2 September	3
1939 from 3 September	4
1941	68
1942	169
1943	239
1944	407
1945	67
1954	3
1964	5

Fatalities by base:

Coudekerke	5
San Stephano	2
Eastchurch	7
Bircham Newton	2
Ed Damer	3
Worthy Down	1
Cottesmore	4
Cranfield	4
Waddington	68
Bottesford/Syerston	122
Langar	250
Spilsby	510
Marham	8

Fatalities by aircraft type (including ground crew members flying on duty):

HP O/100	5
DH.9A	2
Fairey IIIF	7
Gordon	3
Wellesley	1
Battle	7
Manchester	83
Lancaster	851
Canberra	3
Valiant	5

From the above list, it will be seen that in 1944 207 Squadron suffered no less than 41.3% of the total number of casualties over its entire existence, with 7 and 7A (Naval) Squadrons taken into account. Furthermore, when flying from Spilsby the squadron lost 51.7% of the total number of personnel who gave their lives. Deaths in Lancasters accounted for 86.3% of the total number of aircrew fatalities.

WE WILL REMEMBER THEM

Section B – personnel of 207 Squadron and its predecessors who were taken prisoner or avoided capture.

In all, 173 aircrew members were taken prisoner during the Second World War and ten during the First World War, one of whom died in captivity. Evaders totalled 38. An analysis of the bases from which they flew is as follows:

Coudekerke	7 PoW
Ligescourt	3 PoW
Waddington	35 PoW, 3 evaders
Bottesford/Syerston	16 PoW
Langar	19 PoW, 5 evaders
Spilsby	103 PoW, 30 evaders

Section C – Bombs dropped by 207 Squadron between 22 June 1918 and 11 November 1918

June	812 x 112 lb + 23 x 20 lb = 91,404 lbs (40.8 tons, 41.55 tonnes)
July	921 x 112 lb + 235 x 25 lb = 109,027 lbs (48.67 tons, 49.56 tonnes)
August	6 x 1650 lb + 1795 x 112 lb + 609 x 25 lb = 226,165 lbs (100.97 tons, 102.8 tonnes)
September	12 x 1650 lb + 1043 x 112 lb + 581 x 25 lb = 151,141 lbs (67.47 tons, 68.7 tonnes)
October	4 x 1650 lb + 6 x 550 lb + 627 x 112 lb + 337 x 25 lb = 88,549 lbs (39.53 tons, 40.25 tonnes)
November	255 x 112 lb + 79 x 25 lb = 30,535 lbs (13.63 tons, 13.88 tonnes)

Section D – Total tonnage of bombs dropped by 7 (Naval) Squadron and 207 Squadron during the First World War

Base	Tonnage (Imperial)	Tonnage (metric)
Coudekerke	270 tons	274.9 tonnes
Ligescourt	296 tons, 7 cwt., 44 lbs.	301.8 tonnes
Estrée–en–Chausée	21 tons, 8 cwt., 28 lbs.	21.8 tonnes

Section E – The number of different aircraft on charge to 7 (Naval) Squadron and 207 Squadron

Voisin	4 at least
Sopwith 1.1/2 Strutter	5 at least
BE.2c	8
Caudron G.IV	7
Short Bomber	16
HP O/100	27
HP O/400	32
DH.9A	40
Fairey IIIF	47
Gordon Mk.I	54
Vincent Mk.I	4
Wellesley	15
Battle	65
Anson Mk.I	8
Manchester Mk.I	75
Hampden Mk.I	10
Lancaster Mk.I	203
Lancaster Mk.III	74
Lincoln B.2	8
Washington B.1	14
Canberra B.2	21
Valiant B.1	18
Bassett CC.1	10
Pembroke C.1	6
Devon C.2	21

Appendix VII: Roll of Honour – Fatalities, PoWs and Evaders

Part 1: those members of 7 and 7A (Naval) Squadrons and 207 Squadron who lost their lives.

Name	Date	Serial
ABEL, Sgt Leslie Francis	21 January 1944	R5895
ABELL, P/O Douglas Roy RAAF	6 October 1944	ME667
ADAMS, F/O Joseph Edward	6 November 1944	ND555
ADDISON, Sgt William Walter George	28 August 1943	L7278
AITKEN, Sgt William Cuthbertson	21 March 1941	ED627
AKERMAN, Sgt Frederick Samuel	6 August 1942	R5550
ASKRIGG, Sgt Ben	31 August 1941	L7316
ALLAN, F/Sgt James McGregor RCAF	25 November 1942	R5695
ALLEN, Sgt James	13 August 1941	L7381
ALP, F/O Frederick Arthur	13 May 1943	W4938
ANDERSON, Sgt David Angus	31 March 1944	LM436
ANDERSON, F/O John Graham RNZAF	16 November 1944	NF979
ANDERSON, F/Lt Peter Murray RCAF	11 April 1945	ME472
APPLETON, Sgt Robert Mitchell	2 October 1943	DV184
ARCHER, Sgt Albert John Owen	30 January 1944	ED758
ARCHER, F/Sgt Arthur Dorrien	2 October 1943	DV184
ARCHER, AC1 John Richard	10 April 1944	-
ARMOUR, P/O Wilton Garnet RCAF	11 November 1944	PB428
ARNOTT, F/Sgt John Woodrow	20 July 1941	L7310
ATKINS, F/Sgt Milton Wilbur RCAF	11 August 1942	R5499
ATKINSON, Sgt John Wilfred	5 September 1942	R5755
ATKINSON, Sgt Maurice	31 August 1943	W4120
ATKINSON, Sgt Richard Graham	24 March 1944	ME680
ATKINSON, F/Sgt Thomas Donald	4 June 1942	R5847
BACKLOG, P/O Cyril Peter	23 August 1943	ED550
BADGE, P/O Horace	12 July 1943	ED412
BAILEY, Sgt Charles Ronald	30 January 1944	DV371
BAIN, W/Cdr Francis George Levett	8 December 1942	R5570
BAKER, Sgt Frederick Robert William	23 September 1944	PD318
BAKER, F/O John Albert RAAF	11 November 1944	PB428
BALDWIN, Sgt Bernard Henry John	20 February 1944	ME633
BALFOUR, P/O Donald Campbell RAAF	14 January 1944	DV369
BALL, F/O Peter William	22 June 1944	ME827
BALL, Sgt William Alfred Henry	7 November 1942	L7546
BANKS, Sgt Robert Charles	2 March 1945	ME473
BANNERMAN, F/O Douglas Robert RNZAF	21 December 1942	W4191
BARHAM, F/O Douglas Reginald	22 March 1944	ME666
BARKER, Sgt Eric Harry Frederick	26 May 1943	W4919
BARKER, Sgt John Skinner	26 February 1944	W4815
BARKER, Sgt Raymond	4 May 1944	ND575
BARNARD, Cpl Leonard Edward	21 January 1930	J9637
BARNES, Sgt Frederick John Charles	5 September 1942	R5755
BARNES, Sgt Kenneth Victor	22 June 1944	ME683
BARNETT, Sgt Thomas	31 August 1943	W4120
BARRETT, LAC Alfred Gallagher	10 April 1944	-
BARRETT, Sgt Arthur Courtney	8 July 1944	ND866
BASKERVILLE, P/O Norman George RCAF	4 May 1944	ND575
BATE, Sgt Harold	21 December 1942	W4191
BATEMAN, Sgt Lawrence David	25 July 1944	PB294
BATEMAN, Sgt Walter	13 April 1938	K7766
BAYLEY, F/O George Reginald	9 January 1942	L7322
BEATTIE, Thomas	13 August 1941	L7377
BEECH, Sgt James	25 July 1944	PB294
BEER, Sgt Norman Clive RNZAF	18 February 1943	ED330
BELL, Cyril	4 May 1944	ND575
BELL, Sgt Lionel Horace	24 October 1942	W4121
BELL, Sgt Raymond	6 August 1942	R5761
BENN, Sgt John Walter RAAF	12 August 1942	R5760
BENTLEY, Sgt Gordon Joseph	21 December 1942	W4191
BERMINGHAM, F/O Daniel Charles RCAF	16 October 1944	NG143
BINGHAM, W/O John Michael	12 September 1944	LM261
BIRCH, Sgt George Herbert Arthur	10 September 1942	R5628
BIRCH, Sgt Norman	21 March 1941	L7278
BIRCH, F/O Sidney Harold	6 November 1944	ND555
BIRT, F/Sgt George Robert	13 August 1941	L7377
BISHOP, F/Sgt Henry William	14 March 1945	NG399
BISHOP, F/Sgt Leon Eric Gordon RNZAF	11 June 1943	ED537
BISHOP, Sgt Roy	9 April 1943	ED554
BISSET, F/O George Alexander	2 March 1943	ED533
BLACKBURN, LAC Jack	26 March 1943	-
BLAIR, F/Sgt Timothy Clayton RCAF	24 July 1942	R5632
BOAD, F/O Albert Alan	10 March 1944	ND513
BOARDMAN, Sgt Roy	8 December 1942	R5570
BODDY, P/O Howard Bruce RCAF	15 March 1945	LL902
BOLDY, F/Sgt David Adrian	11 July 1942	L7543
BONE, Sgt Henry George	15 February 1943	L7547
BONNER, F/O Harry Frederick Charles	2 December 1943	ED601
BOOTH, Sgt Fred	8 July 1944	ND567
BORE, F/Sgt Stanley Robert	22 June 1944	ME683
BOSWELL, Sgt George William	10 June 1944	ME678
BOTTOMLEY, Sgt George Langdon	26 May 1943	W4919
BOTTRELL, F/O William John	2 January 1944	DV370
BOULTON, W/O Alfred	23 May 1944	ND871
BOWEN, F/Sgt Bryan Victor	12 September 1944	PD267
BOWES, F/O Lyle Edward RAAF	22 June 1944	LM578
BOWES-CAVANAGH, P/O Brian Derek	13 October 1941	L7312
BOWS, Sgt Thomas	26 February 1943	W4815
BOYCE, P/O Charles David RCAF	22 June 1944	LM578
BOYCE, P/O Kenneth Arthur	8 July 1944	LM218
BOYD, AC1 Reginald	15 September 1941	L7318
BOYDON, Sgt Ronald Arthur Blake	21 January 1944	R5895
BOYLE, Sgt Francis Patrick	23 September 1944	PD318
BOYNE, Sgt Alexander John	19 August 1942	R5863
BRADSHAW, Sgt Ronald	23 June 1943	ED692
BREACH, F/Sgt Reginald George Andrew	15 March 1945	LL902
BREMNER, F/O Archibald Ferguson	2 October 1943	DV184
BRETT, P/O Anthony Leonard	15 August 1944	LM263
BRETT, F/Sgt Ronald Oswald Charles RAAF	12 July 1943	ED412
BRIAN, F/O Edward Joseph RCAF	12 September 1944	LM261
BRIGGS, F/O Harry Rowan	10 June 1944	ME678
BRISCO, Sgt Frederick Lionel RCAF	2 December 1943	ED601
BROAD, P/O Harold Douglas	30 January 1944	DV371
BROOKS, F/Sgt John	6 August 1942	R5550
BROPHY, W/O Bernard Anthony RCAF	13 August 1942	R5633
BROWN, Sgt Henry Edward	23 September 1939	-
BROWN, Sgt Richard	2 March 1943	ED533
BROWN, P/O Thomas Deathers	28 August 1942	W4129
BROWN, F/Sgt William	22 June 1941	L7314
BROWNE, Sgt Derek John	6 March 1945	ME386
BROWNE, F/Sgt Michael Vincent	22 June 1941	L7314
BRUCE, F/Sgt Frederick Thomas Robert RAAF	6 April 1944	ME685
BRUMWELL, Sgt Richard Arthur	16 October 1944	NG143
BUCHANAN, F/Lt David Graham RNZAF	18 December 1944	NG144
BUCKLAND, F/Sgt John William James RAAF	31 March 1944	LM436
BUJAC, F/O Bernard Gordon David	10 June 1944	ME678
BURGESS, P/O Hugh Thomas Blakeley RCAF	8 July 1944	ND567
BURGESS, P/O Thomas James RAAF	21 April 1944	ND564
BURNE, F/O Colin	28 July 1943	W4962
BURRELL, Sgt Roy	30 January 1944	ED758
BURT, Sgt Andrew Sweeting	5 March 1945	NG230
BURTON, Sgt Cyril	23 November 1943	E4959
BURTON, Sgt John Bernard	25 November 1942	R5694
BUTTENSHAW, LAC Edward William	17 July 1929	K1758
BUTTERWORTH, Sgt John	8 July 1944	LL902
BUXTON, F/O Gordon	27 April, 1944	LM526
CADMAN, Sgt James Wilfred	14 January 1942	L7309
CADNEY, Sgt William Morrant RCAF	31 August 1941	L7316
CAIN, W/O William Edward	3 March 1943	ED365
CAMERON, W/O Royston Richard	22 March 1945	ME522
CAMPBELL, Sgt John McDougal	22 May 1944	ND522
CAMPLING, LAC Frank	27 January 1936	JR9643
CANNOCK, Sgt George	26 February 1944	W4815
CANT, Sgt William Joseph	2 January 1944	W4892
CANTWELL, P/O Michael James Wallace RCAF	16 July 1944	ME807
CARR, F/Sgt Robert Stonehouse	12 March 1943	L7583
CARTER, Sgt Andrew Joseph	13 October 1941	L7312
CARTER, Sgt Francis Raymond	10 September 1942	R5628
CARTER, LAC Leslie Wilfred	15 September 1941	L7318
CARTWRIGHT, Sgt Eric	24 July 1942	R5632
CAWTHORNE, Cpl Lewis Charles Liversedge	5 November 1944	-
CHALDECOTT, Sgt Eric William John	28 August 1942	W4129
CHALKLIN, Sgt Stanley Kenneth	30 January 1944	DV371
CHALMERS, F/Sgt Ivor Frederick RAAF	29 January 1944	LM366
CHALMERS, Sgt Kenneth Stuart	17 October 1942	L7583
CHANT, Sgt Dennis Vivien	14 October 1941	L7373
CHAPMAN, Sgt Thomas Arnold	20 May 1943	-
CHETNEY, F/Sgt Rolf Arthur RCAF	29 July 1944	ND872
CHIASSON, F/Sgt John Charles RCAF	24 July 1942	R5632
CHOUINIERE, P/O Eugene Edward RCAF	25 November 1942	R5695

Name	Date	Serial
CHURCH, F/O David Campbell RAAF	29 October 1944	LM271
CHURCHOUSE, Sgt David John Kenneth	23 May 1944	LM540
CLADIS, F/Sgt Lionel George	11 August 1942	R5499
CLAPPERTON, Sgt Kenneth William	22 March 1945	ME522
CLARK, P/O Joseph James Richard	20 February 1944	ME633
CLARK, F/O Joseph Norman RNZAF	16 November 1944	NF979
CLARK, Sgt Ronald	2 January 1944	DV370
CLARKE, P/O Arthur Henry RAAF	4 December 1944	PB765
CLARKE, Sgt Harold Frank	24 July 1942	R5632
CLARKE, Sgt Kenneth William	23 September 1944	PD318
CLEARY, F/Sgt William Laurence	6 January 1945	NE168
CLEMENT, Sgt Charles Thomas Leslie	26 February 1944	W4815
CLEMENT, Sgt Harry RCAF	16 August 1943	ED498
CLEMENT, F/Sgt Roger Albert RCAF	28 August 1942	W4129
CLEMENTS, P/O John Russell RCAF	15 September 1941	L7318
CLEWS, AC1 Walter AC1	10 April 1944	-
CLITHERO, F/O Brendan	12 March 1943	L7583
CLOWES, ACW1 Vera Armistace WRAF	1 June 1943	-
CLULOW, F/Sgt George Frederick	31 March 1944	ME805
CLUNAS, F/Sgt Eric Clark RAAF	21 January 1944	R5895
COAKER, Sgt Ronald Lee	15 August 1944	LM263
COAKES, Sgt Albert Edward	13 August 1941	L7381
COATES, P/O Arthur Henry	17 July 1943	DV183
COBDEN, Sgt Walter Theophilus George	6 March 1945	ME386
COCHRANE, Sgt Alexander Wilson	29 April 1943	W4945
COCKIE, Sgt Alastair MacKenzie	10 September 1942	R5628
CODLING, Sgt Ronald	21 January 1944	R5895
COLDICOTT, F/Lt Albert Douglas	13 May 1943	ED418
COLLIN, Sgt Henry Oswald	21 March 1945	PA196
COLLINGS, Sgt Ronald Charles	8 July 1944	ND866
COLLINS, David Norman	27 April 1944	LM526
COLWILL, Sgt William Clifford RCAF	24 October 1942	W4121
COMPTON, Sgt Lewis John	14 October 1941	L7373
CONNOLLY, F/Lt Sylvanus George	27 January 1936	JR9643
CONNOR, Sgt Robert Henry	28 July 1943	W4962
COOK, Sgt Stanley Arthur James	25 May 1943	W5001
COOK, Sgt William Walter Rufus	29 June 1943	ED569
COOKE, F/O David Clifford	12 September 1944	LM261
COOKE, F/Sgt Frank Stewart	26 February 1944	W4815
COOKE, F/O Michael John Hedley	15 March 1945	LL902
COOPER, Sgt Gerald Douglas	8 July 1944	ND567
COOPER, F/Sgt John Stewart	21 October 1941	L7487
CORLESS, F/O Alvin Van Dyke RCAF	22 June 1944	ME683
COSENS, F/O Frank William	15 February 1944	ND510
COSSINS, W/O Reginald Frederick Henry	23 May 1944	ND871
COTTERELL, F/Sgt Anthony Robert	13 August 1941	L7381
COTTRELL, Sgt Norman Richard	31 March 1944	ND568
COWHAM, Sgt Stanley William	29 April 1943	W4945
COX, Sgt Norman McDonald	22 March 1945	ME522
COX, Sgt Ronald William	28 March 1942	R5501
COXON, P/O Geoffrey Lewis	22 September 1943	ED442
CRAIG, Sgt Alexander Milne	16 August 1942	R5509
CRANE, F/Sgt William Edward	18 December 1944	NG144
CROKER, F/Sgt Desmond Rimmer	5 July 1944	ND570
CRONAN, F/Sgt Thomas	18 December 1944	NG144
CROSS, F/Sgt Raymond Jack	4 May 1944	ND575
CRUMP, F/O Ernest Edwin Gordon	15 September 1941	L7318
CRUX, F/Sgt Cecil Charles	18 December 1944	NG144
CUBBON, Sgt William Henry	21 October 1941	L7487
CULLERNE, F/Sgt Allan Percival	11 July 1942	L7543
CULLEY, Sgt Jack	6 August 1942	R5761
CULLINGTON, F/O Augustine Frederick	11 November 1944	PB428
CUMMING, Sgt James Duncan	15 October 1944	LM208
CUNNINGHAM, Sgt John Charles	16 August 1943	ED498
CURSON, Sgt Harold	6 August 1942	R5550
CURTIS, Sgt Maurice Henry James	16 October 1944	NG143
DALGLEISH, F/O Edward	16 July 1944	ME807
DALLEN, F/O Jesse Gray	19 July 1944	ME814
DAMPIER, Sgt Ronald Eric Arthur	9 April 1943	ED554
DANCE, Sgt Raymond Ernest	4 May 1944	ND575
DANGERFIELD, Sgt John Charles RAAF	21 January 1943	W4365
DANZEY, AM2 William Charles	6 December 1917	3115
D'ARCY, P/O John	15 March 1945	LL902
DARKEN, F/Sgt Raymond de Champfleur RAAF	21 January 1943	W4365
DAVEY, Sgt Cecil Albert	21 December 1942	W4191
DAVEY, F/Sgt Jim Boyce RCAF	21 February 1945	PB814
DAVIDSON, LAC Trevor Ewart	10 April 1944	-
DAVIES, Sgt Arthur Haydn	18 October 1943	W4276
DAVIES, Sgt Arthur Henry	12 September 1944	LM261
DAVIES, Sgt David Oswald	24 December 1943	DV188
DAVIES, Sgt Frank Wells	27 April 1943	W4171
DAVIS, Sgt Clifford Francis Charles	31 March 1944	ND568
DAY, F/Sgt Norman Leslie Terrett	4 December 1944	LL968
DAY, F/Sgt Raymond Samuel Louis RCAF	28 July 1943	W4962
DEAN, Sgt George James	21 December 1942	W4191
DE BARDELEBEN, F/O William A. USAAF	2 January 1944	W4892
DEARDEN, Cpl Arnold Delday	9 May 1941	-
DEARMAN, P/O Derrick Roy	21 April 1944	ND564
DE CASAGRANDE, Sgt Raphael Edward	22 June 1944	ME683
DE GARIS, F/O William Sowden RAAF	5 March 1945	NG230
DELATORRE, F/Sgt Melville George RAAF	3 March 1943	ED365
DELLER, Sgt Edwin	6 January 1945	NE168
DERBYSHIRE, P/O James Edward	26 February 1944	W4815
DEWDNEY, Sgt Charles James	21 March 1945	PA196
DICK, Sgt Hugh Robert	13 May 1943	ED418
DICKENSON, F/Sgt Gordon Leonard	6 March 1945	ME386
DICKSON, Sgt Alexander Fernie RCAF	14 October 1941	L7321
DOBLE, F/O Michael Eugene	12 March 1943	L7583
DOCHERTY, Sgt Norman	20 February 1944	ME633
DOUGLAS, Sgt Thomas	17 August 1942	R5616
DOW, F/Sgt John Charles Du Burgh RAAF	23 October 1943	DV243
DRAYTON, F/O Philip Charles Bradley	26 May 1943	W4919
DRYSDALE, Sgt William	5 March 1945	NG230
DUFFY, Sgt Robert	10 April 1944	ME688
DUKE Sgt F/George Henry	11 July 1942	L7543
DUNKLEY, F/O George Cyril RCAF	24 March 1944	ME680
DUNLOP, F/Sgt Leslie Horton	15 February 1944	ND510
DUNN, F/Sgt Ralph Gordon RCAF	22 October 1943	EE175
DYDE, F/Sgt Frederick William	2 October 1943	DV184
DYSON, Sgt John Duncan	31 March 1944	ND568
EASLEY, F/O Gordon	11 August 1942	R5499
EBERT, F/Lt George Henry	6 January 1944	ED586
ECCLESTON, F/Sgt Stanley	16 November 1944	NF979
ECCLESTONE, Sgt Stanley	2 January 1944	DV370
EDGE, Sgt William Henry	5 March 1945	NG230
EDMONDS, F/Sgt Ronald Alfred	24 July 1942	R5867
EDMONDS, F/O Stanley Allan RAAF	10 April 1944	ME688
EDMONDS, F/O Wilfrid Milton RAAF	17 August 1942	R5616
EDMUNDS, P/O Howard Frederick RCAF	19 July 1944	PD210
EDWARDS, Sgt John Francis Patrick	5 July 1944	ND570
EDWARDS, F/Lt Philip Vaughan	27 January 1936	JR9643
EINARSON, F/Sgt Harold Bjorn RCAF	10 September 1942	R5628
ELDER, F/Lt William Alexander Stevenson	25 February 1943	ED356
ELLINGHAM, Sgt Thomas Edward	29 April 1943	W4965
ELLIOTT, F/Sgt John Herbert	11 June 1943	ED537
ELLIS, Sgt Ronald	4 May 1944	ND556
ELLIS, Sgt William Howard	8 December 1942	R5570
ELMES, Sgt Derek Walter	6 August 1944	PD209
EMERY, Sgt Alfred Keith	18 October 1943	W4276
ENNALS, Sgt George Frederick	29 July 1944	ND872
EVANS, F/O Douglas William Henry	13 May 1943	W4938
EVANS, F/Sgt Eric Vincent	22 June 1944	DV360
EVERETT, Sgt Donald Charles	20 February 1944	ME633
EVERITT, F/Sgt Geoffrey Charles	6 August 1942	R5761
EVISON, Sgt Peter	3 March 1943	ED365
EWING, F/Sgt Leslie Ernest	6 November 1944	ND555
FAIRCLOUGH, P/O Ronald	15 March 1945	LL902
FAIRES, F/O Douglas John	22 June 1944	LM578
FALKINGHAM, Sgt Peter	25 May 1943	W5001
FAWCETT, F/Sgt Selwyn	27 April 1944	LM526
FAYLE, Sgt John Stanley RCAF	25 February 1943	ED356
FEAR, Sgt Joseph	8 July 1944	LM218
FELGATE, P/O John Mervyn RAAF	6 October 1944	ME667
FELLOWS, Sgt Joseph Harold	16 July 1944	ME807
FELLS, Sgt Donald	23 August 1943	ED550
FENNELL, F/O Lloyd Richard RCAF	19 July 1944	ME681
FERGUSON, F/Sgt Gordon Joseph RCAF	14 January 1944	LM383
FIELD, Sgt Leonard Alfred	15 February 1944	ND510
FIELDING, F/O Francis Edwin	29 June 1943	ED569
FINDLAY, F/Sgt James	15 October 1944	LM208
FINDLAY, Sgt James Addie	19 July 1944	ME681
FIRTH, F/Sgt Charles Morton	5 July 1944	LM125
FITZGERALD, P/O Arthur Marcus	28 August 1943	ED627
FITZPATRICK, Sgt Thomas	12 August 1942	R5760
FLATT, F/O William Henry RCAF	23 June 1943	ED692
FLECK, Sgt George	5 September 1942	R5755
FLEMING, AC1 Thomas	10 April 1944	-
FLITT, Sgt George Walter	2 March 1945	ME473
FONSECA, P/O Donald Everton RCAF	21 April 1944	ND564
FORBES, Sgt John	6 August 1942	L7385
FORDWYCH, F/Sgt William Dundas	19 August 1942	R5863
FOULDS, F/O Leonard	29 April 1943	W4945
FOX, Sgt Alvin Clarke	3 March 1945	NG204
FREEMAN, Sgt Henry Alfred	22 September 1943	ED442
FREEMAN, Sgt John Anthony	22 May 1944	ND522
FRENCH, F/Sgt Keeble Charles RAAF	28 August 1943	LM334
FROST, Sgt Keith John	26 May 1943	W4919
FRY, W/O David Wyndham	12 August 1942	R5760
FULTON, Sgt Hugh	22 September 1943	ED442

Name	Date	Serial
FURMAN, P/O Russel Max RCAF	17 July 1943	DV183
FURSE, P/O William Walter RAAF	6 October 1944	ME667
GALLAGHER, Sgt Francis Alexander Kevin RAAF	21 January 1943	W4365
GALLAGHER, F/Lt Frederick Whitton	22 June 1944	ME827
GALLIMORE Sgt John James	25 November 1942	R5695
GARDEN, Sgt Alexander	12 March 1943	L7583
GARDINER, F/Sgt John RCAF	21 February 1945	P8295
GARDNER, Sgt Herbert Charles	21 October 1941	L7487
GARDNER, F/Sgt John	12 September 1944	PD267
GAUT, Sgt Richard Arthur	16 July 1944	ME807
GAWTHORPE, Sgt Walter Gordon	18 February 1943	ED330
GENEVER, Sgt Douglas Alan	26 May 1943	W4919
GHISLETTA, Sgt Albert Dennis	23 September 1944	PD318
GIBBS, F/Sgt John William	5 July 1944	EE173
GIBSON, Sgt Eric John	6 December 1944	PD322
GILES, F/Sgt Stanley Frederick	5 March 1945	NG230
GILLESPIE, Sgt John RCAF	27 April 1943	W4171
GLARE, Sgt Geoffrey John	27 April 1943	W4171
GLAZEBROOK, F/O Stanley	11 August 1942	R5499
GOLDIE, Sgt Peter Charles Herbert RAAF	9 January 1942	L7322
GOODMAN, P/O Edwin Arthur	22 June 1944	DV360
GOODSELL, F/Sgt Kenneth Edward	13 August 1943	ED361
GOODWIN, Sgt John	28 August 1943	ED627
GOODWIN, Sgt Stanley Leonard	13 May 1943	W4938
GORDON, F/Sgt James Sidney	29 July 1944	ND872
GOSNEY, P/O Leonard David RCAF	2 January 1944	W4892
GOSSIP, F/O George Hatfeild Digby	24 April 1923	-
GOWAN, F/O Ronald Burtis RCAF	12 September 1944	LM261
GOWER, Sgt Leslie Percy	26 August 1944	PD216
GRACE, AC2 James William	15 September 1941	L7318
GRAHAM, P/O Frederick George RCAF	16 July 1944	ME807
GRAINGER, F/Sgt Athol Richard RAAF	15 February 1943	L7547
GRANBOIS, W/O Maurice Emerson RCAF	21 February 1945	PB295
GRAY, F/Sgt Reginald Wilfred	31 August 1941	L7316
GREEN, Sgt Henry Alfred Lesley	12 August 1942	R5760
GREENHILL, Sgt Bernard Owen	6 January 1944	ED586
GRIFFITHS, Sgt Richard Vivian	9 January 1942	L7322
GRIME, F/Sgt James Douglas	22 March 1945	ME522
GRINT, Sgt Joseph Robert	25 July 1944	PB294
GRUNDY, P/O Eric	21 February 1945	PB814
GUICHARD, W/O James Louis RCAF	25 November 1942	R5695
HAGUE, F/Sgt John	19 July 1944	PD210
HALFPENNY, F/Sgt Arthur	13 August 1941	L7381
HALL, Sgt Albert Frederick	15 October 1944	LM208
HALL, Sgt Colin James Murray	4 June 1942	R5847
HALL, Sgt Eric George	18 December 1944	NG144
HALL, Sgt Ivor Edwin George	26 May 1943	W4919
HALLETT, Sgt Clement Arthur	5 July 1944	LM125
HAMILTON, Sgt Hugh Graham	26 August 1944	PD216
HANKS, Sgt Charles Raymond	10 April 1944	ME688
HANMER, Sgt Vernon Albert	23 September 1944	PD318
HANNAH, W/O Robert Stanley RCAF	25 February 1943	ED356
HANNAN, F/Lt Raymund Joseph	25 November 1942	R5694
HARDING, F/Lt Maurice Frederick Cleave	26 August 1944	PD216
HARDING, Sgt William	18 February 1943	ED330
HARLEY, F/O Edward Vincent	2 December 1943	ED601
HARPER, Sgt Eric Ronald	14 January 1942	L7523
HARRIS, Sgt Alexander Gordon	9 January 1942	L7322
HARRIS, Sgt Walter John	3 January 1943	W4134
HARRISON, W/O William George	23 May 1944	ND871
HART, F/Sgt Kenneth Harry	11 July 1942	L7543
HARTELL, P/O Raymond Raynes	11 August 1942	R5499
HARWOOD, Sgt Frank Briant	21 March 1941	L7278
HASLER, F/O Christopher John	3 December 1954	WH906
HASTINGS, P/O Adam Byers	5 September 1942	R5755
HAWES, F/Sgt William George RAAF	24 July 1942	R5632
HAWKES, P/O William Dick	13 May 1943	ED418
HAWKINS, F/O Frank Bryce RAAF	2 March 1943	ED533
HAWKINS, F/Lt Leslie Richard	6 May 1964	WZ363
HAWORTH, AC1 Frank	10 April 1944	-
HAYES, F/O Gerald	3 December 1954	WH906
HAYLLAR, Sgt William Frederick	25 May 1943	W5001
HAYWARD, P/O Eric Lionel	24 July 1942	R5867
HEALEY, W/O Harold Arthur RCAF	9 April 1943	ED554
HEATH, P/O Allen Frank	23 May 1944	LM540
HEMINGWAY, Sgt Harry Walker	13 March 1941	L7313
HENDERSON, F/Sgt Arthur	2 March 1945	ME473
HENDERSON, F/O Bryan John RAAF	6 December 1944	PD322
HERRIN, F/O Philip Gerard	23 June 1943	ED692
HESKETH, Sgt John	10 March 1944	ND513
HESLOP, Sgt Thomas	10 April 1944	ME688
HETHERINGTON, F/Sgt George Dennis	23 May 1944	LM540
HICKLING, P/O John	31 August 1943	W4120
HIGGINS, Sgt Charles	19 July 1944	PD210
HIGGINS, Sgt Edward	12 July 1943	ED412
HIGGINS, Sgt Thomas Gibson	22 December 1943	DV361
HILLIER, F/Sgt Henry Roy	18 December 1944	PB765
HIND, Sgt Peter Clinch	21 December 1942	W4191
HINGLEY, Sgt Walter	8 December 1942	R5570
HINTON AC2 Percy Charles	11 November 1926	J7610
HODGSON, F/O Peter Noel	6 January 1944	ED586
HOGARTH, Sgt Kenneth Herbert	25 February 1943	ED356
HOGG, Sgt Bennett	21 March 1941	L7178
HOLDING, Sgt John Lockwood	22 September 1943	ED442
HOLLAND, Sgt Frank	2 January 1944	DV370
HOLLAND, Sgt John William Edward	6 August 1942	R5761
HOLLETT, Sgt William Alfred	27 April 1943	W4171
HOLLEY, Sgt Raymond Walter Ernest	3 March 1943	ED365
HOLMES, Sgt Alan John	8 July 1944	ND567
HOLMES, Sgt Ronald William Edward	12 August 1942	R5760
HOLT, F/Sgt Alwyn Evelyn Stuart	19 July 1944	ME681
HOOD, FSL Thomas Samuel Stanley	26 April 1917	3115
HOOPER, Sgt Percival James RNZAF	24 July 1942	R5632
HOPSON, P/O George Edward	25 May 1943	W5001
HORDLEY, F/O Trevor John	8 July 1944	ND567
HORSLEY, Sgt John Herbert Victor	2 October 1943	DV184
HOUBEN, F/Sgt Denis Arthur	22 June 1944	DV360
HOUGHTON, F/Sgt Clifford Henry	6 October 1944	ME667
HOWE, Sgt John Thomas	14 January 1942	L7523
HOWE, Sgt John Thompson	21 January 1943	W4635
HUGHES, Sgt Robert	29 January 1944	LM366
HULL, P/O James Edward	19 September 1939	K9448
HUNT, Sgt Albert John Victor	24 October 1942	W4121
HUNTLY-WOOD, S/Ldr Ian McArtair	3 September 1943	ED832
HURLEY, Sgt Cornelius Michael	8 December 1942	R5570
HUTTON, 2/Lt William Wallace	27 October 1917	3122
HYLAND, F/O Basil Paul Malcolm	27 April 1943	W4171
INGS, F/Lt Gerald Anthony	6 August 1942	R5761
ISAACS, Sgt Ralph	2 March 1943	ED533
IVORY, Sgt Lawrence	22 October 1943	EE175
JACKSON, W/Cdr Ashley Duke	6 January 1944	ED586
JACKSON, P/O Edward Laming	22 October 1943	EE175
JACKSON, F/Sgt Leslie Frederick	22 June 1944	LM578
JACQUES, Sgt Beresford Matthew	8 July 1944	ND866
JAMES, Sgt Alick Michael	22 June 1941	L7314
JAMES, F/O Geoffrey Watkin	14 January 1944	DV191
JENKIN, Sgt Bryant Leonard McKenzie RNZAF	25 November 1942	R5694
JENKINS, W/O Allan Keith RAAF	4 December 1944	LL968
JEPPS, F/Lt Arthur Charles	12 July 1943	ED412
JEWEL, Sgt Edwin Jack	22 June 1944	LL973
JOHNSON, F/O Bernard	3 March 1943	ED365
JOHNSON, Sgt Joseph	22 March 1945	ME522
JOHNSON, Sgt Kenneth Roy	25 February 1943	ED356
JOHNSTON, F/Sgt Alexander RCAF	3 March 1945	NG204
JOHNSTON, Sgt Edward William Hargreaves	14 January 1944	DV191
JOHNSTONE, Sgt Reginald James	25 May 1944	LM543
JONES, Sgt Benjamin Bryn	27 April 1943	W4171
JONES, F/Lt George Leeson	16 July 1944	ME807
JONES, Sgt Howard Cullimore	4 May 1944	ND575
JONES, AC1 Idris Eurfyl	10 April 1944	-
JONES, Sgt Iorworth Beynon	27 April 1943	W4171
JONES, F/Sgt John Elias	9 January 1942	L7322
JONES, Sgt Russell Roy Alwyn RNZAF	4 June 1942	R5847
JONES, Sgt Stanley	31 March 1944	LM436
JONES, F/Sgt Thomas John	26 August 1944	PD216
JOWETT, LAC Leonard	30 March 1944	-
JUDD, W/O William Bruce RAAF	21 March 1945	PA196
KANE, F/Sgt Samuel Forster	13 August 1942	R5633
KEELER, F/O Ervin Leroy RCAF	30 January 1944	ED758
KEIGHTLEY, Sgt Frederick	31 March 1944	LM436
KELLY, Sgt Michael Thomas	10 June 1944	ME678
KELMAN, Sgt William Ronald	30 January 1944	ED758
KENNEDY, Sgt John	6 January 1945	NE168
KENNY, Sgt Philip Reginald	12 August 1942	R5760
KENSETT, Sgt Arthur Frederick Charles	10 September 1942	R5628
KERR, Sgt Stewart Gray	4 June 1942	R5847
KERWIN, F/O Raymond Thomas RAAF	23 September 1944	PD318
KINGSNORTH, Sgt David John	11 June 1943	ED537
KINGSTON, P/O Patrick Noel RAAF	14 January 1944	LM383
KIRKMAN, Sgt Jack	16 August 1943	ED498
KIRKUP, P/O John Elliott	22 October 1943	EE175
KISILOWSKY, P/O Edward RCAF	26 August 1944	PD216
KITE, Sgt Edwin Dennis	22 September 1943	ED442
KLEINBERG, F/O Georges	23 June 1943	ED692
KLEYNHANS, F/Sgt Cornelius William	9 April 1943	EE554
KNIGHT, F/O Kenneth Joseph	3 September 1943	ED832
KYDD, S/Ldr Charles John French	23 June 1941	L7310
LACEY, F/O Arthur Norman	3 March 1945	NG204
LACKIE, Sgt George	22 June 1944	DV360
LAING, F/Sgt Joseph William	15 March 1945	LL902
LAMB, F/Sgt Thomas Leslie	23 May 1944	ND871

Name	Date	Serial
LANGSTONE, Sgt Albert Frederick	4 December 1944	LL968
LAPPIN, Sgt Robert George	19 July 1944	ME681
LARBY, F/O Harold Joseph	22 May 1944	ND522
LARSEN, F/O John Larsenius	31 March 1944	LM436
LA SALLE, Sgt Joseph Daniel Leo RCAF	24 July 1942	R5867
LATHAM, Sgt Alan	31 March 1944	ND568
LAWRIE, Sgt Alexander William	2 January 1944	W4892
LAWSON, F/Lt Edward McMaster RAAF	2 March 1945	ME473
LAWTON, Sgt Thomas Arnold	21 March 1945	PA196
LAYBOURN, Sgt George Wilfred	18 October 1943	W4276
LEA, Sgt Laurence John	4 June 1942	R5847
LEAHY, F/Sgt John Michael	24 July 1942	R5867
LEASON, Sgt John William	13 October 1941	L7312
LEE, F/Sgt John Kennerleigh Barnett	26 November 1942	R5694
LEIGH, P/O Kenneth RCAF	16 October 1944	NG143
LEISK, F/O Colin Murray	3 March 1945	NG204
LEWIS, F/Sgt Arthur Rupert	9 April 1943	ED554
LEWIS Sgt Leonard James	23 November 1943	W4959
LEWIS F/O Raymond Allan RAAF	21 March 1945	PA196
LINEKER, Sgt Ivan Wildman	3 January 1943	W4134
LINFOOT, Sgt John William	26 February 1944	W4815
LINGARD, Sgt Norman Arthur	28 March 1942	R5501
LINKLATER, P/O Ian Alistair Hay	12 March 1943	L7583
LINTON, P/O Leonard Thomas RCAF	20 February 1944	EE126
LISSETTE, W/O Leslie Harry RNZAF	4 May 1944	ND556
LISTER, AC2 Jack	15 September 1941	L7318
LISTER, Sgt Stanley	23 May 1944	ND871
LITCHFIELD, P/O Maurice Jacques	15 February 1944	ND510
LITOLFF, Sgt Bernard Leo	12 March 1943	L7583
LITTLE, Sgt Arthur James	10 March 1944	ND513
LITTLE, F//Sgt Stanley William George	25 July 1944	PB294
LLOYD, Sgt James Thomas	29 June 1943	ED569
LLOYD, Sgt Raymond William	22 June 1944	ME827
LODGE, Sgt Wallace Eugene RAAF	8 December 1942	R5570
LONGMAN, Sgt Francis David Pemberton	19 July 1944	ME681
LONGMATE, Sgt George Stanley	27 April 1944	LM526
LORD, F/O William Winston	2 March 1945	ME473
LOVEDAY, Sgt David Arthur	27 April 1944	LM526
LOVELL, Sgt John Henry RAAF	7 November 1942	L7546
LOVETT, F/O Michael Joseph	4 December 1944	LL968
LOWERY, Sgt John	23 May 1944	LL776
LOWMAN, AC1 William George	2 March 1928	S1195?
LUPTON, Sgt John Thomas	21 February 1945	PB295
LUTON, Sgt John Campbell RAAF	5 September 1942	R5755
LYGO, Sgt Henry John	11 June 1943	ED537
LYNCH, F/Sgt Geoffrey Augustine RAAF	28 August 1943	LM334
McARTHUR, Sgt John	16 August 1942	R5509
McARTHUR, Sgt Ronald Charles	2 June 1944	LM578
McCALLUM, F/Sgt John Francis RCAF	24 October 1942	W4121
McCARTHY, P/O John Justin Neville RNZAF	24 July 1942	R5867
McCULLOCH, Sgt Duncan McMillan	28 July 1943	W4962
McCULLOCH, F/O Hugh John RAAF	28 August 1943	LM334
MacDONALD, P/O George Sinclair RCAF	21 October 1941	L7487
McDONNELL, F/Sgt David Kenneth RAAF	22 June 1944	DV360
McDONNELL, F/O Ian Locheil	11 June 1943	ED537
McDOWELL, S/Ldr Alexander Lyons	22 October 1943	EE175
McILVENEY, Sgt James Gerald	16 November 1944	NF979
McINTOSH, F/O Peter Cameron	25 July 1944	PB294
McINTYRE, F/O Lynden Arnold RCAF	15 October 1944	LM208
MacKAY, P/O Huntley David Shaw Mann Jack	15 August 1944	LM263
McKEITH, Sgt Thomas Elder Charles Kinnoch	23 August 1943	ED550
McKENNA G/Capt Austin Flower	3 September 1943	ED832
MacKENZIE, F/O Donald	21 January 1930	J9637
McKENZIE, Sgt Alfred Henry	16 August 1942	R5509
MACKEY, Sgt Stanley Herbert	2 September 1944	PD267
MacKINNON, Sgt Kenneth Ewan	6 November 1944	ND555
McLEAN, F/Sgt John	29 October 1944	LM271
McLEAN, F/Sgt John Andrew RCAF	17 August 1942	R5616
McLEOD, F/O Alexander Corbett	10 April 1944	ME688
McNAIR, W/O William Archibald RCAF	13 May 1943	ED418
McNAUGHTON, F/O William Ross	19 July 1944	PD210
MacNICOLL, F/Sgt Robert Campbell RCAF	21 February 1945	PB295
MacNISH-PORTER, Sgt John Anthony	22 October 1943	EE175
McPHAIL, Sgt Donald Hugh	14 August 1941	L7377
MacPHERSON, F/O John	10 April 1944	ME688
McQUADE, F/O William	6 December 1944	PD322
McVICAR, Sgt William Brodie	16 August 1942	R5509
McWILLIAMS, Sgt Robert	28 July 1943	W4962
MAGOFFIN, Sgt James Ivan RCAF	22 June 1944	ME683
MAIR, F/O Robert Edward	23 November 1943	W4959

Name	Date	Serial
MAJOR, F/O Denis William	23 May 1944	LL776
MALCOLM, P/O Robert	19 September 1939	K9448
MALE, Sgt Gerald Arthur Harold	23 June 1943	ED692
MALONE, F/Sgt Allan	22 June 1941	L7314
MALONEY, F/Sgt John Benedict	4 December 1944	LL968
MALTMAN, Sgt William Bean	2 March 1928	S1195?
MANN, P/O Arthur	2 December 1943	ED601
MANSER, Sgt Dennis Rodney	6 August 1942	R5761
MARAVAN-WILLIAMS, F/Sgt Thomas Ronald	6 October 1944	ME667
MARGETSON, Sgt George Sidney	9 March 1943	W4172
MARRIOTT, Sgt James Roy	15 October 1944	LM208
MARSDEN, Sgt Joseph	13 March 1941	L7313
MARSH, Sgt Albert William	22 September 1943	ED442
MARSHALL, F/Lt Kenneth	29 July 1944	ND872
MARTIN, Sgt Sydney	2 December 1943	ED601
MARWOOD, Sgt John	8 July 1944	LM129
MASON, P/O Frank	14 October 1941	L7321
MASON, LAC Sidney Creswell	2 March 1928	S1195?
MASSEY, Sgt Thomas Charles	28 March 1942	R5501
MATHISON, Sgt Norman Alan	15 September 1941	L7318
MATSUMOTO, F/Sgt Gerald	21 March 1945	PA196
MATTHEWS, F/O Hugh Vernon	13 March 1941	L7313
MATTHEWS, Sgt Jeffrey	5 July 1944	LM125
MATTOCKS, F/Sgt Bernard Charles	22 May 1944	ND522
MAVILLE, Sgt John Allan	22 June 1941	L7314
MAWSON, F/O Eric	17 July 1943	DV183
MAXTEAD, F/Sgt Charles Henry	20 February 1944	ME633
MELLISH, F/Sgt Richard Lewis RCAF	24 May 1942	R5617
MERCY, Sgt William Trevor	12 September 1944	PD267
MEYER, Sgt Reginald Charles	13 May 1943	W4938
MIDDLETON, F/O John Hartley RAAF	6 October 1944	ME667
MILLER, Sgt Aubrey Harris	6 January 1944	ED586
MILLER, F/O Herbert Victor	3 March 1945	NG204
MILLER, F/Sgt John	8 July 1944	ND866
MILLS, Sgt Derek Arthur	6 August 1944	PD209
MILLS, F/Lt George Arthur	6 May 1964	WZ363
MILLS, Sgt Peter	23 June 1943	ED692
MILLS, Sgt Stanley Harry	10 April 1944	ME688
MILLWARD, P/O Maxwell Benjamin	22 June1944	ME827
MILLWARD, Sgt Norman Robert	23 May 1944	LM540
MILNE, P/O John Joseph RCAF	12 September 1944	LM261
MILNE, F/O Robert Alexander	22 March 1944	ME666
MILNER, F/O Michael Nicholson	8 July 1944	ND866
MIREAULT, Sgt Joseph Francis RCAF	22 June 1944	ME683
MITCHELL, F/O Ivor	29 January 1944	LM366
MITCHELL, Sgt Robert Caven	17 July 1943	DV183
MITCHELL, Sgt Sydney James	28 August 1943	ED627
MOCKFORD, P/O Patrick Alfred Kingsley	29 April 1943	W4945
MOGER, Sgt William Henry	3 January 1943	W4134
MONTGOMERY, F/Lt George Henry	15 October 1944	LM208
MOORE, F/O Arthur	30 January 1944	ED758
MOORE, F/Lt James Gilhume	10 March 1944	ND513
MOORE, Sgt Thomas George	31 August 1943	W4120
MORAN, P/O Ted James RCAF	20 February 1944	ME633
MOREL, Sgt Ronald Henry	18 October 1943	W4276
MOREY, Sgt Jeffrey Thomas	20 February 1944	EE126
MORGAN, Sgt Frank	2 January 1944	W4892
MORRICE, Sgt George John	11 June 1943	ED537
MORRIS, F/O Gordon	5 March 1945	NG230
MORRIS, F/Sgt Ivor James	29 July 1944	ND872
MORRIS-EDWARDS, P/O Denis Victor	19 August 1942	R5863
MORRISH, Sgt John Anthony	14 January 1944	LM383
MORRISON, LAC John	2 March 1945	ME473
MORTIMORE, Sgt George	9 March 1943	W4172
MOULDEN, P/O Eric Henry	10 March 1944	ND513
MOULDING, F/Sgt Ernest	14 October 1941	L7321
MOXLEY, P/O Wilbur Lee RCAF	12 September 1944	LM261
MUIR, F/Lt James Findlay	27 April 1944	LM526
MURPHY, Sgt John Charles RAAF	19 August 1942	R5863
MURRAY, F/O Hugh McWilliam	10 June 1944	ME678
MUSITANO, F/Sgt Grahame Leveson	4 June 1942	R5847
MUSTO, Sgt Clifford William RAAF	11 August 1942	R5499
MYERS, P/O James Henry	23 May 1944	LM540
NEGUS, P/O Bruce Lindsay RAAF	18 October 1943	W4276
NEW, Sgt Norman Charles	10 March 1944	ND513
NEWBOULT, Sgt Ronald	23 September 1944	PD318
NICOLL, F/Lt David Andrew	8 December 1942	R5570
NIPPER, Sgt George Robert	13 May 1943	ED418
NOBLE, Sgt Richard	6 May 1964	WZ363
NORMAN, Sgt Francis Charles Talbot	23 March 1939	L4967
NORMAN, Sgt Robert John	5 July 1944	ND570
NOTTIDGE, P/O John Jephson	13 August 1941	L7377
NUGENT, Sgt James	11 November 1944	PB428
OAK, P/O Albert Alfred	21 February 1945	PB814
OBARD, Sgt Stanley	12 August 1942	R5760
O'BRIEN, Sgt William	17 July 1943	DV183

Name	Date	Serial
O'CONNOR, Sgt Cornelius	23 November 1943	W4959
O'CONNOR, Sgt Michael	21 April 1944	ND564
OGDEN, Sgt Sydney	13 May 1943	W4938
O'MAHONY, Sgt Joseph Clement	2 January 1944	DV370
O'NEILL, Sgt George Clark	22 December 1943	DV361
ORR, Sgt William	24 March 1944	ME680
O'SHEA, Sgt Francis Crohane Joseph	21 February 1945	PB814
OSMER, P/O George William	23 August 1943	ED550
OVERGAAUW, F/Lt Geert Adrianus Cornelis	15 August 1944	LM263
OWEN, Sgt Anthony Guy	15 February 1944	ND510
PAINE, Sgt Kenneth	19 July 1944	ME681
PALMER, Sgt Edward William	8 July 1944	ND866
PANKHURST, Sgt Charles Arthur	24 May 1942	R5617
PARKER, Sgt Harold Colin	20 February 1944	ME633
PARKYN, P/O Alfred Joseph RCAF	25 November 1942	R5695
PASKELL, P/O Lionel Arthur	14 October 1941	L7373
PASSY, Sgt Ian Harry Deare	13 October 1941	L7312
PATERSON, Sgt Andrew Picken	24 May 1942	R5617
PATTERSON, Sgt George Eric	6 January 1945	NE168
PATTISON, Sgt Cecil Vivian	5 September 1942	R5755
PAYNE, P/O Gordon Arthur	6 October 1944	ME667
PAYNE, F/Sgt Leslie Frank	16 October 1944	NG143
PAYTON, Sgt Stanley	23 June 1943	ED692
PEARCEY, P/O Robert George	16 August 1943	ED498
PECK, F/Sgt Charles Woodrow Wilson RCAF	7 November 1942	L7546
PEEL, F/Sgt Edwin	29 July 1944	ND872
PEREZ, F/O Miguel Louis RAAF	6 January 1945	NE168
PERRIN, F/Sgt Arthur John	7 November 1942	L7546
PETERS, F/Sgt Kenneth George	2 March 1943	ED533
PETTY, Sgt Norman Farrar	2 December 1943	ED610
PHELAN, F/O Terrence Benedict RCAF	21 February 1945	PB814
PHILLIPS, F/Sgt Gordon James RCAF	3 March 1945	NG204
PIERCE, Sgt John Dawson Holland	22 June 1944	DV360
PIKE, S/Ldr Dudley George Hart	10 March 1944	ND513
PIPER, Sgt Ernest Raymond Donald	25 November 1942	R5694
PLOWMAN, P/O Arthur Leslie RAAF	11 November 1944	PB428
POINTON, F/O Charles Ellis	30 January 1944	DV371
POLLEY, P/O Gordon Frederick	24 March 1944	ME680
PORTEUS, Sgt Francis William	2 January 1944	DV370
PORTER, F/Lt Robert King	5 July 1942	-
POTTER, F/Sgt Dennis Kilverton	24 October 1942	W4121
PRATT, Sgt Cyril Herbert	28 August 1943	ED627
PRESTON, Sgt Eric Alfred Richard	31 August 1943	W4120
PRESTON, Sgt Jack	13 August 1942	R5633
PRESTON, Sgt Stephen	28 August 1943	ED627
PRINCE, F/O Stanley Frank	17 July 1929	K1758
PUGH, Sgt Kenneth Henry	3 January 1943	W4134
PULMAN, Sgt Arthur	30 January 1944	EE173
QUEEN, Sgt Harold Allen RCAF	31 August 1943	W4120
QUINLAN, F/O Denis John RCAF	17 August 1942	R5616
RACINE, Sgt Cedric	13 August 1942	R5633
RANDLE, AC1 John Thomas Samuel	23 March 1939	L4967
RATTRAY, Sgt Stanley Herbert	14 January 1944	LM383
RAWSON, Sgt Donald William	5 July 1944	ND570
RAY, P/O Howard Stanley RCAF	21 October 1941	L7487
READ, P/O Jack Montague	21 January 1944	R5895
READ, F/Sgt John Thornton	6 April 1944	ME685
READY, F/O Denis William	16 October 1944	NG143
REAY, F/Lt Derek Edward	23 November 1943	W4959
REDGRAVE, Sgt Henry Cecil	13 March 1941	L7313
REEMAN, P/O Edward Arthur	13 August 1941	L7381
REES, W/O Kenneth Royston	29 April 1943	W4945
REID, F/Sgt Donald Alan RAAF	6 December 1944	PD322
REID, Sgt William Martin Ewing	23 August 1943	ED550
REYNOLDS, Sgt Leslie Thomas	28 August 1943	LM334
REYNOLDS, F/O William Cassin RCAF	25 May 1943	W5001
RICHARDS, F/Sgt David Stanley	12 September 1944	PD267
RICHARDSON, Sgt Arthur William	29 June 1943	ED569
RICHARDSON, Sgt John	23 November 1943	DV369
RICHARDSON, Sgt Raymond	2 March 1945	ME473
RIDDLE, P/O Bertram Challis RNZAF	31 March 1944	LM436
RIDING, LAC John Frederick	15 September 1941	L7318
ROBERTS, Sgt Albert	25 November 1942	R5694
ROBERTS, F/Sgt George Henry	14 October 1941	L7373
ROBERTS, Sgt Kenneth	29 July 1944	ND872
ROBERTS, F/O Leone Joseph RCAF	22 October 1943	EE175
ROBERTS, F/Sgt Sydney Douglas Gowshall	24 October 1942	W4121
ROBERTSON, F/O Donald Kerr	7 November 1939	K9238
ROBINSON, Sgt Robert Calderwood	21 April 1944	ND564
ROBSON, Sgt Robert	17 August 1942	R5616
RODDAM, Sgt Arthur	16 August 1942	R5509
ROGERS, Sgt Sam Paul	20 February 1944	EE126
ROLLS, P/O Philip Charles	13 December 1938	K7585
ROPER, Sgt Albert Derrick	5 July 1944	LM125
ROSE, F/Sgt William James	7 November 1942	L7546
ROSS, P/O Donald Wingrove RCAF	10 September 1942	R5628
ROTHERA, Sgt John Patrick	29 January 1944	LM366
ROULLIER, LAC Edward Thomas	10 April 1944	-
ROURKE, AC2 Edward	10 April 1944	-
ROUTLEDGE, Sgt Frank	11 July 1942	L7543
ROWLAND, F/Sgt Arthur	24 July 1942	R5867
ROWLANDS, F/O Richard Gerald RAAF	5 September 1942	R5755
RUCK-KEENE, P/O John Charles Lancelot	21 October 1941	L7487
RUSHBY, Sgt Alfred Sugden	2 December 1943	ED601
RUSHWORTH, Sgt James Donald	16 November 1944	NF979
RUSSELL, F/O Philip Campion Digby RCAF	29 June 1943	ED569
RUSSELL, Sgt Philip Charles Maurice	16 November 1944	NF979
RYALL, F/Sgt Cecil Ernest RAAF	22 December 1943	DV361
RYE, F/Sgt George RCAF	11 November 1944	PB428
SAMUELS, Sgt John Joseph	3 March 1945	NG204
SANDERS, Sgt John	25 November 1942	R5694
SANSOM, Sgt Kenneth Walter	22 June 1944	LM578
SAVAGE, P/O Maurice	26 August 1944	PD216
SAVILLE, Sgt Kenneth	22 September 1943	ED442
SAWYER, P/O John Patrick Anthony RCAF	15 September 1941	L7318
SAYCE, F/Sgt Stanley Walter	6 April 1944	ME685
SAYERS, Sgt Albert Laurie	8 July 1944	LM218
SCOTT, P/O Hugh MacKenzie	2 January 1944	W4892
SCOTT, F/Sgt Ronald Parson	22 June 1944	ME827
SCRAGG, Sgt Denis	29 June 1943	ED569
SEDDON, Sgt James	28 August 1943	LM334
SEDDON, Sgt Richard Gerard	8 July 1944	LM129
SENIOR, W/O John Raymond	6 April 1944	ME685
SEXTON, F/O Murray Kerr RCAF	25 February 1943	ED356
SEYMOUR, Sgt William Rex	9 January 1942	L7322
SHANNON, F/Sgt George Ross	25 July 1944	PB294
SHAPTER, W/O William James Aubrey RCAF	6 August 1942	R5761
SHARP, F/Sgt Edward	4 December 1944	PB765
SHARP, F/O Robert Walter	21 January 1944	R5895
SHATWELL, Sgt Arthur	29 October 1944	LM271
SHAW, F/Sgt Henry Archibald	22 June 1944	LM578
SHAW, F/Sgt John	22 June 1944	LL973
SHAW, F/Sgt Joseph Pickett	22 June 1944	DV360
SHAW, Sgt William	19 July 1944	ME814
SHELLEY, Sgt William Oliver	2 March 1943	ED533
SHEPHERD, Sgt Caleb Stanley Kenneth	6 August 1942	L7385
SHEPHERD, P/O Guy Cecil	23 March 1939	L4967
SHEPHERD, Sgt John Graham	6 January 1945	NE168
SHERGOLD, Sgt Frederick Cyril	22 September 1943	ED442
SHERMAN, W/O Murray RCAF	22 June 1944	ME827
SHIMEILD, Sgt Eric Henry	18 November 1943	DV361
SHIRLEY, P/O Kenneth James	11 July 1942	L7543
SIDEBOTHAM, F/Sgt Fred Thomas Murray	6 January 1944	ED586
SIEBERT, F/Lt John Aloysius	28 March 1941	L7303
SIEVE, F/Sgt Leonard	14 January 1942	L7523
SIMM, P/O Stephen RCAF	26 August 1944	PD216
SIMMONS, F/Sgt Alfred John	6 January 1944	ED586
SIMPSON, F/Sgt Robert Neil	23 May 1944	LM540
SIMPSON, P/O William Egbert RCAF	14 October 1941	L7321
SKELTON, Sgt Thomas Henry	13 May 1943	W4938
SKUCE, P/O Peter Grahame	10 June 1944	ME678
SLATER, Sgt Jack	25 November 1942	R5695
SMART, F/O Trevor Tressler	22 June 1944	LM578
SMETHURST, Sgt Norman Frederick	10 September 1942	R5628
SMITH, Sgt Arthur Edward	2 October 1943	DV184
SMITH, Sgt Arthur William	25 July 1944	PB294
SMITH, Sgt Bernard Murray	19 August 1942	R5863
SMITH, Sgt Donald	24 March 1944	ME680
SMITH, Sgt Francis Bertram	19 July 1944	ME814
SMITH, Sgt Henry George	29 October 1944	LM271
SMITH, Sgt Joe	13 May 1943	ED418
SMITH, F/O John Duncan	21 March 1945	PA196
SMITH, Sgt John Edward Noble	21 April 1944	ND564
SMITH, F/Sgt Leonard Mervyn	24 May 1942	R5617
SMITH, F/Sgt Philip Newbould	8 July 1944	LM218
SMITH, F/O William Michael Ronald	13 August 1941	L7381
SMITH, Sgt William Robert	24 July 1942	R5632
SMURTHWAITE, Sgt Joseph	18 February 1943	ED330
SMYTH, F/Sgt Robert	12 September 1944	PD267
SOLLY, P/O Charles John	22 June 1944	LL973
SOLOMON, 1/Lt Frank B. N. USAAF	2 January 1944	W4892
SOMERS, F/O Bruce Allan RCAF	22 June 1944	ME683
SOUTHWELL, P/O Anthony Jeaffreson	17 August 1942	R5616
SPANNER, F/O Frederick Gordon Charles RCAF	3 September 1943	ED832
SPARKS, F/O William Angus	11 November 1944	PB428
SPEIR, F/O John Garfield RCAF	11 August 1942	R5499
SPENCE, Sgt James Arthur	12 July 1943	ED412

Name	Date	Serial
SPENCER, Sgt Stanley	16 August 1942	R5509
SPICER, Sgt Stanley Oswald	19 August 1942	R5863
SPINDLER, Sgt George Paul	13 October 1941	L7312
STAMP, F/O Charles Edward	8 July 1944	LM129
STANDISH, Sgt John Ward	23 August 1943	ED550
STAPLETON, Sgt Cyril	5 July 1944	LM125
STEAD, F/Sgt Frank Ronald	15 March 1945	LL902
STEEL, Sgt Adam Innes	13 August 1942	R5633
STERRETT, F/Sgt Joseph Roger Lawrence RCAF	21 January 1943	W4365
STEVENS, Sgt William Harry Read	6 November 1944	ND555
STEWART, P/O James Bruce RCAF	30 January 1944	DV371
STODDART, Sgt Thomas William Tremble	26 May 1943	W4919
STONE, F/Sgt Robert James RCAF	16 December 1943	EE141
STOREY Sgt Harold Arthur	11 July 1942	L7543
STRAIN F/Sgt Robert Peter RCAF	7 November 1942	L7546
STREET, F/Lt Denys Oliver	6 April 1944	W4931
STREET, F/Lt Harold Wilbert	21 April 1923	-
STRINGER, F/O Albert William	18 October 1943	W4276
STRINGER, F/Lt John Robert	6 May 1964	WZ363
STRINGER, Sgt Roy Alan	11 June 1943	ED537
STRONG, F/Sgt Thomas William	15 February 1943	L7547
STUART, Sgt Robert Surfleet	13 October 1941	L7312
STUBBS, P/O Leonard Emmerson	17 July 1943	DV183
SUMMERS, P/O Kenneth James	6 November 1944	ND555
SUPKOVITCH, Sgt Alfred	19 July 1944	PD210
SURRIDGE, Sgt John Arthur	10 June 1944	ME678
SUTHERLAND, F/Sgt Allan Cameron RCAF	8 July 1944	LM218
SUTHERLAND, F/Sgt Norman James RNZAF	16 August 1942	R5509
SUTTON, Sgt Alexander Robert	21 January 1943	W4365
SWANN, Sgt Ronald Ezra	14 January 1944	LM383
SWIHURA, F/Sgt Andrew Anthony RCAF	21 February 1945	PB295
SWINTON, F/O William Auld RCAF	15 August 1944	LM263
SYMONS, F/Lt John George	23 May 1944	ND871
TAKLE, Sgt Ernest John	16 December 1943	EE141
TAYLOR, Sgt David Donald RCAF	21 October 1941	L7487
TAYLOR, Sgt George Frederick	11 November 1926	J7610
TAYLOR, S/Ldr George Richard	13 August 1941	L7377
TAYLOR, Sgt Hugh Cowan	28 August 1942	W4129
TAYLOR, F/Sgt John	15 February 1944	ND510
TAYLOR, F/Lt John Gordon	29 January 1944	LM366
THOMAS, F/Sgt Frederick Edward	14 January 1942	L7523
THOMPSON, Sgt George Adam Nichols	30 January 1944	DV371
THOMPSON, Sgt Lewis Reginald	3 March 1943	ED365
THOMPSON, Sgt Peter John	25 November 1942	R5694
THOMPSON, F/Sgt Robert Findye	31 March 1944	ND568
THOMPSON, P/O Roderick John RCAF	24 March 1944	ME680
THORNE, Sgt Jack Wood	4 December 1944	LL968
THORNTON, P/O Jack Hardy RCAF	31 March 1944	ND568
THORPE, P/O Gordon Raston RCAF	31 March 1944	ND568
TIBBS, P/O Rowland	19 July 1944	PD210
TICKLE, F/O Frank Reginald RAAF	16 July 1944	ME807
TILLEN, Sgt Frank Ivan	15 February 1943	L7547
TOMPKINS, Sgt Edward Stanley	13 May 1943	ED418
TOOHILL, Sgt Noel Messines RAAF	9 January 1942	L73232
TOOMEY, Sgt Henry Albert	28 August 1943	ED627
TOPLIS, F/Sgt Jack Thomas	6 January 1944	ED586
TRANMER, F/O William Thomas RCAF	30 January 1944	ED758
TRAVERS, F/O Charles RCAF	21 January 1944	R5895
TRIMBLE, P/O Samuel John RAAF	6 October 1944	ME667
TUDDENHAM, Sgt Russell James Hammond	29 October 1944	LM271
TURNER, Sgt Donald Arthur	29 January 1944	LM366
TURNER, Sgt William Francis	4 December 1944	PB765
TYLER, Sgt George RCAF	29 April 1943	W4945
UNSWORTH, P/O Joseph	14 October 1941	L7321
UPSALL, Sgt Walter	27 April 1944	LM526
VANDERVOORT, W/O William John RCAF	25 November 1942	R5695
VEITCH, Sgt Stanley	22 June 1941	L7314
WADDINGTON, Sgt Kenneth	22 June 1944	ME827
WAKELING, F/O Albert Harry	6 March 1945	ME386
WALKER, Sgt James Roy	21 December 1942	W4191
WALKER, Sgt Maurice Robert	14 January 1942	L7523
WALKER, F/Sgt Thomas Jack	12 March 1943	L7583
WALLACE, W/O William Victor RCAF	3 March 1943	ED365
WALMSLEY, Sgt Arthur	29 October 1944	LM271
WALTER, Sgt Cyril David George	14 October 1941	L7373
WALTON, Sgt Geoffrey Alan	14 January 1944	LM383
WARDLE, Sgt Kethi Harry Hackney	2 January 1944	DV370
WARREN, Sgt Richard Hall	9 March 1943	W4172
WATERMAN, F/Lt Thomas John Davies RCAF	3 September 1943	ED832

Name	Date	Serial
WATHEY, W/O Colin	4 June 1942	R5847
WATKINS, Sgt Cyril Harry	14 March 1945	NG399
WATKINS Sgt Victor Henry John	29 June 1943	ED569
WATSON, Ldg Mech Richard Henry	26 April 1917	3115
WATT, P/O Alick RCAF	15 August 1944	LM263
WATT, P/O Peter Sydney RNZAF	2 January 1944	W4892
WATTS, Sgt Ernest Leslie	22 May 1944	ND522
WATTS, F/Sgt Raymond Oswell RAAF	27 April 1944	ME631
WAYCOTT, W/O William John RAAF	6 April 1944	ME685
WEBB, Sgt Windsor Francis Richard	25 November 1942	R5695
WEBSTER, Sgt John Walter	2 March 1943	ED533
WEEKES, F/O Norman Lennox	19 July 1944	ME681
WELCH, F/O John Richard RAAF	28 August 1943	LM334
WELCH, Sgt Roy Desmond	13 March 1941	L7313
WELLES, F/Lt Francis Christopher	6 May 1964	WZ363
WENSLEY, Sgt Douglas	19 July 1944	ME814
WERNER, F/Lt Roland Leslie RNZAF	22 March 1945	ME522
WESCOMBE, F/Sgt Basil Courtney	14 January 1942	L7523
WEST, F/Sgt Arnold	22 March 1945	ME522
WEST, Sgt Harold John	18 February 1943	ED330
WEST, F/Sgt Henry George	5 July 1944	LM125
WESTBURY, Sgt Claude Raymond	14 January 1942	L7523
WESTMORELAND, Sgt Thomas Fowler	29 January 1944	LM366
WHEELER, F/O George Howard RCAF	25 February 1943	ED356
WHEELER, P/O Reginald Augustus	10 March 1944	ND513
WHEELER, W/Cdr Vashon James	22 March 1944	ME666
WHETTON, Sgt Arthur Herbert	28 August 1943	LM334
WHITAKER, Sgt Denis Edward	9 April 1943	ED554
WHITE, Sgt Alfred William	25 May 1943	W5001
WHITE, Sgt Edward	15 February 1944	ND510
WHITE, Sgt James Stanley	16 August 1943	ED498
WHITE, Sgt Kenneth	15 February 1943	L7547
WHITEHEAD, F/Sgt Arthur John Charles	3 September 1943	ED832
WHITEHEAD, F/Sgt Colin	29 October 1944	LM271
WHITEHEAD, F/Sgt Samuel Lee Roy RCAF	13 May 1943	W4938
WHITEHEAD, F/O William Anderson RCAF	15 October 1944	LM208
WHITEHOUSE, F/O Gordon	3 December 1954	WH906
WHITEHOUSE, Sgt William Leslie	9 April 1943	ED554
WHITEOAK, Sgt Arthur Wilson	13 May 1943	ED418
WHITING, Sgt Donald Henry	13 August 1942	R5633
WHITNEY, F/Sgt William John RCAF	22 October 1943	EE175
WHYTE, Sgt James Logan	18 February 1943	ED330
WICKENS, P/O Thomas Roy	6 November 1944	ND555
WILCOCKSON, Sgt Robert William	16 August 1943	ED498
WILDSMITH, Sgt Percy Arthur	15 August 1944	LM263
WILKINSON, Sgt George	2 March 1945	ME473
WILLES, P/O Sidney Hulbert	4 May 1944	ND575
WILLIAMS, F/Sgt Alfred John Charles	23 November 1943	W5959
WILLIAMS, Sgt Gwilym	24 March 1944	ME680
WILLIAMS, W/O Percy Gordon RCAF	25 February 1943	ED356
WILLIAMS, Thomas Ross	28 November 1939	L8479
WILLIAMSON, P/O Albert John RCAF	19 July 1944	ME814
WILSON, P/O Erwin Curtis RCAF	16 October 1944	NG143
WILSON, Sgt Henry	6 April 1944	ME685
WILSON, F/Sgt James	18 December 1944	NG144
WILSON, Sgt John	30 January 1944	ED758
WILSON, P/O John Horsburgh	5 July 1944	LM125
WILSON, P/O Ronald Sydney	7 November 1942	L7546
WINNING, Sgt Hector	21 February 1945	PB814
WINTER, LAC Harold Francis	15 September 1941	L7318
WITHERS, F/O John Douglas George	22 June 1941	L7314
WITNEY, Sgt George Henry	22 March 1944	ME666
WOOD, W/O Albert Ernest RAAF	5 March 1945	NG230
WOOD, Sgt Denis	30 January 1944	ED758
WOOD, Sgt Derek Anson	28 March 1942	R5501
WOOD, F/Sgt Ivor	9 March 1943	W4172
WOOD, Sgt Norman Leslie	5 July 1944	ND570
WOOD, F/O Peter Guy Campbell	31 August 1941	L7316
WOOD, Sgt Robert	12 July 1943	ED412
WOOD, Sgt Victor Jack	21 January 1943	W4365
WOOD, Sgt Walter Page Laing	13 August 1942	R5633
WOODHOUSE, F/Sgt Roland Reuben	2 October 1943	DV184
WOODHOUSE, Sgt Walter George	24 October 1942	W4121
WOODWARD, Sgt Bertie	19 July 1944	ME814
WOOLLARD, P/O Barrington St.John	16 July 1944	ME807
WOOLLEY, Sgt Arthur Frederick	6 April 1944	ME685
WORTHINGTON, Sgt Denis Leonard	24 July 1942	R5867
WRIGHT, Sgt Arthur Charles	12 July 1943	ED412
WRIGHT, Sgt George Ernest	26 February 1944	W4815
WRIGHT, F/Sgt Lawrence Ritelli	24 October 1942	W4121
WRIGHT, AC1 Thomas	10 April 1944	-
WRIGHT, F/Sgt Thomas Leslie	16 November 1944	NF979
WYPER, Sgt John	4 December 1944	LL968
YEATMAN, AM2 Percy Maurice	26 August 1917	3137
YOUNG, F/O James Lawson	3 September 1943	ED832

Part 2: those members of 7 and 7A (Naval) Squadrons and 207 Squadron who were taken Prisoner of War

Name	Date	Serial
ALLEN, Sgt Geoffrey Ernest RNZAF	15 January 1942	L7309
ALLEN, F/Lt Ralph James	6 December 1943	EE141
ANDREWS, FSL Geoffrey	27 October 1917	3122
ASKEW, Sgt Maurice	20 February 1944	EE126
AUSTIN, F/Sgt Rex Allan RAAF	23 May 1944	LL776
BAKER, Sgt George	8 July 1944	ND567
BALL, W/.O Ernest Gordon	17 August 1941	L7311
BANFIELD Sgt John Kenneth	3 January 1943	W4134
BARHAM, Sgt Leonard Philip	8 July 1944	ME805
BARKER, Capt Edward Richard	11 April 1918	3119
BARNES, Sgt Lawrence James	30 January 1944	EE173
BARNETT, Sgt Arthur Robert	16 September 1942	L7571
BARRE, F/Sgt Robert Frederick RCAF	14 January 1944	DV191
BARRON, Sgt Christopher Norman	3 May 1941	L7379
BATESON, Sgt George William	23 May 1944	LM540
BAYLISS, Lt William Murray Forbes	19 July 1918	C9665
BESTEL, Sgt Emmanuel G Robert RCAF	14 January 1942	L7309
BETTS, Sgt Ivan Frederick	16 September 1942	L7571
BLAKE, Sgt William Leslie	30 March 1943	W4931
BLAKEMAN, F/O George	16 August 1943	ED498
BOON, Sgt John	28 August 1942	W4129
BOOTH, FSL Harold Harman	26 August 1917	3137
BOSWELL, F/Sgt Douglas Hugh	28 August 1942	W4129
BOWSKILL, F/Sgt Thomas RCAF	14 January 1944	LM383
BRINDLE, F/Sgt oseph Alfred	16 December 1943	EE141
BROWN, Sgt Kenneth Walter Charles	30 January 1944	EE173
BUCK, W/O William	8 April 1941	L7302
BUDDEN, W/O Douglas Alfred	8 April 1941	L7302
BURL, F/Sgt Edward William	24 December 1943	DV188
BURNET, P/O Richardson	30 January 1944	EE173
BURNEY, P/O Charles Douglas Ernest	18 February 1943	ED330
BURTON, Sgt Arthur Reginald	18 October, 1943	LM326
CANNING, AM1 Stanley Alfred	26 August 1917	3137
CARMICHAEL, P/O John Archibald RCAF	27 April 1944	ME631
CHAPMAN, Sgt Charles Edward	22 June 1944	LL973
CHEESMAN, F/Sgt Jack Alfred	13 October 1941	L7312
CHINERY, Sgt Walter	23 May 1944	LL776
CHINN, Sgt Albert John	8 July 1944	ME805
COLWILL Sgt Ernest	14 January 1944	DV369
CONNORS, Sgt Brian	14 January 1944	DV191
CRANSTON, F/O Jack Edward	14 March 1945	NG399
CROXTON, Sgt Leo Arthur	29 January 1944	LM366
CURRIE, Sgt John Richard	17 August 1941	L7311
DANZEY, AM2 William Charles (died in captivity 6 December 1917)	26 April 1917	3115
DAWKINS, P/O Gerald Brian	14 January 1942	L7309
DIXON, Sgt Clarence Stewart	15 October 1944	LM123
DOWNEY, F/Sgt Eric William Devere	30 January 1944	DV371
DUDLEY, Sgt Cyril	30 March 1943	W4931
DUFF, Sgt Donald John	18 October 1943	LM326
DUNCAN, W/O Alexander Stuart	3 May 1941	L7379
DUNN, Sgt Eric Floyd	4 December 1944	PB765
DUNSEATH, F/Sgt Joseph	22 March 1944	ME666
EATON, F/O John Gill RAAF	8 February 1945	NN724
EDWARDS, F/O George Grant	22 March 1944	ME666
EDWARDS, P/O Patrick James	14 January 1942	L7309
EKE, F/Sgt Ernest Henry	28 July 1943	W4962
ELD, Sgt Gerald Valentine	30 March 1943	W4931
EXLEY, Sgt Henry Tennyson	27 April 1944	ME631
FISHER, F/Sgt John Eric	8 July 1944	LM129
FLEAR, Sgt Cecil	15 October 1944	LM123
FLETCHER, P/O Arthur Stanley	14 March 1945	NG399
FOMISON, Sgt George Thomas John	28 March 1941	L7303
FOWLER, F/O Leo John RAAF	8 February 1945	NN724
FRASER, P/O John Henderson RCAF	14 January 1944	DV369
GIBB, Sgt George Murray	30 January 1944	EE173
GILDERTHORP, P/O Thomas Robert RAAF	31 August 1941	L7316
GILLETT, F/O Francis Sidney RNZAF	23 May 1944	ND871
GLADDERS, Sgt Thomas Henry	24 December 1943	DV188
GRIFFIN, F/Sgt William Allan RAAF	27 April 1944	ME631
GURNELL, Sgt Peter	28 March 1941	L7303
HAHN, F/O Lloyd George RCAF	18 December 1944	LM671
HALL, Sgt Charles Frank	8 September 1941	L7380
HANNABY, F/Sgt Terence	14 March 1945	NG399
HART, Sgt William	17 August 1941	L7311
HAWKINS, Sgt Raymond Roland	30 January 1944	EE173
HEDGES, Sgt Leslie William	8 April 1941	L7302
HERRON, F/Sgt John David Monroe RAAF	16 September 1942	L7571
HILL, F/O Roy Ernest	4 December 1944	PB765
HOLMES, Sgt John Alexander	22 February 1945	PB814
HOLMEWOOD, F/O Norman Frederick John	23 May 1944	LL776
HOOD-MORRIS, Sgt Robertson Edwin Henry	26 May 1943	W5001
HORNFECK, Sgt Peter Wilfred	6 December 1944	PD322
HOWSE, Albert Arthur Vincent	14 March 1945	NG399
HUDSON, Lt Frederick Herbert	11 April 1918	3119
HUGHES, P/O George Douglas RCAF	28 August 1942	W4129
HYDE, W/Cdr Noel Challis	9 April 1941	L7302
INGANNI, W/O Lewis Lundi	27 April 1944	ME631
INGLIS, Sgt Edward Ross RCAF	5 July 1944	ND570
JARVIS, P/O Walter Dowse	20 February 1944	EE126
JEFFRIES, Sgt Alfred	14 January1944	DV191
JONES, S/Ldr lbert Norman	27 April 1944	ME631
KEARTLAND, P/O Hugh Gerald	17 August 1941	L7311
KEHOE, Sgt Patrick Bishop	14 March 1945	NG399
KEMP, Lt Fred	19 July 1918	C9665
KENT, LM G.A.	27 October 1917	3122
KINGSTON, |gt Douglas	8 September 1941	L7380
KINMOND, 2/Lt David Crichton	11 April 1918	3119
LEE, Sgt Edward Arthur Christopher	3 May 1941	L7379
LEVICK, Sgt Norman Sidney	8 February 1945	NN724
LEWIS, Sgt Derrick	15 October 1944	LM123
LEWIS, F/Lt Wilfred John	8 September 1941	L7380
LISHMAN, Sgt William Garvey RCAF	10 March 1943	W4172
LOAKES, Sgt Peter Gordon	22 June 1944	LL973
McCARTHY, Sgt Thomas Joseph	22 March 1944	ME666
McCARTHY, F/Sgt Walter Joseph RAAF	18 October 1943	LM326
McDOUGAL, Sgt William John Jewell	28 March 1941	L7303
McGREGOR, Sgt Walter Muir	3 May 1941	L7379
McLEAN, Sgt John Scott	18 October 1943	W4276
McLEOD, Sgt Alexander Gordon	18 October 1943	LM326
McLEOD, Sgt Ronald Bruce RCAF	8 September 1941	L7380
McPHERSON, Sgt Alexander James	8 July 1944	ND866
MARSHALL, Sgt Cecil John	31 August 1941	L7422
MARWOOD, Sgt Gordon Kerr	3 January 1943	W4134
MASSEY-SHAW, Sgt Robert Alexander	6 December 1944	PD322
MERCER, F/Sgt John	14 January 1942	L7309
MILLER, F/Sgt Erle Sinclair RCAF	8 September 1941	L7380
MORGAN, F/O Hugh Travers	9 April 1941	L7302
MORRIS, Sgt Eric	17 July 1943	DV183
MOULTON-BARRETT, P/O Gordon Edward	24 December 1943	DV188
MOUNTNEY, Sgt George Frederick	16 September 1942	L7571
NICHOLSON, Sgt James Duncan	16 September 1942	L7571
NUTT, Sgt Bernard Howard	30 March 1943	W4931
OTTEWELL, Sgt Kenneth Alfred William	6 January 1945	NE168
PADDOCK, Sgt Philip Lovelace	20 February 1944	EE126
PANTON, Sgt Samuel Edward	3 May 1941	L7379
PARKER, Sgt Leonard Charles	31 August 1941	L7316
PARSELLE, W/Cdr Thomas Alfred Boyd	26 May 1943	W5001
PEARSON, F/Sgt Sydney Taylor	20 February 1944	EE126
PEEK, Sgt Edward Charles	18 December 1944	LM671
PEPPALL, Sgt Derek John	16 December 1943	EE141
PETTIE, Sgt Harry	28 July 1943	W4962
PHELPS, Sgt Edward Keith	8 July 1944	LM129
PINCHBECK, F/O Derek Edgar	3 May 1941	L7379
POCKNALL, Sgt Sidney George	14 January 1944	DV191
POTTER, F/Sgt John Francis	14 January 1944	DV369
POWELL, Sgt Cottrell Samuel Frederick	8 September 1941	L7380
RAWLINSON, Sgt Bramwell Allenby	30 March 1943	W4931
READ, Sgt Gordon	30 January 1944	EE173
READ, Sgt Jack	17 August 1942	R5616
RICHARDSON, F/Sgt Edward Evelyn Liston	14 January 1944	DV369
ROBERTS, F/O Louis	24 December 1943	DV188
ROBINSON, F/Sgt Ian William RAAF	24 December 1943	DV188
ROBSON, Sgt Peter Charles	28 March 1941	L7303
ROSE, Lt Godfrey	19 July 1918	C9665
ROSS, Sgt Alexander	17 August 1941	L7311
SCOTT, Sgt Herbert Kenneth RCAF	31 August 1943	W4120
SEIBEL, P/O Albert Alexander RCAF	27 April 1944	ME631
SHERLOCK, F/Sgt Joseph	24 December 1943	DV188
SIMPSON, Sgt Maurice Joseph RCAF	22 May 1944	ND522
SMART, F/Sgt Lyle Carman RCAF	14 January 1944	DV369
SMITH, Sgt Arthur Douglas	14 October 1941	L7373
SMITH, Sgt Cecil Rayle RCAF	18 October 1943	LM326
SPENCE, F/Sgt John William RCAF	22 February 1945	PB295
STACEY, F/Sgt Ronald Elwood RCAF	23 May 1944	LL776
STEPHENSON, P/O Eric Hay	16 December 1943	EE141
STONER, Sgt Bernard William	12 September 1944	PD267
STREET, F/Lt Denys Oliver (shot while attempting to escape 6 April 1944)	30 March 1943	W4931

Name	Date	Serial
STROWGER, Sgt Raymond Allen	16 September 1942	L7571
TAYLOR, F/Sgt Geoffrey RAAF	18 October 1943	LM326
TAYLOR, Sgt Herbert	14 January 1944	DV369
TAYLOR, Sgt James Arthur	28 March 1941	L7302
TAYLOR, Sgt James Earl RCAF	30 March 1943	W4931
TAYLOR, Sgt John Foster	6 December 1944	PD322
TICE, Sgt Reginald George Robert	23 May 1944	LL776
TWEDDLE, Sgt Albert	18 December 1944	LM671
VOWLES, Sgt William John	16 December 1943	EE141
WALKER, Sgt Julian George Seymour	23 August 1943	ED550
WALL, P/O George Lawlor RAAF	4 December 1944	PB765
WALSHE, F/O Paul Evan	22 May 1944	ND522
WAPPET, F/Sgt Alexander	17 August 1941	L7311
WARD, Sgt Kenneth Anthony	8 July 1944	LM129
WEBB, Sgt Robert Herbert	18 December 1944	LM671
WELLS, Sgt John	9 April 1941	L7302
WESLEY, Sgt Laurie	4 May 1944	ND556
WETHERILL, F/Sgt William	13 August 1941	L7377
WHITE, F/Lt John Duncan	18 December 1944	LM671
WILLIAMS, Sgt Gabriel Cochrane	17 September 1942	L7571
WILLIS, Sgt Stanley Thomas	14 January 1944	DV191
WINTON, P/O Ronald Sidney	18 December 1944	LM671
WORTHINGTON, Sgt William	18 October 1943	LM326
WULFF, P/O William Henry RAAF	4 December 1944	PB765
WYKES, F/Sgt Aubrey Edward	18 December 1944	LM671
YEO, Sgt Edwin Victor	14 January 1944	DV369
YOUNG, W/O Alfred	22 June 1944	ME827

Part 3: those members of 207 Squadron who were able to avoid capture and return to the United Kingdom

Name	Date	Serial
AITKEN, F/Sgt Leonard	19 July 1944	ME814
ALDERTON, F/O Michael	8 July 1944	ME805
BARTON, Sgt Arthur Edward John	22 June 1944	LL973
BROWN, Sgt Richard	10 March 1943	W4172
BROWN, Sgt William Raymond	8 July 1944	ND567
BROWNHILL, Sgt Gordon Isaiah	10 March 1943	W4172
CARROLL, P/O Howard Bertram	14 October 1941	L7321
CHAPPLE, Sgt John Kenneth	19 July 1944	PD210
CHASTER, F/Sgt James Barry RCAF	3 January 1943	W4134
CHEESMAN, F/Sgt Wesley George	8 February 1945	NN724
CLOWES, F/O William Alsopp	8 July 1944	ME805
COLLINS, Sgt Cecil Victor	11 April 1945	ME472
COPLEY, Sgt Eric Harry	8 February 1945	NN724
COX, Sgt Gilbert Thomas	14 October 1941	L7321
EMENY, Sgt Ronald Thomas	4 May 1944	ND566
EYRE, F/Sgt Stanley Herbert	15 February 1943	L7547
FAGAN, Sgt Alfred Frederick James	8 July 1944	ME805
GILBY, F/O Arthur Eric James	8 July 1944	LM129
HANSON, F/Sgt Stanley Edward	8 February 1945	NN724
HASLAM, Sgt Frank Raymond	22 June 1944	LL973
HAY, Sgt Ernest Arthur Gilbert	8 July 1944	ME805
HEWETT, F/O Cyril Malcolm	11 April 1945	ME472
HOUGHTON, F/Sgt Kenneth Hugh Leslie	14 October 1941	L7373
HUNTLEY, W/O Charles Otto	22 February 1945	PB295
KING, Sgt Philip Norman	4 May 1944	ND556
LARCOMBE, F/O Kenneth Arthur	11 April 1945	ME472
McSWEENEY, P/O Kevin Winston	23 May 1944	LL776
MATTHEWS, Sgt Eric James	11 April 1945	ME472
METCALFE, Sgt Austin England Benet	8 July 1944	ME805
MOSS, St Harry William	21 April 1944	ND564
NICHOL, F/Sgt Alan	8 July 1944	LM218
NICHOL, Sgt Edward	11 April 1945	ME472
PARKINSON, Sgt John Robert	8 July 1944	LM218
PEARL, Sgt John Raymond	11 April 1945	ME472
PITTWOOD, F/Sgt John	4 May 1945	ND556
STOCKFORD, Sgt Nicholas John	4 May 1944	ND556
WHYTE, F/Sgt John Henry Francis RNZAF	14 February 1943	L7547
YOUNG, F/O Ronald William	8 February 1945	NN724

OTHER R.A.F. SQUADRON AND UNITS BOOKS STILL IN PRINT

UNITED IN EFFORT - THE HISTORY OF No.53 SQUADRON
by Jock Manson

Beginning life as a Corps Reconnaissance unit, spotting for the artillery on the Western Front with BE2cs and RE8s, it disbanded at the end of WWI, then reformed in 1937 as an army co-op squadron with Hectors. Re-equipped with Blenheims for strategic reconnaissance, it flew these over France and Germany before transferring to Coastal Command on Hudsons. The only RAF squadron to operate, early in 1942, from the United States and in the Caribbean against U-boats causing havoc along the eastern US seaboard in the absence of any effective anti-submarine aircraft until its arrival. Returning home, it flew Whitleys briefly before receiving Liberators which it operated for the rest of the war from the UK and Iceland on long-range anti-submarine patrols over the North Atlantic. Post-war it became a transport squadron, flying Dakotas, Hastings, Beverleys and finally Belfasts, being the only squadron to use this type. Compiled by the Squadron Association's historian, appendices include a complete Roll of Honour, lists of aircraft used, decorations awarded and details of COs and movements. HARDBACK A4. 144-page. 200 photographs.

SCORPIONS STING - THE HISTORY OF 84 SQUADRON
by Don Neate

A microcosm of the RAF overseas from 1917 to date, beginning with SE5As in France, then DH9As in Iraq and Blenheims in Greece. It next went to Sumatra and India (Vultee Vengeance), before moving to Malaya with Beaufighters and Brigands, the Middle East with Valettas, Beverleys and Andovers and then Cyprus with Wessexes. Hard cover A4. 160pages. 160 photographs.

THE HORNET STRIKES - HISTORY OF NO.213 SQUADRON
by Frank M Leeson

No.213 Squadron started life as the Seaplane Defence Flight on the coast of Flanders and progressed to Pups and Camels for the rest of the Great War. Reformed in March 1937, it again became a single-seat fighter squadron and retained this role throughout the Second World War and in the post-war years.First equipped with Gauntlets, it replaced these with Hurricanes which it flew in France, during the Battle of Britain, with the Desert Air Force in Cyprus, Egypt and Libya, re-equipping with Spitfires and then Mustangs, and flying in Italy until the end of the war. As part of the Middle East Air Force, it received first Tempests and then Vampires before being disbanded in September 1954. Its final reincarnation was as a Canberra-equipped interdiction unit in Germany until disbanded in December 1969. Written by one of the pilots of the Squadron, this is a detailed account of the life and times of a fighter squadron and is copiously illustrated. Hard cover A4. 224 pages, 221 photographs and maps.

RISE FROM THE EAST - THE STORY OF No.247 (CHINA-BRITISH) SQUADRON
by David John Marchant

On its original disbandment in January 1919, after less that one year as a flying boat unit based at Felixstowe, No.247 Squadron was not reformed until early in the Second World War, to become the only RAF squadron to fly Gloster Gladiator biplanes in the Battle of Britain. Starting its new life as a Fighter Flight of No.152 Squadron based at Sumburgh in the Shetland Isles, it moved south to Roborough when the new No.10 (Fighter) Group formed for the protection of Plymouth, the south west ports, naval dockyards and Channel convoys. It was at this time that the flight became No.247 (Fighter) Squadron. The air war in this region was conducted mainly during the hours of darkness, and even when re-equipped with Hawker Hurricanes victories were few. After the Blitz the squadron took on a more offensive role and in 1943 converted to Hawker Typhoons to become part of No.83 Group, the spearhead of the Normandy invasion, and transferred to the 2nd Tactical Air Force. Heavily involved in the drive across Europe, No.247 had a ground attack and army support role. After the European war the squadron returned to the United Kingdom and was re-equipped with Hawker Tempest IIs in preparation for intended service in the Far East but, with the surrender of Japan, No.247 remained with Fighter Command to become the first operational squadron to be equipped with de Havilland Vampire jet aircraft Gloster Meteors and Hawker Hunters later saw service with No.247, which was based at Odiham from 1946, but in a round of defence cuts a change in defence strategy saw the squadron disbanded for the second time late in 1957. Reformed in Yorkshire in 1960 as a Bloodhound ground-to-air missile unit, it finally ceased to exist at the end of 1963. Hard cover A4. 176 pages. 168 photographs.

ROYAL AIR FORCE FLYING TRAINING AND SUPPORT UNITS
by Ray Sturtivant, John Hamlin and James J.Halley

The first complete listing of flying training and support units of the RAF and its predecessor the RFC from 1912 to the present day. Coverage of such units as FTSs, OTUs, CUs, OCUs, as well as many WWI units. Lesser known units include MUs, Repair & Servicing Units, Air Stores Parks, Staging Posts and numbered landing grounds in the UK, 2nd TAF and the Middle East. Cross-references to relevant administrative units such as Commands, Groups, Wings, Bases and Brigades. Aircraft types and examples are given, many with periodic strength or establishment. Comprehensive index of bases. Hard cover A4. 368 pages. 200 photographs.